Making Connections Across the Curriculum

Readings for Analysis

Making Connections Across the Curriculum

Readings for Analysis

Patricia Chittenden
University of California, Los Angeles

Malcolm Kiniry
University of California, Los Angeles

General Editors

Donna Uthus Gregory
University of California, Los Angeles

Ellen Strenski
University of California, Los Angeles

Jennifer Bradley
University of California, Los Angeles

Michael K. Havens
University of California, Davis

Michael Gustin
University of California, Los Angeles

Robert Cullen
University of California, Los Angeles

Sonia Maasik
University of California, Los Angeles

Carol L. Edwards
California State University – Long Beach

A BEDFORD BOOK

St. Martins Press • New York

Library of Congress Catalog Card Number: 85-61295
Copyright © 1986 by St. Martin's Press, Inc.
All rights reserved.

Manufactured in the United States of America

9 8 7 6
f e d c b a

For information, write St. Martin's Press, Inc.,
175 Fifth Avenue, New York, NY 10010
Editorial Offices: Bedford Books of St. Martin's Press,
29 Commonwealth Avenue, Boston, MA 02116

ISBN: 0-312-50666-X

Design and typography: George McLean
Cover design: Anna Post
Cover photo: Tom Norton

Acknowledgments

Page 49: Pieter Brueghel the Elder, *The Fall of Icarus*, 1558. Musées Royaux des Beaux-Arts, Brussels, Belgium.

Page 126: From *Native American Testimony*, edited by Peter Nabokov. New York: Crowell, 1978. Copyright © 1978 by Peter Nabokov. Reprinted by permission of Harold Matson Company Inc.

Page 219: The illustration is from *Internal Structure of the City: Readings on Space and Environment* by Larry S. Bourne. Copyright © 1971 by Oxford University Press. Reprinted by permission.

Page 228: The graph is from *A Communications Theory of Urban Growth* by R. L. Meier. Copyright © 1962 by the MIT Press. Reprinted by permission of the MIT Press.

Bruce Ames, "Mother Nature Is Meaner Than You Think." Reprinted from *Science '84* (July/August, 1984), by permission of *Science '84* Magazine. © 1984 by the American Association for the Advancement of Science.

W. H. Auden, "Musée des Beaux Arts." Copyright 1940 and renewed 1968 by W. H. Auden. Reprinted from *W. H. Auden: Collected Poems*, edited by Edward Mendelson, by permission of Random House, Inc. and Faber and Faber Ltd.

James L. Axtell, "The European Failure to Convert the Indians: An Autopsy." In *Papers of the Sixth Algonquian Conference*, 1974. William Cowan, editor. Canadian Ethnology Service Paper #23, National Museum of Man, Mercury Series. National Museums of Canada, 1975.

Ernest Baker, excerpts from *The Politics of Aristotle*. Edited and translated by Ernest Baker (1946), reprinted by permission of Oxford University Press.

Charles Beals, selections from "Early American Wolf Hunt" by Charles Beals. From *Of Wolves and Men* by Barry Holstun Lopez. Copyright © 1978 Barry Holstun Lopez. Reprinted with the permission of Charles Scribner's Sons.

Barton J. Bernstein, "The Dropping of the A-Bomb." Reprinted by permission of Baron J. Bernstein and *The Center Magazine*, a publication of the Center for the Study of Democratic Institutions.

Bruno Bettelheim, "Oedipal Conflicts and Resolutions: The Knight in Shining Armor and the Damsel in Distress." From *The Uses of Enchantment: The Meaning and Importance*

(Continued on page 647)

Preface for Instructors

Since college writing is largely analytical writing, we've constructed this reader to provide diverse analytical opportunities. We've chosen readings that range widely across the curriculum, clustered them around ten academically representative and socially important topics, and drawn on our separate experiences using these materials in the classroom. Most of the readings are themselves examples of effective analytical writing, yet their main function is to provide contexts for the analytical writing of students.

These chapters are cross-curricular in a special sense. Rather than compile a miscellany of writing from various disciplines, we have sought out topics on which various disciplines converge. The readings reveal important differences among disciplines — in attitude, language, emphasis, and perspective. But they also show that much good academic writing is interdisciplinary and that analytical thinking works in similar ways across the university.

The clusters of readings increase the analytical possibilities. Of course, each selection can be analyzed on its own terms, but two or more selections can also be examined in relation to one another. And, as a group, a chapter's readings can contribute to an informed analysis of a general issue or problem. Too often, students lack either a context in which to read an essay or a critical perspective from which to evaluate it. The clustered readings provide a fuller base of information, and, more importantly, their varying perspectives encourage independent thinking.

The ten chapters have been compiled and edited by teachers who have based entire composition courses on these topics. We think this amplitude makes for flexibility. Some teachers will want to dip into a chapter to look at a single essay or to select a convenient pairing for purposes of comparison. Others may want to assign entire chapters as background for looking at a few pieces in detail. Still others may want to use a chapter in a sustained way — working through all its readings, developing a sequence of intermediate assignments, and arriving at a project requiring student research.

The book's apparatus is meant to enhance this flexibility. The "Considerations" that follow each reading offer ways of approaching that reading on its own. "Connections" questions, which come next, suggest ways of analyzing one text in relation to another. "Further Connections" at the end of each chapter call upon the readings as a group, and "Extensions" suggest promising and manageable research options. All four types of questions have been conceived as writing assignments. Most of the early questions are also adaptable for class discussions, or for work in small groups. We've found that using one or two questions to prompt some preliminary writing is a good way to get students analytically engaged.

Acknowledgments

As teachers in the UCLA Writing Programs, we have benefited from a collegial atmosphere and administrative encouragement. We have appreciated the enthusiasm and example of Executive Director Richard A. Lanham, the program's initiator and presiding influence; the steadiness and flexibility of Carol P. Hartzog, Director who enabled us to develop the sorts of courses represented here; and the high standard set by Mike Rose, director of Freshman English, whose commitment to intellectually challenging assignments has influenced this book throughout.

Besides our general debts, we have accumulated specific ones. For their helpful reviews of the book's readings and apparatus, we'd like to thank Dave Bartholomae, University of Pittsburgh; Patricia Bizzell, College of the Holy Cross; Richard Brucher, University of Maine, Orono; David Jolliffe, University of Illinois at Chicago; Carol MacKay, University of Texas at Austin; and Donald McQuade, University of California at Berkeley. For further suggestions and advice, we'd like to thank Michael Foley, Dan Hawkes, Mark Infusino, Stephen M. Jones, John Klancher, Michael D. Moore, Howard J. Nelson, John Ollinger, Elizabeth Silver, Jack Solomon, Ivan Strenski, Allan J. Tobin, Linda Venis, and Donald J. Ward.

Finally, we'd like to thank the people at Bedford Books, who proved themselves steady and responsive in dealing with an unusual authorial arrangement. Charles H. Christensen and Joan Feinberg were generous, forebearing, incisive, and insistent — at just the right times and places. As managing editor, Elizabeth Schaaf was both patient and resourceful. Nancy Lyman, Christine Rutigliano, Karen Henry, Virginia Creeden, and Steve Scipione were all efficient and helpful in working, transcontinentally, with the pack of us.

Brief Contents

Contents

2 The Origins of the Nuclear Arms Race   *58*

Edited by Donna Uthus Gregory

3   The Frontier Indians   *124*

Edited by Ellen Strenski

This imaginative reconstruction of Indian life before Europeans came to California shows how historical accounts can draw on linguistics, science, and anthropology.

What happened when Indian and European cultures collided? A biologist's statistical interpretation.

A Pueblo anthropologist cautions white historians about misjudging Indian cultures and thereby misunderstanding their history.

In examining the Ojibwa concept of "persons," another anthropologist examines how the structure of a language can reveal the world view of its speakers.

Historical inquiry is not content to describe what people do; it tries to understand how their beliefs help account for what they do. Here a historian offers an overview of Indian and European contact on the East Coast.

An analysis of one tribe's belief system. The Abenaki's understanding of land "ownership," their relationship to the animals they hunted, and their social organization were all based on a coherent mythological conception of their place in the world.

Kopit's play is a dramatic reconstruction of several historical incidents, including the treaty negotiations between the U.S. government and Sitting Bull's Sioux.

7   The Nature of Intelligence   *381*

Edited by Robert Cullen

9 The Impact of Animals *518*

Edited by Sonia Maasik

Introduction for Students

The readings in this book are aimed at good college writing — yours. Its title and subtitle convey the major emphases: "Readings for Analysis" because most college writing is analytical writing; "Making Connections" because connection-making is at the heart of all analysis, whether it be among the parts of a single reading, between one reading and another, or between the text and something else you know or think; "Across the Curriculum" because a writing course that emphasizes making connections can be the best introduction to the many varied fields that college opens up.

The readings in each chapter are grouped about a single topic of interest to several academic fields. Working with a specific topic over a period of time and from varying points of view increases the analytical opportunities. Each reading can be analyzed on its own terms: what does it say, how is it structured, how does it work upon readers? But each reading also can be analyzed in relation to others in the chapter: how does it compare, what does it add to our understanding, which ideas does it help support or refute, how else might it be seen, what else might it help us see better? The more you read in each chapter, the more you learn and the more perspectives you have for viewing. Points of view are apt to vary widely within a single field. No two urban planners, for example, are likely to diagnose the problems of modern cities in quite the same way. But points of view are apt to differ even more sharply and in more interesting ways as we move from one discipline to another — from the way an economic historian, for example, looks at urban problems to the way a social psychologist does.

Academic Points of View: An Illustration

To illustrate the range and variety of points of view within the university, it helps to imagine how a topic might appear from several different academic perspectives. To choose a topic everyone has some interest in, take sex. Sex can occupy a larger or smaller part of our mental landscape, depending on our distance and what else we see. Along academic lines of vision, too, sex can appear relatively inconsequential, or it can loom large. For physicists, mathematicians, astronomers, and geologists — professionally speaking, at least — it is a topic of little interest (though a geologist might object that a successful history of sexual relationships is embedded in several strata of formerly organic rock). For biologists, by contrast, it is a topic impossible to avoid: genetics, ecology, evolution, animal behavior, to say nothing of the direct study of reproductive mechanisms in plants and animals, all entail thinking about sex and its implications. Chemists, on the other hand, are free to ignore sex or study it; some biochemists specialize in such topics as the chemical interaction of egg and sperm, the functioning of human sex hormones like estrogen and testosterone, or the sexual messages transmitted among animals by the molecular formations called pheremones.

The arts approach a topic like sex from diverse points of view. In the visual arts, the nude, for instance, is a traditional subject for painters, who have treated unclothed bodies with every nuance of feeling from adoration to indifference to revulsion. The entire field of sculpture, which until modern times consisted primarily of representations of the human form, is sensitive to sexual interpretations since clothed or unclothed, at rest or astride horses, statues of human figures often have sexual overtones. As with the visual arts, the study of literature can turn frequently toward sexual themes — not only in the vast body of poetry, drama, and fiction for which sexual emotion provides an important current, but in the many other works where it is an unsettling presence. There is also a tendency in some literary criticism to read into apparently nonsexual works — the poetry of Emily Dickinson or the sea fiction of Joseph Conrad — an undercurrent of disguised, perhaps unconscious, sexual feelings. The study of music, by contrast, is less apt to turn toward sexual themes, particularly when the emphasis is placed more on musical forms and techniques than on the lives of composers. But it is difficult to talk about opera, where plots almost always hinge on sexual melodrama and male and female voices continually compete, cooperate, and merge, without taking account of the sexual component.

The social sciences also approach the topic of sex in varied ways. Many psychologists, especially those influenced by Sigmund Freud, see sexuality as the great creative and disruptive force in mental life. Clinical and experimental psychologists are likely to view sex more neutrally, as merely one feature of human behavior, but they find sexual differences between male and female behavior particularly worth studying. Sociologists, whose interests center on how groups influence individuals, stress not so much how sex influences our behavior as how sexual behavior is channeled by social influences like family, marriage, and peer pressure. Anthropologists are more likely to compare the sexual customs of one culture with those of others as part of the general effort to distinguish between behavior common to all humans and behavior bound to particular times and places. Economists are apt to deemphasize sex altogether — partly because for them sexual motives seem unimportant compared to financial ones, but mostly because economists restrict themselves to the more measurable aspects of supply and demand. Still, some sexual matters do lend themselves to economic analysis: prostitution, for example, can be studied like any other business by analyzing the costs and benefits to suppliers and consumers.

Historians, by contrast, may look at sex closely or from a distance: most political historians will turn to a sexual explanation only where absolutely necessary (like the influence upon English politics of King Henry VIII's many wives); cultural historians, by contrast, may see in the general patterns of shifting sexual attitudes indications of meaningful historical change. Similarly, political scientists studying international and national relationships seldom stress sexual themes, while at the grass-roots level "sexual politics" (like office politics) are increasingly taken into account. Finally, women's studies programs, a recent cross-curricular development on many college campuses, draw upon all of these other disciplines in seeking to understand the social consequences of sexual differences.

The ten topics that form the chapters of this book, though not so widely embracing as sex, have been chosen for their social importance and their cross-curricular appeal. Some, like The Dimensions of Power, span numerous academic fields, while others, like The Frontier Indians, are the concern of people in fields that are themselves strongly interdisciplinary. All of the chapters — on power, the nuclear arms race, Indians, cities, work, learning, intelligence, cancer, animals, and the fairy tale — are meant to stimulate interests that cannot be readily confined to a single area of study. Each set of readings is designed to help you think flexibly and forcefully about a complex topic, one capable of stirring good analytical writing.

What do we mean by *analysis?* The word has a wide range of associations in differing academic contexts. A literature student asked to analyze a poem may feel little in common with a chemistry student analyzing an unknown solution or a business student analyzing a management decision. But any analysis fits this general definition: analysis looks at something closely and from an informed point of view, expressing an interpretation which it attempts to defend.

Looking closely is important. To explain how something is structured or how it works, you need to see it in detail. Yet looking closely isn't enough. Imagine examining a detailed image of diseased human blood cells without knowing what you were looking for. An informed point of view enables you to look selectively, passing over some features in order to stress others, letting you judge what you see in the light of what you already know. Still, a knowledgeable general perspective is also not enough. You need some specific perception or idea to focus the rest of what you find important — an interpretation. Most importantly, you need to support that interpretation with persuasive reasoning and evidence. Good analytical writing makes its connections persuasively.

Types of Analysis

Let us describe some of the types of analytic connections you will be asked to make, beginning with single readings and proceeding to readings in combinations. For all types of analysis, you will need to be able to summarize: to distinguish a readings' main ideas from its lesser ones and to connect those main ideas in a brief but accurate restatement. Summaries can be difficult to compose, since they force you to make difficult judgments about which ideas are most important and how they should be connected. For that reason, they can be very valuable to write, even when you do not intend for others to read what you have written. Summaries are also valuable within essays: at openings, they can introduce the material to be analyzed; at key transition points, segments of summary can help reorient readers; at the conclusions of essays, they can consolidate main points. A summary alone, however, is seldom sufficient for analysis; it lacks an independent perception to clarify or defend. When teachers criticize their students for producing "mere summary," they are calling for essays that subordinate summaries to more fully analytical purposes.

One such purpose is to explain a writer's basic thinking. What are the assumptions and reasoning at the center of that writer's argument? Often a single question, if it is central enough, will focus attention on the most fundamental aspects of the writer's argument. In Chapter 6, for example, after reading some of the educational recommendations of the philosopher John Locke, you are asked to explain why Locke favored imposing strict rules upon children. The question is a fundamental one, and answering it enables you to pass over many of Locke's specific recommendations in order to focus instead upon his basic reasoning. Sometimes a writer's assumptions and reasons will be fully laid out in the text; your analytical job will be simply to help a reader see the interconnections. At other times a writer's basic thinking will seem obscure or flimsy; your job then becomes to explain what you find dissatisfying.

Some analyses explain why; others explain how. An essay that focuses upon how a text works is called rhetorical analysis. Simply put, rhetorical analysis means examining a writer's use of language — choices in the organization of material, in sentence structure, in the selection of words. A rhetorical analysis of the selection from Charles Darwin's *The Descent of Man* (in Chapter 9) might focus on the patient ways in which Darwin prepares the reader for his most controversial points. Or a rhetorical analysis might examine how Darwin's use of figures of speech subtly contributes to his purposes, or how his word choices reveal him as a scientist of his own time rather than ours. Better still, a thorough rhetorical analysis might find a way to connect these several strands of observation within one central perception.

Another analytical approach is to concentrate upon a single contributory idea or theme. That idea may not be the writer's main concern, but it is worth examining for the role it plays. Consider two examples. A theme we can find throughout Chapter 2, The Origins of the Nuclear Arms Race, is the troubled relationship between science and politics. An analytic approach to one of the documents in that chapter — for instance, the letter from physicist Niels Bohr to President Roosevelt — might focus on the influence of that theme. A theme we can trace in Chapter 10 is that of transformation. An analytical essay might compare the role played by sudden transformations in several variants of Snow White. Sometimes a thematic analysis will give prominence to a relatively minor feature of the text; in such cases the test is whether that feature can be connected to some larger interpretive issue. For example, an essay examining the recurrent mention of primary colors in "Snow White" might work well if connected to an idea about the clear-cut emotions of fairy tale characters.

Another approach is to analyze a reading from a fresh perspective. By trying out several ways of approaching a text, you can sometimes illuminate it in an unexpected way. For example, an anthropologist's analysis of the significant events in the cancer operation described by Richard Selzer (Chapter 8) might look very different from the report of a fellow doctor: focusing on cultural behavior might suggest a different set of connections among events in the operating room. To discover a fresh point of view, it is not always necessary to go from one discipline to another, but it does help to be playful with ideas. Try out a variety of points of view as you would try several differently tinted glasses before settling on the one you like best or rejecting them all.

Yet another analytic approach is to connect a reading with something else you know. Having read Machiavelli on political power, you might look at the operation of a corporation from a Machiavellian perspective. This type of analysis must maintain a kind of double focus. You need to demonstrate an accurate understanding of the reading, but you also need to choose a topic you know enough about to make interesting connections. Your choice need not fit the frame provided by the reading. In fact, a good analytical essay might demonstrate why Machiavelli has little to tell us about the operation of American business. But if you can find no connection at all between the reading and the topic you have chosen, you had better choose another topic. With a well chosen topic, this strategy of applying something you have read to something you know gives you the freedom to draw imaginatively on your own experience.

One last analytical approach of a text is to evaluate it. Actually, any analysis evaluates. You are evaluating when you select points worth emphasizing or when you defend any connection you have made. But the main point of an evaluative essay is to make judgments about quality. Assignments that ask you to evaluate, critique, or give your opinion force you to take a position about the effectiveness of a text. To evaluate Frederick Taylor's "Principles of Scientific Management" (Chapter 5), you need to arrive at some feeling about whether those principles are adequate. The rest of what you say will be designed to support your judgment. This does not mean you should ignore everything that does not support your opinion, but you will want to convince your reader that the contrary evidence is not sufficient to undermine your position. You will, however, need to treat your topic as one about which it is possible to disagree.

Further Analytic Applications

Up until now, we have been dealing with analyses based upon a single reading; but much academic analysis requires thinking about readings in relation to one another. Academic sophistication often depends on being willing and able to make such connections. Even so, writing about two or more readings is not necessarily any more difficult than writing about one. Most of the nuts-and-bolts work involves the same sorts of operations just described: summarizing texts, explaining their reasoning or rhetoric, tracing themes, adopting fresh perspectives, testing applications, defending opinions. The major difference is that when dealing with more than one reading, whatever else you choose to do in your essay will depend on your basic decision of how to connect the texts. Let us briefly describe three general ways in which readings can be connected.

First, there are the connections between generalization and example, between readings that offer theoretical explanations and those that illustrate or test those explanations. For instance, in the chapter on the urban experience (Chapter 4), social psychologist Stanley Milgram's discussion of city life can be used to analyze the main character in Shirley Jackson's story, "Pillar of Salt."

Applying one text to another is a tried and true analytical method, a method this book gives you plenty of opportunity to exercise. The exercise can become mechanical, however, if you assume that your job is always to find a compatible match between the generalizations and the specifics. Sometimes you may want to show that the theory is inadequate to explain the case or that the evidence better supports different generalizations.

Comparisons offer a second way of connecting texts. Instead of using one text as an instrument to probe another, a comparison treats the texts as equivalents. The data for comparative essays are the points of similarity and contrast you can discover in the readings. Still, collecting and arranging an assortment of these points is not enough. As with other analyses, your main need is to find a purposeful focus, a single idea capable of ordering your points. Sometimes the wording of an assignment will do some of the focusing for you, as when you are asked to compare Machiavelli and Freud's attitudes toward war. At other times the job of focusing the comparison falls entirely on you; you must grapple with the readings long enough to find a solid basis for comparison. In either situation, you will have to decide the direction of your essay. After establishing an initial basis of resemblance, most comparisons go on to bring out important differences. Some very effective comparisons, however, move in the opposite direction: after acknowledging the important ways in which the texts differ, the analysis proceeds to uncover fundamental correspondences.

A third possibility is to treat the texts as contributory evidence in developing your own generalizations. In Chapter 3 you are asked to draw on several historical accounts in developing your explanation of how the French, encountering the Indians, must have regarded their tribal shamans. A good esssay of this type uses the texts in complementary ways, drawing upon the relevant parts of each to support the generalizations. At their most ambitious, such essays construct an original theory from evidence supplied by several texts.

The more readings you deal with, the less you will depend upon a single reading. The topic itself, not just the texts, becomes the object of analysis. In Chapter 7, The Nature of Intelligence, for example, you can respond to the challenge of identifying and addressing the ethical issues raised by brain and computer research. Equipped with more information and exposed to more points of view, you will find you have more of a basis to make your own judgments and to develop your own ideas.

Research brings even further opportunities to make original analytical connections. While it can be intimidating and tiring, research can also be fun, particularly if you have a fairly clear idea of what you are looking for. The best way to keep research manageable is to keep it subordinated to an analytic aim. One managed form of research involves locating a particular book or article and connecting it to your earlier readings. A second type of research employs tools like bibliographies and indexes to search out a select group of readings capable of extending the topic. A third takes you away from the library to "the field," where you can conduct your own observations or experiments and then analyze the results.

Our writing suggestions are arranged to approximate this movement toward analytical independence that we have described. In the "Considerations" that follow each selection, we ask you to think about that reading in isolation. In "Connections," you are asked to think about that reading in relation to previous ones. At the end of each chapter "Further Connections" invite you to think freshly about the topic, making use of the readings you choose. Finally, "Extensions" and the accompanying "Suggestions for Further Reading" send you away from the book in search of further information and insights.

Making Connections Across the Curriculum

Readings for Analysis

1 The Dimensions of Power

Edited by **Patricia Chittenden**

Power — an ugly word. Or is it? Power gives us light, mobility, warmth. When we have power, we control our surroundings. We feel strong; we'll survive after all. But what consoles us, even exhilarates us, can also intimidate us. Power outside ourselves threatens that very confidence in our own ability to do, to act, to accomplish, and even to live.

It's no wonder, then, that we're fascinated by power. We study it eagerly, in a variety of ways. Physical scientists study physical or mechanical power: hydroelectric, solar, nuclear. The history of technology describes the effort to divert more and more of that power for human purposes. And yet when we look at the nuclear crisis and our crowded cities, it appears that we have not yet mastered the natural forces we've tapped.

Nor have we mastered the power of the biological world. We understand photosynthesis to some extent, or at least we harness that power in agriculture. But we don't yet fully understand the power that drives our own bodies, the power source of our own cells. As we grapple with definitions of intelligence and explanations of learning, we note that cancer — biological power gone awry — is on the increase, and we can't seem to stop it. Life scientists try to understand the struggle to survive not only among us humans but among all living organisms: animal, plant, and even the single-cell amoeba.

Social scientists, on the other hand, do concentrate their scientific study on humans. They examine our competition for material or economic resources that will insure the power to survive and more. As we go about our daily work in our urban industrial centers, social scientists discover how we undermined the entire economic basis for survival of the American Indian.

They also explore the subtle structures — the social power structures — we've erected to give ourselves some semblance of security. Social scientists look at our groups (majority and minority), our customs (how we view and treat women), our institutions (schools), all of which hold the power to organize our lives.

Finally, social scientists concern themselves with the more visible and formalized power structures — the political ones — erected between and within nations. In so doing, they try to understand those threats to political structures: the power of influence, the power of terrorism, and the power struggle that has become the nuclear arms race.

Even though, or perhaps because, we haven't mastered the power evident in our surroundings, as scientists and social scientists we talk about it. We communicate our discoveries and our insights through the power of language. We philosophize: about our place in the scheme of the universe (are we doomed to extinction in a nuclear holocaust?), our relation to a supreme power (is our modern urban existence godless?), our links with the rest of nature (are we different from animals?), and our dealings with our fellow humans. Inquirers in the field of the humanities consider the philosophy of power, both earthly and other-worldly. They probe the myths power generates and the way we communicate our ideas about power to other human beings through art and literature.

Power, then, is a concern of physicists, chemists, engineers; microbiologists, botanists, biologists, physicians, psychologists; economists, sociologists, anthropologists, political scientists, historians; philosophers, theologians, folklorists, artists, and writers. We examine power, in one way or another, in all these academic disciplines. By studying power, in turn, we can see some relationships, or connections, among the disciplines.

This chapter attempts to explore the dimensions of power by sampling some of these perspectives. It begins with a pair of selections familiar to most readers: Niccolò Machiavelli and Sigmund Freud view political power from very different angles. Machiavelli details the requisites for the exercise of political power; and Freud examines the ultimate political power — war — in the context of both biology and psychology. These are followed by philosopher Bertrand Russell, who focuses on the power of opinion and the power that shapes opinion. He sees propaganda as preying on the struggle between Reason and Belief in science and also in religion, advertising, and politics.

The next selections move from Elias Canetti's biological analysis of the human pursuit of power to Samuel S. Janus's more traditional social science view of the contest for power. Canetti claims that the human urge for power has its origin in, and is a metaphor for, the basic animal urge for power over prey. Janus posits a more culture-based power struggle, between male and female of the human species, and he examines one response to it in our use of comedy.

The final selections treat the issue of power in literary form. Lewis Carroll applies his logic to the philosophical and practical relationship between language and power. And poets William Carlos Williams, Michael Hamburger, and W. H. Auden ponder the ethical and existential dilemmas created by one particular instance of the pursuit of power.

The Qualities of the Prince

Niccolò Machiavelli

A Prince's Duty Concerning Military Matters

A prince, therefore, must not have any other object nor any other thought, *1*
nor must he take anything as his profession but war, its institutions, and its
discipline; because that is the only profession which befits one who commands; and it is of such importance that not only does it maintain those who
were born princes, but many times it enables men of private station to rise to
that position; and, on the other hand, it is evident that when princes have given
more thought to personal luxuries than to arms, they have lost their state. And
the first way to lose it is to neglect this art; and the way to acquire it is to be
well versed in this art.

Francesco Sforza became Duke of Milan from being a private citizen be- *2*
cause he was armed; his sons, since they avoided the inconveniences of arms,
became private citizens after having been dukes. For, among the other bad effects it causes, being disarmed makes you despised; this is one of those in-
famies a prince should guard himself against, as will be treated below: for between an armed and an unarmed man there is no comparison whatsoever, and
it is not reasonable for an armed man to obey an unarmed man willingly, nor
that an unarmed man should be safe among armed servants; since, when the
former is suspicious and the latter are contemptuous, it is impossible for them
to work well together. And therefore, a prince who does not understand military matters, besides the other misfortunes already noted, cannot be esteemed
by his own soldiers, nor can he trust them.

He must, therefore, never raise his thought from this exercise of war, and in *3*
peacetime he must train himself more than in time of war; this can be done in
two ways: one by action, the other by the mind. And as far as actions are concerned, besides keeping his soldiers well disciplined and trained, he must always be out hunting, and must accustom his body to hardships in this manner; and he must also learn the nature of the terrain, and know how mountains
slope, how valleys open, how plains lie, and understand the nature of rivers
and swamps; and he should devote much attention to such activities. Such
knowledge is useful in two ways: first, one learns to know one's own country
and can better understand how to defend it; second, with the knowledge and
experience of the terrain, one can easily comprehend the characteristics of any
other terrain that it is necessary to explore for the first time; for the hills, valleys, plains, rivers, and swamps of Tuscany, for instance, have certain similar-

*Niccolò Machiavelli (1469–1527) was an Italian author and statesman and one
of the outstanding figures of the Renaissance. He is best known for his controversial Il Principe (The Prince) (1513), excerpted here, which describes the qualities
a prince needs to maintain power.*

ities to those of other provinces; so that by knowing the lay of the land in one province one can easily understand it in others. And a prince who lacks this ability lacks the most important quality in a leader; because this skill teaches you to find the enemy, choose a campsite, lead troops, organize them for battle, and besiege towns to your own advantage.

Philopoemon, Prince of the Achaeans, among the other praises given to him   4
by writers, is praised because in peacetime he thought of nothing except the means of waging war; and when he was out in the country with his friends, he often stopped and reasoned with them: "If the enemy were on that hilltop and we were here with our army, which of the two of us would have the advantage? How could we attack them without breaking formation? If we wanted to retreat, how could we do this? If they were to retreat, how could we pursue them?" And he proposed to them, as they rode along, all the contingencies that can occur in an army; he heard their opinions, expressed his own, and backed it up with arguments; so that, because of these continuous deliberations, when leading his troops no unforeseen incident could arise for which he did not have the remedy.

But as for the exercise of the mind, the prince must read histories and in   5
them study the deeds of great men; he must see how they conducted themselves in wars; he must examine the reasons for their victories and for their defeats in order to avoid the latter and to imitate the former; and above all else he must do as some distinguished man before him has done, who elected to imitate someone who had been praised and honored before him, and always keep in mind his deeds and actions; just as it is reported that Alexander the Great imitated Achilles; Caesar, Alexander; Scipio, Cyrus. And anyone who reads the life of Cyrus written by Xenophon then realizes how important in the life of Scipio that imitation was to his glory and how much, in purity, goodness, humanity, and generosity, Scipio conformed to those characteristics of Cyrus that Xenophon had written about.

Such methods as these a wise prince must follow, and never in peaceful times   6
must he be idle; but he must turn them diligently to his advantage in order to be able to profit from them in times of adversity, so that, when Fortune changes, she will find him prepared to withstand such times.

On Those Things for Which Men, and Particularly Princes, Are Praised or Blamed

Now there remains to be examined what should be the methods and pro-   7
cedures of a prince in dealing with his subjects and friends. And because I know that many have written about this, I am afraid that by writing about it again I shall be thought of as presumptuous, since in discussing this material I depart radically from the procedures of others. But since my intention is to write something useful for anyone who understands it, it seemed more suitable to me to search after the effectual truth of the matter rather than its imagined one. And many writers have imagined for themselves republics and principalities that have never been seen nor known to exist in reality; for there is such

a gap between how one lives and how one ought to live that anyone who abandons what is done for what ought to be done learns his ruin rather than his preservation: for a man who wishes to make a vocation of being good at all times will come to ruin among so many who are not good. Hence it is necessary for a prince who wishes to maintain his position to learn how not to be good, and to use this knowledge or not to use it according to necessity.

Leaving aside, therefore, the imagined things concerning a prince, and taking into account those that are true, I say that all men, when they are spoken of, and particularly princes, since they are placed on a higher level, are judged by some of these qualities which bring them either blame or praise. And this is why one is considered generous, another miserly (to use a Tuscan word, since "avaricious" in our language is still used to mean one who wishes to acquire by means of theft; we call "miserly" one who excessively avoids using what he has); one is considered a giver, the other rapacious; one cruel, another merciful; one treacherous, another faithful; one effeminate and cowardly, another bold and courageous; one humane, another haughty; one lascivious, another chaste; one trustworthy, another cunning; one harsh, another lenient; one serious, another frivolous; one religious, another unbelieving; and the like. And I know that everyone will admit that it would be a very praiseworthy thing to find in a prince, of the qualities mentioned above, those that are held to be good; but since it is neither possible to have them nor to observe them all completely, because human nature does not permit it, a prince must be prudent enough to know how to escape the bad reputation of those vices that would lose the state for him and must protect himself from those that will not lose it for him, if this is possible; but if he cannot, he need not concern himself unduly if he ignores these less serious vices. And, moreover, he need not worry about incurring the bad reputation of those vices without which it would be difficult to hold his state; since, carefully taking everything into account, one will discover that something which appears to be a virtue, if pursued, will end in his destruction; while some other thing which seems to be a vice, if pursued, wlll result in his safety and his well-being.   8

On Generosity and Miserliness

Beginning, therefore, with the first of the above-mentioned qualities, I say that it would be good to be considered generous; nevertheless, generosity used in such a manner as to give you a reputation for it will harm you; because if it is employed virtuously and as one should employ it, it will not be recognized and you will not avoid the reproach of its opposite. And so, if a prince wants to maintain his reputation for generosity among men, it is necessary for him not to neglect any possible means of lavish display; in so doing such a prince will always use up all his resources and he will be obliged, eventually, if he wishes to maintain his reputation for generosity, to burden the people with excessive taxes and to do everything possible to raise funds. This will begin to make him hateful to his subjects, and, becoming impoverished, he will not be much esteemed by anyone; so that, as a consequence of his generosity, having offended many and rewarded few, he will feel the effects of any slight unrest and will be ruined at the first sign of danger; recognizing this and wishing to   9 alter his policies, he immediately runs the risk of being reproached as a miser.

A prince, therefore, unable to use this virtue of generosity in a manner which *10*
will not harm himself if he is known for it, should, if he is wise, not worry
about being called a miser; for with time he will come to be considered more
generous once it is evident that, as a result of his parsimony, his income is
sufficient, he can defend himself from anyone who makes war against him, and
he can undertake enterprises without overburdening his people, so that he comes
to be generous with all those from whom he takes nothing, who are countless,
and miserly with all those to whom he gives nothing, who are few. In our times
we have not seen great deeds accomplished except by those who were considered miserly; all others were done away with. Pope Julius II, although he
made use of his reputation for generosity in order to gain the papacy, then decided not to maintain it in order to be able to wage war; the present King of
France has waged many wars without imposing extra taxes on his subjects,
only because his habitual parsimony has provided for the additional expenditures; the present King of Spain, if he had been considered generous, would
not have engaged in nor won so many campaigns.

Therefore, in order not to have to rob his subjects, to be able to defend him- *11*
self, not to become poor and contemptible, and not to be forced to become rapacious, a prince must consider it of little importance if he incurs the name of
miser, for this is one of those vices that permits him to rule. And if someone
were to say: Caesar with his generosity came to rule the empire, and many
others, because they were generous and known to be so, achieved very high
positions; I reply: you are either already a prince or you are on the way to
becoming one; in the first instance such generosity is damaging; in the second
it is very necessary to be thought generous. And Caesar was one of those who
wanted to gain the principality of Rome; but if, after obtaining this, he had
lived and had not moderated his expenditures, he would have destroyed that
empire. And if someone were to reply: there have existed many princes who
have accomplished great deeds with their armies who have been reputed to be
generous; I answer you: a prince either spends his own money and that of his
subjects or that of others; in the first case he must be economical; in the second he must not restrain any part of his generosity. And for that prince who
goes out with his soldiers and lives by looting, sacking, and ransoms, who controls the property of others, such generosity is necessary; otherwise he would
not be followed by his troops. And with what does not belong to you or to your
subjects you can be a more liberal giver, as were Cyrus, Caesar, and Alexander;
for spending the wealth of others does not lessen your reputation but adds to
it; only the spending of your own is what harms you. And there is nothing that
uses itself up faster than generosity, for as you employ it you lose the means
of *employing it, and you become either poor or despised or, in order to* escape
poverty, rapacious and hated. And above all other things a prince must guard
himself against being despised and hated; and generosity leads you to both one
and the other. So it is wiser to live with the reputation of a miser, which produces reproach without hatred, than to be forced to incur the reputation of
rapacity, which produces reproach along with hatred, because you want to be
considered as generous.

On Cruelty and Mercy
and Whether It Is Better
to be Loved Than to be Feared
or the Contrary

Proceeding to the other qualities mentioned above, I say that every prince　*12*
must desire to be considered merciful and not cruel; nevertheless, he must take
care not to misuse this mercy. Cesare Borgia was considered cruel; nonetheless, his cruelty had brought order to Romagna, united it, restored it to peace
and obedience. If we examine this carefully, we shall see that he was more
merciful than the Florentine people, who, in order to avoid being considered
cruel, allowed the destruction of Pistoia. Therefore, a prince must not worry
about the reproach of cruelty when it is a matter of keeping his subjects united
and loyal; for with a very few examples of cruelty he will be more compassionate than those who, out of excessive mercy, permit disorders to continue,
from which arise murders and plundering; for these usually harm the community at large, while the executions that come from the prince harm one individual in particular. And the new prince, above all other princes, cannot escape the reputation of being called cruel, since new states are full of dangers.
And Virgil, through Dido, states: "My difficult condition and the newness of
my rule make me act in such a manner, and to set guards over my land on all
sides."

Nevertheless, a prince must be cautious in believing and in acting, nor should　*13*
he be afraid of his own shadow; and he should proceed in such a manner, tempered by prudence and humanity, so that too much trust may not render him
imprudent nor too much distrust render him intolerable.

From this arises an argument: whether it is better to be loved than to be　*14*
feared, or the contrary. I reply that one should like to be both one and the other;
but since it is difficult to join them together, it is much safer to be feared than
to be loved when one of the two must be lacking. For one can generally say
this about men: that they are ungrateful, fickle, simulators and deceivers,
avoiders of danger, greedy for gain; and while you work for their good they are
completely yours, offering you their blood, their property, their lives, and their
sons, as I said earlier, when danger is far away; but when it comes nearer to
you they turn away. And that prince who bases his power entirely on their words,
finding himself stripped of other preparations, comes to ruin; for friendships
that are acquired by a price and not by greatness and nobility of character are
purchased but are not owned, and at the proper moment they cannot be spent.
And men are less hesitant about harming someone who makes himself loved
than one who makes himself feared because love is held together by a chain of
obligation which, since men are a sorry lot, is broken on every occasion in which
their own self-interest is concerned; but fear is held together by a dread of
punishment which will never abandon you.

A prince must nevertheless make himself feared in such a manner that he　*15*
will avoid hatred, even if he does not acquire love; since to be feared and not
to be hated can very well be combined; and this will always be so when he

keeps his hands off the property and the women of his citizens and his subjects. And if he must take someone's life, he should do so when there is proper
justification and manifest cause; but, above all, he should avoid the property
of others; for men forget more quickly the death of their father than the loss
of their patrimony. Moreover, the reasons for seizing their property are never
lacking; and he who begins to live by stealing always finds a reason for taking
what belongs to others; on the contrary, reasons for taking a life are rarer and
disappear sooner.

But when the prince is with his armies and has under his command a mul-   *16*
titude of troops, then it is absolutely necessary that he not worry about being
considered cruel; for without that reputation he will never keep an army united
or prepared for any combat. Among the praiseworthy deeds of Hannibal is
counted this: that, having a very large army, made up of all kinds of men, which
he commanded in foreign lands, there never arose the slightest dissention, neither among themselves nor against their prince, both during his good and his
bad fortune. This could not have arisen from anything other than his inhuman
cruelty, which, along with his many other abilities, made him always respected and terrifying in the eyes of his soldiers; and without that, to attain
the same effect, his other abilities would not have sufficed. And the writers of
history, having considered this matter very little, on the one hand admire these
deeds of his and on the other condemn the main cause of them.

And that it be true that his other abilities would not have been sufficient   *17*
can be seen from the example of Scipio, a most extraordinary man not only in
his time but in all recorded history, whose armies in Spain rebelled against
him; this came about from nothing other than his excessive compassion, which
gave to his soldiers more liberty than military discipline allowed. For this he
was censured in the senate by Fabius Maximus, who called him the corruptor
of the Roman militia. The Locrians, having been ruined by one of Scipio's officers, were not avenged by him, nor was the arrogance of that officer corrected, all because of his tolerant nature; so that someone in the senate who
tried to apologize for him said that there were many men who knew how not
to err better than they knew how to correct errors. Such a nature would have,
in time, damaged Scipio's fame and glory if he had maintained it during the
empire; but, living under the control of the senate, this harmful characteristic
of his not only concealed itself but brought him fame.

I conclude, therefore, returning to the problem of being feared and loved,   *18*
that since men love at their own pleasure and fear at the pleasure of the prince,
a wise prince should build his foundation upon that which belongs to him, not
upon that which belongs to others: he must strive only to avoid hatred, as has
been said.

How a Prince Should Keep His Word

How praiseworthy it is for a prince to keep his word and to live by integrity   *19*
and not by deceit everyone knows; nevertheless, one sees from the experience
of our times that the princes who have accomplished great deeds are those who
have cared little for keeping their promises and who have known how to ma-

nipulate the minds of men by shrewdness; and in the end they have surpassed those who laid their foundations upon honesty.

You must, therefore, know that there are two means of fighting: one according to the laws, the other with force; the first way is proper to man, the second to beasts; but because the first, in many cases, is not sufficient, it becomes necessary to have recourse to the second. Therefore, a prince must know how to use wisely the natures of the beast and the man. This policy was taught to princes allegorically by the ancient writers, who described how Achilles and many other ancient princes were given to Chiron the Centaur to be raised and taught under his discipline. This can only mean that, having a half-beast and half-man as a teacher, a prince must know how to employ the nature of the one and the other; and the one without the other cannot endure. *20*

Since, then, a prince must know how to make good use of the nature of the beast, he should choose from among the beasts the fox and the lion; for the lion cannot defend itself from traps and the fox cannot protect itself from wolves. It is therefore necessary to be a fox in order to recognize the traps and a lion in order to frighten the wolves. Those who play only the part of the lion do not understand matters. A wise ruler, therefore, cannot and should not keep his word when such an observance of faith would be to his disadvantage and when the reasons which made him promise are removed. And if men were all good, this rule would not be good; but since men are a sorry lot and will not keep their promises to you, you likewise need not keep yours to them. A prince never lacks legitimate reasons to break his promises. Of this one could cite an endless number of modern examples to show how many pacts, how many promises have been made null and void because of the infidelity of princes; and he who has known best how to use the fox has come to a better end. But it is necessary to know how to disguise this nature well and to be a great hypocrite and a liar: and men are so simpleminded and so controlled by their present necessities that one who deceives will always find another who will allow himself to be deceived. *21*

I do not wish to remain silent about one of these recent instances. Alexander VI did nothing else, he thought about nothing else, except to deceive men, and he always found the occasion to do this. And there never was a man who had more forcefulness in his oaths, who affirmed a thing with more promises, and who honored his word less; nevertheless, his tricks always succeeded perfectly since he was well acquainted with this aspect of the world. *22*

Therefore, it is not necessary for a prince to have all of the abovementioned qualities, but it is very necessary for him to appear to have them. Furthermore, I shall be so bold as to assert this: that having them and practicing them at all times is harmful; and appearing to have them is useful; for instance, to seem merciful, faithful, humane, forthright, religious, and to be so; but his mind should be disposed in such a way that should it become necessary not to be so, he will be able and know how to change to the contrary. And it is essential to understand this: that a prince, and especially a new prince, cannot observe all those things by which men are considered good, for in order to maintain the state he is often obliged to act against his promise, against charity, against humanity, and against religion. And therefore, it is necessary that he have a mind *23* ready to turn itself according to the way the winds of Fortune and the change-ability of affairs require him; and, as I said above, as long as it is possible, he should not stray from the good, but he should know how to enter into evil when necessity commands.

A prince, therefore, must be very careful never to let anything slip from his   24
lips which is not full of the five qualities mentioned above: he should appear, upon seeing and hearing him, to be all mercy, all faithfulness, all integrity, all kindness, all religion. And there is nothing more necessary than to seem to possess this last quality. And men in general judge more by their eyes than their hands; for everyone can see but few can feel. Everyone sees what you seem to be, few perceive what you are, and those few do not dare to contradict the opinion of the many who have the majesty of the state to defend them; and in the actions of all men, and especially of princes, where there is no impartial arbiter, one must consider the final result. Let a prince therefore act to seize and to maintain the state; his methods will always be judged honorable and will be praised by all; for ordinary people are always deceived by appearances and by the outcome of a thing; and in the world there is nothing but ordinary people; and there is no room for the few, while the many have a place to lean on. A certain prince of the present day, whom I shall refrain from naming, preaches nothing but peace and faith, and to both one and the other he is en-tirely opposed; and both, if he had put them into practice, would have cost him many times over either his reputation or his state.

On Avoiding Being Despised and Hated

But since, concerning the qualities mentioned above, I have spoken about   25
the most important, I should like to discuss the others briefly in this general manner: that the prince, as was noted above, should think about avoiding those things which make him hated and despised; and when he has avoided this, he will have carried out his duties and will find no danger whatsoever in other vices. As I have said, what makes him hated above all else is being rapacious and a usurper of the property and the women of his subjects; he must refrain from this; and in most cases, so long as you do not deprive them of either their property or their honor, the majority of men live happily; and you have only to deal with the ambition of a few, who can be restrained without difficulty and by many means. What makes him despised is being considered change-able, frivolous, effeminate, cowardly, irresolute; from these qualities a prince must guard himself as if from a reef, and he must strive to make everyone rec-ognize in his actions greatness, spirit, dignity, and strength; and concerning the private affairs of his subjects, he must insist that his decision be irrevoca-ble; and he should maintain himself in such a way that no man could imagine that he can deceive or cheat him.

That prince who projects such an opinion of himself is greatly esteemed;   26
and it is difficult to conspire against a man with such a reputation and difficult to attack him, provided that he is understood to be of great merit and revered by his subjects. For a prince must have two fears: one, internal, concerning his subjects; the other, external, concerning foreign powers. From the latter he can defend himself by his good troops and friends; and he will always have good

friends if he has good troops; and internal affairs will always be stable when external affairs are stable, provided that they are not already disturbed by a conspiracy; and even if external conditions change, if he is properly organized and lives as I have said and does not lose control of himself, he will always be able to withstand every attack, just as I said that Nabis the Spartan did. But concerning his subjects, when external affairs do not change, he has to fear that they may conspire secretly: the prince secures himself from this by avoiding being hated or despised and by keeping the people satisfied with him; this is a necessary matter, as was treated above at length. And one of the most powerful remedies a prince has against conspiracies is not to be hated by the masses; for a man who plans a conspiracy always believes that he will satisfy the people by killing the prince; but when he thinks he might anger them, he cannot work up the courage to undertake such a deed, for the problems on the side of the conspirators are countless. And experience demonstrates that conspiracies have been many but few have been concluded successfully; for anyone who conspires cannot be alone, nor can he find companions except from amongst those whom he believes to be dissatisfied; and as soon as you have uncovered your intent to one dissatisfied man, you give him the means to make himself happy, since he can have everything he desires by uncovering the plot; so much is this so that, seeing a sure gain on the one hand and one doubtful and full of danger on the other, if he is to maintain faith with you he has to be either an unusually good friend or a completely determined enemy of the prince. And to treat the matter briefly, I say that on the part of the conspirator there is nothing but fear, jealousy, and the thought of punishment that terrifies him; but on the part of the prince there is the majesty of the principality, the laws, the defenses of friends, and the state to protect him; so that, with the good will of the people added to all these things, it is impossible for anyone to be so rash as to plot against him. For, where usually a conspirator has to be afraid before he executes his evil deed, in this case he must be afraid, having the people as an enemy, even after the crime is performed, nor can he hope to find any refuge because of this.

One could cite countless examples on this subject; but I want to satisfy myself with only one which occurred during the time of our fathers. Messer Annibale Bentivogli, prince of Bologna and grandfather of the present Messer Annibale, was murdered by the Canneschi family, who conspired against him; he left behind no heir except Messer Giovanni, then only a baby. As soon as this murder occurred, the people rose up and killed all the Canneschi. This came about because of the good will that the house of the Bentivogli enjoyed in those days; this good will was so great that with Annibale dead, and there being no one of that family left in the city who could rule Bologna, the Bolognese people, having heard that in Florence there was one of the Bentivogli blood who was believed until that time to be the son of a blacksmith, went to Florence to find him, and they gave him the control of that city; it was ruled by him until Messer Giovanni became of age to rule. 27

I conclude, therefore, that a prince must be little concerned with conspiracies when the people are well disposed toward him; but when the populace is hostile and regards him with hatred, he must fear everything and everyone. And well-organized states and wise princes have, with great diligence, taken 28 care not to anger the nobles and to satisfy the common people and keep them contented; for this is one of the most important concerns that a prince has.

Considerations

1. Summarize Machiavelli's views in a one-page essay.
2. Summarize Machiavelli's views in one sentence. Then gather together all the class members' definitions and classify them into several categories. In an essay, describe each category, and explain how it differs from the others. How do you account for the varied perspectives on Machiavelli?
3. Look up the adjective *Machiavellian* in an unabridged dictionary. Then decide if the definition distorts Machiavelli's ideas or describes them accurately. What is the connotation of the term?
4. A *paradox* is a statement which seems self-contradictory yet can be shown to be logically sound. Find several examples of seeming paradoxes in Machiavelli's advice, and explain how he resolves them.
5. Machiavelli is cynical about human nature. (See especially paragraphs 7, 14, 21, 24.) Is cynicism typical, or necessary, in the politician? Explain, using examples from history and/or the contemporary world of politics.
6. Machiavelli counsels that "one must consider the final result." What is the final result he refers to here, and does he suggest that such an end justifies any means? Do you agree?
7. Machiavelli claims that he wants to keep the common people contented. How would he accomplish this? Does this goal make him a humanitarian? Why or why not?
8. How might Machiavelli's advice about political power be extended or applied to our social interactions?
9. Is Machiavelli's advice out of date? Why or why not?

Dear Professor Einstein

Sigmund Freud

Vienna, September 1932

Dear Professor Einstein: When I learned of your intention to invite me to a   *1*
mutual exchange of views upon a subject which not only interested you per-

Sigmund Freud (1856–1939) was the founder of psychoanalysis, and his theories have had a tremendous impact on twentieth-century thought. Here he responds to a letter from Albert Einstein in which Einstein, acting on a proposal from the League of Nations, has invited Freud to offer his views on the causes of war.

sonally but seemed deserving, too, of public interest, I cordially assented. I expected you to choose a problem lying on the borderland of the knowable, as it stands today, a theme which each of us, physicist and psychologist, might approach from his own angle, to meet at last on common ground, though setting out from different premises. Thus the question which you put me — what is to be done to rid mankind of the war menace? — took me by surprise. And, next, I was dumbfounded by the thought of my (of *our*, I almost wrote) incompetence; for this struck me as being a matter of practical politics, the statesman's proper study. But then I realized that you did not raise the question in your capacity of scientist or physicist, but as a lover of his fellow men, who responded to the call of the League of Nations much as Fridtjof Nansen, the Polar explorer, took on himself the task of succoring homeless and starving victims of the World War. And, next, I reminded myself that I was not being called on to formulate practical proposals, but, rather, to explain how this question of preventing wars strikes a psychologist.

But here, too, you have stated the gist of the matter in your letter — and   2
taken the wind out of my sails! Still, I will gladly follow in your wake and content myself with endorsing your conclusions, which, however, I propose to amplify to the best of my knowledge or surmise.

You begin with the relations between Might and Right, and this is assuredly   3
the proper starting point for our inquiry. But, for the term "might," I would substitute a tougher and more telling word: "violence." In right and violence we have today an obvious antinomy. It is easy to prove that one has evolved from the other, and, when we go back to origins and examine primitive conditions, the solution of the problem follows easily enough. I must beg your indulgence if in what follows I speak of well-known, admitted facts as though they were new data; the context necessitates this method.

Conflicts of interest between man and man are resolved, in principle, by the   4
recourse to violence. It is the same in the animal kingdom, from which man cannot claim exclusion; nevertheless men are also prone to conflicts of opinion, touching, on occasion, the loftiest peaks of abstract thought, which seem to call for settlement by quite another method. This refinement is, however, a late development. To start with, brute force was the factor which, in small communities, decided points of ownership and the question which man's will was to prevail. Very soon physical force was implemented, then replaced, by the use of various adjuncts; he proved the victor whose weapon was the better, or handled the more skillfully. Now, for the first time, with the coming of weapons, superior brains began to oust brute force, but the object of the conflict remained the same: one party was to be constrained, by the injury done him or impairment of his strength, to retract a claim or a refusal. This end is most effectively gained when the opponent is definitively put out of action — in other words, is killed. This procedure has two advantages; the enemy cannot renew hostilities, and, secondly, his fate deters others from following his example. Moreover, the slaughter of a foe gratifies an instinctive craving — a point to which we shall revert hereafter. However, another consideration may be set off against this will to kill: the possibility of using an enemy for servile tasks if his spirit be broken and his life spared. Here violence finds an outlet not in slaughter but in subjugation. Hence springs the practice of giving quarter;

but the victor, having from now on to reckon with the craving for revenge that rankles in his victim, forfeits to some extent his personal security.

Thus, under primitive conditions, it is superior force — brute violence, or   5 violence backed by arms — that lords it everywhere. We know that in the course of evolution this state of things was modified, a path was traced that led away from violence to law. But what was this path? Surely it issued from a single verity; that the superiority of one strong man can be overcome by an alliance of many weaklings, that *l'union fait la force*. Brute force is overcome by union, the allied might of scattered units makes good its right against the isolated giant. Thus we may define "right" (i.e., law) as the might of a community. Yet it, too, is nothing else than violence, quick to attack whatever individual stands in its path, and it employs the selfsame methods, follows like ends, with but one difference; it is the communal, not individual, violence that has its way. But, for the transition from crude violence to the reign of law, a certain psychological condition must first obtain. The union of the majority must be stable and enduring. If its sole raison d'être be the discomfiture of some overweening individual and, after his downfall, it be dissolved, it leads to nothing. Some other man, trusting to his superior power, will seek to reinstate the rule of violence and the cycle will repeat itself unendingly. Thus the union of the people must be permanent and well organized; it must enact rules to meet the risk of possible revolts; must step up machinery ensuring that its rules — the laws — are observed and that such acts of violence as the laws demand are duly carried out. This recognition of a community of interests engenders among the members of the group a feeling of unity and fraternal solidarity which constitutes its real strength.

So far I have set out what seems to me the kernel of the matter: the sup-   6 pression of brute force by the transfer of power to a larger combination, founded on the community of sentiments linking up its members. All the rest is mere tautology and glosses. Now, the position is simple enough so long as the community consists of a number of equipollent individuals. The laws of such a group can determine to what extent the individual must forfeit his personal freedom, the right of using personal force as an instrument of violence, to ensure the safety of the group. But such a combination is only theoretically possible; in practice the situation is always complicated by the fact that, from the outset, the group includes elements of unequal power, men and women, elders and children, and very soon, as a result of war and conquest, victors and the vanquished — i.e., masters and slaves — as well. From this time on the common law takes notice of these inequalities of power, laws are made by and for the rulers, giving the servile classes fewer rights. Thenceforward there exist within the state two factors making for legal instability, but legislative evolution, too: First, the attempts by members of the ruling class to set themselves above the law's restrictions and, secondly, the constant struggle of the ruled to extend their rights and see each gain embodied in the code, replacing legal disabilities by equal laws for all. The second of these tendencies will be particularly marked when there takes place a positive mutation of the balance of power within the community, the frequent outcome of certain historical conditions. In such cases the laws may gradually be adjusted to the changed conditions or (as more usually ensues) the ruling class is loath to reckon with the new developments, the result being insurrections and civil wars, a period when law is in abeyance and force once more the arbiter, followed by a new regime of law. There is another factor of constitutional change, which operates in a wholly pacific manner, viz.: the cultural evolution of the mass of the community; this factor, however, is of a different order and can only be dealt with later.

Thus we see that, even within the group itself, the exercise of violence cannot be avoided when conflicting interests are at stake. But the common needs and habits of men who live in fellowship under the same sky favor a speedy issue of such conflicts and, this being so, the possibilities of peaceful solutions make steady progress. Yet the most casual glance at world history will show an unending series of conflicts between one community and another, or a group of others, between large and smaller units, between cities, countries, races, tribes and kingdoms, almost all of which were settled by the ordeal of war. Such wars end either in pillage or in conquest and its fruits, the downfall of the loser. No single all-embracing judgment can be passed on these wars of aggrandizement. Some, like the war between the Mongols and the Turks, have led to unmitigated misery; others, however, have furthered the transition from violence to law, since they brought larger units into being, within whose limits a recourse to violence was banned and a new regime determined all disputes. Thus the Roman conquests brought that boon, the *pax romana*, to the Mediterranean lands. The French kings' lust for aggrandizement created a new France, flourishing in peace and unity. Paradoxical as it sounds, we must admit that warfare well might serve to pave the way to that unbroken peace we so desire, for it is war that brings vast empires into being, within whose frontiers all warfare is proscribed by a strong central power. In practice, however, this end is not attained, for as a rule the fruits of victory are but short-lived, the new-created unit falls asunder once again, generally because there can be no true cohesion between the parts that violence has welded. Hitherto, moreover, such conquests have only led to aggregations which, for all their magnitude, had limits, and disputes between these units could be resolved only by recourse to arms. For humanity at large the sole result of all these military enterprises was that, instead of frequent not to say incessant little wars, they had now to face great wars which, for all they came less often, were so much the more destructive.

Regarding the world of today the same conclusion holds good, and you, too, have reached it, though by a shorter path. There is but one sure way of ending war and that is the establishment, by common consent, of a central control which shall have the last word in every conflict of interests. For this, two things are needed: first, the creation of such a supreme court of judicature; secondly, its investment with adequate executive force. Unless this second requirement be fulfilled, the first is unavailing. Obviously the League of Nations, acting as a Supreme Court, fulfills the first condition; it does not fulfill the second. It has no force at its disposal and can only get it if the members of the new body, its constituent nations, furnish it. And, as things are, this is a forlorn hope. Still we should be taking a very shortsighted view of the League of Nations were we to ignore the fact that here is an experiment the like of which has rarely — never before, perhaps, on such a scale — been attempted in the course of history. It is an attempt to acquire the authority (in other words, coercive influence), which hitherto reposed exclusively in the possession of power, by calling into play certain idealistic attitudes of mind. We have seen that there are two factors of cohesion in a community: violent compulsion and ties of sentiment ("identifications," in technical parlance) between the members of the group. If one of these factors becomes inoperative, the other may still suffice to hold the group together. Obviously such notions as these can only be significant when they are the expression of a deeply rooted sense of unity, shared by all. It is necessary, therefore, to gauge the efficacy of such sentiments. History tells us that, on occasion, they have been effective. For example, the Panhellenic conception, the Greeks' awareness of superiority over their barbarian neighbors, which found expression in the Amphictyonies, the Oracles and Games, was strong enough to humanize the methods of warfare as between Greeks, though inevitably it failed to prevent conflicts between different elements of the Hellenic race or even to deter a city or group of cities from joining forces with their racial foe, the Persians, for the discomfiture of a rival. The solidarity of Christendom in the Renaissance age was no more effective, despite its vast authority, in hindering Christian nations, large, and small alike, from calling the sultan to their aid. And, in our times, we look in vain for some such unifying notion whose authority would be unquestioned. It is all too clear that the nationalistic ideas, paramount today in every country, operate in quite a contrary direction. Some there are who hold that the Bolshevist conceptions may make an end of war, but, as things are, the goal is very far away and, perhaps, could only be attained after a spell of brutal internecine warfare. Thus it would seem that any effort to replace brute force by the might of an ideal is, under present conditions, doomed to fail. Our logic is at fault if we ignore the fact that right is founded on brute force and even today needs violence to maintain it.

I now can comment on another of your statements. You are amazed that it is so easy to infect men with the war fever, and you surmise that man has in him an active instinct for hatred and destruction, amenable to such stimulations. I entirely agree with you. I believe in the existence of this instinct and have been recently at pains to study its manifestations. In this connection may I set out a fragment of that knowledge of the instincts, which we psychoanalysts, after so many tentative essays and gropings in the dark, have compassed? We assume that human instincts are of two kinds: those that conserve and unify, which we call "erotic" (in the meaning Plato gives to *Eros* in his *Symposium*), or else "sexual" (explicitly extending the popular connotation of "sex"); and, secondly, the instincts to destroy and kill, which we assimilate as the aggressive or destructive instincts. These are, as you perceive, the well-known opposites, Love and Hate, transformed into theoretical entities; they are, perhaps, another aspect of those eternal polarities, attraction and repulsion, which fall within your province. But we must be chary of passing overhastily to the notions of good and evil. Each of these instincts is every whit as indispensable as its opposite and all the phenomena of life derive from their activity, whether they work in concert or in opposition. It seems that an instinct of either category can operate but rarely in isolation; it is always blended ("alloyed," as we say) with a certain dosage of its opposite, which modifies its aim or even, in certain circumstances, is a prime condition of its attainment. Thus the instinct of self-preservation is certainly of an erotic nature, but to gain its end this very instinct necessitates aggressive action. In the same way the love instinct, when directed to a specific object, calls for an admixture of the acquisitive instinct if it is to enter into effective possession of that object. It is the difficulty of isolating the two kinds of instinct in their manifestations that has so long prevented us from recognizing them.

If you will travel with me a little further on this road, you will find that human affairs are complicated in yet another way. Only exceptionally does an action follow on the stimulus of a single instinct, which is per se a blend of Eros and destructiveness. As a rule several motives of similar composition concur to bring about the act. This fact was duly noted by a colleague of yours, Professor G. C. Lichtenberg, sometime Professor of Physics at Göttingen; he was perhaps even more eminent as a psychologist than as a physical scientist. He evolved the notion of a "Compass-card of Motives," and wrote: "The efficient motives impelling man to act can be classified like the 32 Winds, and described in the same manner, e.g. *Food-Food-Fame* or *Fame-Fame-Food*." Thus, when a nation is summoned to engage in war, a whole gamut of human motives may respond to this appeal; high and low motives, some openly avowed, others slurred over. The lust for aggression and destruction is certainly included; the innumerable cruelties of history and man's daily life confirm its prevalence and strength. The stimulation of these destructive impulses by appeals to idealism and the erotic instinct naturally facilitates their release. Musing on the atrocities recorded on history's page, we feel that the ideal motive has often served as a camouflage for the lust of destruction; sometimes, as with the cruelties of the Inquisition, it seems that, while the ideal motives occupied the foreground of consciousness, they drew their strength from the destructive instinct submerged in the unconscious. Both interpretations are feasible.

You are interested, I know, in the prevention of war, not in our theories, and I keep this fact in mind. Yet I would like to dwell a little longer on this destructive instinct, which is seldom given the attention that its importance warrants. With the least of speculative efforts we are led to conclude that this instinct functions in every living being, striving to work its ruin and reduce life to its primal state of inert matter. Indeed it might well be called the "death instinct"; whereas the erotic instincts vouch for the struggle to live on. The death instinct becomes an impulse to destruction when, with the aid of certain organs, it directs its action outward, against external objects. The living being, that is to say, defends its own existence by destroying foreign bodies. But, in one of its activities, the death instinct is operative *within* the living being and we have sought to trace back a number of normal and pathological phenomena to this *introversion* of the destructive instinct. We have even committed the heresy of explaining the origin of human conscience by some such "turning inward" of the aggressive impulse. Obviously, when this internal tendency operates on too large a scale, it is no trivial matter, rather a positively morbid state of things; whereas the diversion of the destructive impulse toward the external world must have beneficial effects. Here is, then, the biological justification for all those vile, pernicious propensities which we now are combating. We can but own that they are really more akin to nature than this our stand against them, which, in fact, remains to be accounted for.

All this may give you the impression that our theories amount to a species *12*
of mythology and a gloomy one at that! But does not every natural science lead
ultimately to this — a sort of mythology? Is it otherwise today with your physical science?

The upshot of these observations, as bearing on the subject in hand, is that *13*
there is no likelihood of our being able to suppress humanity's aggressive tendencies. In some happy corners of the earth, they say, where nature brings forth
abundantly whatever man desires, there flourish races whose lives go gently
by, unknowing of aggression or constraint. This I can hardly credit; I would
like further details about these happy folk. The Bolshevists, too, aspire to do
away with human aggressiveness by ensuring the satisfaction of material needs
and enforcing equality between man and man. To me this hope seems vain.
Meanwhile, they busily perfect their armaments, and their hatred of outsiders
is not the least of the factors of cohesion among themselves. In any case, as
you, too, have observed, complete suppression of man's aggressive tendencies
is not in issue; what we may try is to divert it into a channel other than that
of warfare.

From our "mythology" of the instincts we may easily deduce a formula for *14*
an indirect method of eliminating war. If the propensity for war be due to the
destructive instinct, we have always its counteragent, Eros, to our hand. All
that produces ties of sentiment between man and man must serve us as war's
antidote. These ties are of two kinds. First, such relations as those toward a
beloved object, void though they be of sexual intent. The psychoanalyst need
feel no compunction in mentioning "love" in this connection; religion uses
the same language; Love thy neighbor as thyself. A pious injunction easy to
enounce, but hard to carry out! The other bond of sentiment is by way of identification. All that brings out the significant resemblances between men calls
into play this feeling of community, identification, whereon is founded, in large
measure, the whole edifice of human society.

In your strictures on the abuse of authority I find another suggestion for an *15*
indirect attack on the war impulse. That men are divided into leaders and the
led is but another manifestation of their inborn and irremediable inequality.
The second class constitutes the vast majority; they need a high command to
make decisions for them, to which decisions they usually bow without demur.
In this context we would point out that men should be at greater pains than
heretofore to form a superior class of independent thinkers, unamenable to in-
timidation and fervent in the quest of truth, whose function it would be to guide
the masses dependent on their lead. There is no need to point out how little
the rule of politicians and the Church's ban on liberty of thought encourage
such a new creation. The ideal conditions would obviously be found in a community where every man subordinated his instinctive life to the dictates of
reason. Nothing less than this could bring about so thorough and so durable a
union between men, even if this involved the severance of mutual ties of sentiment. But surely such a hope is utterly utopian, as things are. The other indirect methods of preventing war are certainly more feasible, but entail no quick
results. They conjure up an ugly picture of mills that grind so slowly that, before the flour is ready, men are dead of hunger.

As you see, little good comes of consulting a theoretician, aloof from worldly *16* contacts, on practical and urgent problems! Better it were to tackle each successive crisis with means that we have ready to our hands. However, I would like to deal with a question which, though it is not mooted in your letter, interests me greatly. Why do we, you and I and many another, protest so vehemently against war, instead of just accepting it as another of life's odious importunities? For it seems a natural thing enough, biologically sound and practically unavoidable. I trust you will not be shocked by my raising such a question. For the better conduct of an inquiry it may be well to don a mask of feigned aloofness. The answer to my query may run as follows: Because every man has a right over his own life and war destroys lives that were full of promise; it forces the individual into situations that shame his manhood, obliging him to murder fellow men, against his will; it ravages material amenities, the fruits of human toil, and much besides. Moreover wars, as now conducted, afford no scope for acts of heroism according to the old ideals and, given the high perfection of modern arms, war today would mean the sheer extermination of one of the combatants, if not of both. This is so true, so obvious, that we can but wonder why the conduct of war is not banned by general consent. Doubtless either of the points I have just made is open to debate. It may be asked if the community, in its turn, cannot claim a right over the individual lives of its members. Moreover, all forms of war cannot be indiscriminately condemned; so long as there are nations and empires, each prepared callously to exterminate its rival, all alike must be equipped for war. But we will not dwell on any of these problems; they lie outside the debate to which you have invited me. I pass on to another point, the basis, as it strikes me, of our common hatred of war. It is this: we cannot do otherwise than hate it. Pacifists we are, since our organic nature wills us thus to be. Hence it comes easy to us to find arguments that justify our standpoint.

This point, however, calls for elucidation. Here is the way in which I see it. *17* The cultural development of mankind (some, I know, prefer to call it civilization) has been in progress since immemorial antiquity. To this process we owe all that is best in our composition, but also much that makes for human suffering. Its origins and causes are obscure, its issue is uncertain, but some of its characteristics are easy to perceive. It well may lead to the extinction of mankind, for it impairs the sexual function in more than one respect, and even today the uncivilized races and the backward classes of all nations are multiplying more rapidly than the cultured elements. This process may, perhaps, be likened to the effects of domestication on certain animals — it clearly involves physical changes of structure — but the view that cultural development is an organic process of this order has not yet become generally familiar. The psychic changes which accompany this process of cultural change are striking, and not to be gainsaid. They consist in the progressive rejection of instinctive ends and a scaling down of instinctive reactions. Sensations which delighted our forefathers have become neutral or unbearable to us; and, if our ethical and aesthetic ideals have undergone a change, the causes of this are ultimately organic. On the psychological side two of the most important phenomena of culture are, firstly, a strengthening of the intellect, which tends to master our instinctive life, and, secondly, an introversion of the aggressive impulse, with all its consequent benefits and perils. Now, war runs most emphatically counter to the psychic disposition imposed on us by the growth of culture; we are therefore bound to resent war, to find it utterly intolerable. With pacifists like us it is not merely an intellectual and affective repulsion, but a constitutional intolerance, an idiosyncrasy in its most drastic form. And it would seem that the aesthetic ignominies of warfare play almost as large a part in this repugnance as war's atrocities.

How long have we to wait before the rest of men turn pacifist? Impossible *18* to say, and yet perhaps our hope that these two factors — man's cultural disposition and a well-founded dread of the form that future wars will take — may serve to put an end to war in the near future, is not chimerical. But by what ways or by-ways this will come about we cannot guess. Meanwhile, we may rest on the assurance that whatever makes for cultural development is working also against war.

With kindest regards and, should this *exposé* prove a disappointment to you, *19* my sincere regrets.

> Yours,
> Sigmund Freud

Considerations

1. How does Freud, in his letter to Albert Einstein, justify a scientist's speaking out on what he calls a "matter of practical politics" — war? Would a scientist's view on an issue of political power carry any more weight than a layman's? Why or why not?
2. How does Freud see war as biologically justified? Does he see pacifism as biologically justified too? Explain.
3. What does Freud reveal here about the connections between biology and psychology? Does the issue of power make the connections any clearer?
4. Freud claims that every natural science leads to "a sort of mythology." Explain what he means, and in the process try to come up with a good definition of myth. How powerful are the mythologies that science generates?

Connections

1. How does Freud's perspective on war — and fighting — differ from Machiavelli's?
2. Use Freud's views on the biological justifications for war and for pacifism to support or dispute any of the material in Chapter 2, The Origins of the Nuclear Arms Race.

Power over Opinion

Bertrand Russell

It is easy to make out a case for the view that opinion is omnipotent, and
that all other forms of power are derived from it. Armies are useless unless the
soldiers believe in the cause for which they are fighting, or, in the case of mer-
cenaries, have confidence in the ability of their commanders to lead them to
victory. Law is impotent unless it is generally respected. Economic institutions
depend upon respect for the law; consider, for example, what would happen to
banking if the average citizen had no objection to forgery. Religious opinion
has often proved itself more powerful than the State. If, in any country, a large
majority were in favor of Socialism, capitalism would become unworkable. On
such grounds it might be said that opinion is the ultimate power in social affairs.

But this would be only a half-truth, since it ignores the forces which cause
opinion. While it is true that opinion is an essential element in military force,
it is equally true that military force may generate opinion. Almost every European country has, at this moment, the religion which was that of its government in the late sixteenth century, and this must be attributed mainly to the
control of persecution and propaganda by means of the armed forces in the
several countries. It is traditional to regard opinion as due to mental causes,
but this is only true of the immediate causes: in the background, there is usually force in the service of some creed.

Per contra, a creed never has force at its command to begin with, and the
first steps in the production of a widespread opinion must be taken by means
of persuasion alone.

We have thus a kind of see-saw: first, pure persuasion leading to the conversion of a minority; then force exerted to secure that the rest of the community shall be exposed to the right propaganda; and, finally, a genuine belief
on the part of the great majority, which makes the use of force again unnecessary. Some bodies of opinion never get beyond the first stage, some reach the
second and then fail, others are successful in all three. The Society of Friends
has never got beyond persuasion. The other Nonconformists acquired the forces
of the State in the time of Cromwell, but failed in their propaganda after they
had seized power. The Catholic Church, after three centuries of persuasion,
captured the State in the time of Constantine, and then, by force, established
a system of propaganda which converted almost all the pagans and enabled

*Bertrand Russell (1872–1970) was a British philosopher, mathematician, and
social reformer. He studied, then lectured, at Cambridge University, and also taught
at various universities in the United States. In 1950 he was awarded the Nobel
Prize in Literature. Russell was imprisoned for his pacifist beliefs and for civil disobedience on behalf of nuclear disarmament.*

Christianity to survive the Barbarian invasion. The Marxist creed has reached the second stage, if not the third, in Russia, but elsewhere is still in the first stage.

There are, however, some important instances of influence on opinion with-   5
out the aid of force at any stage. Of these the most notable is the rise of science. At the present day, science, in civilized countries, is encouraged by the State, but in its early days this was not the case. Galileo was made to recant, Newton was estopped by being made Master of the Mint, Lavoisier was guillotined on the ground that *"la République n'a pas besoin de savants."* Nevertheless these men, and a few others like them, were the creators of the modern world; their effect upon social life has been greater than that of any other men known to history, not excluding Christ and Aristotle. The only other man whose influence was of comparable importance was Pythagoras, and his existence is doubtful.

It is customary nowadays to decry Reason as a force in human affairs, yet   6
the rise of science is an overwhelming argument on the other side. The men of science proved to intelligent laymen that a certain kind of intellectual outlook ministers to military prowess and to wealth; these ends were so ardently desired that the new intellectual outlook overcame that of the Middle Ages, in spite of the force of tradition and the revenues of the Church and the sentiments associated with Catholic theology. The world ceased to believe that Joshua caused the sun to stand still, because Copernican astronomy was useful in navigation; it abandoned Aristotle's physics, because Galileo's theory of falling bodies made it possible to calculate the trajectory of a cannon-ball; it rejected the story of the flood because geology is useful in mining; and so on. It is now generally recognized that science is indispensable both in war and in peacetime industry, and that, without science, a nation can be neither rich nor powerful.

All this effect on opinion has been achieved by science merely through ap-   7
peal to fact: what science had to say in the way of general theories might be questionable, but its results in the way of technique were patent to all. Science gave the white man the mastery of the world, which he has begun to lose only since the Japanese acquired his technique.

From this example, something may be learned as to the power of Reason in   8
general. In the case of science, Reason prevailed over prejudice because it provided means of realizing existing purposes, and because the proof that it did so was overwhelming. Those who maintain that Reason has no power in human affairs overlook these two conditions. If, in the name of Reason, you summon a man to alter his fundamental purposes — to pursue, say, the general happiness rather than his own power — you will fail, and you will deserve to fail, since Reason alone cannot determine the ends of life. And you will fail equally if you attack deep-seated prejudices while your argument is still open to question, or is so difficult that only men of science can see its force. But if you can prove, by evidence which is convincing to every sane man who takes the trouble to examine it, that you possess a means of facilitating the satisfaction of existing desires, you may hope, with a certain degree of confidence, that men will ultimately believe what you say. This, of course, involves the proviso

that the existing desires which you can satisfy are those of men who have power or are capable of acquiring it.

So much for the power of Reason in human affairs. I come now to another 9 form of un-forceful persuasion, namely, that of the founders of religions. Here the process, reduced to its bare formula, is this: if a certain proposition is true, I shall be able to realize my desires; therefore I wish this proposition to be true; therefore, unless I have exceptional intellectual self-control, I believe it to be true. Orthodoxy and a virtuous life, I am told, will enable me to go to heaven when I die; there is pleasure in believing this, and therefore I shall probably believe it if it is forcibly presented to me. The cause of belief, here, is not, as in science, the evidence of fact, but the pleasant feelings derived from belief, together with sufficient vigor of assertion in the environment to make the belief seem not incredible.

The power of advertisement comes under the same head. It is pleasant to 10 believe in so-and-so's pills, since it gives you hope of better health; it is possible to believe in them, if you find their excellence very frequently and emphatically asserted. Nonrational propaganda, like the rational sort, must appeal to existing desires, but it substitutes iteration for the appeal to fact.

The opposition between a rational and an irrational appeal is, in practice, 11 less clear-cut than in the above analysis. Usually there is *some* rational evidence, though not enough to be conclusive; the irrationality consists in attaching too much weight to it. Belief, when it is not simply traditional, is a product of several factors: desire, evidence, and iteration. When either the desire or the evidence is nil, there will be no belief; when there is no outside assertion, belief will only arise in exceptional characters, such as founders of religions, scientific discoverers, and lunatics. To produce a mass belief, of the sort that is socially important, all three elements must exist in some degree; but if one element is increased while another is diminished, the resulting amount of belief may be unchanged. More propaganda is necessary to cause acceptance of a belief for which there is little evidence than of one for which the evidence is strong, if both are equally satisfactory to desire; and so on.

It is through the potency of iteration that the holders of power acquire their 12 capacity of influencing belief. Official propaganda has old and new forms. The Church has a technique which is in many ways admirable, but was developed before the days of printing, and is therefore less effective than it used to be. The State has employed certain methods for many centuries: the King's head on coins; coronations and jubilees; the spectacular aspects of the army and navy, and so on. But these are far less potent than the more modern methods: education, the press, the cinema, the radio, etc. These are employed to the utmost in totalitarian States, but it is too soon to judge of their success.

I said that propaganda must appeal to desire, and this may be confirmed by 13 the failure of State propaganda when opposed to national feeling, as in large parts of Austria-Hungary before the War, in Ireland until 1922, and in India down to the present time. Propaganda is only successful when it is in harmony with something in the patient: his desire for an immortal soul, for health, for the greatness of his nation, or what not. Where there is no such fundamental reason for acquiescence, the assertions of authority are viewed with cynical skepticism. One of the advantages of democracy, from the governmental point of view, is that it makes the average citizen easier to deceive, since he regards the government as *his* government. Opposition to a war which is not swiftly successful arises much less readily in a democracy than under any other form of constitution. In a democracy, a majority can only turn against the government by first admitting to themselves that they were mistaken in formerly thinking well of their chosen leaders, which is difficult and unpleasant.

Systematic propaganda, on a large scale, is at present, in democratic coun- *14* tries, divided between the churches, business advertisers, political parties, the plutocracy, and the State. In the main, all these forces work on the same side, with the exception of political parties in opposition, and even they, if they have any hope of office, are unlikely to oppose the fundamentals of State propaganda. In the totalitarian countries, the State is virtually the sole propagandist. But in spite of all the power of modern propaganda, I do not believe that the official view would be widely accepted in the event of defeat in war. This situation suddenly gives to a government the kind of impotence that belongs to alien governments opposed by nationalist feeling; and the more the expectation of victory has been used to stimulate warlike ardor, the greater will be the reaction when it is found that victory is unobtainable. It is therefore to be expected that the next war, like the last, will end with a crop of revolutions, which will be more fierce than those of 1917 and 1918 because the war will have been more destructive. It is to be hoped that rulers realize the risk they will run of being put to death by the mob, which is at least as great as the risk that soldiers will run of death at the hands of the enemy.

It is easy to overestimate the power of official propaganda, especially when *15* there is no competition. In so far as it devotes itself to causing belief in false propositions of which time will prove the falsity, it is in as bad a position as the Aristotelians in their opposition to Galileo. Given two opposing groups of States, each of which endeavors to instill the certainty of victory in war, one side, if not both, must experience a dramatic refutation of official statements. When all opposing propaganda is forbidden, rulers are likely to think that they can cause anything to be believed, and so become overweening and careless. Even lies need competition if they are to retain their vigor.

Power over opinion, like all other forms of power, tends to coalescence and *16* concentration, leading logically to a State monopoly. But even apart from war it would be rash to assume that a State monopoly of propaganda must make a government invulnerable. In the long run, those who possess the power are likely to become too flagrantly indifferent to the interests of the common man, as the Popes were in the time of Luther. Sooner or later, some new Luther will challenge the authority of the State, and, like his predecessor, be so quickly successful that it will be impossible to suppress him. This will happen because the rulers will believe that it cannot happen. But whether the change will be for the better it is impossible to foresee.

The effect of organization and unification, in the matter of propaganda as *17* in other matters, is to delay revolution, but to make it more violent when it comes. When only one doctrine is officially allowed, men get no practice in thinking or in weighing alternatives; only a great wave of passionate revolt can dethrone orthodoxy; and in order to make the opposition sufficiently wholehearted and violent to achieve success, it will seem necessary to deny even what was true in governmental dogma. The only thing that will not be denied will be the importance of immediately establishing *some* orthodoxy, since this will be considered necessary for victory. From a rationalist standpoint, therefore, the likelihood of revolution in a totalitarian State is not necessarily a ground for rejoicing. What is more to be desired is a gradual increase in the sense of security, leading to a lessening of zeal, and giving an opening for laziness — the greatest of all virtues in the ruler of a totalitarian State, with the sole exception of nonexistence.

Considerations

1. Summarize Russell's distinction between the power of science and the power of religion and advertising. Examine the basis for these two types of power, that is, the role of both reason and belief in each.
2. Suggest some concrete modern examples of the power of persuasion in religion and advertising, from your own experience if possible, to illustrate the parallels between the two. Include for each the function of desire, evidence, and iteration (frequent repetition).
3. Russell's piece was written in 1938, before World War II. Yet some of his comments on war, on the failure of propaganda, and on turning against the government are applicable to later events — namely, the Vietnam War and Watergate. Explain how these comments might apply to such events.
4. In 1938 Russell said it was "too soon to judge" the success of "modern methods" of propaganda. Can we judge the success now? What's the verdict?

Connections

1. Sigmund Freud is skeptical about the power of an ideal over brute force, and Bertrand Russell about the power of reason alone over desire. How are their views similar, and how do they differ? Have events of the twentieth century justified such pessimism?
2. Look at two articles in Chapter 3, The Frontier Indians: Kenneth Morrison's study of power among the Abenaki Indians and James Axtell's "The European Failure to Convert the Indians." How would Russell see the relation between power and religion among the Abenaki? How would Machiavelli describe the struggle between the Indians and the European priests? What can you conclude?
3. Look at the pieces in Chapter 2, The Origins of the Nuclear Arms Race, then analyze the *propaganda* for one side or the other according to Russell. Evaluate the mixture of rational and irrational appeal; the role of traditional belief; and the degree to which that position is the product of desire, evidence, and iteration.

4. After reading the John Locke and Jean Jacques Rousseau selections in Chapter 6, The Nature of Learning, determine which of the two views would be more consistent with Russell's ideas about propaganda. Explain why.

The Entrails of Power

Elias Canetti

Seizing and Incorporation

The psychology of seizing and incorporating, like that of eating in general, is still completely unexplored. We tend to take the whole process for granted and never reflect on the mysteriousness of much that occurs in the course of it. There is nothing about us which is more strongly primitive. It is something we share with animals, but even this strange fact has not so far made us pay more attention to it.   *1*

The approach, with hostile intent, of one creature to another falls into several distinct acts, each of which has its particular traditional significance. First there is the lying in wait for prey; the prey is marked down long before it is aware of our designs on it. With feelings of pleasure and approval it is contemplated, observed and kept watch over; it is seen as meat whilst it is still alive, and so intensely and irrevocably seen as meat that nothing can deflect the watcher's determination to get hold of it. Already while he is prowling round it he feels that it *belongs* to him. From the moment he selects it as his prey, he thinks of it as incorporated into himself.   *2*

This watching and lying in wait for prey is a state of such peculiar tension that it can acquire a significance of its own independent of circumstances. It is a state which one tends to prolong. Later it may be induced for its own sake, without reference to any immediate prospect of prey. But man does not lie in ambush and turn persecutor with impunity. Anything of this kind which he actively undertakes, he also experiences passively in himself, in exactly the same form, only more strongly, for his greater intelligence is aware of more dangers and doubles the torment of being persecuted.   *3*

Man is not always strong enough to obtain his prey directly. The skill and experience in pursuit which he has acquired have resulted in his developing   *4*

Elias Canetti (b. 1905) was born in Bulgaria and educated in England and Central Europe, earning a Ph.D. from the University of Vienna in 1929. He now lives in London, where he writes plays, novels, and literary criticism. His special interests — he claims — are anthropology, history, psychiatry, philosophy, sociology, psychology, ancient Egyptian civilizations, and the history of religions. This piece is excerpted from his thought-provoking Crowds and Power *(1962).*

all kinds of complicated traps. Often he makes use of the power of transformation which is his specific gift and appears disguised as the animal he is after. He acts it so well that it believes him. This manner of trapping an animal may be termed flattery. The animal is told "I am like you. I am you. You can safely let me come near you."

After the stealthy approach and the leap — treated in another context — the next thing is the first *touching* of the prey. This is perhaps what is feared most. The fingers of the attacker feel what will soon belong to his whole body. Contact through the other senses, sight, hearing and smell, is not nearly so dangerous. With them there can be space between the attacker and the victim and, as long as this space exists, nothing is finally decided and there is still some chance of escape. The sensation of touch, on the other hand, is the forerunner of tasting. The fairytale witch asks her victim to stretch out a finger so that she can feel whether he is fat enough to eat.

The design of one body on the other becomes concrete from the moment of touching. Even at the lowest levels of life this moment has something decisive about it. It contains the oldest terrors; we dream of it, we imagine it, and civilized life is nothing but a sustained effort to avoid it. Whether resistance is continued after this moment, or is given up completely, depends on the ratio of power between the toucher and the touched, or rather on what the latter imagines this ratio to be. Usually he will fight on to try and save his skin and only if the power confronting him appears overwhelming will he abandon the attempt. The touch to which one resigns oneself because all resistance appears hopeless — and particularly so as regards the future — has, in our society, become the *arrest*. The feel of the hand of authority on his shoulder is usually enough to make a man give himself up without having to be actually seized. He cowers and goes quietly. He maintains an appearance of composure, even though it is not everywhere that this is justified by what is likely to happen to him subsequently.

The next stage of approach is the act of seizure. The fingers of the hand form a hollow into which they try to compress part of the creature they touch. They do this without regard to the shape and organic cohesion of the prey. Whether they injure it or not at this stage is irrelevant; it is simply that some part of its body has to be got into the space thus formed as a pledge for the whole. This space within the grasping hand is the anteroom of the mouth and the stomach by which the prey is finally incorporated. With many animals it is the armed mouth itself which does the seizing, instead of hand or claw. Among men the hand which never lets go has become the very emblem of power: "He was delivered into his hands", "He was in their hands", "It is in God's hands." Similar expressions are common in all languages.

For the actual process of seizing what is really important is the *pressure* exerted by the human hand. The fingers close round the object seized; the hollow space into which this has been forced narrows. The aim is to be able to feel it with the whole inner surface of the hand, and to feel it more firmly. The original lightness and delicacy of touch is first extended to a wider area, then strengthened, and finally concentrated until that part of the body which is touched is as firmly compressed as possible. Pressure of this kind came to supersede the habit of using claws to rend the victim. It is true that in some archaic cults the victim was still clawed, but the actors were disguised as animals and what they did was deliberately bestial. For the real job, men came to rely on their teeth.

Pressure can increase until it crushes. Whether it actually reaches this point   *9* or not depends on how dangerous the prey is. If the attacker has had a hard fight to overcome it, if he has been seriously threatened by it, or enraged or injured, he will want to make it pay for this and will press harder than is necessary to make sure of it. But even more than fear or rage, it is contempt which urges him on to crush it. An insect, something so small that it scarcely counts, is crushed because one would not otherwise know what had happened to it; no human hand can form a hollow small enough for it. But, in addition to the desire to get rid of a pest and to be sure it is really disposed of, our behavior to a gnat or a flea betrays the contempt we feel for a being which is utterly defenseless, which exists in a completely different order of size and power from us, with which we have nothing in common, into which we never transform ourselves and which we never fear except when it suddenly appears in crowds. The destruction of these tiny creatures is the only act of violence which remains unpunished even *within* us. Their blood does not stain our hands, for it does not remind us of our own. We never look into their glazing eyes. We do not eat them. They have never — at least not amongst us in the West — had the benefit of our growing, if not yet very effective, concern for life. In brief, they are outlaws. If I say to someone, "I could crush you with one hand," I am expressing the greatest possible contempt. It is as though I were saying "You are an insect. You mean nothing to me. I can do what I like with you and that won't mean anything to me either. You mean nothing to anyone. You can be destroyed with impunity without anyone noticing it. It would make no difference to anyone. Certainly not to me."

The most extreme form of destruction through pressure, that is, *grinding*,   *10* cannot be achieved by the hand, for this is too soft. Grinding requires a great preponderance of weight and hard objects above and below, between which something is ground. If he wants to do this himself, man has to use his teeth. In general we do not think of something living when we speak of grinding; the process is relegated to inorganic nature, the word being most frequently used in connection with natural catastrophes such as the fall of large rocks which grind or pulverize living creatures. The word is used in a figurative sense, but is never taken quite literally. It conveys the idea of a destructive power not really proper to man himself. There is something impersonal about it. The body as such is not capable of grinding and therefore magnanimously renounces it. The most it is capable of is "an iron grip."

It is remarkable what respect this is accorded. The functions of the hand are   *11* so manifold that it is not surprising that there should be a large number of expressions connected with them. But the hand's real glory derives from the *grip*, that central and most often celebrated act of power. The moment of seizing, which is decisive amongst animals as well as amongst men, has always created the strongest impression on men, and their superstitious awe of the great cats of prey, the tiger and the lion, is based upon it. These are the great *seizers* and they do their seizing alone. With them, the lying in wait and watching, the sudden leap, the thrusting in of the claws and the mauling are all still one. The momentum of the action, its pitilessness, the assurance with which it is carried out, the never questioned superiority of the killer, the fact that he can choose whatever he wants as his prey — all this has contributed to his enormous prestige. However we look at it, this is the highest concentration of power and, as such, has made an ineradicable impression on man; all kings have wanted to be lions. It is the very act of seizing and its success which has been admired and praised. The simple exercise of superior strength has been universally regarded as courage and greatness.

The lion does not have to transform himself in order to catch his prey; he remains himself throughout. Before he goes hunting he makes himself known by his roar; he alone can afford to announce his intention loudly and audibly to every creature. This reveals an indestructible arrogance which can never be deflected and which, for this very reason, spreads even greater terror. Power at its core and its apex despises transformation. It is sufficient unto itself and wills only itself. In this form it has always seemed remarkable to man; free and absolute, it exists for nothing and no one except itself. This is the peak of its glory and, to this very day, it seems as though there were nothing which could prevent its reappearance in the same form.   *12*

There is, however, a second act of power which is not quite so glorious but no less essential. Dazzled by the grandeur of the act of seizing we tend to forget that there is something equally important which runs parallel to it, namely, to avoid being seized.   *13*

All the empty space which a man who holds power creates round himself serves this second purpose. Every man, even the least, seeks to prevent anyone else coming too near him. Every form of social life established amongst men expresses itself in distances which allay the ceaseless fear of being seized and caught. Symmetry, which is so striking a feature of many ancient civilizations, derives in part from man's attempt to create uniform distances all round himself. Within these civilizations, safety is based on distances and is also emblematically expressed by them. The ruler on whose existence that of everyone else depends stands furthest and most clearly apart; in this, and not only in his splendor, he is equated with the sun, or, as among the Chinese, with the sky itself, which is even more spacious. Access to him is made difficult, palaces with more and more rooms being built round him. Each gate and each door is heavily guarded so that it is impossible to intrude on him against his will. He, from his remote security, can have anyone seized whatever he may be. But how is anyone to seize him, protected as he is by his hundredfold separation?   *14*

The actual *incorporation* of the prey begins in the mouth. From hand to mouth is the route followed by everything which can be eaten. Among the many creatures which have no arms for grasping, the process is initiated by the mouth itself, by the teeth or by a beak protruding from it.   *15*

The most striking natural instrument of power in man and in many animals is the teeth. The way they are arranged in rows and their shining smoothness are quite different from anything else belonging to the body. One feels tempted to call them the very first manifestation of order and one so striking that it almost shouts for recognition. It is an order which operates as a threat to the world outside, not always visible, but visible whenever the mouth opens, which is often. The substance of the teeth differs from that of all the other visible   *16* parts of the body and would be impressive even if people only had two teeth. They are smooth, hard and unyielding and can be clenched without any change of shape; they make the same effect as well polished and firmly set stones.

From a very early stage man used all kinds of stones as weapons and tools,   *17* but it was a long time before he learnt to polish them to the smoothness of teeth. It is probable that his teeth served him as a model for the improvement of his tools. The teeth of all kinds of large animals had always been useful to him; he might have captured them at the risk of his life and some of the power of the animal which had threatened him still seemed to him to be contained in them. He wore them as trophies and talismans to pass on to others the terror they had once aroused in him. He proudly displayed on his body the scars they had caused; these ranked as badges of honor and were so much desired that they were often artificially produced.

Thus both his own teeth and those of alien and stronger animals affected   *18* man in a wide variety of ways. By their very nature they occupied a position midway between an actual part of the body and a tool. The fact that they could fall out, or be knocked out, made them even more like a tool.

Smoothness and *order*, the manifest attributes of the teeth, have entered into   *19* the very nature of power. They are inseparable from it and, in every manifestation of power, they are the first things to be established. The conjunction began with primitive tools, but, as power grew, these early attributes became more pronounced. The leap from stone to metal was perhaps the most striking move in the direction of increased smoothness. However much stone was polished, the sword, made first of bronze and then of iron, was smoother. The real attraction of metal lies in the fact that it is smoother than anything else. In the machines and vehicles of the contemporary world smoothness has increased and has also become smoothness of performance. Language expresses this very simply; we say "everything is going smoothly," or "functions smoothly"; and we mean by this that some process is completely and undisturbedly within our power. In modern life the bias towards smoothness has spread to fields where it formerly tended to be avoided. Houses and furniture used to be decorated, as were the limbs and bodies of men. Modes of decoration changed, but decoration always existed and was obstinately preserved even after it had lost its symbolical meaning. Today smoothness has conquered our houses, their walls and all the objects we put into them; ornament and decoration are despised and regarded as a sign of bad taste. We speak of function, clarity of line and utility, but what has really triumphed is smoothness, and the prestige of the power it conceals.

The example of modern architecture shows how difficult it is to separate   *20* smoothness from order. Their common history is old, as old as the teeth. The uniformity of the whole row of front teeth and the regular spaces between them stood as models for many different kinds of arrangements. Many of those which we take for granted today may originally have derived from them. The order of military formations, which is artificially created by man himself, is in myth connected with teeth: the soldiers of Cadmus, who sprang from the soil, were sown as dragon's teeth.

There are certainly other instances of order to be seen in nature, that of var-   *21* ious grasses for example, and the more rigid one of trees. But man did not find these in himself as he did teeth; they were not so directly and uninterruptedly linked with his intake of food, and it was not so easy to make use of them. It was the fact that the teeth are used for biting which so emphatically drew man's attention to their order, and the fact that they fall out with unpleasant consequences which made him conscious of the importance of this order.

The teeth are the armed guardians of the mouth and the mouth is indeed a   22 strait place, the prototype of all prisons. Whatever goes in there is lost, and much goes in whilst still alive. Large numbers of animals first kill their prey only in the mouth, and some not even then. The readiness with which the mouth opens in anticipation of prey, the ease with which, once shut, it remains shut, recall the most feared attributes of a prison. It can scarcely be wrong to assume that the mouth did in fact exert a hidden influence on prisons. Primitive man certainly knew other creatures besides whales in whose mouth there was room for him. In this terrible place nothing could thrive, even if there were time to settle there. It is barren and nothing can take root in it. When the gaping maws of dragons had been virtually extirpated, man found a symbolic substitute for them in prisons. In times when these used to be torture chambers they resembled a hostile mouth in many respects. Hell still presents the same appearance today. Prisons, on the other hand, have become puritanical. The smoothness of teeth has conquered the world; the walls of cells are all smooth and even the window opening is small. For the prisoner, freedom is the space beyond the clenched teeth, and these are now represented by the bare walls of his cell.

The narrow gorge through which everything has to pass is, for the few who   23 live so long, the ultimate terror. Man's imagination has been continually occupied by the several stages of incorporation. The gaping jaws of the large beasts which threatened him have pursued him even into his dreams and myths. Voyages of discovery down these jaws were no less important to him than those over the sea, and certainly as dangerous. Some who had given up all hope were pulled living out of the maw of these beasts and bore the marks of their teeth on them for the rest of their lives.

The road that the prey travels through the body is a long one and on the   24 way all its substance is sucked out of it; everything useful is abstracted from it till all that remains is refuse and stench.

This process, which stands at the end of every act of seizing, gives us a clue   25 to the nature of power in general.

Anyone who wants to rule men first tries to humiliate them, to trick them   26 out of their rights and their capacity for resistance, until they are as powerless before him as animals. He uses them like animals and, even if he does not tell them so, in himself he always knows quite clearly that they mean just as little to him; when he speaks to his intimates he will call them sheep or cattle. His ultimate aim is to incorporate them into himself and to suck the substance out of them. What remains of them afterwards does not matter to him. The worse he has treated them, the more he despises them. When they are no more use at all, he disposes of them as he does of his excrement, simply seeing to it that they do not poison the air of his house.

He will not dare to identify all the individual stages of this process even to   27 himself. If he is a braggart he may admit to his familiars that he degrades to the status of animals the men he procures for himself. But, since he does not have his subjects slaughtered in slaughterhouses nor actually use them to feed his body, he will deny that he sucks them dry and digests them; on the contrary, it is he who feeds them. Thus it is easy to overlook the real nature of these processes, particularly as man has learnt to keep animals which he does not kill, or not immediately, since they are of more use to him in other ways.

But, quite apart from the person who wields power and knows how to con- *28* centrate so much in his two hands, the relation of each and every man to his own excrement belongs to the sphere of power. Nothing has been so much part of one as that which turns into excrement. The constant pressure which, during the whole of its long progress through the body, is applied to the prey which has become food; its dissolution and intimate union with the creature digesting it; the complete and final annihiliation, first of all functions and then of everything which once constituted its individuality; its assimilation to something already existing, that is, to the body of the eater — all this may very well be seen as the central, if most hidden, process of power. It is so much a matter of course, so automatic and so far beyond consciousness, that one underrates its importance. One tends to see only the thousand tricks of power which are enacted above ground; but these are the least part of it. Underneath, day in, day out, is digestion and again digestion. Something alien is seized, cut up into small bits, incorporated into oneself, and assimilated. By this process alone man lives; if it ceases, he dies. So much he has always known. But it is clear that *all* the phases of this process, and not only the external and half-conscious ones, must have their correspondence in the psyche. It is not altogether easy to find these correspondences. We shall, however, come on clear traces of them in the course of our enquiry, and shall follow them up. As will be seen, the symptoms of *melancholia* are especially illuminating in this context.

The excrement, which is what remains of all this, is loaded with our whole *29* blood guilt. By it we know what we have murdered. It is the compressed sum of all the evidence against us. It is our daily and continuing sin and, as such, it stinks and cries to heaven. It is remarkable how we isolate ourselves with it; in special rooms, set aside for the purpose, we get rid of it; our most private moment is when we withdraw there; we are alone only with our excrement. It is clear that we are ashamed of it. It is the age-old seal of that power-process of digestion, which is enacted in darkness and which, without this, would remain hidden for ever.

On the Psychology of Eating

Everything which is eaten is the food of power. The hungry man feels empty *30* space within himself. He overcomes the discomfort which this causes him by filling himself with food. The fuller he is the better he feels. The man who can eat more than anyone else lies back satisfied and heavy with food; he is a champion. There are peoples who take such a champion eater for their chief. His full belly seems to them a guarantee that they themselves will never go hungry for long. It is as though he had filled it for all of them. The connection between power and digestion is obvious here.

With other forms of chiefdom the eating capacity of the ruler becomes less *31* significant. It is no longer necessary that his girth should be greater than that of everyone else. But he continues to eat and drink copiously with members of his entourage, and the food and drink he sets before them *belongs to him*. He may not be the largest eater himself, but he owns the largest store of food, the most corn and the most cattle. If he wanted to, he could still always be the champion eater, but he transfers the satisfaction of repletion to his court, to those who eat with him, only reserving for himself the right to be offered everything first. But the king in his character of champion eater has never wholly disappeared. Time and again the role is re-enacted for the benefit of delighted subjects. Ruling groups in general are also prone to gluttony; the feats of the later Romans are proverbial, in this respect, and all families whose power is securely established tend to exhibit themselves in this way and are later imitated and surpassed by those newly arrived.

In many societies the capacity and the passion for extravagance have gone   *32*
as far as formal, ritually ordered orgies of destruction. The most famous of these is the Potlatch of the Indians of north-western America which consisted of great festal assemblies of the whole community, culminating in contests of destruction among the chiefs. Each chief boasted of the amount of property he was prepared to destroy. The one who destroyed most was the victor and enjoyed the greatest fame. Eating more than anyone else presupposes the destruction of animals which belong to the eater. One has the impression that, in the Potlatch, the destroying of other kinds of property is an extension of the destroying of eatables. Thus the chief was able to boast far more than if he had actually had to eat everything, and in addition was spared the physical consequences of doing so.

It may be useful to have a look at eating in general, independent of the eat-   *33*
er's position in the social scale. A certain esteem for each other is clearly evident in all who eat together. This is already expressed by the fact of their *sharing*. The food in the common dish before them belongs to all of them together. Everyone takes some of it and sees that others take some too. Everyone tries to be fair and not to take advantage of anyone else. The bond between the eaters is strongest when it is *one* animal they partake of, one body which they knew as a living unit, or one loaf of bread. But the touch of solemnity in their attitude cannot be explained by this alone; their mutual esteem also means that they will not eat each other. It is true that membership of the same group always carries a guarantee of this, but only in the moment of eating is it convincingly expressed. People sit together, bare their teeth and eat and, even in this critical moment, feel no desire to eat each other. They respect themselves for this, and respect their companions for an abstemiousness equal to their own.

In a *family* the husband contributes food and the wife prepares it for him.   *34*
The fact that he habitually eats what she has prepared constitutes the strongest link between them. Family life is closest where its members frequently eat together. When one thinks of it, the picture one forms is that of parents and children sitting round a table. Everything else seems to be a preparation for this moment. The more often and the more regularly it recurs, the more those who thus eat together feel themselves to be a family. To be accepted at the family table amounts almost to being accepted into the family.

This may be the most appropriate place to say something about the *mother*,   *35* who is the core and very heart of this institution. A mother is one who gives her own body to be eaten. She first nourishes the child in her womb and then gives it her milk. This activity continues in a less concentrated form throughout many years; her thoughts, in so far as she is a mother, revolve round the food the growing child needs. It does not have to be her own child; a strange child may be substituted for her own, or she may adopt one. Her passion is to give food, to watch the child eating and profiting by the food it eats; its growth and increase in weight are her constant aims. Her behaviour appears selfless and is so if one regards her as a separate unit, as one single human being. But what has really happened is that she now has two stomachs instead of one, and keeps control of both. At first she is more interested in the new stomach, and in the new and undeveloped body, than in her own; pregnancy has merely been externalized. The concept which I have put forward of digestion as a central process of power holds for the mother too, but in her case the process is distributed between two bodies and is made clearer and more conscious by the fact that the new body, for whose nourishment she provides, is separated from her own. The mother's power over a young child is absolute, not only because its life depends on her, but also because she herself feels a very strong urge to exercise this power all the time. The concentration of the appetite for domination on such a small organism gives rise to a feeling of superiority greater than that obtaining in any other habitual relationship between human beings.

She is occupied day and night with this domination, and its continuity and 36 the enormous number of details in which it is expressed give it a roundness and perfection which no other kind of power achieves. It is not confined to the giving of orders, for these could not be understood by a very young child. It means that a creature is kept prisoner, even though in this case genuinely for its own advantage; that the mother, though without knowing what is happening, can pass on to it the commands imposed on *her* decades before and which she has since retained intact in herself; that she can enforce *growth* — something to which rulers only approximate by conferring promotions in rank. For the mother, the child combines the qualities of both plants and animals. It allows her the enjoyment of sovereign rights which can otherwise only be exercised separately; like a plant, she can make it grow in accordance with her wishes and, like an animal, she can keep it prisoner and control its movements. It grows under her hands like corn and like a domestic animal it carries out those movements which she permits it; it removes from her part of the long-standing burden of commands which weighs so heavily upon every civilized being and, finally, it grows into a man or a woman, a new and complete person, for whose accession the group in which she lives is permanently indebted to her. There is no intenser form of power. That the role of the mother is not normally seen in this light is due to two facts; first, that what everyone chiefly remembers is the period when this power is *decreasing*, and second, that the sovereign rights of the father are superficially more striking, though in reality far less important.

The family becomes rigid and hard when it excludes others from its meals; 37 those that must be fed provide a natural pretext for the exclusion of others. The hollowness of this pretext is revealed by families which have no children and yet make not the slightest move to share their meal with others. The "family" of two is man's most contemptible creation. But, even where there are children, we may often feel that they are used as a mere cover for naked self-ishness. People save "for the sake of the children" and allow others to starve. What they are really doing is keeping everything for themselves.

Modern man likes eating in restaurants, at separate tables, with his own   *38* little group, for which *he* pays. Since everyone else in the place is doing the same thing, he eats his meal under the pleasing illusion that everyone everywhere has enough to eat. Even sensitive people do not need this illusion afterwards; those who have eaten do not mind stumbling over the hungry.

The eater increases in weight; he is and he feels heavier, and there is a boast   *39* in this: he cannot grow any more, but there, on the very spot, under everyone's eyes, he can increase in weight. This is another reason why people like eating with others; it is a contest in repletion. The satisfaction of repletion, of the moment when nothing more can be absorbed, is part of the goal and pleasure of eating and originally no one was ashamed of it; there might be a large quantity of game which had to be eaten up before it went bad and so everyone ate as much as he could and carried his store of food within him.

Anyone who eats alone renounces the prestige which the process would bring   *40* him in the eyes of others. He bares his teeth simply for the sake of eating, and this impresses no one, for there is no one there to be impressed. But when people eat together, they can all see each other's mouths opening. Everyone can watch everyone else's teeth while his own are in action at the same time. To be without teeth is contemptible and there is a touch of asceticism in refusing to show those that one has. The natural occasion on which to show off one's teeth is when eating with others. Contemporary etiquette requires the mouth to be closed while eating and thus reduces to a minimum the slight threat contained in opening it at all. But we are not yet as harmless as this makes us appear; we eat with knife and fork, that is, with two instruments which could easily be used for attack; everyone has these ready in front of him, or he may even carry them around with him. And the bit of food which we cut off and, as elegantly as possible, shove in our mouths is still called a "bite."

Laughter has been objected to as vulgar because, in laughing, the mouth is   *41* opened wide and the teeth are shown. Originally laughter contained a feeling of pleasure in prey or food which seemed certain. A human being who falls down reminds us of an animal we might have hunted and brought down ourselves. Every sudden fall which arouses laughter does so because it suggests helplessness and reminds us that the fallen can, if we want, be treated as prey. If we went futher and actually ate it, we would not laugh. We laugh *instead* of eating it. Laughter is our physical reaction to the escape of potential food. As Hobbes said, laughter expresses a sudden feeling of superiority, but he did not add that it only occurs when the normal consequences of this superiority do not ensue. His conception contains only half the truth. Perhaps because animals do not laugh, he did not see that our laughter is originally an animal reaction. But neither do animals deny themselves obtainable food if they really want it. Only man has learnt to replace the final stage of incorporation by a symbolic act. It is as though the whole interior process of gulping down food could be summed up and replaced by those movements of the diaphragm which are characteristic of laughter.

The only animal to make a sound really resembling human laughter is the   42
hyena. This sound can be induced by placing food before a captive hyena and
then withdrawing it quickly before the animal has time to snatch it. Here it is
worth remembering that, in freedom, the hyena's food consists of carrion. It is
easy to imagine how often food must have been snatched away from under its
eyes by other animals after its own appetite had been aroused.

Considerations

1. Look up the meaning and origin of the word *incorporation* in an unabridged
   dictionary. How do the parts of the word create Elias Canetti's meaning?
2. What does Canetti help us to see about *corporations* and the operations of
   corporate power?
3. Canetti offers several examples of *synechdoche,* a figure of speech which
   substitutes a part for the whole, to support his contention that "the hand
   which never lets go has become the very emblem of power" (para. 7). Add
   to his list of examples (para. 7), then broaden it to include other parts of the
   body as well: finger, arm, teeth, or whatever else represents the same sort
   of power. Then write a short essay in which you offer this collection of figures of speech to illustrate Canetti's thesis: that seizing and incorporating
   is the ultimate goal — at least symbolically — of power. Try to explain any
   counter-examples by refining or qualifying Canetti's thesis if necessary.
4. Canetti claims that "the king in his character of champion eater has never
   wholly disappeared" (para. 31). Yet in America eating in excess has come
   to represent an absence of power as well, at least of power over the self. Try
   to reconcile this second view of eating — eating as a moral issue — with
   Canetti's claim.
5. How does Canetti's view of the power of the mother and its relation to food
   contribute to an understanding of one stereotype of the ethnic mother? (You
   may need to do some brief research for this.) What factors might complicate
   the explanation of the stereotype?
6. How well does Canetti's view of the power of the mother and its relation to
   food explain the problem of obesity in children? What else might be a cause
   of overweight?
7. One critic says that Canetti "revels in just that kind of generalization social
   scientists are taught to avoid." Draw on your own knowledge of the aims
   and methodology of social science, or read through the *Encyclopaedia Britannica: Macropaedia*'s article on Social Science for a quick review. Decide
   what the critic means, and then decide whether he is right. If he is, is that
   an impediment to our understanding, or interpreting, or believing what Canetti says? Is Canetti trying to be a social scientist?
8. Canetti describes laughter as "originally an animal reaction" (para. 41). In
   fact, throughout his discussion of power he views us more as animals than
   as humans. Is this offensive? Is it valid? How might he strengthen his arguments?
9. Anthropologists believe that cannibalism in Africa, South America, the South

Pacific islands, and the West Indies was almost always a ritual practice. Would Canetti agree? Why or why not?

Connections

1. Canetti suggests that the urge for power in human beings has its origin in — and is a metaphor for — the urge for power over prey, which in turn means sustenance and the continuation of life, or survival. Read the Darwin selection in Chapter 9, The Impact of Animals, and Sigmund Freud's "Dear Professor Einstein" in this chapter. Do these writers support or contradict Canetti's position?
2. Look at mothers in fairytales — for example, in "Snow White" in Chapter 10, The Fairy Tale "Snow White," or in any other fairy tales you know. Do these examples of the mythic mother support or contradict Canetti's view of the mother as intensely powerful? Explain. (You might want to begin by showing how these fairy tale mothers represent the "mythic" mother.)
3. What connection does Canetti, like Freud, suggest between biology and psychology? Does the issue of power here clarify or complicate the connection?
4. Look at the nature-nurture argument raised in the Stephen Jay Gould article in Chapter 7, The Nature of Intelligence. Explain where Canetti would stand on this issue and why.

Humor, Sex, and Power in American Society

Samuel S. Janus

According to Alan King, former President Richard Nixon freely admits that   *1*
his election efforts were hurt by the widespread cynical joke, "Would you buy a used car from this man?" It certainly did not help in his effort to win, and in fact, he lost the election in 1960 to John Kennedy. Some years later it was not surprising, therefore, to find comic Alan King in the prognosticator role again when he warned Americans about Spiro Agnew with "Beware of Greeks accepting gifts." This comment was made a full one and a half years before

Samuel S. Janus (b. 1930) has been Clinical Assistant Professor of Psychiatry at New York Medical College since 1970. His research focuses on human sexuality and the field of humor, the psychology of humor, and drug abuse and politics. This selection first appeared in the American Journal of Psychoanalysis *(1981).*

former Vice President Agnew had to resign his office under fire, a first in American history. Political humor had come of age in America.

The dramatic upsurge in comedy, seen in the huge explosion of interest by   2
the public in comedy performances as well as in the vastly proliferating numbers of young comics and comedy showcase theaters, points to a phenomenon rife with psychosocial implications. Continual world crises from World War II, the Korean War, the Cuban Missile Crisis, Vietnam, the Middle East, and Korea in 1976, and, on the domestic grounds, the incredibly demoralizing aspects of the Watergate affair, have left Americans feeling very vulnerable and impotent, and thus have given rise to the political comedian. Indeed, with the image of former President Nixon tarnished beyond repair — having lived up to the "Tricky Dicky" appellation of the 1960s — and with the image of President Ford as the do-nothing bumbling buffoon, the American public has experienced a severe crisis of loss of confidence. No longer can, or do, Americans sit back with a sense of ease that their elected representatives will competently manage the affairs of state for them. In addition, the recent rash of sex scandals involving Representatives Hayes, Mills, Albert, Howe, Leggett, Wagonner, Grey, and numerous others — and the revelation that their female partners have been forced into sex roles and been paid salaries for such out of government funds — has eroded moral confidence in the Congress to a considerable degree. The American people cannot depend on the strong father figures embodied as heads of state or as protecting idols, nor can they count on them to guarantee a democratically organized society.

These political traumas have caused Americans to experience their own   3
psychosocial crisis, which is expressed in increasing tensions, insecurities, and a new form of realistic paranoia. The mass media, with emphasis on exposure, disclosure, and open reporting, serve to heighten these already disturbing emotions. The public has ceased to focus on the individual's problems and discontents, has turned its eye toward the welfare of society, and attends primarily to the problems on a national level, attacking the villains in power. Because of the instability and uncertainty of the political structure, more than ever does the American public have a need for a catharsis that is increasingly forthcoming from comedic relief. Comedian Van Harris reports that "I see that George Wallace is feeling better; the color is coming back into his neck."

In Shakespeare's great tragedies, the master himself recognized the needs   4
of the audiences and provided for those needs in the form of court jesters and buffoons. The court jesters of the 1970s national and international tragedies are the professional stand-up comedians. Thus, comedy has become an essential catalyst for emotional release and identification. It now provides the essential stabilization of the public's mental state. Dr. Jacob Levine, in a revealing paper entitled "Failure to Understand Humor," has shown that humor appreciation is blocked by deeply personal fears and anxieties. Thus, it is a healthy phenomenon to be able to laugh appropriately, especially to laugh *with* others.

Comedy has a dual function. It not only provides the tension release for the   5
audiences but also serves as the vehicle of power for the performer. Humor, therefore, is seen not only as a defensive posture in the release of tension but as a very effective forum to serve as an aggressive tool. As we will show, the

economy and impact of a good joke cannot be topped by anything, except by a better joke.

The Comedian as Social Commentator

Who are the people who become professional comedians, and what are their 6
motivations for doing so? Humor has traditionally been the language of the oppressed and disenfranchised. Minority groups have always been the underdog, voiceless and impotent. As a comic performer, the underdog can now achieve a personal sense of power and a platform in which to voice his opinions. He can, in addition, now exercise power over a large number of people, the audiences. By relieving their tensions and anxieties, the audiences become receptive to the comic's comments and jokes. The comedian receives his power by becoming the self-appointed voice of the people. A comic-ombudsman, if you will.

Background factors that were important for an understanding of comedians 7
were discussed in a previous paper. Seventy-six were studied in the original work, which has now been expanded to include 85, both men and women. Over 92 percent of men and women in comedy are from blue-collar homes or even lower economic levels. Jews have long dominated the field, with 80 percent of all comics being Jewish, although Jewish representation in the population of the United States is only 3 percent. The waves of immigration from Eastern Europe saw the rise of the "Old Greats" in comedy, such as Berle, Carter, and King, who are all first-generation Americans. Since these people were forced to live in ghettos with deprivation and poverty, suffering and anger became their predominant emotions. The men who were later to become the great comedians were conscious of the real lack of power in their communities; they learned to use humor to allay the anxieties and sufferings in their families and communities, and to usurp power from the traditional local power figures. From this meager beginning, based on their need for personal and psychic survival, developed the field of stand-up comedy, and with it the sense of personal power as well as the power to change tragedy into laughter and perhaps even wring justice from the Establishment.

Does it work? Apparently yes. The Bell Telephone Company was so exer- 8
cised by Lily Tomlin's antics as the brash, abrasive, obnoxious, "typical" representative of the phone company that, after trying unsuccessfully to squelch it, they offered to buy her routine for more than $75,000. In the same way, Mike Preminger's characterization of McDonald's hamburgers was not overly flattering, and it, too, was sought for purchase.

Part of Mike Preminger's routine about McDonald's has him saying: 9

> McDonald's is now starting a home-delivery service. If you are not at home when the delivery comes, they just slide the hamburgers under the door. In case you hadn't noticed, their French fried potatoes also make great toothpicks.

Alan King reports that, after his acid attacks on poor airline service, he is 10
now "treated better than a U.S. senator, and they practically carry me onto the plane."

Ethnic Representation

Other minority groups have also found that, through humor, they can achieve *11*
power and effect a change in society. Barred from other political platforms,
these groups, which are even lower on the economic ladder than the immigrant Jews were, have begun to spawn increasing numbers of successful comedians. Although still few in comedy, the blacks and Puerto Ricans have enhanced their power status through a comedy with a strong ethnic pride. Today
we find black comics scathingly and caustically taking the system apart in their
comedy routines. Men such as Godfrey Cambridge and Richard Pryor do it on
stage. Dick Gregory has become so involved in social issues that he has moved
from the role of a comic commentator to that of a social activist and agitator,
humor being an effective aggressive tool for him.

More recently, we have seen the introduction of Puerto Rican comics. Fred- *12*
die Prinze and Liz Torres have brought voice to, and greater ethnic respect for,
their communities.

An example of this type of humor is the story of Sammy Davis getting on a *13*
bus in the early 1960s in the South and being told to sit in the back. "But," he
replied, "you don't understand. I'm Jewish." To which the driver responded:
"Oh, in that case, get off the bus altogether."

The more caustic humor of Richard Pryor can be heard in his albums, such *14*
as "Is That Nigger Crazy?" One trenchant routine involves a wino declaiming:

> I'm a veteran, boy, I's in World War I. The battle of Chateau Briand. I got mustard
> gas wounds all over my body. Look at that nigger in the middle of the street. A jun-
> kie, look at 'im. Used to be a genius. That narcotic done made you null and void, boy.
> I'm going to help you, boy, 'cause I believe in your potential. That's right, you don't
> know how to deal with the white man, that's your problem. I know how to deal with
> him. That's why I'm in the position I'm in today.

From a white comedian, Van Harris, on ethnic problems: "George Wallace *15*
says that if elected he will have a place in the White House for Shirley Chis-
holm . . . two days a week."

Freddie Prinz, dean of Puerto Rican comics, reported that "there are no Puerto *16*
Rican astronauts, because they figure they'll honk the horn and play the radio
all the way to the moon." A simple expression of his caught the public's imagination, and Freddie rode it to stardom: "That's not my job."

Women

The fact that women in comedy account for, at most, 12 percent of the field, *17*
whereas in all other areas of show business they represent at least 50 percent
of the population, attests to their lack of credibility as a power figure. Acceptance of women in comedy has paralleled the women's movement in the
changing roles and expectations of women in society in general. Still, generally, acceptance of women in comedy is maintained only by women portraying
the traditional stereotyped roles of the naggers and the incompetent, bumbling
domestics. As yet, women do not seem to allay but to increase the anxieties of
an audience when they venture out of the kitchen/bedroom and into the polit-

ical arena in their routines. However, increasing numbers of bold young women are forcing their way into the field as social commentators and are developing audience receptivity. The traditionalists in the field, like Joan Rivers, Phyllis Diller, and Totie Fields, use the subject of being a woman as a joke in itself. Joan Rivers, for example: "You've heard of A cup, B cup, and C cup. Well, you're looking at demitasse." Or the sign her mother put up, saying, "Last girl before Freeway."

In marked contrast is the humor of the radical feminists, exemplified by   *18* Harrison and Tyler: "So the man said to me, 'Come here and get your peaches, honey.' Well . . . they may have been peaches, but they sure were hanging from a dead limb."

The Here and Now

Comedy material reflects changing times and either keeps pace or often leaps   *19* ahead of societal issues. The comedic material embodies that which causes anxiety. Not surprising, then, that the comedy of yesteryear reflected the daily sufferings of the people as well. Its focus was on the nuclear family, work, and also trivia. With the breakdown of the nuclear family structure and the emphasis in society altered, comedy, too, has changed from these features and moved toward the incorporation of the needs of a collective body of people — society as a whole. With the unabating world crises, the public needs a respite from these tensions and anxieties. The essence of comedy has thus changed from everyday domestic issues to increasingly political humor, and, in the uniquely American manner, it is sexualized. For many years the Europeans had led the way in political humor, while the Americans were still listening to Henny Youngman's "Take my wife . . . please," or the definition of ambivalence as "watching your mother-in-law going over a cliff in your brand-new Cadillac." Today it is difficult to find a comedian whose material does not contain political or explicitly sexual material.

Jack Carter reported that "President Ford is the only Ford to ever back into   *20* a country." During the confirmation hearings of Nelson Rockefeller as Vice President, Carter claimed: "One senator asked, 'Mr. Rockefeller, why did you say you only had $30 million dollars, when in reality you have over $250 million?' and Rockefeller replied, 'I thought you meant how much did I have on me.' " Another wit reported at the time that as Vice President, he would wipe out the national debt with his Master Charge card. Comedian David Steinberg said, "Poor Julie Nixon Eisenhower, she has two of the most embarrassing names in American history."

For the first time in American history, President Ford, in his wisdom, saw   *21* fit to hire a full-time comedy writer to aid in writing his political speeches. Ford, a personally unexciting orator, recognized the need of the situation, considering all the heavy rhetoric in his speeches. Robert Orben, the man chosen for the position, had been the publisher of a monthly, "Gag File," which has been subscribed to by virtually every major and minor comic in the United States for over 30 years. So valuable and effective was Mr. Orben in the White House that he was assigned to writing jokes and speeches and, as a result of a major shake-up of speech writers in December 1975, was also appointed to the post of chief speech writer. Lines such as "I'm a Ford, and not an Edsel" are credited to Mr. Orben. Thus, humor is not only used by professional comics as a powerful political tool but is also being employed by the politicos to make their image more acceptable to the American public.

The names of several men stand out as pioneers in the use of politics and   22
social issues in comedy. Will Rogers' political humor brought him acclaim as both a funny man and a social critic. The role of and the persecution of Lenny Bruce in relation to the political structure are legendary. The social commentary of Lenny Bruce was shocking in that it was ahead of its time. But in comparison with today's comedic routines, that commentary would appear mild. Today's top social and political comic is Mort Sahl. Sahl uses the newspapers' headlines on the day of his performance as the basis for his material. He is most vociferous in championing the conspiracy theory and the C.I.A. involvement in the assassination of the late President Kennedy. More recently, his most pungent comment, at the time of the Democratic National Convention in New York City, was: "If you don't like what Jimmy Carter says . . . wait five minutes."

The rapidly changing sexual mores of the times, heralded by the sexual rev-   23
olution, the feminist movement, and the gay activists, are causing a national identity crisis for the average American. Once again, these issues become reflected in humor and are made a bit lighter. Comedy material contains much of the American admixture of politics and sex. The nature of most of the traditional stand-up comedy for years has been sexist. The "tits and ass" jokes, along with the "wives and mothers-in-law" jokes, are fading into an oblivion long overdue. The use of women as scapegoats by men who generally felt impotent in dealing with other men, and who could feel powerful by having at least a woman to dominate, is changing. The women's movement is making both men and women conscious of the relative power distribution between male and female by protesting the role of the woman as scapegoat. Male comedians who insist on sexist material in their routines now play to often hissing audiences. Through the women's movement, men and women have been freed to form a more effective alliance to face the social-political issues that are so pressing. Mixed audiences will tolerate only a minimum of female derogatory or chauvinistic material. Since the comic must reflect the needs of the audience, and since comedy is a potent force, he, too, is reflective of the newer equality.

Gay people, enjoying the endorsement of the American Psychiatric Associ-   24
ation and other prominent groups, assert that homosexuality is an alternate lifestyle. Gays are coming out of the closet and publicly proclaiming their sexual preference.

The American stand-up comic uses the audience's fears and anxieties as   25
comedy material and elicits an audience-performer interaction all its own. The stand-up comedian takes on the role of a lion tamer; he must go out night after night and "knock 'em dead." Comics experience a sense of omnipotence by playing to anxieties, knowing them, and controlling every emotion that an audience expresses. The audience not only shares laughter but walks away with a sense of catharsis and relief that someone has publicly verbalized that which

they secretly fear. Their realistic paranoia has been confirmed by the man of power, and he may even punish the villains.

While humor is a weapon when used aggressively and a palliative when used defensively, it is at all times a potent force. It adapts to, and assimilates from, a culture in which it has been born and developed. Today, humor is predominantly taken directly from social and political issues, and it affects, as well as reflects, the changing attitudes of American society. American humor, like almost any area of major consciousness in American life, is sexualized, as Madison Avenue has learned. Even politics and our political leaders must have sex appeal. Humor and sex are very powerful forces in our society and have a dramatic impact on our politics. The understanding and use of these forces serve to provide to Americans a powerful new tool of consciousness which aids in controlling their personal and collective destinies. The public has learned how these tools have conditioned it to fit the images that this industrialized society has set up for it.   26

Humor, effectively used, is a most potent source of power; it is especially needed and adopted by those who have no other "recognizable" form of power. Minority groups have long seized upon comedy as the expression of their will and power. The ability to *make* a person laugh *with* them, not at them, is a vital one. Humor has become an expression of change and is irreverent as a vehicle of power.   27

Considerations

1. Janus uses the word *catharsis* in paragraph 3 and elsewhere. Check an unabridged dictionary for its related meanings in the fields of medicine, esthetics or literature, and psychiatry. Using these definitions, write a brief explanation of Janus's point.
2. Janus sees women as moving socially from being simple butts of jokes to becoming comedians themselves, and he regards this as a gain in power for women. Explain his point, and then decide whether or not you agree that in this case humor reflects power.
3. Samuel Johnson said, in the eighteenth century, that "nature has given women so much power that the law has very wisely given them little." What power or powers possessed by women (and not by men) might Johnson have been referring to?
4. How does the evolution of ethnic humor parallel — or differ from — the evolution of sexual humor according to the evidence Janus presents?

Connections

1. Compare and contrast the views of Elias Canetti and Samuel S. Janus on the relation of laughter to power.
2. How would Janus's claims about the shift in the focus of comedy in recent

decades suggest a corresponding increase in the importance of Machiavelli's advice? Do you agree?

3. How would Machiavelli modify Janus's view of the male-female power struggle?

4. After reading several selections in Chapter 4, The Urban Experience, determine the extent to which Janus's ideas are focused on, or even derived from, the urban environment.

Humpty Dumpty
Lewis Carroll

However, the egg only got larger and larger, and more and more human: *1*
when she had come within a few yards of it, she saw that it had eyes and a nose and mouth; and, when she had come close to it, she saw clearly that it was HUMPTY DUMPTY himself. "It can't be anybody else!" she said to herself. "I'm as certain of it, as if his name were written all over his face!"

It might have been written a hundred times, easily, on that enormous face.   *2*
Humpty Dumpty was sitting, with his legs crossed like a Turk, on the top of a high wall — such a narrow one that Alice quite wondered how he could keep his balance — and, as his eyes were steadily fixed in the opposite direction, and he didn't take the least notice of her, she thought he must be a stuffed figure, after all.

"And how exactly like an egg he is!" she said aloud, standing with her hands   *3*
ready to catch him, for she was every moment expecting him to fall.

"It's *very* provoking," Humpty Dumpty said after a long silence, looking away   *4*
from Alice as he spoke, "to be called an egg, — *very!*"

"I said you *looked* like an egg, Sir," Alice gently explained. "And some eggs   *5*
are very pretty, you know," she added, hoping to turn her remark into a sort of compliment.

"Some people," said Humpty Dumpty, looking away from her as usual, "have   *6*
no more sense than a baby!"

Lewis Carroll (1832–1898) was born Charles Lutwidge Dodgson, son of a clergyman and one of eleven children, in Victorian England. He was ordained a deacon in the Church of England but did not want to preach; instead he taught mathematics and logic at Oxford University. His mathematical writings did not achieve renown, but his children's books did — although at first he thought of them simply as entertainment and signed them with the pseudonym Lewis Carroll. Among the most popular of these are his Alice books — Alice in Wonderland *and* Through the Looking-Glass *— written for a child he was fond of. This excerpt is from Chapter 6 of* Through the Looking Glass.

Alice didn't know what to say to this: it wasn't at all like conversation, she   *7*
thought, as he never said anything to *her;* in fact, his last remark was evidently
addressed to a tree — so she stood and softly repeated to herself —

> Humpty Dumpty sat on a wall:
> Humpty Dumpty had a great fall.
> All the King's horses and all the King's men
> Couldn't put Humpty Dumpty in his place again.

"That last line is much too long for the poetry," she added, almost out loud,   *8*
forgetting that Humpty Dumpty would hear her.

"Don't stand chattering to yourself like that," Humpty Dumpty said, look-   *9*
ing at her for the first time, "but tell me your name and your business."

"My *name* is Alice, but — "   *10*

"It's a stupid name enough!" Humpty Dumpty interrupted impatiently.   *11*
"What does it mean?"

"Must a name mean something?" Alice asked doubtfully.   *12*

"Of course it must," Humpty Dumpty said with a short laugh: *"my* name   *13*
means the shape I am — and a good handsome shape it is, too. With a name
like yours, you might be any shape, almost."

"Why do you sit out here all alone?" said Alice, not wishing to begin an   *14*
argument.

"Why, because there's nobody with me!" cried Humpty Dumpty. "Did you   *15*
think I didn't know the answer to *that?* Ask another."

"Don't you think you'd be safer down on the ground?" Alice went on, not   *16*
with any idea of making another riddle, but simply in her good-natured anxiety for the queer creature. "That wall is so *very* narrow!"

"What tremendously easy riddles you ask!" Humpty Dumpty growled out.   *17*
"Of course I don't think so! Why, if ever I *did* fall off — which there's no chance
of — but *if* I did — " Here he pursed up his lips, and looked so solemn and
grand that Alice could hardly help laughing. *"If* I *did* fall," he went on, *"the
King has promised me* — ah, you may turn pale, if you like! You didn't think I
was going to say that, did you? *The King has promised me* — *with his very own
mouth* — to — to — "

"To send all his horses and all his men," Alice interrupted, rather unwisely.   *18*

"Now I declare that's too bad!" Humpty Dumpty cried, breaking into a sud-   *19*
den passion. "You've been listening at doors — and behind trees — and down
chimneys — or you couldn't have known it!"

"I haven't, indeed!" Alice said very gently. "It's in a book."   *20*

"Ah, well! They may write such things in a *book,*" Humpty Dumpty said in   *21*
a calmer tone. "That's what you call a History of England, that is. Now, take
a good look at me! I'm one that has spoken to a King, *I* am: mayhap you'll
never see such another: and, to show you I'm not proud, you may shake hands
with me!" And he grinned almost from ear to ear, as he leant forwards (and as
nearly as possible fell off the wall in doing so) and offered Alice his hand. She
watched him a little anxiously as she took it. "If he smiled much more the ends
of his mouth might meet behind," she thought: "and then I don't know *what*
would happen to his head! I'm afraid it would come off!"

"Yes, all his horses and all his men," Humpty Dumpty went on. "They'd   *22* pick me up again in a minute, *they* would! However, this conversation is going on a little too fast: let's go back to the last remark but one."

"I'm afraid I can't quite remember it," Alice said, very politely.   23

"In that case we start afresh," said Humpty Dumpty, "and it's my turn to   24
choose a subject — " ("He talks about it just as if it was a game!" thought Alice.) "So here's a question for you. How old did you say you were?"

Alice made a short calculation, and said "Seven years and six months."   25

"Wrong!" Humpty Dumpty exclaimed triumphantly. "You never said a word   26
like it!"

"I thought you meant 'How old *are* you?' " Alice explained.   27

"If I'd meant that, I'd have said it," said Humpty Dumpty.   28

Alice didn't want to begin another argument, so she said nothing.   29

"Seven years and six months!" Humpty Dumpty repeated thoughtfully. "An   30
uncomfortable sort of age. Now if you'd asked *my* advice, I'd have said 'Leave off at seven' — but it's too late now."

"I never ask advice about growing," Alice said indignantly.   31

"Too proud?" the other enquired.   32

Alice felt even more indignant at this suggestion. "I mean," she said, "that   33
one can't help growing older."

"*One* can't, perhaps," said Humpty Dumpty; "but *two* can. With proper as-   34
sistance, you might have left off at seven."

"What a beautiful belt you've got on!" Alice suddenly remarked. (They had   35
had quite enough of the subject of age, she thought: and, if they really were to take turns in choosing subjects, it was *her* turn now.) "At least," she corrected herself on second thoughts, "a beautiful cravat, I should have said — no, a belt, I mean — I beg your pardon!" she added in dismay, for Humpty Dumpty looked thoroughly offended, and she began to wish she hadn't chosen that subject. "If only I knew," she thought to herself, "which was neck and which was waist!"

Evidently Humpty Dumpty was very angry, though he said nothing for a   36
minute or two. When he *did* speak again, it was in a deep growl.

"It is a — *most* — *provoking* — thing," he said at last, "when a person doesn't   37
know a cravat from a belt!"

"I know it's very ignorant of me," Alice said, in so humble a tone that Humpty   38
Dumpty relented.

"It's a cravat, child, and a beautiful one, as you say. It's a present from the   39
White King and Queen. There now!"

"Is it really?" said Alice, quite pleased to find that she *had* chosen a good   40
subject, after all.

"They gave it me," Humpty Dumpty continued thoughtfully, as he crossed   41
one knee over the other and clasped his hands round it, "they gave it me — for an un-birthday present."

"I beg your pardon?" Alice said with a puzzled air.   42

"I'm not offended," said Humpty Dumpty.   43

"I mean, what *is* an un-birthday present?"   44

"A present given when it isn't your birthday, of course."   45

Alice considered a little. "I like birthday presents best," she said at last.   46

"You don't know what you're talking about!" cried Humpty Dumpty. "How   47
many days are there in a year?"

"Three hundred and sixty-five," said Alice.   *48*

"And how many birthdays have you?"   *49*

"One."   *50*

"And if you take one from three hundred and sixty-five, what remains?"   *51*

"Three hundred and sixty-four, of course."   *52*

Humpty Dumpty looked doubtful. "I'd rather see that done on paper," he   *53*
said.

Alice couldn't help smiling as she took out her memorandum book, and   *54*
worked the sum for him:

$$\begin{array}{r} 365 \\ \underline{1} \\ 364 \end{array}$$

Humpty Dumpty took the book, and looked at it carefully. "That seems to   *55*
be done right — " he began.

"You're holding it upside down!" Alice interrupted.   *56*

"To be sure I was!" Humpty Dumpty said gaily, as she turned it round for   *57*
him. "I thought it looked a little queer. As I was saying, that *seems* to be done
right — though I haven't time to look it over thoroughly just now — and that
shows that there are three hundred and sixty-four days when you might get
un-birthday presents — "

"Certainly," said Alice.   *58*

"And only *one* for birthday presents, you know. There's glory for you!"   *59*

"I don't know what you mean by 'glory,' " Alice said.   *60*

Humpty Dumpty smiled contemptuously. "Of course you don't — till I tell   *61*
you. I meant 'there's a nice knock-down argument for you!' "

"But 'glory' doesn't mean 'a nice knock-down argument,' " Alice objected.   *62*

"When *I* use a word," Humpty Dumpty said, in rather a scornful tone, "it   *63*
means just what I choose it to mean — neither more nor less."

"The question is," said Alice, "whether you *can* make words mean so many   *64*
different things."

"The question is," said Humpty Dumpty, "which is to be master — that's   *65*
all."

Alice was too much puzzled to say anything; so after a minute Humpty   *66*
Dumpty began again. "They've a temper, some of them — particularly verbs:
they're the proudest — adjectives you can do anything with, but not verbs —
however, *I* can manage the whole lot of them! Impenetrability! That's what *I*
say!"

"Would you tell me, please," said Alice, "what that means?"   *67*

"Now you talk like a reasonable child," said Humpty Dumpty, looking very   *68*
much pleased. "I meant by 'impenetrability' that we've had enough of that
subject, and it would be just as well if you'd mention what you mean to do
next, as I suppose you don't mean to stop here all the rest of your life."

"That's a great deal to make one word mean," Alice said in a thoughtful   *69*
tone.

"When I make a word do a lot of work like that," said Humpty Dumpty, "I   *70*
always pay it extra."

"Oh!" said Alice. She was too much puzzled to make any other remark.   *71*

"Ah, you should see 'em come round me of a Saturday night," Humpty   72
Dumpty went on, wagging his head gravely from side to side, "for to get their
wages, you know."

Considerations

1. Humpty Dumpty says "When *I* use a word . . . it means just what I choose
   it to mean — neither more nor less. . . . The question is . . . which is to be
   master — that's all." What's your reaction to this statement? What happens
   when *we're* master, when we hold such power over language? What happens
   when *words* are master? Is Humpty Dumpty really master, as he suggests?
2. Explain the Humpty Dumpty nursery rhyme that Alice quotes in paragraph
   7 as a fable about power.
3. Analyze the conversation between Alice and Humpty Dumpty as a power
   struggle. Is Alice completely outmaneuvered here, or does she find a way of
   asserting her own power?

Connections

1. Analyze according to Bertrand Russell the power of Humpty Dumpty's propaganda: for example, his attempt to persuade Alice of the value of un-
   birthdays.
2. How might Lewis Carroll's use of humor in "Humpty Dumpty" be explained as an assertion of power? Use Elias Canetti, Samuel S. Janus, and
   any other sources that seem appropriate.
3. Humpty Dumpty poses several problems or puzzles to Alice. Look at Robert
   J. Sternberg and Janet E. Davidson's "The Mind of the Puzzler," in Chapter 7, The Nature of Intelligence, and then write an essay analyzing Humpty
   Dumpty's puzzles according to Sternberg and Davidson.
4. After reading several pieces in Chapter 2, The Origins of the Nuclear Arms
   Race, determine the extent to which language issues — the power of words
   and our power over words — contribute to the controversy.
5. Brainstorm to find other power issues that "Humpty Dumpty" raises, and
   connect them to other pieces in this chapter or other chapters in this book.
   For example, power of economy (in words that do more than one thing),
   power of established social roles (Alice as a polite little girl), power of political influence (Humpty Dumpty's supposed relationship to the king), power
   of cooperation, power of eccentricity, power of anger, power of flattery, power
   of statistics, power of faulty reasoning.

Three Poems on Brueghel's *Landscape with the Fall of Icarus*

Pieter Brueghel the Elder (c.1525–1569), an influential Flemish landscape and genre painter, is best known for his allegorical works and his attention to minute detail. Landscape with the Fall of Icarus *is based on a story from Greek mythology. The architect Daedalus, imprisoned by King Minos in the labyrinth, built wings out of wax and feathers for himself and his son Icarus to escape with. But Icarus, exulting in his new power and strength, flew too near the sun; his wings melted, and he fell into the sea.*

Landscape with
the Fall of Icarus

William Carlos Williams

According to Brueghel
when Icarus fell
it was spring

a farmer was plowing
his field   5
the whole pageantry

of the year was
awake tingling
near

the edge of the sea   10
concerned
with itself

sweating in the sun
that melted
the wings' wax   15

unsignificantly
off the coast
there was

a splash quite unnoticed
this was   20
Icarus drowning

William Carlos Williams (1883–1963) was an American poet and physician educated first in Switzerland, then at the University of Pennsylvania, where he received his M.D. degree in 1906. Later he studied pediatrics at the University of Leipzig. He was a practicing physician for more than forty years, but he also attained the stature of one of America's most important — and most original — poets.

Lines on Brueghel's Icarus

Michael Hamburger

The ploughman ploughs, the fisherman dreams of fish;
Aloft, the sailor through a world of ropes
Guides tangled meditations, feverish
With memories of girls forsaken, hopes
Of brief reunions, new discoveries,   5
Past rum consumed, rum promised, rum potential.
Sheep crop the grass, lift up their heads and gaze
Into a sheepish present: the essential,
Illimitable juiciness of things,
Greens, yellows, browns are what they see.   10
Churlish and slow, the shepherd, hearing wings —
Perhaps an eagle's — gapes uncertainly;

Too late. The worst had happened: lost to man,
The angel, Icarus, for ever failed,
Fallen with melted wings when, near the sun   15
He scorned the ordering planet, which prevailed
And jeering, now slinks off, to rise once more.
But he — his damaged purpose drags him down —
Too far from his half-brothers on the shore,
Hardly conceivable, is left to drown.   20

Michael Hamburger (b. 1924) was born in Berlin and moved to England in 1933, where he earned an M.A. from Oxford in 1948. He has won prizes for his translations of literary works from the German but is also a highly regarded poet in his own right.

Musée des Beaux Arts
W. H. Auden

About suffering they were never wrong,
The Old Masters: how well they understood
Its human position; how it takes place
While someone else is eating or opening a window or just walking dully along;
How, when the aged are reverently, passionately waiting   5
For the miraculous birth, there always must be
Children who did not specially want it to happen, skating
On a pond at the edge of the wood:
They never forgot
That even the dreadful martyrdom must run its course   10
Anyhow in a corner, some untidy spot
Where the dogs go on with their doggy life and the torturer's horse
Scratches its innocent behind on a tree.

In Brueghel's *Icarus*, for instance: how everything turns away
Quite leisurely from the disaster; the ploughman may   15
Have heard the splash, the forsaken cry,
But for him it was not an important failure; the sun shone
As it had to on the white legs disappearing into the green
Water; and the expensive delicate ship that must have seen
Something amazing, a boy falling out of the sky,   20
Had somewhere to get to and sailed calmly on.

Considerations

1. William Carlos Williams's poem "Landscape with the Fall of Icarus" has no punctuation. Rewrite the poem in sentences with proper punctuation, then explain your decisions. Are there possibilities other than the ones you've chosen? Are they as reasonable? Compare your prose version with Williams's. Is yours *poetry* in any sense of the word? Explain.
2. Compare and contrast Williams's description of Brueghel's painting with the painting itself.
3. Compare and contrast Williams's, Hamburger's, and Auden's poems on

Wystan Hugh Auden (1907–1973) was born in England, educated at Oxford, and became a U.S. citizen in 1946. After 1948, he divided his time between New York and Europe, and in 1972, he returned to Oxford. He ranks among the major literary figures of the twentieth century. His poems, often written in everyday language, cover subjects as diverse as politics, modern psychology, and Christianity.

Brueghel's *Icarus*. Look especially at language, images and motifs, emphases, important themes, and the relation of each to the painting. What can you conclude?

4. According to the three poets, what ethical and existential dilemmas does the story of Icarus create? How do these involve the issue of power? Do any of the poets offer answers?

5. To what extent is the story of Icarus a fable about power? What is the moral? Has it been illustrated by any historical figures or any modern political figures? Select one or several, and explain.

6. Answer question 5 using personal examples.

7. Francis Bacon, in his essay "Of Goodness," says, "The desire of power in excess caused the angels to fall; the desire of knowledge in excess caused man to fall." What does each part of the quotation refer to specifically? Is this an analogy? Explain how the form of the sentence emphasizes both similarities and differences. Then explain how both these situations in the quotation parallel, yet differ from, the myth of Icarus.

Connections

1. How might Machiavelli's advice be applied to the moral of the Icarus story?

2. How would Sigmund Freud interpret the story of Icarus? Would Elias Canetti agree?

3. Describe the similarities you can see between the nursery rhyme about Humpty Dumpty that Alice recites and the myth of Icarus.

4. Compare and contrast the myth of Icarus and the fairy tale "Snow White" in Chapter 10, The Fairy Tale "Snow White."

5. How would you connect the story of Icarus with the nuclear arms race as represented in Chapter 2, The Origins of the Nuclear Arms Race?

6. After reading C. Wright Mills's essay, "The Ideal of Craftsmanship," in Chapter 5, The Working World, what sort of warning would you say Icarus offers the craftsman?

Further Connections

1. Assemble a list of adjectives that modify *power;* for example, *political, solar, black, financial, nuclear, horse.* Then classify them into types. Write an essay describing each category.

2. Use *Roget's Thesaurus* to make a list of synonyms for the word *power.* Group synonyms into categories and offer a definition for *power* in each category; then sort out the different synonyms within each, focusing on the connotation each word carries.

3. Compare and contrast the definitions of *power* from the perspectives of as

many academic disciplines as you can think of. Use the selections in this chapter and in the whole book and information from your other courses as well.

4. Francis Bacon said, "Knowledge is power." Use the readings in this chapter to explain what he meant.

5. Icarus shows us one consequence of ambition. Another symbol of ambition appears in John Milton's epic poem *Paradise Lost* in which God punishes the angel Satan's greed for power by driving him out of heaven into hell. Satan responds that it is "better to reign in Hell than serve in Heaven" (Book I, line 263). Argue Satan's side of the case for power, offering examples going beyond the religious context; that is, look at social or political situations where Satan's position might make sense. Use any of the readings in this chapter or in other chapters to strengthen your case.

6. Based on your readings in this chapter and in Chapter 4, The Urban Experience, speculate on how easy it would be to acquire and maintain power in an urban setting.

7. Analyze any of the selections in Chapter 5, The Working World, to determine who has power. Explain what sort of power the piece you have selected examines.

8. Read the John Locke selection in Chapter 6, The Nature of Learning. Then decide on the extent to which the relationship between a boy and his tutor resembles a power struggle. What does each side represent? Would Locke be likely to agree with any of the authors in this chapter?

9. How could David H. Hubel, writing on "The Brain" in Chapter 7, The Nature of Intelligence, define *power?*

10. Explain how the treatments described in Chapter 8, The Treatment of Cancer, represent a power struggle. Who are the principals here?

11. After reading the Charles Darwin and Carl Sagan selections in Chapter 9, The Impact of Animals, explain the concept of *animal power.*

12. Where is the power struggle, and who are the principals, according to the fairy tale "Snow White" in Chapter 10? What is at stake, both literally and metaphorically?

Extensions

1. Freud claims that the "love instinct" is behind both the issue of war and peace (in his letter to Einstein in this chapter) and man's compulsion to work (in Freud's *Civilization and Its Discontents*). Read Chapter 5 of *Civilization and Its Discontents* (New York: Norton, 1961) and explain how the love instinct connects such diverse issues.

2. Look at Konrad Lorenz's *On Aggression* and Nikolaas Tinbergen's discussion of fighting in *The Study of Instinct*, and decide how these authors either support or refute Elias Canetti's explanation of power.

3. Do some brief research on anorexia nervosa. Check *Psychological Abstracts* for journal articles, and look at Hilde Bruch's *The Golden Cage* (New York: Random House, 1979) or Salvador Minuchin's *Psychosomatic Families: An-*

orexia Nervosa in Context (Cambridge, Mass.: Harvard University Press, 1978). Review Canetti; then write a paper in which you discuss anorexia as a question of power — in the family, and over one's body.

4. Read O. Weininger's "Dominance in Children," in *Domination: Essays,* edited by Alkis Koutos. Then write a personal essay applying Weininger's ideas to explain that perennial domestic power struggle, sibling rivalry.

5. As a class project, prepare an annotated bibliography on sibling rivalry. Check *Social Sciences Index* and *Sociological Abstracts* for sources. Each annotation should include a summary of the article's content and an evaluation.

6. The issue of power within the family is tricky. Prepare a research paper on the relationships between husbands and wives or between parents and children. Begin with the extensive bibliography in Gerald McDonald's "Family Power" in *Journal of Marriage and the Family* to find appropriate sources. Add to your list of books and articles either R. W. Medlicott's "The Male-Female Balance of Power in the Western Tradition" in *Australian and New Zealand Journal of Psychiatry* (and the Janus article in this chapter) or Alice Miller's *For Your Own Good* — and any other sources you can find.

7. In the Lewis Carroll selection, Alice asks Humpty Dumpty for an interpretation of "The Jabberwocky," a poem she had discovered earlier. Read the poem and Alice's response to it in Chapter 1 of *Through the Looking-Glass;* then interpret the poem for yourself. When you're done, look at Humpty Dumpty's interpretation, and check in *The Annotated Alice* for the notes by Martin Gardner (New York: New American Library). Decide which interpretation of the poem you prefer. Justify your choice, being sure to weigh the issue of the power of, and power over, language.

8. Read John Fowles's *The French Lieutenant's Woman.* Decide which is master — the power of authority of the omniscient novelist, or the "freedom to allow other freedoms to exist." Defend your position.

9. Both Apollodorus and Ovid tell the story of Icarus. Find one translation of each and one summary of the story; for example in *Bulfinch's Mythology* (New York: Modern Library) or Edith Hamilton's *Mythology* (Boston: Little, Brown, 1942). Compare and contrast these three versions, focusing on how each deals with the issue of ambition and power.

10. Read F. Scott Fitzgerald's novel, *The Great Gatsby,* a portrait of the American dream and the self-made man. One critic has called Gatsby "a modern Icarus." Explain what you think he means; then agree or disagree with that position, supporting your stand with evidence from the novel and from the story of Icarus.

11. Look at any one of the twenty-four studies of political power in Leonard Krieger and Fritz Stern's *The Responsibility of Power: Historical Essays in Honor of Hajo Holborn.* Then prepare a brief research paper on your chosen subject, looking at scholarly articles in *Historical Abstracts* or *International Political Science Abstracts,* or *Social Sciences Index* (or all three).

12. Henry Adams, in "The Dynamo and the Virgin," Chapter 25 of *The Education of Henry Adams,* claims that the Virgin, as a religious figure, built — or at least inspired the building of — the cathedral of Notre-Dame at Chartres. Select another example of religious power (for instance, the Cru-

sades, the founding of the state of Israel, Khomeini's revolution in Iran). Write a research paper in which you discuss the extent to which such religion-inspired action is political. Begin with the *New York Times Index* if you choose a fairly current example; check books or journal articles first if you choose a less recent example.

13. Henry Adams also describes pieces of sculpture as symbols of power. Visit a museum and write a report on three pieces of sculpture, explaining how each represents a different type of power.

14. Read Robert N. McMurry's "Power and the Ambitious Executive" in *Harvard Business Review* or some of Anthony Jay's *Management and Machiavelli*. Then determine the extent to which Machiavellian tactics permeate the activities of the business world according to these authors. Does either author distort Machiavelli's ideas?

15. Read Michael Korda's *Power! How to Get It, How to Use It*. Who is his audience? What is wrong with his advice?

Suggestions for Further Reading

Adams, Henry. "The Dynamo and the Virgin," Chapter 25 of *The Education of Henry Adams*. Boston: Houghton Mifflin, 1961. A cultural historian examines both technology and myth as power.

Annas, George J. "Nuclear Power: Safety and Economics" and "Nuclear Power: Psychology and Statistics." *American Journal of Public Health* 73 (1983): 1099–1100, 1327–1328. A professor of public health law discusses some dimensions of nuclear power.

Jay, Anthony. *Management and Machiavelli: An Inquiry into the Politics of Corporate Life*. New York: Holt, Rinehart and Winston, 1968. The corporate world's power play according to the principles of Machiavelli.

Korda, Michael. *Power! How to Get It, How to Use It*. New York: Ballantine, 1975. A handbook of power in the "real" world, with a chapter, "The Power Game."

Krieger, Leonard, and Fritz Stern. *The Responsibility of Power: Historical Essays in Honor of Hajo Holborn*. New York: Doubleday, 1967. A collection of twenty-four studies of political power, covering the formation of sovereign power, the liberal critique of power, and the ethical dilemma of power in the democratic age.

Lorenz, Konrad. *On Aggression*. New York: Harcourt, Brace and World, 1966. Biology and the struggle for power.

McDonald, Gerald W. "Family Power: The Assessment of a Decade of Theory and Research, 1970–1979." *Journal of Marriage and the Family* (November 1980): 841–854. Detailed review article covering theory and research on "family power"; includes an extensive bibliography.

McMurry, Robert N. "Power and the Ambitious Executive." *Harvard Business Review* 51 (1973):140–145. The business executive's actions as part of a political power struggle.

Medlicott, R. W. "The Male-Female Balance of Power in the Western Tradition." *Australian and New Zealand Journal of Psychiatry* 15 (1981): 157–163. History of male-female competition against the background of Greek and Judaeo-Christian thought, with some applications to the present.

Miller, Alice. *For Your Own Good.* New York: Farrar, Straus, and Giroux, 1983. Parental discipline as simply a power play.

Ridolfi, Roberto. *The Life of Machiavelli.* Translated by Cecil Grayson. Chicago: University of Chicago Press, 1963. Background reading on the controversial analyst of political power.

Tinbergen, Nikolaas. *The Study of Instinct.* New York: Oxford University Press, 1951. Includes a thought-provoking section on the fighting instinct.

Weber, Max. *The Theory of Social and Economic Organization.* New York: Oxford University Press, 1947. The noted German sociologist and political economist discusses power, authority, and imperative control.

Weininger, O. "Dominance in Children." In *Domination: Essays,* edited by Alkis Koutos. Toronto: University of Toronto Press, 1975. An "air of survival necessity" characterizes the young child's sense of power over the behavior, actions, and feelings of others, including members of his own family.

2 The Origins of the Nuclear Arms Race

Edited by **Donna Uthus Gregory**

Nuclear weapons entered our world so suddenly that most of us have not had time to grasp their significance. We may never have time: the nuclear arsenals presently in existence could destroy civilization and most of nature. In a single hour, centuries of human history could be ended, leaving a ruined planet as its only testament.

This terrible power has made its way into our world in only the last forty years. In half a lifetime, all of the assumptions our species makes about its continuity, assumptions that underlie our laws, our economic institutions, our philosophies, our art — assumptions once unquestionable about the endurance of the human spirit, the common goal of a just and loving world, the fulfill-ment of hopes — all these have become tenuous. We have not yet had time to understand such an abrupt change.

Scholars and people active in every field of human inquiry have now begun to think about the profound meaning of nuclear weapons for human culture. But only a few of the fields of human knowledge now concerned about nuclear weapons took up the subject in the early 1940s. Nuclear weapons have been a subject of military science, however, even before they were operational, and this military involvement is revealed in the arcane and often inaccessible lan-guage that developed along with the arsenals and the strategies for managing them — language that reminds us constantly that these were once matters we left to a special group of experts.

There are indeed real experts who constitute a professional group called the *national security community*. It includes defense analysts who primarily advise military and government policy makers; like defense matters generally, most of their research is classified. Employed by various institutions such as the Joint Chiefs of Staff (that is, the military), the Department of Defense, the Depart-ment of State, the CIA, independent research institutes called *think tanks*, and the defense industry, they constitute a relatively stable group and are not subject to public critique or the exigencies of popular elections. Until very recently, our legislators were dependent on this small group for most of their information about nuclear weapons and defense strategy. Now, things are changing. People from many fields are studying these issues and writing about them, broadening the base of information for policy makers.

Of course, political science and international law have maintained their long commitment in this area. And the sciences and engineering, which created the technology for making nuclear weapons more efficient, have created surveillance technology as well — the "national technical means" by which compliance with treaties is monitored. From the beginning there have been scientists who played a different role, too. There have been those who took the lead in every early attempt at nuclear disarmament, and they remain involved in both antinuclear education and in political activism today. These efforts are one of the subjects this chapter includes.

Entirely new groups have entered the scene. Physicians have formed activist groups, taking the position that a nuclear war would render their duty to preserve life impossible to perform; therefore, they argue, they can keep their oath by working to prevent a nuclear war from ever occurring. Lawyers have convened under a similar rationale; while the doctors are studying the potential medical consequences to society of a nuclear war, activist lawyers are trying to find a basis in international law for declaring nuclear weapons illegal.

Social scientists, too, are contributing to the multidisciplinary dialogue. Psychologists have long been studying ways conflicts may be resolved without force. They investigate the effects of living under the threat of nuclear devastation and the tendency of foreign policy to reflect the personalities of a nation's leaders: how fear, a desire for superiority, or an unwillingness to "lose face" affect policy decisions, and how these personal characteristics can shape the very nature of *reality* for many policy makers. Both psychologists and linguists are examining ways that the words and meaning of language have changed with the assimilation of nuclear weapons into our culture. Sociologists are interested in how power and authority work in our own society and in Soviet society and how powerful individuals or groups influence decision-making. With economists, they are also studying how nations allocate their resources among social needs and social classes, and they are beginning to define the process of *militarization*. Economists assess both the relative cost-effectiveness of nuclear weapons compared to conventional ones and the strain a militarized economy puts on our resources.

While the physical and social sciences seem to have an equal number of proponents and opponents of nuclear deterrence, those in the humanities tend to be more critical. Historians are examining every aspect of history that relates to nuclear weapons — diplomatic, intellectual, social, biographic — in light of the enormous cultural impact these weapons have had. Anthropologists question whether a nuclear defense system is *objectively* unavoidable or whether certain characteristics in our own culture influence this choice. Philosophy and religious studies look at the ethical question: Can our current policy of nuclear deterrence be justified on moral grounds?

Everyone agrees that a nuclear war must be prevented. What divides us is *how* we can achieve this. Groups like Physicians for Social Responsibility, the Union of Concerned Scientists, and the Nuclear Freeze Movement believe that the way to prevent a nuclear war is to eliminate the potential for one — the weapons. At the very least, they feel, we should reduce the present size of the arsenals on both sides. But other groups believe that the weapons themselves are the best means for avoiding a holocaust. This group includes those who reluctantly accept the philosophy of nuclear deterrence, believing that there is no alternative; for them, nuclear weapons are a necessary evil. As the readings in this chapter show, each group has many reasons for its beliefs. The readings also show that up to now, decision-making power has been in the hands of the people who believe that weapons are the answer. Thus, the arms race proceeds.

The arguments advanced in 1945 are largely those advanced today: they hinge on assessments of the Soviet Union; on the inevitability of power politics; and on appropriate and necessary means for protecting our homeland, our allies, and our "vital interests," such as Middle Eastern oil. How *necessary* is the nuclear evil that is supposed to provide this protection? When do its risks exceed its benefits? These were the fundamental matters of disagreement in 1945 as they are today.

The readings in this chapter take us back to the first attempts at nuclear disarmament — actually, to the attempts to prevent an arms race in the first place. What you will find here is very much like a drama in which the key characters are the physicists who developed the fission process and the bomb. Like prophets, Niels Bohr, Leo Szilard, James Franck, Robert Oppenheimer, and others knew before the bomb was even operational that without international agreements to control nuclear technology, the world would face an arms race of a potentially cataclysmic nature. Their efforts culminated in a proposal delivered at the United Nations in 1945 called the Baruch Plan (named for the man who presented it). The proposal failed. The documents in this chapter invite us to explain that failure.

Nuclear Arms: A Brief History

Randall Forsberg

What is the relationship of the nuclear arms race to the various roles of conventional military forces?　*1*

Most people in the United States believe that the purpose of US nuclear　*2*

Randall Forsberg (b. 1943), while a graduate student in political science at the Massachusetts Institute of Technology, conceived the Nuclear Freeze Initiative — the Freeze — which went before Congress in 1983. She is presently executive director of the Institute for Defense and Disarmament Studies.

weapons is to deter a nuclear attack on the United States by the Soviet Union by threatening retaliation in kind.

This is undoubtedly one of the functions of US nuclear weapons, but it is   3
not the only function, nor the function that motivates the continuation of the nuclear arms race between the United States and the Soviet Union.

The purpose of the on-going nuclear arms race, to the extent that there is   4
any rational purpose, is to back up US uses of conventional armed forces overseas and to deter such uses of Soviet conventional forces. This connection between the roles of nuclear and conventional military forces is illustrated throughout the history of the nuclear arms race.

Initially, the United States developed nuclear weapons because we believed   5
that there might be a nuclear program in Germany during World War II. We wanted to be able to respond to a potential nuclear threat with a nuclear response.

However, toward the end of World War II it became clear that Germany did   6
not have a nuclear program; and that there was no nuclear threat to the Western allies. At that point the US nuclear program did not end. With great momentum, it continued right ahead.

During the four-year wartime Manhattan project, the United States pro-   7
duced enough fissionable uranium and plutonium to make just three nuclear bombs. We tested one of them in the desert, and we used the other two on Hiroshima and Nagasaki.

This use of nuclear weapons had nothing to do with deterring a nuclear at-   8
tack on the United States or anyone else. The United States used nuclear weapons that had been produced for two reasons.

One was to end a conventional war with, it was argued, less loss of life than   9
would occur if the war continued. It was claimed that it might take 500,000 American lives to recapture all of the Pacific islands from the Japanese, in bloody, over-the-beach warfare. The bombs dropped on Hiroshima and Nagasaki killed, immediately, about 100,000 persons each. So nuclear weapons were seen as a means of decreasing death and violence and ending the war more quickly. They were intimately interrelated with the pursuit of conventional warfare goals.

The second reason probably played a great role in the dropping of the sec-   10
ond bomb on Nagasaki. For the bomb on Hiroshima should have been enough (if even that was needed) to make the Japanese sue for total surrender, which were the only terms permitted to them.

The function of the second bomb, if not the first, was to intimidate the So-   11
viet Union: as a precedent for the post-war environment, to make clear that the United States not only had a nuclear monopoly, but was prepared to use it. The demonstration was intended to show that, if the Soviet Union used its conventional forces in a manner objectionable to the United States, the USA would not hesitate to respond with nuclear weapons. Thus, again, nuclear policy was inextricably intertwined with conventional war and power politics.

Post-War Nuclear Policies

During the period from 1945 to 1955 the United States continued to have a   12
virtual monopoly on nuclear weapons. US policy in this period was called

"massive retaliation." Its purpose was to deter Soviet uses of conventional military force by threatening simply to wipe out the major cities of the Soviet Union in response. In 1950 the United States had 300 nuclear bombs on 300 propeller-driven planes. Those were all the nuclear weapons in the world. They were not very many by present day standards; and they might well have been used against population targets because they were, relatively speaking, so few in number.

By 1960, the Soviet Union had acquired nuclear weapons and the means to   13 deliver them to the United States. It had at that time 150 strategic bombers that could reach this country, together with several hundred nuclear missiles and about 500 bombers that could reach Western Europe.

In the interval, the United States had deployed 2000 strategic bombers,   14 loaded, ready-to-go, and aimed at the Soviet Union: 600 B52s and 1400 shorter-range B47s stationed at overseas bases. The USA had also built up a force of about 10,000 tactical nuclear weapons. These are short-range nuclear weapons aimed primarily at military targets: anti-aircraft missiles with nuclear tips; antisubmarine torpedoes with nuclear tips; and surface-to-surface missiles to use on the battlefield against on-coming enemy tank formations, including missiles with a range of 400 miles that would go from West Germany to East Germany, as well as missiles with a range of 70 miles, missiles with a range of 30 miles, and even 8-inch howitzers with a range of 15 miles, for use on the battlefield in West Germany. (The neutron bomb is an antitank weapon that is designed to emit enough radiation not merely to kill the men driving the tanks but to make them die in a matter of minutes or hours rather than days or weeks.)

Accompanying the deployment of tactical nuclear weapons, the United States   15 maintained the policy in effect since the end of World War II of posing a threat of first use of nuclear weapons. If the USA became involved in a conventional war with the Soviet Union, and the war was going against this country, we would be ready (on someone else's territory) to escalate up to the use of our tactical nuclear weapons against Soviet conventional forces.

Until the mid-1960s, the United States still had such a marked superi-   16 ority in both intercontinental and Europe-oriented nuclear weapons that it could continue to pose this threat with some confidence. The USA built up its original strategic missile force much sooner than the Soviet Union did. Both on land and on submarines the main force of invulnerable US missiles was deployed between 1960 and 1967. At that time, the Soviet Union was still relying on its few intercontinental bombers and on 200 vulnerable ICBMs. Neither the Soviet bombers nor the ICBMs were ready to launch, and both could have been destroyed in a preemptive strike.

The Soviet Union first began to acquire nuclear forces that gave it an in-   17 vulnerable, second-strike deterrent in 1965. This is when the USSR started building ICBMs in steel-reinforced concrete underground silos. The Soviet Union deployed 1400 such ICMBs over the period 1965–1971. It started building submarines with long-range missiles deployed in range of the United States only in 1967; and it built up a force of sixty-two strategic submarines between 1967 and 1977.

Thus, it is only in this last 15 years that US cities have become unavoidably   18 hostage to a Soviet missile strike that could take place in half an hour. It is only because we failed to stop the arms race in 1960 that we are exposed to this threat today.

During the last decade there has been widespread recognition of parity be- *19* tween the USA and USSR in nuclear forces. What this means is not that the Soviet Union can match all the esoteric nuclear capabilities of the United States, but that, for the first time, it can match the all-important, "bottom-line" second-strike capability: it can retain the forces to obliterate the USA in a second strike, no matter what sort of counterforce attack the United States undertakes first.

While the Soviet Union was still building up its main generation of stra- *20* tegic missiles, between 1970 and 1977, the United States took out most of the missiles that it had on land and on submarines and replaced them with new missiles with multiple nuclear warheads or MIRVs (multiple, independently-targetable re-entry vehicles).

In 1976, in a program that was perfectly predictable, the USSR started doing *21* the same thing: replacing its main ICBM and submarine-launched missiles with new MIRVed missiles. The Soviet MIRV program has now been completed on land but is still under way on submarines, where it probably will not be completed until 1985.

Effort to Recapture Superiority

The response of the United States to Soviet acquisition of an invulnerable *22* deterrent force over the last 15 years is to try to recapture the clear superiority that it had until the mid-1960s. The attempt to do this is being made by developing and deploying the MX missile, which will have the ability to destroy Soviet ICBMs in their silos; and by adding a new submarine-based missile, the Trident II, and a new type of missile, the cruise missile, which will provide thousands of additional nuclear warheads with precision attack capability.

In addition to these new offensive nuclear forces, the United States already *23* has an extraordinary antisubmarine warfare (ASW) capability built, as described earlier, in response to Soviet conventional submarines. The US ASW capability has been strengthened for operations against strategic submarines. The United States has large sonar towers off the coast of Norway, off the Azores, and off the Japanese Islands. These are attached by cable to a giant computer processing center, which can dampen out all of the other noises in the ocean and leave in only the noises of Soviet submarines. Under good conditions, Soviet submarines can actually be tracked all the way across the Atlantic by means of these sonar towers. Soviet submarines come out of narrow port exits. They are rather poorly designed and noisy. The port exits are surrounded by US, Japanese and British antisub submarines and aircraft.

As a result of this ASW capability, when the United States acquires the MX *24* in the late 1980s, it will be back in a position similar to that of the 1950s and 1960s, when it could threaten a preemptive strike against most Soviet medium-range and intercontinental nuclear forces.

There will be very important differences, though, between the earlier situ- *25* ation and that in 1990. When the USA threatened a preemptive strike earlier, the number of targets (airfields and missile groups) that it would strike was relatively small, a few hundred; and the Soviet Union had no capability to launch its missiles on warning of an incoming attack. Today and in the future that will not be the case. The Soviet generals can now launch their missiles, just as the United States can, when their radar screens show that the opponent's missiles have been launched. In addition, current US counterforce attack scenarios provide for the use of several thousand nuclear warheads against the large Soviet missile forces. The Soviets could send back to the United States a retaliatory attack of equal magnitude.

The effect of even a limited counterforce exchange between the two super-   26 powers, with nuclear warheads directed against the nuclear forces of the opposing side, has been calculated to be between three and twenty million dead in the United States and a like number in the USSR, simply from downwind fallout of the explosions on missile sites.

This is the most easily predictable effect. No one has the faintest notion of   27 what would happen to the global ecology if 4000–8000 nuclear weapons were exploded in a very short space of time.° The ozone layer would be blown away. The fallout would increase the background level of radiation and darken the sky worldwide. Tremendous firestorms would be created. These things combined would create changes in the world's climate which could be cumulative and synergistic. . . .

The main region for nuclear deterrence of conventional war is Europe. But   28 this is a very stable region, in which conventional war between East and West is highly unlikely: both sides have too little to gain and too much to lose. Where conventional war remains quite likely, and thus, where the nuclear backup may actually be believed to play an active role in shaping the course of events, is in the third world. In this sense, the purpose of the on-going nuclear arms race is, from the point of view of the USA, to give the United States greater freedom to intervene in developing countries without risking a conventional challenge on the part of the Soviet Union; and to inhibit Soviet conventional intervention. From the point of view of the USSR, the purpose of trying to match US nuclear developments is to nullify the nuclear factor in global power politics.

The US generals calculate that, if they can show on paper that a direct con-   29 ventional confrontation between the two superpowers could escalate to a local or intercontinental nuclear exchange that would leave the US ahead by some measure, then the Soviet generals will not risk sending in conventional forces in the first place; nor will they feel free to intervene themselves in developing countries where Western stakes are high, which was not the case in Afghanistan.

Considerations

1. In her opening sentence, Randall Forsberg asks, "What is the relationship of the nuclear arms race to the various roles of conventional military forces?" Summarize her answers.

°This article was written in 1982, at least a year before the nuclear winter effect began to be discussed.

2. Divide Forsberg's account into historical periods. For each, summarize the following: the growth in number of weapons and the action-reaction dynamic between the United States and the Soviet Union. (The article was written in 1982; hence, "the last fifteen years" refers to 1967–1982.)

The Dropping of the A-Bomb: How Decisions Are Made When A Nation Is at War

Barton J. Bernstein

I know that Japan is a terribly cruel and uncivilized nation in warfare but I can't bring myself to believe that, because they are beasts, we should ourselves act in the same manner.

–Harry S. Truman
August 10, 1945

On August 6, 1945, the Enola Gay, a B-29, dropped an atomic bomb on Hiroshima, a major Japanese city. That bomb killed at least eighty thousand, injured many more, and, unknown to Americans then, killed some American prisoners of war. Most of the immediate Japanese deaths were from flash burns, blast, and falling debris. Ultimately thousands more died from radiation. "Hiroshima was uniformly and extensively devastated," an American bombing survey later reported. "Practically the entire densely or moderately built-up portion of the city was leveled by blast or swept by fire." Americans enthusiastically welcomed the news of the atomic bombing.   *1*

When President Harry S. Truman announced the atomic destruction of Hiroshima, which he described only as "an important Japanese army base," he warned Japan of "a rain of ruin" unless it surrendered on American terms. Three days later, on the 9th, America dropped another A-bomb, this time on Nagasaki. That bomb killed at least forty-five thousand, injured over fifty thousand, and again killed some allied prisoners of war. The next day, when Japan offered conditional surrender, Truman decided to halt the atomic bombing. He told his Cabinet, according to an associate's diary, "the thought of wiping out another one hundred thousand people was too horrible. He didn't like the idea of killing, as he said, 'all those kids.'" On August 14th, Japan finally surrendered and the third A-bomb, which could have been delivered on the 18th or 19th, was placed in the stockpile.   *2*

Barton Bernstein (b. 1936) is a professor of history at Stanford University. He has written extensively about the history of the nuclear arms race, focusing particularly on the Truman period.

Since 1945, and especially with the renewed anxiety about nuclear war, many   *3*
have asked important questions about the nuclear attacks on Hiroshima and
Nagasaki: Why weren't alternatives first tried? Would they have produced a
speedy Japanese surrender? Why were the bombs used? Why were cities chosen, and why those cities? Weren't American leaders appalled by the likely
Japanese deaths? On the basis of newly available information, some have asked
additional questions: If the war had not ended in mid-August, would Truman
have dropped a third atomic bomb and possibly more? Why didn't the government later admit the nuclear deaths of the POWs?

I

In late 1941, when President Franklin D. Roosevelt launched the top-secret   *4*
A-bomb project, inspired largely by the fear that Germany was also racing to
build the dread weapon, American leaders assumed that the bomb would be a
legitimate weapon in the war. Throughout the war, they never questioned that
assumption. Building on that assumption, they slowly came to define the target as Japan, not Germany, and to plan to use the weapon on a city, not a purely
military installation.

On May 5, 1943, when the evidence was still unclear whether Germany was   *5*
successfully pursuing its A-bomb project, a high-level American committee, including General Leslie Groves, director of the American project, and Vannevar
Bush and James Conant, top scientist-administrators then advising FDR, concluded that the first bomb should be dropped on Japan. "[T]he general view,"
according to the minutes, was that the bomb's "best point of use would be on
a Japanese fleet concentration in the Harbor of Truk." General Wilhelm Styer,
the representative of the War Department, "suggested Tokyo but it was pointed
out that the bomb should be used where, if it failed to go off, it would land in
water of sufficient depth to prevent easy salvage. The Japanese were selected
as they would not be so apt to secure knowledge from it as would the Ger-
mans."

The committee members never discussed in moral terms the issue of select-   *6*
ing a target: Should the bomb be used against a clearly military target, like a
fleet or troops, or against a city, where civilians and industry were intertwined
and thousands of civilians would be killed? In this discussion, the committee
disposed of the issue on narrow tactical grounds—what was the best way of
using the bomb and of keeping the technology secret if the bomb did not explode? Hence, they did not have to face directly the question of whether America should follow Britain and Germany and use "terror" bombing—the intentional killing of civilians.

Apparently, the choice of targets did not receive systematic attention until   *7*
late April, 1945. By then, the war against Germany was nearly over and scientists estimated that the first A-bombs would be ready in August and might
be equivalent to about five thousand tons of TNT. On April 27th, a special Target Committee, including General Groves, General Lauris Norstad, later the
commander of the North Atlantic Treaty Organization, and John Von Neu-
mann, the famous mathematician, considered which Japanese cities would be
good targets.

The good targets were being destroyed, the group lamented. As the minutes 8
stated, "the 20th Air Force is operating primarily to laying waste all the main
Japanese cities, . . . with the prime purpose in mind of not leaving one stone
lying on another."

"Consideration [of targets for the A-bomb] is to be given," they concluded, 9
"to large urban areas of not less than three miles in diameter existing in the
larger populated areas [and the] target and/or aiming point should have a high
strategic value." They wanted the bomb to kill civilians. They picked seventeen places for further study: Tokyo Bay (the port area), Kawasaki, Yokohama,
Nagoya, Osaka, Kobe, Kyoto, Hiroshima, Kure, Yawata, Kokura, Shimosenka,
Yamaguchi, Kumamoto, Fukuoka, Nagasaki, and Sasebo.

Two weeks later, at their meeting on May 10th and 11th, held this time in 10
the Los Alamos Laboratory office of its director, J. Robert Oppenheimer, the
notable physicist, they discussed where to drop the bomb. They talked about
bombing the Emperor's palace but, according to the minutes, agreed "that we
should not recommend it but that any action for this bombing should come
from authorities on military policy." They focused on five targets: Kyoto, Hiroshima, Yokohama, Kokura Arsenal, and Niigata. They rejected Niigata,
classified as only a "B" target, but retained the other four, since Kyoto and
Hiroshima were "AA" targets and Yokohama and Kokura Arsenal "A" targets.

They stressed that "psychological factors in the target selection were of great 11
importance [, especially] obtaining the greatest psychological effect against
Japan and . . . making the initial use sufficiently spectacular for the importance of the weapon to be internationally recognized . . ." Kyoto, the former
Japanese capital, they emphasized, "has the advantage of the people being more
highly intelligent and hence better able to appreciate the significance of the
weapon. Hiroshima has the advantage of being such a size and with possible
focusing from nearby mountains that a large fraction of the city may be destroyed. The Emperor's palace in Tokyo has a greater fame than any other target but is of less strategic value."

When the Target Committee met on May 28th, they revised their list of tar- 12
get cities and selected Kyoto, Hiroshima, and Niigata. They decided the bomb
should be dropped in the center of the city since the industrial areas of each
city were "small, spread on fringes . . . and dispersed."

Three days later, on May 31st, the high-level Interim Committee met to dis- 13
cuss how—not whether—to use the bomb. It was a blue-ribbon panel, appointed by Secretary of War Henry L. Stimson, including Conant and Bush,
the two scientist-administrators; James F. Byrnes, the next Secretary of State;
Karl Compton, the physicist; William L. Clayton, Assistant Secretary of State;
Ralph Bard, Under-Secretary of the Navy; and George Harrison, Stimson's
representative. According to the minutes, Stimson "expressed the conclusion,
on which there was general agreement, that we could not give the Japanese
any warning; that we could not concentrate on a civilian area; but that we
should seek to make a psychological impression on as many inhabitants as
possible. At the suggestion of Dr. Conant, the Secretary [Stimson] agreed that
the most desirable target would be a vital war plant employing a large number of workers and *closely surrounded by workers' houses*." (emphasis added)
Three weeks later, the committee reaffirmed this recommendation.

They were not looking for a way to avoid the use of the bomb, nor did they   *14*
only want to kill civilians. Rather, as a logical extension of the policy of large-
scale strategic bombing, they wished to destroy industrial targets and kill civilians. They saw no reason to discuss the trade-offs between a war plant and
civilians, for the major plants employed many workers and could be selected
to assure that nearby workers' families would also die.

On the 31st, at the Interim Committee lunch, Ernest O. Lawrence, a Nobel   *15*
physicist and inventor of the cyclotron, suggested that America should first try
a warning and noncombat demonstration of the bomb. Others at the lunch table speedily rejected that notion, for the bomb might be a dud and hence the
warning would embarrass the United States and embolden the Japanese, or
Japan might move allied POW's into the target area and the bomb would kill
them. A few weeks later, when some A-bomb scientists recommended a non-
combat demonstration, their proposal was speedily rejected by the four-mem-
ber scientific advisory panel of Lawrence, Oppenheimer, Enrico Fermi, an Italian Nobel laureate in physics, and Arthur Holly Compton, an American Nobel
physicist. They explained, "We can propose no technical demonstration likely
to bring an end of the war; we see no acceptable alternative to direct military
use."

Secretary of War Stimson, though uneasy about the mass killing of civilians   *16*
in the Air Force's area bombing against Japan, was not seeking to avoid the
use of the A-bomb or to drop it on an exclusively military target. On June 6th,
in discussing conventional and atomic bombing with Truman, Stimson revealed the moral tensions in his own thought. "I . . . was anxious about this
feature [area bombing] of the war for two reasons: first, because I did not want
to have the United States get the reputation of outdoing Hitler in atrocities;
and second, I was a little fearful that before we could get ready the Air Force
might have Japan so thoroughly bombed out that the new weapon would not
have a background to show its strength." According to Stimson, Truman
"laughed and said he understood."

To later-day readers, Stimson may seem hypocritical. How could he be sin-   *17*
cerely troubled about area bombing, which killed thousands of enemy citizens,
and yet want to use the A-bomb, which would kill many thousands of citizens?
He was not hypocritical. He was inconsistent. He was torn between an older
morality, which deemed it wrong to try to kill civilians, and a new morality,
which made it an acceptable way of war. He was too close to events, too harried by the need for decisions, and too enamored of the top-secret A-bomb project
to resolve the tension or even to define the problem clearly.

Stimson had compelled the military planners to delete Kyoto, the former   *18*
capital and famous shrine city, from their list of A-bomb targets. Its elimination was not to save lives but to save the shrines. As Stimson recorded in his
diary, Truman agreed strongly that if Kyoto was not eliminated from the targets, "the bitterness which would be caused by such a wanton act [atomic
bombing of the shrines] might make it impossible during the long postwar period to reconcile the Japanese to us in that area rather than to the Russians."
Both men feared that an angered Japan might otherwise ally with the Soviet
Union, and both comfortably accepted the substitution of Nagasaki for Kyoto.

II

On July 16, at Alamogordo, America tested the first A-bomb. It was a great   *19*
success. On the basis of that test, Oppenheimer informed General Groves that
the total energy released by the first bombs on Japan would be equivalent to
between twelve thousand and twenty thousand tons of TNT, and the blast's
power would be between eight thousand and fifteen thousand tons. Because
the bombs would be exploded about a third of a mile in the air, "it is not expected that radioactive contamination will reach the ground," Oppenheimer
wrote, though "lethal radiation will, of course, reach the ground from the bomb
itself." The implication, tucked away in scientific, impersonal language, was
that radiation would help kill residents of the city but not persist very long.

General Groves promptly informed Oppenheimer, "It is necessary to drop   *20*
the first Little Boy [uranium gun weapon] and the first Fat Man [implosion
plutonium weapon] and probably a second one in accordance with our original plans. It may be that as many as three of the latter [will be necessary]."

Truman was then at Potsdam for the conference with Prime Minister Win-   *21*
ston Churchill and Premier Joseph Stalin, a meeting that the President had
delayed a few weeks so that he would know the results of the Alamogordo test.
On July 16th, Truman received the report on Alamogordo that he was anxiously waiting. "Operated on this morning," the coded message announced
"Diagnosis not yet complete but results seem satisfactory and already exceed
expectations." The next day, when more details arrived about the bomb's awesome power, Truman expressed his delight. "The President was evidently very
greatly re-enforced over the message," Stimson happily recorded in his diary.

On the 21st, the President received a full report on the Alamogordo test. The   *22*
blast was equivalent to at least fifteen to twenty thousand tons of TNT, evap-
orating a one-hundred-foot steel tower, leaving a crater with a diameter of 1,200
feet, knocking over at a half-mile a seventy-foot steel tower anchored in concrete, and knocking over observers at six miles. "The effects on the [seventy-
foot] tower indicate," Groves reported, "that, at that distance, unshielded permanent steel and masonry buildings would have been destroyed. I no longer
consider the Pentagon a safe shelter from such a bomb." The bomb would be
more powerful than American experts had foreseen.

So impressed was Truman that he summarized the report in his private di-   *23*
ary. Both Truman and Secretary of State Byrnes "were immensely pleased,"
Stimson noted in his own diary. "The President was tremendously pepped up
by it and spoke to me of it again and again. . . . He said it gave him an entirely new feeling of confidence." Churchill, when he saw the report, stated that
he now understood why Truman had seemed suddenly emboldened at the negotiating table and pushed matters through with a new confidence and authority. The bomb made Truman tougher in negotiating with the Soviets, for,
as he realized, its power might intimidate them.

When Stimson received from Groves the formal military order listing the   *24*
target cities—Hiroshima, Kokura, Niigata, and Nagasaki (replacing Kyoto)—
Truman easily approved the directive. He did not call in other advisers for
consultation. Truman was simply implementing the shared assumption, recently confirmed by the Interim Committee, that the bomb would be used. He

felt no need to discuss alternatives. "The weapon is to be used against Japan between now [July 25th] and August 10th," Truman recorded in his private diary.

"I have told . . . Stimson," Truman wrote in his diary, "to use it so that 25 military objectives and soldiers and sailors are the target and not women and children. Even if the Japs are savages, ruthless, merciless, and fanatic, we as the leader for the common welfare cannot drop the terrible bomb on the old capital [Kyoto] or the new [Tokyo]. He and I are in accord. The target will be a purely military one . . ."

None of the target cities was a purely military one, and in the case of Hi- 26 roshima the aiming point was not a military target but the center of the city itself. Indeed, as the recently declassified documents show, the cities were chosen partly because of their vulnerable populations. The mass killing of civilians was a major goal.

Yet Truman had privately described the targets as "purely military." Why? 27 Probably he was engaging in a necessary self-deception, for he could not admit to himself that the bomb would kill many thousands of civilians. The great power of the weapon and the earlier criteria for the choice of targets made the mass deaths inevitable.

"The attack [on Hiroshima]," according to the official Air Force history, "was 28 directed against a densely built-up area, a mixture of residential, commercial, military, and small industrial buildings. . . . Planners, calculating on a 7,500-foot radius of destruction, thought that a bomb exploding [there] would wreck all important parts of the city except the dock areas. In this they were eminently correct."

World War II had transformed morality. The mass bombings of Dresden, 29 Hamburg, and Tokyo had been designed to destroy morale and industry, and to kill workers and other civilians, all sinews of war, in what had become total war. Most of the citizens of the civilized world—in Germany, Britain, Russia, Japan, and ultimately America—had become inured to the intentional mass killing of civilians.

America had held out longer than Britain or Germany before following such 30 tactics, but by 1945 all the civilized nations at war had adopted such tactics. Very few in America openly protested, and most Americans disregarded their arguments. War had come to justify virtually any weapons and tactics.

III

On July 31, 1945, General Carl Spaatz, commanding general of the Stra- 31 tegic Air Force in the Pacific, anxiously cabled the Pentagon that "prisoner of war sources, not verified by photos, give location of allied prisoner of war camp [near] center of . . . Nagasaki. Does this influence the choice of this target for initial [A-bomb] operation?" Before Washington replied, Spaatz sent a second message, "Hiroshima [according to prisoner of war reports], is the only one of four target cities for [the A-bomb] that does not have allied prisoner of war camps."

General Groves briefly considered substituting Osaka, Amagasaki, and Omuta 32 for Nagasaki. But after drafting that cable, he discarded it and simply replied,

"Targets previously assigned . . . remain unchanged. However, if you consider your information reliable Hiroshima should be given first priority . . . Information available here indicates that there are prisoner of war camps in practically every major Japanese city." The cable concluded by informing Spaatz that the "best available information here" is a special study, most recently revised on July 1st, on the location of POW camps in Japan. That study, as Washington and Spaatz knew, listed a camp within Hiroshima, on the basis of a 1944 British report.

Spaatz decided to disregard that dated British report and thus concluded 33 that Hiroshima was the best target. On the 6th, at 8:15 A.M., forty-five minutes after a previous air-raid alert, with most factory workers on the job and schoolchildren outdoors, "Little Boy" exploded over Hiroshima. Among the many victims were at least eleven Americans, mostly from the crew of the recently downed Lonesome Lady, and maybe as many as twenty-three American POWs. They were not housed in the British-reported camp, which had been closed, but elsewhere in the city.

No American leader expected a speedy Japanese surrender, and so three days 34 later, after scientists had rushed through the night to get the second bomb ready before bad weather set in for a few days, "Fat Man" was ready for delivery. That day, the primary target, Kokura, was clouded over, so Bock's Car, the B-29 carrying the deadly weapon, flew on with its short fuel supply to Nagasaki, the secondary target. The bombardier dropped the weapon at 11:01 A.M.

Because there had been an earlier air-raid warning that morning and the 35 warning of this one came eight minutes *after* "Fat Man," few Japanese had taken cover. Most were at work, at home, or on the streets. The plutonium bomb, equivalent to about twenty-two thousand tons of TNT, destroyed much of the city but did less damage that the comparatively weaker Hiroshima bomb (12,500 tons) because the hills of Nagasaki blunted the impact of the bomb, and fire storms did not rip through the city. Among the areas destroyed was a small POW camp with sixteen Dutch and two Americans. All the Dutch were killed. Allegedly the two Americans escaped injury.

The aiming point for the bomb, according to the mission planning survey, 36 "was placed east of Nagasaki Harbor in the commercial district of the city. Based upon a 7,500 feet radius, it was believed that an accurate blow would destroy the bulk of the city east of the harbor and possibly carry across to the western shore." The bomb had missed this aiming point by more than a mile because the city was clouded over and the bombardier, according to his report, had not found a break in the clouds until the last thirty seconds of the bombing run. Luis Alvarez, a physicist then at Tinian, the Pacific outpost from which Bock's Car had departed, later told Groves that the error was so substantial because the bomb was dropped by radar, contrary to orders, and that the official report concealed this violation of orders.

Regardless of how one explains the bombing error, the fact remains that if 37 the bombardier had erred about two miles in the opposite direction, "Fat Man" would have destroyed a large POW camp, then unknown to planners, with about 1,400 POWs, including 1,290 Americans. If they had been killed, the news would have leaked out after the war and American officials would have been compelled to admit the atomic slaying of allied POWs at Nagasaki.

The Nagasaki bombing was probably unnecessary. There is no evidence that 38 it speeded the end of the war. The bomb did not change the thinking of the militarists in Japan nor lead the Emperor to intervene in the deliberations to ask his ministers to seek peace on the 10th. He was already privately committed to calling for an end to the war. Even after the Nagasaki bombing, the militarists in the Japanese Cabinet opposed the quest for peace until the Emperor pleaded for peace. The available evidence indicates that the war would probably have ended in about the same way, maybe even on the same day, if the second bomb had never been used.

Why was it dropped? The process had been automatic. The second bomb 39 had seemed necessary. American leaders believed that the Hiroshima bomb, Soviet entry into the war on the 8th, and even the second bomb might not produce an imminent Japanese surrender. They even assumed that more A-bombs would be necessary. Above all, they wanted to end the war on acceptable terms before November 1, 1945, the date for the so-called "small" invasion of Japan, with about 775,000 troops and casualties estimated near thirty-one thousand in the first month. No American leader ever considered delaying the second bomb to await the changes in Japanese policy produced by the trip-hammer blows of "Little Boy" on the 6th and Soviet entry on the 8th. The original order to the Air Force had said, "[use bombs] as soon as made ready." The Air Force and the scientists who assembled the bomb in the Pacific eagerly followed those orders.

IV

If the second bomb was almost definitely unnecessary, what about the first 40 bomb? Why was it used? Why weren't alternatives first tried?

Ever since FDR had initiated the secret project, American leaders had as- 41 sumed that the bomb would be used in the war. Truman inherited that assumption and the advisers who shared it. It fit his own inclinations, and he never questioned it.

Because most American leaders were not deeply troubled by the prospective 42 use of the A-bomb, they did not seek alternatives and they easily rejected tactics that later critics would cite as "missed opportunities," as ways of avoiding the combat use of the A-bomb. There were at least four: a warning and non-combat demonstration; pursuit of Japan's peace feelers; a guarantee of the Emperor; and a delay until Soviet entry into the Pacific war.

According to Truman and some key advisers, these tactics risked prolonging 43 the war and making the scheduled invasion of November 1st necessary. Only if Truman and his major advisers had viewed the bomb as a radical evil, as a weapon to be avoided, might they have been tempted to try one or more of these tactics. Instead, they deemed the bomb attractive because it offered a potential bonus: its combat use might intimidate the Soviets and make them more tractable in the postwar period. The quest for retribution—retaliation for Pearl Harbor and the mistreatment of POWs—may have also constituted a subtle influence, for Truman stressed these themes in later justifying his decision.

In view of what we know about the course of events immediately after Hi- 44 roshima, when the Japanese militarists sought to minimize the A-bomb and still wished to continue the war, it is unlikely that a warning and noncombat demonstration or pursuit of peace feelers would have ended the war on American terms in the next few months. Japan's militarists were too obdurate and the peace group too timid. Japan's peace feelers ranged between vague and arrogant, and they never approached American expectations.

Even an American guarantee of the Emperor would not have met the Japanese militarists' demands and might have emboldened these men to hold out for more concessions—no postwar occupation, self-disarmament, and Japanese-conducted trials of their own war criminals. Perhaps Soviet entry would have crushed the militarists' hopes and led them to accept a reasonable peace before November 1st. Such speculation remains "iffy," especially since both the Hiroshima bombing and Soviet entry did not promptly alter the demands of the militarists. They had held out through various meetings even after the Nagasaki bombing, until the Emperor himself had intervened.   *45*

Since the Soviets had promised that they would enter the Pacific war on about August 21st, there would have been only ten weeks for the impact of their entry to produce a Japanese surrender before the scheduled invasion of November 1st. American leaders had not believed that Soviet entry could be so critical and they were unwilling to gamble on its effect by delaying the bomb. Some, like Secretary of State James Byrnes and Secretary of the Navy James Forrestal, even hoped that the war might end before the Soviets could get into it and grab parts of Manchuria. But none ever viewed the A-bomb and Soviet entry as competing ways to end the war. And many viewed the atomic bombings and Soviet entry as essential to speed the end of the war.   *46*

Given the widespread American hatred of the Japanese—spurred by official American propaganda—and the likely anger if Truman had sacrificed American lives to avoid using the bomb in order to save Japanese lives, the President's decision was virtually inevitable. "No man, in our position and subject to our responsibilities, holding in his hand a weapon of such possibilities," Stimson later wrote, "could have failed to use it and afterwards looked his countrymen in the face." It would have been morally unacceptable and politically disastrous, he argued, not to have dropped the A-bomb on Japan.   *47*

V

No American leader had foreseen an imminent Japanese surrender. They assumed that the A-bombs would be powerful supplements to, not substitutes for, large-scale conventional bombing. Accordingly, in the days between the Hiroshima and Nagasaki bombings, the Air Force continued to pound Japan with incendiaries and high explosives. After the Nagasaki bombing, the Air Force continued this "rain of ruin." On August 14th, the day of the Japanese surrender, about one thousand American planes bombed Japan.   *48*

So unexpected was Japan's offer of conditional surrender on the 10th that Stimson was headed at the time to the airport for a much-needed vacation. Abruptly canceling his plans, he rushed to the White House where American leaders split over whether they should accept Japan's conditional surrender, with its stipulation that the imperial system be continued. Urging speedy acceptance, Stimson and Forrestal, the two service secretaries, stressed that they   *49* wished to end the bloodshed. Stimson emphasized that continuation of the Emperor would be useful in guaranteeing the surrender of the Japanese armies. But Secretary of State James Byrnes, a shrewd politician, warned Truman that such a concession, marking a retreat from explicit American terms, could mean "crucifixion of the President." "I cannot understand," Byrnes complained, "why we should go further than we were willing to go at Potsdam when we had no atomic bomb, and Russia was not in the war."

"Let the Japs know unqualifiedly what unconditional surrender means. Let   50
the dirty Japs squeal," one bloodthirsty congressman telegraphed the White House. Of the 170 telegrams sent to the President, 153 urged the harsh terms of unconditional surrender. "No concession [should] be made that will continue the rule of Hirohito," some liberal organizations insisted, for he is "as much a symbol of the super-race theory as Hitler."

Truman, fearful of a political backlash at home, where many linked Hiro-   51
hito and Hitler, refused to accept Japan's single condition. His advisers accordingly phrased an ambiguous message that neither accepted nor rejected continuation of the imperial system. That message briefly shattered the peace coalition in Japan, emboldened some of the militarists, compelled the Emperor to intervene again on behalf of peace, and nearly unleashed a successful military coup. Had General Korechika Anami, Japan's war minister, supported the coup, it probably would have won support from the Japanese Army, and succeeded.

Against the advice of Stimson and Forrestal, Truman decided on the 10th   52
to continue the heavy conventional bombing of Japan's cities. He wanted to pressure the Japanese into accepting America's terms. But he ordered, in the words of an associate, that the A-bomb "is not to be released on Japan without express authority from the President." No longer would the process of dropping A-bombs be automatic.

The third bomb, Groves had reported, "should be ready for delivery . . .   53
after 17 or 18 August." It was a weapon that Truman did not want to use, for, as he explained to his Cabinet, he did not want to kill another one hundred thousand people, including "all those kids." When one prominent Democratic senator pleaded for more A-bombings, Truman replied, "I know that Japan is a terribly cruel and uncivilized nation in warfare but I can't bring myself to believe that, because they are beasts, we should ourselves act in the same manner. For myself, I certainly regret the necessity of wiping out whole populations because of the 'pigheadedness' of [their] leaders . . . I am not going to do it unless it is absolutely necessary."

The use of the third atomic bomb would have been popular in America. If   54
the war had dragged on much beyond the 17th, Truman might have had great difficulty resisting the political pressures for its use. How could he have justified dropping the first two and then explained that new moral doubts deterred him from using a third and even more? It would not have been an easy argument to sell to an often bloodthirsty electorate which had come to hate the Japanese.

Fortunately, Japan accepted America's ambiguous terms and surrendered   55
on August 14th. In their enthusiasm over peace and their anxiety over reconversion, few Americans paid much attention to the continuation of the Japa-

nese imperial system. It never became a political issue in postwar America. Nor did the combat use of the two A-bombs.

Even had Americans learned that the Hiroshima bomb had killed some 56 American POWs, it is unlikely that citizens would have raised political and moral questions about the use of these powerful weapons. American officials, probably anxious about a domestic backlash, concealed the information about the dead POWs. Probably officials did not want to risk unleashing a dialogue that might challenge government decisions, threaten careers, and make future combat use of the A-bomb more difficult. Ironically, just as Truman was morally more concerned about using a third bomb than were most Americans, officials worried unduly after Hiroshima and Nagasaki that citizens might question the A-bombings of Japan. Not for many years would substantial numbers of Americans criticize those momentous actions of 1945.

Considerations

1. Barton J. Bernstein's essay has been carefully written. Notice its structure. What purpose does the introductory section serve? How does the conclusion both reflect and extend the introduction? What pattern has each of the five sections in common?
2. Bernstein's essay is subtitled, "How decisions are made when a nation is at war." Summarize this decision process. Does Bernstein think that such a process operates only when a nation is at war or that it operates at other times, too? Find evidence to support your answer.

Connections

1. Suggest possible relationships between the logic of the "decision-making process" that Bernstein describes and the growth of the American and Soviet nuclear arsenals that Randall Forsberg describes. What evidence in these articles supports one or more of your hypotheses?
2. Both Bernstein and Forsberg are writing as historians, and yet their essays are very different. Forsberg, for example, covers nearly forty years in a very brief essay, while Bernstein's article is over three times as long but covers only a few months. This allows Bernstein to be much more *analytical*. Write an essay defining *analytical* reasoning, and show what is analytical about Bernstein's essay.
3. Find evidence in Bernstein's essay to support or contradict Forsberg's position, that

> . . . the purpose of the on-going nuclear arms race is, from the point of view of the USA, to give the United States greater freedom to intervene in developing countries without risking a conventional challenge on the part of the Soviet Union; and to inhibit Soviet conventional intervention. From the point of view of the USSR, the purpose of trying to match US nuclear developments is to nullify the nuclear factor in global power politics.

Memorandum to President Roosevelt, July 1944

Niels Bohr

It certainly surpasses the imagination of anyone to survey the consequences *1* of the project in years to come, where, in the long run, the enormous energy sources which will be available may be expected to revolutionize industry and transport. The fact of immediate preponderance is, however, that a weapon of an unparalleled power is being created which will completely change all future conditions of warfare.

Quite apart from the question of how soon the weapon will be ready for use *2* and what role it may play in the present war, this situation raises a number of problems which call for most urgent attention. Unless, indeed, some agreement about the control of the use of the new active materials can be obtained in due time, any temporary advantage, however great, may be outweighed by a perpetual menace to human security.

Ever since the possibilities of releasing atomic energy on a vast scale came *3* in sight, much thought has naturally been given to the question of control, but the further the exploration of the scientific problems concerned is proceeding, the clearer it becomes that no kind of customary measures will suffice for this purpose, and that the terrifying prospect of a future competition between nations about a weapon of such formidable character can only be avoided through a universal agreement in true confidence.

In this connection it is particularly significant that the enterprise, immense *4* as it is, has still proved far smaller than might have been anticipated, and that the progress of the work has continually revealed new possibilities for facilitating the production of the active materials and of intensifying their efforts.

The prevention of a competition prepared in secrecy will therefore demand *5* such concessions regarding exchange of information and openness about industrial efforts, including military preparations, as would hardly be conceivable unless all partners were assured of a compensating guarantee of common security against dangers of unprecedented acuteness.

The establishment of effective control measures will of course involve intri- *6* cate technical and administrative problems, but the main point of the argu-

---

Niels Bohr (1885–1962) was an eminent Danish physicist deeply concerned about the risks of an arms race. This memorandum to President Roosevelt warns of the dangers of an arms race a full year before the weapons were completed and used. A month after writing the memo, Bohr met with Roosevelt—another of many attempts by him and other scientists to establish international control over nuclear weapons. He received a Nobel Prize in physics in 1922.

ment is that the accomplishment of the project would not only seem to necessitate but should also, due to the urgency of mutual confidence, facilitate a new approach to the problems of international relationship.

The present moment where almost all nations are entangled in a deadly   7
struggle for freedom and humanity might, at first sight, seem most unsuited for any committing arrangement concerning the project. Not only have the aggressive powers still great military strength, although their original plans of world domination have been frustrated and it seems certain that they must ultimately surrender, but even when this happens, the nations united against aggression may face grave causes of disagreement due to conflicting attitudes toward social and economic problems.

A closer consideration, however, would indicate that the potentialities of the   8
project as a means of inspiring confidence under these very circumstances acquire real importance. Moreover, the present situation affords unique possibilities which might be forfeited by a postponement awaiting the further development of the war situation and the final completion of the new weapon. . . .

In view of these eventualities the present situation appears to offer a most   9
favorable opportunity for an early initiative from the side which by good fortune has achieved a lead in the efforts of mastering mighty forces of nature hitherto beyond human reach.

Without impeding the immediate military objectives, an initiative, aiming   10
at forestalling a fateful competition, should serve to uproot any cause of distrust between the powers on whose harmonious collaboration the fate of coming generations will depend.

Indeed, it would appear that only when the question is raised among the   11
united nations as to what concessions the various powers are prepared to make as their contribution to an adequate control arrangement, will it be possible for any one of the partners to assure himself of the sincerity of the intentions of the others.

Of course, the responsible statesmen alone can have insight as to the actual   12
political possibilities. It would, however, seem most fortunate that the expectations for a future harmonious international co-operation, which have found unanimous expressions from all sides within the United Nations, so remarkably correspond to the unique opportunities which, unknown to the public, have been created by the advancement of science.

Many reasons, indeed, would seem to justify the conviction that an approach with the object of establishing common security from ominous menaces, without excluding any nation from participating in the promising industrial development which the accomplishment of the project entails, will be welcomed, and be met with loyal co-operation in the enforcement of the necessary far-reaching control measures.   13

It is in such respects that helpful support may perhaps be afforded by the   14
world-wide scientific collaboration which for years has embodied such bright promises for common human striving. Personal connections between scientists of different nations might even offer means of establishing preliminary and unofficial contact.

It need hardly be added that any such remark or suggestion implies no underrating of the difficulty and delicacy of the steps to be taken by the states-   15 men in order to obtain an arrangement satisfactory to all concerned, but aims only at pointing to some aspects of the situation which might facilitate endeavours to turn the project to the lasting benefit of the common cause.

Considerations

1. Though Niels Bohr's formulation is vague, he offers at least a general vision of how the world might avoid an arms competition. Describe this vision.
2. Identify some features of Bohr's style that make his memorandum difficult to read. (Bohr was Danish and learned English as a foreign language.)

Connections

1. How well does Niels Bohr's memorandum foreshadow the nuclear arms race as Randall Forsberg describes it?
2. Taking into account what Barton J. Bernstein says about the decision-making process (or lack of one) that led to the targeting decision, rewrite Bohr's memo. If he knew what we now know about the inside operations of governmental decision-making, how would his memo be different?

The Franck Report

James Franck et al.

A Report to the Secretary of War, June 11, 1945

1. Preamble

The only reason to treat nuclear power differently from all other develop-   *1*
ments in the field of physics is the possibility of its use as a means of political pressure in peace and sudden destruction in war. All present plans for the or-

---

James Franck (1882–1964) et al. Many scientists working within the Manhattan Project were concerned about how the weapons they were designing might actually be used and they worried about the prospects of a runaway competition in the production of nuclear arms. Other scientists, however, felt it was not their proper role to offer advice or make moral assessments about political policy. Thus, the action of the Franck group in writing to the Secretary of War, Henry L. Stimson, was surrounded by great controversy.

ganization of research, scientific and industrial development, and publication in the field of nucleonics are conditioned by the political and military climate in which one expects those plans to be carried out. Therefore, in making suggestions for the postwar organization of nucleonics, a discussion of political problems cannot be avoided. The scientists on this Project do not presume to speak authoritatively on problems of national and international policy. However, we found ourselves, by the force of events, during the last five years, in the position of a small group of citizens cognizant of a grave danger for the safety of this country as well as for the future of all the other nations, of which the rest of mankind is unaware. We therefore feel it is our duty to urge that the political problems, arising from the mastering of nuclear power, be recognized in all their gravity, and that appropriate steps be taken for their study and the preparation of necessary decisions. We hope that the creation of the Committee by the Secretary of War to deal with all aspects of nucleonics, indicates that these implications have been recognized by the government. We believe that our acquaintance with the scientific elements of the situation and prolonged preoccupation with its world-wide political implications, imposes on us the obligation to offer to the Committee some suggestions as to the possible solution of these grave problems.

Scientists have often before been accused of providing new weapons for the mutual destruction of nations, instead of improving their well-being. It is undoubtedly true that the discovery of flying, for example, has so far brought much more misery than enjoyment and profit to humanity. However, in the past, scientists could disclaim direct responsibility for the use to which mankind had put their disinterested discoveries. We feel compelled to take a more active stand now because the success which we have achieved in the development of nuclear power is fraught with infinitely greater dangers than were all the inventions of the past. All of us, familiar with the present state of nucleonics, live with the vision before our eyes of sudden destruction visited on our own country, of a Pearl Harbor disaster repeated in thousand-fold magnification in every one of our major cities. *2*

In the past, science has often been able to provide also new methods of protection against new weapons of aggression it made possible, but it cannot promise such efficient protection against the destructive use of nuclear power. This protection can come only from the political organization of the world. Among all the arguments calling for an efficient international organization for peace, the existence of nuclear weapons is the most compelling one. In the absence of an international authority which would make all resort to force in international conflicts impossible, nations could still be diverted from a path which must lead to total mutual destruction, by a specific international agreement barring a nuclear armaments race. *3*

II. Prospects of Armaments Race

It could be suggested that the danger of destruction by nuclear weapons can be avoided — at least as far as this country is concerned — either by keeping our discoveries secret for an indefinite time, or else by developing our nuclear *4* armaments at such a pace that no other nations would think of attacking us from fear of overwhelming retaliation.

The answer to the first suggestion is that although we undoubtedly are at   5 present ahead of the rest of the world in this field, the fundamental facts of nuclear power are a subject of common knowledge. British scientists know as much as we do about the basic wartime progress of nucleonics — if not of the specific processes used in our engineering developments — and the role which French nuclear physcists have played in the pre-war development of this field, plus their occasional contact with our Projects, will enable them to catch up rapidly, at least as far as basic scientific discoveries are concerned. German scientists, in whose discoveries the whole development of this field originated, apparently did not develop it during the war to the same extent to which this has been done in America: but to the last day of the European war, we were living in constant apprehension as to their possible achievements. The certainty that German scientists were working on this weapon and that their government would certainly have no scruples against using it when available, was the main motivation of the initiative which American scientists took in urging the development of nuclear power for military purposes on a large scale in this country. In Russia, too, the basic facts and implications of nuclear power were well understood in 1940, and the experience of Russian scientists in nuclear research is entirely sufficient to enable them to retrace our steps within a few years, even if we should make every attempt to conceal them. Even if we can retain our leadership in basic knowledge of nucleonics for a certain time by maintaining secrecy as to all results achieved on this and associated Projects, it would be foolish to hope that this can protect us for more than a few years.

It may be asked whether we cannot prevent the development of military nu-   6 cleonics in other countries by a monopoly on the raw materials of nuclear power. The answer is that even though the largest now known deposits of uranium ores are under the control of powers which belong to the "western" group (Canada, Belgium and British India), the old deposits in Czechoslovakia are outside this sphere. Russia is known to be mining radium on its own territory; and even if we do not know the size of the deposits discovered so far in the USSR, the probability that no large reserves of uranium will be found in a country which covers one-fifth of the land area of the earth (and whose sphere of influence takes in additional territory) is too small to serve as a basis for security. Thus, we cannot hope to avoid a nuclear armament race either by keeping secret from the competing nations the basic scientific facts of nuclear power or by cornering the raw materials required for such a race.

We now consider the second of the two suggestions made at the beginning   7 of this section, and ask whether we could not feel ourselves safe in a race of nuclear armaments by virtue of our greater industrial potential, including greater diffusion of scientific and technical knowledge, greater volume and efficiency of our skilled labor crops, and greater experience of our management — all the factors whose importance has been so strikingly demonstrated in the conversion of this country into an arsenal of the Allied Nations in the present war. The answer is that all that these advantages can give us is the accumulation of a larger number of bigger and better atomic bombs.

However, such a quantitative advantage in reserves of bottled destructive   8 power will not make us safe from sudden attack. Just because a potential enemy will be afraid of being "outnumbered and outgunned," the temptation for him may be overwhelming to attempt a sudden unprovoked blow — particularly if he should suspect us of harboring aggressive intentions against his security or his sphere of influence. In no other type of warfare does the advantage lie so heavily with the aggressor. He can place his "infernal machines" in advance in all our major cities and explode them simultaneously, thus destroying a major part of our industry and a large part of our population, aggregated in densely populated metropolitan districts. Our possibilities of retaliation — even if retaliation should be considered adequate compensation for the loss of millions of lives and destruction of our largest cities — will be greatly handicapped because we must rely on aerial transportation of the bombs, and also because we may have to deal with an enemy whose industry and population are dispersed over a large territory.

In fact, if the race for nuclear armaments is allowed to develop, the only 9 apparent way in which our country can be protected from the paralyzing effects of a sudden attack is by dispersal of those industries which are essential for our war effort and dispersal of the populations of our major metropolitan cities. As long as nuclear bombs remain scarce (i.e., as long as uranium remains the only basic material for their fabrication), efficient dispersal of our industry and the scattering of our metropolitan population will considerably decrease the temptation to attack us by nuclear weapons.

At present, it may be that atomic bombs can be detonated with an effect 10 equal to that of 20,000 tons of TNT. One of these bombs could then destroy something like 3 square miles of an urban area. Atomic bombs containing a larger quantity of active material but still weighing less than one ton may be expected to be available within ten years which could destroy over ten square miles of a city. A nation able to assign 10 tons of atomic explosives for a sneak attack on this country, can then hope to achieve the destruction of all industry and most of the population in an area from 500 square miles upwards. If no choice of targets, with a total area of five hundred square miles of American territory, contains a large enough fraction of the nation's industry and population to make their destruction a crippling blow to the nation's war potential and its ability to defend itself, then the attack will not pay, and may not be undertaken. At present, one could easily select in this country a hundred areas of five square miles each whose simultaneous destruction would be a staggering blow to the nation. Since the area of the United States is about three million square miles, it should be possible to scatter its industrial and human resources in such a way as to leave no 500 square miles important enough to serve as a target for nuclear attack.

We are fully aware of the staggering difficulties involved in such a radical 11 change in the social and economic structure of our nation. We felt, however, that the dilemma had to be stated, to show what kind of alternative methods of protection will have to be considered if no successful international agreement is reached. It must be pointed out that in this field we are in a less favorable position than nations which are either now more diffusely populated and whose industries are more scattered, or whose governments have unlimited power over the movement of population and the location of industrial plants.

If no efficient international agreement is achieved, the race for nuclear ar-   *12*
maments will be on in earnest not later than the morning after our first demonstration of the existence of nuclear weapons. After this, it might take other
nations three or four years to overcome our present head start, and eight to
ten years to draw even with us if we continue to do intensive work in this field.
This might be all the time we would have to bring about the relocation of our
population and industry. Obviously, no time should be lost in inaugurating a
study of this problem by experts.

III. Prospects of Agreement

The consequences of nuclear warfare, and the type of measures which would   *13*
have to be taken to protect a country from total destruction by nuclear bombing, must be as abhorrent to other nations as to the United States. England,
France and the smaller nations of the European continent, with their congeries
of people and industries would be in a particularly desperate situation in the
face of such a threat. Russia and China are the only great nations at present
which could survive a nuclear attack. However, even though these countries
may value human life less than the peoples of Western Europe and America,
and even though Russia, in particular, has an immense space over which its
vital industries could be dispersed and a government which can order this dis-
persion the day it is convinced that such a measure is necessary — there is no
doubt that Russia, too, will shudder at the possibility of a sudden disintegration of Moscow and Leningrad, almost miraculously preserved in the present
war, and of its new industrial cities in the Urals and Siberia. Therefore, only
lack of mutual trust, and not lack of desire for agreement, can stand in the
path of an efficient agreement for the prevention of nuclear warfare. The
achievement of such an agreement will thus essentially depend on the integrity of intentions and readiness to sacrifice the necessary fraction of one's own
sovereignty, by all the parties to the agreement.

One possible way to introduce nuclear weapons to the world — which may   *14*
particularly appeal to those who consider nuclear bombs primarily as a secret
weapon developed to help win the present war — is to use them without warning on appropriately selected objects in Japan.

Although important tactical results undoubtedly can be achieved by a sud-   *15*
den introduction of nuclear weapons, we nevertheless think that the question
of the use of the very first available atomic bombs in the Japanese war should
be weighed very carefully, not only by military authorities, but by the highest
political leadership of this country.

Russia, and even allied countries which bear less mistrust of our ways and   *16*
intentions, as well as neutral countries may be deeply shocked by this step. It
may be very difficult to persuade the world that a nation which was capable
of secretly preparing and suddenly releasing a new weapon, as indiscriminate
as the rocket bomb and a thousand times more destructive, is to be trusted in
its proclaimed desire of having such weapons abolished by international
agreement. We have large accumulations of poison gas, but do not use them,

and recent polls have shown that public opinion in this country would disapprove of such a use even if it would accelerate the winning of the Far Eastern war. It is true that some irrational element in mass psychology makes gas poisoning more revolting than blasting by explosives, even though gas warfare is in no way more "inhuman" than the war of bombs and bullets. Nevertheless, it is not at all certain that American public opinion, if it could be enlightened as to the effect of atomic explosives, would approve of our own country being the first to introduce such an indiscriminate method of wholesale destruction of civilian life.

Thus, from the "optimistic" point of view — looking forward to an international agreement on the prevention of nuclear warfare — the military advantages and the saving of American lives achieved by the sudden use of atomic bombs against Japan may be outweighed by the ensuing loss of confidence and by a wave of horror and repulsion sweeping over the rest of the world and perhaps even dividing public opinion at home. *17*

From this point of view, a demonstration of the new weapon might best be made, before the eyes of representatives of all the United Nations, on the desert or a barren island. The best possible atomosphere for the achievement of an international agreement could be achieved if America could say to the world, "You see what sort of a weapon we had but did not use. We are ready to renounce its use in the future if other nations join us in this renunciation and agree to the establishment of an efficient control." *18*

After such a demonstration the weapon might perhaps be used against Japan if the sanction of the United Nations (and if public opinion at home) were obtained, perhaps after a preliminary ultimatum to Japan to surrender or at least to evacuate certain regions as an alternative to their total destruction. This may sound fantastic, but in nuclear weapons we have something entirely new in order of magnitude of destructive power, and if we want to capitalize fully on the advantage their possession gives us, we must use new and imaginative methods. *19*

It must be stressed that if one takes the pessimistic point of view and discounts the possibility of an effective international control over nuclear weapons at the present time, then the advisability of an early use of nuclear bombs against Japan becomes even more doubtful — quite independently of any humanitarian considerations. If an international agreement is not concluded immediately after the first demonstration, this will mean a flying start towards an unlimited armaments race. If this race is inevitable, we have every reason to delay its beginning as long as possible in order to increase our head start still further. *20*

The benefit to the nation, and the saving of American lives in the future, achieved by renouncing an early demonstration of nuclear bombs and letting the other nations come into the race only reluctantly, on the basis of guesswork and without definite knowledge that the "thing does work," may far outweigh the advantages to be gained by the immediate use of the first and comparatively inefficient bombs in the war against Japan. On the other hand, it may be argued that without an early demonstration it may prove difficult to *21* obtain adequate support for further intensive development of nucleonics in this country and that thus the time gained by the postponement of an open armaments race will not be properly used. Futhermore one may suggest that other nations are now, or will soon be, not entirely unaware of our present achievements, and that consequently the postponement of a demonstration may serve no useful purpose as far as the avoidance of an armaments race is concerned, and may only create additional mistrust, thus worsening rather than improving the chances of an ultimate accord on the international control of nuclear explosives.

Thus, if the prospects of an agreement will be considered poor in the immediate future, the pros and cons of an early revelation of our possession of nuclear weapons to the world — not only by their actual use against Japan, but also by a prearranged demonstration — must be carefully weighed by the supreme political and military leadership of the country, and the decisions should not be left to the considerations of military tactics alone.   22

One may point out that scientists themselves have initiated the development of this "secret weapon" and it is therefore strange that they should be reluctant to try it out on the enemy as soon as it is available. The answer to this question was given above — the compelling reason for creating this weapon with such speed was our fear that Germany had the technical skill necessary to develop such a weapon and that the German government had no moral restraints regarding its use.   23

Another argument which could be quoted in favor of using atomic bombs as soon as they are available is that so much taxpayers' money has been invested in these Projects that the Congress and the American public will demand a return for their money. The attitude of American public opinion, mentioned earlier, in the matter of the use of poison gas against Japan, shows that one can expect the American public to understand that it is sometimes desirable to keep a weapon in readiness for use only in extreme emergency; and as soon as the potentialities of nuclear weapons are revealed to the American people, one can be sure that they will support all attempts to make the use of such weapons impossible.   24

Once this is achieved, the large installations and the accumulation of explosive material at present earmarked for potential military use will become available for important peacetime developments, including power production, large engineering undertakings, and mass production of radioactive materials. In this way, the money spent on wartime development of nucleonics may become a boon for the peacetime development of national economy.   25

IV. Methods of International Control

We now consider the question of how an effective international control of nuclear armaments can be achieved. This is a difficult problem, but we think it soluble. It requires study by statesmen and international lawyers, and we can offer only some preliminary suggestions for such a study.   26

Given mutual trust and willingness on all sides to give up a certain part of their sovereign rights, by admitting international control of certain phases of   27 national economy, the control could be exercised (alternatively or simultaneously) on two different levels.

The first and perhaps the simplest way is to ration the raw materials — primarily, the uranium ores. Production of nulcear explosives begins with the processing of large quantities of uranium in large isotope separation plants or huge production piles. The amounts of ore taken out of the ground at different locations could be controlled by resident agents of the international Control Board, and each nation could be allotted only an amount which would make large-scale separation of fissionable isotopes impossible.

Such a limitation would have the drawback of making impossible also the development of nuclear power for peacetime purposes. However, it need not prevent the production of radioactive elements on a scale sufficient to revolutionize the industrial, scientific and technical use of these materials, and would thus not eliminate the main benefits which nucleonics promises to bring to mankind.

An agreement on a higher level, involving more mutual trust and understanding, would be to allow unlimited production, but keep exact bookkeeping on the fate of each pound of uranium mined. If in this way, check is kept on the conversion of uranium and thorium ore into pure fissionable materials, the question arises as to how to prevent accumulation of large quantities of such materials in the hands of one or several nations. Accumulations of this kind could be rapidly converted into atomic bombs if a nation should break away from international control. It has been suggested that a compulsory denaturation of pure fissionable isotopes may be agreed upon — by diluting them, after production, with suitable isotopes to make them useless for military purposes, while retaining their usefulness for power engines.

One thing is clear: any international agreement on prevention of nuclear armaments must be backed by actual and efficient controls. No paper agreement can be sufficient since neither this or any other nation can stake its whole existence on trust in other nations' signatures. Every attempt to impede the international control agencies would have to be considered equivalent to denunciation of the agreement.

It hardly needs stressing that we as scientists believe that any systems of control envisaged should leave as much freedom for the peacetime development of nucleonics as is consistent with the safety of the world.

Summary

The development of nuclear power not only constitutes an important addition to the technological and military power of the United States, but also creates grave political and economic problems for the future of this country.

Nuclear bombs cannot possibly remain a "secret weapon" at the exclusive disposal of this country for more than a few years. The scientific facts on which construction is based are well known to scientists of other countries. Unless an effective international control of nuclear explosives is instituted, a race for nuclear armaments is certain to ensue following the first revelation of our possession of nuclear weapons to the world. Within ten years other countries may have nuclear bombs, each of which, weighing less than a ton, could destroy an urban area of more than ten square miles. In the war to which such an armaments race is likely to lead, the United States, with its agglomeration of population and industry in comparatively few metropolitan districts, will be at a disadvantage compared to nations whose populations and industry are scattered over large areas.

We believe that these considerations make the use of nuclear bombs for an early unannounced attack against Japan inadvisable. If the United States were to be the first to release this new means of indiscriminate destruction upon mankind, she would sacrifice public support throughout the world, precipitate the race for armaments and prejudice the possibility of reaching an international agreement on the future control of such weapons. 35

Much more favorable conditions for the eventual achievement of such an agreement could be created if nuclear bombs were first revealed to the world by a demonstration in an appropriately selected uninhabited area. 36

In case chances for the establishment of an effective international control of nuclear weapons should have to be considered slight at the present time, then not only the use of these weapons against Japan, but even their early demonstration, may be contrary to the interests of this country. A postponement of such a demonstration will have in this case the advantage of delaying the beginning of the nuclear armaments race as long as possible. 37

If the government should decide in favor of an early demonstration of nuclear weapons, it will then have the possibility of taking into account the public opinion of this country and of the other nations before deciding whether these weapons should be used against Japan. In this way, other nations may assume a share of responsibility for such a fateful decision. 38

Composed and signed by

> J. Franck
> D. Hughes
> L. Szilard
> T. Hogness
> E. Rabinowitch
> G. Seaborg
> C. J. Nickson

Considerations

1. The Franck Report is a complex argument that is clearly structured and reasoned. Summarize the argument and outline the essay.
2. The authors of the Franck Report show a good deal of interest in the relationship between scientists and politics. Elucidate this issue.
3. The Franck Report's preamble concludes saying, "In the absence of an international authority which would make all resort to force in international conflicts impossible, nations could still be diverted from a path which must lead to total mutual destruction, by a specific international agreement bar-

ring a nuclear armaments race" (para. 3). What are the elements of this proposal? To what extent does it solve the problem posed by a lack of international authority?

4. How does the Franck Report connect the potential bombing of Japanese cities — which would take place about two months from the report's date — and the momentum toward a postwar arms race?

5. How do the authors reason that a nuclear arms race would set us upon "a path which must lead to total mutual destruction"? Assess their reasoning.

Connections

1. What do the authors of the Franck Report mean in the first sentence: "a means of political pressure in peace"? How do other readings in this chapter deal with this theme?

2. How does the Franck Report resemble Niels Bohr's memorandum?

3. The authors of the Franck Report argue against using the bomb on Japanese civilian targets on the grounds that the American public would disapprove. Barton J. Bernstein finds that quite the opposite happened: American public opinion overwhelmingly supported the Japanese bombings. Why does Bernstein think this was so? Why do you suppose the scientists could have been so wrong?

A Petition to the President of the United States

Leo Szilard

July 17, 1945

Discoveries of which the people of the United States are not aware may affect the welfare of this nation in the near future. The liberation of atomic power   *1*

Leo Szilard (1898–1964), a physicist with the Chicago group of Manhattan Project scientists and one of those who signed "The Franck Report," has been called the first moral philosopher of the nuclear age. After the German surrender, the reason for our developing the bomb in the first place had vanished and Szilard questioned U.S. motives in shifting the target from a potentially nuclear nation — Germany — to a decidedly nonnuclear one. Szilard, who founded the Council for a Livable World in 1962, remained active in nuclear disarmament efforts until his death.

which has been achieved places atomic bombs in the hands of the Army. It places in your hands, as Commander-in-Chief, the fateful decision whether or not to sanction the use of such bombs in the present phase of the war against Japan.

We, the undersigned scientists, have been working in the field of atomic 2 power. Until recently we have had no fear that the United States might be attacked by atomic bombs during this war and that her only defense might lie in a counterattack by the same means. Today, with the defeat of Germany, this danger is averted and we feel impelled to say what follows:

The war has to be brought speedily to a successful conclusion and attacks 3 by atomic bombs may very well be an effective method of warfare. We feel, however, that such attacks on Japan could not be justified, at least not unless the terms which will be imposed after the war on Japan were made public in detail and Japan were given an opportunity to surrender.

If such public announcement gave assurance to the Japanese that they could 4 look forward to a life devoted to peaceful pursuits in their homeland and if Japan still refused to surrender, our nation might then, in certain circumstances, find itself forced to resort to the use of atomic bombs. Such a step, however, ought not to be made at any time without seriously considering the moral responsibilities which are involved.

The development of atomic power will provide the nations with new means 5 of destruction. The atomic bombs at our disposal represent only the first step in this direction and there is almost no limit to the destructive power which will become available in the course of their future development. Thus a nation which sets the precedent of using these newly liberated forces of nature for purposes of destruction may have to bear the responsibility of opening the door to an era of devastation on an unimaginable scale.

If after this war a situation is allowed to develop in the world which per- 6 mits rival powers to be in uncontrolled possession of these new means of destruction, the cities of the United States as well as the cities of other nations will be in continuous danger of sudden annihilation. All the resources of the United States, moral and material, may have to be mobilized to prevent the advent of such a world situation. Its prevention is at present the solemn responsibility of the United States — singled out by virtue of her lead in the field of atomic power.

The added material strength which this lead gives to the United States brings 7 with it the obligation of restraint, and if we were to violate this obligation our moral position would be weakened in the eyes of the world and in our own eyes. It would then be more difficult for us to live up to our responsibility of bringing the unloosened forces of destruction under control.

In view of the foregoing, we, the undersigned, respectfully petition: first, that 8 you exercise your power as Commander-in-Chief to rule that the United States shall not resort to the use of atomic bombs in this war unless the terms which will be imposed upon Japan have been made public in detail and Japan, knowing these terms, has refused to surrender; second, that in such an event the question whether or not to use atomic bombs be decided by you in the light of the considerations presented in this petition as well as all the other moral responsibilities which are involved.

Considerations

1. What does Leo Szilard mean by *moral?* How does his meaning compare to your own?
2. What reasons, both explict and implicit, does Szilard give for seeing the targeting of Japanese cities as a moral issue?
3. Do you agree or disagree with Szilard that the use of nuclear weapons should be deliberated in moral terms (that moral considerations ought to be brought to bear upon decisions about nuclear weapons)?

Connections

1. Is Barton J. Bernstein's moral analysis like Leo Szilard's in any important respects? Explain.
2. Szilard was one of the authors of the Franck Report. Where do you find similarities in that report and Szilard's petition to the president of the United States?

Letter and Memorandum, September 11, 1945

Henry L. Stimson

The Secretary of War (Stimson) to President Truman

Washington, September 11, 1945

Dear Mr. President: In handing you today my memorandum about our re-   *1*
lations with Russia in respect to the atomic bomb, I am not unmindful of the
fact that when in Potsdam I talked with you about the question whether we
could be safe in sharing the atomic bomb with Russia while she was still a

---

Henry L. Stimson (1867–1950) was Secretary of War (like our present Secretary of Defense) under presidents Roosevelt and Truman. Although he had been one of the policy makers who set in motion the Manhattan Project and approved the Japanese targeting plans, Stimson, after the war, was convinced by the Franck Report, among other factors, that to risk an arms race would set us on a very dangerous course. In this letter he tries to prevail upon Truman to set American-Soviet cooperation above the temptation to continue American nuclear superiority.

police state and before she put into effect provisions assuring personal rights of liberty to the individual citizen.

I still recognize the difficulty and am still convinced of the importance of   2
the ultimate importance of a change in Russian attitude toward individual liberty but I have come to the conclusion that it would not be possible to use our possession of the atomic bomb as a direct lever to produce the change. I have become convinced that any demand by us for an internal change in Russia as a condition of sharing in the atomic weapon would be so resented that it would make the objective we have in view less probable.

I believe that the change in attitude toward the individual in Russia will   3
come slowly and gradually and I am satisfied that we should not delay our approach to Russia in the matter of the atomic bomb until that process has been completed. My reasons are set forth in the memorandum I am handing you today. Furthermore, I believe that this long process of change in Russia is more likely to be expedited by the closer relationship in the matter of the atomic bomb which I suggest and the trust and confidence that I believe would be inspired by the method of approach which I have outlined.

Faithfully yours,   [Henry L. Stimson]

Memorandum by the Secretary of War (Stimson) to President Truman

[Washington,] 11 September, 1945

Subject: Proposed Action for Control of Atomic Bombs

The advent of the atomic bomb has stimulated great military and probably   4
even greater political interest throughout the civilized world. In a world atmosphere already extremely sensitive to power, the introduction of this weapon has profoundly affected political considerations in all sections of the globe.

In many quarters it has been interpreted as a substantial offset to the growth   5
of Russian influence on the continent. We can be certain that the Soviet government has sensed this tendency and the temptation will be strong for the Soviet political and military leaders to acquire this weapon in the shortest possible time. Britain in effect already has the status of a partner with us in the development of this weapon. Accordingly, unless the Soviets are voluntarily invited into the partnership upon a basis of cooperation and trust, we are going to maintain the Anglo-Saxon bloc over against the Soviet in the possession of this weapon. Such a condition will almost certainly stimulate feverish activity on the part of the Soviet toward the development of this bomb in what will in effect be a secret armament race of a rather desperate character. There is evidence to indicate that such activity may have already commenced.

If we feel, as I assume we must, that civilization demands that some day we   6
shall arrive at a satisfactory international arrangement respecting the control of this new force, the question then is how long we can afford to enjoy our momentary superiority in the hope of achieving our immediate peace council objectives.

Whether Russia gets control of the necessary secrets of production in a min-   7
imum of say four years or a maximum of twenty years is not nearly as impor-

tant to the world and civilization as to make sure that when they do get it they are willing and cooperative partners among the peace loving nations of the world. It is true that if we approach them now, as I would propose, we may be gambling on their good faith and risk their getting into production of bombs a little sooner than they would otherwise.

To put the matter concisely, I consider the problem of our satisfactory re- *8* lations with Russia as not merely connected with but as virtually dominated by the problem of the atomic bomb. Except for the problem of the control of that bomb, those relations, while vitally important, might not be immediately pressing. The establishment of relations of mutual confidence between her and us could afford to await the slow progress of time. But with the discovery of the bomb, they become immediately emergent. These relations may be perhaps irretrievably embittered by the way in which we approach the solution of the bomb with Russia. For if we fail to approach them now and merely continue to negotiate with them, having this weapon rather ostentatiously on our hip, their suspicions and their distrust of our purposes and motives will increase. It will inspire them to greater efforts in an all out effort to solve the problem. If the solution is achieved in that spirit, it is much less likely that we will ever get the kind of covenant we may desperately need in the future. This risk is, I believe, greater than the other, inasmuch as our objective must be to get the best kind of international bargain we can — one that has some chance of being kept and saving civilization not for five or for twenty years, but forever.

The chief lesson I have learned in a long life is that the only way you can *9* make a man trustworthy is to trust him; and the surest way to make him untrustworthy is to distrust him and show your distrust.

If the atomic bomb were merely another more devastating military weapon *10* to be assimilated into our pattern of international relations, it would be one thing. We could then follow the old custom of secrecy and nationalistic military superiority relying on international caution to prescribe *[proscribe?]* the future use of the weapon as we did with gas. But I think the bomb instead constitutes merely a first step in a new control by a man over the forces of nature too revolutionary and dangerous to fit into the old concepts. I think it really caps the climax of the race between man's growing technical power for destructiveness and his psychological power of self-control and group control — his moral power. If so, our method of approach to the Russians is a question of the most vital importance in the evolution of human progress.

Since the crux of the problem is Russia, any contemplated action leading to *11* the control of this weapon should be primarily directed *to* Russia. It is my judgment that the Soviet would be more apt to respond sincerely to a direct and forthright approach made by the United States on this subject than would be the case if the approach were made as a part of a general international scheme, or if the approach were made after a succession of express or implied threats or near threats in our peace negotiations.

My idea of an approach to the Soviets would be a direct proposal after dis- *12* cussion with the British that we would be prepared in effect to enter an arrangement with the Russians, the general purpose of which would be to control and limit the use of the atomic bomb as an instrument of war and so far as possible to direct and encourage the development of atomic power for peaceful and humanitarian purposes. Such an approach might more specifically lead to the proposal that we would stop work on the further improvement in, or manufacture of, the bomb as a military weapon, provided the Russians and the British would agree to do likewise. It might also provide that we would be willing to impound what bombs we now have in the United States provided the Russians and the British would agree with us that in no event will they or we use a bomb as an instrument of war unless all three Governments agree to that use. We might also consider including in the arrangement a convenant with the U.K. and the Soviets providing for the exchange of benefits of future developments whereby atomic energy may be applied on a mutually satisfactory basis for commercial or humanitarian purposes.

I would make such an approach just as soon as our immediate political considerations make it appropriate.   *13*

I emphasize perhaps beyond all other considerations the importance of taking this action with Russia as a proposal of the United States — backed by Great Britain — but peculiarly the proposal of the United States. Action of any international group of nations, including many small nations who have not demonstrated their potential power or responsibility in this war would not, in my opinion, be taken seriously by the Soviets. The loose debates which would surround such proposal, if put before a conference of nations, would provoke but scant favor from the Soviet. As I say, I think this is the most important point in the program.   *14*

After the nations which have won this war have agreed to it, there will be ample time to introduce France and China into the covenants and finally to incorporate the agreement into the scheme of the United Nations. The use of this bomb has been accepted by the world as the result of the initiative and productive capacity of the United States, and I think this factor is a most potent lever toward having our proposals accepted by the Soviets, whereas I am most skeptical of obtaining any tangible results by way of any international debate. I urge this method as the most realistic means of accomplishing this vitally important step in the history of the world.   *15*

Henry L. Stimson

Considerations

1. Throughout his essay Henry L. Stimson shows how thoroughly he believes that "the crux of the problem is Russia" by devoting much discussion to Russia. What specifically was the problem with Russia? What does Stimson tell you explicitly and what must you infer?
2. What, precisely, is Stimson's proposal? Based only on what you can infer about President Truman's position from the letter and memorandum, write a memo from Truman to Stimson explaining why he rejected Stimson's proposal.
3. Stimson says, "The chief lesson I have learned in a long life is that the only way you can make a man trustworthy is to trust him; and the surest way

to make him untrustworthy is to distrust him and show your distrust" (para. 9). Some people think this position is naive and others think it is profound. What do you think, and why?

4. Barton J. Bernstein shows that little if any genuine ethical deliberation went into the plans for targeting Japan. Policy makers seemed unconcerned about this, and most — Stimson, for example — seemed to think they were behaving morally. Why did Secretary of War Stimson believe, as Bernstein says, that it would have been "morally unacceptable" *not* to have dropped the A-bomb on Japan. Do you agree or disagree with Stimson's position?

Connections

1. Why could the bomb be seen as "a substantial offset to the growth of Russian influence on the continent"? What do the essays by Randall Forsberg and Barton J. Bernstein tell you about the political power in possessing the bomb?

2. At one point Henry L. Stimson says that the question is "how long we can afford to enjoy our momentary superiority" (para. 6). What does he conclude? How is his answer like or unlike the position taken by the authors of the Franck Report?

3. Stimson says that the bomb "caps the climax of the race between man's growing technical power for destructiveness and his psychological power of self-control and group control." He calls this latter, psychological dimension our "moral power" (para. 10). What does he mean? Is his meaning of "moral" included in those of the other writers in this chapter or is this a new connotation for this word?

4. Bernstein indicates that Stimson's thinking about bombing Japan was not easy to understand. Review what he says about the Japanese targeting decisions. Based on this glimpse of Stimson's character, on what you know about his role as Secretary of War (Defense), and about the political tensions of the time, write a speculative essay on the following question: Why did Stimson wait until *after* the bombs were used and the Japanese surrendered to make his proposal to Truman?

Letter to Bernard Baruch, June 14, 1946

Dwight D. Eisenhower

The Chief of Staff of the United States Army (Eisenhower) to the United States Representative on the Atomic Energy Commission (Baruch)

SECRET   Washington, 14 June 1946

Dear Mr. Baruch: The Joint Chiefs of Staff have agreed that their views on   *1*
the complex questions raised in your letters of 24 May 1946 can best be dealt
with individually. My personal views follow.

General. I completely agree with you that only through effective interna-   *2*
tional control of atomic energy can we hope to prevent atomic war. Arriving
at the methods for such control is, of course, the difficult task. The national
security requires that those methods be tested and proven before the U.S. can
enter any international agreement limiting the production or use of atomic
bombs.

Approach to the Problem. The procedures outlined in the Acheson report ap-   *3*
pear to offer the most practicable initial steps towards international control,
provided that in the step by step accomplishment of those procedures, the U.S.
does not recede from its position of advantage faster than realistic and practical reciprocal concessions are made by other powerful nations. We must not
further unbalance against us world power relationships.

Inspection, the First Step. An essential primary step is to establish, and prove   *4*
in operation, a system of free and complete inspection. We must satisfy ourselves of complete good faith on the part of the other great powers; their past
and current policies are not altogether reassuring. In this connection, as I understand present atomic energy production techniques, no system of inspection can be expected to guarantee completely against the construction of some
atomic bombs.

---

*Dwight D. Eisenhower (1890–1969) was commander in chief of Allied forces
during World War II and was widely credited with the Allied victory over Germany. After the war, he remained the army chief of staff and was both influential
and highly respected. Eisenhower was first elected President in 1952 and stayed in
office through 1960. In this letter Eisenhower writes to Bernard Baruch, the man
who will present to the United Nations the U.S. proposal for international control
of atomic energy and weapons. The letter reveals much about security thinking at
the time, and amounts to a statement of our bargaining position.*

Preventive Measures. For the present, I am sure you agree that there must be 5
force behind any system for *preventing* aggression. There must exist for deterrent purposes, provisions for *retaliation* in the event other control and prevention devices should fail. Further, the sanctions employed against a willful aggressor by law-abiding nations can be no less effective in character than the weapons the aggressor nation is capable of using. To my mind, this means, for the present, that to *prevent* the use of atomic weapons there must exist the capability of employing atomic weapons against the recalcitrant.

Decisive Weapons in War. Biological, chemical, and other as yet unforeseen 6
weapons may prove no less effective than the atomic bomb, and even less susceptible to control. Another major war may see the use of such destructive weapons, however horrible, including the atomic bomb. The problem of controlling, and finally preventing, the use of atomic bombs (and other decisive weapons) thus becomes the problem of preventing war itself.

The Dilemma. If we enter too hurriedly into an international agreement to 7
abolish all atomic weapons, we may find ourselves in the position of having no restraining means in the world capable of effective action if a great power violates the agreement. Such a power might, in fact, deliberately avoid the use of atomic weapons and embark on aggression with other equally decisive weapons. If, on the other hand, we enter into agreements providing for the maintenance of atomic weapons under international control, we face extraordinary difficulties. First, in providing adequate control and inspection systems and second, the possibility that the national leaders of a totalitarian state, possessing a supply of the weapons, might choose to strike first rather than to compromise. This dilemma, unless other approaches to a solution come to hand, must be solved before we should proceed to any treaty, abolishing atomic weapons.

Fundamental National Interest. The U.S. should be party to no control treaty 8
which militates against our vital security interests. I have touched upon aspects of this scarcely debatable point. However, the fundamental interest and security of the American people is bound up with a solution to the problem you face. We can yield much, even certain points of our sovereignty, to reach this solution. Whether our people could be brought to see this necessity at present is a question. There will exist practical difficulties in keying up the American people to accept even the necessity for immediate preventive military action with conventional weapons in case an aggressor violates measures for inspection and control. Historically, in the face of threats of unmistakable import and seriousness, our practice has been to indulge in wishful thinking rather than to undertake decisive action.

To summarize: 9

a. The existence of the atomic bomb in our hands is a deterrent, in fact, to aggression in the world. We cannot at this time limit our capability to produce or use this weapon.

b. We must move, by steps, toward international control of atomic energy if we are to avoid an atomic war. The Acheson report is a practicable suggestion for an approach to such control. A first step is to *prove* a system of inspection.

c. Atomic weapons are only a part of the problem. There will be other equally

terrible weapons of mass destruction. The whole problem must be solved concurrently with the problem of controlling atomic energy. To control atomic
weapons, in which field we are preeminent, without provision for equally adequate control of other weapons of mass destruction can seriously endanger
our national security.

I will continue to consider this problem and will communicate to you any   *10*
ideas which might assist your difficult decisions.

Sincerely,

Dwight D. Eisenhower

Considerations

1. Under the heading Approach to the Problem, Eisenhower cautions that the
United States must not "recede from its position of advantage" too fast. Why
not? What reasons does he give or imply?

2. In the same passage, Eisenhower says that we must not "unbalance against
us" the power relationships in the world. Examine the meaning of his phrase.
How does he seem to define balance?

3. Under the heading The Dilemma, Eisenhower describes what for him seems
a genuine, logical dilemma. Technically, a dilemma exists when one must
choose between two equally undesirable paths. Some people say that the
situation Eisenhower sees as a dilemma was not really so. Look carefully at
what Eisenhower sees as choices. How might the situation be described and
restructured to eliminate the apparent dilemma? Which structuring do you
prefer and why?

4. What does Eisenhower mean in the concluding paragraph by "preventive
military action" and by "decisive action"? What does he say was the American people's attitude toward such things? How is that attitude the same or
different today?

5. Some aspects of Eisenhower's language make it difficult to grasp precisely
what he means. Examine his language in general and find some examples
of ambiguous or difficult statements. Identify what makes his writing difficult to understand.

Connections

1. Put yourself in Bernard Baruch's shoes: You are reading Eisenhower's memo
as you prepare to present the United States proposal for international control over nuclear weapons to the United Nations. You have been briefed by
Henry L. Stimson, by the president, and by many others, and have formed
some expectations about how the Soviets might react to the American proposal in general. Based on what you know about the Soviets so far, how do
you think they would respond to Eisenhower's insistence that "we cannot
at this time limit our capability to produce or use this weapon"? Why?

2. Read the Macchiavelli section in Chapter 1, The Dimensions of Power. Ap-
praise Eisenhower's position on maintaining American superiority in terms

of the qualities and behavior Macchiavelli designates as appropriate to a leader.

3. Do Stimson and Eisenhower disagree on any fundamental issues? Explain.

The Baruch Plan

Bernard Baruch

Proposals for an International Atomic Development Authority

By the United States Representative to the Atomic Energy Commission[1]

My Fellow Members of the United Nations Atomic Energy Commission, and My Fellow Citizens of the World:

We are here to make a choice between the quick and the dead. *1*

That is our business. *2*

Behind the black portent of the new atomic age lies a hope which, seized *3* upon with faith, can work our salvation. If we fail, then we have damned every man to be the slave of Fear. Let us not deceive ourselves: We must elect World Peace or World Destruction.

Science has torn from nature a secret so vast in its potentialities that our *4* minds cower from the terror it creates. Yet terror is not enough to inhibit the use of the atomic bomb. The terror created by weapons has never stopped man from employing them. For each new weapon a defense has been produced, in

---

Bernard Baruch (1870–1965), a financier, was chosen by President Truman to present the U.S. proposal for international control of nuclear weapons at the United Nations. Baruch was an arrogant man whom the Soviets already knew to be difficult to work with. Baruch's Soviet counterpart was Andrei Gromyko, a statesman who until recently was still centrally involved in American-Soviet arms negotiations.

The United Nations meeting was the first nuclear weapons negotiation meeting, and it did not go well. Five days after Baruch presented the U.S. proposal, Gromyko presented the Soviet response. The Soviets said they would not talk about creation of controls over nuclear materials until the United States first destroyed its existing stockpile of atomic bombs. The United States refused, as Eisenhower had advised, and the talks were stalemated. Shortly after 1949, when the Soviets tested their first atomic bomb, the talks dissolved.

time. But now we face a condition in which adequate defense does not exist.

Science, which gave us this dread power, shows that it *can* be made a giant   5
help to humanity, but science does *not* show us how to prevent its baleful use.
So we have been appointed to obviate that peril by finding a meeting of the
minds and the hearts of our peoples. Only in the will of mankind lies the answer.

It is to express this will and make it effective that we have been assembled.   6
We must provide the mechanism to assure that atomic energy is used for
peaceful purposes and preclude its use in war. To that end, we must provide
immediate, swift, and sure punishment of those who violate the agreements
that are reached by the nations. Penalization is essential if peace is to be more
than a feverish interlude between wars. And, too, the United Nations can prescribe individual responsibility and punishment on the principles applied at
Nürnberg by the Union of Soviet Socialist Republics, the United Kingdom,
France, and the United States — a formula certain to benefit the world's future.

In this crisis, we represent not only our governments but, in a larger way,   7
we represent the peoples of the world. We must remember that the peoples do
not belong to the governments but that the governments belong to the peoples.
We must answer their demands; we must answer the world's longing for peace
and security.

In that desire the United States shares ardently and hopefully. The search   8
of science for the absolute weapon has reached fruition in this country. But she
stands ready to proscribe and destroy this instrument — to lift its use from
death to life — if the world will join in a pact to that end.

In our success lies the promise of a new life, freed from the heart-stopping   9
fears that now beset the world. The beginning of victory for the great ideals
for which millions have bled and died lies in building a workable plan. Now
we approach fulfilment of the aspirations of mankind. At the end of the road
lies the fairer, better, surer life we crave and mean to have.

Only by a lasting peace are liberties and democracies strengthened and   10
deepened. War is their enemy. And it will not do to believe that any of us can
escape war's devastation. Victor, vanquished, and neutrals alike are affected
physically, economically, and morally.

Against the degradation of war we can erect a safeguard. That is the guer-   11
don for which we reach. Within the scope of the formula we outline here there
will be found, to those who seek it, the essential elements of our purpose. Others will see only emptiness. Each of us carries his own mirror in which is reflected hope — or determined desperation — courage or cowardice.

There is a famine throughout the world today. It starves men's bodies. But   12
there is a greater famine — the hunger of men's spirit. That starvation can be
cured by the conquest of fear, and the substitution of hope, from which springs
faith —faith in each other, faith that we want to work together toward salvation, and determination that those who threaten the peace and safety shall be
punished.

The peoples of these democracies gathered here have a particular concern   13
with our answer, for their peoples hate war. They will have a heavy exaction
to make of those who fail to provide an escape. They are not afraid of an in-

ternationalism that protects; they are unwilling to be fobbed off by mouthings about narrow sovereignty, which is today's phrase for yesterday's isolation.

The basis of a sound foreign policy, in this new age, for all the nations here 14 gathered, is that anything that happens, no matter where or how, which menaces the peace of the world, or the economic stability, concerns each and all of us.

That, roughly, may be said to be the central theme of the United Nations. 15 It is with that thought we begin consideration of the most important subject that can engage mankind — life itself.

Let there be no quibbling about the duty and the responsibility of this group 16 and of the governments we represent. I was moved, in the afternoon of my life, to add my effort to gain the world's quest, by the broad mandate under which we were created. The resolution of the General Assembly, passed January 24, 1946 in London, reads:

Section V. Terms of Reference of the Commission
The Commission shall proceed with the utmost despatch and enquire into all phases of the problems, and make such recommendations from time to time with respect to them as it finds possible. In particular the Commission shall make specific proposals:
(a) For extending between all nations the exchange of basic scientific information for peaceful ends;
(b) For control of atomic energy to the extent necessary to ensure its use only for peaceful purposes;
(c) For the elimination from national armaments of atomic weapons and of all other major weapons adaptable to mass destruction;
(d) For effective safeguards by way of inspection and other means to protect complying States against the hazards of violations and evasions.
The work of the Commission should proceed by separate stages, the successful completion of each of which will develop the necessary confidence of the world before the next stage is undertaken. . . .[2]

Our mandate rests, in text and in spirit, upon the outcome of the Conference 17 in Moscow of Messrs. Molotov of the Union of Soviet Socialist Republics, Bevin of the United Kingdom, and Byrnes of the United States of America. The three Foriegn Ministers on December 27, 1945 proposed the establishment of this body.[3]

Their action was animated by a preceding conference in Washington on No- 18 vember 15, 1945, when the President of the United States, associated with Mr. Attlee, Prime Minister of the United Kingdom, and Mr. Mackenzie King, Prime Minister of Canada, stated that international control of the whole field of atomic energy was immediately essential. They proposed the formation of this body. In examining that source, the Agreed Declaration, it will be found that the fathers of the concept recognized the final means of world salvation — the abolition of war. Solemnly they wrote:

We are aware that the only complete protection for the civilized world from the destructive use of scientific knowledge lies in the prevention of war. No system of safeguards that can be devised will of itself provide an effective guarantee against production of atomic weapons by a nation bent on aggression. Nor can we ignore the possibility of and development of other weapons, or of new methods of warfare, which may constitute as great a threat to civilization as the military use of atomic energy.[4]

Through the historical approach I have outlined, we find ourselves here to   *19*
test if man can produce, through his will and faith, the miracle of peace, just
as he has, through science and skill, the miracle of the atom.

The United States proposes the creation of an International Atomic Devel-   *20*
opment Authority, to which should be entrusted all phases of the development
and use of atomic energy, starting with the raw material and including —

1. Managerial control or ownership of all atomic-energy activities potentially
   dangerous to world security.
2. Power to control, inspect, and license all other atomic activities.
3. The duty of fostering the beneficial uses of atomic energy.
4. Research and development responsibilities of an affirmative character intended to put the Authority in the forefront of atomic knowledge and thus
   to enable it to comprehend, and therefore to detect, misuse of atomic energy. To be effective, the Authority must itself be the world's leader in the
   field of atomic knowledge and development and thus supplement its legal
   authority with the great power inherent in possession of leadership in
   knowledge.

I offer this as a basis for beginning our discussion.   *21*

But I think the peoples we serve would not believe — and without faith   *22*
nothing counts — that a treaty, merely outlawing possession or use of the atomic
bomb, constitutes effective fulfilment of the instructions to this Commission.
Previous failures have been recorded in trying the method of simple renunciation, unsupported by effective guaranties of security and armament limitation.
No one would have faith in that approach alone.

Now, if ever, is the time to act for the common good. Public opinion sup-   *23*
ports a world movement toward security. If I read the signs aright, the peoples
want a program not composed merely of pious thoughts but of enforceable
sanctions — an international law with teeth in it.

We of this nation, desirous of helping to bring peace to the world and real-   *24*
izing the heavy obligations upon us arising from our possession of the means
of producing the bomb and from the fact that it is part of our armament, are
prepared to make our full contribution toward effective control of atomic energy.

When an adequate system for control of atomic energy, including the   *25*
renunciation of the bomb as a weapon, has been agreed upon and put into
effective operation and condign punishments set up for violations of the
rules of control which are to be stigmatized as international crimes, we propose that —

1. Manufacture of atomic bombs shall stop;
2. Existing bombs shall be disposed of pursuant to the terms of the treaty; and
3. The Authority shall be in possession of full information as to the know-how
   for the production of atomic energy.

Let me repeat, so as to avoid misunderstanding: My country is ready to make   *26*
its full contribution toward the end we seek, subject of course to our constitutional processes and to an adequate system of control becoming fully effective, as we finally work it out.

Now as to violations: In the agreement, penalties of as serious a nature as   27
the nations may wish and as immediate and certain in their execution as possible should be fixed for —

1. Illegal possession or use of an atomic bomb;
2. Illegal possession, or separation, of atomic material suitable for use in an
   atomic bomb;
3. Seizure of any plant or other property belonging to or licensed by the Authority;
4. Willful interference with the activities of the Authority;
5. Creation or operation of dangerous projects in a manner contrary to, or in
   the absence of, a license granted by the international control body.

It would be a deception, to which I am unwilling to lend myself, were I not   28
to say to you and to our peoples that the matter of punishment lies at the very
heart of our present security system. It might as well be admitted, here and
now, that the subject goes straight to the veto power contained in the Charter
of the United Nations so far as it relates to the field of atomic energy. The Charter
permits penalization only by concurrence of each of the five great powers —
the Union of Soviet Socialist Republics, the United Kingdom, China, France,
and the United States.

I want to make very plain that I am concerned here with the veto power   29
only as it affects this particular problem. There must be no veto to protect those
who violate their solemn agreements not to develop or use atomic energy for
destructive purposes.

The bomb does not wait upon debate. To delay may be to die. The time be-   30
tween violation and preventive action or punishment would be all too short for
extended discussion as to the course to be followed.

As matters now stand several years may be necessary for another country   31
to produce a bomb, *de novo*. However, once the basic information is generally
known, and the Authority has established producing plants for peaceful purposes in the several countries, an illegal seizure of such a plant might permit
a malevolent nation to produce a bomb in 12 months, and if preceded by secret preparation and necessary facilities perhaps even in a much shorter time.
The time required — the advance warning given of the possible use of a bomb
— can only be generally estimated but obviously will depend upon many factors, including the success with which the Authority has been able to introduce
elements of safety in the design of its plants and the degree to which illegal
and secret preparation for the military use of atomic energy will have been
eliminated. Presumably no nation would think of starting a war with only one
bomb.

This shows how imperative speed is in detecting and penalizing violations.   32

The process of prevention and penalization — a problem of profound state-   33
craft — is, as I read it, implicit in the Moscow statement, signed by the Union
of Soviet Socialist Republics, the United States, and the United Kingdom a
few months ago.

But before a country is ready to relinquish any winning weapons it must   34
have more than words to reassure it. It must have a guarantee of safety, not
only against the offenders in the atomic area but against the illegal users of

other weapons — bacteriological, biological, gas — perhaps — why not? — against war itself.

In the elimination of war lies our solution, for only then will nations cease   35
to compete with one another in the production and use of dread "secret" weapons which are evaluated solely by their capacity to kill. This devilish program takes us back not merely to the Dark Ages but from cosmos to chaos. If we succeed in finding a suitable way to control atomic weapons, it is reasonable to hope that we may also preclude the use of other weapons adaptable to mass destruction. When a man learns to say "A" he can, if he chooses, learn the rest of the alphabet too.

Let this be anchored in our minds: 36

Peace is never long preserved by weight of metal or by an armament race.   37
Peace can be made tranquil and secure only by understanding and agreement fortified by sanctions. We must embrace international cooperation or international disintegration.

Science has taught us how to put the atom to work. But to make it work for   38
good instead of for evil lies in the domain dealing with the principles of human duty. We are now facing a problem more of ethics than of physics.

The solution will require apparent sacrifice in pride and in position, but better   39
pain as the price of peace than death as the price of war.

I now submit the following measures as representing the fundamental fea-   40
tures of a plan which would give effect to certain of the conclusions which I have epitomized.

1. *General.* The Authority should set up a thorough plan for control of the   41
field of atomic energy, through various forms of ownership, dominion, licenses, operation, inspection, research, and management by competent personnel. After this is provided for, there should be as little interference as may be with the economic plans and the present private, corporate, and state relationships in the several countries involved.

2. *Raw Materials.* The Authority should have as one of its earliest purposes   42
to obtain and maintain complete and accurate information on world supplies of uranium and thorium and to bring them under its dominion. The precise pattern of control for various types of deposits of such materials will have to depend upon the geological, mining, refining, and economic facts involved in different situations.

The Authority should conduct continuous surveys so that it will have the most complete knowledge of the world geology of uranium and thorium. Only after all current information on world sources of uranium and thorium is known to us all can equitable plans be made for their production, refining, and distribution.

3. *Primary Production Plants.* The Authority should exercise complete man-   43
agerial control of the production of fissionable materials. This means that it should control and operate all plants producing fissionable materials in dangerous quantities and must own and control the product of these plants.

4. *Atomic Explosives.* The Authority should be given sole and exclusive right   44
to conduct research in the field of atomic explosives. Research activities in the

field of atomic explosives are essential in order that the Authority may keep in the forefront of knowledge in the field of atomic energy and fulfil the objective of preventing illicit manufacture of bombs. Only by maintaining its position as the best-informed agency will the Authority be able to determine the line between intrinsically dangerous and non-dangerous activities.

5. *Strategic Distribution of Activities and Materials.* The activities entrusted 45 exclusively to the Authority because they are intrinsically dangerous to security should be distributed throughout the world. Similarly, stockpiles of raw materials and fissionable materials should not be centralized.

6. *Non-Dangerous Activities.* A function of the Authority should be promo- 46 tion of the peace-time benefits of atomic energy.

Atomic research (except in explosives), the use of research reactors, the production of radioactive tracers by means of non-dangerous reactors, the use of such tracers, and to some extent the production of power should be open to nations and their citizens under reasonable licensing arrangements from the Authority. Denatured materials, whose use we know also requires suitable safeguards, should be furnished for such purposes by the Authority under lease or other arrangement. Denaturing seems to have been overestimated by the public as a safety measure.

7. *Definition of Dangerous and Non-Dangerous Activities.* Although a reason- 47 able dividing line can be drawn between dangerous and non-dangerous activities, it is not hard and fast. Provision should, therefore, be made to assure constant reexamination of the questions and to permit revision of the dividing line as changing conditions and new discoveries may require.

8. *Operations of Dangerous Activities.* Any plant dealing with uranium or 48 thorium after it once reaches the potential of dangerous use must be not only subject to the most rigorous and competent inspection by the Authority, but its actual operation shall be under the management, supervision, and control of the Authority.

9. *Inspection.* By assigning intrinsically dangerous activities exclusively to 49 the Authority, the difficulties of inspection are reduced. If the Authority is the only agency which may lawfully conduct dangerous activities, then visible operation by others than the Authority will constitute an unambiguous danger signal. Inspection will also occur in connection with the licensing functions of the Authority.

10. *Freedom of Access.* Adequate ingress and egress for all qualified repre- 50 sentatives of the Authority must be assured. Many of the inspection activities of the Authority should grow out of, and be incidental to, its other functions. Important measures of inspection will be associated with the tight control of raw materials, for this is a keystone of the plan. The continuing activities of prospecting, survey, and research in relation to raw materials will be designed not only to serve the affirmative development functions of the Authority but also to assure that no surreptitious operations are conducted in the raw-materials field by nations or their citizens.

11. *Personnel.* The personnel of the Authority should be recruited on a basis 51 of proven competence but also so far as possible on an international basis.

12. *Progress by Stages.* A primary step in the creation of the system of con- 52

trol is the setting forth, in comprehensive terms, of the functions, responsibilities, powers, and limitations of the Authority. Once a charter for the Authority has been adopted, the Authority and the system of control for which it will be responsible will require time to become fully organized and effective. The plan of control will, therefore, have to come into effect in successive stages. These should be specifically fixed in the charter or means should be otherwise set forth in the charter for transitions from one stage to another, as contemplated in the resolution of the United Nations Assembly which created this Commission.

13. *Disclosures.* In the deliberations of the United Nations Commission on   53
Atomic Energy, the United States is prepared to make available the information essential to a reasonable understanding of the proposals which it advocates. Further disclosures must be dependent, in the interests of all, upon the effective ratification of the treaty. When the Authority is actually created, the United States will join the other nations in making available the further information essential to that organization for the performance of its functions. As the successive stages of international control are reached, the United States will be prepared to yield, to the extent required by each stage, national control of activities in this field to the Authority.

14. *International Control.* There will be questions about the extent of con-   54
trol to be allowed to national bodies, when the Authority is established. Purely national authorities for control and development of atomic energy should to the extent necessary for the effective operation of the Authority be subordinate to it. This is neither an endorsement nor a disapproval of the creation of national authorities. The Commission should evolve a clear demarcation of the scope of duties and responsibilities of such national authorities.

And now I end. I have submitted an outline for present discussion. Our con-   55
sideration will be broadened by the criticism of the United States proposals and by the plans of the other nations, which, it is to be hoped, will be submitted at their early convenience. I and my associates of the United States Delegation will make available to each member of this body books and pamphlets, including the Acheson-Lilienthal report, recently made by the United States Department of State, and the McMahon Committee Monograph No. 1 entitled "Essential Information on Atomic Energy" relating to the McMahon bill recently passed by the United States Senate, which may prove of value in assessing the situation.[5]

All of us are consecrated to making an end of gloom and hopelessness. It   56
will not be an easy job. The way is long and thorny, but supremely worth traveling. All of us want to stand erect, with our faces to the sun, instead of being forced to burrow into the earth, like rats.

The pattern of salvation must be worked out by all for all.   57

The light at the end of the tunnel is dim, but our path seems to grow brighter   58
as we actually begin our journey. We cannot yet light the way to the end. However, we hope the suggestions of my Government will be illuminating.

Let us keep in mind the exhortation of Abraham Lincoln, whose words, ut-   59
tered at a moment of shattering national peril, form a complete text for our deliberation. I quote, paraphrasing slightly:

We cannot escape history. We of this meeting will be remembered in spite of ourselves. No personal significance or insignificance can spare one or another of us. The fiery trial through which we are passing will light us down in honor or dishonor to the latest generation.

We say we are for Peace. The world will not forget that we say this. We know how to save Peace. The world knows that we do. We, even we here, hold the power and have the responsibility.

We shall nobly save, or meanly lose, the last, best hope of earth. The way is plain, peaceful, generous, just — a way which, if followed, the world will forever applaud.

My thanks for your attention.   *60*

NOTES
[1] Bernard M. Baruch, who delivered this address at the opening session of the United Nations Atomic Energy Commission in New York, N.Y., on June 14. The address was released to the press by the U.S. Delegation to the United Nations on the same date.
[2] *Department of State Bulletin* of Feb. 10, 1946, p. 198.
[3] *Department of State Bulletin* of Dec. 30, 1945, p. 1031.
[4] *Department of State Bulletin* of Nov. 18, 1945, p. 781.
[5] Department of State publication 2498; for excerpts from the Acheson-Lilienthal report see *Bulletin* of Apr. 7, 1946, p. 553. The text of the McMahon bill is S. Rept. 1211, 79th Cong.

Considerations

1. The actual stipulations of the proposal are fairly brief, appearing in paragraphs 41–54 and introduced in paragraphs 20, 25, and 27. What functions does the rest of Bernard Baruch's speech serve?
2. Notice some of the language and phrasing of this speech. What effect do words like *hope, faith, salvation, punishment, guerdon,* and *quest* have? What other words strike you as unusual for this kind of situation? Why do you think Baruch chose such words?
3. Look at the discussion of the veto and of punishment for violations. Are these provisions worded in such a way that they apply equally to the United States, Great Britain, and the Soviet Union? Explain.

Connections

1. Compare and contrast the recommendations of the Henry L. Stimson memorandum with the provisions of the Baruch Plan.
2. Niels Bohr, Leo Szilard, and the authors of the Franck Report influenced the shaping of the Baruch Plan. Where do you find evidence of their influence?
3. Both the Franck Report and the Stimson memo declare that only mutual trust between the United States and Soviet Union can make arms negotiations possible and save us from the risks of an arms race. Review these pieces and then describe how Bernard Baruch treats the issue of trust.

Four Historical Views: On the Failure of the Baruch Plan

From "A History of Strategic Arms Limitations"

G. Allen Greb and Gerald W. Johnson

The proposal called for the creation of an international nuclear develop-   *1*
ment authority. This authority would have the power to control all atomic energy activities and to establish inspection procedures not subject to U.N. Security Council veto. The United States promised to dismantle its nuclear bombs
once this agency was established. The Soviet reply, presented by Deputy Foreign Minister Andrei Gromyko, came only five days later; because the United
States enjoyed a nuclear monopoly, the Soviets called for the destruction of
existing atomic arsenals *before* any discussion of inspection and control procedures could take place. This fundamental difference blocked all progress toward any form of arms control or disarmament for a dozen years.

Considerations

1. Does this very brief account of the Baruch Plan explain why the United States
   and the Soviet Union failed to reach an agreement? Does it blame one side
   or the other?

*G. Allen Greb (b. 1948) and Gerald W. Johnson (b. 1928). G. Allen Greb is a
research historian in the Program in Science, Technology, and Public Affairs at
the University of California at San Diego and also serves as the assistant director
of the Institute for Global Conflict and Cooperation. Gerald W. Johnson was part
of the SALT II and Comprehensive Test Ban negotiating teams. This excerpt originally appeared in the* Bulletin of the Atomic Scientists *(January 1984).*

Arms Control and Disarmament

Stockholm International Peace Research Institute

Disarmament Efforts, 1945–1965

On 26 June 1945 the United Nations Charter was signed in San Francisco. *1* The new world organization proclaimed as one of its main purposes and principles the maintenance of international peace and security. In order to promote this purpose the founding members entrusted specific responsibilities for disarmament and the regulation of armaments to the Security Council and the General Assembly, thus providing the legal basis for all further activities in this field.

The Security Council was made responsible for formulating, with the assis- *2* tance of the Military Staff Committee (art. 47), plans to be submitted to the members of the United Nations for the establishment of a system for the regulation of armaments (art. 26). The General Assembly was empowered to consider the principles governing disarmament and the regulation of armaments and to make recommendations about them (art. 11).

When the Charter came into force (24 October 1945), disarmament had al- *3* ready become a serious problem. The dropping of the first atomic bombs (August 1945) confronted the United Nations with the urgent task of establishing control over atomic energy and outlawing the use and production of atomic weapons. Thus the very first resolution passed by the General Assembly (24 January 1946) unanimously established the UN Atomic Energy Commission, consisting of the members of the Security Council, plus Canada (when not a member of the Council). The Commission was asked to draw up plans for the control of atomic energy and for the elimination of atomic weapons and of all other major weapons of mass destruction. In the immediate post-war period disarmament negotiations were almost entirely concerned with these questions.

The United States plan for nuclear disarmament (Baruch Plan) was put for- *4* ward in the Atomic Energy Commission in June 1946. It envisaged the creation of a system for control of atomic energy, with punishment for violation of the rules of operation. This would then be followed by the stopping of the manu-

Stockholm International Peace Research Institute (SIPRI) is dedicated to researching and promoting conditions for world peace. SIPRI publications are one of the most reliable sources of information about the Soviet arsenal and contain updates of arms control and weapons issues as well as topical articles. This essay is from the SIPRI Yearbook, *1968/69.*

facture of bombs and the destruction of all existing bombs. The plan provided that *control must precede prohibition;* and the administration of the control would be free of the veto of permanent members of the Security Council. The suggested degree of inspection and control — probably to be exercised by a body in which Western powers would have the major influence — was unacceptable to the Soviet Union. Furthermore, if at any time the treaty broke down, the United States would have a monopoly of atomic weapons. The Soviet Union's counter-proposal of June 1946 (Gromyko Plan) required signatories to agree not to use atomic weapons, to prohibit the production of them and to destroy all existing stocks. In this plan, *prohibition and destruction would precede control:* consequently, the United States advantage in atomic weapons would be nullified. The Soviet Union modified this position in October 1948, suggesting that the conventions of the prohibition of atomic weapons and on the establishment of international control over atomic energy be brought into operation simultaneously.

It was some time before discussion on conventional armaments began. The   5 Commission for Conventional Armaments, established by the Security Council in 1947 and consisting of its members, did not begin serious work until 1948, after the rejection of the Soviet proposal that conventional and nuclear disarmament be considered together. The Soviet proposal, which then called for reductions in existing forces by a third, was not accepted because in the Western opinion such reduction would preserve the Soviet Union's conventional military superiority. The Western countries were concerned with the relative level of conventional arms, and most immediately with establishing what the existing ratio in fact was.

In this period, then, when the United States had a nuclear monopoly and   6 the Soviet Union was presumed to be superior in conventional weapons, each side was making proposals which preserved its own position while neutralizing the other side's superiority. The two Commissions, failing to agree, adjourned indefinitely in 1950.

Considerations

1. How does the history of the United Nations, described in the first three paragraphs, influence your understanding of the Baruch Plan?
2. Paragraph 4 focuses on the Baruch Plan itself. What information does it add to what you already know? Do its two italicized statements summarize accurately the disagreement between the United States and the Soviet Union? Does the passage blame one country or the other?
3. What do the discussion of conventional weapons and the concluding paragraph add to your understanding?

Connections

1. How does the SIPRI account explain the failure of the Baruch Plan in a different way than the G. Allen Greb and Gerald W. Johnson's account does?

A History of
Lost Opportunities

Alva Myrdal

After 6 and 9 August 1945, when the United States demonstrated the awe-   *1*
some explosive power of the atom at Hiroshima and Nagasaki, governments
realized that fundamental conceptions of war, peace, and security had been
changed radically. From then on it was clear that disarmament efforts were
highly urgent. It was clear to responsible thinkers that efforts should be directed towards the elimination of nuclear weapons, not just limitation and
regulation of what was coming to be called conventional weapons.

The exploding of these atomic bombs was a blow dealt the new world or-   *2*
ganization only a few weeks after the signing of its Charter, 26 June 1945, and
a few months before its first General Assembly met in session in London on 24
January 1946. Its very first resolution, numbered 1 (I), by unanimous decision
established an Atomic Energy Commission with the urgent task of making specific proposals "for the elimination from national armaments of atomic weapons and of all other major weapons adaptable to mass destruction."[1] In pursuing its work the Commission concentrated entirely on nuclear weapons.

Acceptance of this sweeping resolution by all the fifty-one members should   *3*
have opened possibilities for international agreement on this issue of momentous importance. It should have been the right moment to act, as it was still
possible to envisage complete non-nuclear armament. At that time only three
nuclear devices, of varying construction, had been produced and consumed:
one, in the proving grounds of Alamagordo; two having brought death and destruction to Hiroshima and Nagasaki. The opportunity to stop production which
had not yet begun in earnest,[2] was never to recur.

The immediate blame must be laid on the Soviet Union for being such an   *4*
insistent naysayer when the United States, at the first meeting of the UN Atomic
Energy Commission on 14 June 1946, presented a plan for the prohibition of
the manufacture of atomic bombs and for placing all phases of the development and use of atomic energy under an International Authority.[3] But this
seemingly magnanimous plan, known to history as the Baruch Plan, contained
explicit and implicit reservations which as they were revealed raised suspicions and caused resistance on the part of the Russians.

---

*Alva Myrdal (b. 1902) has held many appointments in the Swedish government.
Her book,* The Game of Disarmament: How the United States and Russia Run
the Arms Race *(1982), is one of her many contributions to the literature of social
philosophy, population control, and equality. In 1982 she was awarded the Nobel
Peace Prize.*

Indeed, the Baruch Plan was formulated at a time when U.S. foreign policy 5
was moving towards a more nationalistic Realpolitik.°

With the death of Franklin Roosevelt on 25 April 1945 there passed from the 6
scene an American president who, in spite of basic nationalism and considerable apprehension caused by Stalin's takeover of Eastern Europe, had continued to support the wartime alliance with the Soviet Union and to believe in
the workability of the United Nations. Even after his death his farsighted views
continued to be expressed, as in this memorandum of 11 September 1945 by
Henry Stimson, the Secretary of War, who had been advised by scientists James
Conant and Vannevar Bush:

> Those relations may be perhaps irretrievably embittered by the way in which we ap-
> proach the solution of the bomb with Russia. For if we fail to approach them now
> and merely continue to negotiate with them, having this weapon rather ostenta-
> tiously on our hip, their suspicions and their distrust of our purposes and motives
> will increase.[4]

Before the cold war solidified, a preliminary version of a plan for interna- 7
tional cooperation in the atomic field had been worked out. Robert Oppenheimer was among the participants. A later version, which became known as the
Acheson-Lilienthal Report, had much of the original awareness of the need to
accommodate the Soviet Union. When it was presented publicly over the radio
on 23 April 1946 it stated prophetically that:

> the extremely favored position with regard to atomic devices, which the United States
> enjoys at present, is *only temporary. It will not last.* We must use that advantage now
> to promote international security and to carry out our policy of building a lasting
> peace through international agreement.[5]

But the visionary view gradually dimmed, and each succeeding draft of a 8
proposed plan grew less generous and equitable. As Harry Truman got more
into his presidential stride, the outlook narrowed considerably.[6] Taking the advice of his Secretary of State, James Byrnes, Truman decreed that the plan
should be made more workable and, against Dean Acheson's protests, the old
financier Bernard M. Baruch was chosen. He set about translating the Acheson-Lilienthal Report into terms more workable from the American point of
view.

A major change was the addition of "condign punishment"[7] for violators of 9
a UN treaty that would ban atomic weapons and control production and use
of fissionable material by inspections.[8] At the bottom of the controversy that
opened up in the Commission was the Soviet Union's deep distrust of any actions by the United Nations, which it regarded, then with considerable justification, as being dominated by the United States.

Thus, when Baruch presented his plan to the Commission as "plain, peace- 10
ful, generous, (and) just," the Russians regarded it as considerably less so. The
Baruch plan contained several wise and statesmanlike proposals, but it as-

---

°Power politics: the view that nations always act to increase their own power, that a realistic foreign
policy takes this into account, and that such power politics, being inescapable, necessitate some
brutal acts.

signed obligations to the United States that were extremely vague, while the obligations of the Soviet Union were to be quite strict and harsh. Baruch's insistence on condign punishments and the implied abolition of the veto rights for such extremely important decisions were political elements that wrecked the plan. Moreover, until a UN treaty could be agreed upon and come into force the United States was to retain its monopoly on atomic secrets and it did not promise to end production of new atomic weapons. Under these conditions, the United States was the only nation in a position to impose condign punishment. There was no doubt that the Soviet Union was the only potential violator upon whom punishments might be visited.

> The Soviet Union was undoubtedly doing all in its power to develop nuclear weapons at the moment. . . . If so, the "swift and sure punishment" provision could be interpreted in Moscow only as an attempt to turn the United Nations into an alliance to support a United States threat of war against the USSR unless it ceased its efforts, for only the United States could conceivably administer "swift and sure punishment" to the Soviet Union. This meant certain defeat of the treaty by Soviet veto.[9]

This warning lent some credence to the possibility of the United States with UN support waging preventive war against the Soviet Union before it would have had time to catch up with its nuclear-armed adversary.[10]

In all probability, the Soviet Union had already chosen the alternative course 11 to procure the atomic bomb for itself, although Andrei Gromyko, Soviet delegate to the UN Security Council, immediately countered the Baruch plan with a proposal to destroy all nuclear weapons in existence and cease all production and use of atomic weapons categorically. The United States instead immediately demonstrated its unwillingness to sacrifice its advantage by conducting its first postwar atomic test over Bikini, on 1 July 1946 — seventeen days after Baruch had presented his plan to the Commission and before its relevant technical subcommittee had met.

The political positions of both sides allow us to learn a lot from what hap- 12 pened in the Commission at the dawn of the atomic era about how to negotiate and how not to negotiate disarmament agreements. Besides the politically loaded issue of punishment, the controversy circled around two moot points.

The first concerned the exchange of information. Despite much doubletalk 13 from both sides it was clear that the United States would refuse to share the know-how about the military application of nuclear-fission technologies — that is, the very secret of explosions; nor did it promise to release secrets to the envisaged International Authority. In return, Gromyko stressed the need for a total sharing of all knowledge under the planned Authority. This question of secrecy is a major issue that still befouls disarmament negotiations (Chapter VI, Sections 1–2, and Chapter X).

The second crucial point was the United States insistence on inspections, 14 which a war-weary Russia and a paranoiacally suspicious Stalin were not willing to accept. This would remain an issue bedeviling later disarmament controversies in many fields. Much later Khrushchev, reiterating the criticism that the Baruch plan aimed "to set up an international control organ," said, "We, of course, could not agree to this."[11] In fact, Acheson had argued against using inspection as a means of opening up the Soviet Union:

We should not . . . use the effort for international control of atomic energy to attempt to open up Russian society.[12]

A serious omission in the negotiations was that the world community did   *15* not sit down to reason things out, from the outset, using sincere analyses and a will to construct instead of obstruct. The Baruch plan and the Soviet counterproposals could have served as points of departure in the attempt to settle questions like those of international control of proliferation. Instead, several years were wasted by meandering discourses in the Commission and in the General Assembly when the Commission's reports were discussed. In September 1949 the United States announced that the Soviet Union had exploded an atomic bomb.

NOTES

[1]United Nations, *The United Nations and Disarmament 1945–1970* (New York, 1970), p. 12.

[2]U.S. capabilities for production were, however, in an advanced stage. See George H. Quester, *Nuclear Diplomacy: The First 25 Years* (New York: Dunellen, 1970).

[3]United Nations, *Atomic Energy Commission, Official Records, First Meeting, Friday, 14 June 1946* (New York, 1946).

[4]Dean Acheson, *Present at the Creation: My Years in the State Department* (New York: W. W. Norton, 1967), p. 123. This history is thoroughly documented in Richard G. Hewlett and Oscar E. Anderson, Jr., *A History of the United States Atomic Energy Commission*, vol. 1, *The New World 1939/1946* (University Park: Pennsylvania State University Press, 1962), pp. 427ff.

[5]Acheson, *Present at the Creation*, p. 154; italics in the original. The presentation was made by Dean Acheson and Vannevar Bush, the latter then serving as Director of the Office of Scientific Research and Development.

[6]Rexford G. Tugwell, *Off Course: From Truman to Nixon* (New York: Praeger, 1971); see particularly Part 5 on Truman's "five mistakes": The Bomb, Disarmament Fumble, Containment, Korea, and Assisting the French in Indo-China, pp. 181–222.

Tugwell had been close to Roosevelt from the beginning and throughout his presidency. The tenor of his judgment is reflected in one condensed sentence: "It had taken only two years after Roosevelt's death, and with Truman's management, to turn two great victorious allied powers into aggressive enemies. Russia and China. . . ." (p. 203).

It is still a controversial issue how much American policies towards the Soviet Union changed after Truman's ascendancy to the presidency. Roosevelt had towards the end of his life been deeply disturbed particularly by the Soviet Union's actions towards Poland. But in regard to the problems discussed in the text — on the dropping of the bombs in Japan and the American position towards internationalizing the controls of atomic power — I believe Tugwell's judgment stands.

[7]The matter of sanctions had been discussed by the Acheson committee: "After careful analysis we had concluded that provisions for either 'swift and sure,' or 'condign,' punishment for violation of the treaty were very dangerous words that added nothing to a treaty and were almost certain to wreck any possibility of Russian acceptance of one." Acheson, *Present at the Creation*, p. 155.

[8]For full text of the final and official Baruch statement, see UN, *Atomic Energy Commission, First Meeting, Friday, 14 June 1946*. Also, Chalmers M. Roberts, *The Nuclear Years: The Arms Race and Arms Control, 1945–70* (New York: Praeger, 1970), pp. 123–133.

[9]Acheson, *Present at the Creation*, p. 155.

[10]Such warnings were made repeatedly, e.g., by P. M. S. Blackett, see *Atomic Weapons and East-West Relations* (Cambridge: Cambridge University Press, 1956), pp. 90–92.

[11]Roberts, *The Nuclear Years*, p. 17, quoted from a 1962 interview with American journalists.

[12]Acheson, *Present at the Creation*, p. 152.

Considerations

1. Alva Myrdal frames her discussion by recapturing the sense of urgency that existed in 1945–1946 and stressing the unanimous agreement of the fifty-one United Nations members that nuclear weapons must be eliminated. How

does this context influence Myrdal's treatment of the issue? How does the context anticipate Myrdal's analysis of the Baruch Plan's failure?

2. Why does it make some difference that the United Nations was dominated by the United States?

3. Ultimately, who does Myrdal blame for the failure of the Baruch Plan?

Connections

1. Myrdal quotes from Henry L. Stimson's memo (para. 6). What is her purpose?

The Failure of Liberal Diplomacy

Michael Mandelbaum

You come up to face these terrible issues and you know that what is in almost everybody's heart is a wish for peace, and you want to do *something*. . . .
                                                    – Dwight D. Eisenhower[1]

The Baruch Plan

The first official American approach to the problems that nuclear weapons   *1*
posed was presented to the newly formed United Nations organization in 1946. The allied powers had laid the groundwork for the UN while the Second World War was still in progress. It was the international organization in which American hopes for a peaceful and orderly postwar world rested. The scheme was called the Baruch Plan, after the man President Truman chose to present it, Bernard Baruch — financier, philanthropist, and purveyor of advice to several chief executives. The Baruch Plan called for the creation of an "International Atomic Development Authority" that would take control of "all phases of the

---

Michael Mandelbaum (b. 1946) is the author of The Nuclear Question: The U.S. and Nuclear Weapons 1946–1976 *(1984), written under the auspices of the Center for International Affairs and the Center for Science and International Affairs of Harvard University. He has also written* The Nuclear Revolution: International Politics Before and after Hiroshima *(1981) and* The Nuclear Future *(1983). Currently he serves as research and editorial director at the Lehrman Institute in New York.*

development and use of atomic energy," from the mining of the necessary raw materials to the operation of reactors to the conduct of nuclear research and development.[2] The Baruch Plan proposed to keep atomic bombs out of the hands of sovereign states by placing the means to make them under the supervision of a supranational body. That body would have the power, as Baruch envisioned it, to mete out "immediate, swift and sure punishment" to any nation that attempted to acquire them. The UN had been created as a two-tiered body. In the General Assembly every state had a single vote, and a majority was sufficient to pass any measure. But above the General Assembly stood the Security Council, made up of the most powerful states in the international system, including the United States and the Soviet Union. And any permanent member of the Security Council could defeat a proposal with a negative vote. Baruch stipulated that the new Atomic Development Authority would not report to the Security Council, thereby making its dictates immune to the veto of one of the Council's permanent members.[3]

The Baruch Plan bore the stamp of Niels Bohr's ideas. He was its spiritual father, and his scientific colleagues played important roles in its creation. The substance of the Plan emerged from a series of memoranda, declarations, and reports that scientists helped to shape. It was they who pressed upon government officials the idea of international control, which the Plan incorporated. Indeed, after the war they formed an organization to lobby for this idea.[4]

The scientists had a hand in fashioning important markers on the trail that led from Bohr's vision to the Baruch Plan. At the end of September 1944, Vannevar Bush, chairman of the Manhattan Project's Military Committee, and James Conant, his deputy, both prominent scientists, sent a memorandum to Secretary of War Stimson suggesting that atomic weapons be turned over to some sort of international agency after the war's end.[5] By November of 1945 the war was over, the feasibility and the power of the atomic bomb had been conclusively demonstrated at Hiroshima and Nagasaki, and President Truman was meeting with the Prime Ministers of Great Britain and Canada to consider, among other things, the future of atomic energy. Bush was instrumental in preparing a statement issued in the names of all three leaders declaring their readiness to take steps to put this new force under international control, and calling for the establishment of a UN committee to work out specific steps in this direction. To prepare an American position for this UN inquiry, President Truman appointed a committee headed by Under Secretary of State Dean Acheson and the Chairman of the Tennessee Valley Authority David Lilienthal. Both Bush and Conant sat on the Acheson–Lilienthal panel. The report that the panel produced had a central theme — the international control of atomic energy — and it became, with a few modifications, the Baruch Plan.

The Baruch Plan made a generally favorable impression on the members of the United Nations. There was, however, a notable exception: It did not favorably impress the Soviet Union. Five days after Baruch offered his formula the Soviet delegate, Andrei Gromyko, tabled a counterproposal. It called, initially, for an international convention "prohibiting the production and employment of weapons based on the use of atomic energy."[6] Parties to the convention would promise not to use, produce, or store atomic weapons in the future and to destroy all present stocks within three months from the day the convention entered into force. Gromyko also proposed the creation of two committees under UN auspices; one to work out channels for circulating scientific information, the other to devise a system of safeguards against violating the initial convention. But the safeguards would come only *after* the weapons, which the United States alone then possessed, had been destroyed. And Gromyko made it clear that whatever organization came into being to monitor atomic energy had to include a provision for a veto.[7]

Months of discussion and negotiation followed. But no common ground could be found. Neither side would move far enough from its initial position to accommodate the other. A technical committee was set up, and it issued several reports. The Security Council considered the matter. The General Assembly encouraged the talks to go on. But the deadlock remained unbroken. Finally, in November 1949, more than three years after they had begun, the deliberations of the United States Atomic Energy Committee were discontinued. Their failure had been sealed the month before, on September 23, when the Soviet Union had set off, for the first time, a nuclear explosion of its own.

Even if the Soviets had found the Baruch Plan more attractive than they did, it is not at all clear, in retrospect, that the American government would have been willing to carry out its provisions. The Americans were cautious about revealing the "secrets" of atomic energy and there was a reluctance, strongly felt by members of the Acheson–Lilienthal group and reflected in the rejection of the Soviet counterproposal to the Plan, to divulge useful atomic information before a workable system of international control was in place.[8] Moreover, any agreement on international control would have come under close congressional scrutiny, and the Congress was not happy about the dissemination of the discoveries made by American scientists and their foreign colleagues working under American auspices. The May–Johnson bill for the control of atomic energy, which left open the possibility of military supervision, which made no provision for sharing with other nations what American scientists had learned, and which included criminal penalties for the disclosure of classified information, had been defeated — but only after a spirited political battle.[9] And the McMahon Act, which the Congress had passed in its stead, did not mandate an entirely open-handed approach to nuclear matters. Truman had appointed Baruch as his special representative to the UN meetings in the hope that the financier's stature in the country and in the Congress would help to blunt suspicions of any plan for international control. Public opinion on the subject of atomic energy, although diffuse, uncertain, and susceptible to the influence of political leaders, especially the President, seemed to favor keeping atomic information secret.[10] And the American armed services, which took almost no part in preparing the Baruch Plan, had deep reservations about relinquishing control of a potentially decisive weapon.[11]

The Baruch Plan is important not as an end but as a beginning. It was not the last chance to put the new fearsome power of the atom under international supervision — although it represents the apogee of hope for international control — but the first of many failed attempts to do so. The Baruch Plan, and the Soviet response to it, served as models for the nuclear diplomacy of the next fifteen years. In that period the two sides tabled dozens of schemes and spent hundreds of hours discussing them. Almost all resembled, in crucial respects, the original positions. And this resemblance doomed them. None led to an agreement. Throughout the 1950s nuclear negotiation was a soufflé that never rose, because the United States and the Soviet Union followed the recipe, with the same principle ingredients, that had failed in 1946.

The Nuclear Diplomacy of the 1950s

The Baruch Plan was a liberal proposal. It bore three distinct liberal trade-   *8*
marks that characterized its successors as well. It was, first of all, sweeping in scope, in contrast to the traditional practice of concentrating on a few concrete issues. It was intended to bring all facets of nuclear energy everywhere under international control. Baruch strongly implied that his scheme was to be understood as the first step toward the abolition of *all* weapons.[12] Successor plans had similarly broad goals. Even after both the United States and the Soviet Union had accumulated sizable stockpiles of nuclear weapons, at least rhetorical homage continued to be paid to the goal of "general and complete disarmament." The British and French floated a proposal to that end in 1954 and 1955. In 1959 Soviet Prime Minister Khrushchev called for the abolition of all weapons of war over a period of four years in a speech to the United Nations. And two years later, from the same rostrum, President Kennedy announced a plan for full-scale disarmament.

The Baruch Plan was liberal, as well, in its manner of presentation — before   *9*
the United Nations. Despite Stimson's warning, the task of controlling nuclear energy was entrusted to the international organization that the victors had created at the end of World War II. And even after the glow that surrounded its birth had faded and bright hopes for its success had been tempered by the harsh realities of postwar international politics, the UN remained the principal forum for nuclear diplomacy. Every nation, large or small, thereby received the opportunity to air its views on nuclear weapons.

And the Baruch Plan was most characteristically liberal — and this was the   *10*
most telling point for the future of nuclear diplomacy — in its provision for the dilution of national sovereignty. It required every state to surrender the prerogative of acquiring the most powerful of all weapons, and to submit to the authority, in nuclear matters, of a supranational body. It therefore envisioned a partial transformation of international politics, of the kind that Bohr and his scientific colleagues had anticipated. The transformation was not complete. While an international authority governed all nuclear matters, the rest of the world's business would presumably continue to be transacted by sovereign, independent states. But coexistence between those two ways of doing business might not be easy. Walter Lippmann wrote: ". . . There cannot be a system of world law that is unique for atomic energy and a different and conflicting system for the maintenance of peace."[13]

NOTES

[1] Quoted in Emmett John Hughes, *The Ordeal of Power: A Political Memoir of the Eisenhower Years* (New York: Atheneum, 1965), p. 105.

[2] Quoted in Adam Ulam, *Expansion and Coexistence: The History of Soviet Foreign Policy, 1917–1967* (New York: Praeger, 1968), p. 416. A detailed outline of the proposal appears in Joseph Nogee,

Soviet Policy Towards International Control of Atomic Energy (Notre Dame, Ind.: University of Notre Dame Press, 1961), p. 42.

[3]Lloyd C. Gardner, *Architects of Illusion* (Chicago: Quadrangle Press, 1970), pp. 194–195.

[4]See Alice Kimball Smith, *A Peril and a Hope: The Scientist's Movement in America, 1945–1947* (Chicago: University of Chicago Press, 1965).

[5]*Ibid.*, pp. 13–14.

[6]Bernhard G. Bechhoefer, *Postwar Negotiations for Arms Control* (Washington, D.C.: The Brookings Institution, 1961), p. 44.

[7]Joseph I. Lieberman, *The Scorpion and the Tarantula* (Boston: Houghton Mifflin, 1970), p. 310; Nogee, *op. cit.*, pp. 36–39.

[8]Leniece N. Wu, *The Baruch Plan: U.S. Diplomacy Enters the Nuclear Age.* Prepared for the Subcommittee on National Security Policy and Scientific Developments of the Committee on Foreign Affairs, U.S. House of Representatives (Washington, D.C.: U.S. Government Printing Office, 1972). In his memoirs Vannevar Bush says of the Baruch Plan, "Of course, the approach to the United Nations got nowhere, but we all felt better for the try." Vannevar Bush, *Pieces of the Action* (New York: William Morrow, 1970), p. 298.

[9]Smith, *op. cit.*, p. 129ff.

[10]Wu, *op. cit.*, pp. 21–22.

[11]*Ibid.*, p. 48.

[12]"But before a country is ready to relinquish any winning weapons it must have more than words to reassure it. It must have a guarantee of safety, not only against the offenders in the atomic area but against the illegal uses of other weapons . . . why not? against war itself." Quoted in Lieberman, *op. cit.*, p. 300.

[13]Walter Lippmann, "International Control of Atomic Energy," in Dexter Masters and Katherine Way, editors, *One World or None?* (London: Latimer House, 1947), p. 143.

Considerations

1. Michael Mandelbaum follows his brief description of the Baruch Plan with a discussion about the scientists who influenced it. Why does he do this? What effect does this information have on your understanding of the Baruch Plan and its failure?

2. Mandelbaum cites much evidence supporting the contention that "even if the Soviets had found the Baruch Plan more attractive than they did, it is not at all clear, in retrospect, that the American government would have been willing to carry out its provisions" (para. 6). If the United States was, in fact, unwilling, what would that imply about American motives or expectations in offering the Plan in the first place? Does Mandelbaum seem to approve or disapprove of this unwillingness?

3. What aspects of the Baruch Plan make it a *liberal* proposal? What connotations does *liberal* have for Mandelbaum — is liberal something of which he approves or disapproves? How can you tell?

Connections

1. Mandelbaum structures his discussion differently from Alva Myrdal. Describe some of the differences. What aims do each of the structures suggest?

2. The Franck Report alludes to the need for each nation to relinquish part of its sovereign rights as a necessary step toward international control. What does Mandelbaum say about sovereignty? How does his view of the problem differ from that of the Franck Report?

3. It has been suggested that Truman deliberately sabotaged the intentions of the Baruch Plan and its forerunners. For one thing, although Baruch was already greatly disliked by the Soviets prior to the United Nations meeting, Truman appointed him anyway; moreover, Baruch himself inserted provisions unacceptable to the Soviets — the veto and the context for discussing and meting out punishment. Based on what you now know, what evidence can you find to support the contention that while some people in the US were in earnest about nuclear disarmament, Truman and others actually opposed it? Is the evidence you find convincing? How?

Further Connections

1. Based on a careful examination of Barton Bernstein's methods of reasoning, line of argument, and kind of evidence used to support his analysis, how do you suppose he would account for the failure of the Baruch Plan? Write an essay in which you apply some of Bernstein's methods of analysis and argumentation to the question: Why did the Baruch Plan fail to achieve its announced aim — the negotiation of an international means of controlling atomic energy?
2. Write an essay in which you take a position on the issue: Scientists should/should not assume responsibility for the way society uses their discoveries. Explore some arguments supporting involvement of scientists in political issues and some that disagree with this view.
3. Imagine you are a member of a group promoting nuclear disarmament. Write a paper in which you tell your group what lessons they can learn from the first attempts at nuclear disarmament in 1945 and 1946.
4. Imagine you are the leader of a group promoting continued nuclear deterrence — that is, deterring the Soviets (or anyone else) from using their weapons by maintaining and upgrading our own nuclear arsenal. What can you say about the risks, costs, and benefits of deterrence based on your study of the documents in this chapter?
5. Many of the documents in this section stress the need for mutual trust. Reflect on how individuals can develop and maintain trust both in low tension situations and in more intense conflicts. In what ways might the behavior of individuals illuminate the behavior of nations, and in what ways is the analogy insufficient? Drawing on the materials in this chapter, write an essay about trust.
6. Some people think that personal morality should be a guide to the actions of nations in the international arena; others disagree, believing that it would undesirably affect national defense or that it would be impossible. How do the writers in this chapter approach the issue of personal morality and international policy?
7. It is impossible to prove that stockpiling nuclear weapons has prevented a nuclear war. The claim that deterrence has worked is based on a kind of

faulty causal reasoning that philosophers call a *post hoc* fallacy in which it is assumed that if B happens *after* A, A was the *cause* of B: we have had peace for forty years after the advent of nuclear weapons; therefore, we have had peace because of nuclear weapons.

Find examples of *post hoc* reasoning in the readings in this chapter. Explain why supporters of nuclear deterrence are the people most committed to the proposition that deterrence has worked.

8. What is connoted by the term *arms race?* That is, what does the race metaphor reveal about the way we perceive the military competition between the United States and the Soviet Union? Think of as many kinds of races as you can, and examine some of their qualities. Consider the difference in attitude expressed by the phrase "race toward oblivion" (coined by a former Manhattan Project scientist and arms control negotiator) and the statement, "The arms *competition* is the best form of arms control" (spoken by an economist who believes that unregulated competition in arms, as in economic markets, will result in stability.)

9. All the readings in this section (excluding the excerpts) were written to persuade. Analyze two or three of them. Compare their structures of reasoning and identify the ways they try to convince their audience to adopt their position or proposed course of action.

10. Look at the question of what makes history and historical evidence in Chapter 3, The Frontier Indians. Do the documents on early attempts to prevent an arms race constitute good historical evidence? Explain.

Extensions

1. The Franck Report, in its concern about how the bomb was to be used, argued: "It may be very difficult to persuade the world that a nation which was capable of secretly preparing and suddenly releasing a new weapon . . . is to be trusted in its proclaimed desire of having such weapons abolished by international agreement" (para. 16). Find some detailed accounts of the three-year-long Baruch Plan negotiations. What measures, if any, did Bernard Baruch take to reassure the Soviet Union that our "proclaimed desire" to abolish these weapons was sincere? (You could start by looking at an encyclopedia article on arms control negotiations and consulting its bibliography. See also the Library of Congress subject heading "atomic weapons and disarmament" in the library card catalog.

2. Some of the challenges and conflicts the early atomic scientists faced epitomize those the current culture as a whole faces in the nuclear age. Write a biographical study of one of these scientists and focus on a period in which he had to confront a difficult choice. You should be able to find information about Albert Einstein, Niels Bohr, Robert Oppenheimer, Leo Szilard, and Edward Teller in a good encyclopedia, in your library's card catalog, and in early histories of atomic energy such as *The Advisors* by Herbert York (San Francisco: Freeman, 1976), *Brighter than a Thousand Suns* by Robert Jungk (New York: Harcourt, Brace, 1958), and *The Winning Weapon*

by Greg Herken (New York: Knopf, 1980). Biographical indexes and dictionaries are also very good sources.

3. Recently, the Catholic Bishops of the United States issued a statement about nuclear weapons [the National Council of Catholic Bishops', "Pastoral Letter on War and Peace — The challenge of Peace: God's Promise and Our Response," originally published in *Origins*, vol. 13, no. 1 (May 19, 1983), and now reprinted in many sources]. The bishops examine both the mainstream Christian tradition of the just war and the minority, pacifist tradition that rejects all war. They find that even in the context of a just war, nuclear weapons must be condemned on two grounds: these weapons cannot discriminate sufficiently between soldiers and civilians, and the potential for escalation far outweighs any justification. They conclude that nuclear deterrence can be considered moral *only if deterrence is a step toward nuclear disarmament*. Read the bishops' letter, and some of the material cited in its bibliography on the just war and the pacifist tradition. Write a focused paper on one of the issues.

4. Should matters of state — particularly national defense — be exempted from the kinds of moral considerations that bind individuals? What would the "just war" theory say? What would the pacifist theory say?

5. The policy of the Reagan administration is to maintain nuclear deterrence and to use arms control only to make deterrence stable; there is no official policy that sets nuclear *disarmament* as a goal. Write a letter from the Catholic bishops to the president (see question 3, above) explaining the position the bishops would take toward the administration's policy. Include special consideration of whether there should be arms control efforts and if so, what their goals should be.

6. Recently Dr. George Keyworth, President Reagan's science advisor, said that the Strategic Defense Initiative (SDI or Star Wars) "takes the moral highground away from the supporters of the Nuclear Freeze Initiative," supposedly by making nuclear weapons less effective and therefore less needed and by being defensive, not offensive, in purpose. Research some current periodicals containing arguments both for and against SDI. Write a paper in which you argue that SDI is a moral/immoral proposal.

7. Learn what is in the nuclear weapons treaties between the United States and the Soviet Union and learn something about the process of arriving at these agreements. There is a danger that if SDI is built and deployed, it will abrogate the ABM treaty; if the space-based lasers are activated by internal nuclear explosive devices, the Outer Space Treaty would be abrogated; and if any of these devices were tested, the Test Ban Treaty might also be violated. After studying the negotiation process, decide if there is a significant reason to honor the United States and Soviet nuclear treaties. Take into account the opposing arguments.

8. *Realpolitik* is the theory that power politics must regulate relations between nations. Based on your understanding of issues raised by the atomic bombings of Japan and the conflicts over the possibility of international control of nuclear weapons, do you believe realpolitik is the inevitable reality in international politics? (Consult the *Encyclopedia of the Social Sciences* in preparing your answer.)

9. Louis Ridenour (1911–1959) was an atomic physicist who wrote a one-act play set in the future, after all the industrialized nations have mastered the production and use of atomic power. The play, "Pilot Lights of the Apocalypse," satirizes a runaway arms race and a nuclear holocaust. Read Ridenour's play in *Fortune* (January 1946) or in *The Atomic Age: Scientists in National and World Affairs,* edited by Morton Grodzins and Eugene Rabinowitch (New York: Basic Books, 1963). What is Ridenour's attitude toward his subject. Is he saying, "This is what will happen *if* we fail to prevent an arms race," or "This is what is going to happen because we *will* fail to prevent an arms race"? How can you tell? Justify your position including evidence drawn from this chapter about other scientists' attitudes at the time.

10. If you have seen Stanley Kubrick's film *Dr. Strangelove* (1963), write an essay comparing it to "Pilot Lights." How are the works thematically similar? Identify the authors' attitudes toward their subject matter and compare them. How do you think both pieces would move an audience? To action, to disgust, to scorn, to laughter, to a sense of hopelessness, or to what? What do these works say about American or Soviet culture? Does either take a stand on human nature? On anything aside from the immediate subject of nuclear weapons and policies governing their use?

11. Could Bernard Baruch have had a personal motive for desiring unimpeded nuclear weapons development? Who was he? Who were his friends and associates? What were his values and political attitudes? Did he or his friends stand to profit from a thriving arms industry or from American economic dominance? (Start with a recent biography of Baruch; research some of its references and look up some of his friends in a *Who's Who?* for the period.)

12. What is the history of the early Atomic Energy Commission? Who ran it? How was it involved in the political tensions of its time? Did any of the first directors of the AEC have personal connections to industries or other financial enterprises that would benefit from continued development of either nuclear energy or weapons? (Several histories of the AEC have appeared recently.)

13. Construct a history of hydrogen bomb development focusing on Edward Teller and Robert Oppenheimer. Begin with Herbert York's book, *The Advisors.* What similarities exist between the H-Bomb debate of 1946–1954 and the contemporary MX debate? (*Public Affairs Information Service Bulletin* (PAIS) is a good source for material on public policy debates. Herbert Scoville, Jr., has written extensively on the MX.)

14. What reasons do feminists advance for seeing the arms race as a feminist issue?

15. While the number of weapons has increased, total megatonnage has decreased by half from its 1962 peak. Why? Which is more important, the numbers of weapons or their blast force? What other factors must one take into account to assess whether the arsenals today threaten us more, less, or differently than they did a decade ago? (The SIPRI publications are a good source for finding out about this.) Are we safer now than we were in 1970? In 1960? In 1945?

Suggestions for Further Reading

Aldridge, Robert. *The Counterforce Syndrome: A Guide to U.S. Nuclear Weapons and Strategic Doctrine.* Washington, D.C.: Institute for Policy Studies, 1978. Aldridge's work is a classic popular explanation critical of U.S. policy. See Utgoff and Wohlstetter below for contrasting views.

Ambrose, Stephen E. *Rise to Globalism: American Foreign Policy 1938–1980.* New York: Penguin, 1980. A balanced presentation written for the general reader.

Bechhofer, Bernard G. *Postwar Negotiations for Arms Control.* Washington, D.C.: Brookings Institution, 1961. A detailed history of arms negotiations through the 1950s.

Dellums, Ronald V. *Defense Sense: The Search for a Rational Military Policy.* Cambridge, Mass.: Ballinger, 1983. An excellent anthology of articles aimed at informing the concerned citizen about defense budget issues. Takes an activist position.

Fallows, James. *National Defense.* New York: Random House, 1981. Engaging presentation dealing with general issues. A good, but biased, introduction to the national security debate.

Gaddis, John Lewis. "Containment: Its Past and Future." *International Security* 5:4 (Spring, 1981): 74–102. An excellent overview and analysis of the history of our policy toward the Soviet Union. Somewhat complex.

Gilpin, Robert. *American Scientists and Nuclear Weapons Policy.* Princeton: Princeton University Press, 1962. Examines the role scientists played in attempts to influence national security policy.

Holloway, David. *The Soviet Union and the Arms Race.* New Haven: Yale University Press, 1983. A well-respected study of the arms race from the Soviet side.

National Council of Catholic Bishops. "Pastoral Letter on War and Peace — The Challenge of Peace: God's Promise and Our Response." *Origins* 13:1 (May 19, 1983). The official position of the Catholic church on the ethical status of nuclear deterrence. A rich resource for ethical reflection, with extensive bibliographic references.

Russett, Bruce. *The Prisoners of Insecurity: Nuclear Deterrence, the Arms Race, and Arms Control.* San Francisco: W. H. Freeman, 1983. Russett has studied the domestic and international sources of the arms race.

Schell, Jonathan. *The Fate of the Earth.* Boston: Houghton Mifflin, 1982. An intelligent polemic favoring disarmament, Schell's book is still unique in drawing from the humanistic tradition of western culture rather than from the social-scientific.

SIPRI (Stockholm International Peace Research Institute). *SIPRI Yearbook of World Armaments and Disarmament.* London: Taylor & Francis, annual. An indispensable source for weapons data and current analyses of political issues. (Also comes in an abbreviated edition.)

Sivard, Ruth Leger. *World Military and Social Expenditures.* Washington, D.C.: World Priorities, annual. Sivard's annual publication is an invaluable source of financial data much like the SIPRI publications are for weapons data. Covers expenditures on food, medicine, and education in addition to weapons costs.

Smoke, Richard. *National Security and the Nuclear Dilemma: An Introduction to the American Experience.* New York: Random House, 1984. The best introduction to national security affairs to date; Smoke covers the history of deterrence doctrine, arms control negotiations, the weapons build-ups on both sides. Good bibliography.

Stanford Arms Control Group. *International Arms Control: Issues and Agreements.* Edited by Coit D. Blacker and Gloria Duffy. Stanford: Stanford University Press, 1984. A useful and thorough textbook.

Truman, Harry S. *Memories. Volume II: Years of Trial and Hope, 1946–1952.* New York: Doubleday, 1956. President Truman explains how his administration understood the early nuclear age.

U.S. Department of Defense. *Annual Report to Congress.* Washington, D.C.: United States Government Printing Office, annual. Written at the time the Secretary of Defense presents his annual budget to Congress, the report also contains budget projections for the next five years. The justifications are an important clue to classified U.S. defense strategy.

Walzer, Michael. *Just and Unjust Wars: A Moral Argument With Historical Illustrations.* New York: Basic Books, 1977. A classic statement of the "just war" argument.

Wieseltier, Leon. *Nuclear War, Nuclear Peace.* New York: Holt, Rinehart and Winston, 1983. Frustrated with the polarization between "the party of war" who advocates technological solutions coupled with little or no arms control and "the party of peace" whose members seem to him naive dreamers, Wieseltier argues for a middle ground.

Woito, Robert S., ed. *To End War.* New York: Pilgrim Press, 1982. A rich compilation of essays and annotated bibliographies; indispensable for understanding disarmament efforts and war.

York, Herbert. *The Advisors: Oppenheimer, Teller, and the Superbomb.* San Francisco: W. H. Freeman, 1976. A history of the H-bomb debate from a scientist-insider.

3 The Frontier Indians

Edited by **Ellen Strenski**

Frontiers are areas of intense activity and conflict, whether they are geographic places, like Oklahoma, or more abstract points of contact; for instance, two chemical solutions colliding through a permeable membrane. This chapter considers the collision of Native American Indians with the European invaders, which, from the fifteenth century on, created a frontier moving inward from the coasts. A geographical frontier is still very much evident today; for instance, informally surrounding the Micmacs who live in South Boston or formally encircling reservations. This chapter, however, deals mainly with the early contact between the Indians and the Europeans several centuries ago. What happened between the Indians and the fur traders, missionaries, and settlers? And why did it happen in these ways? It is important for all of us to try to answer these questions. The Indian is a basic and ambiguous symbol in America's culture and national character, as well as a tragic element in America's past.

Whether we like it or not, we are haunted by the Indian. Chief Seattle explained this in 1854 when he spoke to the government representative in Washington Territory who was negotiating with his tribe to buy 2 million acres of Indian land and move them to a small reservation. Chief Seattle said,

> When the last Red Man shall have perished, and the memory of my tribe shall have become a myth among the White Man, these shores will swarm with the invisible dead of my tribe, and when your children's children think themselves alone in the field, the store, the shop, upon the highway, or in the silence of the pathless woods, they will not be alone.

So we owe it to ourselves now, and we owe it to the memory of the Indians who were here first to understand our common past in the land we share.

The main emphasis in this chapter is history — the past. But the past is much more than names, places, dates, and battles. Reading and writing history means trying to understand what happened, why it happened, and even why we think it happened that way. And understanding all this means understanding the people — the Indians and Europeans alike — understanding what they believed, hoped, feared, loved, and wanted — for themselves and for their families. Why did they act towards each other as they did? How did they together, knowingly and unknowingly, create our American past?

History cuts across almost every other discipline. To answer questions about the American past, we need to know how the Indians and Europeans lived, where they built settlements, how they got their food and materials, how they protected themselves against the climate, disease, and their enemies, and what their values were. To answer these questions, we must consider studies dealing with geography, disease, trade, language, psychology, and religion. This chapter, accordingly, presents a sampling of appropriate readings. Some selections are scholarly analyses prepared by academic historians and anthropologists; some selections are themselves primary sources — the kinds of evidence that these scholars study. And yet other readings are more literary and imaginative treatments of this subject.

The chapter begins with "Copper-Colored People in a Golden Land," from *Ishi in Two Worlds: A Biography of the Last Wild Indian in North America.* Theodora Kroeber, the author, was not a professional historian — she was a dancer with a master's degree in psychology. But her imagination and perseverance enabled her to do fine work in history. "The Conflict Between the California Indian and White Civilization," by Sherburne F. Cook, a professor of physiology, takes a different, more abstractly biological approach to human populations, using statistical evidence to measure and compare the effects of two white groups: first, the Spanish missionaries who tried to convert the Indians and passed on epidemic diseases in the process; and second, the Anglo-American gold prospectors and the ranchers and settlers who came after them — by planting crops and grazing cattle, they destroyed the Indians' sources of food.

The third selection is by a professor of anthropology who is also a Pueblo Indian. In "Some Concerns Central to the Writing of 'Indian' History," Alfonso Ortiz recommends a special sensitivity to the Indians' own sense of time, place, and language — all of which can reveal the essential world view that informs their attitudes and behavior toward white "civilization." Ortiz is followed by another anthropologist, A. Irving Hallowell, whose "Ojibwa Ontology, Behavior, and World View" demonstrates how the world view of the Ojibwa is revealed in the structure of their language.

The next reading, "The European Failure to Convert the Indians: An Autopsy," by ethnohistorian James L. Axtell, is a broad overview of Indian-European contact on the east coast of North America. Then, in "The Mythological Sources of Abenaki Catholicism: A Case Study of the Social History of Power," another historian, Kenneth M. Morrison, looks closely at the belief system of the Abenaki, one of these Eastern tribes.

The seventh reading is part of a play, *Indians,* by Arthur Kopit. Kopit's play, based on fact, is a dramatic reconstruction of several historical incidents involving treaty negotiations between the United States and Sitting Bull's Sioux. (Sitting Bull was present at the Battle of the Little Bighorn — "Custer's Last Stand" — and was ultimately assassinated by U.S. agents.) An anonymous

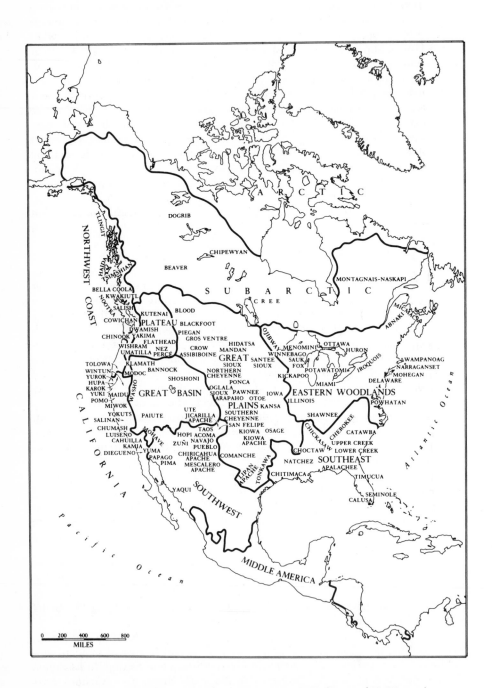

Native American Tribes and Culture Areas, circa 1650. (Bernard H. Wagner)

contemporary newspaper interview with Sitting Bull during treaty negotiations in 1877 — a year after the Battle of the Little Bighorn — follows Kopit's play.

"On the Wigwams and Dwellings of the Gaspesians" by Father Chrestien Le Clercq (1681), and "Letters from an American Farmer" by J. Hector St. John de Crèvecoeur (1782) were written by people living in proximity to the Indians. Le Clercq was a Roman Catholic missionary from France reporting back to his superior in France; de Crèvecoeur was recording his Pennsylvania homesteading experiences in literary form for eventual publication.

Finally, the chapter concludes with a selection from J. W. Jackson's book, *Ethnology and Phrenology as an Aid to the Historian,* published in Europe in 1863. Jackson's claims about Caucasian superiority over other races based on the shape and size of skulls are typical of his time.

Copper-Colored People in a Golden Land

Theodora Kroeber

The stubborn and enduring land of California has changed less than its people. From an aeroplane the "colored counties" are seen spread out like a giant relief map. Mount Shasta looms to the north, Mount Whitney to the south; the Sierra Nevada forms a wall to the east; and beyond Whitney, where the Sierra appears to go underground, the desert takes over. There are the long interior valleys; and there are the tumbled, rough, and wooded Coast Ranges through which rivers and creeks break to the sea. Below, incredible, lies the vast and varied land, its mountains and deserts empty and mute today, while over the accessible valleys and coastal plains a congested and diverse population clusters close to a few centers like wasps around heavy-hanging nests. A constant stream of automobiles, looking from the air like lines of black ants on the march, fills the passes over the Sierra barrier, moving westward to the favored spots. The hills are empty except for lumbering operations wherever there is a good stand of trees; the mining towns of the Mother Lode and the old rancherias are

1

Theodora Kroeber (1897–1979) was not a professional historian — she was a dancer with a master's degree in psychology. "Copper-Colored People in a Golden Land" is taken from the first chapter of Kroeber's book, Ishi in Two Worlds: A Biography of the Last Wild Indian in North America *(1961). Ishi was a Yana Indian who came out of the hills near Mount Lassen, California, in 1911. He was befriended by the anthropologist Alfred Kroeber (the author's husband), who studied and cared for him at the University Museum in San Francisco until Ishi's death from pneumonia in 1916.*

shabby and deserted, or have been taken over by "summer people." The banks of rivers and creeks are empty save for sporadic invasions of fishermen; and the desert is without human occupants except for a citified overflow which follows in the wake of air-cooling installations, swimming pools, and motels.

What would an air view have revealed in the days of the gold rush? The same lines of black ants moving in the same westerly direction over the same passes, on horseback, and in covered wagons drawn by oxen, traveling more slowly than today's immigrants but with the same doggedness as these later ones, heading in part for the same centers, in part stopping in the hill country where ranches, mining camps, and saw and grist mills were scattered along streams and in the forests.   2

Hovering over the same land, but continuing our flight back in time, we view another trek, this one on foot or on mule and horseback, coming up from the south, northward along the rim of the sea. The time is the seventies of the eighteenth century, and the travelers, Spaniards pushing out of Mexico, keeping a sharp eye for a sheltered and sunny and likely spot for mission, rancheria, or presidio as they move slowly on.   3

If we take a last backward flight in time, the Spaniard is no longer seen. This is the time before his coming; the golden land belongs wholly and undisputedly to its native sons and daughters. No lines of black ants move over the high passes or come up from the south in this view. Indeed, we must fly low to see the narrow trails meandering beside a stream, or across country to an oak flat, or up into the hills. At first there seem to be neither houses nor people, but presently a frame with surf fish strung on it to dry on a sunny beach, a clearing in the trees, a thin blue wisp of smoke from a wood fire, serve to guide the eyes to the weathered roof of a low redwood house, to an earth-covered circular house, to a thatched house, to a brush shelter. We see an old woman tending the fire outside a house, a man spearing fish beside a stream, a half-grown boy paddling downstream in a dugout canoe. A young woman, her baby in a basket carrier on her back, gathers wild iris on a hillside; a hunter brings down a deer with bow and arrow. These people step noiselessly over the ground, barefoot or in soft deerskin moccasins, and their naked or near-naked copper-colored bodies blend in semicamouflage against the colors of the earth. Such clothes as they wear, a skirt of shredded bark, a buckskin breechclout, an occasional fur or feather cape, also blend into the natural background. Their voices, whether in ordinary conversation, or in song or prayer or mourning cry, are light-toned, neither harsh nor loud.   4

The high mountains are empty. But people are living in the hills as far up as oak trees grow and wherever manzanita and other berries are abundant, and wherever there are deer; along fish-filled streams; and where a river flows into the sea; and on the desert. Even so unlikely a place as Death Valley has men who call it home.   5

Back on the ground and again in the twentieth century, we turn to maps and estimates and reports to learn something more of these ancestral peoples whom we have glimpsed distantly through time.   6

We have seen that they lived on parts of the land which modern men do not find habitable or attractive, although at no place were their numbers large. The population of Indian California was small: over the whole of the state there were probably no more than a hundred and fifty thousand people, perhaps as   7 many as two hundred and fifty thousand. (In 1860, ten years after the beginning of the gold rush, the white population of the state was already three hundred and ninety thousand.) There are, to be sure, estimates of the pre-conquest population of California which run higher, but the archaeological remains from village and burial sites point to numbers close to those given here. There is no evidence, as there is in the Southwest, in Mexico, in Yucatan of the Mayas, that a once much more numerous people suffered disaster and decimation. Nor do the histories, legends, myths, or stories of any California Indians speak of ancient wholesale famine as do the old as well as the modern chronicles of China and India.

These one or two hundred and fifty thousand native people constituted   8
twenty-one known nationalities, or small nations, which were in turn further separated into subnationalities, and these again into tribes or tribelets to a total number of more than two hundred and fifty — exactly how many more can never be known because of the obliteration in modern times of whole peoples and cultures by Spaniard and Anglo-Saxon alike without record of tribal name or affiliation. Many of these subgroups were of course few in number and inhabited only a small area. Their numbers were almost unbelievably small beside the territorial and population figures for modern nations, but they were nonetheless true nations in their stubbornly individual and boundaried separateness and distinctiveness one from another. . . .

Remains of Dawn Man or of some Dawn-like man, his bones or his stones,   9
are proclaimed from time to time as having been found on the Pacific slope, but if Dawn Man or any of his near relations once lived in California, they have yet to be rediscovered. California's first people so far as is presently known were American Indians, ancestors of today's Indians and in no significant way different from them. And they have been in California a long time; by our standards of mobility and compared with our brief history, immemorially long. . . .

What, then, of the Digger Indians who are supposed to have been the ab-   10
origines of California, to have spoken a guttural language, and to have managed barely to maintain a miserable existence by eating the roots which they dug from the unfriendly land with that most generic of tools, the wooden digging stick? Alas, the Diggers are a frontier legend, like the Siwash Indians of the Northwest, Siwash being a blanket term growing out of a mishearing of the word *sauvage*, the French trappers' designation for Indian. Nor was there a Digger language amongst all the babel of tongues.

There is another frontier legend which dies hard: that the hills and streams   11
and valleys of California yielded a grudging and sorry living to their native sons and daughters. The Spaniards and Mexicans did not so misunderstand the golden land, in part because they were never wholly detached from the soil in thinking or occupation, and in part because California is not unlike much of Mexico and Spain. The Forty-niners, veteran contenders against mountains, high plains, and deserts, were without interest in the land as such, which appeared to them inhospitable, dry, barren. In the course of their continental trek, they had come to look upon food not as something to be grown or harvested, but as meat to be shot on the hoof, and as flour, sugar, coffee, and beans to be carried as part of one's pack and replaced in "Frisco" or Sacramento or at some other urban center.

The legend may have been prolonged in defiance of known fact through in-   12 ertia, legends easily becoming habits which are hard to break, and through its usefulness in salving a not quite good conscience over the taking of land and lives. If the land was lean and the lives miserable then the wrong done was so much the less, or no wrong at all.

The term Digger continued to be used to refer to Indians other than those 13 one knew. I have heard my grandmother, who came to Amador County to teach school in the early 1850's, and became a rancher's wife there, speak affectionately and correctly of her Miwok Indian neighbors, and disapprovingly of the strange Digger Indians who from time to time used to wander in from a distance asking for work or perhaps only for food. Digger remains to this day a term of derogation, like "nigger."

Digger also defines however crudely and inadequately, one occupation of 14 California Indians which the Forty-niners must have seen over and over again. The Indians did no planting, being hunters, fishermen, gatherers, and harvesters of grains and seeds and fruits and roots which grew wild in their natural habitat and uncultivated state — diggers if you will. The digging stick was used, customarily in the hands of women who were forever going off into the hills or meadows for maidenhair and sword ferns, for squaw grass and pine root, for redbud and hazel, and for all the stems and plants and grasses which they wanted for making baskets. And the digging stick, as will be seen, helped them in season to get some of the fresh vegetables of which they were fond. Only the aberrant Mohaves and Yumas, who live on the Colorado River, have always been agriculturists of sorts. That is, they planted many of their food stuffs — not like the hard-working and true farmers of the Southwest: the Hopi, Zuni, and Rio Grande pueblo Indians — but like the people of ancient Egypt, by dropping the seeds of corn and beans and squash into the red ooze exposed by the seasonal flooding and retreat of the river, and allowing the crops to grow under the blazing sun with a minimum of attention from the planters. But the Colorado River Indians were different also — and fortunate — in having no Forty-niners. . . .

The great staple food of the California Indian was acorn flour made into mush 15 or bread. The acorn, of which some half dozen or more edible varieties were recognized, meant to Indians what rice means to Cantonese Chinese, or maize to Mexicans. After acorns came salmon, fresh or dried and in large variety; and after salmon, deer meat, again fresh or dried. Other fish were of course eaten, and game larger and smaller than deer, and for the coastal people there was added all the rich variety of seafood. Ducks and geese were much liked. Pine nuts, hazel nuts, buckeye, manzanita berries, wild raspberry, huckleberry, plum grape, elderberry, barberry, and thimbleberry were enjoyed in season, and some of them were dried and stored. There were sage and tarweed and clarkia seeds, and a host of other seeds small and large and, in season, the earth-oven roasted roots of the camas, annis, tiger lily, and brodiaea were a welcome addition. Certain grubs and worms were roasted as delicacies; also grasshoppers as in modern Mexico. Snakes were not eaten, nor so far as is known, were frogs.

But far deeper than food preferences and response to climate is the psycho- 16 logical set of the California cultures. To judge by their descendants, the ancestral California Indians who made the Far West their permanent home had found their way in the first place, and stayed on, in order to realize an ideal of a separatist and static arrangement of life. The most conspicuous feature of this life, at least to our view, is the preference for a small world intimately and minutely known, whose utmost boundaries were within reach by boat or on foot, a few days journey at most. Outside worlds were known to exist, of course. A man knew certain of his neighbors, sometimes when the neighbor's tongue had dialectic relation to his own so close that communication came readily, or sometimes when two worlds shared adjoining stretches of the same river, for example, and were similar enough in their ways to feel some identification even though they spoke different languages, as with the Yurok and Karok Indians along the Klamath River. But anything, everything that belonged within a man's own world, including its corpus of legendary event going back to the most ancient times, was better known and was more important than any person, place, or happening across the border.

By and large, no one voluntarily left his own and familiar world for a strange   17
one. It was terrifying and dangerous to enter a community as a stranger. You were properly suspect, the inference being that your own people had put pressure on you to leave because of some crime you were guilty of. At best you would be without family or friends or influence or status, and forced to learn to speak a foreign language, if you were allowed to remain at all. There was always the chance that you would be killed, or ordered to move on.

The California Indian was, in other words, a true provincial. He was also an   18
introvert, reserved, contemplative and philosophical. He lived at ease with the supernatural and the mystical which were pervasive in all aspects of life. He felt no need to differentiate mystical truth from directly evidential or "material" truth, or the supernatural from the natural: one was as manifest as the other within his system of values and perceptions and beliefs. The promoter, the boaster, the aggressor, the egoist, the innovator, would have been looked at askance. The ideal was the man of restraint, dignity, rectitude, he of the Middle Way. Life proceeded within the limits of known and proper pattern from birth through death and beyond. Its repetitive rhythm was punctuated with ritual, courtship, dance, song, and feast, each established according to custom going back to the beginning of the world, an event which, along with subsequent events having to do with setting the way of life, was well known and fully recounted in the people's oral but elaborate and specific histories.

It was not an easy life, but it was a good one. The hunting and fishing and   19
gathering, the endless labor of preparation of foods and hides, the making of baskets, tools, and implements and the always vexing problem of storage, required the industry and skill of both sexes and of young and old; but there was some choice and there was seasonal and ritual variety. There were lean times, but the lean like the fat times were shared with family, friends, and tribe. Life was as it had always been.

Considerations

1. Write a paragraph explaining the connection between history and legend. In your paragraph explain how history and legend are similar and how they are different. Use Theodora Kroeber's information about the Digger Indians

to illustrate your explanation of *legend* and her own information about the lives of California Indians before the arrival of the Europeans to illustrate *history*.

2. Write a paragraph explaining why the information in this reading is generally considered history and not legend. If *you* consider it legend, write a paragraph arguing that Kroeber's information about the early California Indians is itself legend.

3. Do you get the feeling that Kroeber liked the early California Indians and their life? How can you tell? Write a paragraph about her point of view and quote the exact phrases that illustrate this sympathy. Explain how her choice of words are clues for the reader and reveal her personal attitude towards the topic.

4. What does *provincial* mean? Write a short definition of several sentences. Kroeber claims that the California Indian was a "true provincial." Write a paragraph in which you use Kroeber's information to illustrate your own definition of *provincial*.

The Conflict Between the California Indian and White Civilization

Sherburne F. Cook

Certain similarities and differences in the Indian response emerge with respect to the mission type of culture, to the pre-American settlers of Latin extraction, and to the Yankee invasion after the Mexican War.   1

The fundamental clue to success in interracial competition is the change in   2 population. Under the relatively favorable control of the missions the natives suffered considerable diminution. From the mission records it is ascertained that approximately 53,600 Indians underwent conversion. At the end of the mission period (1834) there were 14,900 left, a reduction of 72 per cent. This signifies a mean annual reduction of 0.9 per cent. The six wild tribes which came into direct contact with the California civil and military civilization be-

---

Sherburne F. Cook (1896–1974) was a professor emeritus of physiology at the University of California. Taking a biological approach in this article, Cook studies the California Indians as a human population reacting to radical changes in its environment. Cook's meticulous statistical work in the 1930s and 1940s upset many people because it revealed how the Spanish missionaries and the Anglo-American prospectors and settlers had systematically destroyed a whole civilization.

tween 1800 and 1848 were reduced from approximately 58,900 to 35,950, or 0.8 per cent annually. The surviving mission Indians together with the remainder of the wild tribes which were subjected to Anglo-American influence from 1848 to 1865 diminished from 72,000 to 23,000, a mean annual depletion of 2.9 per cent. From these figures alone, it is apparent that the impact of the settlement from the United States was three times as severe as that of pre-American colonization.

The triad of factors which brings about a decline in population is war, disease, and starvation. In the missions, war was of negligible consequence. A study of expeditions and sporadic fighting shows that for the six wild tribes mentioned above, roughly 11.5 per cent of the decline may be attributed to casualties suffered in armed conflict. The corresponding value for the period after 1848 is 8.6 per cent. Hence, although the absolute effect of warfare was greater in the American period, its relative influence on population decline was substantially the same as in the years of Ibero-American domination. *3*

The relative effect of disease was also quite uniform, since in the missions, in the valley before 1848, and generally after 1848, approximately 60 per cent of the decline may be attributed to this cause. Such a result is not surprising, since most of the mortality was due to introduced epidemic maladies and the action of these upon a nonimmune population is entirely independent of the culture which introduces them. It is probable that the spread of disease was intensified in the missions by the crowded living conditions there but, on the other hand, this factor may have been nullified by the hygienic, sanitary, and curative measures adopted by the missionaries. *4*

The effect of dietary maladjustment cannot be evaluated in strictly numerical terms. This factor operates on both birth rate and death rate; moreover, very few persons actually died of direct starvation. In the missions the subsistence level seems to have been low, and, because of a tendency to rely upon cereal crops, there may have been vitamin and mineral deficiencies. The nonconverted Indians encountered the problem of depletion rather than alteration of diet. Until 1848, the reduction of food supply was not serious because the few settlers in the interior did not materially alter the natural flora and fauna. After the gold rush, however, the universal conversion of fertile valleys into farms, the widespread cattle ranching on the hills, and the pollution of the streams all combined to destroy the animal and plant species used for food. The transition to a white dietary, although ultimately accomplished, was rendered difficult by economic and social obstacles. During the interim a great deal of malnutrition was present. From the nutritional standpoint, therefore, the natives suffered most under Anglo-Saxon domination. *5*

Certain quasicultural items were undoubtedly significant in intensifying the effect of the primary lethal factors. Among these were, in particular, labor and sex relations. In the missions a great deal of unrest and maladjustment was caused by the current system of forced labor and of drastically restricted liberty in sex matters. In both these, the basic difficulty was not physical but emotional and was derived from the compulsion which forced activity into new and unaccustomed channels. Under the Americans, compulsion was of a different character, but even more disruptive in its effects. The native was compelled to labor by economic necessity rather than by personal command. In *6* acquiring the tools and the facility for work he was obstructed by a hostile society, rather than aided by a paternal government. Hence his progress was slow and his entire material welfare — diet and health —suffered in consequence. From the sexual inhibitions of the mission environment he was carried by the Americans to the most violent and brutal excesses and his women subjected to universal outrage. The hatred and despair thus generated found expression in still further retardation of his material adjustment.

On the whole, therefore, and for many causes, the conflict of the native with the settlers from the United States was characterized by far greater violence than the conflict with the invaders from Latin America. This violence was reflected in greater relative population decline and in more difficult adjustment in all material respects under the American occupation.

Considerations

1. Draw and label a circular graph divided into pie-shaped wedges representing the relative proportion of Indian deaths attributable to disease. Write a paragraph explaining the information represented by the graph.
2. Sherburne F. Cook compares and contrasts the effect on the California Indians of two main groups of Europeans: the Spanish missionaries and settlers before 1848 and the Yankee Anglo-Americans after 1848. Cook uses three main categories to sort out, analyze, and organize his data (war, disease, and starvation), and then he adds two more categories (labor and sex relations).

   a. Fill in this formal outline of Cook's article. Write one sentence for each item in the outline. Find the necessary details in Cook's article.

   Thesis: The impact of the settlement from the United States was three times as severe as that of pre-American colonization.

   Introduction (statistics)
      I. War
         A. Spanish
         B. Yankee
      II. Disease
         A. Spanish
         B. Yankee
      III. Diet
         A. Spanish
         B. Yankee
      IV. Labor
         A. Spanish
         B. Yankee
       V. Sex Relations
         A. Spanish
         B. Yankee
   Conclusion

3. Write a summary of Cook's article by condensing the information in your outline. Use sentence combining techniques to reduce the number of words.
4. Write a second outline of Cook's article. Again, try to find enough information in Cook's article to write one sentence for each item in the outline. However, this time use the second possible pattern for organizing a comparison/contrast essay, that is, the pattern that Cook himself did not choose.

Thesis: The impact of the settlement from the United States was three times as severe as that of pre-American colonization.

Introduction
  I. Pre-American Spanish colonization: missionaries and settlers
     A. War
     B. Disease
     C. Diet
     D. Labor
     E. Sex Relations
  II. Yankee Anglo-Americans
     A. War
     B. Disease
     C. Diet
     D. Labor
     E. Sex Relations
5. Now write a comparison/contrast essay on the effect of Europeans on the California Indians. Use Cook's information, but organize it according to the second outline. Paraphrase Cook's information whenever possible. When you need to quote Cook's exact words, enclose them within quotation marks.

Connections

1. Sherburne F. Cook, like Theodora Kroeber, treats the California Indians, but in very different ways. Write an essay comparing and contrasting these two passages — not the information itself, but the ways in which Kroeber and Cook present this information.
2. Criticize or defend the statement: Cook's article is more scientific than Kroeber's.

Some Concerns Central to the Writing of "Indian" History

Alfonso Ortiz

Historians and other scholars, Indian and non-Indian, concerned with the   *1*
writing of new, more truthful Indian histories should begin with and continually be concerned with Indian traditions. One very important reason is that, as we would learn from any good traditionalist, Indian traditions usually exist more in space, in a specific place, than in time. It is no accident that some of us who happen to be Indians as well as scholars place the word *space* before *time* when we write. I am thinking of my own first book in this case, which I subtitled *Space, Time Being and Becoming in a Pueblo Society*. It is no accident at all, because Indian traditions exist in, and are primarily to be understood in relation to, space; they belong to the place where the people exist or originated. This is certainly a characteristic of all North American horticultural societies, and it applies as well to many nomadic groups. Any historians who overlook this fact run the risk of proceeding into the writing of Indian history without taking the most sublime of Indian values into consideration, a totally self-defeating enterprise. And, unfortunately, too much of what has heretofore passed as Indian history reflects this lack of awareness of the distinctiveness of Indian cultural traditions viewed as realities deeply rooted in the soils of the peoples' respective homelands. Indeed, some realities, most notably the sacred, have little meaning except in the context of their spatial referents. When shorn of these spatial referents, they are likewise shorn of their moral force and a large portion of their range of meanings; hence, of their explanatory value.

I would like to give a few examples of the kind of things which have their   *2*
richest, fullest range of meanings only in the context of the place where they occur, the place where the people live or originate. This is not to say, let me hasten to add, that the historian necessarily has to go to the place and tour every rock, mountain, lake, or whatever in which traditional events are said to have occurred. I only mean to suggest that historians need to develop a sensitivity to certain tribal traditions that have a bearing on a people's past, present, and aspirations for the future, to wit, on their history, which have no meaning apart from where they occur.

Each example concerns my own native Pueblo traditions. A vivid example   *3*
of the importance of space in sacred contexts has to do with Pueblo traditional dances and ceremonies. When powwows and other commercially inspired dancing opportunities off the reservations first began to appear in the Southwest, instead of taking their own traditional dances to these gatherings, Pueblo

Alfonso Ortiz (b. 1939) is a professor of anthropology at the University of New Mexico in Albuquerque. He is a Pueblo Indian.

people would don Plains Indian buckskin and war bonnets and perform dances they had learned from Plains Indian neighbors. Not only were their own traditional sacred dances rigidly locked into the seasonal cycle, but they could not be performed outside of a given sacred space within a Pueblo because it was believed that the dance would not only lose all its efficacy, but that it would have no meaning whatsoever outside of that sacred space. The reason they believed so is that a ceremonial occasion is viewed metaphorically as being like a plant. When the date for the ceremony is set, it is believed that a crack appears in the earth where the seed of the dance has sprouted. The song-composing and practice sessions in preparation for the dance are viewed as being analogous to the stages of growth of the plant. The day of the dance itself is considered the day when the plant bears fruit. Hence, through these powerful earth-bound metaphors the Pueblo peoples reinforced their sense of, and commitment to, the particular places they inhabit. They found it difficult to even think of these locale-centered ceremonies as having any meaning apart from the earth which gave them their being.

Recently, however, some ingenious individual in one of the Tewa Pueblos   4
suggested that it did not really matter where the middle performances of a sacred dance occurred, as long as it began and ended within the Pueblo. By this suggestion, the plant that is the dance could be viewed as both sprouting and bearing fruit within a particular Pueblo's sacred space, while it could be taken elsewhere for the middle stages of its growth cycle. Still, however, when this is done, these middle stages are not regarded as having any religious meaning whatsoever. This is how those Pueblos which do export religious dances rationalize their doing so. The more traditional Pueblos have not accepted this rationale, however, so they do not permit their dances to be performed either out of context on the seasonal calendar or outside of their sacred space within the Pueblo.

The remaining two examples concern oral traditions of the Tewa. When I   5
was recording historical narratives, myths, legends, and folklore, I was impressed frequently by the fact that the further away a series of events receded into time, say over a century, the more likely they were to be framed into sets of four. For instance, there was a time when the Navajo people and my own people had a lot of skirmishes with one another. When Tewa elders spoke about skirmishes with the Navajos which took place over a century ago, they would say that the battle took place four days march away, and that it lasted four days. For another example, an expression frequently used in Tewa oral traditions is "when it has been four times," which is used to convey both a sense of time and a sense of space simultaneously. It signifies both when a time span of four days has passed or when a spatial distance of four days travel has passed. Like the four-day battle, the four times of this expression is not to be taken literally. There is so much of four of this, and four of that, and four of the other thing that this is obviously not history in the sense that we as scholars understand it.

Similarly, anything which occurred outside of the four sacred mountains of   6
the Tewa world — quite a vast distance — is likely to be rendered into a nu-

merical formula of twelve in Tewa oral tradition. One would say that it was twelve days march away, because it was so far that it was convenient and meaningful to remember the distance in that way. It was meaningful because in the Tewa genesis the migration from the northern boundary of the Tewa world to the present Tewa villages took place in twelve steps. Hence, anything which involved going to that boundary or beyond was conveniently remembered in spatial or temporal units of twelve, while anything which occurred within the four sacred mountains was remembered in units of four.

What is clearly happening in these brief examples is that the Tewa were   7
persistently attempting to turn time into space, to anchor historical events onto meaningful spatial referents, which could be used as mnemonic devices to aid the Tewa in recalling what they thought to be the essential meanings of those events. That these essential meanings were shorn of their historical referents is due to the, by now, obvious fact that the dominant metaphor governing Tewa existence is spatial rather than temporal. All of this is not to deny that time is important; rather, it is time in its linear, historical dimension that is unimportant. The kind of time the Tewa, and other Pueblo people as well, attempt to be a part of is cyclical, rhythmic time, time viewed as a series of endlessly repeating cycles, on the model of the seasons or, again, plants. This use of space as a dominant metaphor and the understanding of time in its cyclical dimension is true, as well, of a large number, perhaps even all, of traditional native North American cultures.

This tendency to spatialize time presents problems in the writing of Indian   8
history because, as we know, historians tend to do exactly the opposite, to turn space into time. That is to say, instead of understanding experience primarily in terms of the places in which events occurred, historians and Western scholars in general tend to understand events primarily in terms of when they occurred. At the extreme, some historians will take simultaneous circumstances which differ because they occur in distinct places, and turn these distinct circumstances into a historical progression. In the history of Indian-white relations, this leads to statements such as one made by Philip Barbour[1] as recently as 1964 that the time of contact, "a gulf of a hundred centuries . . . separated Algonkian from European" (1964:123). This, and more common, less extreme examples of turning space into time, does grave injustice to essential dimensions of Indian reality.

There is yet another admonition to be made based upon these Tewa examples. It is that most Western scholars would term what happened in these examples a process of mythologization, and dismiss them at that, believing that they have no relevance to the historical enterprise. That is to say, most scholars would say that beyond the reach of a few generations, historical events occurring among the Tewa tend to be rendered into convenient pre-existing cognitive categories so that they can be remembered in a way that is meaningful in terms of tribal tradition. Not only would the designation of this process as one of mythologization represent an attempt to impose a temporal frame on these experiences and descriptions, but precisely in the process of so doing it would misrepresent them. Hence, just to say that these events were being mythologized and to let it go at that would be to demean and patronize them, as

well as to preclude the possibility of understanding them. And only by understanding them can we begin to describe Indian perceptions of their past.

I have used just these few examples of patterns or tendencies toward ren-   9
dering events into numerical formulae anchored onto spatial referents, but there
are many such phenomena to be found when one assumes a tradition-sensitive
perspective in the writing of Indian history. And phenomena such as these are
precisely at the cutting edge of the challenge in the writing of Indian history.
For historians to venture into this area, they would, at the very least, have to
develop a deeper sensitivity to, and respect for, the tenacity of Indian cultures
in America. Hopefully, the time will also come when some historians who are
not Indian will take the time to learn to speak an Indian language, or at least
learn to read those which are now being written. Unfortunately, these latter
are not too many, nor are they being written down fast enough. The importance of learning an Indian language cannot be overemphasized, for it is the
most reliable way to enter a people's world, to understand how they impose
meaning and order upon their experience. Until then, this dialogue we speak
of as hopefully constituting the Indian history of the future just will not occur.

On the other hand, I must say that it bothers me when I hear Indian people   10
and Indian scholars saying "if we choose to believe that we came up out of a
hole in the ground, that is our business." It bothers me, but it should bother
historians more, for it shows that some Indian people have come to distrust
historians to the extent that they feel a need to assert total sovereignty over
their traditions and their past. I agree that they have every right to believe as
they wish, but they should not call such beliefs "history." The kind of truth
that is communicated by tribal traditions postulating a prior existence in one
of four worlds beneath this one, beneath a lake or in a mountain or whatever,
is of another order. The word that comes the closest to describing this kind of
truth, a truth which is of critical importance to Indian traditions, is "metaphorical." The truth and the reality is not of an historical order, but of a metaphorical one.

It seems to me that this notion of metaphorical truth is essential for under-   12
standing many tribal traditions. For example, the horticultural societies of the
aboriginal southwest uniformly postulated their ultimate beginnings as being
within the earth. In their traditions of genesis some state that the people moved
up vertically through multiple (usually four) underworld homes before finally
emerging onto this, the earth-surface world. Other tribes postulate a single underworld home. In each case, however, they perceive their lives as proceeding
upward from within the earth on the analogy of plant life. I do not believe they
are claiming that at some distant time in the past the original group of ancestors actually grew up out of the earth like plants. Rather, I believe that such
statements reflect their recognition of the profound truth that *all* life, human
and animal as well as plant, ultimately derives from the earth and returns to
the earth.

The place which a given one of these tribes postulates as its original point   13
of entry into this world, usually a lake or a mountain or both together, there-

fore assumes a special aura of sanctity for the members of that tribe. Such a place of emergence serves as a master, all-encompassing condensation symbol of a people's whole being and identity, the anchor of their very existence. Hence, when they say that they have their beginnings in a particular spot on the landscape I understand them to mean that they have a special relationship with that place, and that they cannot be understood apart from it because it gives them their very sense of being as a people, from one generation to the next. Understood in these ways we can see that the claims of such tribal traditions as those under discussion here are not unreasonable, childlike, foolish, or merely pretty allegories, all of which they have been called in the past. These traditions make splendid sense, but the sense is not of a historical or literal order. Hence, to keep the debate on that level is quite to miss the point. Neither are these kinds of traditions irrelevant to the historian's task if he or she is to represent a given tribe's view of reality accurately and fully. The challenge, again, is to understand the categories in terms of which a given people think about their past, insofar as said categories give them a distinctive outlook on the past and thus bear upon the historical enterprise. All of this merely underscores the desirability of developing a greater sensitivity toward, and respect for, tribal traditions, and of learning Indian languages.

There is another tendency when non-Indians write "Indian history" which 14 has long bothered me and upon which I would like to comment. I refer to the implicit "up from darkness" strain of thought in these writings, the view of the inevitability of "enlightenment" or "progress." This kind of thinking is unfortunate, and I admit that it exists as much in anthropology as in history. In anthropology this is represented by the evolutionary school of thought, a school which was especially prominent in this country during the last decades of the nineteenth century and the early decades of the twentieth. The result of this kind of thinking in anthropology has been a legacy of age-area and culture area studies characterized by a laundry-list approach to the collection of data. It is unfortunate, first, because studies characterized by and guided by these kinds of theoretical and methodological biases read like the yellow pages of a small town telephone book. More importantly, it is unfortunate because it leads to the familiar tendency to turn space into time upon which I have commented above. The age-area and culture area notions are quite pristine examples of this relentless linearity or historicity, if you will, of scholarly thought as regards Indian cultures and traditions. It tends to take things which must first be understood as cycles, as repeatable rhythms, happening in a concrete place, and instead render them into arbitrary linear sequences. This is what I mean by the notion of turning space into time, and it is a very dangerous enterprise, for it misrepresents Indian realities as being something other than what they actually are.

I have yet to encounter a tribal tradition in which there is anything re- 15 motely resembling the notion of progress. It is a distortion when people who deify a notion like progress and regard it as inevitable write about Indian people with the assumption that they, too, are caught up in and with the notion of progress. Historians and anthropologists who write in this vein treat Indian tribal peoples as if they were also grinding, inevitably, inexorably, up the step-ladder of progressive enlightenment and toward greater complexity. To insist on perceiving something that is not there is again to distort the true experiences of these peoples.

Something else that I often encounter in the historical literature written about   *16* Indians is a catalogue of "contributions" Indian people have purportedly made to some other entity, whether it be to the society of their conquerors or to Western civilization generally. I have no quarrel with the movement today to acknowledge the rightful role of Indian peoples in the formation of the American character and in changes in Europe as well. However, I find the attitude shown by many who pursue these types of studies to be that subordinate, colonized peoples exist solely to make contributions to the onrushing monolithic monster that is Western civilization. What are cited as contributions by Indian people to Western civilization are actually stealings and borrowing in large part. This attitude is part and parcel of the "up from darkness" strain of thinking and the deification of progress. Clearly we have to get beyond the inherent dangers these attitudes pose and return to a recognition of the more modest notion that perhaps we Indian people who survived with the essences of our cultures intact really want to make contributions first and foremost to the continued survival and perpetuation of these cultures, rather than to something called "civilization," which is, after all, alien to our traditional cultures, and usually antagonistic to them as well. I will not go into a disquisition on the materialistic basis from which this and other attitudes arise, but it would be a useful exercise if someone would do so.

It has been implicit in all the comments made here today that we do need   *17* to understand why so many Indians now seem to find it necessary to say: "You, whitey, you ripped me off, therefore I am not going to let you come onto my reservation;" furthermore, I am going to write my own history and do my own thing." I believe there has been adequate provocation and justification for taking this point of view in the past, but to continue such a split between Indians and historians would be tragic, for it would preclude a new dialogue, a kind of creative mutually rewarding partnership between Indians and sympathetic historians. Before the situation can be remedied, historians must accept and concede that the "partnership" of the past was so one-sided that it caused Indian people to say "to hell with what has gone on before, we are going to do our own thing." The challenge is primarily for those non-Indian American historians who are interested in forging a new partnership to understand how and why things between Indians and historians deteriorated to the point that some among Indian people find it necessary to say "no more whitey."

I have one more concrete suggestion; but first, a prefatory observation. I am   *18* impressed by the number of very, very conservative people in American history writing about Indian/white relations. I thought we had them all in anthropology, but it increasingly appears to me not to be so. One manifestation of this is an overweening preoccupation with the very distant past. To me it is paradoxical that American historians dealing with Indian/white relations position themselves predominantly in the Colonial, Treaty, Allotment, or, at closest in time to the present, the Reservation Periods. Despite the large number of studies that fall temporally within these early periods, I am amazed at the absence or paucity of good literature on the post-1934 Reorganization Period, otherwise known as the Indian New Deal, and succeeding years. I do not understand this preoccupation of American historians with the earliest centuries of Indian/white contact, the colonial period, and the earliest decades of American nationhood; truly I do not understand it, for the very people who concern themselves with early origins and the founding of the republic are the ones most reluctant to talk to tribal elders who also deal with the origins, the beginning of the beginning of all beginnings. The tribal elders deal with the beginning in what I have termed, in the language of scholarship, a metaphorical way; historians deal with it through documents, though I will not go so far as to say they do it in a literal way, because the more I read history, the more I am convinced that history is modern man's mythology. Even the best of Western historical writing has no more meaning and no more truth value than what we have heretofore been pleased to term, with no little air of condescension, Indian mythology.

The danger is that our near exclusive preoccupation with the distant past *19* continues to render Indian experiences of the present or Indian aspirations for the future opaque. It makes history, as it has made much of anthropology, a continuing handmaiden of the colonial enterprise. That has always been sad, and it continues to an unfortunate degree even now. It consigns the diverse Indian peoples and Indian experiences on this land into the shadows of history. Indian peoples must come out of these shadows before we are to have, all of us, a truly honest American history. If one side is rendered opaque, by being seen as mute, witless, and hence, irrelevant for the purposes of dialogue, there can be no honest American history. It is a good thing to get on with in the next two hundred years of our national existence, I think, since we are at this milestone in the history of our mutual coexistence on this land we call America.

NOTE
[1]Barbour, Philip. *The Three Worlds of Captain John Smith*, Boston: Houghton Mifflin, 1964.

Considerations

1. Write a paragraph explaining what Alfonso Ortiz means when he refers to the " 'up from darkness' strain of thinking" (para. 14). Why does it bother him?
2. Ortiz claims that "history is modern man's mythology" (para. 18). Write a paragraph in which you define *mythology*, give an example of your own of a modern myth about Indians, and then explain how your example fits the definition. You might think, for example, about how we celebrate Thanksgiving.
3. Ortiz refers to Indian tribal traditions and says Indians "should not call such beliefs 'history' " (para. 11). Write a paragraph in which you explain why not.
4. Do you think there is any tradition we believe in and also call *history*? Write

a paragraph answering this question including an example to illustrate your answer.

5. Ortiz complains about the attitude that "subordinate, colonized peoples exist solely to make contributions to the onrushing monolithic monster that is Western civilization" (para. 16). He writes "I will not go into a disquisition on the materialistic basis from which this and other attitudes arise, but it would be a useful exercise if someone would do so" (para. 16). Write an essay in which you analyze the materialistic basis of these attitudes.

Connections

1. Do you think Alfonso Ortiz would approve of Theodora Kroeber or Sherburne Cook, or with one more than the other? Write a short essay defending your choice.
2. Ortiz refers to his own native Pueblo traditions. Based on any of the systems for classifying folk tales presented in Chapter 10, The Fairy Tale Snow White, explain why Indian lore, like Ortiz's traditions, does or does not fit that definition of *folklore*. If you think Indian traditions *do* fit a definition of folklore, then explain how and to what extent. If you think Indian traditions *do not* fit such a definition, explain these definitions as an inappropriate Western European-American system.

Ojibwa Ontology, Behavior, and World View
A. Irving Hallowell

In this paper I have assembled evidence, chiefly from my own field work on   *1*
a branch of the Northern Ojibwa, which supports the inference that in the metaphysics of being found among these Indians, the action of persons provides the major key to their world view.

While in all cultures "persons" comprise one of the major classes of objects   *2*
to which the self must become oriented, this category of being is by no means limited to *human* beings. In Western culture, as in others, "supernatural" beings

A. Irving Hallowell (1892–1974) was a social worker in Philadelphia for a number of years before getting his Ph.D. degree in anthropology. He did very distinguished and influential fieldwork among the Ojibwa, which is described in this excerpt from a paper he wrote about his experiences.

are recognized as "persons," although belonging, at the same time, to an other than human category. But in the social sciences and psychology, "persons" and human beings are categorically identified. This identification is inherent in the concept of "society" and "social relations." In Warren's *Dictionary of Psychology* "person" is defined as "a human organism regarded as having distinctive characteristics and social relations." The same identification is implicit in the conceptualization and investigation of social organization by anthropologists. Yet this obviously involves a radical abstraction if, from the standpoint of the people being studied, the concept of "person" is not, in fact, synonymous with human being but transcends it. The significance of the abstraction only becomes apparent when we stop to consider the perspective adopted. The study of social organization, defined as human relations of a certain kind, is perfectly intelligible as an objective approach to the study of this subject in any culture. But if, in the world view of a people, "persons" as a class include entities other than human beings, then our objective approach is not adequate for presenting an accurate description of "the way a man, in a particular society, sees himself in relation to all else." A different perspective is required for this purpose. It may be argued, in fact, that a thoroughgoing "objective" approach to the study of cultures cannot be achieved solely by projecting upon those cultures categorical abstractions derived from Western thought. For, in a broad sense, the latter are a reflection of our cultural subjectivity. A higher order of objectivity may be sought by adopting a perspective which includes an analysis of the outlook of the people themselves as a complementary procedure. It is in a world view perspective, too, that we can likewise obtain the best insight into how cultures function as wholes.

The significance of these differences in perspective may be illustrated in the case of the Ojibwa by the manner in which the kinship term "grandfather" is used. It is not only applied to human persons but to spiritual beings who are persons of a category other than human. In fact, when the collective plural "our grandfathers" is used, the reference is primarily to persons of this latter class. Thus, if we study Ojibwa social organization in the usual manner, we take account of only one set of "grandfathers." But if we adopt a world view perspective no dichotomization appears. In this perspective "grandfather" is a term applicable to certain "person objects," without any distinction between human persons and those of an other-than-human class. [3]

Any discussion of "persons" in the world view of the Ojibwa must take cognizance of the well known fact that the grammatical structure of the language of these people, like all their Algonkian relatives, formally expresses a distinction between "animate" and "inanimate" nouns. These particular labels, of course, were imposed upon Algonkian languages by Europeans; it appeared to outsiders that the Algonkian differentiation of objects approximated the animate-inanimate dichotomy of Western thought. Superficially this seems to be the case. Yet a closer examination indicates that, as in the gender categories of other languages, the distinction in some cases appears to be arbitrary, if not extremely puzzling, from the standpoint of common sense or in a naturalistic frame of reference. Thus, substantives for some, but not all — trees, sun-moon (*gtzis*), thunder, stones, and objects of material culture like kettle and pipe — are classified as "animate." [4]

If we wish to understand the cognitive orientation of the Ojibwa, there is an   5
ethno-linguistic problem to be considered: What is the meaning of animate in
Ojibwa thinking? Are such generic properties of objects as responsiveness to
outer stimulation — sentience, mobility, self-movement, or even reproduction
— primary characteristics' attributed to all objects of the animate class irrespective of their categories as physical objects in our thinking? Is there evidence to substantiate such properties of objects independent of their formal
linguistic classification? It must not be forgotten that no Ojibwa is consciously
aware of, or can abstractly articulate the animate-inanimate category of his
language, despite the fact that this dichotomy is implicit in his speech. Consequently, the grammatical distinction as such does not emerge as a subject
for reflective thought or bear the kind of relation to individual thinking that
would be present if there were some formulated dogma about the generic
properties of these two classes of objects.

Since stones are grammatically animate, I once asked an old man: Are *all*   6
the stones we see about us here alive? He reflected a long while and then replied, "No! But *some* are." This qualified answer made a lasting impression on
me. And it is thoroughly consistent with other data that indicate that the Ojibwa
are not animists in the sense that they dogmatically attribute living souls to
inanimate objects such as stones. The hypothesis which suggests itself to me is
that the allocation of stones to an animate grammatical category is part of a
culturally constituted cognitive "set." It does not involve a consciously formulated theory about the nature of stones. It leaves a door open that our orientation on dogmatic grounds keeps shut tight. Whereas we should never expect a stone to manifest animate properties of any kind under any circumstances,
the Ojibwa recognize, *a priori*, potentialities for animation in certain classes of
objects under certain circumstances. The Ojibwa do not perceive stones, in
general, as animate, any more than we do. The crucial test is experience. Is
there any personal testimony available? In answer to this question we can say
that it is asserted by informants that stones have been seen to move, that some
stones manifest other animate properties, and, as we shall see, Flint is represented as a living personage in their mythology.

Considerations

1. Assume your younger brother or sister in another city has been assigned this
   reading for a first-year anthropology course. Your brother or sister writes
   asking you for help in understanding what Hallowell is getting at. Write a
   short letter explaining the importance of Hallowell's ideas.
2. In the first paragraph, Hallowell claims that "the action of persons provides
   the major key" to the world view of the Ojibwa. What word do you think
   provides the major key to the world view of present-day Americans (money,
   love, sex, ambition . . .)? Is there some one special word in American English that is especially revealing about our values and sense of our place in
   the universe? Write a paragraph proposing your word (and the concept it
   represents), and defend your choice with examples.

Connections

1. In the first reading, Theodora Kroeber claims that the early California Indians did not voluntarily leave their own familiar world. She explains the disadvantages of doing so: "At best you would be without family or friends or influence or status, and forced to learn to speak a foreign language . . ." (para. 17). Assume that you are A. Irving Hallowell, and use his observations to explain Kroeber's point about learning to speak a foreign language. Write a paragraph outlining why an Indian would think the prospect of learning a different language so terrifying.
2. Write a short essay explaining why Alfonso Ortiz would approve of Hallowell's article.

The European Failure to Convert the Indians: An Autopsy

James L. Axtell

The European campaigns to convert the American natives began with mixed   *1*
feelings. On the one hand, the Indians were believed to be fearsome savages and barbarians, without religion, civility, reason, or even humanity. This meant to some colonists, largely new arrivals unacquainted with the Indians, that the effort to convert them was time lost. But most Europeans, especially those at home, believed that "it is not the nature of men, but the education of men, which makes them barbarous and uncivill." (Gray 1609: [Clv-]-C2r) According to Father Le Jeune, the Jesuit Superior in Quebec, it was optimism such as this that caused a "great many people in France [to] imagine that all we have to do is to open our mouths and utter four words, and behold, a Savage is converted." (JR 9:91)

The European ambivalence about the Indians gave rise to a complex pro-   *2*
gram of conversion. While the Indians were felt to be educable, their savage condition was not felt to be fertile ground for the holy seeds of Christianity. As late as 1770, it was said that "the most sensible Writers on this Subject" felt that it was necessary to "civilize Savages before they can be converted to

---

James L. Axtell (b. 1941) is a professor of history at the College of William and Mary in Williamsburg, Virginia. Author of The European and the Indian: Essays in the Ethnohistory of Colonial North America *(New York: Oxford University Press, 1981), Axtell is known for his distinguished work on cultural interaction.*

Christianity; & that in order to make them *Christians*, they must first be made *Men*." (Johnson 7:506)

In implying that the Indians were not yet "Men," Europeans usually meant one of three things. The first meaning was that the Indians were the children of the human race, their passions still largely unrestrained by reason. The second meaning also emphasized the Indians' passions, but gave them a much less charitable interpretation. Rather than innocent children, the Indians in this view were little better than animals, almost incapable of reason and enslaved by the "most brutal passions." (JR 66:221) As late as 1721 Cotton Mather advised the commissioners of a missionary society that "to *Humanize* these Miserable *Animals*, and in any measure to *Cicurate* [tame] them & *Civilize* them, were a work of no little Difficulty; and a Performance little short of what One of our most famous *Physicians* esteemed the *Greatest Cure* that ever himself had wrought in all his Practice; *To bring an Idiot unto the Use of Reason*." (Mather 1721:28–29)

The third and most common meaning, however, was simply that the Indians had not mastered the "Arts of civil Life & Humanity," which is to say, the classical liberal arts. (Johnson 5:511) In the European hierarchy of knowledge, Theology was the queen of the sciences and Philosophy her handmaiden. To approach Theology, the guardian of Christian Truth, one had to first master the seven liberal arts, the arts of humane living, much as one would progress through the trivium and quadrivium of a medieval university. While civilized Europeans could be assumed to have acquired those arts through education or social osmosis, the Indians were thought to lack them totally. Therefore, as the Récollet friars proposed upon coming to Canada in 1615, the Indians were to be "regulated by French laws and modes of living" in order to render them capable of understanding the "profound mysteries" of Christianity, "for all that concerns human and civil life is a mystery for our Indians in their present state, and it will require more expense and toil to render them men than it has required to make whole nations Christian." (Le Clercq 1881 I:214)

The Récollets' prediction was prophetic, for the task the Europeans had set themselves was monumental. It was nothing less than to try to persuade the members of a stone-age culture, at home in the forest, to allow themselves to be transformed — mentally, morally, and materially — into denizens of an urban-agrarian culture whose mores they considered ridiculous and whose politico-economic system they regarded as destructive of individual liberty and inimical to charity and justice, all this to enable them to embrace a religion they found dangerous and unreasonable. In short, nomadic hunters (or so all Indians were thought to be) were to be made into sedentary farmers or schoolmasters by teaching them — largely in sedentary schools — how to dress, talk, eat, think, and pray like Europeans.

As it turned out, neither European culture —French or English — was fully equal to the task, but one was better prepared than the other. If anyone had a fighting chance of converting the Indians, it was the French. Unlike their English neighbors to the south, the French in Canada were not interested in settling a commonwealth of farmers, with their insatiable appetite for new land. They were intent only upon the fur trade, which depended wholly upon the well-being and friendship of the Indian trappers and middlemen. To secure the trust and allegiance of their Indian partners required a tactful blend of cultural toleration, personal flexibility, and endurance, traits which the French alone among the North American colonists seemed to possess in abundance.

While their cultural character and situation undoubtedly accounted for much   7
of the advantage the French enjoyed over their English rivals, the French missionaries, particularly the Jesuits, also possessed several characteristics that gave them an edge in the contest of conversion. The first characteristic they shared with their countrymen: the uncommon ability to acculturate themselves to the Indians' way of life in order to win their trust for the task ahead. Unlike the Dominicans and Franciscans within their own church and the Puritans and Anglicans without, the Jesuits articulated and practised a brand of cultural relativism, without, however, succumbing to ethical neutrality. Their world-wide technique was to "assume 'a thousand masks,' being all things to all men and with 'holy cunning' accepting the limitations imposed by the local situation. Rather than destroy and condemn what they found, they tried to reshape and reorient existing practices and beliefs in order to establish a common ground on which to begin conversion." (Duignan 1958: 726) As Father Vimont put it in 1642, "to make a Christian out of a Barbarian is not the work of a day. . . . A great step is gained when one has learned to know those with whom he has to deal; has penetrated their thoughts; has adapted himself to their language, their customs, and their manner of living; and, when necessary, has been a Barbarian with them, in order to win them over to Jesus Christ." (JR 27:207–209) In large measure, the Jesuits' success was gained not by expecting less of their converts, as the English accused, but by accepting more.

Yet the Jesuits enjoyed other advantages, some owing to the nature of their   8
religion, others to the nature of their vocation. The English Puritans were hampered in their missionary efforts by an ecclesiastical polity that restricted the ministry to those specifically called by an individual congregation of the elect. A minister without a congregation, no matter how holy or how learned he was, was simply a man without the ministry. He could not administer the sacraments of baptism and communion — the only two they recognized — or gather a formal church. Furthermore, despite evangelical assertions to the contrary, the Puritan minister was effectively prevented from winning new souls to Christ by being tied to the needs and wishes of his small flock. Unless the unregenerate happened to wander into his congregation on the Sabbath — and understood English — the minister was not likely to encounter many potential converts. "By their principles," an Anglican visitor criticized, "no Nation can or could ever be converted." (Lechford 1833:80)

By contrast, the Puritans themselves recognized that "*the Romanists* have   9
their singular Advantages, in the *Circumstances of their Clergy, to go to and fro in the Earth, and walk up and down in it,* everywhere seeking whom they may seduce, and bring under their strong Delusions." (Mayhew 1727: xiv) Organized hierarchically in an international order in 1534, the Jesuits quickly became the intellectual shock-troops of the Counter-Reformation, freed from parish work to attack heresy and paganism wherever it flourished. One of their greatest assets, besides an iron code of obedience and self-sacrifice, was their rigorous classical education, which was acknowledged by friends and enemies alike to be the best in Europe. After several years at a LaFlèche, the Jesuit had

few equals in his ability to dissect an opponent's arguments, to draw upon a fund of classical, patristic, and Biblical allusion, and to construct a logically and rhetorically compelling argument for his own faith.

But equally impressive was his linguistic aptitude gained from an exhaus-   *10* tive apprenticeship in the classical languages. As every missionary would soon discover, a finely tuned ear and a mastery of comparative linguistics was among his most valuable assets in the Indian Babel of the New World. Unfortunately, the English saw the connection too infrequently or too late. For example, when Father Sébastien Râle attacked the Latin style and theological ineptitude of a Harvard-educated minister sent to Maine to steal his converts, the governor of Massachusetts protested to the Jesuit: "Certainly you Cannot Suppose the Main or principal Qualification of a Gospel Minister, or Missionary among a Barbarous Nation . . . to be an Exact Scholar as to the Latin Tongue." (Willis 9:372) We can be sure that he didn't, but to a former professor of rhetoric who had mastered the Abenaki vocabulary and most of its intricate pronunciation in five months, had written an Abenaki dictionary and catechism, and had become fluent in three other Indian languages, the question must have seemed naive.

Another advantage that Catholicism held over Protestantism, especially the   *11* stark Puritan variety, was that Catholicism was essentially a religion of the liturgy, of colorful and affective ceremony, based on daily habits of prayer and worship. Protestantism, on the other hand, was a religion of the Book, a highly rationalistic effort to understand the inscrutable will of God, distracted by a minimum of human observances. While both forms of Christianity were ultimately based on the Scriptures, Catholicism had always embraced the human emotions, while Protestantism, in emphasizing Adam's fall from grace, held them at arm's length. Accordingly, the Protestant's trademark was the sermon — long, abstract, and loaded with Scriptural proofs — which assumed on its audience's part a good deal of cultural sophistication and formal education. The Catholic's trademark was the Mass, which appealed to the communicant's senses with candles, bells, vestments, incense, and the familiar sonorities of Latin chants and responses. It was the Catholic's affective ceremonies, ceremonies which resembled native religious observances in color, drama, and participation and appealed to the Indians' practical intelligence — that stood the best chance of bridging the cultural chasm that lay between the two races.

But ritual is only one part of religion; a religion without a doctrinal foun-   *12* dation would not deserve the name. Here as well Catholicism accorded more with Indian belief than did Protestantism. In emphasizing God's omnipotent will, the Puritans believed that salvation could not be earned by an exemplary life or good works; only a free gift of God could confer grade and election upon a sinner. Catholics, on the other hand, believed that *only* good works and a virtuous life could bind religion and morality and accommodate both to fallible human beings. While the Indians originally entertained no well-defined idea of heaven or salvation in an afterlife, they found more sense in the possibility of earning their future condition than in having it given or denied them regardless of a lifetime of intentions and actions. This difference clearly inflected Lahontan's ironical lament to his Huron companion that "the Son of God is willing to save all the *English* by his Blood and Merits. And thus you see that they are happier than the *French*, of whom God has requir'd good Works that they scarce ever mind, and who are doom'd to everlasting Flames, if their evil Actions run counter to the [Ten] Commandments of God." (Lahontan 1905:547–48)

And yet at the end of nearly two centuries of effort, both the French and the English were forced to admit that they had largely failed to convert the Indians to Christianity and civilization. The reasons are not difficult to find. In fact, they are so plentiful and so overwhelming that we should rather wonder how the Europeans achieved as much success as they did. The usual explanations — those most commonly given by contemporaries in a spirit of half-hearted expiation — pointed to the regrettable but inevitable results of contact with European culture: disease (to which the Indians had no immunities), war (fomented by European trade competition and exacerbated by European firearms), alcohol (for whose use the Indians had no cultural sanctions), and the immoral example of false Christians (who, instead of raising the Indians' sights to a higher level, "reduce[d] them to civility"). Cotton Mather spoke for many when he confessed that the Europeans had "very much *Injured* the *Indians . . .* by *Teaching* of them, *Our Vice*. We that should have learn'd them to *Pray*, have learn'd them to Sin." (Mather 1690:27)   13

While no one would deny that these external forces did much to undermine the conversion process — the dead make poor converts — we should emphasize the traits within Indian culture itself that impeded first the civilizing and then the Christianizing attempts of the Europeans.   14

As we've seen, the Europeans began their conversion efforts with high hopes. Their ultimate goal was to lead the Indians to Christianity, but they felt that only civilized people could fully appreciate and benefit from Christ's mercy. So with equal optimism, they set out to convert the Indians to their peculiar cultural life-styles through the educational agencies they knew best — schools. Both the Récollets and the Jesuits established seminaries for Indian children during the first years of their missions, but within five years each had folded for lack of funds and students. It was just as well and the French learned a valuable lesson from their failures. For despite outmoded orders from Paris, the colonists and missionaries in Canada soon gave over the unrealistic attempt to civilize the Indians and concentrated on the difficult enough mission of trying to Christianize them. Through a concentration of time, money, and effort, they made greater progress than if they had continued to attempt the impossible.   15

Unfortunately, the English missionaries were incurable idealists, largely because so few had ever lived with the Indians long enough to take a hard look at their culture and their character. Consequently, long after the French had shifted their efforts to the religious conversion of adults, the English — Puritan and Anglican alike — were still trying to civilize Indian children by packing them off to schools, often far from home. The result was predictable: "we have no examples," wrote Hector de Crèvecoeur in 1782, "of even one of those Aborigines having from choice become Europeans." (Crèvecoeur 1912:215)   16

The contemporary explanation for this failure did not advance beyond simple cultural stereotyping. "I have seen, in a number of instances," said Mary   17

Jemison, a white woman who lived most of her life with the Iroquois, "the effects of education upon some of our Indians, who were taken when young, from their families, and placed at school before they had had an opportunity to contract many Indian habits, and there kept till they arrived at manhood; but I have never seen one of those but what was an Indian in every respect after he returned. Indians must and will be Indians," she asserted, "in spite of all the means that can be used for their cultivation in the sciences and the arts." (Seaver 1961: 56) Frances Slocum, another white Indian, invested the explanation with adage status when she told her English brothers, "It is very easy to make an Indian out of a white man, but you cannot make a white man out of an Indian." (Meginness 1891: 196)

While the adage served as a convenient rationalization for the colonists' sin- *18* gular lack of success in converting the Indians to the English way of life, it does nothing to reveal the actual reasons for that failure. Mary Jemison gave the essential clue when she said that Indian *boys* were sent to colonial *schools*. What the English did not seem to have learned was that Indian boys "love[d] liberty" and abhor[red] restraint" of any kind, which fostered a healthy sense of pride in their status as junior hunters and warriors. (JR 44: 259) To be cooped up in a sedentary school at the most active time of their lives was simply insupportable. Moreover, the education they were given was useless to Indian society, it ordained their inability to live in English society, and was so difficult to acquire that most of them gave up in despair before it was ever completed. Sir William Johnson, the English Superintendant of Indian Affairs, thought that Indian students "are put to Schools too [late?] & sent home too Soon to their people, whose Political Maxim, Spartanlike, is to discountenance all Arts but War, holding all other knowledge as unworthy the dignity of man & as tending to enervate & divert them from those pursuits on which they conceive their Liberty & Happiness depends. These Sentiments," he concluded, "constantly instilled into the Minds of Youth & Illustrated by Examples drawn from the Contemptible State of the domesticated Tribes Leave lasting impressions & can hardly be defeated by an ordinary School Education." (Johnson 12: 954–55) It was, in short, the wrong method for the wrong people at the wrong time.

The failure of the English to civilize the Indians could not have a better ep- *19* itaph than the report made in 1796 by two Boston commissioners of a missionary society. "An Indian youth has been taken from his friends, and conducted to a new people, whose modes of thinking and living, whose pleasures and pursuits are totally dissimilar to those of his own nation. His new friends profess love to him, and a desire for his improvement in human and divine knowledge, and for his eternal salvation; but at the same time endeavour to make him sensible of his inferiority to themselves. To treat him as an equal would mortify their own pride, and degrade themselves in the view of their neighbours. He is put to school; but his fellow [English] students look on him as being an inferior species. He acquires some knowledge, and is taught some ornamental and perhaps useful accomplishments; but the degrading memorials of his inferiority, which are continually before his eyes, remind him of the manners and habits of his own country, where he was once free and equal to his associates. He sighs to return to his friends; but there he meets with the most bitter mortification. He is neither a white man nor an Indian; as he had no character with us, he has none with them. If he has strength of mind suffi- cient to renounce all his acquirements, and resume the savage life and man- ners, he may possibly be again received by his countrymen; but the greater probability is, that he will take refuge from their contempt in the inebriating draught; and when this becomes habitual, he will be guarded from no vice, and secure from no crime. His downward progress will be rapid, and his death premature." "Such has been the fate of several Indians," the report continued, "who have had the opportunity of enjoying an English or a French education, and have returned to their native country. Such persons must either entirely renounce their acquired habits, and resume the savage life; or, if they live among their countrymen, they must be despised, and their death will be unla- mented." (Belknap and Morse 1798: 29–30) Reluctantly, the commissioners would have agreed with Mark Twain's serious quip that "soap and education are not as sudden as a massacre, but they are more deadly in the long run."

When the soaring hopes of the Europeans had been scaled down by failure,   20 there was still the difficult task of converting the Indians to Christianity. But here too Indian culture placed innumerable obstacles in the way. Once the high hurdle of language was cleared, the first and most apparent obstacle was the Indian shaman and his native followers. The professional contest between the shaman and the priest has all the earmarks of great drama. Pitting one kind of magic and power against another, the priest sought to win the people's alle- giance to Christianity by discrediting the symbol and spokesman of their na- tive religion. By their possession of printed truths (which initially impressed the members of that oral culture), a scientific understanding of Nature (whereby a magnet could be used to attract a following away from a divination rite), and an unrelenting questioning of the habitual (which no cultural practice can long survive), the Jesuits eventually wore down the shaman's prestige and estab- lished their own. But not without formidable resistance. Native customs en- joyed a long life well after many of the Indians had accepted the form if not the spirit of Christianity. Priests were ridiculed, insulted, berated, threatened, and even killed by pagan factions, and their new converts were subjected to similar indignities. Under such pressure, the Jesuits had "greater trouble in keeping [their] Christians than in acquiring them." (JR 25: 113)

The rivalry between pagan and Christian factions was carried even to the   21 marriage bed. The Catholic priests, of course, regarded monogamous marriage as one of the seven sacraments and divorce as anathema. The Indians, on the other hand, had been "for many ages in possession of" — as Father Vimont put it — "a complete brutal liberty, changing wives when they pleased — taking only one or several, according to their inclination." Understandably, "conjugal continence and the indissolubility of marriage, seemed to them the most seri- ous obstacles in the progress of the Gospel." (JR 18: 125) "This will be a stum- bling block," Father Le Jeune predicted. (JR 10:63) And so it was.

Young converts had their chastity tempted so often that, as one Huron said,   22 "I dread meeting women as I would an Iroquois." (JR 23: 165) They also found it difficult to find Indian spouses, as Father Le Jeune noted in 1638 when he resolved not to "hasten their baptism, because this would render it almost im- possible for them to find wives. . . . Until we have a village that is entirely

devoted to God, the marriages of our new Christians will occasion us difficulty." (JR 15: 125) As late as 1644 Father Vimont was still complaining that
"of all the Christian laws which we propound to them, there is not one that
seems so hard to them as that which forbids polygamy, and does not allow
them to break the bonds of lawful marriage . . . They no longer look upon
Christian marriage as an aid and comfort of human life, but as a servitude full
of vexation and bitterness. It is this that prevents most of the infidels from accepting the Faith, and has caused some to lose it who already embraced it."
(JR 25: 247–49)

The Christian way of life offered many other stumbling blocks for the Indi- 23
ans. Lenten fasting at the end of winter scarcity (even though the Sorbonne
declared the beaver to be a fish for religious purposes); discriminating between
people after death when in life they had been equals; burying the dead facing
east when the land of the dead lay west; pretending that Christians professed
the one true faith when missionaries from many denominations hawked their
spiritual wares; confining people in the "yoke of God" on the Sabbath when
the struggle for life required a full week; being obsessed by death and the afterlife, especially by the palpable threat of eternal torture by fire — all these
practices and more seemed simply unreasonable to a people who had been raised
in a religious tradition that was better adapted to the natural and social world
in which they lived.

While the Indians could have raised many objections to Christianity from 24
their cultural traditions — and often did when pushed far enough, usually only
sachems, speakers, or shamans chose to lock minds with the Europeans on their
own dialectical turf. Most simply deployed the ultimate Indian weapon against
aggressive Europeans, a weapon that has frustrated the best laid plans of white
men for four centuries. It doesn't have one name because it's made of many
things, so I'll let contemporaries describe it. Father Hennepin put it this way:
"That people, though so barbarous and rude, have a piece of civility peculiar
to themselves; for a man would be accounted very impertinent if he contra-
dicted anything that is said in their council, and if he does not approve the
greatest absurdity therein proposed. Notwithstanding this seeming approbation, they believe what they please and no more, and therefore 'tis impossible
to know when they are really persuaded of those things you have mentioned
to them, which I take to be one of the greatest obstructions to their conversion.
For their civility hindering them from making any objection, or contradicting
what is said to them, they seem to approve it, though perhaps they laugh at it
in private, or else never bestow a moment to reflect upon it, such being their
indifference to a future life." (Belknap 1877: 41–42) In describing the obstacles
to the conversion of the Ottawas, Father Allouez put a less charitable interpretation on it: "Dissimulation, which is natural to those Savages, and a certain
spirit of acquiescence, in which the children in that country are brought up,
make them assent to all that is told them; and prevent them from ever showing any opposition to the sentiments of others, even though they may know
that what is said to them is not true. To this dissimulation must be added
stubbornness and obstinacy in following entirely their own thoughts and
wishes." (JR 52: 203–205)

Either way, it was an outgrowth of the basic Indian toleration of other re- 25 ligions and the correspondent wish to pursue their own. "The *French* in general take us for Beasts," Adario told Lahontan, "the Jesuits Brand us for impious, foolish and ignorant Vagabonds. And to be even with you, we have the same thoughts of you; but with this difference, that *we* pity you without offering invectives." (Lahontan 1905: 570) It was true, as Lahontan knew; but being French, he persisted, like his countrymen, in the attempt to change the Indians. For the Europeans were never listening when the Indians asked, with mounting despair, "Do you not see that, as we inhabit a world so different from yours, there must be another heaven for us, and another road to reach it?" (Charlevoix 1870 II: 79)

REFERENCES CITED

Belknap, Jeremy. 1877. Letter to Ebenezer Hazard, 13 March 1780, *Collections of the Massachusetts Historical Society*, 5th series, vol. 2, pp. 41–43.

Belknap, Jeremy, and Jedidiah Morse. 1798. "The Report of a Committee of the Board of Correspondents of the Scots Society for Propagating Christian Knowledge, Who Visited the Oneida and Mohekunuh Indians in 1796, "*Collections of the Massachusetts Historical Society*, 1st series, vol. 5, pp. 12–32.

Charlevoix, Pierre de. 1870. *History and General Description of New France*, translated by John Gilmary Shea, New York, 6 vols.

Crèvecoeur, J. Hector St. John de. 1912. *Letters from an American Farmer* (1782), London: Everyman.

Duignan, Peter. 1958. "Early Jesuit Missionaries: A Suggestion for Further Study," *American Anthropologist*, vol. 60, no. 4, pp. 725–732.

Gray, Robert. 1609. *A Good Speed to Virginia*, London.

JR. 1896–1901. *The Jesuit Relations and Allied Documents*, edited by Reuben Gold Thwaites, Cleveland, 73 vols.

Johnson, Sir William. 1921–65. *The Papers of Sir William Johnson*, edited by James Sullivan *et al.*, Albany, 14 vols.

Lahontan, Baron de. 1905. *New Voyages to North-America* (1703), edited by Reuben Gold Thwaites, Chicago.

Lechford, Thomas. 1833. *Plain Dealing: or, Newes from New-England* (1642), in *Collections of the Massachusetts Historical Society*, 3rd series, vol. 3.

Le Clercq, Chrétien. 1881. *The First Establishment of the Faith in New France*, translated by John Gilmary Shea, New York, 2 vols.

Mather, Cotton. 1690. *The Way to Prosperity*, Boston. 1721. *India Christiana*, Boston.

Mayhew, Experience. 1727. *Indian Converts*, London.

Meginness, John Franklin. 1891. *Biography of Frances Slocum, The Lost Sister of Wyoming*, Williamsport, Pa.

Seaver, James E. 1961. *A Narrative of the Life of Mrs. Mary Jemison* (1823), edited by Allen W. Trelease, New York.

Willis, William, *et al.* (editors). 1869–1916. *Documentary History of the State of Maine, Collections of the Maine Historical Society*, 2nd series, 24 vols.

Considerations

1. Write a paragraph defending James L. Axtell's rather surprising title, surprising for a formal academic publication. Why is *autopsy* such a good word? Think of at least three reasons to include in your paragraph and illustrate them.

2. List all the differences between the English and the French missionaries as Axtell describes them.

3. In his second-to-last paragraph, Axtell refers to "the ultimate Indian weapon against aggressive Europeans, a weapon that has frustrated the best laid plans of white men for four centuries. It doesn't have one name because it's made

of many things. . . . ." If you were forced to come up with one name, one word, what would you choose to describe this ultimate Indian weapon? Write a paragraph proposing this one word and defending your choice with illustrations and explanation.

Connections

1. The Indian, Adario, asked the French Baron de Lahontan this question: "Do you not see that, as we inhabit a world so different from yours, there must be another heaven for us, and another road to reach it?" (para. 25) Acknowledging this different world requires "a world view perspective." Write a paper explaining A. Irving Hallowell's "Ojibwa Ontology, Behavior, and World View." Begin with a definition of *ontology* and then connect this definition to Hallowell's thesis. What is the main difference between the world the Ojibwa Indians inhabit and the world Anglo-Americans inhabit? What evidence does Hallowell give to support this thesis? Why, according to James L. Axtell, does it matter?
2. Alfonso Ortiz writes, "The importance of learning an Indian language cannot be overestimated, for it is the most reliable way to enter a people's world, to understand how they impose meaning and order upon their experience" (para. 10). Write a short essay, using the Hallowell text about the Ojibwa and the example of Father Sébastien Râle — the Jesuit missionary mentioned by Axtell — to illustrate Ortiz's point.
3. The European attempt to convert the Indians can be seen as a power struggle. Refer to the Machiavelli piece in Chapter 1, The Dimensions of Power, and then write an essay explaining this attempt to convert the Indians as a power struggle.

The Mythological Sources of Abenaki Catholicism: A Case Study of the Social History of Power

Kenneth M. Morrison

I. The Mythological Paradigm

Undeniably, religious power was widely shared within the egalitarian Abenaki   1
societies. Even well-known shamans found their authority questioned, ridiculed, and sometimes even challenged. But more to the point, while individuals wielded power, power itself was always an instrument either for social good
or communal malaise. Legitimate power — whether that of the hunter, warrior, shaman, or of any persons engaged in socially productive domestic tasks
— existed only for the people's welfare. Power might be abused, but ideally it
was sensitive to the needs of the small-scale Abenaki communities; as their
mythology demonstrates, among the Abenaki, community and religious practice were co-extensive.

The Abenakis' experience of post-contact events was rooted in their social   2
ideals — normative values so intense that folkloric accounts record the changing implications of their mythically-given religious order. Although concepts
of historical periodization may very well violate Abenaki thought about historical process, distinct types of moral challenge to their social solidarity characterize at least general trends in Abenaki history as the oral accounts establish. For example, mythic treatments of the original Abenaki condition
distinguish between that formative time and all others. . . . Shamanistic traditions fall into three temporal categories: the mythical age when such powers
flourished, and the historical period, and a time closely related to the present.
Thus, while the Abenaki themselves may not have thought of temporal categories in linear terms, the idea that their history falls into three general periods has some utility at least in defining particular kinds of moral struggle.
Their present time of trouble began at European contact when, suddenly, their
ethical order met new problems which tested its integrity. The present era
evolved from a middle period in which the Abenaki explored basic kinship values and applied them to preserve moral unity among their growing and ex-

*Kenneth M. Morrison currently teaches American Indian Religions in the De-
partment of Religious Studies, Arizona State University; previously he taught Indian history at UCLA. He is the author of* The Embattled Northeast *(published
by the University of California Press in 1984) and is now working on several projects in American Indian religious history.*

panding population. This central age rests in turn on a pivotal time of mythic transformation in which the world was cast into its present physical, biological, social, and moral condition. The great persons of the mythical period established the fundamental moral direction of Abenaki history.

Abenaki mythology does not describe the creation of the world itself. Instead, the physical world and the various beings who live above, upon, or under it are taken as givens. Yet the myths described a world which has a dynamism only dimly perceived in the second and third ages. Plasticity formed the world in the mythic age: living presences whose essence as persons was more important than their specific forms enlivened basic matter. The myths do not describe any polarity between good and evil: rather such moral qualities rest only in the singular actions of persons. Nevertheless, the Abenaki people found the mythic age challenging. Human beings had not yet found their proper place in a world peopled by hostile beings in their plant, animal, and even inanimate guises. Some beings, however, worked for the Abenakis' well-being, and their altruism grounded the events of the mythic period. This was especially true of Gluskabe, the central figure of Abenaki mythology, whose acts made the world hospitable for the Abenaki peoples.

Abenaki mythology describes a system of social dynamics which was quite different from the mythic assumptions of European world-views. In the Abenakis' mythic age, men and animals were not co-operative, but they were essentially alike. There was no Abenaki Adam to name animals, and thus to give human beings dominion over them. In the primary age, men and animals shared the same nature, and they lived with, and married one another, without distinction. Similarly, the Abenaki had no belief comparable to the Hebraic-Christian fall from grace; human sin did not shatter the amity of the initial world. Gluskabe shared no character traits with Adam. Gluskabe exposed the evil exercise of power for all to see, and he established an ethical system which could contain it. Adam did neither.

Gluskabe taught the Abenaki that evil came from disordered social relations, and their mythology encapsulated that understanding. Evil power was inherent in the world, and it had to be countered. In a Passamaquoddy account, Gluskabe had an evil twin brother, Malsum, the Wolf. Unlike Gluskabe, who was born naturally, Malsum thrust himself into the world through his mother's flesh, killing her in the process. Gluskabe's first positive act for humankind occurred when he killed his obstreperous brother. In a Penobscot myth, Gluskabe had three brothers who were intensely jealous of him, but he vanquished them in games which tested their respective powers.

Orphaned, even Gluskabe had to learn the powers of good and evil from his grandmother, Woodchuck, who raised him. Gluskabe was an exuberant adolescent, well-intentioned but not always aware of his impact on the world. While Woodchuck easily taught Gluskabe to hunt, to fish, and to make snowshoes, she had more trouble with moral concepts. For example, Gluskabe carried his concern for his grandmother's welfare to enthusiastic extremes. To make food readily available for Woodchuck, he seized all the animals and trapped all of the fish behind a huge weir. Woodchuck appreciated the help but scolded Gluskabe for his excesses: If all the animals and fish were dead, she asked, "what will our descendants in the future do to live?" Gluskabe repaired his error and learned his lesson. Woodchuck proclaimed proudly: "He will be a great magician. He will do great wonders for our descendants as he goes on. . . ." In their awareness of his personal growth, Gluskabe dignified the Abenakis' sense of their own faltering struggle toward responsible power.

Gluskabe did become more judicious as he matured. The world was full of beings who did as they pleased without concern for people's welfare. As one tale says of Lox: "Now he was a great magician, though little to other folks' good." Gluskabe set about transforming the world and forcing such persons to conform to the moral purposefulness of human activity. He cajoled the giant bird, Culloo, to flap his wings less vigorously to moderate the winds. Gluskabe stole tobacco from Grasshopper who had refused to share it with people. With the help of Summer, Gluskabe overcame the worst effects of Winter. He examined the animals to be sure that they could not take unfair advantage of human beings. Some of them, like hostile Squirrel and Beaver, were too large, and Gluskabe reduced them to their present size. In all that he accomplished, Gluskabe modified the world to human measure.

He did a great deal more. In order to ensure the happiness of the people, Gluskabe showed them proper moral conduct, teaching them the rules that should govern their relations with other-than-human persons, as well as with each other. Gluskabe taught magnanimity as the primary ethical principle. Seven of his neighbours kidnapped his grandfather and left Gluskabe to die. Determined upon revenge, Gluskabe caught the culprits, but then he perceived that they were frightened. "Because he is good natured. . . ." the myth recounts, "he pities and forgives them." Such social responsibility and freely-exercised compassion were the keys to Gluskabe's power. The strict rules requiring the Abenaki to be generous with one another have their source in Gluskabe's example. A. I. Hallowell noted similarly of the Ojibwa that their moral stress on hospitality "is illustrated by the fact that other-than-human persons share their power with human beings." Morality and social mutuality were synonymous for the Abenaki peoples.

The moral principles of social cooperation which Gluskabe taught suffused Abenaki culture. For example, the Abenaki derive both their concept of land "ownership," and indirectly their social organization, from Gluskabe. Among the Penobscots, Maliseets and Passamaquoddies, one myth relates that once a giant frog held all of the world's water in its belly. When the frog refused to consider the people's plight, Gluskabe slew him and released the water which flows in northeastern streams and rivers. Many of the people could not control their thirst and rushing into the water were transformed into aquatic animals — lobsters, crabs, eels, whales, frogs, yellow perch, and sturgeon. The survivors took the names of their altered relatives' new forms and chose hunting territories adjacent to the new watercourses. The extended Abenaki kinship group — human and animal alike — remained bonded despite persistent differences in outward appearance. The Penobscots used a special word to describe the intimacy which continued to exist between humans and their animal kin: the term *ntu 'tem* "my spouse's parents," or in another sense "my partner of a strange race," referred to animal relatives. The term also suggests, Dr. Peter Paul observes, the family lines related through intermarriage.

The *ntu 'tem* relationships expressed with everyday immediacy the interests 10 which humans and other-than-human persons shared in the middle age of Abenaki history. When Gluskabe left the world, his power — *ktaha 'ndo* — continued as the "source of dynamics" of Abenaki life. Once Gluskabe completed his world transformation for Abenaki habitation, the world became much less fluid. Yet the myths embody a practical sense of the individual's enduring responsibility for the social welfare of the human group and its animal relatives. Gluskabe had not intended to establish a world order in which collective struggle was no longer necessary; rather, "he wanted to show the man that he must not always wait for spiritual help, but do the things with his own labour, only appealing to spiritual power when necessity requires it." In fact, in the second age, the Abenaki faced unprecedented tensions as their numbers increased and the people dispersed across the land. Gluskabe had demonstrated the fundamental principles of moral solidarity but he "did not recommend any system of organization under which the people might live." The Abenaki found their way in confronting perplexity: in the middle age they learned through trial and error, and with the aid of No-chi-gar-neh the spirit of the air, to use medicinal plants, to heed the dream spirits of sleep and trance, and to wield shamanistic powers of transformation and communication with animals. "You shall be great men among your people," No-chi-gar-neh said to the first shamans, "because your works shall bring great comfort to yourselves [and] also to all your people, for you shall be useful to them." No-chi-gar-neh also added an ominous admonition which defined the moral parameters of Abenaki experience:

> Being great, great must be your care in keeping yourselves in this greatness. You must never allow yourselves to become so small as to use your power upon or against your brother on any contention. Do not abuse one another with this power . . . because whoever abuses this power shall lose it.

The shamans linked the first and second ages of Abenaki history. While ordinary people lost much of their power to change form and to speak with other-than-human persons, the *made 'olinouk*, the shamans, had power to bridge the resulting void between humans and other persons. The shamanistic relationship with a *baohi· 'gan*, or spirit helper, retained and funneled power from the mythical era. The shaman considered a *baohi· 'gan* as part of himself and such interpersonal solidarity moulded shamanistic power, as it had Gluskabe's.   *11*

The shamans remembered and recorded the Abenaki cosmos. They recounted the mythic past and through esoteric rituals repaired other-worldly relations. They also integrated the bonds between ordinary and other-than-human persons into the entire ritualistic structure by interpreting the dreams in which such persons appeared. The shaman's medicinal powers stemmed from the same concern for interpersonal relations. The Abenaki, along with other Algonkians, believed that social disorder caused disease. The shamans either placated or thwarted malevolent persons, or indicated to the afflicted person and his relatives the means to ease some interpersonal affront.   *12*

Slowly in the middle age, the institutional structures of the Abenaki world emerged from this human/non-human sociality which bound man and other persons to mutual responsibility and obligation. Tribal myth, folklore, and practical experience recounted the essential ties between man and other beings and warned of dreadful consequences for failure to respect the integrity of both   *13* other-than-human and human persons. Complex prohibitions and a positive sense that the two worlds were intimately connected gave meaning to the Abenaki food cycle. Ritual surrounded hunting, fishing and agricultural activities. The Abenaki explained to the animal or plant that the taking of life was necessary. He carefully prepared himself to hunt, summoning personal power to ensure success, and he ritually acknowledged the life he took. Abenaki subsistence activities were thus sacral practices; the welfare of the hunting band depended on the proper social orientation of the individual.

These religious convictions continued to inform Abenaki life, even after their 14
present age began with European contact. At that time, the Abenakis' long-established moral order found itself beset by continuous and cumulative challenge, if only because of the mythological assumption that 'every stranger was a potential magical antagonist.' While neither European sources nor Abenaki traditions expose adequately the moral impact of the early contact years on the Abenaki societies, they do indicate generally the Abenakis' internal struggle to deal constructively with a greatly expanded world. Both French and English documents report widespread warfare between the Algonkians and the Iroquois of the St. Lawrence River valley, and even among the Algonkians of coastal New England and Atlantic Canada intertribal hostilities predominated. Although these events cannot be precisely reconstructed, Penobscot Abenaki traditions suggest that internal disagreements were as important as intertribal economic competition for control of the European fur trade. Until European contact, Penobscot traditions relate, Abenaki shamans had "never showed among themselves any other kind of feeling only that was kind and brotherly"; thereafter shamanistic rivalries rent the moral unity of the Abenaki peoples.

In their initial effort to gauge the nature of the European intruders, the 15
Abenaki chose some noted shamans "to watch the strange people's movements." The selection of these observers unfortunately sparked vicious disagreements among the Abenaki; shamans who had not been chosen for public service succumbed to jealousy, and they "began to agitate the minds of their friends to discord, each of them having a large influence among the people, [and] the whole country was thrown into different bands." Ignoring their elders who "advised peace and harmony," the disappointed shamans moved aggressively against their rivals, despite No-chi-gar-neh's warning that power abused would be lost. Among the Kennebec Abenaki the shamans not only used their powers to kill the English settlers of the 1607 Popham colony, they also threatened to inflict sickness on any of their countrymen who collaborated with the newcomers.

The third age of Abenaki history thus began with the people divided, with 16
intense shamanistic rivalries, and with the fundamental principles of power violated. To their own way of thinking, precisely these departures from tradition made the Abenaki especially vulnerable to two external contact factors, liquor and disease, which added to the inexorable erosion of the kinship solidarity which Gluskabe had taught. Admittedly, the Abenaki were physiologically incapable of resisting European diseases but, had they been morally united, they might have weathered the crisis of faith which followed. Although many

people morally resisted, the traditionalists could not challenge the personal and social disruptions which sickness and drinking unleashed. The illnesses, they knew were symptomatic of their moral decline, and drinking was a vivid pantomime of the larger, internal social disorders. After European settlement, the Abenaki became more aware of violations of their mythically based social order and increasingly reeled before the consequences.

Considerations

1. Kenneth M. Morrison refers to the "mythically based social order" (para. 16) of the Abenaki. Is our present-day American society mythically based? Write an essay answering this question and identifying the myth you perceive our society to be based on.
2. In many ways the Abenaki's central mythological figure, Gluskabe, is similar to Jesus in the Christian Bible. Make a list of similarities between Gluskabe and Jesus, and another list of differences between the two figures. Then write two paragraphs, one comparing the two figures, and one contrasting them.
3. Morrison claims that the Abenaki Indians derive their concept of land ownership from the mythological person, Gluskabe. Write a short paragraph explaining why Morrison puts quotation marks around the term *ownership*.
4. Write a paragraph explaining the connection between the mythological person Gluskabe and the Abenaki's concept of land ownership.
5. Where do you think present-day Anglo-Americans get their concept of land ownership? Write a paragraph in which you present your hunch. Start with this hunch (also called a hypothesis) about the origin of contemporary American attitudes towards land ownership and then write several more sentences of evidence to help prove your point.

Connections

1. The seventeenth-century French saw Indian shamans as frauds and jugglers. How did the Indians see the shaman? Write a paragraph explaining the shaman as a medical healer. Draw on the articles by Kenneth M. Morrison and James L. Axtell for evidence to support your answer.
2. Write a paragraph contrasting the Abenaki Indians' beliefs about the beginnings of the world with the Pueblo Indians' beliefs as Alfonso Ortiz describes them.
3. Refer to Chapter 10, The Fairy Tale Snow White, and then explain whether or not you think the Abenaki stories about Gluskabe are fairy tales.

Chronology for a Dreamer

Arthur Kopit

1846   William F. Cody born in Le Claire, Iowa, on February 26.

1866   Geronimo surrenders.

1868   William Cody accepts employment to provide food for railroad workers; kills 4,280 buffaloes. Receives nickname "Buffalo Bill."

1869   *Buffalo Bill, the King of the Border Men*, a dime novel by Ned Buntline, makes Buffalo Bill a national hero.

1872   Expedition west in honor of Grand Duke Alexis of Russia, Buffalo Bill as guide.

1876   Battle at the Little Big Horn; Custer killed.

1877   Chief Joseph surrenders.

1878   Buffalo Bill plays himself in *Scouts of the Plains*, a play by Ned Buntline.

1879   Wild Bill Hickok joins Buffalo Bill on the stage.

1883   Sitting Bull surrenders, is sent to Standing Rock Reservation.

1883   "Buffalo Bill's Wild West Show" gives first performance, is great success.

1885   Sitting Bull allowed to join Wild West Show, tours with company for a year.

1886   United States Commission visits Standing Rock Reservation to investigate Indian grievances.

1890   Sitting Bull assassinated, December 15.

1890   Wounded Knee Massacre, December 25.

The play derives, in part, from this chronology but does not strictly adhere to it.–A.K.

Arthur Kopit (b. 1937) is an American playwright who, in 1960, may have written the play with the longest title: Oh Dad, Poor Dad, Mamma's Hung You in the Closet and I'm Feelin' So Sad: A Pseudoclassical Farce in a Bastard French Tradition. Indians *is a dramatic reconstruction, based in part upon contemporary documents, of several historical incidents. Scenes 2 and 11 present a portion of the hearings conducted in 1886 by a U.S. Commission investigating Indian grievances. Sitting Bull, chief of the Sioux, had been present at the Battle of the Little Big Horn — Custer's Last Stand — in 1876; he was ultimately assassinated by U.S. agents in 1890.*

Scenes 2 and 11 from *Indians*

Scene 2

(Light up on SITTING BULL. *He is dressed simply — no feathered headdress. It is winter.)*

SITTING BULL

I am Sitting Bull! . . . In the moon of the first snow-falling, in the year half   *1*
my people died from hunger, the Great Father sent three wise men . . . to investigate the conditions of our reservation, though we'd been promised he would come himself.

(Lights up on SENATORS LOGAN, MORGAN, *and* DAWES; *they are flanked by armed* SOLDIERS. *Opposite them, in a semicircle, are* SITTING BULL'*s people, all huddling in tattered blankets from the cold.)*

SENATOR LOGAN

Indians! Please be assured that this committee has not come to punish you or   *2*
take away any of your land but only to hear your grievances, determine if they are just. And if so, remedy them. For we, like the Great Father, wish only the best for our Indian children.

(The SENATORS *spread out various legal documents.)*

SITTING BULL

They were accompanied by . . . my friend, William Cody —   *3*
(Enter BUFFALO BILL, *collar of his overcoat turned up for the wind.)*
in whose Wild West Show I'd once appeared . . .
*(*BUFFALO BILL *greets a number of the* INDIANS.*)*
in exchange for some food, a little clothing. And a beautiful horse that could do tricks.

SENATOR MORGAN

Colonel Cody has asked if he might say a few words before testimony begins.   *4*

SENATOR LOGAN

We would be honored.   *5*

BUFFALO BILL

(To the INDIANS.*)*
My . . . brothers.   *6*
(Pause.)
I know how disappointed you all must be that the Great Father isn't here; I apologize for having said I thought I . . . could bring him.
(Pause.)
However! The three men I *have* brought are by far his most trusted personal representatives. And I promise that talking to them will be the same as . . .
(Pause. Softly.)
. . . talking to him.
(Long pause; he rubs his eyes as if to soothe a headache.)
To . . . Sitting Bull, then . . .
(He stares at SITTING BULL.*)*
. . . I would like to say that I hope you can overlook your . . . disappointment.

And remember what is at *stake* here. And not get angry . . . or too impatient.
(Pause.)
Also, I hope you will ask your people to speak with open hearts when talking
to these men. And treat them with the same great respect I have always . . .
shown . . . to you, for these men have come to *help* you and your people. And
I am afraid they may be the only ones left, now, who can.

SITTING BULL

And though there were many among us who wanted to speak first: men like   7
Red Cloud! And Little Hawk! And He-Who-Hears-Thunder! And Crazy Horse!
Men who were great warriors, and had counted many coups! And been with
us at the Little Big Horn when we *KILLED CUSTER!* . . .
(Pause.)
I would not let them speak. . . . For they were like me, and tended to get an-
gry, easily.
(Pause.)
Instead, I asked the *young* man, John Grass, who had never fought at all, but
had been to the white man's school at Carlisle. And *thought* he understood . . .
something . . . of their ways.

BUFFALO BILL

Sitting Bull would like John Grass to speak first.   8

LOGAN

Call John Grass.   9

BUFFALO BILL

John Grass! Come forward.   10

(Enter JOHN GRASS *in a black cutaway many sizes too small for him. He wears an
Indian shirt. Around his neck is a medal.)*

JOHN GRASS

Brothers! I am going to talk about what the Great Father told us a long time   11
ago. He told us to give up hunting and start farming. So we did as he said, and
our people grew hungry. For the land was suited to grazing not farming, and
even if we'd been farmers, nothing could have grown. So the Great Father said
he would send us food and clothing, but nothing came of it. So we asked him
for the money he had promised us when we sold him the Black Hills, thinking,
with this money we could *buy* food and clothing. But nothing came of it. So
we grew ill and sad. . . . So to help us from this sadness, he sent Bishop Marty,
to teach us to be Christians. But when we told him we did not wish to be
Christians but wished to be like our fathers, and dance the sundance, and fight
bravely against the Shawnee and the Crow! And pray to the Great Spirits who
made the four winds, and the earth, and made man from the dust of this earth,
Bishop Marty hit us! . . . So we said to the Great Father that we thought we
would like to go *back* to hunting, because to live, we needed food. But we found
that while we had been learning to farm, the buffalo had gone away. And the
plains were filled now only with their bones. . . . Before we give you any more
of our land, or move from here where the people we loved are growing white
in their coffins, we want you to tell the Great Father to give us, who still live,
what he promised he would! *No more than that.*

SITTING BULL

I prayed for the return of the buffalo!   12

(*Lights fade to black on everyone but* BUFFALO BILL.
Distant gunshot heard offstage.
Pause.
Two more gunshots.
Lights to black on BUFFALO BILL.)

Scene 11

(*Lights up on reservation, as when last seen.*
The INDIANS *are laughing; the* SENATORS, *rapping for silence.*)
    SENATOR DAWES
What in God's name do they think we're doing here?   *13*
    BUFFALO BILL
(*To* SITTING BULL.)
Please! You must tell them to stop this *noise!*   *14*
    SITTING BULL
You told us you would bring the Great Father.   *15*
    BUFFALO BILL
I told you! He couldn't come! It's not my fault! Besides, these men are the Great *16*
Father's representatives! Talking to them is like talking to him!
    SITTING BULL
If the Great Father wants us to believe he is wise, why does he send us men *17*
who are *stupid?*
    BUFFALO BILL
They're *not* stupid! They just don't see things the way *you* do!   *18*
    SITTING BULL
Yes. Because they are stupid.   *19*
    BUFFALO BILL
They're *not stupid!*   *20*
    SITTING BULL
Then they must be blind. It is the only other explanation.   *21*
    BUFFALO BILL
All right. Tell me. Do *you* understand them?   *22*
    SITTING BULL
Why should I want to understand men who are stupid?   *23*
    BUFFALO BILL
Because if you *don't*, your people will *starve to death*.   *24*
(*Long pause.*)
All right. . . . Now. Let me try to explain some . . . *basics.*
(*To the* SENATORS.)
Well, as you've just seen, the Indian can be hard t' figure. What's one thing t'
us is another t' him. For example, farmin'. Now the *real* problem here is not
poor soil. The real problem's plowin'. Ya see, the Indian believes the earth is
sacred and sees plowin' as a sacrilegious act. Well, if ya can't get 'em t' plow,
how can ya teach 'em farmin'? Impossible. Fertile land's another problem. There
just ain't much of it, an' what there is, the Indians prefer to use for pony racin'.
Naturally, it's been explained to 'em how people can race ponies anywhere,
but they *prefer* the fertile land. They say, if their ancestors raced ponies there,

that's where *they* must race. . . . Another difficult problem is land itself. The majority of 'em, ya see, don't understand how land can be owned, since they believe the land was made by the Great Spirits for the benefit of everyone. So, when we do buy land from 'em, they think it's just some kind o' temporary loan, an' figure we're kind o' foolish fer payin' good money for it, much as someone 'ud seem downright foolish t' us who paid money fer the sky, say, or the ocean. Which . . . causes problems.

(Pause.)

Well, what I'm gettin' at is *this:* if *their* way o' seein' is hard fer *us* t' follow, ours is just as hard fer *them*. . . . There's an old Indian legend that when the first white man arrived, he asked some Indians for enough land t' put his blanket down onto fer the night. So they said yes. An' next thing they knew, he'd unraveled this blanket till it was one long piece o' thread. Then he laid out the thread, an' when he was done, he'd roped off a couple o'square miles. Well, the Indian finds that sort o' behavior hard t' understand. That's all I have t' say. Maybe, if you think about it, some good'll finally come from all this. I dunno.

SENATOR MORGAN

Thank you. We *shall* think about it. And hope the Indians think about it, too.   *25*
And cause no more disturbances like the one just now. . . . Ask Sitting Bull if he has anything to say.

BUFFALO BILL

Sitting Bull.   *26*

SITTING BULL

Of course I will speak if they desire me to. I suppose it is only such men as   *27*
they desire who may say anything.

SENATOR LOGAN

Anyone here may speak. If you have something to say, we will listen. Other-   *28*
wise, sit down.

SITTING BULL

Tell me, do you know who I am, that you talk as you do?   *29*

BUFFALO BILL

SITTING BULL, PLEASE!   *30*

(Long pause.)

SITTING BULL

I wish to say that I fear I spoke hastily just now. In calling you . . . stupid. For   *31*
my friend William Cody tells me you are here with good intentions. So I ask forgiveness for my unthinking words, which might have caused you to wreak vengeance on my people for what was not their doing, but *mine, alone.*

SENATOR LOGAN

We are pleased you speak so . . . sensibly. You are . . . forgiven.   *32*

SITTING BULL

I shall tell you, then, what I want you to say to the Great Father for me. And I   *33*
shall tell you everything that is in my heart. For I know the Great Spirits are looking down on me today and want me to tell you everything that is in my heart. For you are the only people now who can help us.

(Pause.)

My children . . . are dying. They have no warm clothes, and their food is gone. The old way is gone. No longer can they follow the buffalo and live where they wish. I have prayed to the Great Spirits to send us back the buffalo, but I have

not yet seen any buffalo returning. So I know the old way is gone. I think . . . my children must learn a *new* way if they are to live. Therefore, tell the Great Father that if he wishes us to live like white men, we will do so.
(Stunned reaction from his Indians. He silences them with a wave of his hand.)
For I know that if that pleases him, we will benefit. I am looking always to the benefit of my children, and so, want only to please the Great Father. . . . Therefore, tell him for me that I have never yet seen a white man starving, so he should send us food so we can live like the white man, as he wants. Tell him, also, we'd like some healthy cattle to butcher — I wish to kill three hundred head at a time. For that is the way the white man lives, and we want to please the Great Father and live the same way. Also, ask him to send us each six teams of mules, because that is the way the white men make a living, and I want my children to make as good a living. I ask for these things only because I was advised to follow your ways. I do not ask for anything that is not needed. Therefore, tell him to send each person here a horse and buggy. And four yokes of oxen and a wagon to haul wood in, since I have never yet seen a white man dragging wood by hand. Also, hogs, male and female, and male and female sheep for my children to raise from. If I leave anything out in the way of animals that the white men have, it is a mistake, for I want every one of them! For we are great Indians, and therefore should be no less great as white men. . . . Furthermore, tell him to send us warm clothing. And glass for the windows. And toilets. And clean water. And beds, and blankets, and pillows. And fur coats, and gloves. And hats. And *pretty silk ties*. As you see, I do not ask for anything that is not needed. For the Great Father has advised us to live like white men, so clearly, this is how we should live. For it is your doing that we are here on this reservation, and it is not right for us to live in poverty. And be treated like beasts. . . . That is all I have to say.

SENATOR LOGAN

I want to say something to that man before he sits down, and I want all the   34
Indians to listen very carefully to what I'm going to tell him. . . . Sitting Bull,
this committee invited you to come here for a friendly talk. When you talked,
however, you insulted them. I understand this is not the first time you have
been guilty of such an offense.

SITTING BULL

Do you know who I am that you talk the way you do?   35

SENATOR LOGAN

I know you are Sitting Bull.   36

SITTING BULL

Do you really not recognize me? Do you really not know who I am?   37

SENATOR LOGAN

I said, I know you are Sitting Bull!   38

SITTING BULL

You know I am Sitting Bull. But do you know what *position* I hold?   39

SENATOR DAWES

We do not recognize any difference between you and other Indians.   40

SITTING BULL

Then I will tell you the difference. So you will never ever make this mistake   41
again. I am here by the will of the Great Spirits, and by their will I am a chief.
My heart is red and sweet, and I know it is sweet, for whatever I pass near tries

to touch me with its tongue, as the bear tastes honey and the green leaves lick the sky. If the Great Spirits have chosen anyone to be leader of their country, know that it is not the Great Father; *it is myself.*

SENATOR DAWES

WHO IS THIS CREATURE? 42

SITTING BULL

I will show you. 43

(He raises his hand. The INDIANS *turn and start to leave.)*

SENATOR LOGAN

Just a minute, Sitting Bull! 44

(SITTING BULL *stops.*)

Let's get something straight. You said to this committee that you were chief of 45 all the people of this country and that you were appointed chief by the Great Spirits. Well, I want to say that you were *not* appointed by the Great Spirits. Appointments are not made that way. Furthermore, I want to say that you are arrogant and stupidly proud, for you are not a great chief of this country or any other; that you have no following, no power, no control, and no right to any control.

SITTING BULL

I wish to say a word about my not being a chief, having no authority, being 46 proud —

SENATOR LOGAN

You are on an Indian reservation merely at the sufferance of the Government. 47 You are fed by the Government, clothed by the Government; your children are educated by the Government, and all you have and are today is because of the Government. I merely say these things to notify you that you cannot insult the people of the United States of America or its committees. And I want to say to the rest of you that you must learn that you are the equals of other men and must not let this one man lead you astray. You must stand up to him and not permit him to insult people who have come all this way just to help you. . . . That is all I have to say.

SITTING BULL

I wish to say a word about my not being a chief, having no authority, being 48 proud, and considering myself a great man in general.

SENATOR LOGAN

We do not care to talk with you any more today. 49

SENATOR DAWES

Next Indian. 50

SITTING BULL

I said, I wish to speak about my having no authority, being not a chief, and — 51

SENATOR LOGAN

I said, we've heard enough of you today! 52

(SITTING BULL *raises his hand; the* INDIANS *leave.*

SITTING BULL *stares at* CODY.)

SITTING BULL

If a man is the chief of a great people, and has lived only for those people, and 53 has done many great things for them, *of course he should be proud!*

(He exits.

Lights fade to black.)

Considerations

1. Arthur Kopit's selection begins with "Chronology for a Dreamer." What is a *chronology*? Write a paragraph defining *chronology* and *history* and explain the similarities and differences between them.
2. Much of Kopit's script is taken word for word from congressional records. Write a short essay in which you explain why this play is or is not good history writing.

Connections

1. Read the selection by Studs Terkel in Chapter 5, The Working World. Given the insights in this passage, to what extent do you think Arthur Kopit's play, like Terkel's interviews, is legitimate history? If you think the Kopit selection and the Terkel selection are not comparable, then explain why not.
2. After reading Chapter 4, The Urban Experience, try to determine the reason(s) why Indian cultures face such troubles adapting to urban life. Use testimony from John Grass, Buffalo Bill, and Sitting Bull (as Kopit records it in his play) as evidence to help prove your point.

Interview with Sitting Bull
New York Herald, November 16, 1877

Fort Walsh, Northwest Territory,
October 17, 1877.

The conference between Sitting Bull and the United States Commissioners   *1*
was not, as will presently be seen, the most interesting conference of the day. Sitting Bull and his chiefs so hated the "Americans," especially the American officers, that they had nothing for them but the disdain evinced in the speeches I have reported to you. After the talk with Generals Terry and Lawrence the Indians retired to their quarters.

But through the intercession of Major Walsh, Sitting Bull was persuaded at   *2*
nightfall to hold a special conference with me. It was explained to him that I was not his enemy, but that I was his good friend. He was told by Major Walsh that I was a great paper chief who talked with a million tongues to all the people in the world. Said the Major: "This man is a man of wonderful medicine; he speaks and the people on this side and across the great water open their ears and hear him. He tells the truth; he does not lie. He wishes to make the world know what a great tribe is encamped here on the land owned by the White Mother. He wants it to be understood that her guests are mighty warriors. The Long Haired Chief (alluding to General Custer) was his friend. He

wants to hear from you how he fought and whether he met death like a brave."

"Agh-howgh!" (It is well) said Sitting Bull.   *3*

He finally agreed to come, after dark, to the quarters which had been as-   *4*
signed to me, on the condition that nobody should be present except himself,
his interlocutor, Major Walsh, two interpreters and the stenographer I had employed for the occasion.

Sitting Bull As He Appears

At the appointed time, half-past eight, the lamps were lighted, and the most   *5*
mysterious Indian chieftain who ever flourished in North America was ushered
in by Major Walsh, who locked the door behind him. This was the first time
that Sitting Bull had condescended, not merely to visit but to address a white
man from the United States. During the long years of his domination he had
withstood, with his bands, every attempt on the part of the United States government at a compromise of interests. He had refused all proffers, declined any
treaty. He had never been beaten in a battle with United States troops: on the
contrary, his warriors had been victorious over the pride of our army. Pressed
hard, he had retreated, scorning the factions of his bands who accepted the
terms offered them with the same bitterness with which he scorned his white
enemies.

Here he stood, his blanket rolled back, his head upreared, his right mocca-   *6*
sin put forward, his right hand thrown across his chest.

I arose and approached him, holding out both hands. He grasped them cor-   *7*
dially.

"How!" said he.   *8*

"How!"   *9*

And now let me attempt a better portrait of Sitting Bull than I was able to   *10*
despatch to you at headlong haste by the telegraph. He is about five feet ten
inches high. He was clad in a black and white calico shirt, black cloth leggings,
and moccasins, magnificently embroidered with beads and porcupine quills.
He held in his left hand a foxskin cap, its brush drooping to his feet.

I turned to the interpreter and said — "Explain again to Sitting Bull that he   *11*
is with a friend."

The interpreter explained.   *12*

"Banee!" said the chief, holding out his hand again and pressing mine.   *13*

Major Walsh here said: "Sitting Bull is in the best mood now that you could   *14*
possibly wish. Proceed with your questions and make them as logical as you
can. I will assist you and trip you up occasionally if you are likely to irritate
him."

Then the dialogue went on. I give it literally.   *15*

"I Am No Chief."

"You are a great chief," said I to Sitting Bull, "but you live behind a cloud.   *16*
Your face is dark; my people do not see it. Tell me, do you hate the Americans
very much?"

A gleam as of fire shot across his face.   *17*

"I am no chief."   *18*

This was precisely what I expected. It will dissipate at once the erroneous *19*
idea which has prevailed that Sitting Bull is either a chief or a warrior.

"What are you?"   *20*

"I am," said he, crossing both hands upon his chest, slightly nodding and *21*
smiling satirically, "a man."

"What does he mean?" I inquired, turning to Major Walsh.   *22*

"He means," responded the Major, "to keep you in ignorance of his secret if *23*
he can. His position among his bands is anomalous. His own tribes, the Uncpapas, are not all in fealty to him. Parts of nearly twenty different tribes of
Sioux besides a remnant of the Uncpapas, abide with him. So far as I have
learned he rules over these fragments of tribes, which compose his camp of
2,500, including between 800 and 900 warriors, by sheer compelling force of
intellect and will. I believe that he understands nothing particularly of war or
military tactics, at least not enough to give him the skill or the right to command warriors in battle. He is supposed to have guided the fortunes of several
battles, including the fight in which Custer fell. That supposition, as you will
presently find, is partially erroneous. His word was always potent in the camp
or in the field, but he has usually left to the war chiefs the duties appertaining
to engagements. When the crisis came he gave his opinion, which was accepted as law."

"What was he, then?" I inquired, continuing this momentary dialogue with *24*
Major Walsh. "Was he, is he, a mere medicine man?"

"Don't for the world," replied the Major, "intimate to him, in the questions *25*
you are about to ask him, that you have derived the idea from me, or from any
one, that he is a mere medicine man. He would deem that to be a profound
insult. In point of fact he is a medicine man, but a far greater, more influential
medicine man than any savage I have ever known. . . . He speaks. They listen
and they obey. Now let us hear what his explanation will be."

A Savage Companion

"You say you are no chief?"   *26*

"No!" with considerable hauteur.   *27*

"Are you a head soldier?"   *28*

"I am nothing — neither a chief nor a soldier."   *29*

"What? Nothing?"   *30*

"Nothing."   *31*

"What, then, makes the warriors of your camp, the great chiefs who are here *32*
along with you, look up to you so? Why do they think so much of you?"

Sitting Bull's lips curled with a proud smile.   *33*

"Oh, I used to be a kind of a chief, but the Americans made me go away *34*
from my father's hunting ground."

"You do not love the Americans?"   *35*

You should have seen this savage's lips.   *36*

"I saw to-day that all the warriors around you clapped their hands and cried *37*
out when you spoke. What you said appeared to please them. They liked you.

They seemed to think that what you said was right for them to say. If you are not a great chief, why do these men think so much of you?"

At this Sitting Bull, who had in the meantime been leaning back against the   38
wall, assumed a posture of mingled toleration and disdain.

"Your people look up to men because they are rich; because they have much   39
land, many lodges, many squaws?"

"Yes."   40

"Well, I suppose my people look up to me because I am poor. That is the   41
difference."

In this answer was concentrated all the evasiveness natural to an Indian.   42

"What is your feeling toward the Americans now?"   43

He did not even deign an answer. He touched his hip where his knife was.   44

I asked the interpreter to insist on an answer.   45

"Listen," said Sitting Bull, not changing his posture but putting his right   46
hand out upon my knee. "I told them today what my notions were — that I
did not want to go back there. Every time that I had any difficulty with them
they struck me first. I want to live in peace."

"Have you an implacable enmity to the Americans? Would you live with   47
them in peace if they allowed you to do so; or do you think that you can only
obtain peace here?"

"I Bought Them."

"The White Mother° is good."   48
"Better than the Great Father?"   49
"Howgh!"   50

And then, after a pause, Sitting Bull continued; — "They asked me to-day   51
to give them my horses. I bought my horses, and they are mine. I bought them
from men who came up the Missouri in macinaws. They do not belong to the
government; neither do the rifles. The rifles are also mine. I bought them; I
paid for them. Why I should give them up I do not know. I will not give them
up."

"Do you really think, do your people believe, that it is wise to reject the   52
proffers that have been made to you by the United States Commissioners? Do
not some of you feel as if you were destined to lose your old hunting grounds?
Don't you see that you will probably have the same difficulty in Canada that
you have had in the United States?"

"The White Mother does not lie."   53

"Do you expect to live here by hunting? Are there buffaloes enough? Can   54
your people subsist on the game here?"

"I don't know; I hope so."   55

"If not, are any part of your people disposed to take up agriculture? Would   56
any of them raise steers and go to farming?"

"I don't know."   57

"What will they do, then?"   58

°Canada, technically Queen Victoria.

"As long as there are buffaloes that is the way we will live."   *59*
"But the time will come when there will be no more buffaloes."   *60*
"Those are the words of an American."   *61*

Poisoned With Blood

"How long do you think the buffaloes will last?"   *62*

Sitting Bull arose. "We know," said he, extending his right hand with an   *63* impressive gesture, "that on the other side the buffaloes will not last very long. Why? Because the country there is poisoned with blood — a poison that kills all the buffaloes or drives them away. It is strange," he continued, with his peculiar smile, "that the Americans should complain that the Indians kill buffaloes. We kill buffaloes, as we kill other animals, for food and clothing, and to make our lodges warm. They kill buffaloes — for what? Go through your country. See the thousands of carcasses rotting on the Plains. Your young men shoot for pleasure. All they take from dead buffalo is his tail, or his head, or his horns, perhaps, to show they have killed a buffalo. What is this? Is it robbery? You call us savages. What are they? The buffaloes have come North. We have come North to find them, and to get away from a place where people tell lies."

To gain time and not to dwell importunately on a single point, I asked Sit-   *64* ting Bull to tell me something of his early life. In the first place, where he was born?

"I was born on the Missouri River; at least I recollect that somebody told   *65* me so — I don't know who told me or where I was told of it."

"Of what tribe are you?"   *66*
"I am an Uncpapa."   *67*
"Of the Sioux?"   *68*
"Yes; of the great Sioux Nation."   *69*
"Who was your father?"   *70*
"My father is dead."   *71*
"Is your mother living?"   *72*
"My mother lives with me in my lodge."   *73*

"Great lies are told about you. White men say that you lived among them   *74* when you were young; that you went to school; that you learned to write and read from books; that you speak English; that you know how to talk French?"

"It is a lie."   *75*
"You are an Indian?"   *76*
(Proudly) "I am a Sioux."   *77*

Then, suddenly relaxing from his hauteur, Sitting Bull began to laugh. "I   *78* have heard," he said, "of some of these stories. They are all strange lies. What I am I am," and here he leaned back and resumed his attitude and expression of barbaric grandeur. . . .

Adieu King Bull

As Sitting Bull rose to go I asked him whether he had the stomach for any   *79* more battles with the Americans. He answered: —

"I do not want any fight."   *80*

"You mean not now?"   *81*
He laughed quite heartily.   *82*
"No; not this winter."   *83*
"Are your young braves willing to fight?"   *84*
"You will see."   *85*
"When?"   *86*
"I cannot say."   *87*
"I have not seen your people. Would I be welcome at your camp?"   *88*
After gazing at the ceiling for a few moments Sitting Bull responded: —   *89*
"I will not be pleased. The young men would not be pleased. You came with   *90*
this party (alluding to the United States Commissioners) and you can go back
with them. I have said enough."
With this Sitting Bull wrapped his blanket around him and, after gracefully   *91*
shaking hands, strode to the door. Then he placed his fox-skin cap upon his
head and I bade him adieu.

Considerations

1. List all the features of a television interview that make it distinctive and
   different from other television shows; for example, the purpose of the interview, the kinds of questions asked, their length, the ways personalities are
   revealed, etc.
2. In a short essay, compare this newspaper interview from 1877 with today's
   typical television interview. How are they similar? Use the example you
   thought of in question 1 to illustrate your points about current television
   interviews.
3. Do you think this newspaper correspondent did a good job interviewing Sitting Bull? Make a list of five additional questions you wish the correspondent had asked Sitting Bull. Then next to each question, suggest a reason
   that the question was not asked.

Connections

1. Which reading is truer history — Arthur Kopit's present-day theatrical reconstruction or this newspaper interview by an eyewitness? Write an essay
   defending your choice.
2. Given your sense of Sitting Bull as he is portrayed in Kopit's play and in
   this interview, write a paragraph about Sitting Bull intended for a young
   person's (age 10–14) encyclopedia.
3. Look at your paragraph for question 2 above. Have you stuck to facts? Have
   you included any value judgments? Underline any words or phrases about
   Sitting Bull that reveal how you feel. If you can find any such words, write
   a letter to the editor of the encyclopedia telling her or him why you think
   these words should stay in your paragraph even though encyclopedias are
   supposed to present factual information.

4. Write a paragraph arguing the case that this newspaper interview shares a dramatic quality with Kopit's play and could be properly described as theatrical. In other words, what do these two pieces have in common?

On the Wigwams and Dwellings of the Gaspesians [Micmacs]

Father Chrestien Le Clercq

Since these people live without society and without commerce, they have 1 neither cities, towns, nor villages, unless, indeed, one is willing to call by these names certain collections of wigwams having the form of tents, very badly kept, and just as badly arranged.

Their wigwams are built of nothing but poles, which are covered with some 2 pieces of bark of the birch, sewed one to another; and they are ornamented, as a rule, with a thousand different pictures of birds, moose, otters and beavers, which the women sketch themselves with their paints. These wigwams are of a circular form, and capable of lodging fifteen to twenty persons; but they are, however, so made that with seven or eight barks a single one is constructed, in which from three to four fires are built. They are so light and portable, that our Indians roll them up like a piece of paper, and carry them thus upon their backs wheresoever it pleases them, very much like the tortoises which carry their own houses. They follow the ancient custom of our first fathers, who remained encamped in a place only so long as they found there the means of subsistence for their families and their herds. In the same manner, also, our Gaspesians decamp when they no longer find the means to subsist in the places where they are living; for, having neither animals to feed, nor lands or fields to cultivate, they are obliged to be almost always wanderers and vagabonds, in order to seek food and other commodities necessary to life. It is the business of the head of the family, exclusively over all others, to give orders that camp be made where he pleases, and that it be broken when he wishes. This is why, on the eve of departure, he goes in person to trace the road which is to be taken, and to choose a place suitable and ample for the encampment. From this place he removes all the useless wood, and cuts off the branches which could be in the way. He smooths and opens out a road to make it easy for the women to

Father Chrestien Le Clercq was a Roman Catholic missionary from France. In this letter of 1681, he is reporting back to his superior in Europe.

drag over the snow on their toboggans, the trifle of furniture and of luggage which comprises their housekeeping outfit. He marks out, also all by himself, the plan of the wigwam, and throws out the snow with his snowshoes until he has reached the ground, which he flattens and chops in pieces until he has removed all the frozen part, so that all of the people who compose his family may lodge in the greatest possible comfort. This done, he then cuts as many poles as he considers suitable, and plants them in a circle around the border of the hollow which he has made in the earth and the snow — always in such a manner, however, that the upper ends come together in a point, as with tents or belfrys. When this is finished, he makes preparations for hunting, from which he does not return until the wigwam has been completely put in order by the women, to whom he commits the care thereof during his absence, after assigning to each one her particular duty. Thus some of the women go to collect branches of fir, and when they place the barks upon the poles: others fetch dry wood to make the fire: others carry water for boiling the kettle, or in order to have the supper ready when the men return from the hunt. The wife of the head of the family, in the capacity of mistress, selects the most tender and most slender of the branches of fir for the purpose of covering all the margin inside the wigwam, leaving the middle free to serve as a common meeting-place. She then fits and adjusts the larger and rougher of the branches to the height of the snow, and these form a kind of little wall. The effect is such that this little building seems much more like a camp made in the spring than one made in winter, because of the pleasing greenness which the fir keeps for a long time without withering. It is also her duty to assign his place to each one, according to the age and quality of the respective persons and the custom of the nation. The place of the head of the family is on the right. He yields it sometimes, as an honour and courtesy to strangers, whom he invites to stop with him, and to repose upon certain skins of bears, of moose, of seal, or upon some fine robes of beaver, which these Indians use as if they were Turkey carpets. The women occupy always the first places near the door, in order to be all ready to obey, and to serve promptly when they are ordered. There are very great inconveniences in these kinds of wigwams; for, aside from the fact that they are so low that one cannot readily stand upright in them, and must of necessity remain always seated or lying down, they are moreover, of a coldness which cannot be described, whilst the smoke which one is necessarily obliged to endure in the company of these barbarians is something insufferable.

All these hardships, without doubt, are not the least of the mortifications 3 which are endured by the missionaries, who, after the example of Saint Paul, in order to be all things to all men so that they may gain these people to JESUS-CHRIST, do not fail, despite so many discomforts, to work without ceasing at the conversion of these poor pagans.

I pass without mention several other methods of camping which are in use 4 among our Gaspesians, because there is nothing about them more important than that they cause extreme suffering in those who follow the Indians in the woods, and that they are all equally mean and miserable. But however that may be, the Indians esteem their camps as much as, and even more than, they do the most superb and commodious of our houses. To this they testified one day to some of our gentlemen of Isle Percée, who, having asked me to serve them as interpreter in a visit which they wished to make to these Indians in order to make the latter understand that it would be very much more advantageous for them to live and to build in our fashion, were extremely surprised when the leading Indians, who had listened with great patience to everything I had said to him on behalf of these gentlemen, answered me in these words: "I am greatly astonished that the French have so little cleverness, as they seem to exhibit in the matter of which thou has just told me on their behalf, in the effort to persuade us to convert our poles, our barks, and our wigwams into those houses of stone and of wood which are tall and lofty, according to their account, as these trees. Very well! But why now," continued he, "do men of five to six feet in height need houses which are sixty to eighty? For, in fact, as thou knowest very well thyself, Patriarch — do we not find in our own all the conveniences and the advantages that you have with yours, such as reposing, drinking, sleeping, eating, and amusing ourselves with our friends when we wish? This is not all," said he, addressing himself to one of our captains, "my brother, hast thou as much ingenuity and cleverness as the Indians, who carry their houses and their wigwams with them so that they may lodge wheresoever they please, independently of any seignior whatsoever? Thou art not as bold nor as stout as we, because when thou goest on a voyage thou canst not carry upon thy shoulders thy buildings and thy edifices. Therefore it is necessary that thou preparest as many lodgings as thou makest changes of residence, or else thou lodgest in a hired house which does not belong to thee. As for us, we find ourselves secure from all these inconveniences, and we can always say, more than thou, that we are at home everywhere, because we set up our wigwams with ease wheresoever we go, and without asking permission of anybody. Thou reproachest us, very inappropriately, that our country is a little hell in contrast with France, which thou comparest to a terrestrial paradise, inasmuch as it yields thee, so thou sayest, every kind of provision in abundance. Thou sayest, of us also that we are the most miserable and most unhappy of all men, living without religion, without manners, without honour, without social order, and, in a word, without any rules, like the beasts in our woods and our forests, lacking bread, wine, and a thousand other comforts which thou hast in superfluity in Europe. Well, my brother, if thou dost not yet know the real feelings which our Indians have towards thy country and towards thy nation, it is proper that I inform thee at once. I beg thee not to believe that, all miserable as we seem in thine eyes, we consider ourselves nevertheless much happier than thou in this, that we are very content with the little that we have; and believe also once for all, I pray, that thou deceivest thyself greatly if thou thinkest to persuade us that thy country is better than ours. For if France, as thou sayest, is a little terrestrial paradise, art thou sensible to leave it? And why abandon wives, children, relatives, and friends? Why risk thy life and thy property every year, and why venture thyself with such risk, in any season whatsoever, to the storms and tempests of the sea in order to come to a strange and barbarous country which thou considerest the poorest and least fortunate of the world? Besides, since we are wholly convinced of the contrary, we scarcely take the trouble to go to France, because we fear, with good reason, lest we find little satisfaction there, seeing, in our own experience, that those who are natives thereof leave it every year in order to enrich themselves on our shores. We believe, further, that you are also incomparably poorer than we, and that you are only simple journeymen, valets, servants, and slaves, all masters and grand captains though you may appear, seeing that you glory in our old rags and in our miserable suits of beaver which can no longer be of use to us, and that you find among us, in the fishery for cod which you make in these parts, the wherewithal to comfort your misery and the poverty which oppresses you. As to us, we find all our riches and all our conveniences among ourselves, without trouble and without exposing our lives to the dangers in which you find yourselves constantly through your long voyages. And, whilst feeling compassion for you in the sweetness of our repose, we wonder at the anxieties and cares which you give yourselves night and day in order to load your ship. We see also that all your people live, as a rule, only upon cod which you catch among us. It is everlastingly nothing but cod — cod in the morning, cod at midday, cod at evening, and always cod, until things come to such a pass that if you wish some good morsels, it is at our expense; and you are obliged to have recourse to the Indians, whom you despise so much, and to beg them to go a-hunting that you may be regaled. Now tell me this one little thing, if thou hast any sense: Which of these two is the wisest and happiest — he who labours without ceasing and only obtains, and that with great trouble, enough to live on, or he who rests in comfort and finds all that he needs in the pleasure of hunting and fishing? It is true," added he, "that we have not always had the use of bread and of wine which your France produces; but, in fact, before the arrival of the French in these parts, did not the Gaspesians live much longer than now? And if we have not any longer among us any of those old men of a hundred and thirty to forty years, it is only because we are gradually adopting your manner of living, for experience is making it very plain that those of us live longest who, despising your bread, your wine, and your brandy, are content with their natural food of beaver, of moose, of waterfowl, and fish, in accord with the custom of our ancestors and of all the Gaspesian nation. Learn now, my brother, once for all, because I must open to thee my heart: there is no Indian who does not consider himself infinitely more happy and more powerful than the French." He finished his speech by the following last words, saying that an Indian could find his living everywhere, and that he could call himself the seigneur and the sovereign of his country, because he could reside there just as freely as it pleased him with every kind of rights of hunting and fishing, without any anxiety, more content a thousand times in the woods and in his wigwam than if he were in palaces and at the tables of the greatest princes of the earth.

No matter what can be said of this reasoning, I assert, for my part, that I should consider these Indians incomparably more fortunate than ourselves, and that the life of these barbarians would even be capable of inspiring envy, if they had the instructions, the understanding, and the same means for their salvation which God has given us that we may save ourselves by preference over so many poor pagans, and as a result of His pity; for, after all, their lives are not vexed by a thousand annoyances as are ours. They have not among them those situations or offices, whether in the judiciary or in war, which are sought among us with so much ambition. Possessing nothing of their own, they are consequently free from trickery and legal proceedings in connection with inheritances from their relatives. The names of serjeant, of attorney, of clerk, of judge, of president are unknown to them. All their ambition centers in surprising and killing quantities of beavers, moose, seals, and other wild beasts in order to obtain their flesh for food and their skins for clothing. They live in very great harmony, never quarrelling and never beating one another except in drunkenness. On the contrary, they mutually aid one another in their needs with much charity and without selfseeking. There is continual joy in their wigwams. The multitude of their children does not embarrass them, for, far from being annoyed by these, they consider themselves just that much the more fortunate and richer as their family is more numerous. Since they never expect that the fortunes of the children will be larger than those of their fathers, they are also free from all those anxieties which we give ourselves in connection with the accumulation of property for the purpose of elevating children in society and in importance. Hence it comes about that nature has always preserved among them in all its integrity that conjugal love between husband and wife which ought never to suffer alteration through selfish fear of having too many children. This duty, which in Europe is considered too onerous, is viewed by our Indians as very honourable, very advantageous, and very useful, and he who has the largest number of children is the most highly esteemed of the entire nation. This is because he finds more support for his old age, and because, in their condition of life, the boys and girls contribute equally to the happiness and joy of those who have given them birth. They live, in fact, together — father and children — like the first kings of the earth, who subsisted at the beginning of the world by their hunting and fishing, and on vegetables and sagamite, or stew, which was, in my opinion, like the pottage which Jacob asked of Esau before giving him his benediction.

Considerations

1. Make a numbered list of the steps necessary to build a wigwam, as described by Father Chrestien Le Clercq. Now write two sets of instructions, in chronological order, which detail the steps in building a wigwam. Prepare one set of instructions for a seventeenth-century Micmac man who is the head of his family. Prepare the other set of instructions for a woman in this family. Prepare and include at least one diagram to illustrate your instructions.

2. Father Le Clercq quotes a Micmac Indian who tries to explain why the Indians view themselves as "infinitely more happy and more powerful than the French" (para. 4). Make a numbered list of the separate reasons the Indian gives to support his position. Add another list of additional reasons that Father Le Clercq provides to support the Indian's reasoning. Now assume you are in a debate representing the Indian argument. Prepare one paragraph summing up the Indian side. You can use Father Le Clercq's reasons as well as those of the Micmac Indians, but in order to be convincing, you must synthesize them and present them logically.

Connections

1. Look back at James L. Axtell's article, particularly his analysis of the differences between the Roman Catholic and the Protestant missionaries. Then write an essay comparing and contrasting the French Catholic missionaries and the English Protestant missionaries. In what ways were they similar, in what ways different? Use Father Le Clercq as an example of a French Roman Catholic missionary.
2. To what extent would Alfonso Ortiz approve of Le Clercq?
3. Would Le Clercq approve of Ortiz? Explain your answer.

Letter from an American Farmer

J. Hector St. John de Crèvecoeur

Distresses of a Frontier Man

The difficulty of the language, the fear of some great intoxication among the   *1*
Indians, finally the apprehension lest my younger children should be caught by that singular charm, so dangerous at their tender years, are the only considerations that startle me. By what power does it come to pass that children who have been adopted when young among these people can never be prevailed on to readopt European manners? Many an anxious parent have I seen last war who at the return of the peace went to the Indian villages where they knew their children had been carried in captivity, when to their inexpressible sorrow they found them so perfectly Indianized that many knew them no longer, and those whose more advanced ages permitted them to recollect their fathers and mothers absolutely refused to follow them and ran to their adoptive parents for protection against the effusions of love their unhappy real parents lavished on them! Incredible as this may appear, I have heard it asserted in a thousand instances, among persons of credit. In the village of —— , where I purpose to go, there lived, about fifteen years ago, an Englishman and a Swede, whose history would appear moving had I time to relate it. They were grown to the age of men when they were taken; they happily escaped the great punishment of war captives and were obliged to marry the squaws who had saved their lives by adoption. By the force of habit, they became at last thoroughly naturalized to this wild course of life. While I was there, their friends sent them a considerable sum of money to ransom themselves with. The Indians, their

---

J. Hector St. John de Crèvecoeur (1735–1813) was a European settler who came to Pennsylvania to homestead. In this literary letter, which he intended to publish, Crèvecoeur reveals to a fictional friend his worries about his children. He fears they might prefer the Indian way of life to their own traditions.

old masters, gave them their choice, and without requiring any consideration, told them that they had been long as free as themselves. They chose to remain, and the reasons they gave me would greatly surprise you: the most perfect freedom, the ease of living, the absence of those cares and corroding solicitudes which so often prevail with us, the peculiar goodness of the soil they cultivated, for they did not trust altogether to hunting — all these and many more motives which I have forgot made them prefer that life of which we entertain such dreadful opinions. It cannot be, therefore, so bad as we generally conceive it to be; there must be in their social bond something singularly captivating and far superior to anything to be boasted of among us; for thousands of Europeans are Indians, and we have no examples of even one of those aborigines having from choice become Europeans! There must be something more congenial to our native dispositions than the fictitious society in which we live; or else why should children, and even grown persons, become in a short time so invincibly attached to it? There must be something very bewitching in their manners, something very indelible and marked by the very hands of Nature. For, take a young Indian lad, give him the best education you possibly can, load him with your bounty, with presents, nay with riches, yet he would secretly long for his native woods, which you would imagine he must have long since forgot; and on the first opportunity he can possibly find, you will see him voluntarily leave behind all you have given him and return with inexpressible joy to lie on the mats of his fathers. Mr. —— some years ago received from a good old Indian, who died in his house, a young lad of nine years of age, his grandson. He kindly educated him with his children and bestowed on him the same care and attention in respect to the memory of his venerable grandfather, who was a worthy man. He intended to give him a genteel trade, but in the spring season when all the family went to the woods to make their maple sugar, he suddenly disappeared, and it was not until seventeen months after that his benefactor heard he had reached the village of Bald Eagle, where he still dwelt. Let us say what we will of them, of their inferior organs, of their want of bread, etc., they are as stout and well made as the Europeans. Without temples, without priests, without kings, and without laws, they are in many instances superior to us; and the proofs of what I advance are that they live without care, sleep without inquietude, take life as it comes, bearing all its asperities with unparalleled patience, and die without any kind of apprehension for what they have done or for what they expect to meet with hereafter. What system of philosophy can give us so many necessary qualifications for happiness?

Considerations

1. Crèvecoeur calls his writing *letters,* but he was not writing to anyone in particular. Such letters were a well-known literary device of the eighteenth century, and Crèvecoeur did succeed in publishing his letters.

   First underline the words and phrases that give clues that this is not a real letter. Then think about what kinds of words these are. (They illustrate at least two different kinds of clues.) Using the two kinds of clues, write a paragraph explaining why you suspect that this letter was not a real letter addressed to a personal friend but part of a published book.

2. Rewrite the information in this passage as a real letter from Crèvecoeur to one of his relatives in Europe.

Connections

1. James L. Axtell quotes part of Crèvecoeur's letter as evidence to support his own point about European residential schools for Indians:

> The result was predictable: "we have no examples," wrote Hector de Crèvecoeur in 1782, "of even one of those Aborigines having from choice become Europeans" [para. 16].

Evaluate the effectiveness of this quotation. Write a paragraph in which you approve or disapprove of Axtell's use of Crèvecoeur's letter. Considering the context of the rest of the quotation in Crèvecoeur's letter, is Axtell's use legitimate? Could Axtell have chosen a more suitable comment from Crèvecoeur's letter to make this point?

2. Crèvecoeur worried that his children might be tempted to run away and join the Indians. In his second sentence, he asks, "By what power does it come to pass, that children who have been adopted when young among these people, can never be prevailed on to readopt European manners?" Write a short paragraph in which you explain to Crèvecoeur why he is right to worry and what this power is, as you understand it from the readings so far.

3. Crèvecoeur claims about the Indians that "there must be in their social bond something singularly captivating, and far superior to anything to be boasted of among us." Write a short essay, drawing on any of the previous readings for examples, in which you explain what that something was.

Ethnology and Phrenology as an Aid to the Historian

J. W. Jackson

The Aborigines

The Red-man is manifestly a lower type than the Caucasian. He represents   *1*
humanity at an earlier stage of development. His osseous structure is less harmonious, his muscular less powerful, and his nervous less complex and re-

---

J. W. Jackson has fortunately faded into obscurity; nothing seems to be known about him other than his book, published in 1863.

fined. His brain demonstrates that he is not allied to the intellectual races, the anterior lobe being deficient in the requisite power for abstract thought or creative imagination. He has the tall stature, the slender form, the high features, and lofty coronal region of the Caucasian, combined, in most cases, with the high cheek bones, and other indications of a not remote Mongolic relationship. He is daring, chivalrous, and eloquent, a keen observer, quick in his perceptions, fertile in resources, cautious in the formation, but persistent in the execution of his enterprises. His language is complex, his figures of speech bold and imaginative, and his entire framework of mind not that of a primitive savage, but rather that of a warrior caste, reduced, by isolation and a combination of untoward circumstances, to the condition of hunters, after having enjoyed for centuries the high culture and refined training of an heroic phase of civilization. This is more especially the case with the chiefs, and applies rather to the tribes of the Northern than the Southern division of the continent; and among the former is more true of those east of the Rocky Mountains than of those to the West of that boundary. Are these characteristics the results of a Caucasian graft on a Mongolic basis, of a long-past colonial infusion, now thoroughly absorbed and assimilated? Or are they the indication that we have here the barbarized remnants of a noble race, the rude *debris* of an ancient colonial civilization, reduced not only socially and intellectually, but ethnically, almost to a level with the aborigines?

Whatever may be the origin, however, of the model North American Indian — whether purely an aborigine, or in part a colonist — his organization is in strict accordance with his character. Powerfully developed in the region of Firmness and Self-Esteem, with very considerable Conscientiousness and a fair share of Caution, the cranium slopes almost continuously from the first to his unusually prominent perceptive faculties, which thus altogether preponderate over the reflectives. The domestic affections are rather deficient, the occipital region being small. Combativeness is strongly, and Destructiveness, together with Secretiveness, powerfully developed. These proportions are united with a brain of fully average volume, and combined with a temperament perhaps the most eminently fibrous in the world. We have thus, then, little difficulty in understanding how this noble savage, in his better moods, can be so dignified; in his sterner, so cruel and revengeful. As a conqueror, so unrelenting; as the conquered, so unyielding — ever ready to endure what he is always prepared to inflict. Haughty, yet polite in his manners; stern, yet faithful in his friendships; cold and self-possessed in his loves; his gentler emotions are habitually restrained by a sense of dignity, the warrior triumphing over the father and the husband. His enthusiasm is reserved for war and the chase, and his admiration is bestowed upon valour rather than beauty. He has, indeed, no proper sympathy with the softer sex, and cannot make the remotest approach to a right understanding of the character of woman, and would rather win his wife by a military raid than by the delicate attentions of a devoted and gallant lover. With senses of sight and hearing so acute that they remind one of some especial animal gifts, rather than of harmonious human endowments, he has yet little aptitude for acquiring systematic knowledge. His faculties are admirable as far as they go, but their range is decidedly limited. He dwells wholly in the concrete, the abstract is altogether beyond him. He relies upon his own indi-

2

viduality rather than on the collective knowledge or power of the community. He is great in isolation, feeble in union. He is heroic and even ennobled as a savage, but he is incapable of civilization. There is not sufficient susceptibility and flexibility in his nature to admit of the ready reception of new ideas and the easy adoption of alien habits. He perishes in the process of transmutation. He is too effectually developed as a hunter to permit of his suddenly submitting to the steady labor demanded by modern civilization. He degenerates under attempted improvement. A hero in the wigwam, he sinks into an idle sot in the village. Thus it would seem that he is largely destined to extinction, that over vast spaces the Red-man must perish before the pale faces, and leave but the faint echo of heroic deeds, that, in their intrinsic excellence as feats of daring or endurance, might, doubtless, match with anything in romantic legend or classic story.

Anglo-Saxon Colonies

The great colonial success of the American continent is to be found, how- 3
ever, in the English settlements of the North, which, as the United States, have
achieved a rapidity of advancement in wealth, population, culture, and all the
moral and material resources of civilization, perfectly unexampled in ancient
or modern times. This is, no doubt, due principally to the superior character
of the immigrant race, derived chiefly from the most vigorous stock of the Old
Continent. In part it may also be attributed to climatic and telluric influences
in their reaction on the humanity of different zones, for the Indians of the North
were, beyond question, far more manly and heroic than those of the South.
These aborigines, moreover, were neither numerous or civilized enough to mingle
effectually with the invaders, whose blood, consequently, remained practically
pure. The progressive and prosperous condition of the mother country also could
not fail to react most beneficially on her colonial offshoots, both prior and subsequent to their independence, as, conversely, the decadence of Spain could
not but most disastrously affect the interests of her colonial extensions. In truth,
Britain is the especial colonial empire of the day, and her dependencies, whether
east or west, north or south, are, consequently, the great successes of the time.

Considerations

1. Referring to the Indian, J. W. Jackson concludes, "Thus it would seem that
   he is largely destined to extinction. . . ." Write a paragraph explaining how
   Jackson makes it seem that it is the Indians' fault that they have almost
   died out.
2. Jackson's ideas seem ridiculous to most people today. But some probably
   still believe such ideas are true of certain groups other than the Indians.
   Write a paragraph in which you identify a modern-day group of people who
   believe in Jackson's approach and explain how their beliefs are connected
   to Jackson's ideas.

Connections

1. Write a paragraph explaining how J. W. Jackson's comments about Indians illustrate Alfonso Ortiz's main complaints.
2. Read the selections by Charles Darwin and by Carl Sagan on the intelligence of animals in Chapter 9, The Impact of Animals. Then write an essay reconstructing what you think Darwin *or* Sagan would think of Jackson's argument.
3. Refer to the selection by Stephen Jay Gould in Chapter 7, The Nature of Intelligence. To what extent can you find parallels between Jackson's ideas and the system of eugenics in Singapore that Gould describes?

Further Connections

1. Alfonso Ortiz says "I do not understand this preoccupation of American historians with the earliest centuries of Indian/white contact, the colonial period, and the earliest decades of American nationhood; truly I do not understand it. . . ." (para. 18) Write a paragraph explaining to Ortiz why such an understanding is so important. Include two examples of this early contact from the other readings.
2. A. Irving Hallowell (and others) have remarked on the ways Indians connected disease with immoral social behavior. Explain how this connection made sense to a frontier Indian. Draw on at least three readings to find evidence supporting this Indian interpretation of serious illness.
3. Calvin Martin (see Suggestions for Further Reading) quotes Frank G. Speck who refers to Micmac hunting as "a holy occupation." Kenneth M. Morrison refers in the same way to these subsistence activities as "sacral practices." Why not call Micmac hunting a superstitious occupation? Write a short essay justifying Speck's or Morrison's phrases.
4. Historian Anthony F. C. Wallace has written about Iroquois warfare in *The Death and Rebirth of the Seneca.* (see Suggestions for Further Reading). Monitor your own immediate reactions to this information from Wallace (p. 46): "The bodies of captives who had been tortured to death were sometimes eaten ceremonially." Write a paragraph describing and explaining your own first personal response to this data. Then wait a while and write another paragraph recommending a different, more scholarly response to the same information.
5. Look at Elias Canetti's piece in Chapter 1, The Dimensions of Power. Then determine the extent to which the Indian practice of cannibalism and torture is explained by Canetti's thesis.
6. Historian Calvin Martin has claimed dramatically that "If our histories of the North American fur trade are to be full and accurate they will have to reconcile themselves to the stark fact that once upon a time man and an-

imals talked with one another on this continent. Why they ceased their conversation is a question for the ethnohistorian to ponder." (*Keepers of the Game,* p. 156)

Write a paragraph in which you explain the technical meaning of the term *fact* and either justify or criticize Martin for calling this conversation between Indians and animals a fact. Support your position with examples from any of the readings in this book.

7. Write an essay in which you ponder at least three reasons why the Indians ceased their conversation with the animals (see question 6). You might want to consult Martin's own book or his initial article (see Bibliography) to find suitable evidence to support your points. (Suggested length: 5 paragraphs one introductory paragraph, one paragraph for each reason, and one concluding paragraph.)

8. James L. Axtell, at the end of his article, quotes an Indian who asked, "Do you not see that, as we inhabit a world so different from yours, there must be another heaven for us, and another road to reach it?"

Think about the Indian world and brainstorm features that you remember from the readings. Then group or cluster these items together into several main categories. Now check the readings to supplement your stock of brainstormed information.

9. Write an essay in which you compare and contrast the most significant differences between our world and the frontier Indians' world. There are many possible differences, so in your introduction be sure to justify why you think the ones you chose are the most significant differences.

10. Write a short essay in which you use information from any readings in this book to criticize and counter J. W. Jackson's claims about the Indians' limited thinking ability in *Ethnology and Phrenology as an Aid to the Historian.* Try to demolish Jackson as logically and elegantly as you can.

11. The following terms have the same denotations, but different connotations: *aborigine, Indian, Native American, redskin, savage.* Rank these terms from favorable to unfavorable.

Now write five short paragraphs, one for each term, beginning with the one you consider the most derogatory. For each term explain who might use such a word and when it would be an appropriate choice, if at all. Also, identify any possible disadvantages in using the term, for instance, in meaning or in its effect on the reader.

12. Follow the same procedure you used in question 11 for the following group: *colonist, homesteader, invader, settler, white.*

Extensions

1. Marshall Sahlins has claimed in *Stone Age Economics* (Chicago: Aldine, 1972) that nomadic hunters, like many frontier Indians, were "the Original Affluent Society." They enjoyed leisure, plentiful food, and freedom from fear of scarcity. Sahlins says that to understand tribal economies, we must abandon the entrepreneurial and individualistic conception of economy as a means-end relationship. "Economy becomes a category of culture rather

than behavior, in a class with politics or religion rather than rationality or product: the material life-process of society instead of the need-satisfying activities of individuals."

Find examples in at least three chapter readings to help you write a paragraph supporting the statement that "the Frontier Indians were the 'original affluent society' in Sahlins' terms."

2. How is Sahlins' understanding of the term *economy* different from a classical analysis of the marketplace, and how is it a better explanation for the Indians' life? Write a short essay answering these questions.

3. Calvin Martin says that a Micmac shaman sometimes "functioned as a psychotherapist." Take notes on the entry for "psychotherapy" in *The International Encyclopedia of Psychiatry, Psychology, Psychoanalysis, and Neurology* and the entry on "shamanism" in the *Encyclopaedia Britannica*. Then using this information write an essay explaining how a Shaman functioned as a psychotherapist.

4. Alfonso Ortiz has written that "even the best of Western historical writing has no more meaning and no more truth value than . . . Indian mythology." Using a specific example of what you consider to be the best of Western historical writing, write an essay in which you agree or disagree with Ortiz.

5. It has been said that Henry Wadsworth Longfellow's "Hiawatha" is *the* poem of the American Indian. Find out who this fifteenth century Mohawk chief was, read Longfellow's poem, and write an essay assessing Longfellow's use of Indian material.

6. Listen to a recording of Edward McDowell's *Indian Suite* (composed in 1891–1892; first performed in 1896). Write an essay analyzing the extent to which this suite is really "Indian." Bear in mind that the first collection of American Indian melodies was obtained in the field in 1880 by Theodore Baker and published in 1882.

7. Sacajawea has had more public statues erected to her than any other American woman. Read the entry on Sacajawea in the *Dictionary of American Biography*. Write a paragraph explaining why she has been regarded as such an important national public figure and defend or criticize this emphasis.

8. According to Ortiz, "the importance of learning an Indian language cannot be overemphasized, for it is the most reliable way to enter a people's world, to understand how they impose meaning and order upon their experience." Write an essay examining the Sapir-Whorf hypothesis. To begin your research, see Benjamin Lee Whorf, *Language, Thought, and Reality*, John B. Carroll, ed. (New York: Wiley, 1956). In your essay include information identifying Edward Sapir, Benjamin Lee Whorf, what Whorf was trying to accomplish among the Hopi Indians, what Whorf claimed as results of this work, and finally, what criticisms have been leveled at the Sapir-Whorf hypothesis. Where do you stand?

9. Gary B. Nash, an eminent historian, has written in *Red, White, and Black: The Peoples of Early America* (Englewood Cliffs, N.J.: Prentice-Hall, 1982) that "In the national imagination and in popular history warfare has always stood out as the crucial element in Indian-white relations. But three

aspects of the acculturative process — disease, trade, and religion — deserve much greater emphasis. Of the three, trade is especially important." (p. 310)

Write a paragraph explaining why the three aspects Nash mentions deserve greater emphasis than does war.

10. Write an essay in which you agree or disagree that of the three factors Nash specifies in question 10, above, trade is the most important.

11. Calvin Martin has written in *Keepers of the Game:*

> Late in the 1960s the North American Indian acquired yet another stereotypic image in the popular mind: the erstwhile "savage," the "drunken" Indian, the "vanishing" Indian, was conferred the title of the "ecological" (i.e., conservationist-minded) Indian. Propped up for everything that was environmentally sound, the Indian was introduced to the American public as the great high priest of the Ecology Cult. Depending upon one's point of reference, this might appear to be another crass commercial gimmick, a serious case of misread or ignored history, or a logical outgrowth of the conservation movement. Actually it was some of all three.

Choosing commercialism, bad history, or the conservation movement as the focus, write an essay explaining what Martin means and how the factor you have chosen has contributed to this stereotyping of the Indian as the "great high priest of the Ecology Cult." Use the *Social Science Index,* the *Humanities Index,* or the *Public Affairs Information Services Bulletin* to locate at least one appropriate article for evidence supporting and illustrating your essay.

12. According to Harvard paleontologist Stephen Jay Gould in *The Mismeasure of Man* (New York: Norton, 1981):

> Many primary-school curriculums of the late nineteenth century were reconstructed in the light of recapitulation. Several school boards prescribed the *Song of Hiawatha* in early grades, reasoning that children passing through the savage state of their ancestral past, would identify with it. (p. 114)

Look up *recapitulation* in the *Dictionary of Anthropology* or the *Encyclopedia of Anthropology*. Write a paragraph defining what it means and explaining how it applies to our thinking about North American Indians and to humankind in general.

13. Write a paragraph explaining how J. W. Jackson's comments about Indians are a typical example of recapitulation.

14. Chief Joseph of the Nez Percé said the following words when he surrendered to Generals O. O. Howard and Nelson A. Miles in 1877. This speech is often published in anthologies of poetry, each sentence beginning a new line. Write an essay explaining why this speech can be considered a poem. In your answer, provide a short definition of poetry, list its special characteristics, and use Chief Joseph's speech to illustrate these characteristics.

> I am tired of fighting. Our chiefs are killed. Looking Glass is dead. Toohulhulsote is dead. The old men are all dead. It is the young men who say yes and no. He who led the young men is dead. It is cold and we have no blankets. The little children are freezing to death. My people, some of them, have run away to the

hills and have no blankets, no food; no one knows where they are — perhaps freezing to death. I want to have time to look for my children and see how many of them I can find. Maybe I will find them among the dead. Hear me, my chiefs. I am tired; my heart is sick and sad. From where the sun now stands I will fight no more forever.

15. There is much debate about where the North American Indians came from and how long they had been on the American continent before the Europeans came. For example, here is a letter to Dear Abby (*Los Angeles Times,* July 19, 1984):

> Dear Abby: I learned in school that when Columbus discovered America, the American Indians were already here, but I would like to know where the Indians came from.
>
> Likes to Learn (12 years old)

Dear Abby answers this question by consulting the *Encyclopaedia Britannica:*

> Dear Likes: The *Encyclopaedia Britannica* says that the North American Indians probably migrated to the Americas from Asia. About 15,000 to 25,000 years ago they crossed from northeast Asia to the Bering Strait. By the time the Europeans arrived in the fifteenth century, waves of these Asiatic migrants had spread over the Americas.

But where did the *Encyclopaedia Britannica* get its information? Write a short report identifying the main problems scholars face on this issue, for example, explaining the Pleistocene ice advance, identifying the animal migration that people followed, dating procedures, justifying the evidence, such as charcoal or tools. End your report by summing up what seems the most plausible explanation to you and how you would answer the 12-year-old, agreeing or not with Dear Abby.

16. Prepare a series of paragraphs, each one briefly answering the 12-year-old's question from question 15 about where the Indians come from. In each paragraph, answer as one of the following: a linguist, a geographer or a geologist, a zoologist or medical doctor, a historian or an anthropologist, a Pueblo Indian (see Alfonso Ortiz's selection in this chapter), an Abenaki Indian (see Kenneth M. Morrison's selection in this chapter), or a member of the Church of Jesus Christ of the Latter Day Saints (a Mormon). Identify your evidence, provide one quotation from a relevant source, and explain why your evidence proves your answer.

17. The writer of the letter to Dear Abby (see question 15) learned that Columbus discovered America (in 1492). Write a short essay analyzing this as the sort of Western eurocentric myth that Alfonso Ortiz dislikes. For each of its terms, propose an alternative and justify your suggestions:

> Columbus — Columbus was not the first European to land on the North American continent. (Who?)
>
> discovered — North America was already there and other Europeans knew about it. (Who?) Moreover, Columbus thought he had reached somewhere else. (Where?)
>
> America — Columbus landed on several islands (present-day Cuba, Haiti, and the Bahamas). "America" refers to someone else entirely (Who?)

in 1942 — This system of dating depends on the Christian tradition. There are other systems to date events. (What?)

Suggestions for Further Reading

Axtell, James L. "Some Thoughts on the Ethnohistory of Missions." *Ethnohistory* 29(1982):35–41. Here Axtell asks a key question about social and cultural continuity among natives as a result of conversion attempts by missionaries.

Berkhofer, Robert F. *The White Man's Indian: Images of the American Indian from Columbus to the Present.* New York: Knopf, 1978. A very readable, empathetic account of the ways whites have perceived Indians and an analysis of the reasons why this should be so.

Coe, Ralph T. *Sacred Circles: Two Thousand Years of North American Art.* London: Arts Council of Great Britain, 1976. This bicentennial exhibit catalogue is full of wonderful reproductions of Indian art and illuminating commentary on the pipes, headdresses, blankets, pots, carvings, etc.

Farb, Peter. *Man's Rise to Civilization as Shown by the Indians of North America from Primeval Times to the Coming of the Industrial State.* New York: Avon, 1969. A controversial, but very readable book about many North American tribes. It is controversial because it takes a cultural evolutionary approach, which is not universally accepted by scholars.

Gill, Sam. D. *Native American Religions. An Introduction.* Belmont, Cal.: Wadsworth, 1982. An outsider's extremely sympathetic account of a variety of Indian forms of worship, spiritual practices, myths, ceremonies, traditional rites, social institutions — all of which are now protected by Public Law 95–341, which the U.S. Congress passed in 1978.

Guillemin, Jeanne. *Urban Renegades: The Cultural Strategy of American Indians.* New York: Columbia University Press, 1975. This project began as an academic sociological treatment of the ways modern Micmac Indians live in and around Boston. To do her research, however, Guillemin had to live among the Micmac and began to appreciate the unique dimensions of their culture.

Levi-Strauss, Claude. "The Sorcerer and his Magic." In *Structural Anthropology*, vol. I, pp. 167–185. New York: Basic Books, 1963. A poignant, thought-provoking analysis of skeptical Quesalid, a Kwakiutl shaman from the Pacific Northwest, who knew his techniques for healing sick people were tricks even though they seemed to work. Both Quesalid and Levi-Strauss ask why the techniques work.

Martin, Calvin. "The European Impact on the Culture of a Northeastern Algonquian Tribe: An Ecological Interpretation." *William and Mary Quarterly* 13(January 1974):3–26. This article was published while Martin was still a graduate student. His research addressed the question of why the frontier Indians systematically killed too many of the animals on which they depended for their lives and livelihood. He found that the Europeans had disrupted the Indian relationship to the land which had been "suffused with religious considerations."

————. *Keepers of the Game: Indian-Animal Relationships and the Fur Trade.* Berkeley and Los Angeles: University of California Press, 1979. Here Martin elaborates his thesis that European disease, Christianity, and the fur trade with its accompanying technology, were responsible for the corruption of the Indian relationship to the land.

Nabokov, Peter, ed. *Native American Testimony. An Anthology of Indian and White Relations. First Encounter to Dispossession.* New York: Thomas Y. Crowell, 1978. This is a collection of stories, speeches, recorded memories of many Indians, famous and not so well known.

Ortiz, Alfonso. *The Tewa World: Space, Time, Being and Becoming in a Pueblo Society.* Chicago: University of Chicago Press, 1969. Ever since they were "discovered" 400 years ago by the Spanish, the Tewa have been nominally Roman Catholic. But they took their own religion underground and have maintained it to this day, carefully guarding their ceremonies and inner life against the Anglo-American world. This scholarly work by an Indian who was born in a Tewa Pueblo in New Mexico reveals an inside view.

Rosen, Kenneth, ed. *Man to Send Rain Clouds: Contemporary Stories by American Indians.* New York: Viking, 1974. N. Scott Momaday, one of the authors, was a Kiowa Indian who won a Pulitzer Prize for his novel *House Made of Dawn.* Fiction by Indians themselves is an excellent way to find out "what is going on in the minds and hearts of American Indians today. . . ."

Vaughan, Alden T. "From White Man to Redskin: Changing Anglo-American Perceptions of the American Indian." *American Historical Review* 87(October 1982):917–953. A fascinating analysis of color metaphors (red, white, black) that convey ideas about race and ethnicity. Vaughan traces the ways European settlers developed color labels to describe Indians — white, olive, tawny, russet, brown, yellow, and, eventually, red.

Wallace Anthony F. C. *The Death and Rebirth of the Seneca.* New York: Vintage, 1972. According to Wallace, "This book tells the story of the late colonial and early reservation history of the Seneca Indians [one of the Iroquois peoples], and of the prophet Handsome Lake, his visions, and the moral and religious revitalization of an American Indian society that he and his followers achieved in the years around 1800."

4 The Urban Experience

Edited by **Jennifer Bradley**

Though legends often characterize Americans as creatures of great open spaces, the building of large communities has shaped much of what makes us a nation. Today more than 90 percent of our people live in urban areas, and that fact powerfully affects how Americans think and interact with others. Whether or not you live in a city, much of what you have become proceeds from city life.

For centuries the city has attracted both theorists, who were interested in the ideal and purpose of large centralized communities, and empiricists, who used observation and historical analysis to describe actual cities. Other people have been more activist and prescriptive than theoretical and descriptive; they built great cities and implemented the policies that governed the citizens. But even the most practical of city builders is never very far away from theory and empiricism. Thus, when Pierre L'Enfant laid out the plan for the new United States capital, Washington City, he relied on both the eighteenth-century theoretical ideal of balance and order and a thorough study of the design of Paris. Urban theory, urban analysis, and urban administration have always depended on one another's insights and methods.

This interpenetration of values and interests has found expression in one of the newest academic disciplines. Though discourse about cities is ages old, urban studies has become a profession only during this century. The American city in particular is a relatively recent experiment, so it is appropriate that Americans have been very active in this recently developed interdisciplinary study. Because a city is its design, its environmental impact, and its people, urban scholars combine sophisticated methods in aesthetics, environmental studies, and human services. University departments of urban studies require expertise from the traditional disciplines of philosophy, sociology, psychology, history, economics, public administration, political science, architecture, geography and cartography, geology, engineering, biological sciences, and communications studies — a wide range of scholarly interests.

Accordingly, urban scholars do not work in a vacuum. Enter any American university school of urban studies or any municipal department of planning and development — or even a private planning consultant's office — and you will see people of various academic backgrounds working as a team. Does your city require a new senior citizens' housing project? At the very least, you will need architects, landscape planners, and professionals in health care services, traffic control, and waste management. Do you and your neighbors wish to preserve an important architectural landmark? You will probably employ art historians, environmentalists, lawyers, and zoning specialists. Does the university plan to study ethnic diversity in a particular community? The urban studies department will call on the services of statisticians, linguists, anthropologists and sociologists, cartographers, and specialists in housing and education. In a sense, then, the study of urban life replicates the city environment itself: it has a dense and richly varied population, and if it is to progress, it requires mutual reliance and cooperation.

Hence the selections in this chapter demonstrate a variety of approaches to the urban environment. First, Robert F. Kennedy assumes an ideal of city living as he catalogues forces that compromise that purpose. Two pieces describe the views of ancient Mediterranean cultures about city life, the classical Greek city-state and the Judeo-Christian interpretations of the city. Next, several contemporary urban scholars present results of their work on city growth, Jane Jacobs arguing from an economic perspective, John W. Reps from American history, Howard J. Nelson from geography, and Stanley Milgram from social psychology. These approaches range from the most sweeping and general to more individual responses. Finally, because personal experience emerges most visibly in literary treatments of urban life, the chapter ends with a short story and a poem. Yet even here, comparing Shirley Jackson's protagonist and Walt Whitman's speaker, you see again an ancient vision of the city — the dialogue between the ideal and the real.

By viewing the city in light of various traditional disciplines and by observing the work of recent urbanologists, you become aware of the basic values, interpretations, and writing conventions of each discipline; like an urban planner, you use and synthesize various analytical tools as you analyze the American city; and ultimately, you analyze your own American experience.

Urban Crises in America

Robert F. Kennedy

Aristotle wrote that the city "should be such as may enable the inhabitants   1
to live at once temperately and liberally in the enjoyment of leisure." If we add
the objective of rewarding and satisfying work, we have a goal worthy of the
effort and energy of this entire generation of Americans.

Therefore, the city is not just housing and stores. It is not just education and   2
employment, parks and theaters, banks and shops. It is a place where men should
be able to live in dignity and security and harmony, where the great achievements of modern civilization and the ageless pleasures afforded by natural
beauty should be available to all.

If this is what we want — and this is what we must want if men are to be   3
free for that "pursuit of happiness" which was the earliest promise of the
American Nation — we will need more than poverty programs, housing programs, and employment programs, although we will need all of these. We will
need an outpouring of imagination, ingenuity, discipline, and hard work un-
matched since the first adventurers set out to conquer the wilderness. For the
problem is the largest we have ever known. And we confront an urban wilderness more formidable and resistant and in some ways more frightening than
the wilderness faced by the pilgrims or the pioneers.

The beginning of action is to understand the problem. We know riots are a   4
problem. We know that poverty is a problem. But underneath these problems
and all the others are a series of converging forces which rip at the fabric of
life in the American city. . . .

Five Forces Which Disrupt the City

One great problem is sheer growth — growth which crowds people into slums,   5
thrusts suburbs out over the countryside, burdens to the breaking point all our
old ways of thought and action — our systems of transport and water supply
and education, and our means of raising money to finance these vital services.

A second is destruction of the physical environment, stripping people of   6
contact with sun and fresh air, clean rivers, grass and trees — condemning them
to a life among stone and concrete, neon lights and an endless flow of automobiles. This happens not only in the central city, but in the very suburbs where

*After taking a Harvard law degree, Robert F. Kennedy (1925–1968) was counsel
in the U.S. Department of Justice and to governmental committees on investigation and improper activities. He served as attorney general in the cabinet of his
brother, President John F. Kennedy, and was later a senator from New York. He
was a leading candidate in the presidential primary elections when he was assassinated in Los Angeles.*

people once fled to find nature. "There is no police so effective," said Emerson, "as a good hill and a wide pasture . . . where the boys . . . can dispose of their superfluous strength and spirits." We cannot restore the pastures; but we must provide a chance to enjoy nature, a chance for recreation, for pleasure and for some restoration of that essential dimension of human existence which flows only from man's contact with the natural world around him.

A third is the increasing difficulty of transportation adding concealed, un-   7
paid hours to the workweek; removing men from the social and cultural amenities that are the heart of the city; sending destructive swarms of automobiles across the city, leaving behind them a band of concrete and poisoned atmosphere. And sometimes — as in Watts° — our surrender to the automobile has so crippled public transport that thousands literally cannot afford to go to work elsewhere in the city.

A fourth destructive force is the concentrated poverty and racial tension of   8
the urban ghetto — a problem so vast that the barest recital of its symptoms is profoundly shocking:

> Segregation is becoming the governing rule: Washington is only the most prominent example of a city which has become overwhelmingly Negro as whites move to the suburbs; many other cities are moving along the same road — for example, Chicago, which, if present trends continue, will be over 30 percent Negro in 1975. The ghettoes of Harlem and Southside and Watts are cities in themselves, areas of as much as 350,000 people.
> Poverty and unemployment are endemic: from one-third to one-half of the families in these areas live in poverty; in some, male unemployment may be as high as 40 percent; unemployment of Negro youths nationally is over 25 percent.
> Welfare and dependency are pervasive: one-fourth of the children in these ghettoes, as in Harlem, may receive Federal Aid to Dependent Children; in New York City, ADC alone costs over $20 million a month; in our five largest cities, the ADC bill is over $500 million a year.
> Housing is overcrowded, unhealthy, and dilapidated: the last housing census found 43 percent of urban Negro housing to be substandard; in these ghettoes, over 10,000 children may be injured or infected by rat bites every year.
> Education is segregated, unequal, and inadequate: the high school dropout rate averages 70 percent; there are academic high schools in which less than 3 percent of the entering students will graduate with an academic diploma.
> Health is poor and care inadequate: infant mortality in the ghettoes is more than twice the rate outside; mental retardation among Negroes caused by inadequate prenatal care is more than seven times the white rate; one-half of all babies born in Manhattan last year will have had no prenatal care at all; deaths from diseases like tuberculosis, influenza, and pneumonia are two to three times as common as elsewhere.

Fifth is both cause and consequences of all the rest. It is the destruction of   9
the sense, and often the fact, of community, of human dialog, the thousand invisible strands of common experience and purpose, affection and respect which tie men to their fellows. Community is expressed in such words as neighbor-

---

°Watts: Black neighborhood in Los Angeles.

hood, civic pride, friendship. It provides the life-sustaining force of human warmth and security, a sense of one's own human significance in the association and companionship of others.

Considerations

1. "Urban Crises in America" is part of Robert F. Kennedy's testimony before the Senate Committee on Government Operations in 1966. Speculate on Kennedy's rationale for organizing the five destructive forces in this order.
2. Analyze Kennedy's rhetorical effect by focusing on two devices of writing:
   a. *metaphor* — What metaphorical expressions does Kennedy use, and how do the literal meanings contribute to the points he is making?
   b. *statistics* — At what points does Kennedy use facts and figures, and why?

The Polis
Aristotle

The end of the state is not mere life; it is, rather a good quality of life. [If   *1* mere life were the end], there might be a state of slaves, or even a state of animals; but in the world as we know it any such state is impossible, because slaves and animals do not share in true felicity and free choice. Similarly, it is not the end of the state to provide an alliance for mutual defense against all

The Politics *of Aristotle (384–322* B.C.) *is one of the prime texts of Western theories of government. Because of Aristotle's importance as a philosopher, it is easy to forget that his method was invariably inductive. That is, though Aristotle spoke with authority, that authoritative voice depends on much research and thought. And though Aristotle believed in his own culture's central values and traditions, he and his assistants collected plans of government (constitutions) from many parts of the world. Only after careful analysis did he classify the observable data and describe the ideal political order.*

Aristotle did not know the modern metropolis or the nation-state; he assumed the city-state, or polis, *as a standard. All of Greece might share a common language, religion, and racial heritage, but each of the city-states had its own geographical limits, economic independence, defense capability, and system of laws. Though some philosophers believed that this standard had evolved merely because of convention and convenience, Aristotle perceived it as entirely natural. But by natural he did not mean instinctual or impulsive; for Aristotle, it is the nature of people to rise above instinct, and in a community of mutually-dependent, responsible citizens, people achieve their natural human state. This for Aristotle was the purpose of the* polis.

injury, or to ease exchange and promote economic intercourse. If that had been the end, the Etruscans and the Carthaginians would be in the position of belonging to a single state; and the same would be true of all peoples who have commercial treaties with one another. But it is the cardinal issue of goodness or badness in the life of the polis which always engages the attention of any state that concerns itself to secure a system of laws well obeyed. The conclusion which clearly follows is that any polis which is truly so called, and is not merely one in name, must devote itself to the end of encouraging goodness. Otherwise, a political association sinks into a mere alliance, which only differs in space from other forms of alliance where the members live at a distance from one another. Otherwise, too, law becomes a mere covenant — or (in the phrase of the Sophist Lycophron) "a guarantor of men's rights against one another" — instead of being, as it should be, a rule of life such as will make the members of a polis good and just.

It is clear, therefore, that a polis is not an association for residence on a   2
common site, or for the sake of preventing mutual injustice and easing exchange. These are indeed conditions which must be present before a polis can exist; but the presence of all these conditions is not enough, in itself, to constitute a polis. What constitutes a polis is an association of households and clans in a good life, for the sake of attaining a perfect and self-sufficing existence. A polis is constituted by the association of families and villages in a perfect and self-sufficing existence; and such an existence, in our definition, consists in a life of true felicity and goodness.

In the light of this general preface, and bearing in mind our previous dis-   3
cussion . . . . , we may now embark on the rest of our theme. The first question which arises is, "What are the necessary bases for the construction of an ideal state?" An ideal constitution is bound to require an equipment appropriate to its nature. We must therefore assume, as its basis, a number of ideal conditions, which must be capable of fulfilment as well as being ideal. These conditions include, among others, a citizen body and a territory. The primary factor necessary, in the equipment of a state, is the human material; and this involves us in considering the quality, as well as the quantity, of the population naturally required. The second factor is territory; and here too we have to consider quality as well as quantity. Most men think that the happiness of a state depends on its being great. They may be right; but even if they are, they do not know what it is that makes a state great or small. They judge greatness in numerical terms, by the size of the population; but it is capacity, rather than size, which should properly be the criterion. States, like other things, have a function to perform; and the state which shows the highest capacity for performing the function of a state is therefore the one which should be counted greatest. In the same way Hippocrates would naturally be described as "greater" (not as a man, but as a doctor) than somebody who was superior in point of bodily size.

The initial stage of the state may therefore be said to require such an initial   4
amount of population as will be self-sufficient for the purpose of achieving a good way of life in the shape and form of a political association. A state which exceeds this initial amount may be a still greater state; but such increase of

size, as has already been noticed, cannot continue indefinitely. What the limit of increase should be is a question easily answered if we look at the actual facts. The activities of a state are partly the activities of its governors, and partly those of the governed. The function of governors is to issue commands and give decisions. [The function of the governed is to elect the governors.] Both in order to give decisions in matters of disputed rights, and to distribute the offices of government according to the merit of candidates, the citizens of a state must know one another's characters. Where this is not the case, the distribution of offices and the giving of decisions will suffer. Both are matters in which it is wrong to act on the spur of the moment; but that is what obviously happens where the population is overlarge. These considerations indicate clearly the optimum standard of population. It is, in a word, "the greatest surveyable number required for achieving a life of self-sufficiency."

Similar considerations apply also to the matter of territory. So far as the 5 *character* of the soil is concerned, everybody would obviously give the preference to a territory which ensured the maximum of self-sufficiency; and as that consists in having everything, and needing nothing, such a territory must be one which produces all kinds of crops. In point of *extent* and size, the territory should be large enough to enable its inhabitants to live a life of leisure which combines liberality with temperance. As for the general lie of the land, it is easy to make the suggestion (though here a number of questions arise on which the advice of military experts ought to be taken) that the territory of a state should be difficult of access to enemies, and easy of egress for its inhabitants. What was said above of the population — that it should be such as to be surveyable — is equally true of the territory. A territory which can be easily surveyed is also a territory which can be easily defended. The ideal position for the central city should be determined by considerations of its being easy of access both by land and by sea. [Two matters are here involved.] The first, which has already been mentioned, is that the city should be a common military center for the dispatch of aid to all points in the territory. The second is that it should also be a convenient commercial center, where the transport of food supplies, timber for building, and raw materials for any other similar industry which the territory may possess, can easily be handled.

On this follows that, if states need property, property nevertheless is not a 6 part of the state. It is true that property includes a number of animate beings, as well as inanimate objects. But the state is an association of equals, and only of equals; and its object is the best and highest life possible. The highest good is felicity; and that consists in the energy and perfect practice of goodness. But in actual life this is not for all; some may share in it fully, but others can only share in it partially or cannot even share at all. The consequence is obvious. These different capacities will issue in different kinds and varieties of states, and in a number of different constitutions. Pursuing felicity in various ways and by various means, different peoples create for themselves different ways of life and different constitutions.

It remains for us now to enumerate *all* the elements necessary for the exis- 7 tence of the state. Our list of these elements will include what we have called the "parts" of the state as well as what we have termed its "conditions." To make such a list we must first determine how many services a state performs; and then we shall easily see how many elements it must contain. The first thing to be provided is food. The next is arts and crafts; for life is a business which needs many tools. The third is arms: the members of a state must bear arms in person, partly in order to maintain authority and repress disobedience, and partly in order to meet any threat of external aggression. The fourth thing which has to be provided is a certain supply of property, alike for domestic use and for military purposes. The fifth (but, in order of merit, the first) is an establishment for the service of the gods, or, as it is called, public worship. The sixth thing, and the most vitally necessary, is a method of deciding what is demanded by the public interest and what is just in men's private dealings. These are the services which every state may be said to need. A state is not a mere casual group. It is a group which, as we have said, must be self-sufficient for the purposes of life; and if any of these services is missing it cannot be totally self-sufficient. A state should accordingly be so constituted as to be competent for all these services. It must therefore contain a body of farmers to produce the necessary food; craftsmen; a military force; a propertied class; priests; and a body for deciding necessary issues and determining what is the public interest.

Considerations

1. Summarize the purposes Aristotle assigned to the *polis* (the city-state).
2. At what points does Aristotle appear to be anticipating and responding to his audience's conceptions about the city-state?
3. Using the standards of excellence for your own composition class, grade Aristotle's essay and defend your evaluation orally or in wirting.

Connections

1. You recall that Robert F. Kennedy refers to Aristotle in his testimony at the Ribicoff hearings. Using "Urban Crises in America," show which of Aristotle's purposes for the *polis* are fulfilled by the modern city and which purposes are not.
2. Review the descriptions of native North American culture in Chapter 3, The Frontier Indians. Then write an Aristotelian analysis of traditional Indian communities. In other words, had Aristotle known about these communities, to what extent would he have accepted them as demonstrations of the ideal *polis?*

The City in the Bible

Ronald D. Pasquariello,
Donald W. Shriver, Jr., and
Alan Geyer

The Bible is not the only source to which Jews and Christians turn for giv-   *1*
ing an account of themselves and their points of view. But it is a particularly
important source, for it records the earliest surviving memories of these religious communities. In different periods of Western history, Christians have
understood the biblical tradition from various points of view.

Ever since Augustine's great work, *The City of God*, theologians have been   *2*
well aware that the murderer Cain is credited with being the builder of the
first mundane city, while Abel, a farmer, "built none." One way of reading all
the rest of the Bible is to highlight the judgments and the destructions that
God brings upon human cities — Babel, Sodom, Gomorrah, Jericho, Ninevah,
Babylon, Rome. Each of these cities is famous in the biblical narrative for its
idolatry against the true God and its oppressions to the people of God. Each
becomes a symbol of the dangers of city life to the life of fidelity to the Kingdom of God. In this part of the biblical perspective, cities are sinful places.
Prophets like Amos condemn them as places where the poor are oppressed,
commerce supplants community, and the old life of the desert people gives way
to the settled life with all its temptations of idolatry.

Among biblical interpreters, none has pursued this negative view of the city   *3*
as one theme of the Bible with more drastic consistency than Jacques Ellul.
His book, *The Meaning of the City*, set out to discover "what the Bible reveals
concerning the city." He concludes from his study, "From the first book in the
Bible to the last there is the same judgment of the city" — the same negative
judgment.[1] Everywhere in the Bible Ellul finds the human city as the place of
idolatry, oppression, and opposition of human power to the power of God.
Typical of the Ellulian reading of the urban theme in the scriptures are the
following excerpts from the book:[2]

The very fact of living in a city directs a man down an inhuman road.

It was in slavery that Israel and the city were bound together. . . . Never again will
the cities built by the chosen people be an act of the chosen people. . . . And the pro-

Ronald D. Pasquariello (b. 1939), Donald W. Shriver, Jr. (b. 1927), and Alan
Geyer (b. 1931) are all theologians concerned with contemporary social ethics.
Pasquariello is a senior fellow in urban policy at the Churches' Center for Theol-
ogy and Public Policy in Washington, D.C. Shriver, an ordained minister, is pres-
ident of Union Theological Seminary in New York City, where he is also professor
of applied Christianity. Geyer is executive director of the Churches' Center for The-
ology and Public Policy and is a specialist in world peace and disarmament.

phesies of those long-haired prophets who were a constant reminder of the innocence of the nomadic life as opposed to urban life were based on that first apprenticeship: Israel bound herself to slavery, and even more, to the land of sorrow and sin by the cities she built, cities that were always the imitation of what she had learned in Egypt. . . .

The spiritual power of the city must . . . clash with the spirit of grace. Such is the central problem that the city represents for Israel. Such is the problem for every man who wants to live by the grace of Christ.

All that is said about Babylon can be applied to every other city. . . .

The Scriptures affirm that the agent of war is the great city. There is no such thing as a great agricultural war. A rural people is never a ravenous people.

The message of the cross must be carried to the center of man's autonomy. It must be established where man is most clearly a wild beast. . . . Christ's sending his disciples out into the cities of Israel is their most dangerous mission, for it is directed against the heart of the world's power and betrayal.

In Matthew's text we see Jesus speaking differently to the multitude than to the city. The multitude, the crowd! Such is the form of life in the city. Man can be nothing but a crowd in the city. . . . He has no silent zone; he lives in a perpetual noise that eliminates any isolation, any meditation, any authentic contact.

Can anyone change the evil city? Yes, says Ellul. Ultimately God promises   4
a New Jerusalem, a new creation where humans at last are delivered from their idolatry. The old urban vision of humans has been abolished. . . . In the meantime,

> . . . it is no holy world. Let there be no confusion: there is no use expecting a New Jerusalem on earth. Jerusalem will be God's action, absolutely free, unforeseeable, transcendent . . . from this very city [God] is going to make the new Jerusalem. Thus we can observe God's strange progress: Jerusalem becomes Babylon, Babel is restored to the status of a simple city, and this city becomes the city of the living God.[3]

Jews and Christians who read their Bibles through the spectacles of Jacques   5
Ellul will be looking from an angle of vision different from ours. We attempt no reasoned refutation of his vision here. Simply, our problem with his approach to the Bible is its one-dimensioned insistence on shaping its message to his theological predispositions. Absent from his reading is an appreciation for the mixed righteousness and corruption in David, the founder and first king of Jerusalem; the combination of judgment and hope for historic eighth-century Jerusalem in the prophecies of the First Isaiah; the almost-physical hope for restoration of his beloved city in the later prophecies of Jeremiah; the meaning of the contrast between the prophet Nahum (gleeful over the destruction of Nineveh) and Jonah (who is required by God to preach repentance to that city); the fact that the early church begins in Jerusalem, that the early churches were primarily urban in location, that Paul put a high value upon his Roman citizenship and his vocation for preaching the gospel in Rome; and the possibility that theological ambivalence towards human cities is a better summation of "the" biblical view than theological condemnation.

We believe that ambivalence is the better summation. We resist Ellul's penchant for a dialectic that verges on dualism — God's grace over against the constructs of humans. We read the Bible as a book full of the same confusing mixture of good and evil that we detect every day in cities where we live. *Empirically* claims like "The very fact of living in cities directs a man down an inhuman road" and "A rural people is never a ravenous people" are absurd. Jews who left the ghettoes of Russia in the late nineteenth century to come to America left a rural culture dominated by "ravenous" anti-semitism; and they found, even in the steaming East Side of New York City, a degree of blessing that was not in absolute contrast to the ancient liberation from Egypt. The world of human cities, and God's relation to them, is more complex, less single-dimensioned than Ellul's account of the Bible permits. We need not be captive to his way of interpreting the Jewish and Christian heritages.   6

On the other hand, we would not want our angle of vision to be mistaken   7
for typical, liberal American confidence in the goodness and the promise of human achievement as represented by the city. A tendency towards this confidence was evident in the 1965 book by Harvey Cox, *The Secular City.* In one important point of theological and biblical interpretation, Cox agrees with Ellul: from the Exodus to the cross of Jesus, God was at work "secularizing" the traditional "holy times and places" of human culture. After the Exodus and after the resurrection of Jesus, no one has an excuse for worshipping in an urban temple as the holy place to find God or living on a rural patch of earth as the only place to remain human.

The modern secular city, says Cox, is an embodiment and a celebration of   8
change, mobility, open human futures. In resonance with the experience of many Americans, Cox points out that rural and small town living has its own slaveries. Even the anonymity of city life can be a stage in the loosening of old, suffocating identities imposed by small town culture upon its inhabitants.

> The contemporary urban region represents an ingenious device for vastly enlarging the range of human communication and widening the scope of individual choice. Urbanization thus contributes to the freedom of man.

> The Gospel . . . means a summons to choice and answerability. . . . In the historical process itself man meets the One who calls him into being as a free deciding self, and knows that neither his past history nor his environment determines what he does. In the anonymity of modern culture, far from the fishbowl of town life, modern man experiences both the terror and the delight of human freedom more acutely. . . . The God of the Gospel is the One who wills freedom and responsibility, who points towards the future in hope. The Law, on the other hand, includes any cultural phenomenon which holds men in immaturity, in captivity to convention and tradition. The Law is enforced by the weight of human opinion; the Gospel is the activity of God creating new possibilities in history. . . . From this perspective, urbanization can be seen as a liberation from some of the cloying bondages of preurban society. It is the chance to be free.[4]

Cox would also agree with Ellul that out in the wilderness the Israelites were   9
closer to their Lord than when they flirted with the "lords" (the Baalim) of Canaan. The latter were stationary gods-of-the-land. They were immobile, but Yahweh "went before" his people. "He moved wherever he wanted to."

This was a crucial victory for the Yahwist faith, since the historical character of Is- rael's vision of life depends on Yahweh's stalwart refusal to be a hearthgod of some home-sweet-home.

Similarly, and more radically, the early Christians believed in the ascension of the resurrected Jesus, with the implication that now "Jesus is mobile." The Spirit that raised him from the dead still "goes before" the faithful disciples, who on earth have "no lasting city" (Hebrews 13:14). "They were essentially travellers." As such, they often founded their earliest churches in the cities rather than the less mobile rural countryside of the Roman Empire. "Mobile man," in Cox's view,

> . . . is less tempted than the immobile to demote Yahweh into a baal. He will usually not idolatrize any town or nation. He will not be as likely to see the present economic and political structure as the unambigious expression of how things always have been and always should be. He will be more open to change, movement, newness. There is no reason why Christians should deplore the accelerating mobility of the modern me- tropolis. The Bible does not call man to renounce mobility, but "to go to a place that I will show you" (Genesis 12:1). Perhaps the mobile man can even hear with less static a message about a man who was born during a journey, spent his first years in exile, was expelled from his own home town, and declared that he had no place to lay his head. High mobility is no assurance of salvation, but neither is it an obstacle to faith.[5]

On the whole, the contrast between the Ellul and the Cox perspectives on *10* the biblical "meaning of the city" is stark. Rather than a symbol of human idolatry, the secular city for Cox is a symbol of a human step of obedience to God, the on-the-move ruler of history. Rather than being an inhuman oppres- sor of individuality and community among humans, the city is "the common- wealth of maturity and interdependence."[6] Rather than deluding humans about their capacity to live with no thought of their Creator, the modern city is a summons from the Creator to the responsible use of God-given powers. Rather than being an occasion for new enslavement of the weak by the powerful, the city can be understood as the context of a great gospel summons to new hu- man effort "to come to terms with the new historical reality" of urban, secular society and with "the formulation of ways to live more equitably with other human beings in a system of increasing reciprocity."[7]

[We] would not encourage any reader to side with one or the other of two *11* such contrasting ways for reading the Bible and the experience of modern hu- mans in their cities. Each such perspective calls our attention to something real, and from each we have important truth to learn. On the whole, we would warn against the danger of one-sided exegesis, of which we suspect Ellul to have been guilty, or lopsided emphasis on the liberating side of the modern urban experience, into which Cox sometimes fell. Indeed, the Bible's contri- bution to our understanding is richer, more complex, and more illuminating than any of our interpretations, including the one to follow here. That is why we are all well-advised to keep reading this ancient book, in the confidence shown by John Robinson as he bade farewell to the America-bound Pilgrims in 1620: "God has yet more light to break forth from his Holy Word."

Our "light," in the following, is derived from a view of the Bible and the *12* views of those Bible scholars that accentuate two-sided ambivalence concerning human cities in relation to the City of God. This ambivalence is found in the Bible itself, in our experience of cities, and in our own disposition to entertain hope rather than despair for them. We are sympathetic, for example, with the views of an Old Testament scholar like Bernhard Anderson, who has concluded that the story of the Tower of Babel° is not about the city, but about unity and diversity. The story needs to be understood in terms of the creation theology that precedes it. Humans are not condemned for their pride and creativity, but because of their intention to gather people into a centralized location, thereby resisting God's purpose that they should multiply, fill the earth and subdue it.[8] Anderson claims that to see the city, on the basis of the Babel story, as the locus of evil in human history is an insufficiently contextual interpretation.

Sodom and Gomorrah, on the other hand, were condemned for a sin much   13
worse than the [licentiousness] that is often associated with their name. They were condemned for inhospitality towards strangers, perhaps the greatest moral offense in desert countries. In Bedouin cultures, the desert was the common enemy. Survival was always at stake. Among Bedouins, even one's enemy was to be protected and treated with hospitality while he was within a host's tent. Prophets like Amos demanded that Israel remember the abiding principles of fidelity to its Lord and its own humanity revealed in the Exodus-liberation of the nation. Here was no romantic longing for a rural lifestyle but an insistence that neighborliness to strangers belonged to cities, too.

Babylon is frequently criticized in the Bible, no doubt because its rulers   14
dominated the Middle East for long periods of biblical history. While Babylon is accused of all types of urban immorality, the underlying evil is her worship of false gods. The essence of Israelite identity is the worship of one, true God, Yahweh. Babylon's blandishments to idolatry cause its condemnation. (See Isaiah 46:1–13.)

Babylon appears again in the Book of Revelation, where it is a symbol of   15
Rome. Here, as in the prophets, it is criticized for its pride and immorality, but it is ultimately condemned for its cult of emperor worship, a case once more of setting up false gods before the one true God. (See Revelation 17:1–14.)

Throughout the Bible, God's love for the city is never in doubt: "On the holy   16
mount stands the city he founded; the Lord loves the gates of Zion more than all the dwelling places of Jacob" (Psalm 87:1–2). Even in judgment, always tempered with a vision of redemption, God's love is present. God is at work in the city throughout history, redeeming creation.

In *A Theological Word Book of the Bible*,[9] Alan Richardson has written under   17
the entry *city:*

> The equivocal attitude of the Bible towards the culminating point of human social organization, the city, constitutes a good example of the biblical dialectical point of

---

°Babel: City condemned by God for trying to build a tower that would reach into the heavens; citizens were punished with the loss of their common language.

view. On the one hand, a city may be a lovely and noble place: the earthly Jerusalem is to be God's dwelling place. . . . On the other hand, cities may become the habitation of all that is vile, oppressive and horrible in human life. . . .

The Bible is equivocal in its attitude toward the city. The biblical images [18] contain a realistic assessment of what the city is and what it is supposed to be. Yet the equivocal attitude does not apply to God's ultimate purpose for the city nor to the city as the people of God. Throughout the biblical narrative God's love for the city is never in doubt. . . . We cannot sit back in judgment or apathy toward the city. The biblical message is clear: God is at work in the city redeeming his creation. If those of us who see ourselves as God's people are to be part of that new creation, then we must join in that process.

NOTES
[1] *The Meaning of the City* (Grand Rapids, Mich.: Eerdmans, 1970), pp. 7–8.
[2] Ibid., pp. 22, 24–25, 41, 50, 51, 83, and 125.
[3] Ibid., p. 171.
[4] *The Secular City* (New York: Macmillan, 1965), pp. 40, 47.
[5] Ibid., pp. 56–58.
[6] Ibid., p. 116.
[7] Ibid., p. 123.
[8] Bernhard Anderson, "The Babel Story: Paradigm of Human Unity and Diversity," in Andrew M. Greeley and Gregory Baum, *Ethnicity* (New York: Seabury Press, 1977), pp. 66–67.
[9] Alan Richardson, *A Theological Word Book of the Bible* (London: SCM Press, 1950), p. 49.

Considerations

1. What is the purpose of "The City in the Bible"? That is, do authors Pasquariello, Shriver, and Geyer present propositions of fact and write to convince the audience that their description is true or valid, or do they present propositions of action and write to prescribe some action? Or is their purpose more complicated?
2. According to "The City in the Bible," what features do the books of Jacques Ellul and Harvey Cox share, and what is their central disagreement? As you summarize the major comparisons and contrasts between these two aruments, be sure to take into account Pasquariello, Shriver, and Geyer's own thesis about the Biblical meaning and treatment of the city.

Connections

1. Does Robert F. Kennedy's approach and purpose in "Urban Crises in America" place him as an ally of Ellul, of Cox, of the authors, or of none of these writers?
2. Look up the words *telos* and *teleology*, terms often used by philosophers and theologians. Use these definitions to analyze how the classical Greek view of the city (Aristotle's *polis*) and the Biblical view (according to Pasquariello, Shriver, and Geyer) are each teleological. In addition, compare the two versions of *telos*.

Cities and the Wealth of Nations

Jane Jacobs

Nations are political and military entities, and so are blocs of nations. But   *1*
it doesn't necessarily follow from this that nations are also the salient entities
of economic life or that they are particularly useful for probing the mysteries
of economic structure, the reasons for the rise and decline of wealth. Indeed,
the failures of national governments to force economic life to do their bidding
suggest that nations are essentially irrelevant to promoting economic success.
It also affronts common sense, if nothing else, to think of entities as disparate
as, say, Singapore and the United States, or Ecuador and the Soviet Union, or
the Netherlands and Canada, as economic analogues. All they really have in
common is the political fact of sovereignty.

Once we remove the blinders that mislead us into assuming that nations are   *2*
economic units and try looking at the economic world as it is rather than as a
dependent artifact of politics, we see that most nations are grab bags of very
different economies, of rich regions and poor ones.

We see, too, that among all the various types of economies, those of cities   *3*
are unique in their power to shape the economies of other settlements, including ones far removed geographically. To take a simple and small example, consider the forces at work on the economy of a single hamlet, a little cluster of
stone houses perched high in the Cévennes Mountains, in south central France,
one of the poorest parts of that country. The hamlet, Bardou, found its way
into my Toronto morning paper because it is so charming, having become a
kind of Shangri-la for writers, musicians, artists, and craftsmen fleeing the cities of Europe, the United States, and Canada in search of beauty and a cheap,
quiet place in which to work.

Bardou has a long history. Some two thousand years ago, when Gaul be-   *4*
came a province of Rome, the site was linked to the imperial economy by roads
terminating at a collection of iron mines nearby. The iron was taken elsewhere
to be shaped into swords, lances, chisels, hinges, ploughs, wheel rims, cauld-
rons, and the many other items for which iron was useful at the time. Where
it went for manufacturing is now unknown. A logical guess is the foundries in
Nîmes, an extremely ancient city that had become a metropolis of this part of

*Though Jane Jacobs (b. 1916) never attended college, she is a successful writer
and editor. An active apologist for the conservation of city architecture, she has
long criticized conventional urban planning and renewal. Jacobs believes instead
that the natural evolution of city environments is the basis of modern civilization.
These themes run throughout her three most celebrated works,* The Death and Life
of Great American Cities *(1961),* The Economy of Cities *(1969), and* Cities and
the Wealth of Nations *(1984).*

Gaul in pre-Roman times, or it might have been carried to Lugdunum, now Lyon, which also has an ancient tradition as a metalworking center and which was the hub of the Roman road system in Gaul. Wherever the foundry was, the metal was in sufficient demand there to justify mine roads so well engineered and so solidly built that, though they have gone largely untended and unrepaired for some fifteen centuries, they still serve admirably as hikers' trails. The mines and the roads were abandoned when economic life in this part of Gaul disintegrated, probably in the fourth century.

The area then reverted to wilderness, unpopulated, as far as has been dis- 5 covered, until the sixteenth century, when squatters — landless peasants pushed up from the valley and slopes below — built themselves the stone houses of the present-day hamlet. They scratched out little garden plots among the rocks, gathered chestnuts and probably caught game in the surrounding forests, and on their poor and rocky soil pursued as well as they could the subsistence arts they had inherited from economies of the distant past more creative than their own. Lifetime after lifetime, nothing changed.

Then, abruptly, in the 1870s, a radical change began to take place. Word 6 somehow arrived that a more desirable life was to be found far away. Perhaps the information percolated back from army recruits who had been stationed in Paris or who had passed through there in the aftermath of the Franco-Prussian War, or perhaps it came from migrants who had left villages on the mountains' lower slopes. Paris had been drawing in rural migrants for untold generations; the word was very late in reaching Bardou, but once a few venturesome souls left to find city work, a slow but almost total exodus ensued. By 1900, half the population had departed. During the following forty years, everybody left except for three families.

In 1966, when two hikers happened by on the old Roman roads, the ruins 7 sheltered only one aged man. The hikers bought the hamlet from him and from such descendants of former inhabitants as they and their lawyers could trace. The new owners moved in and invited kindred spirits to join them and help pay expenses. In this incarnation, Bardou has a changing core of year-round residents who live on their savings or by selling their works to publishers and other customers in the city. Holiday renters and campers are welcomed, along with the income they bring. Residents and vacationers alike live chiefly on imported food, of course, and they import nearly all their other necessities, too; but they make a virtue of getting along without such amenities as electricity, telephones, and hot water.

Bardou is an example, in microcosm, of a "passive economy," meaning an 8 economy that does not create economic change itself but instead responds to forces unloosed in distant cities. Time and again, like a toy on a string, Bardou has been jerked by some *external* economic energy or other. In ancient times, the site was exploited for its iron and then abandoned. In modern times, it was depopulated when distant city jobs attracted its people and then was repopulated by city people. The string-pulling was not gentle. But when cities and city people left Bardou alone, had no use for it, the place either had no economy whatsoever, as when it was a wilderness, or else had a subsistence economy that remained unchanging.

We could beat our brains out trying to explain Bardou's economic history 9 in terms of its own attributes, right down to compiling statistics on the probable average yield of chestnuts, the tools used there, the quantity and quality of iron taken out and of that remaining, the man-hours required to build a house, the nature of the soil, the annual rainfall, and so on — and none of this would enlighten us at all as to why and how Bardou's economy took the twists and turns it actually did. On that subject, the local clues stand mute, for the clues that in reality explain Bardou's economic history are to be found in distant city markets, city jobs, city technology (which built the new water system and the old roads), city work transplanted, city capital. To understand both the changes that occurred in Bardou and why there were periods when nothing changed, we must look to clues that do not define Bardou in any way *except as they have acted upon Bardou.*

At first thought it may seem like hairsplitting to differentiate between jerks   10
administered to Bardou by various cities and jerks administered by entities we can choose to call, instead, the Roman Empire, France, the European Economic Community, and the international economy. But it is not hairsplitting. The reality is that those jerks were administered to Bardou by particular cities. All around Bardou lies something called "the French national economy," but that has not been what put Bardou through its economic twists and turns. Why be fuzzy about these things if we can be specific? Rome, perhaps Nîmes or Lyon, Paris, and the various cities from which Bardou's current population of artists, writers, and vacationers have come — these cities are the salient economic entities that have shaped and reshaped Bardou.

Distinctions between city economies and the potpourris as we call national   11
economies are not only useful for getting a grip on realities; they are of the essence where practical attempts to reshape economic life are concerned. For example, the failure to make such distinctions is directly responsible for many wildly expensive economic debacles in backward countries. These have resulted from failing to observe that the little understood but economically indispensable function of import replacing or import substitution is specifically a city function, and from thinking of it fuzzily as something a "national economy" can be made to do. . . . Cities grow and become economically versatile by replacing goods that they once imported with goods that they make themselves, . . . blindness to this ordinary reality is the source of much confusion in our economic thinking in general, as well as the source of much nonsense, waste, and lost opportunity for development.

Cities that significantly replace imports replace not only finished goods but,   12
concurrently, many, many items of producers' goods and services — that is, those sold not to consumers but to other producers. They do it in swiftly emerging, logical chains. For example, first comes the local processing of fruit preserves that were formally imported; then comes the production of jars or other packaging materials, formerly imported, for which there was no local market of producers until the first step had been taken. Or, first comes the assembly of formerly imported pumps, for which parts are imported; then comes the making of parts, for which metal is imported; then, possibly, comes the smelting of metal for these and other import replacements. The process pays for itself as it goes along. When Tokyo began producing bicycles, first came

repair work cannibalizing imported bicycles, then came the manufacture of some of the parts most in demand for repair work, then came the manufacture of more parts, and finally came the assembly of whole, Tokyo-made bicycles. And almost as soon as Tokyo began exporting bicycles to other Japanese cities, some of those customer cities began much the same process of replacing bicycles imported from Tokyo.

A city's production of goods for export — the work that pays for the imports 13 — helps the city's import-replacing process. For example, an enterprise that electroplates tableware for export can also electroplate metal chair and table legs, and thus can play a part in locally producing furniture that has formerly been imported. Or, better yet, workers can break away from the parent plant and set up a second plant, but this time they will be working in a furniture-making enterprise rather than for a tableware company. I say "better yet" because now there are two establishments, not one, to help carry out the import-replacing process.

Import replacing has always been a *city* process, for good, practical reasons. 14 In the first place, replacing imports is impossible to achieve economically, skillfully, and flexibly — that is, in ways suitable to the time and place — except in a settlement that is already versatile enough at production to possess the necessary foundation for the new work. Cities can build up that kind of versatility, often very rapidly, in part as a result of their already existing export work (if it is reasonably diversified), in part as a result of their previous simpler achievements in import replacing, and in part as a result of the complex symbiotic relationships formed among their various producers. In the second place, city markets — whether of consumers or of producers — are at once diverse and concentrated. These two qualities of the local market make economically feasible the local production of many kinds of goods and services that would not be feasible in rural places, company towns, or little market towns.

Proponents of economic specialization would of course attack the idea that 15 import replacing is economically constructive. Specialization, they would argue, represents the division of labor on a regional or an international scale; division of labor is efficient; and, therefore, specialized economies form and persist because the arrangement is efficient. Adam Smith, for one, believed this.

The argument has two major flaws. In the first place, the reasoning is cir- 16 cular. It assumes that a result — in this case, efficiency — is its own cause. One might as well say that rain is beneficial to plants and that that is why it rains. The second flaw in the argument is that specialized economies are not efficient in any case. That is why they are commonly poor or else subsidized. To be sure, their specialties are sometimes (not always) efficiently produced. But that is not the same as saying these economies are efficient. An economy that contains few different niches for people's differing skills, interests, and imaginations is not efficient. An economy that is unresourceful and unadaptable is not efficient. An economy that can fill few of the needs of its own people and producers is not efficient.

Economic life develops by grace of innovating; it expands by grace of im- 17 port replacing. These two master economic processes are closely related, both being functions of city economies. Furthermore, successful import replacing often entails adaptations in design, materials, or methods of production, and these require innovating and improvising, especially of producer's goods and services.

Any settlement that becomes proficient at import replacing *becomes* a city.   *18*
And any city that repeatedly achieves explosive episodes of import replacing keeps its economy up-to-date and keeps itself capable of generating streams of innovative export work. Why "explosive episodes"? In real life, whenever import replacing occurs to a significant extent, it occurs in explosive episodes, because it works as a chain reaction. The process feeds itself and, once well under way in a given city, does not cease until all the imports that it is economically feasible to replace at that time and in that place have been replaced. Once an episode is over, a city must build up new funds of potentially replaceable imports, mostly the products of other cities, if it is to experience another chain reaction. The process vastly enlarges city economies as well as diversifies them, and causes cities to grow in spurts. The growth is by no means all net growth, however. Much import replacing, especially in already large cities, merely compensates for the loss of older work. Cities are forever losing older work: some of it because former customer cities take to replacing imports themselves, and even become competitive producers of the items they formerly imported; some because well-established enterprises, after having first developed in the symbiotic city nest, transplant their operations to distant places; some because old work, together with many old enterprises, grows obsolete.

Whenever a city replaces imports with its own production, other settle-   *19*
ments, mostly other cities, lose sales to it. However, other settlements — either the ones that have lost export sales or different ones — gain an equivalent value of *new* export work. This is because an import-replacing city does not import less than it otherwise would. Rather, it shifts to other purchases in lieu of what it no longer needs from outside. Since the city has everything it formerly had, plus its complement of new and different imports, economic life as a whole expands by grace of this process. Indeed, as far as I can see, city import replacing is at the root of all economic expansion.

It is important, if we are to understand the rise and decline of wealth, for   *20*
us to be specific about how expansion occurs and of what it consists. The expansion that derives from city import replacing consists specifically of five forms of growth: abruptly enlarged city markets for new and different imports, consisting largely of goods from rural areas and of innovations being produced in other cities; abruptly increased numbers and kinds of jobs in the import-replacing city; new uses of technology, particularly to increase rural productivity; increased transplants of city work into non-urban locations as older, expanding enterprises are crowded out; and the growth of city capital.

These five great forces exert far-reaching effects outside of import-replacing   *21*
cities as well as within them, ultimately affecting even the remotest places, like Bardou.

Considerations

1. Many urbanologists rely on empirical statistical studies of discrete city environments. Jane Jacobs does not. What rhetorical techniques and modes of development does she use instead?

2. What common assumptions about economic forces does Jacobs aim to dispel in "Cities and the Wealth of Nations"? At what points does she refer directly or indirectly to those who disagree with her, and how does she time those references in her essay?
3. Define *import replacing* and trace its normal process, explaining why, in Jacob's opinion, it is a specifically urban process.
4. What persuasive advantages does Jacobs gain by giving so much attention to the village of Bardou? What disadvantages does she risk?

Connections

1. Compare Jacobs's apparent research methods with those of Robert F. Kennedy and Aristotle.
2. Living in the fourth century B.C., Aristotle could not imagine the nation-state and certainly not the concept of modern internationalism. Compare his ideas about the economic life of the city with those of Jacobs.

Towns, Time, and Tradition: The Legacy of Planning in Frontier America

John W. Reps

By the middle of the nineteenth century the basic pattern of urban settle-   *1*
ment east of the Mississippi had been established. Virtually all of what were
to become the major cities of an increasingly urban nation had begun as planned
communities: Boston, New York, Philadelphia, Baltimore, Washington, Pittsburgh, Buffalo, Cleveland, Detroit, Chicago, Cincinnati, Indianapolis, St. Louis,
and New Orleans. Not all had been planned with skill, and in every case the
explosive growth of these urban centers was soon to outrun the bounds of their
original borders. In each of these, as well as in dozens of planned cities of smaller
size, something of the heritage of its planned beginnings remains. In many, in-

---

John W. Reps (b. 1921) has concentrated his urban studies career on the history of American cities. Educated in the United States and England, he has worked as a practicing urban planner in Boston and in Ithaca, New York, and is professor of city and regional planning at Cornell. His books include The Making of Urban America: A History of City Planning in the United States *(1965),* Town Planning in Frontier America *(1980), and* The Forgotten Frontier: Urban Planning in the American West Before 1890 *(1981).*

deed most, the character and quality of the first settlement forms prescribed by their founders exceeds in merit the accretions of the later nineteenth century and of our own era.

We are now entering a new period of American urbanization. By the year 2000 current projections indicate that we will develop as much additional land for urban purposes as we did in the first 400 years of city building from 1565 to 1965. In addition, we are setting about the complex task of reconstructing the blighted and congested centers of our existing cities. Increasingly the effort to create a better life will focus on the issues of city growth and control of the urban environment, along with attempts to grapple with the nagging social problems of poverty and racial segregation.   2

The American philosopher George Santayana once observed that those who are ignorant of history are condemned to re-live it. What are the lessons to be learned from our planning experience during the first period of frontier development as we approach the new frontier of making our cities habitable for ourselves and succeeding generations? Let us try to sum up our failures and our achievements during that remarkable era of our history when we laid the foundation for an urban civilization.   3

We must not let national pride warp our perspective. The North Atlantic proved a major barrier to the transplanting of town planning techniques and concepts which were highly developed in Europe at the beginning of colonization and which continued to advance and change in the centuries to follow. The resources of colonial settlers pitted against the difficulties of a harsh and often hostile environment permitted little more than the minimum requirements of town life let alone the amenities or embellishments which were commonplace in seventeenth- and eighteenth-century Europe.   4

Compare, for example, the Quebec of Champlain with the Charleville of its founder, Duke Charles III. Both date from 1608. Quebec consisted of Champlain's crude "Habitation" and a tiny grid of streets hugging the banks of the St. Lawrence River. Charleville embodied all the theories of Renaissance formal planning, with its elaborate hierarchy of streets and open squares on which fronted carefully scaled buildings all making up a sophisticated composition in civic design. Not until 1791, with L'Enfant's Baroque° plan for Washington, did American urban planners produce a large-scale example of what had long been established as a standard plan form in Europe.   5

Or, contrast the development pattern of the West End of London in the mid-eighteenth century with the plan of Savannah and its multiple squares. While the plan forms are essentially similar, the differences between them in the third dimension were striking. Fronting the London squares stood elegant and restrained terrace houses of urbane dignity and harmonious proportions. Lining the squares of frontier Savannah were the simplest of huts and cabins. Not for nearly a century did Savannah attain something of the character of even the least imposing of Georgian London's squares. The lag between city planning practice in Europe and what occurred in the colonial empires of North America was thus substantial.   6

°Baroque: Artistic style characterized by curves and loops.

The reasons for these differences between colony and mother country are   7
readily understandable. The strangeness of the environment, the slowness of
communications, the absence of traditions, the lack of institutional patterns,
and the necessity to create anew even the most elementary of urban services
and facilities — all contributed to prevent the speedy and complete transfer to
the New World of what had been learned about city planning in the old. Today
these inhibiting factors have vanished, yet one can argue that in comparison
with such remarkably well-ordered European cities as Stockholm and Amster-
dam we still lag far behind European practice in urban planning. No longer
do we have the excuse of limited physical resources; indeed, their very abundance may contribute to our urban physical disarray. Yet in a sense we still
act like primitive colonials, helpless to put into practice the latest lessons of
how to arrange cities in patterns which are both functional and beautiful.

Our failure to achieve an urban order fitting for the time and within our   8
capabilities may well stem from attitudes toward the city developed in our
swaddling years. America was peopled by Europeans who were hungry for land.
In a seemingly limitless continent the most insatiable appetites could be satisfied. For a time fear of Indian attack combined with old habits of settlement
to promote the development of compact agricultural villages. But when the
natives were overcome and when the boundless extent of the land became apparent, the old associations of village and town life gave way to a quite different agricultural settlement pattern of isolated farmsteads. As early as 1623 in
Plymouth Governor Bradford regretfully described these events:

> For now as their stocks increased . . . there was no longer any holding them to-
> gether, but now they must of necessitie goe to their great lots; they could not other
> wise keep their katle; and having oxen growne, they must have land for plowing and
> tillage. And no man now thought he could live, except he had catle and a great deale
> of ground to keep them; all striving to increase their stocks. By which means they
> were scatered all over the bay,° quickly, and the town, in which they lived compactly
> till now, was left very thine, and in a short time allmost desolate. . . . And this, I
> fear, will be the ruine of New-England.

For a good many Americans it was rural life which represented the ideal.   9
The town was something from which to escape. The Jeffersonian notion of an
agrarian democracy represents an old and deep feeling in American culture
which has its manifestation today in the attempt to find in endless suburbia
the freedoms which our ancestors sought on the western frontier of settlement.
It is perhaps a permissible exaggeration to state that today's urban sprawl began in seventeenth-century Plymouth.

One feature of American planning in the frontier era is the almost total ab-   *10*
sence of three-dimensional design. This is not to say that effective bits of town-
scape were unknown — countless New England villages testify to the care taken
by early settlers in the siting of individual buildings. For the most part, however, towns were conceived of in only two dimensions. The example of Williamsburg is virtually unique. Here was a town in which the plan of streets

---

°bay: Lands along the shores of Cape Cod Bay.

and building sites was developed as part of a larger vision of the future which included the location, size, and elevational treatment of its major structures. This approach to total urban design is the great lesson which Williamsburg has to teach — not the plan itself, the architectural style of its buildings, or the layout of its gardens. These belong to another era, and mere imitation of their dimensions and appearance is an insult to the integrity of colonial designers. Many of the shortcomings of the nation's cities today have resulted from earlier failures to realize that the third dimension of architecture is a vital ingredient of urban planning.

Another characteristic of American town planning was the widespread use   *11* of the gridiron or checkerboard pattern. As in virtually all other periods of wholesale colonization in world history, early colonial and later frontier towns were planned mainly on a geometric pattern of rectangular blocks, straight streets, and right-angle intersections. As the plan form most economical to survey, quickest to build, and easiest to understand, it is not surprising that the orthogonal system prevailed. For European visitors this feature of the American scene was novel and, at first impression, desirable. Thus, Francis Baily, noting the "perfect regularity" of Philadelphia and Baltimore was moved to comment, "This is a plan of which the Americans are very fond, and I think with reason, as it is by far the best way of laying out a city. All the modern-built towns in America are on this principle." However, what may have at first seemed like a vision of a new world of urban rationality all too quickly blurred into an impression of sterile dullness. By the time Baily reached Cincinnati his infatuation with the grid had given way to disenchantment:

> I have taken occasion to express my approbation of the American mode of laying out their new towns, in a general way, in straight lines; but I think that oftentimes it is a sacrifice of beauty to prejudice, particularly when they persevere in making all their streets cross each other at right angles, *without any regard to the situation of the ground*, or the face of the surrounding country: whereas, these ought certainly to be taken into consideration, in order that a town may unite both utility and beauty; and, with a little attention to this, a town might still preserve the straight line, and yet avoid that disgusting appearance which many of the new towns in America make.[2]

The seeds of senseless mechanized and unimaginative town planning which   *12* was to characterize much of the nineteenth century were sown in colonial soil. Yet not all gridiron plans of the frontier era of American urban development were of this quality. One thinks of New Haven, with a generous one-ninth of the original town left as an open green; or of Savannah, with its multiple squares breaking the monotony of the grid; or of Jeffersonville, with its alternating pattern of open squares and building blocks. Even Philadelphia's original plan contained the five squares laid out by Penn, the largest intended as a town center and the four smaller as recreation grounds. And Williamsburg demonstrates that the orthogonal plan is not incompatible with an atmosphere of formality and dignity.

It was less the first gridiron plans, which, in most cases were too modest in   *13* size to be offensively dull, than the later extensions of cities that violated good sense in community planning. Without regard to topography or, more importantly, failing to include in the additions of the city some of the open spaces of the original design, these new areas mechanically repeated almost endlessly the grid street system without any relieving features. Savannah stands almost alone as an exception to this dreary tradition.

The reasons are not difficult to identify. Planning of towns and development *14* of land, in the beginning a community enterprise, fell into the hands of individuals and corporations whose almost sole aim was private profit. Even if the proper skills and sensibilities had been present, there was little incentive to plan well when mediocre planning, or worse, yielded generous financial returns. Moreover, as most communities abandoned responsibility for town planning to individuals they failed to create adequate legal and administrative institutions for the public control of private land development.

Our present urban land policy has scarcely departed from this position. Most *15* important decisions about the timing of development, its location, and its design remain in private hands, tempered only mildly by regulations supposedly intended to protect the public interest. Because memories are short and historical perspective lacking, our generation regards this as the American tradition. So it is, but it is not the only tradition of our town planning history, nor has it proved the most effective.

The examples of Annapolis, Williamsburg, Savannah, Washington, and many *16* of the nineteenth-century planned state capital cities remind us that public initiative and investment for the planning of cities once served to create an urban environment superior in quality to that of the present when measured against available financial and intellectual resources. The history of modern American city planning since the turn of the century can be read as an attempt, faltering and so far largely ineffective, to recapture that earlier tradition which placed the planning of towns as a responsibility of the community at large.

If American urban history has anything to contribute to the modern world *17* aside from mere antiquarian enjoyment it is that good cities — beautiful, as well as safe and efficient — will arise only when it is the city itself that assumes the obligation for its own destiny.

NOTES

[1] William Bradford, *History of Plymouth Plantation*, W. T. David, ed. (New York, 1908), pp. 293–294.

[2] Francis Baily, *Journal of a Tour in Unsettled Parts of North America in 1796 & 1797* (London, 1856), pp. 105, 226–227.

Considerations

1. According to John W. Reps, what are the major differences between the developmental patterns of the American city and those of the European city? Take into account the process of city planning as well as the appearance of city plans. Write up a summary or a detailed outline.
2. Does Reps seem to favor spontaneous or planned urban development? Use specific references to his article to defend your conclusions.

Connections

1. Analyze John Reps's article in light of Aristotle's description of the *polis:* To what extent does the history of American town and city planning as described by Reps reflect the ideal of the *polis?* (You may want also to review Robert F. Kennedy's brief summary of city purpose at the beginning of "Urban Crises in America.")
2. In paragraph 9, Reps briefly describes the American agrarian tradition. Compare that view of city life with the view of Jacques Ellul as summarized in "The City in the Bible."
3. Briefly compare the departure of Bardou residents as Jane Jacobs speculates on it in "Cities and the Wealth of Nations" (par. 6) with the movement of Plymouth colonists as described by Reps (par. 8).

The Form and Structure of Cities: Urban Growth Patterns

Howard J. Nelson

The casual observer, in today's era of extensive travel, is perhaps first struck　*1* by the unique features of individual American cities. These characteristics that give each city a personality are often attributable to the distinctive historic past: the compact, hilly, water-encircled site of San Francisco, the level lake plain of Chicago, the charming Vieux Carre section of New Orleans, or the open squares in the street pattern of Savannah. But the more perceptive traveler soon begins to notice a repetitive pattern in the form and structure of our cities, and becomes almost instinctively aware of a kind of "normal" location of specialized districts, and of associations of activities within them. For, in fact, American cities have developed a highly stylized arrangement and characteristic, repetitive interrelations among the specialized areas that constitute their urban anatomy. . . .

. . . Formal models of city structure have been constructed by sociologists,　*2* economists, and geographers. Three of the most famous of these constructs follow.

A professor in the department of geography at UCLA, Howard J. Nelson (b. 1919) has published numerous scholarly works on urban geography and several important popular studies of Los Angeles. Larry S. Bourne (b. 1939) is on the faculty at the University of Toronto.

The earliest (1923) and best known of the classic models is the concentric circle or zonal hypothesis of Ernest W. Burgess.[1] The essence of this model is that as a city grows it expands radially from its center to form a series of concentric zones. Using Chicago as an example, Burgess identified five of these. In the center of the city was Zone I, the *central business district* or CBD. The heart of the CBD contained department stores, style shops, office buildings, clubs, banks, hotels, theaters, and civic buildings. Encircling it was a wholesale district. Zone II, the *zone in transition*, surrounded the CBD, and comprised an area of residential deterioration as the result of encroachments from the CBD. It consisted of a factory district as an inner belt, and an outer belt of declining neighborhoods, rooming house districts, and generally blighted residences. In many American cities of the 1920s, this area was the home of numerous first generation immigrants. Zone III, the *zone of independent workingman's homes*, was the next broad ring, at the time largely inhabited by second generation immigrants, and characterized in Chicago by the "two-flat" dwelling. Beyond this ring was located Zone IV, the *zone of better residences*. Here lived the great middle-class of native born Americans in single family residences or apartments. Within this area, at strategic places, were local business centers, which Burgess implied might be likened to satellite CBD's. Zone V, the *commuter's zone*, lay beyond the area of better residences, and consisted of a ring of encircling small cities, towns, and hamlets. These were, in the main, dormitory suburbs, with the men commuting to jobs in the CBD.   3

The operating mechanism of the concentric circle model was the growth and radial expansion of the city, with each zone having a tendency to expand outward into the next. Burgess assumed a city with a single center, a heterogeneous population, a mixed commercial and industrial base, as well as economic competition for the highly-valued, severely limited central space. He explicitly recognized "distorting factors," such as site, situation, natural and artificial barriers, the survival of the earlier use of the district, and so on. But he argued that to the extent of which the spatial structure of a city is determined by radial expansion, the concentric zones of his model will appear. Given the limited data available, the Burgess model was a remarkably astute description of the American city of the time.   4

A second model of the growth and spatial structure of American cities was formulated by Homer Hoyt in 1939 and is known as the wedge or sector theory.[2] Hoyt analyzed the distribution of residential neighborhoods of various qualities, as defined by rent levels, and found that they were neither distributed randomly nor in the form of concentric circles. High rental areas, for example, tended to be located in one or more pie-shaped sectors, and did not form a complete circle around the city. Intermediate rental areas normally were sectors adjacent to a high rent area. Further, different types of residential areas usually grew outward along distinct radii, and new growth on the arc of a given sector tended to take on the character of the initial growth in that sector. In summary, Hoyt argued that "if one sector of the city first develops as a high, medium, or low rental residential area, it will tend to retain that character for long distances as the sector is extended outward through the process of the city's growth."   5

Although no geometric pattern can be superimposed upon a city to deter-   6 mine the position of high and low rent sectors, some generalizations can be made about their location. The area occupied by the highest income families tends to be on high ground, or on a lake, river, or ocean shore, along the fastest existing transportation lines, and close to the country clubs or parks on the periphery. The low income families tend to live in sectors situated farthest from the high rent areas, and are normally located on the least desirable land alongside railroad, industrial, or commercial areas. Rental areas are not static. Occupants of houses in the low rent categories tend to move out in bands from the center of the city, mainly by filtering into the houses left behind by the higher income groups, or in newly constructed shacks on the fringe of the city, usually in the extension of the low rent section. It is felt by some that because Hoyt's model takes into account both distance and direction from the center of the city, it is an improvement on the earlier Burgess effort.

A third model, the multiple nuclei, was formulated by Chauncy Harris and   7
Edward Ullman in 1945 as a modification of the two previous models.[3] They argue that the land use pattern of a city does not grow from a single center, but around several distinct nuclei. In some cases these nuclei, elements around which growth takes place, have existed from the origin of the city, but others may develop during the growth of the city. Their numbers vary from city to city, but the larger the city the more numerous and specialized are the nuclei.

Urban nuclei attracting growth might include the original retail district, a   8
port, a railroad station, a factory area, a beach, or, in today's city, an airport. The authors identify a number of districts that have developed around individual nuclei in most large American cities. The *central business* district usually includes, or is adjacent to the original retail area. The *wholesale and light manufacturing* district is normally located along railroad lines, adjacent to, but not surrounding the CBD. The *heavy industrial* district is near the present or former edge of the city, where large tracts of land and rail or water transportation are available. *Residential* districts of several classes are identified with high-class districts on desirable sites, on well drained, high land, and away from nuisances, such as noise, odors, smoke, and railroad lines, the low-class districts near factories and railroad districts. Finally, *suburbs* and *satellites*, either residential or industrial, are characteristic of American cities. Suburbs are defined as lying adjacent to the city, with satellites farther away with little daily commuting to the central city.

The rise of separate nuclei and differentiated districts is thought to result   9
from a combination of four factors. (1) Certain activities require specialized facilities, i.e., a retail district needs intracity accessibility, a port requires a harbor. (2) Certain like activities group together because they profit from linkages. For example, retail activities may cluster to facilitate comparison shopping and financial institutions may locate in close clusters to make easy face to face communication by decision makers. (3) Certain unlike activities are detrimental to each other. Thus extensive users of land, such as bulk storage yards, are not compatable with retail functions requiring dense pedestrian traffic. (4) Certain activities are unable to afford the high rents of the most desirable sites — low class housing is seldom built on view lots.

Models such as these which emerge from the process of analysis and gen-   10
eralization do not conform to the reality of any city. But anyone familiar with

large or medium sized American cities will recognize many elements of each model in the vast majority of our urban areas. Obviously, too, they are not mutually exclusive, for the latter two models are both modifications of the concentric circle theory. Even in Hoyt's concept, residential areas expand outward concentrically. There has been extensive statistical testing of these models in recent years with no conclusive results. They remain as valuable conceptual tools for analyzing the modern city, and provide a basis for cross-cultural urban comparisons.

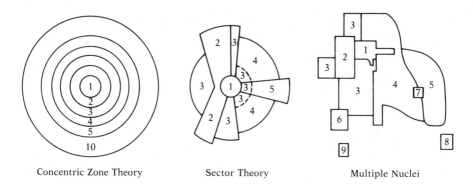

| Concentric Zone Theory | Sector Theory | Multiple Nuclei |

District:

1. Central Business District
2. Wholesale Light Manufacturing
3. Low-class Residential
4. Medium-class Residential

5. High-class Residential
6. Heavy Manufacturing
7. Outlying Business District
8. Residential Suburb

9. Industrial Suburb
10. Commuters' Zone

Three Generalizations of the Internal Structure of Cities

Source: Larry S. Bourne, ed., *Internal Structure of the City: Readings on Space and Environment* (New York: Oxford University Press, 1971), p. 71.

NOTES

[1] First presented as a paper in 1923, Burgess restated his hypothesis at somewhat greater length five years later. Ernest W. Burgess, "Urban Areas," in T. V. Smith and L. D. White, eds., *Chicago: An Experiment in Social Science Research* (Chicago: University of Chicago Press, 1929), pp. 114–123. An excellent review of the Burgess model is Leo F. Schnore, "On the Spatial Structure of Cities in the Two Americas," in Philip M. Hauser and Leo F. Schnore, eds., *The Study of Urbanization* (New York: John Wiley and Sons, Inc., 1965), pp. 347–398.

[2] Homer Hoyt, *The Structure and Growth of Residential Neighborhoods in American Cities* (Washington, D.C.: Federal Housing Administration, 1939).

[3] Chauncy D. Harris and Edward L. Ullman, "The Nature of Cities," *Annals* of the American Academy of Political and Social Science, CCXLII (November 1945), 7–17.

Considerations

1. Compare the three classic patterns of city structure.
2. For what kind of reader is Howard J. Nelson writing (sophisticated or naive, interested, or apathetic, etc.)? Use details from the article to defend your answer.

3. Ernest W. Burgess acknowledged that site, situation, and natural barriers can disrupt his regular concentric circle model of city structure. Work with a group to enumerate some specific disruptive geophysical factors; then write up an individual or collective report.

Connections

1. Compare Nelson's purpose for composing this article with that of Robert F. Kennedy in "Urban Crises in America." Alternatively, or in addition, compare the organizational structure of the two selections.
2. To what extent does any of the three classic patterns of urban development allow for the necessary "elements" of city life that Aristotle enumerates?
3. Twenty-five years after he formulated the sector model of city structure, Homer Hoyt declared that he had based his theory on pre-1930 data, and accordingly, in 1964 he took into account more recent changes in American cities. The "classical models" of urban growth, he said, can be distorted by any of these five dynamic changes: (1) common dependence on the private automobile; (2) new zoning statutes which regulate land use, allow condemnation of property, and provide monetary compensation for condemnations; (3) deterioration of the downtown central business district (CBD); (4) building booms financed by borrowing from banks and insurance companies; and (5) federal aid to urban redevelopment. To what extent can any of these changes in urban policy and everyday life provide an answer to John W. Reps's call for the American city to assume responsibility for its own development (para. 17)?

The Experience of Living in Cities

Stanley Milgram

When I first came to New York it seemed like a nightmare. As soon as I got off the train at Grand Central I was caught up in pushing, shoving crowds on 42nd Street. Sometimes people bumped into me without apology; what really frightened me was

The best-known work of social psychologist Stanley Milgram (b. 1933) focuses on human aggression. He has explored this theme in authority and obedience behaviors, in television violence, and in urban psychology. Widely published, Milgram has also produced a film and taught at Harvard and Yale. Currently he is a professor at the City University of New York Graduate Center.

to see two people literally engaged in combat for possession of a cab. Why were they so rushed? Even drunks on the street were bypassed without a glance. People didn't seem to care about each other at all.

This statement represents a common reaction to a great city, but it does not tell the whole story. Obviously cities have great appeal because of their variety, eventfulness, possibility of choice, and the stimulation of an intense atmosphere that many individuals find a desirable background to their lives. Where face-to-face contacts are important, the city offers unparalleled possibilities. It has been calculated by the Regional Plan Association (1) that in Nassau County, a suburb of New York City, an individual can meet 11,000 others within a 10-minute radius of his office by foot or car. In Newark, a moderate-sized city, he can meet more than 20,000 persons within this radius. But in midtown Manhattan he can meet fully 220,000. So there is an order-of-magnitude increment in the communication possibilities offered by a great city. That is one of the bases of its appeal and, indeed, of its functional necessity. The city provides options that no other social arrangement permits. But there is a negative side also, as we shall see.

Granted that cities are indispensable in complex society, we may still ask what contribution psychology can make to understanding the experience of living in them. What theories are relevant? How can we extend our knowledge of the psychological aspects of life in cities through empirical inquiry? If empirical inquiry is possible, along what lines should it proceed? In short, where do we start in constructing urban theory and in laying out lines of research?

Observation is the indispensable starting point. Any observer in the streets of midtown Manhattan will see (i) large numbers of people, (ii) a high population density, and (iii) heterogeneity of population. These three factors need to be at the root of any sociopsychological theory of city life, for they condition all aspects of our experience in the metropolis. Louis Wirth (2), if not the first to point to these factors, is nonetheless the sociologist who relied most heavily on them in his analysis of the city. Yet, for a psychologist, there is something unsatisfactory about Wirth's theoretical variables. Numbers, density, and heterogeneity are demographic facts but they are not yet psychological facts. They are external to the individual. Psychology needs an idea that links the individual's *experience* to the demographic circumstances of urban life.

One link is provided by the concept of overload. This term, drawn from systems analysis, refers to a system's inability to process inputs from the environment because there are too many inputs for the system to cope with, or because successive inputs come so fast that input A cannot be processed when input B is presented. When overload is present, adaptations occur. The system must set priorities and make choices. A may be processed first while B is kept in abeyance, or one input may be sacrificed altogether. City life, as we experience it, constitutes a continuous set of encounters with overload, and of resultant adaptations. Overload characteristically deforms daily life on several levels, impinging on role performance, the evolution of social norms, cognitive functioning, and the use of facilities.

The concept has been implicit in several theories of urban experience. In 1903 Georg Simmel (3) pointed out that, since urban dwellers come into contact with vast numbers of people each day, they conserve psychic energy by becoming acquainted with a far smaller proportion of people than their rural counterparts do, and by maintaining more superficial relationships even with these acquaintances. Wirth (2) points specifically to "the superficiality, the anonymity, and the transitory character of urban social relations."

One adaptive response to overload, therefore, is the allocation of less time   6
to each input. A second adaptive mechanism is disregard of low-priority inputs. Principles of selectivity are formulated such that investment of time and energy are reserved for carefully defined inputs (the urbanite disregards the drunk sick on the street as he purposefully navigates through the crowd). Third, boundaries are redrawn in certain social transactions so that the overload system can shift the burden to the other party in the exchange; thus, harried New York bus drivers once made change for customers, but now this responsibility has been shifted to the client, who must have the exact fare ready. Fourth, reception is blocked off prior to entrance into a system; city dwellers increasingly use unlisted telephone numbers to prevent individuals from calling them, and a small but growing number resort to keeping the telephone off the hook to prevent incoming calls. More subtly, a city dweller blocks inputs by assuming an unfriendly countenance, which discourages others from initiating contact. Additionally, social screening devices are interposed between the individual and environmental inputs (in a town of 5000 anyone can drop in to chat with the mayor, but in the metropolis organizational screening devices deflect inputs to other destinations). Fifth, the intensity of inputs is diminished by filtering devices, so that only weak and relatively superficial forms of involvement with others are allowed. Sixth, specialized institutions are created to absorb inputs that would otherwise swamp the individual (welfare departments handle the financial needs of a million individuals in New York City, who would otherwise create an army of mendicants continuously importuning the pedestrian). The interposition of institutions between the individual and the social world, a characteristic of all modern society, and most notably of the large metropolis, has its negative side. It deprives the individual of a sense of direct contact and spontaneous integration in the life around him. It simultaneously protects and estranges the individual from his social environment.

Many of these adaptive mechanisms apply not only to individuals but to   7
institutional systems as well, as Meier (4) has so brilliantly shown in connection with the library and the stock exchange.

In sum, the observed behavior of the urbanite in a wide range of situations   8
appears to be determined largely by a variety of adaptations to overload. I now deal with several specific responses to overload, which make for differences in the tone of city and town.

Social Responsibility

The principal point of interest for a social psychology of the city is that moral   9
and social involvement with individuals is necessarily restricted. This is a direct and necessary function of excess of input over capacity to process. Such restriction of involvement runs a broad spectrum from refusal to become involved in the needs of another person, even when the person desperately needs

assistance, through refusal to do favors, to the simple withdrawal of courtesies (such as offering a lady a seat, or saying "sorry" when a pedestrian collision occurs). In any transaction more and more details need to be dropped as the total number of units to be processed increases and assaults an instrument of limited processing capacity.

The ultimate adaptation of an overloaded social environment is to totally   *10* disregard the needs, interests, and demands of those whom one does not define as relevant to the satisfaction of personal needs, and to develop highly efficient perceptual means of determining whether an individual falls into the category of friend or stranger. The disparity in the treatment of friends and strangers ought to be greater in cities than in towns; the time allotment and willingness to become involved with those who have no personal claim on one's time is likely to be less in cities than in towns.

Bystander intervention in crises. The most striking deficiencies in social re-   *11* sponsibility in cities occur in crisis situations, such as the Genovese murder in Queens. In 1964, Catherine Genovese, coming home from a night job in the early hours of an April morning, was stabbed repeatedly, over an extended period of time. Thirty-eight residents of a respectable New York City neighborhood admit to having witnessed at least part of the attack, but none went to her aid or called the police until after she was dead. Milgram and Hollander, writing in *The Nation* (5), analyzed the event in these terms:

> Urban friendships and associations are not primarily formed on the basis of physical proximity. A person with numerous close friends in different parts of the city may not know the occupant of an adjacent apartment. This does not mean that a city dweller has fewer friends than does a villager, or knows fewer persons who will come to his aid; however, it does mean that his allies are not constantly at hand. Miss Genovese required immediate aid from those physically present. There is no evidence that the city had deprived Miss Genovese of human associations, but the friends who might have rushed to her side were miles from the scene of her tragedy.
>
> Further, it is known that her cries for help were not directed to a specific person; they were general. But only individuals can act, and as the cries were not specifically directed, no particular person felt a special responsibility. The crime and the failure of community response seem absurd to us. At the time, it may well have seemed equally absurd to Kew Gardens residents that not one of the neighbors would have called the police. A collective paralysis may have developed from the belief of each of the witnesses that someone else must surely have taken that obvious step.

Latané and Darley (6) have reported laboratory approaches to the study of   *12* bystander intervention and have established experimentally the following principle: the larger the number of bystanders, the less the likelihood that any one of them will intervene in an emergency. Gaertner and Bickman (7) of The City University of New York have extended the bystander studies to an examination of help across ethnic lines. Blacks and whites, with clearly identifiable accents, called strangers (through what the caller represented as an error in telephone dialing), gave them a plausible story of being stranded on an outlying highway without more dimes, and asked the stranger to call a garage. The experimenters found that the white callers had a significantly better chance of obtaining assistance [from white subjects] than the black callers. This suggests that ethnic allegiance may well be another means of coping with overload: the city dweller can reduce excessive demands and screen out urban heterogeneity by responding along ethnic lines; overload is made more manageable by limiting the "span of sympathy."

In any quantitative characterization of the social texture of city life, a necessary first step is the application of such experimental methods as these to field situations in large cities and small towns. Theorists argue that the indifference shown in the Genovese case would not be found in a small town, but in the absence of solid experimental evidence the question remains an open one. *13*

More than just callousness prevents bystanders from participating in altercations between people. A rule of urban life is respect for other people's emotional and social privacy, perhaps because physical privacy is so hard to achieve. And in situations for which the standards are heterogeneous, it is much harder to know whether taking an active role is unwarranted meddling or an appropriate response to a critical situation. If a husband and wife are quarrelling in public, at what point should a bystander step in? On the one hand, the heterogeneity of the city produces substantially greater tolerance about behavior, dress, and codes of ethics than is generally found in the small town, but this diversity also encourages people to withhold aid for fear of antagonizing the participants or crossing an inappropriate and difficult-to-define line. *14*

Moreover, the frequency of demands present in the city gives rise to norms of noninvolvement. There are practical limitations to the Samaritan impulse in a major city. If a citizen attended to every needy person, if he were sensitive to and acted on every altruistic impulse that was evoked in the city, he could scarcely keep his own affairs in order. *15*

Willingness to trust and assist strangers. We now move away from crisis situations to less urgent examples of social responsibility. For it is not only in situations of dramatic need but in the ordinary, everyday willingness to lend a hand that the city dweller is said to be deficient relative to his small-town cousin. The comparative method must be used in any empirical examination of this question. A commonplace social situation is staged in an urban setting and in a small town—a situation to which a subject can respond by either extending help or withholding it. The responses in town and city are compared. *16*

One factor in the purported unwillingness of urbanites to be helpful to strangers may well be their heightened sense of physical (and emotional) vulnerability—a feeling that is supported by urban crime statistics. A key test for distinguishing between city and town behavior, therefore, is determining how city dwellers compare with town dwellers in offering aid that increases their personal vulnerability and requires some trust of strangers. Altman, Levine, Nadien, and Villena (8) of The City University of New York devised a study to compare the behaviors of city and town dwellers in this respect. The criterion used in this study was the willingness of householders to allow strangers to enter their home to use the telephone. The student investigators individually rang doorbells, explained that they had misplaced the address of a friend nearby, and asked to use the phone. The investigators (two males and two females) made 100 requests for entry into homes in the city and 60 requests in the small towns. The results for middle-income housing developments in Manhattan were compared with data for several small towns (Stony Point, Spring Valley, Ramapo, *17*

Table 1 Percentage of Entries Achieved by Investigators for City and Town Dwellings (see text)

Experimenter	Entries achieved (%)	
	City*	Small town†
Male		
No. 1	16	40
No. 2	12	60
Female		
No. 3	40	87
No. 4	40	100

*Number of requests for entry, 100. †Number of requests for entry, 60.

Nyack, New City, and West Clarkstown) in Rockland County, outside of New York City. As Table 1 shows, in all cases there was a sharp increase in the proportion of entries achieved by an experimenter when he moved from the city to a small town. In the most extreme case the experimenter was five times as likely to gain admission to homes in a small town as to homes in Manhattan. Although the female experimenters had notably greater success both in cities and in towns than the male experimenters had, each of the four students did at least twice as well in towns as in cities. This suggests that the city-town distinction overrides even the predictably greater fear of male strangers than of female ones.

The lower level of helpfulness by city dwellers seems due in part to recognition of the dangers of living in Manhattan, rather than to mere indifference or coldness. It is significant that 75 percent of all the city respondents received and answered messages by shouting through closed doors and by peering out through peepholes; in the towns, by contrast, about 75 percent of the respondents opened the door. 18

Supporting the experimenters' quantitative results was their general observation that the town dwellers were noticeably more friendly and less suspicious than the city dwellers. In seeking to explain the reasons for the greater sense of psychological vulnerability city dwellers feel, above and beyond the differences in crime statistics, Villena (8) points out that, if a crime is committed in a village, a resident of a neighboring village may not perceive the crime as personally relevant, though the geographic distance may be small, whereas a criminal act committed anywhere in the city, though miles from the city dweller's home, is still . . . located within the city; thus, Villena says, "the inhabitant of the city possesses a larger vulnerable space." 19

Civilities. Even at the most superficial level of involvement—the exercise of everyday civilities—urbanites are reputedly deficient. People bump into each other and often do not apologize. They knock over another person's packages and, as often as not, proceed on their way with a grumpy exclamation instead of an offer of assistance. Such behavior, which many visitors to great cities find distasteful, is less common, we are told, in smaller communities, where traditional courtesies are more likely to be observed. 20

In some instances it is not simply that, in the city, traditional courtesies are 21 violated; rather, the cities develop new norms of noninvolvement. These are so well defined and so deeply a part of city life that *they* constitute the norms people are reluctant to violate. Men are actually embarrassed to give up a seat on the subway to an old woman; they mumble "I was getting off anyway," instead of making the gesture in a straightforward and gracious way. These norms develop because everyone realizes that, in situations of high population density, people cannot implicate themselves in each others' affairs, for to do so would create conditions of continual distraction which would frustrate purposeful action.

In discussing the effects of overload I do not imply that at every instant the   22
city dweller is bombarded with an unmanageable number of inputs and that his responses are determined by the excess of input at any given instant. Rather, adaptation occurs in the form of gradual evolution of norms of behavior. Norms are evolved in response to frequent discrete experiences of overload; they persist and become generalized modes of responding.

Overload on cognitive capacities: anonymity. That we respond differently   23
toward those whom we know and those who are strangers to us is a truism. An eager patron aggressively cuts in front of someone in a long movie line to save time only to confront a friend; he then behaves sheepishly. A man is involved in an automobile accident caused by another driver, emerges from his car shouting in rage, then moderates his behavior on discovering a friend driving the other car. The city dweller, when walking through the midtown streets, is in a state of continual anonymity vis-à-vis the other pedestrians.

Anonymity is part of a continuous spectrum ranging from total anonymity   24
to full acquaintance, and it may well be that measurement of the precise degrees of anonymity in cities and towns would help to explain important distinctions between the quality of life in each. Conditions of full acquaintance, for example, offer security and familiarity, but they may also be stifling, because the individual is caught in a web of established relationships. Conditions of complete anonymity, by contrast, provide freedom from routinized social ties, but they may also create feelings of alienation and detachment.

Empirically one could investigate the proportion of activities in which the   25
city dweller or the town dweller is known by others at given times in his daily life and the proportion of activities in the course of which he interacts with individuals who know him. At his job, for instance, the city dweller may be known to as many people as his rural counterpart. However, when he is not fulfilling his occupational role—say, when merely traveling about the city—the urbanite is doubtless more anonymous than his rural counterpart.

Limited work on anonymity has begun. Zimbardo (9) has tested whether the   26
social anonymity and impersonality of the big city encourage greater vandalism than do small towns. Zimbardo arranged for one automobile to be left for 64 hours near the Bronx campus of New York University and for a counterpart to be left for the same number of hours near Stanford University in Palo Alto. The license plates on the two cars were removed and the hoods were opened, to provide "releaser cues" for potential vandals. The New York car was stripped of all movable parts within the first 24 hours, and by the end of 3 days was only a hunk of metal rubble. Unexpectedly, however, most of the destruction occurred during daylight hours, usually under the scrutiny of observers, and

the leaders in the vandalism were well-dressed . . . adults. The Palo Alto car was left untouched.

Zimbardo attributes the difference in the treatment accorded the two cars 27 to the "acquired feelings of social anonymity provided by life in a city like New York," and he supports his conclusions with several other anecdotes illustrating casual, wanton vandalism in the city. In any comparative study of the effects of anonymity in city and town, however, there must be satisfactory control for other confounding factors: the large number of drug addicts in the city like New York; the higher proportion of slum-dwellers in the city; and so on.

Another direction for empirical study is investigation of the beneficial ef- 28 fects of anonymity. The impersonality of city life breeds its own tolerance for the private lives of the inhabitants. Individuality and even eccentricity, we may assume, can flourish more readily in the metropolis than in the small town. Stigmatized persons may find it easier to lead comfortable lives in the city, free of the constant scrutiny of neighbors. To what degree can this assumed difference between city and town be shown empirically? Judith Waters (10), at the City University of New York, hypothesized that avowed homosexuals would be more likely to be accepted as tenants in a large city than in small towns, and she dispatched letters from homosexuals and from heterosexual individuals to real estate agents in cities and towns across the country. The results of her study were inconclusive. But the general idea of examining the protective benefits of city life to the stigmatized ought to be pursued.

Role behavior in cities and towns. Another product of urban overload is the 29 adjustment in roles made by urbanites in daily interactions. As Wirth has said (2): "Urbanites meet one another in highly segmental roles. . . . They are less dependent upon particular persons, and their dependence upon others is confined to a highly fractionalized aspect of the other's round of activity." This tendency is particularly noticeable in transactions between customers and individuals offering professional or sales services. The owner of a country store has time to become well acquainted with his dozen-or-so daily customers, but the checker of a busy supermarket, serving hundreds of customers a day, barely has time to toss the green stamps into one customer's shopping bag before the next customer confronts him with his pile of groceries.

Meier, in his stimulating analysis of the city (4), discusses several adapta- 30 tions a system may make when confronted by inputs that exceed its capacity to process them. Meier argues that, according to the principle of competition for scarce resources, the scope and time of the transaction shrink as customer volume and daily turnover rise. This, in fact, is what is meant by the "brusque" quality of city life. New standards have developed in cities concerning what levels of services are appropriate in business transactions (see Fig. 1).

McKenna and Morgenthau (11), in a seminar at The City University of New 31 York, devised a study (i) to compare the willingness of city dwellers and small-town dwellers to do favors for strangers that entailed expenditure of a small amount of time and slight inconvenience but no personal vulnerability, and (ii) to determine whether the more compartmentalized, transitory relationships of the city would make urban salespersons less likely than small-town salespersons to carry out, for strangers, tasks not related to their customary roles.

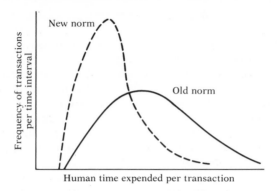

Figure 1 Changes in the Demand for Time for a Given Task When the Overall Transaction Frequency Increases in a Social System

Source: R. L. Meier, *A Communications Theory of Urban Growth* (Cambridge, Mass.: MIT Press, 1962).

To test for differences between city dwellers and small-town dwellers, a   32
simple experiment was devised in which persons from both settings were asked
(by telephone) to perform increasingly onerous favors for anonymous strangers.

Within the cities (Chicago, New York, and Philadelphia), half the calls were   33
to homemakers and the other half to salespersons in women's apparel shops;
the division was the same for the 37 small towns of the study, which were in
the same states as the cities. Each experimenter represented herself as a long-
distance caller who had, through error, been connected with the respondent by
the operator. The experimenter began by asking for simple information about
the weather for purposes of travel. Next the experimenter excused herself on
some pretext (asking the respondent to "please hold on"), put the phone down
for almost a full minute, and then picked it up again and asked the respondent
to provide the phone number of a hotel or motel in her vicinity at which the
experimenter might stay during a forthcoming visit. Scores were assigned the
subjects on the basis of how helpful they had been. McKenna summarizes her
results in this manner:

> People in the city, whether they are engaged in a specific job or not, are less helpful
> and informative than people in small towns; . . . People at home, regardless of where
> they live, are less helpful and informative than people working in shops.

However, the absolute level of cooperativeness for urban subjects was found   34
to be quite high, and does not accord with the stereotype of the urbanite as
aloof, self-centered, and unwilling to help strangers. The quantitative differences obtained by McKenna and Morgenthau are less great than one might have
expected. This again points up the need for extensive empirical research in
rural-urban differences, research that goes far beyond that provided by the few
illustrative pilot studies presented here. At this point we have very limited evidence on differences in the quality of social encounters in city and small town.

But the research needs to be guided by unifying theoretical concepts. As I 35
have tried to demonstrate, the concept of overload helps to explain a wide variety of contrasts between city behavior and town behavior: (i) the differences
in role enactment (the tendency of urban dwellers to deal with one another in
highly segmented, functional forms, and of urban sales personnel to devote
limited time and attention to their customers); (ii) the evolution of urban norms
quite different from traditional town values (such as the acceptance of noninvolvement, impersonality, and aloofness in urban life); (iii) the adaptation of
the urban dweller's cognitive processes (his inability to identify most of the
people he sees daily, his screening of sensory stimuli, his development of blasé
attitudes toward deviant or bizarre behavior, and his selectivity in responding
to human demands); and (iv) the competition for scarce facilities in the city
(the subway rush, the fight for taxis, traffic jams, standing in line to await services). I suggest that contrasts between city and rural behavior probably reflect the responses of similar people to very different situations, rather than
intrinsic differences in the personalities of rural and city dwellers. The city is
a situation to which individuals respond adaptively.

REFERENCES

(1) *The New York Times* (15 June 1969).
(2) L. Wirth, *Amer. J. Soc.* 44, 1 (1938). Wirth's ideas have come under heavy criticism by contemporary city planners, who point out that the city is broken into neighborhoods, which fulfill many of
the functions of small towns. See, for example, H. J. Gans, *People and Plans: Essays on Urban Problems and Solutions* (Basic Books, New York, 1968); J. Jacobs *The Death and Life of Great American
Cities* (Random House, New York, 1961); G. D. Suttles, *The Social Order of the Slum* (Univ. of Chicago
Press, Chicago, 1968).
(3) G. Simmel, *The Sociology of Georg Simmel*, K. H. Wolff, Ed. (Macmillan, New York, 1950) [En-
glish translation of G. Simmel, *Die Grossstadte und das Geistesleben Die Grossstadt* (Jansch, Dresden,
1903)].
(4) R. L. Meier, *A Communications Theory of Urban Growth* (MIT Press, Cambridge, Mass., 1962).
(5) S. Milgram and P. Hollander, *Nation* 25, 602 (1964).
(6) B. Latané and J. Darley, *Amer. Sci.* 57, 244 (1969).
(7) S. Gaertner and L. Bickman (Graduate Center, The City University of New York), unpublished
research.
(8) D. Altman, M. Levine, M. Nadien, J. Villena (Graduate Center, The City University of New
York), unpublished research.
(9) P. G. Zimbardo, paper presented at the Nebraska Symposium on Motivation (1969).
(10) J. Waters (Graduate Center, The City University of New York), unpublished research.
(11) W. McKenna and S. Morgenthau (Graduate Center, The City University of New York), unpublished research.

Considerations

1. Stanley Milgram goes to some trouble to emphasize the value to the psychologist of objective data ("psychological facts," "quantitative characteristics," and "[empirical] data"); but he does allow subjective, impressionistic testimony about city environments. List the experiments and methods
   he describes according to objective and subjective classifications. Alternatively, classify the experiments and their methods according to any other
   principles that seem relevant to his article.
2. Study the behavior of a person or group at some public place (store, street
   corner, park, restaurant, subway or bus, taxi rank, public telephone, li-

brary, bank, etc.); write down in your journal what you observe. You may wish to expand your data base by sharing descriptions among members of a small group. Determine which of your descriptions Milgram might classify as objective data and which as general impressionistic observations. Annotate your journal accordingly.

3. Speculate on Milgram's possible reactions to your observations: do your assumptions suggest urban tone and experience or small-town tone and experience? Write a brief report.

4. Restrict your observations of public places to your college campus. Using Milgram's suggestions, write an analysis of your observations. Would Milgram categorize your college as a city environment or as a small-town environment? If your conclusions surprise you, account for the discrepancy between your previous informal impressions and your later analysis.

Connections

1. Pretend that Stanley Milgram had followed Robert F. Kennedy as a witness at the Ribicoff hearings. What might Milgram have said about the "destruction of . . . community" that Kennedy describes?

2. In *The Origin of Consciousness in the Breakdown of the Bicameral Mind* (Boston: Houghton Mifflin, 1977), Julian Jaynes has written that "civilization is the art of living in cities of such size that everyone does not know everyone else." Develop an essay comparing the possible reactions of Milgram and Aristotle to Janes's definition.

3. Analyze Milgram's article from a theological perspective: how might Ronald Pasquariello, Donald Shriver, and Alan Geyer respond to Milgram's suggestions about overload? Alternatively, speculate on Harvey Cox's possible responses to Milgram.

4. In "Alienated Labor" (reprinted in Chapter 5, The Working World), Karl Marx explains the worker's alienation from the product of labor, from the act of production, and from other people. Using Marx's essay as a model, analyze the data (*not* the conclusions) in Milgram's article; that is, perform a Marxian analysis of the actions and reactions that Milgram describes.

Pillar of Salt

Shirley Jackson

For some reason a tune was running through her head when she and her   *1*
husband got on the train in New Hampshire for their trip to New York; they
had not been to New York for nearly a year, but the tune was from further
back than that. It was from the days when she was fifteen or sixteen, and had
never seen New York except in movies, when the city was made up, to her, of
penthouses filled with Noel Coward° people; when the height and speed and
luxury and gaiety that made up a city like New York were confused inextricably with the dullness of being fifteen, and beauty unreachable and far in the
movies.

"What *is* that tune?" she said to her husband, and hummed it. "It's from   *2*
some old movie, I think."

"I know it," he said, and hummed it himself. "Can't remember the words."   *3*

He sat back comfortably. He had hung up their coats, put the suitcases on   *4*
the rack, and had taken his magazine out. "I'll think of it sooner or later," he
said.

She looked out the window first, tasting it almost secretly, savoring the ex-   *5*
treme pleasure of being on a moving train with nothing to do for six hours but
read and nap and go into the dining-car, going farther and farther every minute from the children, from the kitchen floor, with even the hills being incredibly left behind, changing into fields and trees too far away from home to be
daily. "I love trains," she said, and her husband nodded sympathetically into
his magazine.

Two weeks ahead, two unbelievable weeks, with all arrangements made, no   *6*
further planning to do, except perhaps what theatres or what restaurants. A
friend with an apartment went on a convenient vacation, there was enough
money in the bank to make a trip to New York compatible with new snow suits
for the children; there was the smoothness of unopposed arrangements, once
the initial obstacles had been overcome, as though when they had really made
up their minds, nothing dared stop them. The baby's sore throat cleared up.
The plumber came, finished his work in two days, and left. The dresses had

---

°Noel Coward (1899–1973), British actor and playwright known for his wit, sophistication, and ur-
banity.

---

*Shirley Jackson (1919–1965) wrote novels, short stories, and TV scripts. Her
most famous work is "The Lottery" and* The Haunting of Hill House. *Critics applauded her mystery and comic fiction, which portrays both the horror and the
humor of ordinary life. Though Jackson's work often took her to New York City,
her primary residence for much of her adult life was the town of North Benning-
ton, Vermont.*

been altered in time; the hardware store could be left safely, once they had found the excuse of looking over new city products. New York had not burned down, had not been quarantined, their friend had gone away according to schedule, and Brad had the keys to the apartment in his pocket. Everyone knew where to reach everyone else; there was a list of plays not to miss and a list of items to look out for in the stores—diapers, dress materials, fancy canned goods, tarnish-proof silverware boxes. And, finally, the train was there, performing its function, pacing through the afternoon, carrying them legally and with determination to New York.

Margaret looked curiously at her husband, inactive in the middle of the   7
afternoon on a train, at the other fortunate people traveling, at the sunny country outside, looked again to make sure, and then opened her book. The tune was still in her head, she hummed it and heard her husband take it up softly as he turned a page in his magazine.

In the dining-car she ate roast beef, as she would have done in a restaurant   8
at home, reluctant to change over too quickly to the new, tantalizing food of a vacation. She had ice cream for dessert but became uneasy over her coffee because they were due in New York in an hour and she still had to put on her coat and hat, relishing every gesture, and Brad must take the suitcases down and put away the magazines. They stood at the end of the car for the interminable underground run, picking up their suitcases and putting them down again, moving restlessly inch by inch.

The station was a momentary shelter, moving visitors gradually into a world   9
of people and sound and light to prepare them for the blasting reality of the street outside. She saw it for a minute from the sidewalk before she was in a taxi moving into the middle of it, and then they were bewilderingly caught and carried on uptown and whirled out on to another sidewalk and Brad paid the taxi driver and put his head back to look up at the apartment house. "This is it, all right," he said, as though he had doubted the driver's ability to find a number so simply given. Upstairs in the elevator, and the key fit the door. They had never seen their friend's apartment before, but it was reasonably familiar—a friend moving from New Hampshire to New York carries private pictures of a home not erasable in a few years, and the apartment had enough of home in it to settle Brad immediately in the right chair and comfort her with instinctive trust of the linen and blankets.

"This is home for two weeks," Brad said, and stretched. After the first few   10
minutes they both went to the windows automatically: New York was below, as arranged, and the houses across the street were apartment houses filled with unknown people.

"It's wonderful," she said. There were cars down there, and people, and the   11
noise was there. "I'm so happy," she said, and kissed her husband.

They went sight-seeing the first day; they had breakfast in an Automat and   12
went to the top of the Empire State Building. "Got it all fixed up now," Brad said, at the top. "Wonder just where that plane hit."

They tried to peer down on all four sides, but were embarrassed about ask-   13
ing. "After all," she said reasonably, giggling in a corner, "if something of mine got broken I wouldn't want people poking around asking to see the pieces."

"If you owned the Empire State Building you wouldn't care." Brad said.   14

They traveled only in taxis the first few days, and one taxi had a door held *15*
on with a piece of string; they pointed to it and laughed silently at each other,
and on about the third day, the taxi they were riding in got a flat tire on
Broadway and they had to get out and find another.

"We've only got eleven days left," she said one day, and then, seemingly *16*
minutes later, "we've already been here six days."

They had got in touch with the friends they had expected to get in touch *17*
with, they were going to a Long Island summer home for a week end. "It looks
pretty dreadful right now," their hostess said cheerfully over the phone, "and
we're leaving in a week ourselves, but I'd never *forgive* you if you didn't see it
once while you were here." The weather had been fair but cool, with a definite
autumn awareness, and the clothes in the store windows were dark and already hinting at furs and velvets. She wore her coat every day, and suits most
of the time. The light dresses she had brought were hanging in the closet in
the apartment, and she was thinking now of getting a sweater in one of the big
stores, something impractical for New Hampshire, but probably good for Long
Island.

"I have to do some shopping, at least one day," she said to Brad, and he *18*
groaned.

"Don't ask me to carry packages," he said. *19*

"You aren't up to a good day's shopping," she told him, "not after all this *20*
walking around you've been doing. Why don't you go to a movie or something?"

"I want to do some shopping myself," he said mysteriously. Perhaps he was *21*
talking about her Christmas present; she had thought vaguely of getting such
things done in New York; the children would be pleased with novelties from
the city, toys not seen in their home stores. At any rate she said, "You'll probably be able to get to your wholesalers at last."

They were on their way to visit another friend, who had found a place to *22*
live by a miracle and warned them consequently not to quarrel with the appearance of the building, or the stairs, or the neighborhood: All three were bad,
and the stairs were three flights, narrow and dark, but there was a place to live
at the top. Their friend had not been in New York long, but he lived by himself
in two rooms, and had easily caught the mania for slim tables and low book-
cases which made his rooms look too large for the furniture in some places,
too cramped and uncomfortable in others.

"What a lovely place," she said when she came in, and then was sorry when *23*
her host said, "Some day this damn situation will let up and I'll be able to
settle down in a really decent place."

There were other people there; they sat and talked companionably about *24*
the same subjects then current in New Hampshire, but they drank more than
they would have at home and it left them strangely unaffected; their voices
were louder and their words more extravagant; their gestures, on the other hand,
were smaller, and they moved a finger where in New Hampshire they would
have waved an arm. Margaret said frequently, "We're just staying here for
a couple of weeks, on a vacation," and she said, "It's wonderful, so *exciting*,"
and she said, "We were *terribly* lucky; this friend went out of town just at the
right . . . ."

Finally the room was very full and noisy, and she went into a corner near a   25
window to catch her breath. The window had been opened and shut all evening, depending on whether the person standing next to it had both hands free;
and now it was shut, with the clear sky outside. Someone came and stood next
to her, and she said, "Listen to the noise outside. It's as bad as it is inside."

He said, "In a neighborhood like this someone's always getting killed."   26

She frowned. "It sounds different than before. I mean, there's a different sound   27
to it."

"Alcoholics," he said. "Drunks in the streets. Fighting going on across the   28
way." He wandered away, carrying his drink.

She opened the window and leaned out, and there were people hanging out   29
the windows across the way shouting, and people standing in the street looking up and shouting, and from across the way she heard clearly, "Lady, lady."
They must mean me, she thought, they're all looking this way. She leaned out
farther and the voices shouted incoherently but somehow making an audible
whole, "Lady, your house is on fire, lady, lady."

She closed the window firmly and turned around to the other people in the   30
room, raising her voice a little. "Listen," she said, "they're saying the house is
on fire." She was desperately afraid of their laughing at her, of looking like a
fool while Brad across the room looked at her blushing. She said again, "The
house is on *fire*," and added, "They say," for fear of sounding too vehement.
The people nearest to her turned and someone said, "She says the house is on
fire."

She wanted to get to Brad and couldn't see him; her host was not in sight   31
either, and the people all around were strangers. They don't listen to me, she
thought, I might as well not be here, and she went to the outside door and
opened it. There was no smoke, no flame, but she was telling herself, I might
as well not be here, so she abandoned Brad in panic and ran without her hat
and coat down the stairs, carrying a glass in one hand and a package of matches
in the other. The stairs were insanely long, but they were clear and safe, and
she opened the street door and ran out. A man caught her arm and said,
"Everyone out of the house?" and she said, "No, Brad's still there." The fire
engines swept around the corner, with people leaning out of the windows
watching them, and the man holding her arm said, "It's down here," and left
her. The fire was two houses away; they could see flames behind the top windows, and smoke against the night sky, but in ten minutes it was finished and
the fire engines pulled away with an air of martyrdom for hauling out all their
equipment to put out a ten-minute fire.

She went back upstairs slowly and with embarrassment, and found Brad   32
and took him home.

"I was so frightened," she said to him when they were safely in bed, "I lost   33
my head completely."

"You should have tried to find someone," he said.   34

"They wouldn't listen," she insisted. "I kept telling them and they wouldn't   35
listen and then I thought I must have been mistaken. I had some idea of going
down to see what was going on."

"Lucky it was no worse," Brad said sleepily.   36

"I felt trapped," she said. "High up in that old building with a fire; it's like   *37*
a nightmare. And in a strange city."

"Well, it's all over now," Brad said.   *38*

The same faint feeling of insecurity tagged her the next day; she went shop-   *39*
ping alone and Brad went off to see hardware, after all. She got on a bus to go
downtown and the bus was too full to move when it came time for her to get
out. Wedged standing in the aisle she said, "Out, please," and, "Excuse me,"
and by the time she was loose and near the door the bus had started again and
she got off a stop beyond. "No one *listens* to me," she said to herself. "Maybe
it's because I'm too polite." In the stores the prices were all too high and the
sweaters looked disarmingly like New Hampshire ones. The toys for the children filled her with dismay; they were so obviously for New York children:
hideous little parodies of adult life, cash registers, tiny pushcars with imitation fruit, telephones that really worked (as if there weren't enough phones in
New York that really worked), miniature milk bottles in a carrying case. "We
get our milk from cows," Margaret told the salesgirl. "My children wouldn't
know what these were." She was exaggerating, and felt guilty for a minute,
but no one was around to catch her.

She had a picture of small children in the city dressed like their parents,   *40*
following along with a miniature mechanical civilization, toy cash registers in
larger and larger sizes that eased them into the real thing, millions of clatter-
ing jerking small imitations that prepared them nicely for taking over the large
useless toys their parents lived by. She bought a pair of skis for her son, which
she knew would be inadequate for the New Hampshire snow, and a wagon for
her daughter inferior to the one Brad could make at home in an hour. Ignoring
the toy mailboxes, the small phonographs with special small records, the kid-
die cosmetics, she left the store and started home.

She was frankly afraid by now to take a bus; she stood on the corner and   *41*
waited for a taxi. Glancing down at her feet, she saw a dime on the sidewalk
and tried to pick it up, but there were too many people for her to bend down,
and she was afraid to shove to make room for fear of being stared at. She put
her foot on the dime and then saw a quarter near it, and a nickel. Someone
dropped a pocketbook, she thought, and put her other foot on the quarter,
stepping quickly to make it look natural; then she saw another dime and another nickel, and a third dime in the gutter. People were passing her, back and
forth, all the time, rushing, pushing against her, not looking at her, and she
was afraid to get down and start gathering up the money. Other people saw it
and went past, and she realized that no one was going to pick it up. They were
all embarrassed, or in too much of a hurry, or too crowded. A taxi stopped to
let someone off, and she hailed it. She lifted her feet off the dime and the quarter,
and left them there when she got into the taxi. This taxi went slowly and bumped
as it went; she had begun to notice that the gradual decay was not peculiar to
the taxis. The buses were cracking open in unimportant seams, the leather seats
broken and stained. The buildings were going, too—in one of the nicest stores
there had been a great gaping hole in the tiled foyer, and you walked around
it. Corners of the buildings seemed to be crumbling away into fine dust that
drifted downward, the granite was eroding unnoticed. Every window she saw

on her way uptown seemed to be broken; perhaps every street corner was pep-
pered with small change. The people were moving faster than ever before; a
girl in a red hat appeared at the upper side of the taxi window and was gone
beyond the lower side before you could see the hat; store windows were so terribly bright because you only caught them for a fraction of a second. The people seemed hurled on in a frantic action that made every hour forty-five minutes long, every day nine hours, every year fourteen days. Food was so elusively
fast, eaten in such a hurry, that you were always hungry, always speeding to
a new meal with new people. Everything was imperceptibly quicker every
minute. She stepped into the taxi on one side and stepped out the other side
at her home; she pressed the fifth-floor button on the elevator and was coming
down again, bathed and dressed and ready for dinner with Brad. They went
out for dinner and were coming in again, hungry and hurrying to bed in order
to get to breakfast with lunch beyond. They had been in New York nine days;
tomorrow was Saturday and they were going to Long Island, coming home
Sunday, and then Wednesday they were going home, really home. By the time
she had thought of it they were on the train to Long Island; the train was broken, the seats torn and the floor dirty; one of the doors wouldn't open and the
windows wouldn't shut. Passing through the outskirts of the city, she thought,
It's as though everything were traveling so fast that the solid stuff couldn't stand
it and were going to pieces under the strain, cornices blowing off and windows
caving in. She knew she was afraid to say it truly, afraid to face the knowledge
that it was a voluntary neck-breaking speed, a deliberate whirling faster and
faster to end in destruction.

On Long Island, their hostess led them into a new piece of New York, a house   42
filled with New York furniture as though on rubber bands, pulled this far,
stretched taut, and ready to snap back to the city, to an apartment, as soon as
the door was opened and the lease, fully paid, had expired. "We've had this
place every year for simply ages," their hostess said. "Otherwise we couldn't
have gotten it *possibly* this year."

"It's an awfully nice place," Brad said. "I'm surprised you don't live here   43
all year round."

"Got to get back to the city *some* time," their hostess said, and laughed.   44

"Not much like New Hampshire," Brad said. He was beginning to be a little   45
homesick, Margaret thought; he wants to yell, just once. Since the fire scare
she was apprehensive about large groups of people gathering together; when
friends began to drop in after dinner she waited for a while, telling herself they
were on the ground floor, she could run right outside, all the windows were
open; then she excused herself and went to bed. When Brad came to bed much
later she woke up and he said irritably, "We've been playing anagrams. Such
crazy people." She said sleepily, "Did you win?" and fell asleep before he told
her.

The next morning she and Brad went for a walk while their host and hostess   46
read the Sunday papers. "If you turn to the right outside the door," their hostess said encouragingly, "and walk about three blocks down, you'll come to our
beach."

"What do they want with our beach?" their host said. "It's too damn cold   47
to do anything down there."

"They can look at the *water*," their hostess said.   *48*

They walked down to the beach; at this time of year it was bare and wind-   *49*
swept, yet still nodding hideously under traces of its summer plumage, as though
it thought itself warmly inviting. There were occupied houses on the way there,
for instance, and a lonely lunchstand was open, bravely advertising hot dogs
and root beer. The man in the lunchstand watched them go by, his face cold
and unsympathetic. They walked far past him, out of sight of houses, on to a
stretch of grey pebbled sand that lay between the grey water on one side and
the grey pebbled sand dunes on the other.

"Imagine going swimming here," she said with a shiver. The beach pleased   *50*
her; it was oddly familiar and reassuring and at the same time that she realized this, the little tune came back to her, bringing a double recollection. The
beach was the one where she had lived in imagination, writing for herself dreary
love-broken stories where the heroine walked beside the wild waves; the little
tune was the symbol of the golden world she escaped into to avoid the everyday dreariness that drove her into writing depressing stories about the beach.
She laughed out loud and Brad said, "What on earth's so funny about this
Godforsaken landscape?"

"I was just thinking how far away from the city it seems," she said falsely.   *51*

The sky and the water and the sand were grey enough to make it feel like   *52*
late afternoon instead of midmorning; she was tired and wanted to go back,
but Brad said suddenly, "Look at that," and she turned and saw a girl running
down over the dunes, carrying her hat, and her hair flying behind her.

"Only way to get warm on a day like this," Brad remarked, but Margaret   *53*
said, "She looks frightened."

The girl saw them and came toward them, slowing down as she approached   *54*
them. She was eager to reach them but when she came within speaking distance the familiar embarrassment, the not wanting to look like a fool, made
her hesitate and look from one to the other of them uncomfortably.

"Do you know where I can find a policeman?" she asked finally.   *55*

Brad looked up and down the bare rocky beach and said solemnly, "There   *56*
don't seem to be any around. Is there something we can do?"

"I don't think so," the girl said. "I really need a policeman."   *57*

They go to the police for everything, Margaret thought, these people, these   *58*
New York people, it's as though they had selected a section of the population
to act as problem-solvers, and so no matter what they want they look for a
policeman.

"Be glad to help you if we can," Brad said.   *59*

The girl hesitated again. "Well, if you *must* know," she said crossly, "there's   *60*
a leg up there."

They waited politely for the girl to explain, but she only said, "Come *on*,   *61*
then," and waved to them to follow her. She led them over the dunes to a spot
near a small inlet, where the dunes gave way abruptly to an intruding head of
water. A leg was lying on the sand near the water, and the girl gestured at it
and said, "There," as though it were her own property and they had insisted
on having a share.

They walked over to it and Brad bent down gingerly. "It's a leg all right,"   *62*
he said. It looked like part of a wax dummy, a death-white wax leg neatly cut

off at top-thigh and again just above the ankle, bent comfortably at the knee
and resting on the sand. "It's real," Brad said, his voice slightly different. "You're
right about that policeman."

They walked together to the lunchstand and the man listened unenthusiast-   63
ically while Brad called the police. When the police came they all walked out
again to where the leg was lying and Brad gave the police their names and
addresses, and then said, "Is it all right to go on home?"

"What the hell you want to hang around for?" the policeman inquired with   64
heavy humor. "You waiting for the rest of him?"

They went back to their host and hostess, talking about the leg, and their   65
host apologized, as though he had been guilty of a breach of taste in allowing
his guests to come on a human leg; their hostess said with interest, "There was
an arm washed up in Bensonhurst, I've been reading about it."

"One of these killings," the host said.   66

Upstairs Margaret said abruptly, "I suppose it starts to happen first in the   67
suburbs," and when Brad said, "What starts to happen?" she said hysterically,
"People starting to come apart."

In order to reassure their host and hostess about their minding the leg, they   68
stayed until the last afternoon train to New York. Back in their apartment again
it seemed to Margaret that the marble in the house lobby had begun to age a
little; even in two days there were new perceptible cracks. The elevator seemed
a little rusty, and there was a fine film of dust over everything in the apartment. They went to bed feeling uncomfortable, and the next morning Margaret
said immediately, "I'm going to stay in today."

"You're not upset about yesterday, are you?"   69

"Not a bit," Margaret said. "I just want to stay in and rest."   70

After some discussion Brad decided to go off again by himself; he still had   71
people it was important to see and places he must go in the few days they had
left. After breakfast in the Automat Margaret came back alone to the apartment, carrying the mystery story she had bought on the way. She hung up her
coat and hat and sat down by the window with the noise and the people far
below, looking out at the sky where it was grey beyond the houses across the
street.

I'm not going to worry about it, she said to herself, no sense thinking all the   72
time about things like that, spoil your vacation and Brad's too. No sense worrying, people get ideas like that and then worry about them.

The nasty little tune was running through her head again, with its burden   73
of suavity and expensive perfume. The houses across the street were silent and
perhaps unoccupied at this time of day; she let her eyes move with the rhythm
of the tune, from window to window along one floor. By gliding quickly across
two windows, she could make one line of the tune fit one floor of windows, and
then a quick breath and a drop down to the next floor; it had the same number
of windows and the tune had the same number of beats, and then the next floor
and the next. She stopped suddenly when it seemed to her that the windowsill
she had just passed had soundlessly crumpled and fallen into fine sand; when
she looked back it was there as before but then it seemed to be the windowsill
above and to the right, and finally a corner of the roof.

No sense worrying, she told herself, forcing her eyes down to the street, stop   74 thinking about things all the time. Looking down at the street for long made her dizzy and she stood up and went into the small bedroom of the apartment. She had made the bed before going out to breakfast, like any good housewife, but now she deliberately took it apart, stripping the blankets and sheets off one by one, and then she made it again, taking a long time over the corners and smoothing out every wrinkle. *"That's* done," she said when she was through, and went back to the window. When she looked across the street the tune started again, window to window, sills dissolving and falling downward. She leaned forward and looked down at her own window, something she had never thought of before, down to the sill. It was partly eaten away; when she touched the stone a few crumbs rolled off and fell.

It was eleven o'clock; Brad was looking at blowtorches by now and would 75 not be back before one, if even then. She thought of writing a letter home, but the impulse left her before she found paper and pen. Then it occurred to her that she might take a nap, a thing she had never done in the morning in her life, and she went in and lay down on the bed. Lying down, she felt the building shaking.

No sense worrying, she told herself again, as though it were a charm against 76 witches, and got up and found her coat and hat and put them on. I'll just get some cigarettes and some letter paper, she thought, just run down to the corner. Panic caught her going down in the elevator; it went too fast, and when she stepped out in the lobby it was only the people standing around who kept her from running. As it was, she went quickly out of the building and into the street. For a minute she hesitated, wanting to go back. The cars were going past so rapidly, the people hurrying as always, but the panic of the elevator drove her on finally. She went to the corner, and, following the people flying along ahead, ran out into the street, to hear a horn almost overhead and a shout from behind her, and the noise of brakes. She ran blindly on and reached the other side where she stopped and looked around. The truck was going on its appointed way around the corner, the people going past on either side of her, parting to go around her where she stood.

No one even noticed me, she thought with reassurance, everyone who saw 77 me has gone by long ago. She went into the drugstore ahead of her and asked the man for cigarettes; the apartment now seemed safer to her than the street— she could walk up the stairs. Coming out of the store and walking to the corner, she kept as close to the buildings as possible, refusing to give way to the rightful traffic coming out of the doorways. On the corner she looked carefully at the light; it was green, but it looked as though it were going to change. Always safer to wait, she thought, don't want to walk into another truck.

People pushed past her and some were caught in the middle of the street 78 when the light changed. One woman, more cowardly than the rest, turned and ran back to the curb, but the others stood in the middle of the street, leaning forward and then backward according to the traffic moving past them on both sides. One got to the farther curb in a brief break in the line of cars, the others were a fraction of a second too late and waited. Then the light changed again and as the cars slowed down Margaret put a foot on the street to go, but a taxi swinging wildly around her corner frightened her back and she stood on the curb again. By the time the taxi had gone the light was due to change again and she thought, I can wait once more, no sense getting caught out in the middle. A man beside her tapped his foot impatiently for the light to change back; two girls came past her and walked out into the street a few steps to wait, moving back a little when cars came too close, talking busily all the time. I ought to stay right with them, Margaret thought, but then they moved back against her and the light changed and the man next to her charged into the street and the two girls in front waited a minute and then moved slowly on, still talking, and Margaret started to follow and then decided to wait. A crowd of people formed around her suddenly; they had come off a bus and were crossing here, and she had a sudden feeling of being jammed in the center and forced out into the street when all of them moved as one with the light changing, and she elbowed her way desperately out of the crowd and went off to lean against a building and wait. It seemed to her that people passing were beginning to look at her. What do they think of me, she wondered, and stood up straight as though she were waiting for someone. She looked at her watch and frowned, and then thought, What a fool I must look like, no one here ever saw me before, they all go by too fast. She went back to the curb again but the green light was just changing to red and she thought, I'll go back to the drugstore and have a Coke, no sense going back to that apartment.

The man looked at her unsurprised in the drugstore and she sat and ordered   79
a Coke but suddenly as she was drinking it the panic caught her again and she thought of the people who had been with her when she first started to cross the street, blocks away by now, having tried and made perhaps a dozen lights while she had hesitated at the first; people by now a mile or so downtown, because they had been going steadily while she had been trying to gather her courage. She paid the man quickly, restrained an impulse to say that there was nothing wrong with the Coke, she just had to get back, that was all, and she hurried down to the corner again.

The minute the light changes, she told herself firmly; there's no sense. The   80
light changed before she was ready and in the minute before she collected herself traffic turning the corner overwhelmed her and she shrank back against the curb. She looked longingly at the cigar store on the opposite corner, with her apartment house beyond; she wondered, How do people ever manage to get there, and knew that by wondering, by admitting a doubt, she was lost. The light changed and she looked at it with hatred, a dumb thing, turning back and forth, back and forth, with no purpose and no meaning. Looking to either side of her slyly, to see if anyone were watching, she stepped quietly backward, one step, two, until she was well away from the curb. Back in the drugstore again she waited for some sign of recognition from the clerk and saw none; he regarded her with the same apathy as he had the first time. He gestured without interest at the telephone; he doesn't care, she thought, it doesn't matter to him who I call.

She had no time to feel like a fool, because they answered the phone im-   81
mediately and agreeably and found him right away. When he answered the phone, his voice sounding surprised and matter-of-fact, she could only say miserably, "I'm in the drugstore on the corner. Come and get me."

"What's the matter?" He was not anxious to come.   82

"Please come and get me," she said into the black mouthpiece that might   83
or might not tell him, "please come and get me, Brad. *Please.*"

Considerations

1. What does Margaret expect from her holiday in New York? For each of her plans and expectations that you list, chart the reality that she eventually experiences.
2. After finishing the story, review it to find the spot where you first suspected that Margaret's visit would not be an entirely satisfying one. What in Shirley Jackson's writing led you to make this inference? Compare your own reading experience with that of other readers.
3. Jackson's title alludes to the story of Lot's wife (Genesis 19:15–26). After reading the Biblical account, evaluate the appropriateness of this allusion to the overall plot of Jackson's story.
4. In *Transcultural Nursing* (Englewood Cliffs, N.J.:Prentice-Hall, 1976), medical anthropologist Pamela J. Brink traces four predictable phases of culture shock: (1) *honeymoon*—delight in new surroundings; (2) *alienation*—depression and anxiety because of strange surroundings; (3) *acceptance*—adjustment to values, customs, and pace of current surroundings; and (4) *reacculturation*—acceptance so total that returning to the indigenous culture would cause another culture shock. To what extent and in what ways does Margaret experience culture shock as Brink describes it?

Connections

1. Look back at your list of Margaret's expectations about New York. (If you like, you may add Brad's expectations to this list.) Which of these would Aristotle recognize as benefits of city living?
2. How might Aristotle or Jacques Ellul explain Margaret's eventual paralysis?
3. One episode in "Pillar of Salt" describes Margaret and Brad's visit to a part of Long Island that has a residential density not much different from that of their New England hometown. Use selections by Howard J. Nelson or Jane Jacobs or other previous readings in this chapter to suggest why such an outlying area could present a city experience to an out-of-towner.
4. In what ways do Stanley Milgram's descriptions of city experience explain Margaret's trouble adapting to the metropolis?

Crossing Brooklyn Ferry°

Walt Whitman

1

Flood-tide below me! I see you face to face!
Clouds of the west—sun there half an hour high—I see you also face to face.

Crowds of men and women attired in the usual costumes, how curious you are
    to me!
On the ferry-boats the hundreds and hundreds that cross, returning home, are
    more curious to me than you suppose,
And you that shall cross from shore to shore years hence are more to me, and
    more in my meditations, than you might suppose.   5

2

The impalpable sustenance of me from all things at all hours of the day,
The simple, compact, well-join'd scheme, myself disintegrated, every one dis-
    integrated yet part of the scheme,
The similitudes of the past and those of the future,
The glories strung like beads on my smallest sights and hearings, on the walk
    in the street and the passage over the river,
The current rushing so swiftly and swimming with me far away,   10
The others that are to follow me, the ties between me and them,
The certainty of others, the life, love, sight, hearing of others.

Others will enter the gates of the ferry and cross from shore to shore,
Others will watch the run of the flood-tide,
Others will see the shipping of Manhattan north and west, and the heights of
    Brooklyn to the south and east,   15

°Until the Brooklyn Bridge was completed in 1883, the ferry provided public transport between Manhattan and Brooklyn.

---

*Through his long career as poet, newspaper editor, and army nurse, Walt Whit-
man (1819–1892) traveled widely across America. He visited many cities and studied
the features of urban life through direct observation. Much of his time he spent
conversing with city dwellers and participating in their everyday activities. Hence
his poetry combines ordinary speech patterns with resonant oratory. In this voice
Whitman was best able to express his faith in democracy and to personify a visionary who could rise above conventional life.*

Others will see the islands large and small;
Fifty years hence, others will see them as they cross, the sun half an hour high,
A hundred years hence, or ever so many hundred years hence, others will see
      them,
Will enjoy the sunset, the pouring-in of the flood-tide, the falling-back to the
      sea of the ebb-tide.

3

It avails not, time nor place—distance avails not,   20
I am with you, you men and women of a generation, or ever so many genera-
      tions hence,
Just as you feel when you look on the river and sky, so I felt,
Just as any of you is one of a living crowd, I was one of a crowd,
Just as you are refresh'd by the gladness of the river and the bright flow, I was
      refresh'd.
Just as you stand and lean on the rail, yet hurry with the swift current, I stood
      yet was hurried,   25
Just as you look on the numberless masts of ships and the thick-stemm'd pipes
      of steamboats, I look'd.

I too many and many a time cross'd the river of old,
Watched the Twelfth-month° sea-gulls, saw them high in the air floating with
      motionless wings, oscillating their bodies,
Saw how the glistening yellow lit up parts of their bodies and left the rest in
      strong shadow,
Saw the slow-wheeling circles and the gradual edging toward the south,   30
Saw the reflection of the summer sky in the water,
Had my eyes dazzled by the shimmering track of beams,
Look'd at the fine centrifugal spokes of light round the shape of my head in the
      sunlit water,
Look'd on the haze on the hills southward and south-westward,
Look'd on the vapor as it flew in fleeces tinged with violet,   35
Look'd toward the lower bay to notice the vessels arriving,
Saw their approach, saw aboard those that were near me,
Saw the white sails of schooners and sloops, saw the ships at anchor,
The sailors at work in the rigging or out astride the spars,
The round masts, the swinging motion of the hulls, the slender serpentine pen-
      nants,   40
The large and small steamers in motion, the pilots in their pilot-houses,
The white wake left by the passage, the quick tremulous whirl of the wheels,
The flags of all nations, the falling of them at sunset,
The scallop-edged waves in the twilight, the ladled cups, the frolicsome crests
      and glistening,

°Twelfth-month: The Quaker name for December.

The stretch afar growing dimmer and dimmer, the gray walls of the granite
    storehouses by the docks,   *45*
On the river the shadowy group, the big steam-tug closely flank'd on each side
    by the barges, the hay-boat, the belated lighter,
On the neighboring shores the fires from the foundry chimneys burning high
    and glaringly into the night,
Casting their flicker of black contrasted with wild red and yellow light over the
    tops of houses, and down into the clefts of streets.

4

These and all else were to me the same as they are to you,
I loved well those cities,° loved well the stately and rapid river,   *50*
The men and women I saw were all near to me,
Others the same—others who look back on me because I look'd forward to them,
(The time will come, though I stop here to-day and to-night.)

5

What is it between us?
What is the count of the scores or hundreds of years between us?   *55*

Whatever it is, it avails not—distance avails not, and place avails not,
I too lived, Brooklyn of ample hills was mine,
I too walk'd the streets of Manhattan island, and bathed in the waters around
    it,
I too felt the curious abrupt questionings stir within me,
In the day among crowds of people sometimes they came upon me,   *60*
In my walks home late at night or as I lay in my bed they came upon me,
I too had been struck from the float forever held in solution,
I too had receiv'd identity by my body,
That I was I knew was of my body, and what I should be I knew I should be
    of my body.

6

It is not upon you alone the dark patches fall,   *65*
The dark threw its patches down upon me also,
The best I had done seem'd to me blank and suspicious,
My great thoughts as I supposed them, were they not in reality meagre?
Nor is it you alone who know what it is to be evil,
I am he who knew what it was to be evil,   *70*
I too knitted the old knot of contrariety,
Blabb'd, blush'd, resented, lied, stole, grudg'd,
Had guile, anger, lust, hot wishes I dared not speak,

°those cities: Until 1895, Brooklyn was a separate municipality.

Was wayward, vain, greedy, shallow, sly, cowardly, malignant,
The wolf, the snake, the hog, not wanting in me,   *75*
The cheating look, the frivolous word, the adulterous wish, not wanting,
Refusals, hates, postponements, meanness, laziness, none of these wanting,
Was one with the rest, the days and haps° of the rest,
Was call'd by my nighest name by clear loud voices of young men as they saw
      me approaching or passing,
Felt their arms on my neck as I stood, or the negligent leaning of their flesh
      against me as I sat,   *80*
Saw many I loved in the street or ferry-boat or public assembly, yet never told
      them a word,
Lived the same life with the rest, the same old laughing, gnawing, sleeping,
Play'd the part that still looks back on the actor or actress,
The same old role, the role that is what we make it, as great as we like,
Or as small as we like, or both great and small.   *85*

7

Closer yet I approach you,
What thought you have of me now, I had as much of you—I laid in my stores
      in advance,
I consider'd long and seriously of you before you were born.

Who was to know what should come home to me?
Who knows but I am enjoying this?   *90*
Who knows, for all the distance, but I am as good as looking at you now, for
      all you cannot see me?

8

Ah, what can ever be more stately and admirable to me than mast-hemm'd
      Manhattan?
River and sunset and scallop-edg'd waves of flood-tide?
The sea-gulls oscillating their bodies, the hay-boat in the twilight, and the be-
      lated lighter?
What gods can exceed these that clasp me by the hand, and with voices I love
      call me promptly and loudly by my nighest name as I approach?   *95*
What is more subtle than this which ties me to the woman or man that looks
      in my face?
Which fuses me into you now, and pours my meaning into you?

We understand then do we not?
What I promis'd without mentioning it, have you not accepted?
What the study could not teach—what the preaching could not accomplish is   *100*
      accomplish'd, is it not?

°haps: Chance events.

9

Flow on, river! flow with the flood-tide, and ebb with the ebb-tide!
Frolic on, crested and scallop-edg'd waves!
Gorgeous clouds of the sunset! drench with your splendor me, or the men and
    women generations after me!
Cross from shore to shore, countless crowds of passengers!
Stand up, tall masts of Mannahatta!° stand up, beautiful hills of Brooklyn!   *105*
Throb, baffled and curious brain! throw out questions and answers!
Suspend here and everywhere, eternal float of solution!
Gaze, loving and thirsting eyes, in the house or street or public assembly!
Sound out, voices of young men! loudly and musically call me by my highest
    name!
Live, old life! play the part that looks back on the actor or actress!   *110*
Play the old role, the role that is great or small according as one makes it!
Consider, you who peruse me, whether I may not in unknown ways be looking
    upon you.
Be firm, rail over the river, to support those who lean idly, yet haste with the
    hasting current;
Fly on, sea-birds! fly sideways, or wheel in large circles high in the air;
Receive the summer sky, you water, and faithfully hold it till all downcast eyes
    have time to take it from you!   *115*
Diverge, fine spokes of light, from the shape of my head, or any one's head, in
    the sunlit water!
Come on, ships from the lower bay! pass up or down, white-sail'd schooners,
    sloops, lighters!
Flaunt away, flags of all nations! be duly lower'd at sunset!
Burn high your fires, foundry chimneys! cast black shadows at nightfall! cast
    red and yellow light over the tops of the houses!
Appearances, now or henceforth, indicate what you are,   *120*
You necessary film, continue to envelop the soul,
About my body for me, and your body for you, be hung our divinest aromas,
Thrive, cities—bring your freight, bring your shows, ample and sufficient rivers,
Expand, being than which none else is perhaps more spiritual,
Keep your places, objects than which none else is more lasting.   *125*

You have waited, you always wait, you dumb, beautiful ministers,
We receive you with free sense at last, and are insatiate henceforward,
Not you any more shall be able to foil us, or withhold yourselves from us,
We use you, and to not cast you aside—we plant you permanently within us,
We fathom you not—we love you—there is perfection in you also,   *130*
You furnish your parts toward eternity,
Great or small, you furnish your parts toward the soul.

°Mannahatta: An Indian word for Manhattan.

Considerations

1. Outline the poem's ideas; what is the progression of thought in "Crossing Brooklyn Ferry"?
2. One useful way to study the structure and purpose of a poem is to inventory (list and classify) its salient images and diction. What are its various degrees of light and dark? Where are references to nature, to manufactured objects, and to human beings? Look for the specific as compared to the general, and for the concrete as compared to the abstract. Which objects or terms are specialized or erudite, and which are ordinary or popular? Which terms and images are used repeatedly in the poem? As you collect and share your inventories, be sure to consider the effects of these devices and how they contribute to the poem's meaning.
3. Study Walt Whitman's poetic rhetoric. Where does Whitman speak *to* other men and women, and where does he speak *about* them?
4. A poem, like an essay, is built of sentences, and Whitman's can sometimes be complicated. Which sentences are declarative? which imperative? In addition, which rhetorical questions assume a yes/no answer? which a more complicated response?
5. Two interesting devices in this poem are *anaphora* (the repetition of words and phrases at beginnings of clauses, sentences, or lines) and *anastrophe* (unusual arrangement of words within phrases and sentences). Find examples of these devices, and suggest Whitman's reasons for using them. What would the poem lose without them?
6. In line 126, the speaker addresses "dumb, beautiful ministers." In terms of urban study, what are these ministers?

Connections

1. In his way, Walt Whitman was as forward-looking as Robert F. Kennedy was. Compare the two men's statements and inferences about the future of the American city.
2. Aristotle says in "The Polis" that "the highest good is felicity; and that consists in the energy and perfect practice of goodness" (para. 6). To what extent would Whitman endorse these statements?
3. As Ronald Pasquariello, Donald Shriver, and Alan Geyer have said, ambivalent attitudes toward the city are in no way new. Some people see the city as "a lovely and noble place"; others view it as "the habituation of all that is evil" (para. 17). Catalogue references in Whitman's poem along this continuum of city-as-hell to city-as-demi-paradise. (Why does Whitman include both points of view?)
4. Pretend that Whitman had been a subject in one of the experiments Stanley Milgram describes. Name the experiment and, using inferences from "Crossing Brooklyn Ferry," describe how Whitman might have behaved in the experimental situation.

5. Contrast the reactions of Whitman's speaker to the cityscape with those of Shirley Jackson's protagonist Margaret. What in the situations and characters of these two individuals might cause their differing reactions?

Further Connections

1. After studying the pieces in this unit, write an extended definition of the term *American city.*
2. In "Urban Crises in America," Robert F. Kennedy says that "destruction of . . . community" spirit is "both cause and consequence" (para. 9) of the four other disruptive urban forces: growth, ruination of the environment, transportation problems, and poverty and racial tension. After you have read the selections in this unit, make a list or construct a chart of specific theory and observable data that substantiate or offer alternative explanations to Kennedy's statement of this two-way causal relationship.
3. As educator Dwight W. Hoover points out, academic disciplines study the cityscape differently. Use the following 22 definitions to debate the question: Does your college campus qualify as a city?

> *Geography*
>
> City as a central, interdependent place with identifiable social features
> City as a result of land patterns and water resources
>
> *Urban Planning*
>
> City as a provider of essentials and amenities to the citizenry
>
> *Literature and Painting*
>
> City as a metaphor for other things
> City as a repository for myths about the American Dream
> City as a cluster of traits that demonstrate urbanity
>
> *Architecture and Design*
>
> City as a physical container for the populace
> City as a spatial organization of shapes and forms
>
> *Theology and Philosophy*
>
> City as an expression of human responsibility and freedom
> City as a teleological symbol
>
> *Sociology and Anthropology*
>
> City as an institution and groups of institutions
> City as a socially stratified structure
> City as a promoter of social role
>
> *Political Science*
>
> City as a corporate legal body
> City as conflict and resolution of conflict, as order and awareness of the possibility of disorder

City as a formal organization establishing and guarding policy
City as a statement of ideals of the elite class
City as a center of pluralism

Economics

City as a producer and distributor of resources based on market conditions

City as an economic unit allocating limited resources while endeavoring to maximize benefits

Biology

City as an extended community of beings, some related genetically but most not

Chemistry

City as a complex and temporary order of atoms, molecules, and cell structures

4. Recall your reading of Chapter 1, The Dimensions of Power, to describe how one can obtain and maintain power in a specifically urban setting. (The selection by Machiavelli will be especially useful.)
5. Use animal characters to construct a tale about urban life. You may want to consult Chapter 9, The Impact of Animals, for information, and you may model your story on the patterns of folk lore as seen in Chapter 10, The Fairy Tale Snow White.
6. Articles by Charles Darwin and Carl Sagan (reprinted in Chapter 9, The Impact of Animals) suggest that humans retain a biological urge to contend with rivals or to seek out and master prey. In what ways does the modern American urban environment thwart this urge? In what ways does it allow or even stimulate it?
7. Epidemiological studies like those mentioned in Chapter 8, The Treatment of Cancer, show that building the metropolis may create medical risks as well as technological and cultural advantages. In pieces by Robert F. Kennedy, Stanley Milgram, and Shirley Jackson, you have read about the violence and mental illness that cities can cause. Now speculate about the ways that urban environments are also conducive to physical illness. Brainstorm with a team and share ideas with the whole class. You may then want to organize the collections of ideas in order to write a summary report of these speculations.

Extensions

1. To gain control of urban studies terminology, study this vocabulary:
   a. *Metropolitan* and *urban* are two adjectives denoting "city." Briefly, compare their etymologies and present meanings.
   b. Use the *Oxford English Dictionary* to study and record the etymology and meaning of *city*.
   c. Compare the modern term *megalopolis* to the words in (a) and (b).
   d. Define the terms *cosmopolitan* and *urbane*.

e. What is the etymology of the word *citizen?*
What implications do these definitions suggest? That is, what connotations have cities had for English speakers?

2. Read a standard history of an American metropolis. Use your reading to write your own short history of one of the urban problems Robert F. Kennedy pinpoints in his remarks at the Ribicoff hearings.

3. Select an American city and study its map in light of Howard J. Nelson's description of the classic developmental models. Write an essay in which you suggest which of the three models this city seems to demonstrate: concentric zones, sectors, or multiple nodes. Alternatively, point out the factors that make this city impossible to classify in terms of these models.

4. Research the history of an American city to determine its earliest plan. (In the first paragraph of "Towns, Time, and Tradition," John W. Reps offers a list of fruitful choices.) A good place to begin your work is Reps's own history *The Making of Urban America*, but you will also want to check other local histories and books about city planning. Write an essay comparing the original city plan to the current map. To what factors (economic, geographic, or meteorlogical, political, commercial, etc.) would you attribute the similarities or differences?

5. Reps says that a number of American cities were not "planned with skill" but that many an original design "exceeds in merit" its later development. Prepare a written or oral presentation arguing that the original plan of the city you researched for question 4 was inferior or superior to that city's eventual development.

6. Propose an advertisement for investing in or moving to a specific American city; thinking of what makes for effective business and public relations, advertise any period in the city's history. First, research what the city had to offer at the time. Then choose an advertising medium appropriate to the audience and the period. Write a memo to members of your class or prepare an oral briefing in which you defend your ad's appeal; alternatively, draft the copy of the advertisement itself.

7. Social historian Anselm L. Strauss offers this advice to urban planners:

> Cities might well be studied, contemporaneously and historically, in terms of their icons. These are important—at least for various groups within a given city—for helping to set the city's style, for bringing a sense of belonging to citizens, for representing a city to outsiders, even for giving direction to planning and to the evolution of its institutions. The symbolism of Washington for the nation, and the prominence of its icons (the Capitol, the White House, and so on) is an obvious instance. . . . What is needed for the development of urban theory is a series of cumulative studies of different types of icons, for different cities, and for different populations within those cities. And since the meanings of these icons are never static, we need a focus on change also: for instance, it would be interesting to know what happened in Brooklyn just before and after the Dodgers left.

Use a dictionary to find out the traditional meanings of *icon* and *iconography*, terms important in religious studies and art history as well as in urban studies. Then select a single icon for a city you have researched or know well (or for your college, even if it is not an urban campus). Write an essay defending your choice.

8. Using Strauss's suggestion, compare two similar icons from two different cities, a past and a present icon from the same city, or two different population groups' probable interpretations of iconography for a single city.

9. In "The Form and Structure of Cities," Howard J. Nelson refers to the "personality" of cities such as San Francisco, New Orleans, and Savannah, Georgia. Anselm L. Strauss notes that Chicago has long been called an "adolescent," while nearby Milwaukee, which is no older, seems "settled" and "middleaged." And in 1981, a *Time* magazine article argued that to people from Dallas, Houston seems "loud" and "boorish" while Houstonians find Dallas "dull" and "snobbish." Select one American city and write a description personifying its appearnace, energy level, interests, attitudes, age, etc. What kind of person would your city be if it were a single human being? Alternatively, personify a college campus.

10. Editor Ralph K. Andrist has written that "technology created the modern city. The New York or New Orleans of four or five decades before the Civil War was not basically different from the Rome of fifteen hundred years earlier." According to Andrist, the "great change" is technological. Support or refute Andrist's contention by using library materials. Begin your search with articles from specialized encyclopedias or general histories of urban or technological development.

11. As part of his further work on the quality of urban experience (not reprinted in The Urban Experience), Stanley Milgram has suggested researching people's impressions about specific cities. Devise a research design that polls the impressions of a sizable sample of people on your campus or in your community. You might ask about the atmosphere of one or more cities: tempo and pace, density, level of activity, diversity, degree of cleanness, temperament of citizens (tolerance, courtesy, etc.), ease of mobility, physical beauty, or cultural contributions. Write up your experiment's hypothesis, procedures, and conclusions.

12. Another type of survey you could design is quantitative. Compose a multiple-choice survey of popular myths about a city, or ask respondents to give true or false answers to statements you have written.

13. Select an American city and research one of its particular problems of geophysical landscape (threats such as hurricanes, tornados, earthquakes, flood, and drought). Check both general histories and recent periodical literature. Prepare an essay or an oral presentation suggesting ways that citizens have adjusted or may adjust to this hazard.

14. In *Jazz City*, author Leroy Ostransky says, "The early history of cities . . . is often important in showing the spirit in which a particular city was formed. . . . It may be a 'frontier' spirit, or one of laissez-faire, or simply one of great lawlessness." Select a city well known for some cultural contribution: music, literature, art, law, education, etc. Show how the general history of the city—its social life, neighborhood structure, commerce, geographical situation, major purpose and "spirit"—affected the development of this cultural contribution.

15. In "Urban Crises in America," Robert F. Kennedy points out "the destruction of the sense, and often the fact, of community" (para. 9). He also lists some symptoms of the lack of access to urban services and separation from

the power base. Choose one group (Blacks, Latinos, American Indians, another ethnic minority, the working class, women, the elderly, the handicapped, etc.), and research its traditional lack of power in American cities. Write an essay presenting the causes, symptoms, and effects of this political disenfranchisement; point out how it might be or has been ameliorated or corrected.

16. Two prominent notions about the cause of urban crime are (1) that ordinary citizens feel anonymous and alienated from other citizens and (2) that those with power to shape metropolitan life are corrupted by their power. Read one of the novels or short stories listed below. Write an essay showing to what extent the characterization and plot dramatizes the city's effect on class estrangement and class conflict.

Sholom Asch, *East River*
Saul Bellow, *Seize the Day*
Stephen Crane, *Maggie, a Girl of the Streets, George's Mother*
John Dos Passos, *Manhattan Transfer*
Theodore Dreiser, *Sister Carrie*
F. Scott Fitzgerald, *This Side of Paradise*
William Dean Howells, *A Hazard of New Fortunes, The Rise of Silas Lapham*
Frank Norris, *McTeague*
Thomas Pynchon, *The Crying of Lot 49*
Henry Roth, *Call It Sleep*
Damon Runyan, "Guys and Dolls" (collection of short stories)
Betty Smith, *A Tree Grows in Brooklyn*
Dan Wakefield, *Going All the Way*
Edith Wharton, *The House of Mirth, The Age of Innocence*
Thrya Samter Winslow, "A Cycle of Manhattan"
Thomas Wolfe, *Of Time and the River*
Anzia Yezierska, *Bread Givers*

17. Be utopian: describe what you believe to be the ideal American urban environment for the 1980s. Given what Kennedy, Milgram, and others have written, you need not describe an actual place.

18. Defend in writing your choice of one actual American city as the quintessence of the American urban experience. Especially useful from this chapter will be articles by Kennedy, Reps, Nelson, Milgram, and Whitman, but you will also need some research. You might, for example, begin by using the *Readers' Guide to Periodical Literature* to find out what criteria are used to select "all-American cities" and what cities have been selected in the recent past. Once you choose a city, use aids such as the Public Affairs Information Service (PAIS), the *Social Science Index*, the *New York Times Index*, and other guides to specialized publications.

Suggestions for Further Reading

Andrist, Ralph K. "The City of Tomorrow." In *Looking Forward: Life in the Twentieth Century as Predicated in the Pages of American Magazines from 1895 to 1905,* edited by Ray Brousseau, pp. 8–41. New York: American Heritage, 1970. Interpretive text accompanies a compilation of articles and illustrations.

Cox, Harvey. *The Secular City.* New York: Macmillan, 1965. A theologian's argument that technology and communications have created the modern city, which both requires and allows humans to act maturely and responsibly.

Gelfant, Blanche Housman. *The American City Novel.* Norman, Okla.: University of Oklahoma Press, 1954. Literary criticism focusing on the first four decades of this century.

Greenbie, Barrie B. *Spaces: Dimensions of the Human Landscape.* New York: Yale, 1981. An ecological study with references to the biological sciences; many photographs.

Hall, Peter. *The World Cities.* New York: McGraw-Hill, 1966. Helpful for setting the American metropolis in the context of international urban geography.

Jacobs, Jane. *The Death and Life of Great American Cities.* New York: Random House, 1961.

Lynch, Kevin. *The Image of the City.* Cambridge, Mass.: MIT Press, 1960. Employs perception theories to describe urban form and architecture.

Marx, Leo. *The Machine in the Garden: Technology and the Pastoral Ideal in America.* New York: Oxford, 1964. A classic of literary and cultural criticism; traces the development of American cities as one expression of the pastoral ideal.

Mumford, Lewis. *Sticks and Stones: A Study of American Architecture and Civilization.* New York: Dover, 1954. One of the most accessible of the author's many influential works about urban theory and design.

Ostransky, Leroy. *Jazz City: The Impact of Our Cities on the Development of Jazz.* Englewood Cliffs, N.J.: Prentice-Hall, 1978. Traces effects of "nonjazz" urban history on this peculiarly American musical style.

Reps, John W. *The Making of Urban America: A History of City Planning in the United States.* Princeton: Princeton University Press, 1965. A rich compendium of information, covering the period up to 1910; many maps.

Strauss, Anselm L. *Images of the American City.* Glencoe, Ill.: Free Press, 1961. An anthology of short pieces, most of them the reactions of individuals to particular cities.

Suttles, Gerald D. *The Social Order of the Slum: Ethnicity and Territory in the Inner City.* Chicago: University of Chicago Press, 1968. A salient sociological study of moral and behavioral standards.

Taylor, Lisa, ed. *Cities: The Forces That Shape Them.* New York: Cooper-Hewitt Museum, 1982. A useful, fully illustrated, large format anthology of short pieces; covers many academic fields.

Warner, Sam Bass. *The Urban Wilderness.* New York: Harper and Row, 1972. An important historical study.

Yeates, M. and B. Gardner. *The North American City,* 3rd ed. New York: Harper and Row, 1980. Includes information about Canadian city planning.

5 The Working World

Edited by *Michael K. Havens*

Although it takes up about half our waking hours, we usually take work for granted. Even if we criticize our own job or dream about another we'd like, most of us never take the time to think systematically about work: its history, its possibilities, its abuses. And while we may at first assume that people work only to pay the bills, upon reflection most of us have higher aspirations for work. We may aspire to personal fulfillment by developing a skill and perfecting a product, or we may wish that our work could help improve society, making life richer for all. Thinking about these goals forces us to confront the barriers — social, political, psychological — that keep us from realizing work's highest potential.

Work is often a topic for academic inquiry, though usually at a distance. Some of that distance may result from the broad scope that many disciplines employ in studying work. For economists, work may primarily mean variables in a complex equation describing the flow of money and its results — employment, productivity, or investment figures. For business students, planning to manage other people's work often involves studying how to organize tasks efficiently or negotiate workers' demands. Labor relations courses bring together insights from psychology, law, history, and politics. Also casting a wide net, anthropologists note the ways work fits into a culture, distinguishing patterns like hunting, gathering, or farming, and the influences work has on everything from art to housing. Anthropological description of the life led by a regional or ethnic group — ethnography — inevitably describes the role work plays in that culture. Social historians combine such descriptions, usually in broad outlines, to study the way that patterns of work have shifted over the centuries. And political scientists analyze the ways systems of government interact with work patterns. So important is this interaction that there is a special subdiscipline that studies it: political economy. For instance, it is impossible to understand nineteenth-century American politics without acknowledging the industrial revolution, its mechanizing and standardizing of labor and the great monopolies that resulted from this process.

On the micro, or more local and personal level, work is studied by psychologists who look at the effects of a given kind of work on individuals: the factory versus the field, invention versus repetition. Psychologists also provide the tools for the delicate games of give and take that make up labor relations. Studies of particular groups emerge from disciplines like urban studies where economic, environmental, and psychological effects of working in a city are analyzed. The work available shapes a city, like the steel industry shaped, then abandoned Pittsburgh; but the people of a city also change the work that develops, like the ready supply of immigrants continues to shape work in Los Angeles or New York. For women's studies in particular the question of opportunity or limitation arises in considering the work done (and not done) by women. The role of women in a given culture, political system, or social milieu is often pictured succinctly in a description of the work they do. For instance, the restriction of women's work to cooking and bearing and nurturing children provides an important insight into a culture, whether it simply exists in a prehistoric culture or is part of the ideology like the Nazi proclamation that women's work is *kirche, küche, and kinder* (church, kitchen, and children).

The fulfillment and frustration of work emerge in their most unguarded, personal terms in oral history, practiced most often by journalists but also by sociologists and historians. The interviews show events through the eyes of those who live them; so, for instance, an account of agricultural work by a farmer gives a more sensuous and emotional view than the abstract analyses of political science or social theory do. But by editing and assembling these personal accounts, the author determines their context and thus a great part of their meaning. Imaginative fiction is perhaps the freest of all descriptions of work: the writer can give us the intimate view of the first person account but can also interject social or political theory, history, even the details of economic data. In modern fiction the interchange between individual psychology and social context is often pictured in the experiences of work.

This chapter, then, offers the opportunity to read, think, and write about work. But whose work, and why? Primarily we'll be looking at labor, whether industrial, agricultural, or service, rather than at management or professional work. Managers control either labor or capital, while professionals purvey or apply the fruits of academic study (*professional* is a flexible term, usually referring to highly trained people like doctors and lawyers and today to technical experts in many fields). But we could not enjoy the life we do without laborers. Farming and basic manufacturing both depend on manual laborers. Without wheat for morning toast, without a car to drive to the office, the lawyer or manager would quickly become a laborer out of necessity. Labor supports and makes possible all other types of work.

A good place to start our study of work is with the now famous collection of interviews by journalist and oral historian Studs Terkel: three interviews from *Working* present relatively familiar American work in the words of those who do it. Mike Lefevre articulates the personal goals so many workers dream about and the anger that routine labor elicits from so many. Executive secretary Anne Bogan might well work in the head office with Lefevre's employers, and associating with the male executives gives her feelings of power and success. Barbara Herrick, an advertising executive, could be responsible for the ad account of that same company. While she makes truly important decisions, and is paid commensurately, her role in the competitive world of business has brought conflicts along with her success.

Neither of Terkel's working women, though, faces quite the same array of choices and problems as the women in new factories in developing countries described by Barbara Ehrenreich and Annette Fuentes in "Life on the Global Assembly Line." The "new" work these women do — its possibilities and its barricades — grows out of a society like that described by anthropologist Guillermo de la Peña. His ethnographic sketch presents the Figueroa family, whose working life resembles that still lived by a majority of the world's people, a rural life based on access to the land. Far from the Figueroa family, but as new to industrial labor as hi-tech factory work is to the Third World women, the American Velvet Company, described by Paul Dickson, represents the enormous changes in the organization and control coming to more and more jobs in developed nations. At American Velvet, workers and owners have begun to cooperate, both in defining and pursuing goals.

The connections between these diverse working worlds — from the industrial shop floor to the sleek corporate office to the hot field growing corn and chilis — are formulated in theories ventured by various disciplines. Three articles in this chapter represent such theories: in "The Ideal of Craftsmanship," sociologist C. Wright Mills describes a historical ideal of work that promises to extend individual skills to their potential. In contrast, management theorist Frederick Taylor suggests that maximum wages for workers and maximum profits for owners should be the motivating principle for organizing work. Taylor's utilitarian view of work motivation contrasts sharply with that offered by Karl Marx, that human nature is centered on the impulse to productive work and that satisfying this impulse should be the primary goal of political and social arrangements. Marx details how this impulse to creativity has been commandeered by a political and economic system making wealth for a few at the expense of many. But it is perhaps novelist William O'Rourke's fictional fish factory that captures the depth and ambiguity of human work most inclusively: the potential revealed in its degradation, its surprising connections to foreign political systems and passage into terrifying realms of imagination, its immediacy and its utter distance from our everyday lives.

Interviews from *Working*

Studs Terkel

Mike Lefevre

It is a two-flat dwelling, somewhere in Cicero, on the outskirts of Chicago. He is thirty-seven. He works in a steel mill. On occasion, his wife Carol works as a waitress in a neighborhood restaurant; otherwise, she is at home, caring for their two small children, a girl and a boy.

At the time of my first visit, a sculpted statuette of Mother and Child was on the floor, head severed from body. He laughed softly as he indicated his three-year-old daughter: "She Doctor Spock'd it."

I'm a dying breed. A laborer. Strictly muscle work . . . pick it up, put it   1
down, pick it up, put it down. We handle between forty and fifty thousand pounds of steel a day. (Laughs) I know this is hard to believe — from four hundred pounds to three- and four-pound pieces. It's dying.

You can't take pride any more. You remember when a guy could point to a   2
house he built, how many logs he stacked. He built it and he was proud of it. I don't really think I could be proud if a contractor built a home for me. I would be tempted to get in there and kick the carpenter in the ass (laughs), and take the saw away from him. 'Cause I would have to be part of it, you know.

It's hard to take pride in a bridge you're never gonna cross in a door you're   3
never gonna open. You're mass-producing things and yo·· never see the end result of it. (Muses) I worked for a trucker one time. And ι goι this tiny satisfaction when I loaded a truck. At least I could see the truck depart loaded. In a steel mill, forget it. You don't see where nothing goes.

I got chewed out by my foreman once. He said, "Mike, you're a good worker   4
but you have a bad attitude." My attitude is that I don't get excited about my job. I do my work but I don't say whoopee-doo. The day I get excited about my job is the day I go to a head shrinker. How are you gonna get excited about pullin' steel? How are you gonna get excited when you're tired and want to sit down?

It's not just the work. Somebody built the pyramids. Somebody's going to   5
build something. Pyramids, Empire State Building — these things just don't happen. There's hard work behind it. I would like to see a building, say, the

(Louis) Studs Terkel (b. 1912) completed law school and worked in civil service and as a stage actor before beginning his career in radio and television broadcasting. His programs featured low-key, personal talks with a great variety of people. His books are similarly informal; they include Giants of Jazz *(1957),* Hard Times *(1970), and* The Good War *(1984). His most popular book so far,* Working *(1974), contains the interviews with Mike Lefevre, Anne Bogan, and Barbara Herrick.* Working *has also been made into a popular musical.*

Empire State, I would like to see on one side of it a foot-wide strip from top to bottom with the name of every bricklayer, the name of every electrician, with all the names. So when a guy walked by, he could take his son and say, "See, that's me over there on the forty-fifth floor. I put the steel beam in." Picasso can point to a painting. What can I point to? A writer can point to a book. Everybody should have something to point to.

It's the not-recognition by other people. To say a woman is *just* a housewife 6
is degrading, right? Okay. *Just* a housewife. It's also degrading to say *just* a laborer. The difference is that a man goes out and maybe gets smashed.

When I was single, I could quit, just split. I wandered all over the country. 7
You worked just enough to get a poke, money in your pocket. Now I'm married and I got two kids . . . (trails off). I worked on a truck dock one time and I was single. The foreman came over and he grabbed my shoulder, kind of gave me a shove. I punched him and knocked him off the dock. I said, "Leave me alone. I'm doing my work, just stay away from me, just don't give me the with-the-hands business."

Hell, if you whip a damn mule he might kick you. Stay out of my way, that's 8
all. Working is bad enough, don't bug me. I would rather work my ass off for eight hours a day with nobody watching me than five minutes with a guy watching me. Who you gonna sock? You can't sock General Motors, you can't sock anybody in Washington, you can't sock a system.

A mule, an old mule, that's the way I feel. Oh yeah. See. (Shows black and 9
blue marks on arms and legs, burns.) You know what I heard from more than one guy at work? "If my kid wants to work in a factory, I am going to kick the hell out of him." I want my kid to be an effete snob. Yeah, mm-hmm. (Laughs.) I want him to be able to quote Walt Whitman, to be proud of it.

If you can't improve yourself, you improve your posterity. Otherwise life isn't 10
worth nothing. You might as well go back to the cave and stay there. I'm sure the first caveman who went over the hill to see what was on the other side — I don't think he went there wholly out of curiosity. He went there because he wanted to get his son out of the cave. Just the same way I want to send my kid to college.

I work so damn hard and want to come home and sit down and lay around. 11
But I gotta get it out. I want to be able to turn around to somebody and say, "Hey, fuck you." You know? (Laughs.) The guy sitting next to me on the bus too. 'Cause all day I wanted to tell my foreman to go fuck himself, but I can't.

So I find a guy in a tavern. To tell him that. And he tells me too. I've been 12
in brawls. He's punching me and I'm punching him, because we actually want to punch somebody else. The most that'll happen is the bartender will bar us from the tavern. But at work, you lose your job.

This one foreman I've got, he's a kid. He's a college graduate. He thinks he's 13
better than everybody else. He was chewing me out and I was saying, "Yeah, yeah, yeah." He said, "What do you mean, yeah, yeah, yeah. Yes, *sir.*" I told him, "Who the hell are you, Hitler? What is this *"Yes, sir"* bullshit? I came here to work, I didn't come here to crawl. There's a fuckin' difference." One word led to another and I lost.

I got broke down to a lower grade and lost twenty-five cents an hour, which 14
is a hell of a lot. It amounts to about ten dollars a week. He came over — after

breaking me down. The guy comes over and smiles at me. I blew up. He didn't know it, but he was about two seconds and two feet away from a hospital. I said, "Stay the fuck away from me." He was just about to say something and was pointing his finger. I just reached my hand up and just grabbed his finger and I just put it back in his pocket. He walked away. I grabbed his finger because I'm married. If I'd been single, I'd a grabbed his head. That's the difference.

You're doing this manual labor and you know that technology can do it. *15* (Laughs.) Let's face it, a machine can do the work of a man; otherwise they wouldn't have space probes. Why can we send a rocket ship that's unmanned and yet send a man in a steel mill to do a mule's work?

Automation? Depends how it's applied. It frightens me if it puts me out on *16* the street. It doesn't frighten me if it shortens my work week. You read that little thing: what are you going to do when this computer replaces you? Blow up computers. (Laughs.) Really. Blow up computers. I'll be goddamned if a computer is gonna eat before I do! I want milk for my kids and beer for me. Machines can either liberate man or enslave 'im, because they're pretty neutral. It's man who has the bias to put the thing one place or another.

If I had a twenty-hour workweek, I'd get to know my kids better, my wife *17* better. Some kid invited me to go on a college campus. On a Saturday. It was summertime. Hell, if I had a choice of taking my wife and kids to a picnic or going to a college campus, it's gonna be the picnic. But if I worked a twenty-hour week, I could go do both. Don't you think with that extra twenty hours people could really expand? Who's to say? There are some people in factories just by force of circumstance. I'm just like the colored people. Potential Einsteins don't have to be white. They could be in cotton fields, they could be in factories.

The twenty-hour week is a possibility today. The intellectuals, they always *18* say there are potential Lord Byrons, Walt Whitmans, Roosevelts, Picassos working in construction or steel mills or factories. But I don't think they believe it. I think what they're afraid of is the potential Hitlers and Stalins that are there too. The people in power fear the leisure man. Not just the United States. Russia's the same way.

What do you think would happen in this country if, for one year, they ex- *19* perimented and gave everybody a twenty-hour week? How do they know that the guy who digs Wallace today doesn't try to resurrect Hitler tomorrow? Or the guy who is mildly disturbed at pollution doesn't decide to go to General Motors and shit on the guy's desk? You can become a fanatic if you had the time. The whole thing is time. That is, I think, one reason rich kids tend to be fanatic about politics: they have time. Time, that's the important thing.

It isn't that the average working guy is dumb. He's tired, that's all. I picked *20* up a book on chess one time. That thing laid in the drawer for two or three weeks, you're too tired. During the weekends you want to take your kids out. You don't want to sit there and the kid comes up: "Daddy, can I go to the park?" You got your nose in a book? Forget it.

I know a guy fifty-seven years old. Know what he tells me? "Mike, I'm old *21* and tired *all* the time." The first thing happens at work: When the arms start moving, the brain stops. I punch in about ten minutes to seven in the morning.

I say hello to a couple of guys I like, I kid around with them. One guy says good morning to you and you say good morning. To another guy you say fuck you. The guy you say fuck you to is your friend.

I put on my hard hat, change into my safety shoes, put on my safety glasses, *22* go to the bonderizer. It's the thing I work on. They rake the metal, they wash it, they dip it in a paint solution, and we take it off. Put it on, take it off, put it on, take it off, put it on, take it off. . . .

I say hello to everybody but my boss. At seven it starts. My arms get tired *23* about the first half-hour. After that, they don't get tired any more until maybe the last half-hour at the end of the day. I work from seven to three thirty. My arms are tired at seven thirty and they're tired at three o'clock. I hope to God I never get broke in, because I always want my arms to be tired at seven thirty and three o'clock. (Laughs.) 'Cause that's when I know that there's a beginning and there's an end. That I'm not brainwashed. In between, I don't even try to think.

If I were to put you in front of a dock and I pulled up a skid in front of you *24* with fifty hundred-pound sacks of potatoes and there are fifty more skids just like it, and this is what you're gonna do all day, what would you think about — potatoes? Unless a guy's a nut, he never thinks about work or talks about it. Maybe about baseball or about getting drunk the other night or he got laid or he didn't get laid. I'd say one out of a hundred will actually get excited about work.

Why is it that the communists always say they're for the workingman, and *25* as soon as they set up a country, you got guys singing to tractors? They're singing about how they love the factory. That's where I couldn't buy communism. It's the intellectuals' utopia, not mine. I cannot picture myself singing to a tractor, I just can't. (Laughs.) Or singing to steel. (Singsongs.) Oh whoop-dee-doo, I'm at the bonderizer, oh how I love this heavy steel. No thanks. Never happen.

Oh yeah, I daydream. I fantasize about a sexy blonde in Miami who's got *26* my union dues. (Laughs.) I think of the head of the union the way I think of the head of my company. Living it up. I think of February in Miami. Warm weather, a place to lay in. When I hear a college kid say, "I'm oppressed," I don't believe him. You know what I'd like to do for one year? Live like a college kid. Just for one year. I'd love to. Wow! (Whispers) Wow! Sports car! Marijuana! (Laughs.) Wild, sexy broads. I'd love that, hell yes, I would.

Somebody has to do this work. If my kid ever goes to college, I just want *27* him to have a little respect, to realize that his dad is one of those somebodies. This is why even on — (muses) yeah, I guess, sure — on the black thing. . . . (Sighs heavily.) I can't really hate the colored fella that's working with me all day. The black intellectual I got no respect for. The white intellectual I got no use for. I got no use for the black militant who's gonna scream three hundred years of slavery to me while I'm busting my ass. You know what I mean? (Laughs.) I have one answer for that guy: go see Rockefeller. See Harriman. Don't bother me. (Laughs).

After work I usually stop off at a tavern. Cold beer. Cold beer right away. *28* When I was single, I used to go into hillbilly bars, get in a lot of brawls. Just to explode. I got a thing on my arm here (indicates scar). I got slapped with a bicycle chain. Oh, wow! (Softly) Mmm. I'm getting older. (Laughs.) I don't explode as much. You might say I'm broken in. (Quickly) No, I'll never be broken in. (Sighs.) When you get a little older, you exchange the words. When you're younger, you exchange the blows.

When I get home, I argue with my wife a little bit. Turn on TV, get mad at   29
the news. (Laughs.) I don't even watch the news that much. I watch Jackie Gleason. I look for any alternative to the ten o'clock news. I don't want to go to bed angry. Don't hit a man with anything heavy at five o'clock. He just can't be bothered. This is his time to relax. The heaviest thing he wants is what his wife has to tell him.

When I come home, know what I do for the first twenty minutes? Fake it. I   30
put on a smile. I got a kid three years old. Sometimes she says, "Daddy, where've you been?" I say, "Work." I could have told her I'd been in Disneyland. What's work to a three-year-old kid? If I feel bad, I can't take it out on the kids. Kids are born innocent of everything but birth. You can't take it out on your wife either. This is why you go to a tavern. You want to release it there rather than do it at home. What does an actor do when he's got a bad movie? I got a bad movie every day.

I don't even need the alarm clock to get up in the morning. I can go out   31
drinking all night, fall asleep at four, and bam! I'm up at six — no matter what I do. (Laughs.) It's a pseudo-death, more or less. Your whole system is paralyzed and you give all the appearance of death. It's an ingrown clock. It's a thing you just get used to. The hours differ. It depends. Sometimes my wife wants to do something crazy like play five hundred rummy or put a puzzle together. It could be midnight, could be ten o'clock, could be nine thirty.

What do you do weekends?   32

Drink beer, read a book. See that one? *Violence in America.* It's one of them   33
studies from Washington. One of them committees they're always appointing. A thing like that I read on a weekend. But during the weekdays, gee . . . I just thought about it. I don't do that much reading from Monday through Friday. Unless it's a horny book. I'll read it at work and go home and do my homework. (Laughs.) That's what the guys at the plant call it — homework. (Laughs.) Sometimes my wife works on Saturday and I drink beer at the tavern.

I went out drinking with one guy, oh, a long time ago. A college boy. He was   34
working where I work now. Always preaching to me about how you need violence to change the system and all that garbage. We went into a hillbilly joint. Some guy there, I didn't know him from Adam, he said, "You think you're smart." I said, "What's your pleasure?" (Laughs.) He said, "My pleasure's to kick your ass." I told him I really can't be bothered. He said, "What're you, chicken?" I said. "No, I just don't want to be bothered." He came over and said something to me again. I said, "I don't beat women, drunks or fools. Now leave me alone."

The guy called his brother over. This college boy that was with me, he came   35
nudging my arm, "Mike, let's get out of here." I said, "What are you worried about?" (Laughs.) This isn't unusual. People will bug you. You fend it off as

much as you can with your mouth and when you can't, you punch the guy out.

It was close to closing time and we stayed. We could have left, but when   36
you go into a place to have a beer and a guy challenges you — if you expect to
go in that place again, you don't leave. If you have to fight the guy, you fight.

I got just outside the door and one of these guys jumped on me and grabbed   37
me around the neck. I grabbed his arm and flung him against the wall. I grabbed
him here (indicates throat), and jiggled his head against the wall quite a few
times. He kind of slid down a little bit. This guy who said he was his brother
took a swing at me with a garrison belt. He just missed and hit the wall. I'm
looking around for my junior Stalin (laughs), who loves violence and everything. He's gone. Split. (Laughs.) Next day I see him at work. I couldn't get
mad at him, he's a baby.

He saw a book in my back pocket one time and he was amazed. He walked   38
up to me and he said, "You read?" I said, "What do you mean, I read?" He
said, "All these dummies read the sports pages around here. What are you doing
with a book?" I got pissed off at the kid right away. I said, "What do you mean,
all these dummies? Don't knock a man who's paying somebody else's way
through college." He was a nineteen-year-old effete snob.

Yet you want your kid to be an effete snob?   39

Yes. I want my kid to look at me and say, "Dad, you're a nice guy, but you're   40
a fuckin' dummy." Hell yes, I want my kid to tell me that he's not gonna be
like me. . . .

If I were hiring people to work, I'd try naturally to pay them a decent wage.   41
I'd try to find out their first names, their last names, keep the company as small
as possible, so I could personalize the whole thing. All I would ask a man is a
handshake, see you in the morning. No applications, nothing. I wouldn't be
interested in the guy's past. Nobody ever checks the pedigree on a mule, do
they? But they do on a man. Can you picture walking up to a mule and saying,
"I'd like to know who his granddaddy was?"

I'd like to run a combination bookstore and tavern. (Laughs.) I would like   42
to have a place where college kids came and a steelworker could sit down and
talk. Where a workingman could not be ashamed of Walt Whitman and where
a college professor could not be ashamed that he painted his house over the
weekend.

If a carpenter built a cabin for poets, I think the least the poets owe the   43
carpenter is just three or four one-liners on the wall. A little plaque: Though
we labor with our minds, this place we can relax in was built by someone who
can work with his hands. And his work is as noble as ours. I think the poet
owes something to the guy who builds the cabin for him.

I don't think of Monday. You know what I'm thinking about on Sunday night?   44
Next Sunday. If you work real hard, you think of a perpetual vacation. Not
perpetual sleep. . . . What do I think of on a Sunday night? Lord, I wish the
fuck I could do something else for a living.

I don't know who the guy is who said there is nothing sweeter than an un-   45
finished symphony. Like an unfinished painting and an unfinished poem. If he
creates this thing one day — let's say, Michelangelo's Sistine Chapel. It took

him a long time to do this, this beautiful work of art. But what if he had to create this Sistine Chapel a thousand times a year? Don't you think that would even dull Michelangelo's mind? Or if da Vinci had to draw his anatomical charts thirty, forty, fifty, sixty, eighty, ninety, a hundred times a day? Don't you think that would even bore da Vinci?

Way back, you spoke of the guys who built the pyramids, not the pharoahs, the   46
unknowns. You put yourself in their category?

Yes. I want my signature on 'em, too. Sometimes, out of pure meanness,   47
when I make something, I put a little dent in it. I like to do something to make it really unique. Hit it with a hammer. I deliberately fuck it up to see if it'll get by, just so I can say I did it. It could be anything. Let me put it this way: I think God invented the dodo bird so when we get up there we could tell Him, "Don't you ever make mistakes?" and He'd say, "Sure, look." (Laughs.) I'd like to make my imprint. My dodo bird. A mistake, *mine*. Let's say the whole building is nothing but red bricks. I'd like to have just the black one or the white one or the purple one. Deliberately fuck up.

This is gonna sound square, but my kid is my imprint. He's my freedom.   48
There's a line in one of Hemingway's books. I think it's from *For Whom the Bell Tolls*. They're behind the enemy lines, somewhere in Spain, and she's pregnant. She wants to stay with him. He tells her no. He says, "if you die, I die," knowing he's gonna die. But if you go, I go. Know what I mean? The mystics call it the brass bowl. Continuum. You know what I mean? This is why I work. Every time I see a young guy walk by with a shirt and tie and dressed up real sharp, I'm lookin' at my kid, you know? That's it.

Anne Bogan

We're on the thirty-second floor of a skyscraper, the office of a corporation president. She is his private secretary. The view of the river, railroad yards, bridges, and the city's skyline is astonishing.

"I've been an executive secretary for eight years. However, this is the first time I've been on the corporate end of things, working for the president. I found it a new experience. I love it and I feel I'm learning a lot."

I become very impatient with dreamers. I respect the doers more than the   49
dreamers. So many people, it seems to me, talk about all the things they want to do. They only talk without accomplishing anything. The drifters are worse than the dreamers. Ones who really have no goals, no aspirations at all, just live from day to day. . . .

I enjoy one thing more than anything else on this job. That's the association   50
I have with the other executives, not only my boss. There's a tremendous difference in the way they treat me than what I've known before. They treat me more as . . . on the executive level. They consult me on things, and I enjoy this. It stimulates me.

I know myself well enough to know that I've always enjoyed men more than   51
women. Usually I can judge them very quickly when I meet a woman. I can't

judge men that quickly. I seek out the few women I think I will enjoy. The others, I get along with all right. But I feel no basic interest. I don't really enjoy having lunch with them and so on.

You can tell just from conversation what they talk about. It's quite easy. It's 52 also very easy to tell which girls are going to last around the office and which ones aren't. Interest in their work. Many of them aren't, they just don't dig in. They're more interested in chatting in the washroom. I don't know if that's a change from other years. There's always been some who are really not especially career-minded, but they have to give a little bit and try a little harder. The others get by on as little as possible.

I feel like I'm sharing somewhat of the business life of the men. So I think 53 I'm much happier as the secretary to an executive than I would be in some woman's field, where I could perhaps make more money. But it wouldn't be an extension of a successful executive. I'm perfectly happy in my status.

She came from a small town in Indiana and married at eighteen. She had graduated from high school and began working immediately for the town's large company. "My husband was a construction worker. We lived in a trailer, we moved around a lot. There's a lot of community living in that situation and I grew pretty tired of it. You can get involved, you can become too friendly with people when you live too close. A lot of time can be wasted. It was years before I started doing this."

I have dinner with businessmen and enjoy this very much. I like the back- 54 ground music in some of these restaurants. It's soothing and it also adds a little warmth and doesn't disturb the conversation. I like the atmosphere and the caliber of people that usually you see and run into. People who have made it.

I think if I've been at all successful with men, it's because I'm a good lis- 55 tener and interested in their world. I enjoy it, I don't become bored with it. They tell me about their personal life too. Family problems, financial, and the problems of raising children. Most of the ones I'm referring to are divorced. In looking through the years they were married, I can see this is what probably happened. I know if I were the wife, I would be interested in their work. I feel the wife of an executive would be a better wife had she been a secretary first. As a secretary, you learn to adjust to the boss's moods. Many marriages would be happier if the wife would do that.

Barbara Herrick

She is thirty; single. Her title is script supervisor/producer at a large advertising agency; working out of its Los Angeles office. She is also a vice president. Her accounts are primarily in food and cosmetics. "There's a myth: a woman is expected to be a food writer because she is assumed to know those things and a man doesn't. However, some of the best copy on razors and Volkswagens has been written by women."

She has won several awards and considerable recognition for her commercials. "You have to be absolutely on target, dramatic and fast. You have to be aware of legal restrictions. The FTC gets tougher and tougher. You must understand budgetary matters: will it cost a million or can it be shot in a studio in one day?"

She came off a Kansas farm, one of four daughters. "During high school, I worked as a typist and was an extremely good one. I was compulsive about doing every tiny job very well." She graduated from the University of Missouri. According to Department of Labor statistics, she is in the upper one percent bracket of working women.

In her Beverly Hills apartment are paintings, sculpted works, recordings (classic, folk; jazz, and rock), and many books, most of them obviously well thumbed.

Men in my office doing similar work were being promoted, given raises and 56
titles. Since I had done the bulk of the work, I made a stand and was promoted too. I needed the title, because clients figured that I'm just a face-man.

A face-man is a person who looks good, speaks well, and presents the work. 57
I look well, I speak well, and I'm pleasant to have around after the business is over with — if they acknowledge me in business. We go to the lounge and have drinks. I can drink with the men but remain a lady. (Laughs.)

That's sort of my tacit business responsibility, although this has never been 58
said to me directly. I know this is why I travel alone for the company a great deal. They don't anticipate any problems with my behavior. I equate it with being the good nigger.

On first meeting, I'm frequently taken for the secretary, you know, traveling 59
with the boss. I'm here to keep somebody happy. Then I'm introduced as the writer. One said to me after the meeting was over and the drinking had started, "When I first saw you, I figured you were a — you know. I never knew you were the person *writing* this all the time." (Laughs.) Is it a married woman working for extra money? Is it a lesbian? Is it some higher-up's mistress?

I'm probably one of the ten highest paid people in the agency. It would cause 60
tremendous hard feelings if, say, I work with a man who's paid less. If a remark is made at a bar — "You make so much money, you could buy and sell me" — I toss it off, right? He's trying to find out. He can't equate me as a rival. They wonder where to put me, they wonder what my salary is.

Buy and sell me — yeah, there are a lot of phrases that show the reversal of 61
roles. What comes to mind is swearing at a meeting. New clients are often very uptight. They feel they can't make any innuendoes that might be suggestive. They don't know how to treat me. They don't know whether to acknowledge me as a woman or as another neuter person who's doing a job for them.

The first time, they don't look at me. At the first three meetings of this one 62
client, if I would ask a direction question, they would answer and look at my boss or another man in the room. Even around the conference table. I don't attempt to be — the glasses, the bun, and totally asexual. That isn't the way I am. It's obvious that I'm a woman and enjoy being a woman. I'm not overly provocative either. It's the thin, good nigger line that I have to toe.

I've developed a sixth sense about this. If a client will say, "Are you mar- 63
ried?" I will often say yes, because that's the easiest way to deal with him if he needs that category for me. If it's more acceptable to him to have a young, attractive married woman in a business position comparable to his, terrific. It doesn't bother me. It makes me safer. He'll never be challenged. He can say, "She'd be sensational. I'd love to get her. I could show her what a real man is, but she's married." It's a way out for him.

Or there's the mistress thing: well, she's sleeping with the boss. That's ac- 64 ceptable to them. Or she's a frustrated, compulsive castrator. That's a category. Or lesbian. If I had short hair, wore suits, and talked in a gruff voice, that would be more acceptable than I am. It's when I transcend their labels, they don't quite know what to do. If someone wants a quick label and says, "I'll bet you're a big women's libber, aren't you?" I say, "Yeah, yeah." They have to place me.

I travel a lot. That's what gets very funny. We had a meeting in Montreal.   65
It was one of those bride's magazines, honeymoon-type resorts, with heart-shaped beds and the heated pool. I was there for three days with nine men. All day long we were enclosed in this conference room. The agency account man went with me. I was to talk about the new products, using slides and movies. There were about sixty men in the conference room. I had to leave in such a hurry, I still had my gaucho pants and boots on.

The presentation went on for an hour and a half. There was tittering and   66
giggling for about forty minutes. Then you'd hear the shift in the audience. They got interested in what I was saying. Afterwards they had lunch sent up. Some of them never did talk to me. Others were interested in my life. They would say things like, "Have you read *The Sensuous Woman?*" (Laughs.) They didn't really want to know. If they were even more obvious, they probably would have said, "Say, did you hear the one about the farmer's daughter?" I'd have replied, "Of course, I'm one myself."

The night before, there was a rehearsal. Afterwards the account man sug-   67
gested we go back to the hotel, have a nightcap, and get to bed early. It was a 9:00 A.M. meeting. We were sitting at the bar and he said, "Of course, you'll be staying in my room." I said. "What? I have a room." He said, "I just assumed. You're here and I'm here and we're both grown up." I said, "You assumed? You never even asked me whether I wanted to." My feelings obviously meant nothing to him. Apparently it was what you *did* if you're out of town and the woman is anything but a harelip and you're ready to go. His assumption was incredible. . . .

The excuse I gave is one I use many times. "Once when I was much younger   68
and innocent, I slept with an account man. The guy turned out to be a bastard. I got a big reputation and he made my life miserable because he had a loose mouth. And even though you're a terrifically nice guy and I'd like to sleep with you, I feel I can't. It's my policy. I'm older and wiser now. I don't do it. You have to understand that." It worked. I could never say to him, "You don't even understand how you insulted me."

It's the always-have-to-please conditioning. I don't want to make any ene-   69
mies. Only of late, because I'm getting more secure and I'm valued by the agency, am I able to get mad at men and say, "Fuck off!" But still I have to keep egos unruffled, smooth things over . . . I still work with him and he never mentioned it again.

He'll occasionally touch my arm or catch my eye: We're really sympatico,   70
aren't we baby? There may be twelve men and me sitting at the meeting and they can't call on one of the girls or the receptionist, he'd say, "Let's have some coffee, Barbara. Make mine black." I'm the waitress. I go do it because it's easier than to protest. If he'd known my salary is more than his I doubt that he'd have acted that way in Denver — or here.

Part of the resentment toward me and my salary is that I don't have a mort- *71*
gage on a home in the Valley and three kids who have to go to private schools
and a wife who spends at Saks, and you never know when you're going to lose
your job in this business. Say, we're having a convivial drink among peers and
we start grousing. I'm not allowed to grouse with the best of them. They say,
"Oh, you? What do you need money for? You're a single woman. You've got
the world by the balls." I hear that all the time. . . .

Clients. I get calls in my hotel room: "I want to discuss something about *72*
production that didn't go right." I know what that means. I try to fend it off.
I'm on this tightrope. I don't want to get into a drunken scene ever with a client
and to literally shove him away. That's not going to do me any good. The only
smart thing I can do is avoid that sort of scene. The way I avoid it is by suggesting an early morning breakfast meeting. I always have to make excuses: "I
drank too much and my stomach is really upset, so I couldn't do it right now.
We'll do it in the morning." Sometimes I'd like to say, "Fuck off, I know what
you want."

*"I've had a secretary for the last three years. I hesitate to use her . . . I won't
ask her to do typing. It's hard for me to use her as I was used. She's bright and
could be much more than a secretary. So I give her research assignments, things
to look up, which might be fun for her. Rather than just say, 'Here, type this."*

*"I'm an interesting figure to her. She says, 'When I think of Women's Lib I
don't think of Germaine Greer or Kate Millett. I think of you.' She sees my life as
a lot more glamorous than it really is. She admires the externals. She admires the
apartment, the traveling. We shot two commercials just recently, one in Mexico,
one in Nassau. Then I was in New York to edit them. That's three weeks. She takes
care of all my travel details. She knows the company gave me an advance of well
over a thousand dollars. I'm up in the fine hotels, travel first class. I can spend
ninety dollars at a dinner for two or three. I suppose it is something — little Barbara from a Kansas farm and Christ! look where I am. But I don't think of it,
which is a funny thing."*

It used to be the token black at a big agency was very safe because he al- *73*
ways had to be there. Now I'm definitely the token woman. In the current economic climate, I'm one of the few writers at my salary level getting job offers.
Unemployment is high right now among people who do what I do. Yet I get
calls: "Will you come and write on feminine hygiene products?" Another, involving a food account: "We need you, we'll pay you thirty grand and a contract. Be the answer for Such-an'-such Foods." I'm ideal because I'm young
enough to have four or five solid years of experience behind me. I know how
to handle myself or I wouldn't be where I am.

I'm very secure right now. But when someone says to me, "You don't have *74*
to worry," he's wrong. In a profession where I absolutely cannot age, I cannot
be doing this at thirty-eight. For the next years, until I get too old, my future's
secure in a very insecure business. It's like a race horse or a show horse. Although I'm holding the job on talent and responsibility, I got here partly because I'm attractive and it's a big kick for a client to know that for three days

in Montreal there's going to be this young brunette, who's very good, mind you. I don't know how they talk about me, but I'd guess: "She's very good, but to look at her you'd never know it. She's a knockout."

I have a fear of hanging on past my usefulness. I've seen desperate women *75* out of jobs, who come around with their samples, which is the way all of us get jobs. A lot of women have been cut. Women who had soft jobs in an agency for years and are making maybe fifteen thousand. In the current slump, this person is cut and some bright young kid from a college, who'll work for seven grand a year, comes in and works late every night.

Talk about gaps. In a room with a twenty-two year-old, there are areas in *76* which I'm altogether lost. But not being a status-quo-type person, I've always thought ahead enough to keep pace with what's new. I certainly don't feel my usefulness as a writer is coming to an end. I'm talking strictly in terms of physical aging. (Laughs.) It's such a young business, not just the consumer part. It's young in terms of appearances. The client expects agency people, especially on the creative end, to dress a certain way, to be very fashionable. I haven't seen many women in any executive capacity age gracefully. . . .

The part I hate — it's funny. (Pause.) Most people in the business are de- *77* lighted to present their work and get praise for it — and the credit and the laughter and everything in the commercial. I always hate that part. Deep down, I feel demeaned. Don't question the adjectives, don't argue, if it's a cologne or a shampoo. I know, 'cause I buy 'em myself. I'm the biggest sucker for buying an expensively packaged hoax thing. Face cream at eight dollars. And I sell and convince.

I used Erik Satie music for a cologne thing. The clients didn't know Satie *78* from Roger Williams. I'm very good at what I do, dilettantism. I go into my act: we call it dog and pony time, show time, tap dance. We laugh about it. He says, "Oh, that's beautiful, exactly right. How much will it cost us?" I say, "The music will cost you three grand. Those two commercials you want to do in Mexico and Nassau, that's forty grand. There's no way I can bring it in for less." I'm this young woman, saying, "Give me forty thousand dollars of your money and I will go away to Mexico and Nassau and bring you back a commercial and you'll love it." It's blind faith.

Do I ever question what I'm selling? (A soft laugh.) All the time. I know a *79* writer who quit a job equivalent to mine. She was making a lot of money, well thought of. She was working on a consumer finance account. It's blue collar and black. She made this big stand. I said to her, in private, "I agree with you, but why is this your test case? You've been selling a cosmetic for years that is nothing but mineral oil and women are paying eight dollars for it. You've been selling a cake mix that you know is so full of preservatives that it would kill every rat in the lab. Why all of a sudden . . . ?"

If you're in the business, you're in the business, the fucking business! You're *80* a hustler. But because you're witty and glib . . . I've never pretended this is the best writing I can do. Every advertising writer has a novel in his drawer. Few of them ever do it.

I don't think what I do is necessary or that it performs a service. If it's a *81* very fine product — and I've worked on some of those — I love it. It's when you get into that awful area of hope, cosmetics — you're just selling image and a hope. It's like the arthritis cure or cancer — quackery. You're saying to a lady, "Because this oil comes from the algae at the bottom of the sea, you're going to have a timeless face." It's a crock of shit! I know it's part of my job, I do it. If I made the big stand my friend made, I'd lose my job. Can't do it. I'm expected to write whatever assignment I'm given. It's whorish. I haven't written enough to know what kind of writer I am. I suspect, rather than a writer, I'm a good reader. I think I'd make a good editor. I have read so many short stories that I bet you I could turn out a better anthology than anybody's done yet, in certain categories. I remember, I appreciate, I have a feeling I could. . . .

POSTSCRIPT: *Shortly afterward she was battling an ulcer.*   82

Considerations

1. Does Mike Lefevre object to working or does he just want a different kind of work? Back up your opinion with quotations from his interview.
2. Summarize Lefevre's complaints about his job; then summarize the elements of his work he feels proud or enthusiastic about. For a longer essay, explore whether these frustrations and fulfillments stem from the same ideals of work.
3. Summarize Anne Bogan's reasons for feeling so content with her job.
4. Bogan doesn't give any concrete details of the work she does day-to-day. What does that tell us about her attitude toward work? Back up your speculations with references to things she does talk about.
5. Studs Terkel includes a few details of Anne Bogan's personal history. How do those details help us understand the feelings Bogan voices about her job?
6. Is Barbara Herrick basically happy with her job? Be sure to back up your opinion with specific evidence from her interview.
7. If Barbara Herrick were to describe an ideal job, what elements would she include? For each element you mention in this ideal job, give the evidence from her interview that suggests she would value it.
8. Herrick says that what she does is not "necessary" work. What does she mean by that? Illustrate by referring to specific details of her job. You may also refer to other kinds of work she might consider unnecessary.
9. For Barbara Herrick, what is more important in determining her attitude to her job: the content of her job, the actual work itself, or the context of work, its social status and prestige? Base your response on specific points in her interview.

Connections

1. Anne Bogan likes to associate with male executives, but she probably would not feel the same enthusiasm about working with Mike Lefevre. What does this tell you about her aspirations for work? You may want to analyze whether these aspirations represent those of a large segment or class of American workers.
2. Barbara Herrick certainly fits the description of a successful executive. Do

you think Anne Bogan would be as happy working for Herrick as she is in her present job? Develop your answer by referring to specific words and phrases each woman uses in her interview.

3. Read carefully the interviews with Anne Bogan and Barbara Herrick. Their reasons for satisfaction and dissatisfaction on the job are very different. Describe those reasons, looking for social as well as psychological explanations for them. How do the reasons these workers give for their opinions of work relate to their being women?

The Figueroa Family

Guillermo de la Peña

Trinidad Figueroa (1888–1952) — a Tlayacapan farmer — had four children: Arturo (b. 1920), Manuel (b. 1923), Ana (b. 1925), and Pablo (b. 1928). He divided his land between only two of his sons, Manuel and Pablo. Arturo, however, is also a farmer — and a prosperous one. I will describe the expansion and division of Trinidad's farm, and then the life careers of his sons.   *1*

Trinidad's Farm: Expansion and Division

In 1925 Trinidad was confirmed as the owner of a plot of 2.4 hectares situated to the north of Tlayacapan. This plot had belonged to his father. By 1938 his holding had increased to 4.4 hectares, with the addition of three plots of irrigated *ejido°* land which had been granted to him and his children (0.7 hectares to Trinidad, 0.8 to Arturo, and 0.5 to Manuel). All the land was controlled by Trinidad, as both sons were "family children." Arturo married in 1940, but remained with his wife in his father's household; Trinidad gradually let him take charge of some farming decisions. Manuel married in 1941, and in 1943 he moved to another house in the neighborhood and set up an independent farm with his small *ejido* plot plus 1.4 hectares given to him by his father.   *2*

Before Manuel received his inheritance, Arturo had taken a paid job as a part-time officer of the *Banco Ejidal* in the rice program. It was considered that   *3*

°ejido: Cooperative land distributed by the Mexican Government.

Guillermo de la Peña (b. 1943) is a professor of anthropology at the Universidad Autónoma Metropolitana in Mexico City. He has served as a researcher and editor for several of Mexico's leading anthropological and historical institutions, published in journals such as Nexos, Controversia, *and* Communidad, *and co-authored* Ensayos Sobre El Sur de Jalisco (Essays About South Jalisco).

because he had a supplementary income, he did not need more land of his own. Also Trinidad wanted Arturo to continue working on his own farm now that he had good connections in the rice business. In 1945, Ana married an *ejidatario,°* and went to live with him without any inheritance. Pablo, the youngest son, married a girl from the *barrio* of Santiago (the Figueroas were from El Rosario) in 1946. His father-in-law gave them a house in that *barrio* to live in, so Pablo too left his father's household. With his move, Pablo inherited one hectare of private land. Trinidad gave him this rather than the *ejido* land, because he wanted to continue growing rice with Arturo. Trinidad and Arturo were left with their irrigated *ejidos* (1.5 hectares altogether) and with Arturo's salary from the bank — which seemed sufficient at the time. In 1952 Trinidad died. His *ejido* plot was inherited by his wife Herminia and administered by Arturo, who lived with her. With Herminia's death in 1962, this plot was inherited by Pablo, who was at that time the only son with no *ejido* land of his own. Neither Arturo nor Manuel could legally inherit the *ejido*, as no person is — at least in theory — entitled to rights over more than one *ejido* plot. Arturo was then left with his own 0.8 hectares of *ejido*, and inherited his mother's house.

Arturo's Farming Career

Arturo had left primary school in 1932, after finishing the fourth grade, to work on his father's land, where, apart from some chillies, beans and pumpkins for domestic consumption, maize was the main annual crop. In 1936 he became an *ejidatario*, though his plot was worked as part of the parental farm. In 1943, when the bank launched its program for rice cultivation, the family started growing rice in their *ejidos*, and Arturo was appointed local officer for the town of Tlayacapan. He keeps the office to this day. His functions include keeping a record of those *ejidatarios* who are potential rice growers, collecting loans from the bank branch in Cuautla, and distributing them among the *ejidatarios*. After the harvest, he has to weigh the rice, contact the buyers, and pay the producers. His yearly salary is 3 percent of the total value of sales, plus expenses. By local standards it is high. The job involves work only at the beginning and the end of the season, and it provides him with a secure annual income. In 1944 and 1945 he used part of his salary to buy new steel ploughs and a pair of mules for himself and his father. 4

Arturo was appointed to this job by the representative of the bank in Cuautla. He was recommended for it by the local *comisario ejidal,°* who was a friend of his father, and by the municipal president, who said that Arturo could read and write, and that he had proved capable in responsible posts — he had already held various public offices. Thus Arturo's job in the rice program from the age of twenty-three has to be understood within the broader context of an active political career, which made him widely known and trusted in Tlayacapan. In 1940, when he was twenty, the municipality made him *ayudante,°* 5

°ejidatario: An owner of *ejido* land.
°comisario ejidal: Local commissioner of *ejido* land.
°ayudante: An honorary municipal office given to young people contributing to the growth of the community.

again because of his literacy — which at the time was still rare among adults — and also due to his father's friendship ties with the authorities. In the following year he became *juez menor* (assistant magistrate for civil matters). Later, in 1949, he was appointed *regidor* (treasurer) of the *municipio*.° In addition, his network of relationships was widened and reinforced by his active involvement in *mayordomias*,° in which he participated from his early youth; he reached the top of the hierarchy three times.

1940–41   *Ayudante municipal*
1941–42   *Juez menor*
1943–   Rice officer in the *ejido*
1944–45   First *mayordomo*° of Our Lady of Guadalupe
1946–47   *Padrino*° of the Santo Niño
1949–50   Regidor
1956–57   First *mayordomo* of the Santo Niño
1970–   Officer of the CONASUPO°

Up to 1952, then, Arturo was a popular figure, but he was not very success-   6
ful financially, as he shared household expenses with his parents and had a family of his own to support. From 1941 to 1952, six children were born to Arturo, of whom two died shortly after birth. In 1952, after the death of Arturo's father, one of his children became severely ill, and Arturo had to borrow money from a Cuautla moneylender to take him to a Mexico City clinic. It was to clear this debt that Arturo first went as a seasonal migrant to the U.S.A., taking advantage of the opportunities given to Mexican agricultural workers by both the national and the American governments. He then repeated the trip every year without neglecting his irrigated plots or his bank job. During his years of seasonal migration Arturo managed to keep part of the profit of his Tlayacapan resources, thanks to careful planning and with the help of his brother Pablo. He would work in the fields until September, and then leave the crop of rice (or sugar cane, if the refinery had asked him to grow it) in Pablo's care; he then would spend from September to December working in the United States and come back in time for the harvest and to fulfill his office duties for the bank. Pablo received half the profit from Arturo's fields.

In 1962, Arturo's mother died, and Pablo became the holder of his father's   7
ejido. At the time, the government was restricting permits to cross the border. However, this coincided with the tomato boom in the area; Manuel — Arturo's brother — was already growing tomatoes and doing very well. So Arturo decided to stay in Tlayacapan and try his luck at the new crop. He used his savings from seasonal migration to rent one hectare of private land and to buy equipment. The harvest was successful and sold well; the following year Arturo rented two hectares, on which he grew maize and tomatoes. From 1962

°*municipio:* Town.
°*mayordomias* Administration of local religious festivals.
°*mayordomo:* Administrator.
°*Padrino:* Godfather (here, an honorary title for a religious festival).
°*CONASUPO:* Mexican national agricultural cooperative.

on Arturo has not had to migrate and has been able to continue renting land — in 1971 he was renting 2.8 hectares of irrigated *ejido* plus 3.4 hectares of private land. He has twice — in 1967 and 1970 — failed in the tomato harvest; but he has been able to compensate the loss from his earnings in other products and from his bank salary. In addition, he has been able to bypass middlemen, and his brother Manuel owns a lorry which they use for transportation.

Arturo never bought any land, as he reckoned that to buy one hectare would cost him more than to rent ten. He could not really afford to buy land until the end of the 1960s. In addition, none of his children need land at present as all the older ones have non-agricultural occupations. During the 1950s, Arturo had access to only a small potion of the *ejido* (which was further reduced when his mother died), and encouraged his children to continue their education and find occupations outside agriculture. Three of them, Laura (b. 1941), Emilio (b. 1946), and Alberta (b. 1954), got government grants to study in education colleges in Cuernavaca and Tlaxcala and became teachers; only Laura has returned to the household and teaches in Nepopoalco. The other two live in Veracruz and Tlaxcala respectively. Another son, Luis, became an industrial worker in Cuernavaca; he lives with Arturo and commutes daily to his job. (Arturo's daughter married and left the household in 1968, and the two younger sons are at the local primary school.) As a result, Arturo has never been able to use any labor from within the household; but on the other hand he has no obligation to give land to his older sons if they get married, and his household expenses have been reduced. In addition, the salaries of two of his children, Laura and Luis, provide extra cash for the household. At the end of the 1960s, Arturo's economic success was patent in the material improvements he had made to his house, which had a new tiled roof, a gas cooker, a television set, a record player and other items of bedroom and living room furniture.

In 1970 Arturo gained yet another opportunity of acquiring cash when the government-owned CONASUPO (Comisión Nacional de Suministros Populares) opened a store in Tlayacapan to provide fertilizer at cheaper prices throughout the Highlands. He was appointed local officer. This job took half of his time; but he nevertheless continued to farm using hired labor. In 1971 the local CONASUPO store failed to receive any supply of fertilizer, so Arturo's job was interrupted; but he used the occasion to start a splendid business in retailing fertilizer and chemicals privately. Most farmers of the region buy the chemicals for the following season in January or February, when they have some cash from crop sales and chemicals are in good supply. In 1971, however, many farmers failed to buy at the usual time, because the government agricultural officer in Cuautla had promised them low-interest loans — both in cash and in fertilizer — from the National Agrarian Bank. The loans never materialized; in May, when people tried to get chemicals in Cuautla, prices had risen by 20 percent. Arturo saw the opportunity of using the contacts he had made with private and State fertilizer producers during his years with the Ejido Bank and CONASUPO. He started buying chemicals on credit directly from the factories in Mexico City, transporting them in his brother's lorry and in hired vehicles, and selling them in the region at a price much cheaper than in Cuautla, but high enough to make a profit. The operation continued throughout the whole season: in November, Arturo estimated his commercial gains to be 40,000 pesos. He is planning to buy some land from the profits "just in case any of the children need land after all. . . ."

Pablo Figueroa's Farming Career

Pablo's economic life, in contrast to that of his brothers, has never been very *10* successful. Immediately after his marriage in 1946, he inherited a house through his wife, and one hectare of land from his father, and lived quietly on that until 1952, when Arturo asked him to help in the *ejido*.

Pablo has never migrated. Before 1952, he did not have much household ex- *11* penditure, and did not feel any pressure to seek extra income. From 1952 to 1962 he had access to extra income from administering his brother's farm; this committed him to staying in Tlayacapan. After 1962 he obtained control of his father's *ejido*. But as time went by, Pablo became less and less able to save money. His household expenditure grew as family increased: from 1947 to 1965 his wife bore him nine children. His farming practices have always been on the conservative side — he has used his *ejido* plot for sugar cane and rice, and his private land for maize and beans. It was not until 1967, when two of his sons were helping in the fields, that he decided to grow tomatoes, and then only 0.3 hectares. In 1968 he grew 0.5 hectares of tomatoes, and has continued growing that amount in subsequent years. In 1971 he rented 0.4 hectares of private land, expanding his farm for the first time.

Also in contrast to his brothers, Pablo's public life has been very limited. *12* The only major ceremonial office he has held was in 1965, when he became first *mayordomo* of Santiago. He has never held any political office.

Four of Pablo's children have already left school without going beyond pri- *13* mary level, and all except one married daughter live in the household. It seems predictable that when his sons get married, Pablo's small farm will be divided up.

Considerations

1. Compare Arturo's Figueroa's success with his brother Pablo's relatively static career. Describe the influences unique to each brother's work and those which they share.
2. Economists talk about the means of production, the resources necessary for productive work. What is the dominant means of production in Tlayacapan life, and how does it influence the work the Figueroas do? Describe these influences in as much detail as you can, based on the reading.
3. In the Afterword to *A Legacy of Promises*, author Guillermo de la Peña makes the following statement: "In Mexico — as elsewhere — the function of the State is the maintenance of the existing order, i.e. the maintenance of social inequality." Can you see or infer any evidence in support of this statement from the account of the Figueroa families' careers?
4. Many writers have thought education would free workers from the physical and mental brutalities of rural life. Reflect on the agricultural work done

by the Figueroa family and then write an essay on the value of education in improving life for the rural worker. Focus on specific problems that education might or might not solve.

Connections

1. Imagine a *Working* interview with Arturo Figueroa. Compare and contrast his testimony to that of Mike Lefevre. Back up your speculations with references to both readings.
2. Although Arturo Figueroa has achieved great success in the context of his society, certain details in this ethnography reveal a gulf between the physical quality of life in his rural Mexico and that in the urban United States. Separating these details into comparable classes, contrast the Figueroas' rural life in Mexico with the urban lives of American workers interviewed (Lefevre, Bogan, Herrick). You may also use any evidence you find in Chapter 4, The Urban Experience.

Life on the Global Assembly Line

Barbara Ehrenreich
and Annette Fuentes

In Ciudad Juárez, Mexico, Anna M. rises at 5 A.M. to feed her son before starting on the two-hour bus trip to the maquiladora (factory). He will spend the day along with four other children in a neighbor's one-room home. Anna's husband, frustrated by being unable to find work for himself, left for the United States six months ago. She wonders, as she carefully applies her new lip gloss, whether she ought to consider herself still married. It might be good to take a night course, become a secretary. But she seldom gets home before eight at night, and the fac-

Barbara Ehrenreich (b. 1941) writes and consults widely on health policies, especially those affecting women. She writes a regular column for the New York Times, *is a contributing editor of* Ms. *magazine, and is a fellow at the Institute for Policy Studies. Annette Fuentes (b. 1957) studies and writes about women around the world. Her book,* Sisterhood Is Global, *is an anthology of writings by women in seventy countries about their economic, social, and political status. She has written for* The Village Voice, Jump Cut, *and* Ms. *and is now an editor of* City Limits *magazine.*

tory, where she stitches brassieres that will be sold in the United States through J. C. Penney, pays only $48 a week.

In Penang, Malaysia, Julie K. is up before the three other young women with whom she shares a room, and starts heating the leftover rice from last night's supper. She looks good in the company's green-trimmed uniform, and she's proud to work in a modern, American-owned factory. Only not quite so proud as when she started working three years ago — she thinks as she squints out the door at a passing group of women. Her job involves peering all day through a microscope, bonding hair-thin gold wires to a silicon chip destined to end up inside a pocket calculator, and at 21, she is afraid she can no longer see very clearly.

Every morning, between four and seven, thousands of women like Anna and Julie head out for the day shift. In Ciudad Juárez, they crowd into *ruteras* (rundown vans) for the trip from the slum neighborhoods to the industrial parks on the outskirts of the city. In Penang they squeeze, 60 or more at a time, into buses for the trip from the village to the low, modern factory buildings of the Bayan Lepas free trade zone. In Taiwan, they walk from the dormitories — where the night shift is already asleep in the still-warm beds — through the checkpoints in the high fence surrounding the factory zone.   1

This is the world's new industrial proletariat: young, female, Third World. Viewed from the "first world," they are still faceless, genderless "cheap labor," signaling their existence only through a label or tiny imprint — "made in Hong Kong," or Taiwan, Korea, the Dominican Republic, Mexico, the Philippines. But they may be one of the most strategic blocs of womanpower in the world of the 1980s. Conservatively, there are 2 million Third World female industrial workers employed now, millions more looking for work, and their numbers are rising every year. Anyone whose image of Third World women features picturesque peasants with babies slung on their backs should be prepared to update it. Just in the last decade, Third World women have become a critical element in the global economy and a key "resource" for expanding multinational corporations.   2

It doesn't take more than second-grade arithmetic to understand what's happening. In the United States, an assembly-line worker is likely to earn, depending on her length of employment, between $3.10 and $5 an hour. In many Third World countries, a woman doing the same work will earn $3 to $5 a *day*. According to the magazine *Business Asia*, in 1976 the average hourly wage for unskilled work (male or female) was 55 cents in Hong Kong, 52 cents in South Korea, 32 cents in the Philippines, and 17 cents in Indonesia. The logic of the situation is compelling: why pay someone in Massachusetts $5 an hour to do what someone in Manila will do for $2.50 a day? Or, as a corollary, why pay a male worker anywhere to do what a female worker will do for 40 to 60 percent less?   3

And so, almost everything that can be packed up is being moved out to the Third World; not heavy industry, but just about anything light enough to travel — garment manufacture, textiles, toys, footwear, pharmaceuticals, wigs, appliance parts, tape decks, computer components, plastic goods. In some industries, like garment and textile, American jobs are lost in the process, and the biggest losers are women, often black and Hispanic. But what's going on is much   4 more than a matter of runaway shops. Economists are talking about a "new international division of labor," in which the process of production is broken down and the fragments are dispersed to different parts of the world. In general, the low-skilled jobs are farmed out to the Third World, where labor costs are minuscule, while control over the overall process and technology remains safely at company headquarters in "first world" countries like the United States and Japan.

The American electronics industry provides a classic example: circuits are 5 printed on silicon wafers and tested in California; then the wafers are shipped to Asia for the labor-intensive process by which they are cut into tiny chips and bonded to circuit boards; final assembly into products such as calculators or military equipment usually takes place in the United States. Garment manufacture too is often broken into geographically separated steps, with the most repetitive, labor-intensive jobs going to the poor countries of the southern hemisphere. Most Third World countries welcome whatever jobs come their way in the new division of labor, and the major international development agencies — like the World Bank and the United States Agency for International Development (AID) — encourage them to take what they can get.

So much any economist could tell you. What is less often noted is the *gender* 6 breakdown of the emerging international division of labor. Eighty to 90 percent of the low-skilled assembly jobs that go to the Third World are performed by women — in a remarkable switch from earlier patterns of foreign-dominated industrialization. Until now, "development" under the aegis of foreign corporations has usually meant more jobs for men and — compared to traditional agricultural society — a diminished economic status for women. But multinational corporations and Third World governments alike consider assembly-line work — whether the product is Barbie dolls or missile parts — to be "women's work."

One reason is that women can, in many countries, still be legally paid less 7 than men. But the sheer tedium of the jobs adds to the multinationals' preference for women workers — a preference made clear, for example, by this ad from a Mexican newspaper: *We need female workers; older than 17, younger than 30; single and without children; minimum education primary school, maximum education one year of preparatory school [high school]: available for all shifts.*

It's an article of faith with management that only women can do, or will 8 do, the monotonous, painstaking work that American business is exporting to the Third World. Bill Mitchell, whose job is to attract United States businesses to the Bermudez Industrial Park in Ciudad Juárez told us with a certain macho pride: "A man just won't stay in this tedious kind of work. He'd walk out in a couple of hours." The personnel manager of a light assembly plant in Taiwan told anthropologist Linda Gail Arrigo: "Young male workers are too restless and impatient to do monotonous work with no career value. If displeased, they sabotage the machines and even threaten the foreman. But girls? At most, they cry a little."

In fact, the American businessmen we talked to claimed that Third World 9 women genuinely enjoy doing the very things that would drive a man to assault and sabotage. "You should watch these kids going into work," Bill Mitchell told us. "You don't have any sullenness here. They smile." A top-level management consultant who specializes in advising American companies on where to relocate their factories gave us this global generalization: "The [factory] girls genuinely enjoy themselves. They're away from their families. They have spending money. They can buy motorbikes, whatever. Of course it's a regulated experience too — with dormitories to live in — so it's a healthful experience."

What is the real experience of the women in the emerging Third World industrial work force? The conventional Western stereotypes leap to mind: You can't really compare, the standards are so different. . . . Everything's easier in warm countries. . . . They really don't have any alternatives. . . . Commenting on the low wages his company pays its women workers in Singapore, a Hewlett-Packard vice-president said, "They live much differently here than we do. . . ." But the differences are ultimately very simple. To start with, they have less money.   10

The great majority of the women in the new Third World work force live at or near the subsistence level for one person, whether they work for a multinational corporation or a locally owned factory. In the Philippines, for example, starting wages in U.S.-owned electronics plants are between $34 to $46 a month, compared to a cost of living of $37 a month; in Indonesia the starting wages are actually about $7 a month less than the cost of living. "Living," in these cases, should be interpreted minimally: a diet of rice, dried fish, and water — a Coke might cost a half-day's wages — lodging in a room occupied by four or more other people. Rachael Grossman, a researcher with the Southeast Asia Resource Center, found women employees of U.S. multinational firms in Malaysia and the Philippines living four to eight in a room in boardinghouses, or squeezing into tiny extensions built onto squatter huts near the factory. Where companies do provide dormitories for their employees, they are not of the "healthful," collegiate variety implied by our corporate informant. Staff from the American Friends Service Committee report that dormitory space is "likely to be crowded, with bed rotation paralleling shift rotation — while one shift works, another sleeps, as many as twenty to a room." In one case in Thailand, they found the dormitory "filthy," with workers forced to find their own place to sleep among "splintered floorboards, rusting sheets of metal, and scraps of dirty cloth."   11

Wages do increase with seniority, but the money does not go to pay for studio apartments or, very likely, motorbikes. A 1970 study of young women factory workers in Hong Kong found that 88 percent of them were turning more than half their earnings over to their parents. In areas that are still largely agricultural (such as parts of the Philippines and Malaysia), or places where male unemployment runs high (such as northern Mexico), a woman factory worker may be the sole source of cash income for an entire extended family.   12

But wages on a par with what an 11-year-old American could earn on a paper route, and living conditions resembling what Engels found in nineteenth-century Manchester are only part of the story. The rest begins at the factory gate. The work that multinational corporations export to the Third World is not only the most tedious, but often the most hazardous part of the production process. The countries they go to are, for the most part, those that will guar-   13 antee no interference from health and safety inspectors, trade unions, or even free-lance reformers. As a result, most Third World factory women work under conditions that already have broken or will break their health — or their nerves — within a few years, and often before they've worked long enough to earn any more than a subsistence wage.

Consider first the electronics industry, which is generally thought to be the *14* safest and cleanest of the exported industries. The factory buildings are low and modern, like those one might find in a suburban American industrial park. Inside, rows of young women, neatly dressed in the company uniform or T-shirt, work quietly at their stations. There is air conditioning (not for the women's comfort, but to protect the delicate semiconductor parts they work with), and high-volume piped-in Bee Gees hits (not so much for entertainment, as to prevent talking).

For many Third World women, electronics is a prestige occupation, at least *15* compared to other kinds of factory work. They are unlikely to know that in the United States the National Institute on Occupational Safety and Health (NIOSH) has placed electronics on its select list of "high health-risk industries using the greatest number of toxic substances." If electronics assembly work is risky here, it is doubly so in countries where there is no equivalent of NIOSH to even issue warnings. In many plants toxic chemicals and solvents sit in open containers, filling the work area with fumes that can literally knock you out. "We have been told of cases where ten to twelve women passed out at once," an AFSC field worker in northern Mexico told us, "and the newspapers report this as 'mass hysteria.' "

In one stage of the electronics assembly process, the workers have to dip the *16* circuits into open vats of acid. According to Irene Johnson and Carol Bragg, who toured the National Semiconductor plant in Penang, Malaysia, the women who do the dipping "wear rubber gloves and boots, but these sometimes leak, and burns are common." Occasionally, whole fingers are lost. More commonly, what electronics workers lose is the 20/20 vision they are required to have when they are hired. Most electronics workers spend seven to nine hours a day peering through microscopes, straining to meet their quotas.

One study in South Korea found that most electronics assembly workers de- *17* veloped severe eye problems after only one year of employment: 88 percent had chronic conjunctivitis; 44 percent became nearsighted; and 19 percent developed astigmatism. A manager for Hewlett-Packard's Malaysia plant, in an interview with Rachael Grossman, denied that there were any eye problems: "These girls are used to working with 'scopes.' We've found no eye problems. But it sure makes me dizzy to look through those things."

Electronics, recall, is the "cleanest" of the exported industries. Conditions *18* in the garment and textile industry rival those of any nineteenth-century sweatshop. The firms, generally local subcontractors to large American chains such as J. C. Penney and Sears, as well as smaller manufacturers, are usually even more indifferent to the health of their employees than the multinationals. Some of the worst conditions have been documented in South Korea, where the garment and textile industries have helped spark that country's "economic miracle." Workers are packed into poorly lit rooms, where summer temperatures rise above 100 degrees. Textile dust, which can cause permanent lung damage, fills the air. When there are rush orders, management may require forced overtime of as much as 48 hours at a stretch, and if that seems to go beyond the limits of human endurance, pep pills and amphetamine injections are thoughtfully provided. In her diary (originally published in a magazine now banned by the South Korean government) Min Chong Suk, 30, a sewing-machine operator, wrote of working from 7 A.M. to 11:30 P.M. in a garment factory: "When [the apprentices] shake the waste threads from the clothes, the whole room fills with dust, and it is hard to breathe. Since we've been working in such dusty air, there have been increasing numbers of people getting tuberculosis, bronchitis, and eye diseases. Since we are women, it makes us so sad when we have pale, unhealthy, wrinkled faces like dried-up spinach. . . . It seems to me that no one knows our blood dissolves into the threads and seams, with sighs and sorrow."

In all the exported industries, the most invidious, inescapable health hazard   19
is stress. On their home ground United States corporations are not likely to sacrifice productivity for human comfort. On someone else's home ground, however, anything goes. Lunch breaks may be barely long enough for a woman to stand in line at the canteen or hawkers' stalls. Visits to the bathroom are treated as privilege; in some cases, workers must raise their hands for permission to use the toilet, and waits up to a half hour are common. Rotating shifts — the day shift one week, the night shift the next — wreak havoc with sleep patterns. Because inaccuracies or failure to meet production quotas can mean substantial pay losses, the pressures are quickly internalized; stomach ailments and nervous problems are not unusual in the multinationals' Third World female work force. In some situations, good work is as likely to be punished as slow or shoddy work. Correspondent Michael Flannery, writing for the AFL–CIO's *American Federationist*, tells the story of 23-year-old Basilia Altagracia, a seamstress who stitched collars onto ladies' blouses in the La Romana (Dominican Republic) free trade zone (a heavily guarded industrial zone owned by Gulf & Western Industries, Inc.):

"A nimble veteran seamstress, Miss Altagracia eventually began to earn as   20
much as $5.75 a day. . . . 'I was exceeding my piecework quota by a lot.' . . . But then, Altagracia said, her plant supervisor, a Cuban emigré, called her into his office. 'He said I was doing a fine job, but that I and some other of the women were making too much money, and he was being forced to lower what we earned for each piece we sewed.' On the best days, she now can clear barely $3, she said. 'I was earning less, so I started working six and seven days a week. But I was tired and I could not work as fast as before.' " Within a few months, she was too ill to work at all.

As if poor health and the stress of factory life weren't enough to drive women   21
into early retirement, management actually encourages a high turnover in many industries. "As you know, when seniority rises, wages rise," the management consultant to U.S. multinationals told us. He explained that it's cheaper to train a fresh supply of teenagers than to pay experienced women higher wages. "Older" women, aged 23 or 24, are likely to be laid off and not rehired.

We estimate, based on fragmentary data from several sources, that the mul-   22
tinational corporations may already have used up (cast off) as many as 6 mil-

lion Third World workers — women who are too ill, too old (30 is over the hill in most industries), or too exhausted to be useful any more. Few "retire" with any transferable skills or savings. The lucky ones find husbands.

The unlucky ones find themselves at the margins of society — as bar girls,   23 "hostesses," or prostitutes.

At 21, Julie's greatest fear is that she will never be able to find a husband. She knows that just being a "factory girl" is enough to give anyone a bad reputation. When she first started working at the electronics company, her father refused to speak to her for three months. Now every time she leaves Penang to go back to visit her home village she has to put up with a lecture on morality from her older brother — not to mention a barrage of lewd remarks from men outside her family. If they knew that she had actually gone out on a few dates, that she had been to a discotheque, that she had once kissed a young man who said he was a student . . . Julie's stomach tightens as she imagines her family's reaction. She tries to concentrate on the kind of man she would like to marry: an engineer or technician of some sort, someone who had been to California, where the company headquarters are located and where even the grandmothers wear tight pants and lipstick — someone who had a good attitude about women. But if she ends up having to wear glasses, like her cousin who worked three years at the "scopes," she might as well forget about finding anyone to marry her.

One of the most serious occupational hazards that Julie and millions of   24 women like her may face is the lifelong stigma of having been a "factory girl." Most of the cultures favored by multinational corporations in their search for cheap labor are patriarchal in the grand old style: any young woman who is not under the wing of a father, husband, or older brother must be "loose." High levels of unemployment among men, as in Mexico, contribute to male resentment of working women. (Ironically, in some places the multinationals have increased male unemployment — for example, by paving over fishing and farming villages to make way for industrial parks.) Add to all this the fact that certain companies — American electronics firms are in the lead — actively promote Western-style sexual objectification as a means of insuring employee loyalty: there are company-sponsored cosmetics classes, "guess whose legs these are" contests, and swim-suit-style beauty contests where the prize might be a free night *for two* in a fancy hotel. Corporate-promoted Westernization only heightens the hostility many men feel toward any independent working women — having a job is bad enough, wearing jeans and mascara to work is going too far.

Anthropologist Patricia Fernandez, who has worked in a *maquiladora* her-   25 self, believes that the stigmatization of working women serves, indirectly, to keep them in line. "You have to think of the kind of socialization that girls experience in a very Catholic — or, for that matter, Muslim — society. The fear of having a 'reputation' is enough to make a lot of women bend over backward to be 'respectable' and ladylike, which is just what management wants." She points out that in northern Mexico, the tabloids delight in playing up stories of alleged vice in the *maquiladoras* — indiscriminate sex on the job, epidemics of venereal disease, fetuses found in factory rest rooms. "I worry about this because there are those who treat you differently as soon as they know you have a job at a *maquiladora*," one woman told Fernandez. "Maybe they think that if you have to work, there is a chance you're a whore."

And there is always a chance you'll wind up as one. Probably only a small   26 minority of Third World factory workers turn to prostitution when their working days come to an end. But it is, as for women everywhere, the employment of last resort, the only thing to do when the factories don't need you and traditional society won't — or, for economic reasons, can't — take you back. In the Philippines, the brothel business is expanding as fast as the factory system. If they can't use you one way, they can use you another.

Considerations

1. What motivations for work are assumed by those people creating the jobs Barbara Ehrenreich and Annette Fuentes report? Are these legitimate assumptions?
2. Summarize the work problems of women on the global assembly line, as reported by Ehrenreich and Fuentes. Illustrate each problem you mention and draw them all together in a careful thesis statement.

Connections

1. Barbara Ehrenreich and Annette Fuentes relate some attitudes toward work common among modern Third World women, and they describe how these attitudes shape their lives. Compare these attitudes to those of women workers in the United States (you may want to use Anne Bogan and Barbara Herrick as examples). What similarities and differences can you perceive? Do you see any reasons that might help explain the patterns you discover?
2. Would the working women described by Ehrenreich and Fuentes be likely to live in the Tlayacapan society where the Figueroas live? If not, what changes would have to occur before this society included such work options?
3. Governments appear to play varying roles in shaping the work described thus far in the readings: for the three American workers, the Figueroa family in rural Mexico, and the factory women in developing countries. Citing specific evidence from each article, compare and contrast the role of government in the lives of these three groups of workers.

American Velvet: "That Crazy Place in Connecticut"

Paul Dickson

From 1892, when the Wimpfheimer family moved its textile manufacturing   *1*
business into Stonington, Connecticut, until the early 1940s, labor-management relations at the American Velvet Company were bad. Jacques D.
Wimpfheimer, the current president of the company and the fourth generation
of his family in the business, says that relationship ". . . was one of suspicion,
industrial strife, and unrest that now and then led to stoppages and strikes."

A low point was reached in 1938, when the workers, represented by the Tex-   *2*
tile Workers Union of America, began a sixteen-month strike triggered by
management's attempt to get the weavers to increase their work load from two
to four looms per person. From the company's position, the situation was a
grim one, presenting only three alternatives: to sell out and quit, move South
where labor was cheap and unions weak, or stay and somehow work out a solution. Most of the family opted to sell out, but one man, Clarence Wimpfheimer (the father of the present president), chose to stay, and bought out the other
interests. After the takeover, a very uneasy truce was negotiated with the union,
based on a one-year contract. Jacques Wimpfheimer describes what happened
next: "My father was anxious to try some ideas which I do not believe he could
have articulated at the time. They were much more instinct than anything else."

The most immediate change that took place was that management became   *3*
local and involved—ending absentee ownership. The owner and his top depu-
ties were present in the plant all the time, asking questions, accepting suggestions from the workers, and sharing information with them and their union. A
few of the old-time bosses were unable to accept either this proximity or collaboration with the workforce, and had to be let go.

However, the most important new element in the relationship was not in-   *4*
stituted until the second contract was negotiated with the union a year later
(in 1940). This element was profit sharing. It had been offered in the first contract but was immediately rejected by the membership of the local as a management trick. What got it accepted was an interesting concession the company made to break a deadlock in which the union wanted another one-year
contract and the company, for the purpose of business stability, wanted a three-
year one. The company told the union, which was still cool to the idea, that if
it had accepted the first plan a year earlier each worker would have gotten an

---

Paul Dickson (b. 1939) is a writer specializing in American culture, especially future visions of it.

extra $.11 on every dollar that they had earned during the year, a revelation which began to warm the union's attitude. Then the company made an unusual offer: If the union would accept a three-year contract with profit sharing, the company would pay each worker the extra $.11 on the dollar for the whole previous year even though it was not in the contract. The union agreed, and the 1940 contract became the basis for a new and lasting relationship.

Today, the results of that 1940 relationship (which has developed considerably over the years) are stunning. Few companies anywhere in the nation can match them. There have been no strikes, work stoppages, disputes which have had to go to outside arbitration since 1940, and there has been no year in which the company has lost money. The profits shared with the employees have ranged from a low of 5 percent to high of 39 percent of an individual's wages. Base pay for the workers is the highest in the industry, and the company itself has grown to be the largest in the velvet industry. As for the issue which prompted the 1938 strike, over the years, the union and management have agreed to changes which have changed the weaver's workload from two to eight looms. As for the rates of turnover and absenteeism—key barometers of management effectiveness—the company's are far below the national and area norms, despite the presence nearby of companies in high technology like General Dynamics, which pay more, and despite the fact that working in an eighty-year-old textile mill is anything but glamorous. All of this is especially significant in the face of the experience of the last thirty years, which has seen a large share of the textile mills in New England either gone bankrupt or gone South. . . .

The company is located on a tree-lined side street in the picture-postcard village of Stonington on the Connecticut shore, a few miles from Mystic Seaport. Its main building looks like scores of other aging, red, industrial sites in its part of the country. I arrived there on a September morning in 1973 just in time to observe part of the company's morning routine: the 8:45 meeting. The routine actually starts at 8:00 A.M., when the managers of the business fan out through the plant to talk with some of the four hundred employees on a random basis, mostly to ask questions and get suggestions. At 8:45, the officers, department heads, the union president, and at least one other union member meet in Wimpfheimer's large wood-paneled office. This daily meeting is an informal occasion, where the first order of business is the company but where first names are used and digressions tolerated. (There was some banter about how bad the weather was the day I was there.) Wimpfheimer, who is outwardly relaxed and friendly but firm, is clearly in charge of the meeting.

The meeting began with Wimpfheimer going over the previous day's production figures, making announcements and opening the day's mail and passing it around the circle. The mail reading is a practice that was established to give labor and management immediate insight into what is going right or wrong with the company in the form of customer complaints, purchasing problems, and new sales orders. Next, in clockwise order around the assembled circle, each person in the room had the floor to bring up problems and items of general interest. A few had nothing to say this particular morning, while others dwelt on major and minor concerns. Vice-President Herbert Schell, Jr.; mentioned that there might be tough sledding ahead with an expected shortage of rayon, and said that he was looking into solutions. On the other hand, Hank Marquette, who is in charge of maintenance, addressed himself to the problem of "guano on cars" resulting from birds which were congregating on a large tank next to the parking lot. He estimated that it would cost nine hundred dollars to build a barricade. The group consensus, for the moment at least, was to look into less costly alternatives, such as the one Wimpfheimer suggested, which was to get a couple of cats to act as a deterrent force.

Once everyone had been heard from, Wimpfheimer again took the floor and   8 asked why production was down for the week. Harold Main, a vice-president, said that the cause was clearly from absenteeism due to illness. At this point, Wimpfheimer asked union president Frances Ainsworth if she thought anything could be done. "If they're really sick, we can't do anything," she replied. "If not, I'll come down on them." Next a short pep talk: Wimpfheimer pointed out that, at the moment, the company could sell all it could make, and that with profit sharing down everyone had to work to get production up. The final item on the agenda was the daily conference call to the New York sales office to see what was going on there. The only problem that morning was a lost shipment; once it was agreed that the problem would be looked into from both ends, the meeting was over.

By all accounts, the morning meeting is a very important element in the   9 way this company operates. "Some are more important than others," says Vice-President Schell, "because in many of them, major problems are solved before the day really gets going, but even the less important meetings are important because they show that labor-management collaboration is not just something for crisis situations." Schell and Wimpfheimer both point out that nothing is held back from the union and that the union, in turn, is just as frank. Wimpfheimer says, "We have lots of arguments but few real problems." The meetings also serve the purpose of addressing and correcting minor grievances before they become major ones. Schell sums it up: "By including the union in the business of the company, we have evolved to a point where I can truly say that neither party suspects the other of hiding its true motives."

The morning meeting is not the only collaborative institution at this com-   10 pany whose president brags of "scads of committees." Safety matters are discussed and resolved jointly, as are quality problems, which are ironed out in the Seconds Committee. Workers participate in the selection of new equipment and the design of workspaces. Over the years, an unusual group called "the Pops committee" evolved, which is made up of the present and former presidents of the local union, who are called together on occasion to discuss new ideas and long-range plans with management.

Of this assortment of committees, the most important is the Profit Sharing   11 Council, which meets every few months after work for dinner and drinks. Each department is represented by two workers, a foreman and a member of management. The council serves as an informal session in which suggestions are discussed on improving profits and making the most of the profit-sharing system itself. The system, incidentally, is quite straightforward. Each year, 27 percent of the company's profits before taxes are distributed to the workers. One-third is automatically paid out among the workers in cash—two-thirds cash if requested—with the remainder put into a trust fund payable to individual workers at retirement, disability, or death. This is *in addition* to the company's regular pension plan, which is paid for entirely by the company. A person with more than ten years' service with the company can take his full share out of the trust if he leaves for reasons other than retirement, and a person with less than ten years can take half the amount. Investments made by the trust are tended by another committee, this one composed of two members of management and two union representatives.

The officials of the company are both proud of and enthusiastic about the   *12* system. Significantly, this feeling is shared by both the present and the previous elected presidents of Local 110 with whom I met independently. Former president Joe Sposato feels that the key to the system is communications, and that without it profit sharing would be just another element of the pay system. "If either side stopped communicating, we'd slide back into the Stone Age in a few days," he says, "but I don't think that this will happen because we all like the system we have now, which is that anyone can say what he wants— and has the right to say it." Charlie Gencarella, another former president, feels that another strength of the system is that it can settle 90 percent of all labor-management problems quickly through the morning meetings and other direct contacts. "When we show the bosses that a foreman is wrong, they just go down and work it out with him." Frances Ainsworth adds that the system is a good one for the local because things go so well at American Velvet that Local 110 can handle its own affairs without having continually to call in the parent organization. "The International likes us," she adds, "and I think they'd like to have more locals like ours."

All three of these union leaders are quick to point out that there are things   *13* that need improvement in the company. Sposato feels that the company training program is poorly administered and needs upgrading. All three were in agreement that they were going to have to push for a change in the trust fund rules which would allow an employee to have the right to have his or her money taken out of stocks and bonds and put into a savings account at age fifty-five rather than age sixty in order to allow the person to better protect his share from the fluctuations of the stock market. Other problems had been solved. One was the union's displeasure when pension funds were put into the stocks of European companies—a policy which was felt to be bad for American labor. "We screamed like hell," says Gencarella, "and they stopped."

Nonetheless, their overall feelings about profit sharing and the retirement   *14* plan were generally very favorable. Sposato points out, "This is not just any profit-sharing plan we have here, but one which we are directly involved in. We are given the kind of information that lets us know as much as management does about the fortunes of the company, and we have the right to examine the books anytime we want." The consensus among these three was that the workers, for their part, understand and work with the system. "We work hard to prevent wasted velvet because that's lost money to us as well as to the company," says one, and another adds, "It's the company's business to warn people about too much absence or goofing off, but we'll talk to them too because they're hurting their co-workers."

The more one talks with the people at American Velvet, the more it is dem-   *15*

onstrated just how far it is from the norm in terms of employer-employee relations. Some of the evidence seems downright otherworldly. For instance, the
last contract was negotiated in two minutes; both sides were aware of what
the company could handle and what was an equitable increase for the workers. Gone was the normally obligatory tug of war in which the union asked for
more than it knew it could get and the company offered less than it could afford to give. At American Velvet, both sides agreed right off that a twenty-cent-
an-hour increase seemed about right. What is more, management is routinely
invited to the union's annual party, and Wimpfheimer recently turned some
heads in textile industry when he got invited to participate in a conference held
by the International in New York. "It was a dull meeting, but a significant
event," he says.

Although those in American Velvet do not see their experience as an exper-   16
iment but rather an effective and practical way of working, the company is
always testing new ideas. Some work and others don't. One that flopped was
a recent attempt to turn over the hiring process to the employees in the department where there was a vacancy. The plan bogged down when two ethnic
groups which are heavily represented in the workforce (Italians and Portuguese) began to argue over how many from each group should be hired. At the
time of my visit, a more manageable committee of worker representatives was
being set up to do the hiring. On the other hand, some years back, the company's salesmen successfully tested the idea of pooling their commissions to
protect each other from erratic and seasonal markets. Prior to the pooling, the
salesman who had developed customers for velvet in the Christmas novelty
market, for instance, had a few good months—and a much tougher time for the
rest of the year. The men liked the pooling, and the practice is still in force.

The question raised earlier, and which now begs for an answer, is whether   17
a situation such as that at American Velvet can be established in other operations. Representatives of both labor and management at American Velvet were
unanimous in their belief that it could and should. Although Wimpfheimer has
done little to push his system—for one thing, he doesn't have the time to do
it—he did write twice to Richard Nixon during his first Administration, when
the President was grappling with the question of national productivity.
Wimpfheimer's idea was that his company's experience would be worth studying for national lessons, but all he got was a form letter saying that his first
letter had been received and no answer at all to his second. There seems to be
little reason to doubt that other companies should be able to come up with
similarly successful systems. In fact, there *are* others already who have come
up with highly workable systems that blend the "piece-of-the-action" factor
implicit in profit sharing with some other innovative mechanisms for labor-
management collaboration. . . .

According to the Profit Sharing Research Foundation, there were 122,962   18
plans in operation in the United States in 1972, involving some 9,000,000
American workers. This compares dramatically to the 3,565 plans in 1949, the
20,117 in 1959, and even the 86,957 in 1969. Today, little companies have them
as well as big ones such as Xerox, Sears, Texas Instruments, and Hewlett-
Packard. Profit-sharing plans are fairly common in certain other areas of the

economy: one of three retail firms, wholesale distributors, and banks, for example, pass on some of their profits to their employees. Individual plans range from those which are excellent, equitable, and invite greater involvement with the organization to those thrown together solely to take advantage of the fact that payments are tax deductible and are therefore better than other forms of special compensation. The tax break aside, many see their plans as a means of morale building, strengthening loyalty, and bringing the employee closer to management's goal of greater profits and productivity through enlightened self-interest. It apparently works, because several major studies have shown that profits and organizational health increase when some of the profits are given away.

Considerations

1. Write an imaginary *Working* interview with one or more of the following people from "American Velvet": a beginning laborer recently hired, the union shop steward, or Clarence Wimpfheimer.
2. What element or elements are key to the improved labor relations at American Velvet? In a careful thesis statement, describe this element and how it helped at American Velvet. Then describe the details of the improvement.

Connections

1. Would Mike Lefevre be happier working at American Velvet than at his current job? Cite specific improvements Mike would appreciate at American Velvet, as well as any ideas he would not find fulfilled there.
2. Could any of the reforms instituted in American Velvet improve the rural working life of people like the Figueroas? Describe both the conditions you feel could and those that could not be changed, discussing to what extent the American Velvet model does or does not apply to Tlayacapan society.
3. Compare and contrast the scenario presented by Barbara Ehrenreich and Annette Fuentes with the story of American Velvet. Evaluate whether the American model could improve working life for women on "the global assembly line," and describe why such changes are or are not likely to occur soon.

Alienated Labor

Karl Marx

We shall begin with a contemporary economic fact. The worker becomes all   *1*
the poorer the more wealth he produces, the more his production increases in
power and volume. The worker becomes an ever cheaper commodity the more
commodities he creates. As the world of things increases in value, the human
world becomes devalued. For labor not only produces commodities; it makes
a commodity of the work process itself, as well as the worker—and indeed at
the same rate as it produces goods.

This means simply that the object produced by man's labor—its product—   *2*
now confronts him in the shape of an alien thing, a power independent of the
producer. The product of labor is labor given embodiment in a material form;
this product is the objectification of labor. The performance of work is thus at
the same time its objectification. In the sphere of political economy, the performance of work appears as a material loss, a departure from reality for the
worker; objectification appears both as deprivation of the object and enslavement to it; and appropriation of the product by others as alienation.

The reduction of labor to a mere commodity—in short, the dehumanization   *3*
of work—goes so far that the worker is reduced to the point of starving to death.
So remote from life has work become that the worker is robbed of the real things
essential not only for his existence but for his work. Indeed, work itself becomes something which he can obtain only with the greatest difficulty and at
intervals. And so much does appropriation of his product by others appear as
alienation that the more things the worker produces, the fewer can he possess
and the more he falls under the domination of the wealth he produces but cannot enjoy—capital.

All these consequences flow from the fact that the worker is related to the   *4*
product of his labor as to an alien thing. From this premise it is clear that the
more the worker exerts himeslf, the more powerful becomes the world of things
which he creates and which confront him as alien objects; hence the poorer he
becomes in his inner life, and the less belongs to him as his own. It is the same
with religion. The more man puts into God, the less he retains in himself. The
worker puts his life into the things he makes; and his life then belongs to him
no more, but to the product of his labor. The greater the worker's activity,
therefore, the more pointless his life becomes. Whatever the product of his labor, it is no longer his own. Therefore, the greater this product, the more he is
diminished. The alienation of the worker from his product means not only that

*Karl Marx (1818–1883) was born in Trier, Prussia (now in West Germany), the
son of a wine merchant. He completed a Ph.D. in philosophy but soon devoted full
time to writing and organizing for radical working-class political causes. This
fragmentary piece was written in 1844, but lay unpublished until 1927.*

his labor becomes an impersonal object and takes on its own existence, but that it exists outside himself, independently, and alien to him, and that it opposes itself to him as an autonomous power. The life which he has conferred on the object confronts him in the end as a hostile and alien force.

Let us now look more closely at the phenomenon of objectification and its result for the worker: alienation and, in effect, divorce from the product of his labor. To undersand this, we must realize that the worker can create nothing without nature, without the sensuous, external world which provides the raw material for his labor. But just as nature provides labor with means of existence in the sense of furnishing raw material which labor processes, so also does it provide means for the worker's physical subsistence. Thus the more the worker by his labor appropriates the external, sensuous world of nature, the more he deprives himself of the means of life in two respects: first, that the sensuous external world becomes progressively detached from him as the medium necessary to his labor; and secondly, that nature becomes increasingly remote from him as the medium through which he gains his physical subsistence. 5

In both respects, therefore, the worker becomes a slave of things; first, in that labor itself is something he obtains—that is, he gets work; and secondly, in that he obtains thereby the physical means of subsistence. Thus, things enable him to exist, first as a worker, and secondly, as one in bondage to physical objects. The culmination of this process of enslavement is that only as a worker can he maintain himself in his bondage and only as a bondsman to things can he find work. 6

In the laws of political economy, the alienation of the worker from his product is expressed as follows: the more the worker produces, the less he has to consume; the more value he creates, the more valueless, the more unworthy he becomes; the better formed is his product, the more deformed becomes the worker; the more civilized his product, the more brutalized becomes the worker; the mightier the work, the more powerless the worker; the more ingenious the work, the duller becomes the worker and the more he becomes nature's bondsman. 7

Political economy conceals the alienation inherent in labor by avoiding any mention of the evil effects of work on those who work. Thus, whereas labor produces miracles for the rich, for the worker it produces destitution. Labor produces palaces, but for the worker, hovels. It produces beauty, but it cripples the worker. It replaces labor by machines, but how does it treat the worker? By throwing some workers back into a barbarous kind of work, and by turning the rest into machines. It produces intelligence, but for the worker, stupidity and cretinism. 8

Fundamentally, the relationship of labor to the product of labor is the relationship of the worker to the object of his production. The relationship of property owners to the objects of production and to production itself is only a consequence of his primary relationship, and simply confirms it. We shall consider this other aspect later. When we ask, then, what is the essential relationship of labor, we are concerned with the relationship of the worker to production. 9

Thus far we have considered only one aspect of the alienation of the worker, 10 namely, his relationship to the product of his labor. But his estrangement is manifest not only in the result, but throughout the work process—within productive activity itself. How could the worker stand in an alien relationship to the product of his activity if he were not alienated in the very act of production? The product after all is but the résumé of his activity, of production. Hence if the product of labor is alienation, production itself must be active alienation—the alienation of the product of labor merely sums up the alienation in the work process itself.

What then do we mean by the alienation of labor? First, that the work he   *11* performs is extraneous to the worker, that is, it is not personal to him, is not part of his nature; therefore he does not fulfill himself in work, but actually denies himself; feels miserable rather than content, cannot freely develop his physical and mental powers, but instead becomes physically exhausted and mentally debased. Only while not working can the worker be himself; for while at work he experiences himself as a stranger. Therefore only during leisure hours does he feel at home, while at work he feels homeless. His labor is not voluntary, but coerced, forced labor. It satisfies no spontaneous creative urge, but is only a means for the satisfaction of wants which have nothing to do with work. Its alien character therefore is revealed by the fact that when no physical or other compulsion exists, work is avoided like the plague. Extraneous labor, labor in which man alienates himself, is a labor of self-sacrifice, of mortification. Finally, the alienated character of work for the worker is shown by the fact that the work he does is not his own, but another's, and that at work he belongs not to himself, but to another. Just as in religion the spontaneous activity of human imagination, of the human brain and heart, is seen as a force from outside the individual reacting upon him as the alien activity of gods or devils, so the worker's labor is no more his own spontaneous activity; but is something impersonal, inhuman and belonging to another. Through his work the laborer loses his identity.

As a result, man—the worker—feels freely active only in his animal func-   *12* tions—eating, drinking, procreating, or at most in his dwelling and personal adornment—while in his human and social functions he is reduced to an animal. The animal becomes human, and the human becomes animal. Certainly eating, drinking and procreating are also genuinely human functions; but abstractly considered, apart from all other human activities and regarded as ultimate ends in themselves, they are merely animal functions.

We have considered the alienation of practical human activity or labor from   *13* two aspects. First, the relationship of the worker is the product of labor as an alien object which dominates him. This relationship implies at the same time a relationship to the sensuous external world of nature as an alien and hostile world. Second the relationship of labor to the act of production within the work process. This is the relationship of the worker to his own activity as something alien, and not belonging to him; it is activity as misery, strength as weakness, creation as emasculation; it is the worker's own physical and mental energy, his personal life (for what is life but activity?) as an activity which is turned against himself, which neither depends on nor belongs to him. Here we have self-alienation as opposed to alienation from things.

And now we see that yet a third aspect of alienated labor can be deduced   *14* from the two already considered. For man is a creature of his species *[Gat-tungswesen]* not only because in practice and in theory he adopts mankind as the object of his creation—indeed his field is the whole of nature—but also because within himself he, one man, represents the whole of mankind and therefore he is a universal and a free being.

The life of the species, for man as for animals, has its physical basis in the   *15* fact that man, like animals, lives on nature; and since man is more universal than animals, so too the realm of nature on which he lives is more universal. Just as plants, animals, stones, the air, light, etc. theoretically form a part of human consciousness, as subjects for natural science and art, providing man with intellectual and spiritual nourishment from the non-human world—nourishment which he must first prepare and transform before he can enjoy and absorb it—so too this non-human world is a practical part of human life and activity, since man also subsists physically on nature's products in the form of food, heat, clothing, shelter, etc. The universality of man in practice is seen in the universality which makes the whole of nature conceivable as man's inorganic body, since nature is first, his direct means of existence, and second, the raw material, the field, the instrument of his vital activity. Nature is man's inorganic body, that is, nature apart from the human body itself. To say that man lives on nature means that nature is his body with which he must remain in constant and vital contact in order not to die. And to say that man's physical and spiritual life is linked to nature is simply an expression of the interdependence of all natural forces, for man himself is part of nature.

Just as alienated labor separates man from nature and from himself—his   *16* own active functions and life activity—so too it alienates him from the species, from other men. It degrades all the life of the species and makes some cold and abstract notion of individual life and toil into the goal of the entire species, whose common life also then becomes abstract and alienated.

What happens in the end is that man regards his labor—his life-activity, his   *17* productive life—merely as a means of satisfying his drive for physical existence. Yet productive life is the real life of the species. We live in order to create more living things. The whole character of a species is evident in its particular type of life-activity; and free, conscious activity is the generic character of human beings. But alienated labor reduces this area of productive life to a mere means of existence.

Among animals there is no question of regarding one part of life as cut off   *18* from the rest; the animal is one with its life-activity. Man, on the other hand, makes his life-activity the object of his conscious will; and this is what distinguishes him from animals. It is because of this free, conscious activity that he is a creature of his species. Or perhaps it is because he is a creature of his species that he is a conscious being, that he is able to direct his life-activity; and that he treats his own life as subject matter and as an object of his own determination. Alienated labor reverses this relationship: man, the self-conscious being, turns his chief activity—labor, which should express his profound essence—into a mere means of physical existence.

In manipulating inorganic nature and creating an objective world by his   *19* practical activity, man confirms himself as a conscious creature of his species, that is, as a member of his whole species, a being who regards the whole of mankind as involved in himself, and himself as part of mankind. Admittedly animals also produce, building, as do bees, ants or beavers, their nests or dens. But animals produce only for their own immediate needs or for those of their young. Animal production is limited, while man's production is universal. The animal produces only under compulsion of direct physical need, while man produces even when free from physical need, and only truly produces or creates when truly free from such need. Animals produce or reproduce only themselves, while man reproduces the whole of nature. Whatever animals produce—nests or food—is only for their own bodies; but man's creations supply the needs of many species. And whereas animals construct only in accordance with the standards and needs of their kind, man designs and produces in accordance with the standards of all known species and can apply the standards appropriate to the subject. Man therefore designs in accordance with the laws of beauty.

Thus it is precisely in shaping the objective world that man really proves 20 himself as a creature of his species; for in this handiwork resides his active species-life. By means of man's productivity, nature appears to him as his work and his reality. The true object of man's labor therefore is the objectification of man's species-life—his profound essence; for in his labor man duplicates himself not merely intellectually, in consciousness, but also actively, in reality; and in the world that he has made man contemplates his own image. When, therefore, alienated labor tears away from man the object of his production, it snatches from his species-life—the essence of his being—and transforms his advantage over animals into a disadvantage, insofar as his inorganic body, nature, is withdrawn from him.

Hence, in degrading labor—which should be man's free, spontaneous activ- 21 ity—to a mere means of physical subsistence, alienated labor degrades man's essential life to a mere means to an end. The awareness which man should have of his relationship to the rest of mankind is reduced to a state of detachment in which he and his fellows become simply unfeeling objects. Thus alienated labor turns man's essential humanity into a non-human property. It estranges man from his own human body, and estranges him from nature and from his own spiritual essence—his human being.

An immediate consequence of man's estrangement from the product of his 22 labor is man's estrangement from man. When man confronts himself, he confronts other men. What characterizes his relationship to his work, to the product of his labor, and to himself also characterizes his relationship to other men, their work, and the products of their labor.

In general, the statement that man is alienated from the larger life of his 23 species means that men are alienated from each other and from human nature. Man's self-estrangement—and indeed all his attitudes to himself—first finds expression in his relationship to other men. Thus in the relationship of alienated labor each man's view of his fellows is determined by the narrow standards and activities of the work place.

We started with an economic fact, the separation of the worker from the 24 means of production. From this fact flows our concept of alienated or estranged labor; and in analyzing this concept, we merely analyzed a fact of political economy.

Let us now see how alienated labor appears in real life. If the product of my   *25*
labor is alien to me, if it confronts me as an alien power, to whom then does
it belong? If my own activity belongs not to me, but is an alien, forced activity,
to whom does it then belong? It must belong to a being other than me. Who
then is this being?

Is it the gods? In ancient times the major productive effort was evidently in   *26*
the service of the gods—for example, temple building in Egypt, India, Mexico;
and the product of that effort belonged to the gods. But the gods were never
the lords of labor. Neither was nature ever man's taskmaster. What a contradiction it would be if man—as he more and more subjugated nature by his
labor, rendering divine miracles superfluous by the wonders of industry—if man
were then to renounce his pleasure in producing and his enjoyment of the
product merely in order to continue serving the gods.

Hence, the alien being to whom labor and the product of labor belong, in   *27*
whose service labor is performed and for whose enjoyment the product of labor serves—this being can only be man himself. So, if the product of labor does
not belong to the worker, if it confronts him as an alien power, this must mean
that it belongs to a man other than the worker. If the worker's activity is a
torment to him, it must be a source of enjoyment and pleasure to another man.
Neither the gods nor nature but only man himself can be this alien power over
men.

Let us consider our earlier statement that man's relation to himself first be-   *28*
comes objectified, embodied and real through his relation to other men. Therefore, if he is related to the product of his objectified labor as to an alien, hostile, powerful and independent object, then he is related in such a way that
someone else is master of this object—someone who is alien, hostile, powerful
and independent of him. If his own activity is not free, then he is related to it
as an activity in the service, and under the domination, coercion and yoke, of
another man.

The alienation of man from himself and from nature appears in his rela-   *29*
tionships with other men. Thus religious self-alienation necessarily appears in
the relationship between laymen and priest—or—since we are here dealing with
the spiritual world—between laymen and intercessor. In the everyday, practical world, however, self-alienation manifests itself only through real, practical
relationships between men. The medium through which alienation occurs is
itself a practical one. As alienated laborer, man not only establishes a certain
relationship to the object and process of production as to alien and hostile
powers; he also fixes the relationship of other men to his production and to his
product; and the relationship between himself and other men. Just as he turns
his own product into something not belonging to him; so he brings about the
domination of the non-producer over production and its product. In becoming
alienated from his own activity, he surrenders power over that activity to a
stranger.

So far we have considered this alienated relationship only from the work-   *30*
er's standpoint. Later we shall also consider it from the standpoint of the non-
worker, since through the process of alienating his labor the worker brings forth
another man who stands outside the work process. The relationship of the worker

to work also determines the relationship of the capitalist—or whatever one chooses to call the master of labor—to work. Private property thus is essentially the result, the necessary consequence of alienated labor and of the extraneous relationship of the worker to nature and to himself. Hence private property results from the phenomenon of alienated labor—that is, alienated labor alienated life and alienated man.

Considerations

1. Karl Marx mentions four aspects of alienation. Describe each, explaining how he feels they grow from one another. To illustrate what these aspects of alienation mean, you may draw on the interviews, on current events, or on your own experience as a worker.
2. In paragraphs 16–23, Marx discusses what he considers the essence of the human species, or human "species-life," as distinguished from other animals' lives. Analyze this passage carefully and discuss what kinds of work and working arrangements Marx might commend as fulfilling or furthering this "species-life." The interviews may provide you with examples, both favorable and unfavorable, by suggesting the jobs that discontented workers long for.

Connections

1. Karl Marx wrote primarily about industrial laborers, the proletariat, people like Mike Lefevre and the women on the global assembly line. Drawing on the Lefevre interview, the Barbara Ehrenriech and Annette Fuentes selection, and on the sketch of the Figueroa family, discuss whether Marx's theory of alienation applies only to industrial laborers or to agricultural laborers and peasant farmers as well.
2. The American Velvet Company adopted changes which seem to have satisfied most of its workers. Do you think these changes solve the basic problem of worker alienation as Marx describes it?
3. Marx's theory of alienation was developed as he observed workers in a stage of economic history we now call early monopoly capitalism, or the Industrial Revolution. Of all the working contexts described in this chapter, that of women in Third World nations comes closest to the economic structure Marx analyzed. Explain Marx's theory of alienation by illustrations from the Ehrenreich and Fuentes article. If you can't find evidence for one or more points, note that also, explaining why you think the theory doesn't fit this reality.
4. After analyzing Marx's concept of the human "species-life," compare Charles Darwin's thoughts on the relation between humans and other animals in the selection from *The Descent of Man* in Chapter 9, The Impact of Animals. Specify precisely where Marx and Darwin agree and where they disagree.

The Principles of Scientific Management

Frederick W. Taylor

The principal object of management should be to secure the maximum   *1*
prosperity for the employer, coupled with the maximum prosperity for each
employee.

The words "maximum prosperity" are used, in their broad sense, to mean   *2*
not only large dividends for the company or owner, but the development of
every branch of the business to its highest state of excellence, so that the prosperity may be permanent.

In the same way maximum prosperity for each employee means not only   *3*
higher wages than are usually received by men of his class, but, of more importance still, it also means the development of each man to his state of maximum efficiency, so that he may be able to do, generally speaking, the highest
grade of work for which his natural abilities fit him, and it further means giving him, when possible, this class of work to do.

It would seem to be so self-evident that maximum prosperity for the em-   *4*
ployer, coupled with maximum prosperity for the employee, ought to be the
two leading objects of management, that even to state this fact should be unnecessary. And yet there is no question that, throughout the industrial world,
a large part of the organization of employers, as well as employees, is for war
rather than for peace, and that perhaps the majority on either side do not believe that it is possible so to arrange their mutual relations that their interests
become identical.

The majority of these men believe that the fundamental interests of em-   *5*
ployees and employers are necessarily antagonistic. Scientific management, on
the contrary, has for its very foundation the firm conviction that the true interests of the two are one and the same; that prosperity for the employer cannot exist through a long term of years unless it is accompanied by prosperity
for the employee, and *vice versa;* and that it is possible to give the workman
what he wants most—high wages—and the employer what he wants—a low
labor cost—for his manufacturers. . . .

These principles appear to be so self-evident that many men may think it   *6*
almost childish to state them. Let us, however, turn to the facts, as they actually exist in this country and in England. The English and American peoples
are the greatest sportsmen in the world. Whenever an American workman plays
baseball, or an English workman plays cricket, it is safe to say that he strains

*Frederick W. Taylor (1856–1915) began as a laborer in a Philadelphia machine
shop, moving rapidly into management. Generally regarded as the founder of systematic programs for managing labor, Taylor presented these ideas to businessmen
across the country and eventually to Congress.*

every nerve to secure victory for his side. He does his very best to make the largest possible number of runs. The universal sentiment is so strong that any man who fails to give out all there is in him in sport is branded as a "quitter," and treated with contempt by those who are around him.

When the same workman returns to work on the following day, instead of using every effort to turn out the largest possible amount of work, in a majority of the cases this man deliberately plans to do as little as he safely can—to turn out far less work than he is well able to do—in many instances to do not more than one-third to one-half of a proper day's work. And in fact if he were to do his best to turn out his largest possible day's work, he would be abused by his fellow-workers for so doing, even more than if he had proved himself a "quitter" in sport. Underworking, that is, deliberately working slowly so as to avoid doing a full day's work, "soldiering," as it is called in this country, "hanging it out," as it is called in England, "ca canae," as it is called in Scotland, is almost universal in industrial establishments, and prevails also to a large extent in the building trades; and the writer asserts without fear of contradiction that this constitutes the greatest evil with which the working-people of both England and America are now afflicted. . . .   7

Why is it, then, in the face of the self-evident fact that maximum prosperity can exist only as the result of the determined effort of each workman to turn out each day his largest possible day's work, that the great majority of our men are deliberately doing just the opposite, and that even when the men have the best of intentions their work is in most cases far from efficient?   8

There are three causes for this condition, which may be briefly summarized as: 9

First. The fallacy, which has from time immemorial been almost universal among workmen, that a material increase in the output of each man or each machine in the trade would result in the end in throwing a large number of men out of work.   10

Second. The defective systems of management which are in common use, and which make it necessary for each workman to soldier, or work slowly, in order that he may protect his own best interests.   11

Third. The inefficient rule-of-thumb methods, which are still almost universal in all trades, and in practicing which our workmen waste a large part of their effort.   12

This paper will attempt to show the enormous gains which would result from the substitution by our workmen of scientific for rule-of-thumb methods.   13

To explain a little more fully these three causes: 14

First. The great majority of workmen still believe that if they were to work at their best speed they would be doing a great injustice to the whole trade by throwing a lot of men out of work, and yet the history of the development of each trade shows that each improvement, whether it be the invention of a new machine or the introduction of a better method, which results in increasing the productive capacity of the men in the trade and cheapening the costs, instead of throwing men out of work make in the end work for more men.   15

The cheapening of any article in common use almost immediately results in a largely increased demand for that article. Take the case of shoes, for instance. The introduction of machinery for doing every element of the work which   16 was formerly done by hand has resulted in making shoes at a fraction of their former labor cost, and in selling them so cheap that now almost every man, woman, and child in the working-classes buys one or two pairs of shoes per year, and wears shoes all the time, whereas formerly each workman bought perhaps one pair of shoes every five years, and went barefoot most of the time, wearing shoes only as a luxury or as a matter of the sternest necessity. In spite of the enormously increased output of shoes per workman, which has come with shoe machinery, the demand for shoes has so increased that there are relatively more men working in the shoe industry now than every before. . . .

A great deal has been and is being constantly said about "sweat-shop" work   17
conditions. The writer has great sympathy with those who are overworked, but on the whole a greater sympathy for those who are *underpaid*. For every individual, however, who is overworked, there are a hundred who intentionally underwork—greatly underwork—every day of their lives, and who for this reason deliberately aid in establishing those conditions which in the end inevitably result in low wages. And yet hardly a single voice is being raised in an endeavor to correct this evil.

As engineers and managers, we are more intimately acquainted with these   18
facts than any other class in the community, and are therefore best fitted to lead in a movement to combat this fallacious idea by educating not only the workmen but the whole of the country as to the true facts. And yet we are practically doing nothing in this direction, and are leaving this field entirely in the hands of the labor agitators (many of whom are misinformed and misguided), and of sentimentalists who are ignorant as to actual working conditions.

Second. As to the second cause for soldiering—the relations which exist be-   19
tween employers and employees under almost all of the systems of management which are in common use—it is impossible in a few words to make it clear to one not familiar with this problem why it is that the *ignorance of employers* as to the proper time in which work of various kinds should be done makes it for the interest of the workman to "soldier,"

The writer therefore quotes herewith from a paper read before The Ameri-   20
can Society of Mechanical Engineers, in June, 1903, entitled "Shop Management," which it is hoped will explain fully this cause for soldiering:

"This loafing or soldiering proceeds from two causes. First, from the natural   21
instinct and tendency of men to take it easy, which may be called natural soldiering. Second, from more intricate second thought and reasoning caused by their relations with other men, which may be called systematic soldiering.

"There is no question that the tendency of the average man (in all walks of   22
life) is toward working at a slow, easy gait, and that it is only after a good deal of thought and observation on his part or as a result of example, conscience, or external pressure that he takes a more rapid pace.

"There are, of course, men of unusual energy, vitality, and ambition who   23
naturally choose the fastest gait, who set up their own standards, and who work hard, even though it may be against their best interests. But these few uncommon men only serve by forming a contrast to emphasize the tendency of the average.

"This common tendency to 'take it easy' is greatly increased by bringing a   24 number of men together on similar work and at a uniform standard rate of pay by the day.

"Under this plan the better men gradually but surely slow down their gait   25
to that of the poorest and least efficient. When a naturally energetic man works for a few days beside a lazy one, the logic of the situation is unanswerable. 'Why should I work hard when that lazy fellow gets the same pay that I do and does only half as much work?' . . .

"The natural laziness of men is serious, but by far the greatest evil from   26
which both workmen and employers are suffering is the *systematic soldiering* which is almost universal under all of the ordinary schemes of management and which results from a careful study on the part of the workmen of what will promote their best interests.

"The writer was much interested recently in hearing one small but experi-   27
enced golf caddy boy of twelve explaining to a green caddy, who had shown special energy and interest, the necessity of going slow and lagging behind his man when he came up to the ball, showing him that since they were paid by the hour, the faster they went the less money they got, and finally telling him that if he went too fast the other boys would give him a licking.

"This represents a type of *systematic soldiering* which is not, however, very   28
serious, since it is done with the knowledge of the employer, who can quite easily break it up if he wishes.

"The greater part of the *systematic soldiering*, however, is done by the men   29
with the deliberate object of keeping their employers ignorant of how fast work can be done.

"So universal is soldiering for this purpose that hardly a competent work-   30
man can be found in a large establishment, whether he works by the day or on piece work, contract work, or under any of the ordinary systems, who does not devote a considerable part of his time to studying just how slow he can work and still convince his employer that he is going at a good pace.

"The causes for this are, briefly, that practically all employers determine   31
upon a maximum sum which they feel it is right for each of their classes of employees to earn per day, whether their men work by the day or piece.

"Each workman soon finds out about what this figure is for his particular   32
case, and he also realizes that when his employer is convinced that a man is capable of doing more work than he has done, he will find sooner or later some way of compelling him to do it with little or no increase of pay. . . .

"It is, however, under piece work that the art of systematic soldiering is   33
thoroughly developed; after a workman has had the price per piece of the work he is doing lowered two or three times as a result of his having worked harder and increased his output, he is likely entirely to lose sight of his employer's side of the case and become imbued with a grim determination to have no more cuts if soldiering can prevent it. Unfortunately for the character of the workman, soldiering involves a deliberate attempt to mislead and deceive his employer, and thus upright and straightforward workmen are compelled to become more or less hypocritical. The employer is soon looked upon as an antagonist, if not an enemy, and the mutual confidence which should exist between a leader and his men, the enthusiasm, the feeling that they are all working for the same end and will share in the results is entirely lacking.

"The feeling of antagonism under the ordinary piece-work system becomes   *34*
in many cases so marked on the part of the men that any proposition made by
their employers, however reasonable, is looked upon with suspicion, and soldiering becomes such a fixed habit that men will frequently take pains to restrict the product of machines which they are running when even a large increase in output would involve no more work on their part."

Third. As to the third cause for slow work, considerable space will later in   *35*
this paper be devoted to illustrating the great gain, both to employers and em-
ployés, which results from the substitution of scientific for rule-of-thumb
methods in even the smallest details of the work of every trade. The enormous
saving of time and therefore increase in the output which it is possible to effect
through eliminating unnecessary motions and substituting fast for slow and
inefficient motions for the men working in any of our trades can be fully realized only after one has personally seen the improvement which results from a
thorough motion and time study, made by a competent man. . . .

It is not here claimed that any single panacea exists for all of the troubles   *36*
of the working-people or of employers. As long as some people are born lazy or
inefficient, and others are born greedy and brutal, as long as vice and crime
are with us, just so long will a certain amount of poverty, misery, and unhap-
piness be with us also. No system of management, no single expedient within
the control of any man or any set of men can insure continuous prosperity to
either workmen or employers. Prosperity depends upon so many factors entirely beyond the control of any one set of men, any state, or even any one
country, that certain periods will inevitably come when both sides must suffer,
more or less. It is claimed, however, that under scientific management the intermediate periods will be far more prosperous, far happier, and more free
from discord and dissension. And also, that the periods will be fewer, shorter
and the suffering less. And this will be particularly true in any one town, any
one section of the country, or any one state which first substitutes the principles of scientific management for the rule of thumb.

That these principles are certain to come into general use practically   *37*
throughout the civilized world, sooner or later, the writer is profoundly convinced, and the sooner they come the better for all the people.

Considerations

1. Frederick W. Taylor asserts that the maximum prosperity for both workers
   and owners occurs when workers produce their maximum output at work.
   Does he mean by this that workers and owners will reap equal benefits from
   increased production? Analyze Taylor's article to discover exactly what he
   means by *maximum prosperity.* You may need to look carefully at several
   other key terms in the article as well.
2. Summarize Taylor's principles for scientific management, trying to envision briefly how each principle would be carried out in practice.
3. What assumptions about human nature does Taylor make here? Are the same
   assumptions made about all classes of people? You may organize your re-

sponse by listing and discussing each assumption or by looking first at the assumptions for one class and then at those for another class.

Connections

1. What does Frederick W. Taylor assume as the motivation for work? How important does this motivation seem for the workers interviewed and described in this chapter? Do not assume this motivation applies equally to all workers, but distinguish their motives carefully.
2. After having defined Taylor's assumptions about the motivation for work, ask whether other theorists in this chapter would agree with his assumptions. If some would disagree, on what grounds would they do so?
3. Economists usually weigh three elements (at least) in determining the value of a product: the raw materials, the equipment and plant used to process them, and the labor necessary to complete the processing. Read Frederick Taylor's and Karl Marx's essays and decide what balance of these three elements (materials, plant, labor) each thinks determines the value of a product.
4. Would Taylor approve the changes made at American Velvet? Support your opinion with details from both Taylor's theory and the American Velvet story.

The Ideal of Craftsmanship
C. Wright Mills

Craftsmanship as a fully idealized model of work gratification involves six *1* major features: There is no ulterior motive in work other than the product being made and the processes of its creation. The details of daily work are meaningful because they are not detached in the worker's mind from the product of the work. The worker is free to control his own working action. The craftsman is thus able to learn from his work; and to use and develop his capacities and skills in its prosecution. There is no split of work and play, or work and culture. The craftsman's way of livelihood determines and infuses his entire mode of living.

C. Wright Mills (1916–1962) was a popular sociologist who taught for many years at Columbia University. He is best known for works documenting contemporary American power relations. This excerpt comes from White Collar: The American Middle Class (1951), *the first major study of its kind.*

I. The hope in good work, William Morris remarked, is hope of product and   *2*
hope of pleasure in the work itself; the supreme concern, the whole attention,
is with the quality of the product and the skill of its making. There is an inner
relation between the craftsman and the thing he makes, from the image he first
forms of it through its completion, which goes beyond the mere legal relations
of property and makes the craftsman's will-to-work spontaneous and even exuberant.

Other motives and results—money or reputation or salvation—are subor-   *3*
dinate. It is not essential to the practice of the craft ethic that one necessarily
improves one's status either in the religious community or in the community
in general. Work gratification is such that a man may live in a kind of quiet
passion "for his work alone."

II. In most statements of craftsmanship, there is a confusion between its   *4*
technical and aesthetic conditions and the legal (property) organization of the
worker and the product. What is actually necessary for work-as-craftsmanship,
however, is that the tie between the product and the producer be psychologically possible; if the producer does not legally own the product he must own
it psychologically in the sense that he knows what goes into it by way of skill,
sweat, and material and that his own skill and sweat are visible to him. Of
course, if legal conditions are such that the tie between the work and the worker's material advantage is transparent, this is a further gratification, but it is
subordinate to that workmanship which would continue of its own will even
if not paid for.

The craftsman has an image of the completed product, and even though he   *5*
does not make it all, he sees the place of his part in the whole, and thus understands the meaning of his exertion in terms of that whole. The satisfaction
he has in the result infuses the means of achieving it, and in this way his work
is not only meaningful to him but also partakes of the consummatory satisfaction he has in the product. If work, in some of its phases, has the taint of tra-
vail and vexation and mechanical drudgery, still the craftsman is carried over
these junctures by keen anticipation. He may even gain positive satisfaction
from encountering a resistance and conquering it, feeling his work and will as
powerfully victorious over the recalcitrance of materials and the malice of things.
Indeed, without this resistance he would gain less satisfaction in being finally
victorious over that which at first obstinately resists his will.

George Mead has stated this kind of aesthetic experience as involving the   *6*
power "to catch the enjoyment that belongs to the consummation, the outcome, of an undertaking and to give to the implements, the objects that are
instrumental in the undertaking, and to the acts that compose it something of
the joy and satisfaction that suffuse its successful accomplishment."

III. The workman is free to begin his work according to his own plan and,   *7*
during the activity by which it is shaped, he is free to modify its form and the
manner of its creation. In both these senses, Henri De Man observed, "plan
and performance are one," and the craftsman is master of the activity and of
himself in the process. This continual joining of plan and activity brings even
more firmly together the consummation of work and its instrumental activi-

ties, infusing the latter with the joy of the former. It also means that his sphere of independent action is large and rational to him. He is responsible for its outcome and free to assume that responsibility. His problems and difficulties must be solved by him, in terms of the shape he wants the final outcome to assume.

IV. The craftsman's work is thus a means of developing his skill, as well as   8
a means of developing himself as a man. It is not that self-development is an ulterior goal, but that such development is the cumulative result obtained by devotion to and practice of his skills. As he gives it the quality of his own mind and skill, he is also further developing his own nature; in this simple sense, he lives in and through his work, which confesses and reveals him to the world.

V. In the craftsman pattern there is no split of work and play, of work and   9
culture. If play is supposed to be an activity, exercised for its own sake, having no aim other than gratifying the actor, then work is supposed to be an activity performed to create economic value or for some other ulterior result. Play is something you do to be happily occupied, but if work occupies you happily, it is also play, although it is also serious, just as play is to the child. "Really free work, the work of a composer, for example," Marx once wrote of Fourier's notions of work and play, 'is damned serious work, intense strain.' The simple self-expression of play and the creation of ulterior value of work are combined in work-as-craftsmanship. The craftsman or artist expresses himself at the same time and in the same act as he creates value. His work is a poem in action. He is at work and at play in the same act.

"Work" and "culture" are not, as Gentile has held, separate spheres, the first   10
dealing with means, the second with ends in themselves; as Tilgher, Sorel, and others have indicated, either work or culture may be an end in itself, a means, or may contain segments of both ends and means. In the craft model of activity, "consumption" and "production" are blended in the same act; active craftsmanship, which is both play and work, is the medium of culture; and for the craftsman there is no split between the worlds of culture and work.

VI. The craftsman's work is the mainspring of the only life he knows; he   11
does not flee from work into a separate sphere of leisure; he brings to his nonworking hours the values and qualities developed and employed in his working time. His idle conversation is shop talk; his friends follow the same lines of work as he, and share a kinship of feeling and thought. The leisure William Morris called for was "leisure to think about our work, that faithful daily companion. . . ."

In order to give his work the freshness of creativity, the craftsman must at   12
times open himself up to those influences that only affect us when our attentions are relaxed. Thus for the craftsman, apart from mere animal rest, leisure may occur in such intermittent periods as are necessary for individuality in his work. As he brings to his leisure the capacity and problems of his work, so he brings back into work those sensitivities he would not gain in periods of high, sustained tension necessary for solid work.

"The world of art," wrote Paul Bourget, speaking of America, "requires less   13 self-consciousness—an impulse of life which forgets itself, the alternation of dreamy idleness with fervid execution." The same point is made by Henry James, in his essay on Balzac, who remarks that we have practically lost the faculty of attention, meaning . . . "that unstrenuous, brooking sort of attention required to produce or appreciate works of art." Even rest, which is not so directly connected with work itself as a condition of creativity is animal rest, made secure and freed from anxiety by virtue of work done—in Tilgher's words, "a sense of peace and calm which flows from all well-regulated, disciplined work done with a quiet and contented mind."

Considerations

1. Consulting a good unabridged dictionary, compare the definitions of *craft* and *craftsmanship* with C. Wright Mills's article. Describe the similarities and differences you discover. Do the differences say anything about the changes in society since the Renaissance?
2. Mills's essay is taken from his book entitled *White Collar*. Define *white collar* work. What changes does Mills's essay suggest for the traditional distinction between white and blue collar work?
3. What assumptions does Mills (or, perhaps, the society from which the idea of craft grew) make about human nature? Discuss each assumption by referring to one of the six ideals of craft.

Connections

1. C. Wright Mills describes an older ideal of work, that of craftsmanship. Where can we find *craft* in modern work options? Use the interviews and your own work experiences to illustrate your point. You may want to conclude by observing where craft can still be found today. What does its scarcity say in the modern world?
2. To what degree does the work of computer programming, as discussed in Chapter 7, The Nature of Intelligence, meet the requirements for a craft as described by Mills?
3. Describe how well Mills's ideals of craftsmanship are fulfilled by the work arrangements at the American Velvet company.
4. Clearly, the work of women on the global assembly line does not meet Mills's criteria of craft. Describe the social, political, and economic conditions responsible for keeping these ideals unfulfilled for the women workers. Be sure to tie your descriptions into Mills's six criteria.
5. Compare and contrast Karl Marx's and Mills's theories. Can they be seen as complementary, one describing fulfillment and the other frustration of the same ideals? In other words, would fulfilling Mills's ideals of craft solve the problems of alienation as described by Marx?

The Maggot Principle

William O'Rourke

I do two things each day that I hate to do. I go to sleep and I wake up. *1*
Knowing this, it is not as easy to rail against that which I do that I have no
wish to do. We are all extorted by chance, though the guise makes a difference,
and it is not unusual to come to a place and find yourself engaged in an enterprise opposite your original intentions.

A small town is different from a large city in that any grotesques you see, *2*
you are likely to see again, as in a recurrent bad dream. And this is not even a
small town, but a summer resort, the bait on the tip of this hook of New England. When winter comes, those who remain are the stragglers any traveling
thing leaves behind. You may think of touring circuses, fairs, religious zealots
with tent compounds, or a retreating army, and that is close to the situation.
There is a meanness in the shut-up buildings: plywood over the windows as if
the glass has grown cataracts. What makes people stay is the same inclination
that brings them to the lip of an extinct volcano or a notable man's grave.

Through the winter there is only one institution that functions; it is the Fish *3*
Factory. It appears another ruin, cited for extinction. Listing walls notwithstanding, it still prospers within. The building is kept together by what it is:
three floors of cold storage is its center and the ice gives solid structure. If the
freezers were shut off, it is said by those who have worked there longest, the
building would collapse. The ice is like anger, which steadies men.

The employees of the Fish Factory have a grim cheerfulness that comes to *4*
people who are glad to have a job, any job. The manager who hired me, seeing
drawn across my face a map of Midwestern industry, advised me to take other
employment, if I could find it, though his expression was that of the only gro-
cer in town who tells you to buy your produce elsewhere if you don't like the
price.

The stench, the unskinned odor, though never gotten used to, becomes fa- *5*
miliar and then unrecognized. My training began in the packing room, where
lobster tails are weighed and sorted and put in packages ready for stores. One
thousand frozen lobster tails smell like caged white mice. Stainless steel tables, a cement floor, Toledo scales, gray plastic pans, and cartons of frozen
lobster tails from South Africa. Who packed these across the Atlantic? I won-

*William O'Rourke (b. 1945) was born in Chicago and educated at the Univer-
sity of Missouri and Columbia University. He is the author of* The Harrisburg 7
and the New Catholic Left *(1972); the novel* The Meekness of Isaac *(1974), which
won a New York State Council on the Arts CAPS award; and the novel* Idle Hands
(1981). He is the editor of On the Job: Fiction About Work by Contemporary
American Writers *(1977), from which this story comes. Currently he is an assistant professor in the department of English at the University of Notre Dame.*

der as I crack a block of frozen lobster tails across the edge of the table. It shatters, an ancient clay pot filled with coins, into fifty little tails.

Could any machine equal the chaotic precision of four people sorting lob-   6
ster tails? Flinging them, after checking their weight, into eight stainless steel pans, separated in two by wooden dividers. The air is as full of flying lobster tails as the sky above Kennedy Airport is with planes.

Casey, an aging lesbian, who does the final weighing, has masculinized every   7
woman in the room by circumcising their names. Alice is Al, Lucy is Lu, Freida is Fred. Casey is boss of the radio, a tiny plastic thing that sits on a crate. Its cord snakes up the wall to a high socket as if the music coming from it held it erect like a summoned cobra.

Frozen lobster tails hit pans sounding like cutlery dropped in a sink. The   8
windows are covered with polyethylene; a few late summer flies cling to it. Furry, they evolve short cilia against the cold; and it is cold in the large room. A heater suspended from the ceiling comes on at intervals suddenly, like a man bolting up from troubled sleep.

There are the stuffers, usually four, lobster tails piled in front of them. The   9
tails come wrapped in cellophane, and the stuffers put them into boxes and then onto a conveyor belt that brings them to two elderly women who select an additional lobster tail from one of the pans I and another have been filling, which will bring the weight up to what is marked on the box. From there to Casey and then through a machine that seals the ends of the cardboard boxes. The air is filled with the smell of melting wax. An old man, Sammy, takes them into the freezer, where they wait to be shipped out. On the wall is taped the record amount of lobster tails ever to be packed in a day.

Four of us, poker-faced, stand around a table, dealing lobster tails into pans.   10
Each tail is given an inspection, a multiplicity of single observations of identical articles. Having seen each for a second, you have seen one for eight hours. The dark brown carapace which is spotted with reds and greens is no longer a crustacean's but an insect's. The white meat of the lobster is the starch inside a withered twig. The little fins folded over in death across its belly are the hands of children in their abbreviated coffins.

At the end of the day, when the room is filled with fluorescent light, a gid-   11
diness sets in, a hilarity takes over. After a spurt of feverish activity, crackling laughter. I have seen it happen elsewhere, this spasm of silent activity ended by laughter. The infirm have it, the insane and the employed.

"Oh, look at this, Casey," a small Portuguese woman says upon finding a   12
lobster tail brown with eggs. The women gather around her as around a newborn. "They should have thrown her back in, the damn fisherman," Casey says, "I've seen them sit on the dock during summer and scrib off the eggs so they could sell them. They'll kill them all off." The women continue to coo over the lobster, halved as ever the babe would have been if Solomon had carried out his intentions.

I keep forgetting these are corpses. Dismembered ones at that, since they're   13
frozen, hard little shards of ice. Sometimes, through excessive handling and being in a lot that is unpacked but not repacked, and then returned to the freezer

to come out again and not find its way into a finished package, they get to be a little limp. But these are supposed to be terminally discarded.

There is a break at ten after beginning at eight in the morning. The men go   *14* for coffee, the women into a room that has benches. The packing room empties and takes on a coldness that is present whenever humans depart, like a fire gone completely out.

There is an hour for lunch. Atop a nearby firehouse a siren screams out noon.   *15* A generator that is hooked up to nothing, and its wail is mechanized frustration. It gives a split-second warning of its coming, a mere electrical click, and as I walk away from the factory to a luncheonette I put my gloved hands up to my ears. It takes fifteen steps for it to end. Every day at noon; a reminder, a flag at half-mast; whatever machines are buried in me mourn with it.

I worry for the first week that my work in the Fish Factory will brand me.   *16* That the stink will be too odious to those not directly involved with the work. That my uniform of boots and sweaters and coarse coat with a cap pulled over my hair will ostracize me, make me stand out, put the town off-limits. But the populace surprises me and takes no notice. Even when I get to the luncheonette, the stools next to me are not vacated, even though I smell of death and flounder. Soon I have no sense of shame.

Walking the one main street of town, I see the daily grotesques. The man   *17* with his hair shaved away from two sullen lumps that show the remains of their stitches like the teeth marks a child leaves playfully on your arm. Some hack's proud work, though I cannot know what ill caused the surgery, though the man has an addled smile. The main street of town is the common recreation area for a number of lost homes. There is the man with the nervous disorder who has to generate more stationary thrust than a Saturn rocket before he can propel himself ten feet. Then he rests against the fender of a car. He once asked me a question and spoke so fast that I had to learn to listen to him. By slowing down his speech, a seventy-eight record to thirty-three-and-a-third, I could understand him. But then the only answer his question required was "No." By the time I reach the luncheonette the parade is half over, though usually at the counter there is a gentle spastic who is having a cup of coffee, continually stirring his sugar, sounding all the while through my desiccated meal like he is calling a meeting to order.

The Fish Factory system can assimilate anyone immediately. Without no-   *18* tice, one afternoon the packing room emptied out and we filed through the door, up narrow steps attached to the outside of the building. High tide is in, right up to the pilings which begin where the building stops. There is a long wharf extending into the bay. Next to the Fish Factory is a boat-restoring yard, and a large fishing boat lies beached on its side, a peeling underbelly exposed like an obese patient waiting for an injection. The steps we climb continue over the roof and up to a high third floor to which I have never come. From here everything is motionless, stilled by distance, and silent except for the squalls of the gulls who perch around and along a track that descends to the wharf. There is a large cage that is run on cable, ascending now, loaded with fresh fish. The trap slams against a metal tank and then the load of fish drops. Hollow sounds, distant, far-off explosions. The cage descends again as we enter the room, leaving the gulls to rip the fish that make a path of carcasses underneath the cage's track.

Machinery, water on the floor, mounds of ice go undiminished in the cold. *19* Cartons thrown down a hole in the ceiling; Dominic, the foreman, herds his gang together, the old women beside the conveyor, herring comes over the elevated ridge on one belt like an unexpected assault and flops into cartons that are to hold fifty pounds each. They are sent down over rollers to be weighed and then transferred to carts, and when fifteen are stacked they are hauled to the freezer. I lift them from the weighing table to the carts. Round silver scales stick to my black gloves. Soon they are covered by this soft mail. The boxes of herring get backed up. "Stop the belt!" Dominic yells. Herring spills over the filled boxes onto the floor, sounding like strokes of a tired whipping. They are scooped up later with a shovel. It is hard work and doesn't slow down unless the belts stop. During the pause my wrists ache, the delayed burning that cold produces when you just start to get warm. The body gets used to it, new rhythms are learned. I keep forgetting the fish are dead, I pay such little attention to them, lost to the rapid motions that are required to keep up. They do not have whites to their eyes, but are clear. All their small mouths are open. Thousands and thousands of herring. My feet slip on the ones fallen around me. The iron wheels of the cart flatten them. My heels gash open orange bellies. I get used to the queasy footing.

Three young men are clustered around the end of the initial conveyor belt. *20* They wear thick aprons and gloves, shoving boxes just filled down the line. At times they find an odd fish among the school of herring and they are discarded into one large box. The monster box. They look like excited physicians throwing spare organs back over their shoulders.

Sarge trips the cage, releasing fish into the tank. There is a fury behind the *21* work that is always present during a siege. The long whine of the steel cable, the crash of the cage against metal, the thud of two hundred pounds of herring. They drop onto the fish below, which are continually slithering out a small opening onto the conveyor belt. In their convex and concave mesh they resemble the race of the sperm for the egg, down the narrow channel, each forcing the other with helpless collaborators' weight. Cattle do the same thing in their stalls that lead to slaughterhouses. A Judas goat is not necessary in every case. Confined numbers can cause deadly momentum.

We get caught up. Over two hundred barrels of herring packed. Dominic, *22* now bored with driving the crew, descends to the floor beneath and I wander over to see the beginnings of the process of which I am the end. I pass the monster box like a cemetery a young boy encounters unavoidably at night on his way home. A spiny fish that still breathes like a tattered bellows. A starfish adhering to a pink stingray like a sea spider. A squid twisted around a scup. Kelp forms a reticule around the ooze. The monster box: a synopsis of a nightmare.

There is a tank into which large cod have been thrown that were caught *23* with the herring. One cod has already been gutted. Its emptied carcass, which is now nothing but a wide flat head and a long handle of backbone, stretches out on the cement like a lost shovel you find rotting in the ground after a winter's snow has gone and uncovered it. The two filleted sections rest atop a crate. They are washed off and very white.

In the tank are the sleek cod, so huge they seem after the herring which never *24* got beyond eight inches. Big-mouthed, an olive-drab color without any of the iridescence of the herring. Some of the cod have, stuck halfway out of their mouths, three or four half-swallowed herring. Death has prevented the cod from consuming them. A macabre *in flagrante delicto*. Stories to inspire chastity in my high-school youth leap to mind like spawning salmon. During a Retreat, a gray priest telling of two "fornicating youths in the back seat of a car, crushed by a brakeless truck, found by their parents and the authorities still locked in their carnal embrace, their sin embossed in death, their guilt preserved as surely as by the lava of Vesuvius. . . ."

I pick up one of the cod from whose mouth four half-swallowed herring pro- *25* trude, and in death his startled eyes give back some excuse of innocence, like all the heads at that boys' school seemed to want to extend by the amused and shocked shaking of their heads. *Somebody stuffed them in my mouth. I can't even breathe. . . .*

I try to pull one herring out by its tail, till its reluctance overwhelms me, *26* so tenacious is their graved epoxy, and I drop the cod back in the tank. I had begun to get an erection.

It is seven-fifty in the morning and I am the first to leave tracks in the snow. *27* As I come around the corner of the pump house a man leans out the window and pours a coffee can full of steaming water over a pipe's frozen valve.

May, an old woman who is very short and whenever she looks at you to speak *28* she turns her head, so it appears she's looking at you from around some non-existent corner, says to me as I weigh lobster, "Maybe they'll give us medals depending on how many lobsters we get done."

How could people have worked eighteen hours a day? The same incompre- *29* hension as a soldier has viewing the armor of a knight. Finally five o'clock comes; it is terrible; the death wish of killing time. We file from the room each day like surgeons who keep losing their patients under the knife.

The men who assemble near a truck in the early morning, cold vapors seep- *30* ing from their youths, the departing cast of their slumbering hopes, come rubbing their hands, standing near the empty trailer like seconds who arrive early for a duel in order to survey the clearing.

The resignation of men before they take to their jobs. It is the same, regard- *31* less of the task, as long as it is one they have resigned themselves to. Shrugged shoulders, jokes made, sour as coffee grinds that collapse garbage bags. They shame reluctance by action. We are used to earth's passings, its relays, its handings-over.

So we load the truck. The freezer door swings open onto the loading dock. *32* Aluminum tracks are set up down the middle of the empty trailer, the truck driver and myself at the far end. An airconditioning unit sticks out, for this truck carries perishables, the cold air channeled down the length of the trailer by a canvas tube that hangs close to the ceiling. It is primitive but works, something Archimedes would have figured out. The truckdriver and I do not introduce ourselves, but the speed with which we handle the cartons describes us to one another, the archaic dance of manual labor. Midway, he tells me his name and asks for mine, and because I am ten years younger than he and youth will be forgiven most anything, he overlooks the length of my hair, and because I will take eight cartons to his seven (a subtle dowry I have to pay because it is *his* truck). The others he has met before and for the sake of good comradeship they recall him, or if not exactly him, a truckdriver they did remember, as if it is good enough to say kind things about a member of the species if not the exact individual.

The truck fills up completely, a queen bee brimming with eggs, and for a 33
while we are somber with the idea of procreation, stacking the cartons, but it wanes.

"Boy, whoever it is that runs that coffee place, is that a man or a woman?" 34
the truckdriver asks.

I reply it is indeed a woman but in a voice full of regret at her mannishness, 35
the same tone a hunter uses when he speaks of a favorite coon dog that has lost the ability to follow the scent. With this cleared up, other testings go on, exchanged assurances in the muted air of the trailer as we pile up frozen whiting.

"You don't exactly clean up around here," Sammy had said. Clean up. Hy- 36
giene. Money douche. Five-dollar ablutions.

Sarge talks like a motor that will never quite turn over. Short, breathy sen- 37
tences that end completely before they are finished, then start up again, only to end. He tells about an old man who would pay money for your socks, the mangier the better, which he would stuff into his mouth. Sarge makes movements with his hand like he's tossing peanuts in between his teeth. The truckdriver tells about a friend of his who would walk twenty miles through a blizzard if he knew there was a sure piece of ass waiting for him. Sarge, because of his excited speech, seems to bubble, telling about a retarded girl who has to be taken out of school because she would remove her clothes in class.

"Slap. Her titties." Sarge using his hands like there's fluttering wash hang- 38
ing below his chest. "Hump. Around in. The aisles." Sarge juggling his three hundred pounds around the loading dock as if he were offering his thrusting middle to a fire hydrant. Common men load trucks and we are common men.

Who saw the first one? Behind me, at the table of stuffers, someone says 39
quietly, "Is that a maggot?" Lippy, who sounds like Radio Free Europe jammed by the Russians, replies, "Naaaahissparrtaadulobstir," and brushes aside whatever it is.

It is a bad day for lobster packing; the law of averages had given us the 40
wrong sizes, too many big ones, too many small ones, not enough medium-sized and the correct weight was hard to come by. A computer could figure the variations possible to get four separate lobster tails to weigh out to 6.8 ounces and it is easy if you have all different sizes; but a preponderance of one will impede the natural selection, and boxes are rejected, and the race of 6.8-ounce

boxes of Cap'n Ahab's South African Lobster Tails will die out, disappear from the face of the earth, if the balance in sizes is not restored. Boxes would come back and be emptied out, repacked and sent back again — not many, but just enough to make it a bad day, like yesterday, when the same thing happened. There was a box of lobster tails that had been put back in the freezer the day before that had begun to thaw out and so there would be today.

"Look," Casey let out with an unaccustomed girlish screech, "there *are* 41 maggots!" She held up a blue box on which could be seen a small silhouette climbing along one wall, like a mountain climber descending a sheer cliff.

The stuffers pushed aside the pile of lobster tails, and there on the top of 42 that stainless-steel table are about a dozen maggots. Maggots! Though on top of the bright silver table they look like shoots of wild rice. Their backs hump like babies flexing little fists.

"It's these loose ones," Casey yells, holding up an almost completely thawed 43 lobster tail that bends over in her hand like a man collapsed across barbed wire.

"I told Dominic they were getting no good, but he wanted to get rid of them," 44 Casey goes on exultantly, glad to have her day's grumblings vindicated. Maggots in the lobster tails! That'll show them!"

Maggots. An American housewife, fresh from Food World, comes into her 45 kitchen, puts down her brown sacks, takes off her car coat, sets aside her new checkbook which pictures in color the first A-Bomb explosion on each check, and gets out a box of Cap'n Ahab's Apartheid Lobster Tails, tearing its quick-zip opener to thaw out her hors d'oeuvres for tonight's pre-bridge dinner party, and out crawls a maggot. Her throat parches. She steps back, irises widening. She puts out a hand to reach for the absolute axis that Food World spins on, and finds it gone! Stumbling, only to knock over her Osterizer, which trips the switch that sets growling her disposal, and finding nothing to cling to as the terror of that vision becomes entire and lucid, cracking open an evil that falls onto her Teflon mind like a black egg, she grabs her Arctic Chest's door handle, reeling, swings it open and collapses at its feet, slowly being covered with ice cubes from the mini-igloo-icemaker till she revives.

What must she think we are? We who have packed MAGGOTS into her lobster 46 tails. That our factory is a geodesic dome of cobwebs. Our lobsters hauled in fetid garbage cans. She sees not ground zero, but the periphery, the sores, the ooze, the tracks left by the skittering rats which imprint the new cuneiform on the clay tablets of Mesopotamia!

But all the while, it is just our Fish Factory. Quiet as a battlefield when they 47 come to strip the weapons from the dead. Clean, brightly lit, the cement floor washed as spotlessly as front walks by summer gardeners. And on the silver table the dozen grains of wild rice.

Casey is still yelling, vilifying Dominic, as if he is the First Cause, the un- 48 caused cause, the harborer of spontaneous generation.

I hear a faint rambunctious tapping. I look over to the window covered with 49 cloudy plastic, and trapped in there are several hairy flies. One of whose knocking against that plastic sounds as proud as an old man who has been accused of being the impregnator of a young girl thought to be virginal. A Joseph fly.

Dominic comes through the door, his upper and lower jaw meshing badly, 50 the missing teeth cause his bite to be sinister. He grumbles against the elements, that it is not his fault, that it is the general policy to use lobster tails if they have thawed out a bit, possibly exposed to contamination by our little club of flies. He rips open sealed cartons and discovers no maggots in them, but Casey takes a box and finds a maggot perched on a tail.

Dominic's broken face for a minute resembles Robert McNamara's as he stares   *51* at the pile of boxes ready to be taken into the freezer. A whole day's work! His brow knits into an abacus, cost accounting, tabulating, the number of employees, wages, hours worked, cost of recycling, and makes the humane, the only decision: Check all the boxes! Open them up and check them and repack them all. He continues to mutter against the cosmos and quits the room, a king who chooses not to see the execution he has just decreed.

We all set to the sealed boxes. Savagely tearing them open, transfixed smiles   *52* as we ravage the work we did, a chance to open what we heretofore had only been able to close. The battered boxes we empty lay at our feet like the fruit that falls too soon from the tree and is trampled by the pickers. Young men grunt as they rip into large cartons which contain the smaller baby-blue boxes. The first minutes of this are elating, then the dark zeal abates and the monotony that is our true condition reclaims us. No other maggots are discovered.

Casey looks at the rising pyramid of repacked cartons with a bitterness that   *53* I know can only mean she let one contaminated box through, to lurk on the shelf of Food World, under the frosty breath of their air conditioning which continually bathes the produce with a white eminence like the red glow of a sacristy lamp. The unsuspecting mother will pick it out and take it into her home and finally unwrap for herself a putrescence that even if hell were our three floors of freezers could not be preserved forever from her gaze. We deal in perishables.

The repacking resumes its usual pace. Any lobster tail that is even partially   *54* thawed is discarded. The work is done. The day over. Sammy hauls the last load into the freezer.

"Maybe we should tell the Board of Health," May whispers around her in-   *55* visible corner, but the refrain is not picked up. If someone tells, and they do something about it, if they close this place down, then we won't have jobs, and anyway, nothing really happened. The maggots were here, but they didn't get through; the maggots didn't get into Food World. If they got into Food World and crawled along America's kitchen counter that would be one thing, but they were stopped *here*, where they began. At the Fish Factory.

Considerations

1. What is the maggot principle that the story is named for? Detail how it works in the Fish Factory and how the author implies that it extends elsewhere?
2. Look for the recurring images in the story — metaphors, similes, adjectives — especially those associated with the Fish Factory. What do they tell you about the narrator's attitude toward work?
3. When first reading "The Maggot Principle," the opening paragraph may seem

a somewhat funny or odd philosophical abstraction. After reading the story, decide how these abstractions connect to the story, how they take form in the concrete details of life at the Fish Factory.

Connections

1. How does the narrator of "The Maggot Principle" fight the boredom of routine which Mike Lefevre complains about? Refer to specific problems Lefevre complains of and the specific tactics the narrator uses.
2. After determining what you think the maggot principle is, decide how this principle connects work in America to work in other countries, such as the work described in "The Figueroa Family," "Life on the Global Assembly Line," or other work suggested by "The Maggot Principle."
3. Does the work in the Fish Factory share any characteristics with other work described in this chapter? Describe specific details from each piece, telling what they have in common.
4. Among the other workers described and interviewed in this chapter, which views work most like the narrator of "The Maggot Principle"? Give specific passages to back up your comparison.
5. After determining what you think the maggot principle is, decide if this principle explains any of the discontent or frustration experienced by the American workers described and interviewed in this chapter. Refer to specific comments or descriptions to establish this connection.

Further Connections

1. Some of the workers interviewed and described in this chapter are obviously more fulfilled in their work than others. Write an essay grouping these people into more and less satisfied workers, describing for each group what seems to explain their satisfaction or dissatisfaction.
2. What does mechanization have to do with the quality of work available today? You'll need to narrow and specify your field of discussion here, and choose your examples carefully. For example, you could focus on mechanization in agricultural work, in industrial work, or in a single country, such as Mexico.
3. Using the interviews in which workers seem basically dissatisfied, develop a classification for the problems these workers have. Then ask whether labor unions could do anything to solve these problems. You may want to consult current literature on unions.
4. In explaining the self-chastisement of unemployed people, Frank Trippett claims that "the nation has not relinquished its basic view of work as sacred and worklessness as sin" (*Time*, Jan. 18, 1982, p. 90). Based on your

readings in this chapter, do you think this view of work and worklessness is limited to the United States? Or is it rooted somewhere deeper in Western civilization, or even in human nature?

5. Agricultural workers' lives differ in significant ways from the lives of industrial or white collar workers. Drawing on articles from this chapter, compare two or three of these work categories. You will need to narrow your comparison to a specific topic you can manage. You may want to use theoretical treatments as well as the interviews and descriptions. For example, you could compare the life of steel worker Mike Lefevre with secretary Anne Bogan or with farmer Arturo Figueroa.

6. Sociologist Amitai Etzioni has written that defining the *project*, or central concern of a society, helps us understand that society's work. So, for instance, the project of many Third World nations is growing food to survive; the project of the United States during World War II was to defeat the Axis powers. Drawing on articles in this chapter and on other sources if you wish, define the central project of modern American society.

7. In light of the evidence from Chapter 4, The Urban Experience, how do the development of work and urban life influence one another?

8. Read Jane Jacobs's article in Chapter 4, The Urban Experience. How are the economic dimensions discussed there connected to work?

9. Given the evidence in Chapter 8, The Treatment of Cancer, what connections can you see between modern work and the increasing occurrence of cancer?

10. After reading about power in Chapter 1, The Dimensions of Power, write an essay exploring the power struggle between workers and owners. Refer to specific workers' experiences to support your thesis and to one or more theories if you wish.

Extensions

1. A serious labor problem in the United States is currently arousing fierce debate: the hiring of undocumented workers (illegal aliens) for wages and under conditions below accepted standards. The labor unions argue that this takes jobs from U.S. citizens. Social workers point out that it leads to exploitation of the illegals. And many farmers and factory owners argue that they must have this cheap labor to survive. Read current positions, including the continuing Congressional debate, on this difficult problem. Analyze these positions, and then propose a policy to mediate the real needs of all parties involved. You might begin your search by consulting the *Public Affairs Information Service (PAIS)*, the *New York Times Index*, and the *Monthly Catalogue of Government Documents*.

2. Karl Marx says in "Alienated Labor," "The product of labor is labor given embodiment in a material form; this product is the objectification of labor" (para. 2). Research the philosophical background for this statement in the work of the German idealist Georg Wilhelm Friedrich Hegel. How is Marx drawing on Hegel when he makes this claim? Do any of the inter-

views in this chapter suggest that this claim might be more than a purely abstract one? Or does is it belong exclusively to nineteenth-century German philosophy? You may want to consult a good overview of Hegel, such as chapters 9–11, volume VII, of Frederick Copleston's *History of Philosophy*, or chapters 3–4, volume II, in John Plamenatz's *Man and Society* (in particular, the chapter titled "The Social and Political Philosophy of Hegel"). You could consult one of the many books on Marx and Hegel or at least the articles on Hegel and Marx in the *Encyclopedia of Philosophy*.

3. In Chapters 4 and 5 of his last major work, *Civilization and Its Discontents*, Sigmund Freud gives a hypothetical history of the beginnings of work, explaining why and how people first began to work together. This history seems quite different than the one Marx would propose, were he asked about it. Read Marx's "Alienated Labor" carefully and develop the hypothetical history of work's origins you think he would offer. Then contrast this history with Freud's. Finally, decide which history you find more convincing.

4. In his article, "Alienation Under Capitalism" (pp. 120–151 of his book, *The Sane Society*), psychologist Erich Fromm describes two kinds of economic systems: one based on use and one on consumption. Explain what he says about this important contrast. Decide whether the economy you live in is dominated by use or by consumption motives.

5. Frederick W. Taylor says that workers are wrong to assume that increased productivity will destroy jobs in the industry in question. He offers the shoe industry as a counter-example to this assumption. What historical evidence can you find to confirm or contradict Taylor's argument here? Have industrialists ever used increased productivity to cut labor costs and thus eliminated jobs? Or has increased productivity usually resulted in more jobs? The shoe industry, the steel industry, or a more hi-tech industry, like semiconductors, would be examples to study. You could begin your search by consulting the *Directory of Industry Data Sources* and then the *Business Periodicals Index* under the key words *labor productivity*.

6. Find John McDermott's book, *The Crisis in the Working Class, and Some Arguments for a New Labor Movement*. McDermott discusses why trade unions do not seem to be solving workers' basic problems. Looking into current labor statistics, try to confirm or contradict McDermott's conclusion that labor unions have effectively organized workers only in those industries that can easily pass on costs to consumers. Sources for these statistics might include the *Public Affairs Information Service (PAIS)*, the *Monthly Catalogue of Government Documents*, or *American Statistics Index*.

7. In the oral history, *Not Working*, by Harry Maurer, unemployed people describe their feelings about being unable to work. Drawing on a few of these interviews, or on interviews you conduct with unemployed people, decide how unemployment affects your understanding of work motivation. Focusing on what the unemployed workers seem to miss will be important here.

8. In "Deindustrialization and the Abandonment of Community," Barry Bluestone describes one of the social costs of deindustrialization, or plant closing: modern American workers have become a "nation of migrants." Research current news articles, films, television programs, or a combination of these, looking for images of the modern American worker. How is

this migratory character treated in these media? Are solutions to the problem being offered? You may begin your search by consulting the *New York Times Index* or articles in *Time* and *Newsweek* you find listed in the *Readers' Guide.*

9. One reason to justify the multinationals' use of Third World women as cheap labor is that the populations of these countries are "outgrowing [their] agricultural capacity," and so the women need an economic alternative (AID staffer Emmy Simmons, as reported by Barbara Ehrenreich and Annette Fuentes further along in their article). Check this claim with the evidence presented elsewhere on Third World agriculture. Has expanding population really been responsible for the changing patterns in Third World agriculture? You will probably need to consider the connections between agricultural and industrial development in these nations. How do these developments affect the choices workers in these nations have? Two good sources to begin with are Erick P. Eckholm's study, "The Dispossessed of the Earth: Land Reform and Sustainable Development," and Gilbert Goodman's book, *The Poverty of Nations.* You could also search in the *Public Affairs Information Service (PAIS)* and *Predicasts International.*

10. Pick one or two multinational corporations to study. Using both government and industry data, trace the moves your chosen corporation(s) have made since World War II (or some shorter period if that is justified). Where have they created jobs and where have they eliminated them? As far as you can tell, what relation have these moves had to labor issues? Three good sources for beginning your research are the *Business Periodicals Index*, the *Wall Street Journal Index*, and *Predicasts International.*

11. Research current experiments in worker participation, often called *economic democracy*, and choose a few that most interest you. Do you think economic democracy would solve the problem of alienation as Marx describes it? You may begin your research by looking in the *Business Periodicals Index* under these key words: *participative management, team work, quality circles,* and *employee ownership.*

12. American music is a rich source for images of work. Find several songs that deal with the working life, and carefully detail the scene they describe. You'll want to limit yourself somehow: by period (music of the Great Depression, or contemporary music), by musical genre (blues, folk, country), or even by composer or group (Leadbelly, Woody Guthrie, or the Grateful Dead).

13. The increasing number of women working, as well as the increasing variety of work they do, is among the most dramatic shifts in recent American society. Find data reporting these changes. Then write an essay categorizing the major ways in which womens' work options have changed in the United States. You may begin searching for this data in the *Monthly Catalogue of Government Documents* or if it is available, the *American Statistics Index.*

14. Strategies for managing work are evolving today, even where current definitions of ownership remain unchanged. Find data reporting these changing management plans. Then write an essay describing new management options. Clark Kerr and Jerome Rosow's anthology, *Work in America: The*

Decade Ahead and the key words in the *Business Periodicals Index,* listed in question 11, will provide a good start for your research.

15. Ehrenreich and Fuentes describe the practice of "using up" young women in Third World labor markets — laying them off before they accrue any seniority benefits. Investigate practices common in hiring American teenagers to see if this practice is used here as well (fast food restaurants are often accused of this). Then compare and contrast the employment practices in the different nations. The *Business Periodicals Index* and *Business Abstracts* will give you a start on this research.

16. The nineteenth-century writer William Morris was associated with a revival in the English crafts movement. Research this historical revival, then describe the ideals of work that Morris and his circles were attempting to teach and fulfill.

17. Further on in their article excerpted in this chapter Ehrenreich and Fuentes describe the roles international financial institutions (the World Bank, the United Nations Industrial Development Organization, etc.), and governments of both developing and developed nations play in shaping work on the global assembly line. Find their article in its entirety; originally printed in *Ms.* magazine, vol. 9, pp. 52–59 (January, 1981), reprinted in *The Crisis in American Institutions* (1979), eds. Jerome H. Skolnick and Elliot Curie, pp. 373–389, and in its fullest form published as a booklet, *Women in the Global Factory* (Boston: South End Press, 1983). Then find details of the governmental and international decisions regarding industries moving to Third World nations. Try to confirm or contradict the claims made by Ehrenreich and Fuentes by referring to these decisions. The *Public Affairs Information Service* will be a good place to start this research.

Suggestions for Further Reading

Applegath, John. *Working Free: Practical Alternatives to the 9 to 5 Job.* New York: AMACON, 1982. An exploration of alternative work individuals can develop for themselves.

Bluestone, Barry, and Bennett Harrison. *The Deindustrialization of America: Plant Closings, Community Abandonment,* and *the Dismantling of Basic Industry.* New York: Basic Books, 1982. A detailed account of capital mobility, which is changing work all over the world by moving jobs.

Collins, Joseph. *What Difference Could a Revolution Make: Food and Farming in the New Nicaragua.* 2nd ed. San Francisco: Institute for Food and Development Policy, 1985. A study of work in an agriculturally-based society soon after a popular revolution.

Dahl, Robert A. *A Preface to Economic Democracy.* Berkeley: University of California Press, 1985. An empirical and philosophical defense suggesting that only work-place democracy can truly reconcile the demands of liberty, justice, and efficiency.

Eckholm, Erick P. "The Dispossessed of the Earth: Land Reform and Sustainable Development." Washington, D.C.: Worldwatch Institute, 1979. A short paper exploring the ways in which access to the land affects the work and health of the most marginal workers, landless peasants.

Fromm, Erich. "Alienation Under Capitalism." in *The Sane Society*, pp. 120–151. New York: Holt, Rinehart, and Winston, 1955. Reprinted in *Man Alone*, edited by Eric and Mary Josephson, pp. 56–73. New York: Dell, 1962. Another look at alienation, discussing the psychological effects of its modern form.

Garson, Barbara. *All the Livelong Day: The Meaning and Demeaning of Routine Work*. New York: Penguin, 1977. Interviews with workers, offering more interviewer analysis than in Studs Terkel's *Working*.

Goodman, Gilbert. *The Poverty of Nations*. Ann Arbor, Mich.: Ann Arbor Press, 1960.

Halperin, Rhoda, and James Dow, eds. *Peasant Livelihood: Studies in Economic Anthropology and Cultural Ecology*. New York: St. Martin's Press, 1977. Several studies demonstrating anthropological method in the study of peasant work.

Jackall, Robert, and Henry M. Levin, eds. *Worker Cooperatives in America* Berkeley: University of California Press, 1984. A variety of studies investigating this growing phenomenon in American work.

Kerr, Clark, and Jerome M. Rosow, eds. *Work in America: The Decade Ahead*. New York: Van Nostrand Reinhold, 1979. These articles investigate ways in which work has changed and will change in the near future.

Laslett, Peter. "The Sovereignty of the Family." *The Listener* 63 (April 7, 1960):607–709. Reprinted as "The World We Have Lost" in *Man Alone*, edited by Eric and Mary Josephson. New York: Dell, 1962. A look at the ways in which family and work have differently engaged as society and economy have changed.

Maurer, Harry. *Not Working: An Oral History of the Unemployed*. New York: Holt, Rinehart, and Winston, 1979. These interviews include people who are not working for all kinds of reasons: being fired, being laid off, even having independent wealth.

McDermott, John. *The Crisis in the Working Class, and Some Arguments for a New Labor Movement*. Boston: South End Press, 1980. A discussion of where labor unions have failed in their purpose and promise.

The Nature
6 of Learning

Edited by **Michael Gustin**

The *tabula rasa* has served since Aristotle's time as a metaphor for the unformed mind of a child. Indeed, this view has found a strong loyal following through several centuries of philosophers, educators, and psychologists. But equally committed opponents have perceived children's minds in quite different ways and have developed methods for training those minds based on their perceptions. This controversy still simmers in the twentieth century; Aristotle's *tabula rasa* has lost the force of unquestioned authority but remains a handy metaphor, allowing us to speak generally of that systematic transmission of knowledge which we call education.

Modern developmental psychologists examine many aspects of a child's growth and transformation into an adult. However, the study of cognitive development has perhaps the most intriguing implications for parents, educators, and students — those most closely concerned with the knowledge that is scribbled on each of our blank slates. The breadth of this topic's appeal is revealed by the selections included in this chapter, authored by philosophers and psychologists concerned with child rearing and education. Of course, the ultimate source of relevance must be you, the reader. As college undergraduates, you have already endured over a dozen years of education influenced by the issues illustrated in these readings. The selections in this chapter cover the historical background of child study and some significant trends in twentieth-century developmental psychology.

The first two readings are excerpts from John Locke's *Some Thoughts Concerning Education* (1693) and Jean-Jacques Rousseau's *Émile* (1762). These texts contain more than advice about the intellectual training advised for aristocratic young men of the time; they are worth attention for at least two reasons: (1) while Rousseau was among the first thinkers to outline various stages of a young person's mental growth, Locke adhered to the established notion that a child was merely a miniature undisciplined adult; (2) some modern psychologists, such as Howard Gardner, acknowledge that Locke and Rousseau prefigure a twentieth-century split in developmental psychology between the environmental learning and cognitive structuralist schools.

The remaining selections offer an opportunity to explore writings of some modern psychologists exemplifying the opposing views suggested in the Locke and Rousseau passages. John B. Watson and B. F. Skinner, two of the most prominent figures in American behavioral psychology, reflect some concerns of environmental learning theorists. The articles by Jean Piaget and Bärbel Inhelder represent the most influential work by cognitive structuralists. Howard Gardner's "Unfolding or Teaching: On the Optimal Training of Artistic Skills" concludes the chapter, allowing the reader to draw together some of the theoretical strands outlined in earlier selections.

From *Some Thoughts Concerning Education*

John Locke

Playing in the *open Air*, has but this one Danger in it, that I know; and that *1* is, That when he is hot with running up and down, he should sit or lie down on the cold or moist Earth. This, I grant, and drinking cold Drink, when they are hot with Labour or Exercise, brings more People to the Grave, or to the Brink of it, by Fevers, and other Diseases, than any Thing I know. These Mischiefs are easily enough prevented whilst he is little, being then seldom out of sight. And if during his Childhood, he be constantly and rigorously kept from sitting on the Ground, or drinking any cold Liquor, whilst he is hot, the Custom of Forbearing grown into Habit, will help much to preserve him, when he is no longer under his Maid's or Tutor's Eye. This is all I think can be done in the Case. For, as Years increase, Liberty must come with them; and in a great many Things he must be trusted to his own Conduct; since there cannot al-

John Locke (1632–1704) published Some Thoughts Concerning Education *in 1693, after he had spent several years as tutor for the first Earl of Shaftesbury's family. This work presents several concepts central to Locke's thinking about educating children. First, he saw the importance of habit as central. Since the child's mind is a* tabula rasa, *he can only learn by constant repetition — that is, by developing sound habits. Moreover, intellectual discipline must begin early in the child's life and impulses should be stifled. Because Locke viewed the child as a miniature adult, he believed the child could only mature in a carefully controlled environment. And finally, such careful control can only be regulated by a superbly qualified tutor.*

ways be a Guard upon him, except what you have put into his own Mind by good Principles, and established Habits, which is the best and surest, and therefore most to be taken Care of. For, from repeated Cautions and Rules, never so often inculcated, you are not to expect any thing either in this, or any other Case, farther than Practice has established them into Habits. . .

Not being permitted to *drink* without eating, will prevent the Custom of   2
having the Cup often at his Nose; a dangerous Beginning, and Preparation to *Good-fellowship.* Men often bring Habitual Hunger and Thirst on themselves by Custom. And if you please to try, you may, though he be weaned from it, bring him by Use, to such a Necessity again of *Drinking* in the Night, that he will not be able to sleep without it. It being the Lullaby used by Nurses, to still crying Children. I believe Mothers generally find some Difficulty to wean their Children from *Drinking* in the Night, when they first take them home.[1] Believe it, Custom prevails as much by Day as by Night; and you may, if you please, bring any One to be Thirsty every Hour.

I once lived in an House, where to appease a froward Child, they gave him   3
Drink as often as he cried; so that he was constantly bibbing: And tho' he could not speak, yet he drunk more in twenty four Hours than I did. Try it when you please, you may with Small, as well as with Strong Beer, drink your self into a Drought. The great Thing to be minded in Education is, what *Habits* you settle: And therefore in this, as all other Things, do not begin to make any Thing *customary,* the Practice whereof you would not have continue, and increase. It is convenient for Health and Sobriety, to *drink* no more than Natural Thirst requires: And he that eats not Salt Meats, nor drinks Strong Drink, will seldom thirst between Meals, unless he has been accustomed to such unseasonable *Drinking.* . . .

As the Strength of the Body lies chiefly in being able to endure Hardships,   4
so also does that of the Mind. And the great Principle and Foundation of all Vertue and Worth, is placed in this, That a Man is able to *deny himself* his own Desires, cross his own Inclinations, and purely follow what Reason directs as best, tho' the Appetite lean the other way.[2]

The great Mistake I have observed in People's breeding their Children has   5
been, that this has not been taken Care enough of in its *due Season;* That the Mind has not been made obedient to Discipline, and pliant to Reason, when at first it was most tender, most easy to be bowed. Parents, being wisely ordain'd by Nature to love their Children, are very apt, if Reason watch not that natural Affection very warily, are apt, I say, to let it run into Fondness. They love their little ones, and 'tis their Duty: But they often, with them, cherish their Faults too. They must not be crossed forsooth; they must be permitted to have their Wills in all things; and they being in their Infancies not capable of great Vices, their Parents think they may safely enough indulge their little Irregularities, and make themselves Sport with that pretty Perverseness, which they think well enough becomes that innocent Age. But to a fond Parent, that would not have his Child corrected for a perverse Trick, but excused it, saying, it was a small Matter; *Solon* very well replied, Ay, but Custom is a great one. . . .

And here give me Leave to take Notice of one thing I think a Fault in the   6
ordinary Method of Education; and that is, The Charging of Children's Memories, upon all Occasions, with *Rules* and Precepts, which they often do not understand, and constantly as soon forget as given.[1] If it be some Action you would
have done, or done otherwise; whenever they forget, or do it awkardly, make
them do it over and over again, till they are perfect: Whereby you will get these
two Advantages; *First,* To see whether it be an Action they can do, or is fit to
be expected of them. For sometimes Children are bid to do Things, which, upon
Trial, they are found not able to do; and had need be taught and exercised in,
before they are required to do them. But it is much easier for a Tutor to command, than to teach. *Secondly,* Another Thing got by it will be this; That by
repeating the same Action, till it be grown habitual in them, the Performance
will not depend on Memory or Reflection, the Concomitant of Prudence and
Age, and not of Childhood; but will be natural in them. Thus bowing to a
Gentleman when he salutes him, and looking in his Face, when he speaks to
him, is by constant Use as natural to a well-bred Man, as breathing; it requires
no Thought, no Reflection. Having this way cured in your Child any Fault, it
is cured for ever: And thus one by one you may weed them out all, and plant
what Habits you please.

I have seen Parents so heap *Rules* on their Children, that it was impossible   7
for the poor little ones to remember a tenth Part of them, much less to observe
them. However they were either by Words or Bows corrected for the Breach of
those multiplied and often very impertinent Precepts. Whence it naturally followed, that the Children minded not, what was said to them; when it was evident to them, that no Attention, they were capable of, was sufficient to preserve them from Transgression, and the Rebukes which followed it.

Let therefore your *Rules* to your Son, be as few as is possible, and rather fewer   8
than more than seem absolutely necessary. For if you burden him with many
Rules, one of these two things must necessarily follow; that either he must be
very often punished, which will be of ill consequence, by making Punishment
too frequent and familiar; or else you must let the Transgressions of some of
your Rules go unpunished, whereby they will of course grow contemptible, and
your Authority become cheap to him. Make but few *Laws,* but see they be well
observed, when once made. Few Years require but few Laws, and as his Age
increases, when one Rule is by Practice, well established, you may add another.

But pray remember, Children are *not* to be *taught by Rules,* which will be   9
always slipping out of their Memories. What you think necessary for them to
do, settle in them by an indispensible Practice, as often as the Occasion returns; and if it be possible, make Occasions. This will beget Habits in them,
which, being once established, operate of themselves easily and naturally,
without the Assistance of the Memory. But here let me give two Cautions,
1. The one is, that you keep them to the Practice, of what you would have grow
into a Habit in them, by kind Words, and gentle Admonitions, rather as minding them of what they forget, than by harsh Rebukes and Chiding, as if they
were wilfully guilty. 2dly, Another thing you are to take care of, is, not to endeavour to settle too many Habits at once, lest by Variety you confound them,

and so perfect none. When constant Custom has made any one thing easy and natural to them, and they practise it without Reflection, you may then go on to another.

This Method of teaching Children by a repeated Practice, and the same Ac-   *10*
tion done over and over again, under the Eye and Direction of the Tutor, till they have got the Habit of doing it well, and not by relying on *Rules* trusted to their Memories, has so many Advantages, which way ever we consider it, that I cannot but wonder (if ill Customs could be wonder'd at in any thing) how it could possibly be so much neglected. I shall name one more that comes now in my way. By this Method we shall see, whether what is requir'd of him be adapted to his Capacity, and any way suited to the Child's natural Genius and Constitution: for that too must be consider'd in a right Education. We must not hope wholly to change their Original Tempers, nor make the Gay Pensive and Grave, nor the Melancholy Sportive, without spoiling them. God has stampt certain Characters upon Men's Minds, which, like their Shapes, may perhaps be a little mended; but can hardly be totally alter'd, and transform'd into the contrary.

He therefore, that is about Children, should well study their Natures and   *11*
Aptitudes, and see by often Tryals, what turn they easily take, and what becomes them; observe what their Native Stock is, how it may be improved, and what it is fit for: He should consider what they want: whether they be capable of having it wrought into them by Industry, and incorporated there by Practice; and whether it be worth while to endeavour it. For in many Cases, all that we can do, or should aim at, is to make the best of what Nature has given, to prevent the Vices and Faults to which such a Constitution is most inclined, and give it all the Advantages it is capable of. . . .

But to return to our Method again. Though I have mentioned the Severity   *12*
of the Father's Brow, and the Awe settled thereby in the Mind of Children when young, as one main Instrument, whereby their Education is to be managed; yet I am far from being of an Opinion, that it should be continued all along to them, whilst they are under the Discipline and Government of Pupilage. I think it should be relaxed, as fast as their Age, Discretion, and Good-Behaviour could allow it, even to that degree, that a Father will do well, as his Son grows up, and is capable of it, to *talk familiarly* with him; nay, *ask his advice, and Consult* with him, about those things wherein he has any knowledge, or understanding. By this, the Father will gain two things, both of great moment. The one is, That it will put serious Considerations into his Son's Thoughts, better than any Rules or Advices he can give him. The sooner you *treat him as a Man*, the sooner he will begin to be one: And if you admit him into serious Discourses sometimes with you, you will insensibly raise his Mind above the usual Amusements of Youth, and those trifling Occupations which it is commonly wasted in. For it is easie to observe, that many Young Men continue longer in the Thoughts and Conversation of School-Boys, than otherwise they would; because their Parents keep them at that distance, and in that low Rank, by all their Carriage to them.

. . . One fit to Educate and Form the Mind of a Young Gentleman, is not   *13*
every where to be found; and that more than ordinary Care is to be taken in

the Choice of him, or else you may fail of your End. The Character of a Sober Man and a Scholar, is, as I have above observ'd, what every one expects in a Tutor. This generally is thought enough and is all that Parents commonly look for. But when such an one has emptied out into his Pupil all the Latin, and Logick, he has brought from the University, will that Furniture make him a fine Gentleman? Or can it be expected, that he should be better Bred, better Skill'd in the World, better Principled in the Grounds and Foundations of true Vertue and Generosity, than his young *Tutor* is?

To form a young Gentleman as he should be, 'tis fit his *Governour* should *14* himself be well bred, understand the Ways of Carriage, and Measures of Civility in all the Variety of Persons, Times and Places; and keep his Pupil, as much as his Age requires, constantly to the Observation of them. This is an Art not to be learnt, nor taught by Books. Nothing can give it but good Company, and Observation joyn'd together. The Taylor may make his Cloathes Modish, and the Dancing-master give fashion to his Motions; yet neither of these, though they set off well, make a well-bred Gentleman; No, though he have Learning to boot; which, if not well-managed, makes him more impertinent and intolerable in Conversation. Breeding is that, which sets a Gloss upon all his other good qualities, and renders them useful to him, in procuring him the Esteem and Good Will of all that he comes near. Without good Breeding his other Accomplishments make him pass but for Proud, Conceited, Vain, or Foolish.

Courage in an ill-bred Man, has the Air, and scapes not the Opinion of Bru- *15* tality: Learning becomes Pedantry; Wit Buffoonry; Plainness Rusticity; Good Nature Fawning. And there cannot be a good quality in him which want of Breeding will not warp, and disfigure to his Disadvantage. Nay, Vertue and Parts, though they are allowed their due Commendation, yet are not enough to procure a Man a good Reception, and make him Welcome whereever he comes. No body contents himself with rough Diamonds, and wears them so, who would appear with Advantage. When they are polish'd, and set, then they give a lustre. Good qualities are the Substantial Riches of the Mind, but 'tis good Breeding sets them off: And he that will be acceptable, must give Beauty as well as Strength to his Actions. Solidity, or even Usefulness, is not enough: A graceful Way and Fashion, in every thing, is that which gives the Ornament and Liking. And in most cases the manner of doing is of more Consequence, than the thing done; And upon that depends the Satisfaction or Disgust wherewith it is received. This therefore, which lies not in the putting off the Hat, nor making of Complements; but in a due and free composure of Language, Looks, Motion, Posture, Place, etc. suited to Persons and Occasions, and can be learn'd only by Habit and Use, though it be above the capacity of Children, and little ones should not be perplex'd about it, yet it ought to be begun, and in a good measure learn'd by a young Gentleman whilst he is under a Tutor, before he comes into the World upon his own Legs: For then usually it is too late to hope to reform several habitual indecencies, which lie in little things. For the Carriage is not as it should be, till it is become Natural in every Part; falling, as Skilful Musicians' Fingers do, into Harmonious Order without Care and without Thought. If in Conversation a Man's Mind be taken up with a sollicitous watchfulness about any part of his Behaviour; instead of being mended by it, it will be constrain'd, uneasie and ungraceful.

Besides, this part is most necessary to be form'd by the Hands and Care of *16* a *Governour:* Because, though the Errors committed in Breeding are the first that are taken notice of by others, yet they are the last that any one is told of. . . .

Besides being well Bred, the *Tutor* should know the World well; The Ways, 17 the Humors, the Follies, the Cheats, the Faults of the Age he is fallen into, and particularly of the Country he lives in. These he should be able to shew to his Pupil, as he finds him capable; teach him Skill in Men, and their Manners; pull off the Mask, which their several Callings, and Pretences cover them with; and make his Pupil discern what lies at the bottom, under such appearances; That he may not, as unexperienced young Men are apt to do, if they are unwarn'd, take one thing for another, judge by the out-side, and give himself up to shew, and the insinuation of a fair Carriage, or an obliging Application;° A Governour should teach his Scholar to guess at, and beware of the Designs of Men he hath to do with, neither with too much Suspicion, nor too much Confidence; but as the young Man is by Nature most inclin'd to either side, rectifie him and bend him the other way. He should Accustom him to make as much as is possible a true Judgement of Men by those Marks, which serve best to shew, what they are, and give a Prospect into their inside; which often shews it self in little things, especially when they are not in Parade, and upon their Guard. He should acquaint him with the true State of the World, and dispose him to think no Man better or worse, wiser or foolisher, than really he is. Thus by safe and insensible degrees, he will pass from a Boy to a Man; which is the most hazardous step in all the whole course of Life. This therefore should be carefully watch'd, and a young Man with great Diligence handed over it; and not, as now usually is done, be taken from a *Governour*'s Conduct, and all at once thrown into the World under his own, not without manifest Danger of immediate Spoiling; there being nothing more frequent, than Instances of the great Loosness, Extravagancy and Debauchery, which young Men have run into as soon as they have been let loose from a severe and strict Education: Which I think may be chiefly imputed to their wrong way of Breeding, especially in this Part: for having been Bred up in a great Ignorance of what the World truly is, and finding it a quite other thing, when they come into it, than what they were taught it should be, and so imagin'd it was, are easily perswaded, by other kind of Tutors, which they are sure to meet with, that the Discipline they were kept under, and the Lectures were read to them, were but the Formalities of Education, and the Restraints of Childhood; that the Freedom belonging to Men, is to take their Swing in a full Enjoyment of what was before forbidden them. They shew the young Novice the World full of fashionable and glittering Examples of this every where, and he is presently dazled with them. My young Master failing not to be willing to shew himself a Man, as much as any of the Sparks of his Years, lets himself loose to all the Irregularities he finds in the most Debauch'd; and thus courts Credit and Manliness, in the casting off the Modesty, and Sobriety, he has till then been kept in; and thinks it Brave, at his first setting out, to signalize himself in running counter to all the Rules of Vertue, which have been Preach'd to him by his Tutor.

°obliging Application: Flattering obsequiousness. [Locke's note]

The shewing him the World, as really it is, before he comes wholly into it,   *18*
is one of the best means, I think, to prevent this Mischief. He should by degrees
be inform'd of the Vices in fashion and warn'd of the Applications and Designs
of those, who will make it their Business to corrupt him. He should be told the
Arts they use, and the Trains° they lay; and now and then have set before him
the Tragical or Ridiculous Examples of those, who are Ruining, or Ruin'd this
way. The Age is not like to want Instances of this Kind, which should be made
Land-marks to him; that by the Disgraces, Diseases, Beggary, and Shame of
Hopeful young Men thus brought to Ruin, he may be precaution'd, and be made
see, how those joyn in the Contempt and Neglect of them that are Undone, who
by Pretences of Friendship and Respect lead them into it, and help to prey upon
them whilst they were Undoing; That he may see, before he buys it by a too
dear Experience, that those who perswade him not to follow the Sober Advices
he has received from his *Governours*, and the Counsel of his own Reason, which
they call being govern'd by others, do it only, that they may have the government of him themselves; and make him believe, he goes like a Man of himself,
by his own Conduct, and for his own Pleasure, when, in truth, he is wholly as
a Child led by them into those Vices, which best serve their Purposes. This is
a Knowledge which, upon all Occasions, a *Tutor* should endeavour to instill,
and by all Methods try to make him comprehend, and throughly relish.

I know it is often said, That to discover to a young Man the Vices of the Age,   *19*
is to teach them him. That I confess is a good deal so, according as it is done;
and therefore requires a discreet Man of Parts, who knows the World, and can
judge of the Temper, Inclination and weak side of his Pupil. This farther is to
be remembered, that it is not possible now (as perhaps formerly it was) to keep
a young Gentleman from Vice, by a total Ignorance of it; unless you will all his
Life mue° him up in a Closet, and never let him go into Company. The longer
he is kept thus hood-wink'd, the less he will see, when he comes abroad into
open Day-light, and be the more expos'd to be a prey to himself, and others.
And an old Boy° at his first appearance, with all the gravity of his Ivy-bush
about him, is sure to draw on him the Eyes and Chirping of the whole Town
Volery,° Amongst which, there will not be wanting some Birds of Prey, that
will presently be on the Wing for him.

°Trains: Traps, snares. [Locke's note]
°mue: A hawking term (mew) for a cage or coop for hawks when moulting. Note the use of hawking
    references: mue, hood-wink'd, chirping, Volery, Birds of Prey, wing. [Locke's note]
°old Boy: A young man with the naïveté and simplicity of a boy. [Locke's note]
°This metaphor is taken from the appearance of an owl or other bird of prey when he leaves his ivy-
    bush and is followed by smaller birds who delight in belittling him. [Locke's note]

NOTES

[1] *home:* From their wet-nurses, who suckled the children for some time, often for as much as eighteen months to two years. This practice can be understood when the large number of births per family in the seventeenth century is considered; though the mortality rate whittled the size of the nuclear
family down to a mean size of about 4–4½ persons. Of course the higher the social rank (which meant
better economic and hygienic conditions), the more children that could be expected to survive birth;
and the more servants to look after the children a gentleman could afford. It was not uncommon for
a gentleman of an income similar to Edward Clarke's to employ from five to ten servants, depending
on the number of children he had.

[2] This is essentially a stoical principle which received great emphasis in the long neoclassical period which grew from the sixteenth-century humanist effort to reestablish Stoicism as a respectable
philosophical position.

[2]This is essentially a stoical principle which received great emphasis in the long neoclassical period which grew from the sixteenth-century humanist effort to reestablish Stoicism as a respectable philosophical position.

Considerations

1. Does John Locke approve of imposing rules upon children? Why or why not?
2. What is the difference between a rule and a habit?
3. After answering the previous two questions, write a short essay summarizing Locke's views on the subject of habit.
4. Locke discusses at length the qualities of a suitable tutor. Make a list of the qualities he deems most desirable. Then write an essay which summarizes these qualities and explains Locke's purpose in treating this topic in such detail.

From *Émile*

Jean-Jacques Rousseau

The only habit which a child should be allowed to form is that of forming   *1*
none; he should not be carried in one arm more than the other; he should not
be accustomed to hold out his right hand oftener than his left, or to use one
more than the other; he should not want to eat, to sleep, or to do anything, at
stated hours; he should not mind being left alone, whether by day or night.
Prepare him early for the enjoyment of liberty and the exercise of his powers;
leave his body its natural habits; enable him always to be master of himself
and, as soon as he acquires a will, always to carry out its dictates.

As soon as a child begins to distinguish objects, a careful choice should be   *2*
made of those which are presented to him. Every new object is naturally interesting to a child. His weakness makes him afraid of everything which he
does not recognize: accustom him to see new objects without being affected by
them and you destroy this timidity. Children who are brought up in neat houses,
where cobwebs are carefully swept away, are always afraid of spiders, and often
continue to fear them when they grow up; but I never knew a peasant, man or
woman, afraid of a spider.

Jean-Jacques Rousseau (1712–1778) published Émile *in 1762. In this work he
discusses the intellectual and moral development of an imaginary boy guided through
the different stages of growth by a dedicated tutor. The excerpts reproduced here
illustrate some of the features of Rousseau's thought that contrast sharply with
the established notions (represented by John Locke) about childhood and education.*

Why, then, should not the education of a child begin before it can speak or   3
understand, since even the choice of the objects which are presented to its gaze
is enough to make it either timid or courageous? I would have them accustomed to seeing new objects — ugly, repulsive, and uncommon animals — but
by degrees and at a distance, till they grow used to them, and, seeing others
handle them, venture to do so themselves. . . .

During infancy, when memory and imagination are still inactive, a child at-   4
tends only to those sensations which actually affect his senses with pain or
pleasure. His sensations are the raw material of his ideas; by supplying sensations in the right order we therefore prepare his memory to present them in
the same order to his understanding: but, as he is at present capable of attending only to sensations, it is enough for a time to show him clearly the connection between these sensations and the objects which excite them. He wants to
touch and handle everything which he sees: do not check this restlessness; it
is a necessary apprenticeship to learning. It is thus that he must learn to distinguish heat and cold, hardness and softness, weight and lightness, and to judge
of size, shape, and other sensible qualities. These lessons he learns by looking,
touching, and listening, but above all by comparing sight with touch and by
estimating with the eye the sensations which would be given to the fingers.

It is by movement that we discover the existence of external objects, and by   5
our own movements that we acquire the idea of extension. It is because a child
has no such idea that he stretches out his hand in the same way to lay hold of
an object that is within reach and another which is a hundred yards distant.
. . . Take care therefore if you wish him to judge distance to change his position frequently, and to carry him from place to place in such a way as to make
him realize the change of position. When once he begins to realize the difference, your method must be changed; you must now carry him only where you
please, not where he pleases: for when he is no longer deceived by his senses,
the efforts of which I have been speaking change their motive.

Love childhood; look kindly on its play, its pleasures, its lovable instincts. . . .   6
You will perhaps reply, "This is the time to correct the evil tendencies of   7
human nature. It is in childhood, when our pains are least felt, that they should
be multiplied, to diminish their number when we arrive at years of discretion." But who has told you that such an arrangement is in your power? Or
that all the fine instruction with which you load the weak mind of a child will
not one day be more pernicious than useful to him? . . . As mankind has its
place in the world, so has childhood its place in human life; we should consider the man in the man and the child in the child. To assign to each his separate place and keep him in it, to regulate human passions by human nature,
is all that we can do for his well-being. The rest depends on external circumstances which are not under our control. . . .

No Reasoning with Children

Locke's great maxim was to reason with children; and it is the most popu-   8
lar method at the present day. Its success does not appear to recommend it;

for my own part, I have never seen anyone so silly as those children with whom they have reasoned so much. Of all man's faculties, Reason, which is a combination of the rest, is developed last and with greatest difficulty; yet this is the faculty which we are asked to use for the development of the earlier. It is the climax of a good education to form a man who is capable of reason; and we propose to educate a young child by means of his reason! This is beginning where we ought to end, and making of the finished product an instrument in its own manufacture. . . .

Watch a cat, the first time it comes into a room. It looks about and peers   9
into every hole and corner; it is not still for a moment till it has carefully examined everything in the room. A child does the same when he begins to walk.
. . . Our first impulses urge us to measure ourselves with our environment, to discover in objects any sensible qualities which might concern us. Men's first study is a sort of experimental physical science relative to self-preservation.
. . . While children's supple and delicate organs can adjust themselves to the physical world, while their senses are still exempt from illusions — this is the time to train these senses and organs in their proper functions, this is the time to teach them to recognize the sensible relations of things to themselves. As everything that enters the human mind comes through the senses, the first kind of reasoning in man is a kind of sensational reasoning, which serves as a basis for intellectual reason. Our first instructors in science are our feet, hands, and eyes. . . .

Locke, amid a number of manly and sensible rules, falls into a contradiction   10
which we should not expect in so exact a reasoner. Though advising that children should take cold baths in the heat of summer, he is against their drinking cold water when they are warm, or sitting on the damp ground. . . . I shall never be persuaded that our natural appetites are misguided, and that we may not satisfy them without endangering our lives. If this were really the case, the human race would have been destroyed hundreds of times before it had learned the precautions which were necessary for self-preservation. . . .

Children require much sleep because they take much exercise. . . . The time   11
for rest is pointed out by nature as the night. It is a certain observation that our sleep is more tranquil and agreeable when the sun is below the horizon.
. . . Hence the most healthy habit is certainly to rise and to go to bed with the sun; it follows that in this latitude man as well as animals requires in general more sleep in winter than in summer. But civilized life is not sufficiently simple and free from accident for us to think of accustoming a child to uniformity, to such an extent as to make it necessary for him. He ought without doubt to subject himself to rules; but the chief rule is to be able to break the others without risk when occasion requires. . . . Leave him at first without restraint to the law of nature; but never forget that in society we are obliged to put ourselves above that law. He must be able to sit up late and to rise early, to be waked unexpectedly out of sleep, and occasionally to sit up all night without inconvenience. By beginning early and by proceeding gently and gradually, we may thus train his constitution to bear conditions which might destroy it if he were subjected to them only after it has been already formed.

Considerations

1. What habits does Jean-Jacques Rousseau endorse for young children?
2. How do objects in the environment influence a child's mental growth?

Connections

1. Both John Locke and Jean-Jacques Rousseau address the value of inculcating habit in the behavior of very young children. Construct an essay comparing their views.
2. Rousseau takes issue with Locke's stern warning that children should be forbidden to drink cold water when they are warm. Why? What does Rousseau believe educators (parents and tutors) should do about children's impulses? Write a brief essay addressing these questions.
3. Examine Chapter 1, The Dimensions of Power. After glancing through its readings, write an essay analyzing both Locke and Rousseau's views of the tutor/student relationship as a power struggle.

Conditioned Emotional Reactions

John B. Watson and Rosalie Rayner

In recent literature various speculations have been entered into concerning   *1*
the possibility of conditioning various types of emotional response, but direct
experimental evidence in support of such a view has been lacking. If the theory
advanced by Watson and Morgan to the effect that in infancy the original emotional reaction patterns are few, consisting so far as observed of fear, rage and
love, then there must be some simple method by means of which the range of
stimuli which can call out these emotions and their compounds is greatly increased. Otherwise, complexity in adult response could not be accounted for.
These authors without adequate experimental evidence advanced the view that
this range was increased by means of conditioned reflex factors. It was sug-

*John B. Watson (1878–1958) is often called the founder of American behavior-
ism. This 1920 study, co-authored by Rosalie Rayner, illustrates Watson's preoccupation with predicting and controlling behavior as well as his allegiance to the
principles of classical conditioning as developed by Ivan Pavlov.*

gested there that the early home life of the child furnishes a laboratory situation for establishing conditioned emotional responses. The present authors have recently put the whole matter to an experimental test.

Experimental work has been done so far on only one child, Albert B. This infant was reared almost from birth in a hospital environment; his mother was a wet nurse in the Harriet Lane Home for Invalid Children. Albert's life was normal: he was healthy from birth and one of the best developed youngsters ever brought to the hospital, weighing twenty-one pounds at nine months of age. He was on the whole stolid and unemotional. His stability was one of the principal reasons for using him as a subject in this test. We felt that we could do him relatively little harm by carrying out such experiments as those outlined below. 2

At approximately nine months of age we ran him through the emotional tests that have become a part of our regular routine in determining whether fear reactions can be called out by other stimuli than sharp noises and the sudden removal of support. Tests of this type have been described by the senior author in another place. In brief, the infant was confronted suddenly and for the first time successively with a white rat, a rabbit, a dog, a monkey, with masks with and without hair, cotton wool, burning newspapers, etc. A permanent record of Albert's reactions to these objects and situations has been preserved in a motion picture study. Manipulation was the most usual reaction called out. *At no time did this infant ever show fear in any situation.* These experimental records were confirmed by the casual observations of the mother and hospital attendants. No one had ever seen him in a state of fear and rage. The infant practically never cried. 3

Up to approximately nine months of age we had not tested him with loud sounds. The test to determine whether a fear reaction could be called out by a loud sound was made when he was eight months, twenty-six days of age. The sound was that made by striking a hammer upon a suspended steel bar four feet in length and three-fourths of an inch in diameter. The laboratory notes are as follows: 4

> One of the two experimenters caused the child to turn its head and fixate her moving hand; the other, stationed back of the child, struck the steel bar a sharp blow. The child started violently, his breathing was checked and the arms were raised in a characteristic manner. On the second stimulation the same thing occurred, and in addition the lips began to pucker and tremble. On the third stimulation the child broke into a sudden crying fit. This is the first time an emotional situation in the laboratory has produced any fear or even crying in Albert.

We had expected just these results on account of our work with other infants brought up under similar conditions. It is worth while to call attention to the fact that removal of support (dropping and jerking the blanket upon which the infant was lying) was tried exhaustively upon this infant on the same occasion. It was not effective in producing the fear response. This stimulus is effective in younger children. At what age such stimuli lose their potency in producing fear is not known. Nor is it known whether less placid children ever lose their fear of them. This probably depends upon the training the child gets. It is well known that children eagerly run to be tossed into the air and caught. 5

On the other hand it is equally well known that in the adult fear responses are called out quite clearly by the sudden removal of support, if the individual is walking across a bridge, walking out upon a beam, etc. There is a wide field of study here which is aside from our present point.

The sound stimulus, thus, at nine months of age, gives us the means of test-   6
ing several important factors. I. Can we condition fear of an animal, *e.g.*, a white rat, by visually presenting it and simultaneously striking a steel bar? II. If such a conditioned emotional response can be established, will there be a transfer to other animals or other objects? III. What is the effect of time upon such conditioned emotional responses? IV. If after a reasonable period such emotional responses have not died out, what laboratory methods can be devised for their removal?

I. The establishment of conditioned emotional responses. At first there was   7
considerable hesitation upon our part in making the attempt to set up fear reactions experimentally. A certain responsibility attaches to such a procedure. We decided finally to make the attempt, comforting ourselves by the reflection that such attachments would arise anyway as soon as the child left the sheltered environment of the nursery for the rough and tumble of the home. We did not begin this work until Albert was eleven months, three days of age. Before attempting to set up a conditioned response we, as before, put him through all of the regular emotional tests. *Not the slightest sign of a fear response was obtained in any situation.*

The steps taken to condition emotional responses are shown in our labora-   8
tory notes.

11 Months 3 Days

1. White rat suddenly taken from the basket and presented to Albert. He began to reach for rat with left hand. Just as his hand touched the animal the bar was struck immediately behind his head. The infant jumped violently and fell forward, burying his face in the mattress. He did not cry, however.

2. Just as the right hand touched the rat the bar was again struck. Again the infant jumped violently, fell forward and began to whimper.

In order not to disturb the child too seriously no further tests were given for one week.

11 Months 10 Days

1. Rat presented suddenly without sound. There was steady fixation but no tendency at first to reach for it. The rat was then placed nearer, whereupon tentative reaching movements began with the right hand. When the rat nosed the infant's left hand, the hand was immediately withdrawn. He started to reach for the head of the animal with the forefinger of the left hand, but withdrew it suddenly before contact. It is thus seen that the two joint stimulations given the previous week were not without effect. He was tested with his blocks immediately afterwards to see if they shared in the process of conditioning. He began immediately to pick them up, dropping them, pounding them, etc. In the remainder of the tests the blocks were given frequently to quiet him and

to test his general emotional state. They were always removed from sight when the process of conditioning was under way.

2. Joint stimulation with rat and sound. Started, then fell over immediately to right side. No crying.

3. Joint stimulation. Fell to right side and rested upon hands, with head turned away from rat. No crying.

4. Joint stimulation. Same reaction.

5. Rat suddenly presented alone. Puckered face, whimpered and withdrew body sharply to the left.

6. Joint stimulation. Fell over immediately to right side and began to whimper.

7. Joint stimulation. Started violently and cried, but did not fall over.

8. Rat alone. *The instant the rat was shown the baby began to cry. Almost instantly he turned sharply to the left, fell over on left side, raised himself on all fours and began to crawl away so rapidly that he was caught with difficulty before reaching the edge of the table.*

This was as convincing a case of a completely conditioned fear response as could have been theoretically pictured. In all seven joint stimulations were given to bring about the complete reaction. It is not unlikely had the sound been of greater intensity or of a more complex clang character that the number of joint stimulations might have been materially reduced. Experiments designed to define the nature of the sounds that will serve best as emotional stimuli are under way.   *9*

II. When a conditioned emotional response has been established for one object, is there a transfer? Five days later Albert was again brought back into the laboratory and tested as follows: *10*

11 Months 15 Days

1. Tested first with blocks. He reached readily for them, playing with them as usual. This shows that there has been no general transfer to the room, table, blocks, etc.

2. Rat alone. Whimpered immediately, withdrew right hand and turned head and trunk away.

3. Blocks again offered. Played readily with them, smiling and gurgling.

4. Rat alone. Leaned over to the left side as far away from the rat as possible, then fell over, getting up on all fours and scurrying away as rapidly as possible.

5. Blocks again offered. Reached immediately for them, smiling and laughing as before.

The above preliminary test shows that the conditioned response to the rat had carried over completely for the five days in which no tests were given. The question as to whether or not there is a transfer was next taken up.

6. Rabbit alone. The rabbit was suddenly placed on the mattress in front of him. The reaction was pronounced. Negative responses began at once. He leaned as far away from the animal as possible, whimpered, then burst into tears. When the rabbit was placed in contact with him he buried his face in the mattress,

then got up on all fours and crawled away, crying as he went. This was a most convincing test.

7. The blocks were next given him, after an interval. He played with them as before. It was observed by four people that he played far more energetically with them than ever before. The blocks were raised high over his head and slammed down with a great deal of force.

8. Dog alone. The dog did not produce as violent a reaction as the rabbit. The moment fixation occurred the child shrank back and as the animal came nearer he attempted to get on all fours but did not cry at first. As soon as the dog passed out of his range of vision he became quiet. The dog was then made to approach the infant's head (he was lying down at the moment). Albert straightened up immediately, fell over to the opposite side and turned his head away. He then began to cry.

9. The blocks were again presented. He began immediately to play with them.

10. Fur coat (seal). Withdrew immediately to the left side and began to fret. Coat put close to him on the left side, he turned immediately, began to cry and tried to crawl away on all fours.

11. Cotton wool. The wool was presented in a paper package. At the end the cotton was not covered by the paper. It was placed first on his feet. He kicked it away but did not touch it with his hands. When his hand was laid on the wool he immediately withdrew it but did not show the shock that the animals or fur coat produced in him. He then began to play with the paper, avoiding contact with the wool itself. He finally, under the impulse of the manipulative instinct, lost some of his negativism to the wool.

12. Just in play W. put his head down to see if Albert would play with his hair. Albert was completely negative. Two other observers did the same thing. He began immediately to play with their hair. W. then brought the Santa Claus mask and presented it to Albert. He was again pronouncedly negative.

11 Months 20 Days

1. Blocks alone. Played with them as usual.

2. Rat alone. Withdrawal of the whole body, bending over to left side, no crying. Fixation and following with eyes. The response was much less marked than on first presentation the previous week. It was thought best to freshen up the reaction by another joint stimulation.

3. Just as the rat was placed on his hand the rod was struck. Reaction violent.

4. Rat alone. Fell over at once to left side. Reaction practically as strong as on former occasion but no crying.

5. Rat alone. Fell over to left side, got up on all fours and started to crawl away. On this occasion there was no crying, but strange to say, as he started away he began to gurgle and coo, even while leaning far over to the left side to avoid the rat.

6. Rabbit alone. Leaned over to left side as far as possible. Did not fall over. Began to whimper but reaction not so violent as on former occasions.

7. Blocks again offered. He reached for them immediately and began to play. All of the tests so far discussed were carried out upon a table supplied with

a mattress, located in a small, well-lighted dark-room. We wished to test next whether conditioned fear responses so set up would appear if the situation were markedly altered. We thought it best before making this test to freshen the reaction both to the rabbit and to the dog by showing them at the moment the steel bar was struck. It will be recalled that this was the first time any effort had been made to directly condition response to the dog and rabbit. The experimental notes are as follows:

8. The rabbit at first was given alone. The reaction was exactly as given in test (6) above. When the rabbit was left on Albert's knees for a long time he began tentatively to reach out and manipulate its fur with forefingers. While doing this the steel rod was struck. A violent fear reaction resulted.

9. Rabbit alone. Reaction wholly similar to that on trial (6) above.

10. Rabbit alone. Started immediately to whimper, holding hands far up, but did not cry. Conflicting tendency to manipulate very evident.

11. Dog alone. Began to whimper, shaking head from side to side, holding hands as far away from the animal as possible.

12. Dog and sound. The rod was struck just as the animal touched him. A violent negative reaction appeared. He began to whimper, turned to one side, fell over and started to get up on all fours.

13. Blocks. Played with them immediately and readily.

On this same day and immediately after the above experiment Albert was *11* taken into the large well-lighted lecture room belonging to the laboratory. He was placed on a table in the center of the room immediately under the skylight. Four people were present. The situation was thus very different from that which obtained in the small dark room.

1. Rat alone. No sudden fear reaction appeared at first. The hands, however, were held up and away from the animal. No positive manipulatory reactions appeared.

2. Rabbit alone. Fear reaction slight. Turned to left and kept face away from the animal but the reaction was never pronounced.

3. Dog alone. Turned away but did not fall over. Cried. Hands moved as far away from the animal as possible. Whimpered as long as the dog was present.

4. Rat alone. Slight negative reaction.

5. Rat and sound. It was thought best to freshen the reaction to the rat. The sound was given just as the rat was presented. Albert jumped violently but did not cry.

6. Rat alone. At first he did not show any negative reaction. When rat was placed nearer he began to show negative reaction by drawing back his body, raising his hands, whimpering, etc.

7. Blocks. Played with them immediately.

8. Rat alone. Pronounced withdrawal of body and whimpering.

9. Blocks. Played with them as before.

10. Rabbit alone. Pronounced reaction. Whimpered with arms held high, fell over backward and had to be caught.

11. Dog alone. At first the dog did not produce the pronounced reaction. The hands were held high over the head, breathing was checked, but there was no

crying. Just at this moment the dog, which had not barked before, barked three times loudly when only about six inches from the baby's face. Albert immediately fell over and broke into a wail that continued until the dog was removed. The sudden barking of the hitherto quiet dog produced a marked fear response in the adult observers!

From the above results it would seem that emotional transfers do take place. *12* Furthermore it would seem that the number of transfers resulting from an experimentally produced conditioned emotional reaction may be very large. In our observations we had no means of testing the complete number of transfers which may have resulted.

III. The effect of time upon conditioned emotional responses. We have al- *13* ready shown that the conditioned emotional response will continue for a period of one week. It was desired to make the time test longer. In view of the imminence of Albert's departure from the hospital we could not make the interval longer than one month. Accordingly no further emotional experimentation was entered into for thirty-one days after the above test. During the month, however, Albert was brought weekly to the laboratory for tests upon right and left-handedness, imitation, general development, etc. No emotional tests whatever were given and during the whole month his regular nursery routine was maintained in the Harriet Lane Home. The notes on the test given at the end of this period are as follows:

1 Year 21 Days

1. Santa Claus mask. Withdrawal, gurgling, then slapped at it without touching. When his hand was forced to touch it, he whimpered and cried. His hand was forced to touch it two more times. He whimpered and cried on both tests. He finally cried at the mere visual stimulus of the mask.

2. Fur coat. Wrinkled his nose and withdrew both hands, drew back his whole body and began to whimper as the coat was put nearer. Again there was the strife between withdrawal and the tendency to manipulate. Reached tentatively with left hand but drew back before contact had been made. In moving his body to one side his hand accidentally touched the coat. He began to cry at once, nodding his head in a very peculiar manner (this reaction was an entirely new one). Both hands were withdrawn as far as possible from the coat. The coat was then laid on his lap and he continued nodding his head and whimpering, withdrawing his body as far as possible, pushing the while at the coat with his feet but never touching it with his hands.

3. Fur coat. The coat was taken out of his sight and presented again at the end of a minute. He began immediately to fret, withdrawing his body and nodding his head as before.

4. Blocks. He began to play with them as usual.

5. The rat. He allowed the rat to crawl towards him without withdrawing. He sat very still and fixated it intently. Rat then touched his hand. Albert withdrew it immediately, then leaned back as far as possible but did not cry. When the rat was placed on his arm he withdrew his body and began to fret,

nodding his head. The rat was then allowed to crawl against his chest. He first began to fret and then covered his eyes with both hands.

6. Blocks. Reaction normal.

7. The rabbit. The animal was placed directly in front of him. It was very quiet. Albert showed no avoiding reactions at first. After a few seconds he puckered up his face, began to nod his head and to look intently at the experimenter. He next began to push the rabbit away with his feet, withdrawing his body at the same time. Then as the rabbit came nearer he began pulling his feet away, nodding his head, and wailing "da da." After about a minute he reached out tentatively and slowly and touched the rabbit's ear with his right hand, finally manipulating it. The rabbit was again placed in his lap. Again he began to fret and withdrew his hands. He reached out tentatively with his left hand and touched the animal, shuddered and withdrew the whole body. The experimenter then took hold of his left hand and laid it on the rabbit's back. Albert immediately withdrew his hand and began to suck his thumb. Again the rabbit was laid in his lap. He began to cry, covering his face with both hands.

8. Dog. The dog was very active. Albert fixated it intensely for a few seconds, sitting very still. He began to cry but did not fall over backwards as on his last contact with the dog. When the dog was pushed closer to him he at first sat motionless, then began to cry, putting both hands over his face.

These experiments would seem to show conclusively that directly conditioned emotional responses as well as those conditioned by transfer persist, although with a certain loss in the intensity of the reaction, for a longer period than one month. Our view is that they persist and modify personality throughout life. It should be recalled again that Albert was of an extremely phlegmatic type. Had he been emotionally unstable probably both the directly conditioned response and those transferred would have persisted throughout the month unchanged in form. *14*

IV. "Detachment" or removal of conditioned emotional responses. Unfortunately Albert was taken from the hospital the day the above tests were made. Hence the opportunity of building up an experimental technique by means of which we could remove the conditioned emotional responses was denied us. Our own view, expressed above, which is possibly not very well grounded, is that these responses in the home environment are likely to persist indefinitely, unless an accidental method for removing them is hit upon. The importance of establishing some method must be apparent to all. Had the opportunity been at hand we should have tried out several methods, some of which we may mention. (1) Constantly confronting the child with those stimuli which called out the responses in the hopes that habituation would come in corresponding to "fatigue" of reflex when differential reactions are to be set up. (2) By trying to "recondition" by showing objects calling out fear responses (visual) and simultaneously stimulating the erogenous zones (tactual). We should try first the lips, then the nipples and as a final resort the sex organs. (3) By trying to "recondition" by feeding the subject candy or other food just as the animal is shown. This method calls for the food control of the subject. (4) By building up "constructive" activities around the object by imitation and by putting the hand *15* through the motions of manipulation. At this age imitation of overt motor activity is strong, as our present but unpublished experimentation has shown.

Incidental Observations

(a) Thumb sucking as a compensatory device for blocking fear and noxious stimuli. During the course of these experiments, especially in the final test, it was noticed that whenever Albert was on the verge of tears or emotionally upset generally he would continually thrust his thumb into his mouth. The moment the hand reached the mouth he became impervious to the stimuli producing fear. Again and again while the motion pictures were being made at the end of the thirty-day rest period, we had to remove the thumb from his mouth before the conditioned response could be obtained. This method of blocking noxious and emotional stimuli (fear and rage) through erogenous stimulation seems to persist from birth, onward. Very often in our experiments upon the work adders with infants under ten days of age the same reaction appeared. When at work upon the adders both of the infants arms are under slight restraint. Often rage appears. They begin to cry, thrashing their arms and legs about. If the finger gets into the mouth crying ceases at once. The organism thus apparently from birth, when under the influence of love stimuli is blocked to all others. This resort to sex stimulation when under the influence of noxious and emotional situations, or when the individual is restless and idle, persists throughout adolescent and adult life. Albert, at any rate, did not resort to thumb sucking except in the presence of such stimuli. Thumb sucking could immediately be checked by offering him his blocks. These invariably called out active manipulation instincts. It is worthwhile here to call attention to the fact that Freud's conception of the stimulation of erogenous zones as being the expression of an original "pleasure" seeking principle may be turned about and possibly better described as a compensatory (and often conditioned) device for the blockage of noxious and fear and rage producing stimuli. [16]

(b) Equal primacy of fear, love and possibly rage. While in general the results of our experiment offer no particular points of conflict with Freudian concepts, one fact out of harmony with them should be emphasized. According to proper Freudians sex (or in our terminology, love) is the principal emotion in which conditioned responses arise which later limit and distort personality. We wish to take sharp issue with this view on the basis of the experimental evidence we have gathered. Fear is as primal a factor as love in influencing personality. Fear does not gather its potency in any derived manner from love. It belongs to the original and inherited nature of man. Probably the same may be true of rage although at present we are not so sure of this. [17]

The Freudians twenty years from now, unless their hypotheses change, when they come to analyze Albert's fear of a seal skin coat — assuming that he comes to analysis at that age — will probably tease from him the recital of a dream which upon their analysis will show that Albert at three years of age attempted to play with the pubic hair of the mother and was scolded violently for it. (We are by no means denying that this might in some other case condition it). If the analyst has sufficiently prepared Albert to accept such a dream when found as an explanation of his avoiding tendencies, and if the analyst has [18] the authority and personality to put it over, Albert may be fully convinced that the dream was a true revealer of the factors which brought about the fear.

It is probable that many of the phobias in psychopathology are true condi-   *19* tioned emotional reactions either of the direct or the transferred type. One may possibly have to believe that such persistence of early conditioned responses will be found only in persons who are constitutionally inferior. Our argument is meant to be constructive. Emotional disturbances in adults cannot be traced back to sex alone. They must be retraced along at least three collateral lines — to conditioned and transferred responses set up in infancy and early youth in all three of the fundamental human emotions.

Considerations

1. Why was Albert chosen for the experiment?
2. What were the four goals of the experiment?
3. How many joint stimulations were required before the experimenters were successful? How did they know success had come?
4. What effect did changing the testing environment from the dark lab to the well-lighted lecture hall have?
5. The experimenters regretted that they had no time to "detach" the emotional responses which had been conditioned into Albert. Summarize the methods they would have used to extinguish Albert's newly acquired phobias.
6. John Watson changed careers about 1920 and went on to become one of the founders of modern advertising. In essay form, speculate about some of the ways techniques of classical conditioning could be used by advertisers.

Connections

1. What would John Locke think of John Watson's methods for conditioning emotional reactions? Could this type of conditioning be used to establish desirable habits? Could it be adapted to an educational curriculum?
2. At one point in Watson and Rayner's lengthy case study we learn that the experimental environment was changed to see whether Baby Albert responded to different lighting conditions. What would Jean-Jacques Rousseau say about this type of manipulation?

Baby In a Box

B. F. Skinner

In that brave new world which science is preparing for the housewife of the   *1*
future, the young mother has apparently been forgotten. Almost nothing has
been done to ease her lot by simplifying and improving the care of babies.

When we decided to have another child, my wife and I felt that it was time   *2*
to apply a little laborsaving invention and design to the problems of the nursery. We began by going over the disheartening schedule of the young mother,
step by step. We asked only one question: Is this practice important for the
physical and psychological health of the baby? When it was not, we marked it
for elimination. Then the "gadgeteering" began.

The result is an inexpensive apparatus in which our baby daughter has now   *3*
been living for eleven months. Her remarkable good health and happiness and
my wife's welcome leisure have exceeded our most optimistic predictions, and
we are convinced that a new deal for both mother and baby is at hand.

We tackled first the problem of warmth. The usual solution is to wrap the   *4*
baby in half-a-dozen layers of cloth — shirt, nightdress, sheet, blankets. This
is never completely successful. The baby is likely to be found steaming in its
own fluids or lying cold and uncovered. Schemes to prevent uncovering may
be dangerous, and in fact they have sometimes even proved fatal. Clothing and
bedding also interfere with normal exercise and growth and keep the baby from
taking comfortable postures or changing posture during sleep. They also encourage rashes and sores. Nothing can be said for the system on the score of
convenience, because frequent changes and launderings are necessary.

Why not, we thought, dispense with clothing altogether — except for the   *5*
diaper, which serves another purpose — and warm the space in which the baby
lives? This should be a simple technical problem in the modern home. Our solution is a closed compartment about as spacious as a standard crib. The walls
are well insulated, and one side, which can be raised like a window, is a large
pane of safety glass. The heating is electrical, and special precautions have been
taken to insure accurate control.

After a little experimentation we found that our baby, when first home from   *6*
the hospital, was completely comfortable and relaxed without benefit of clothing at about 86° F. As she grew older, it was possible to lower the temperature
by easy stages. Now, at eleven months, we are operating at about 78°, with a
relative humidity of 50 per cent.

Raising or lowering the temperature by more than a degree or two will pro-   *7*

---

*B. F. Skinner (b. 1904) has dominated the field of behavioral psychology for
some time. Although he first became famous for his work with operant conditioning in experiments involving rats and pigeons, he has been deeply involved in
learning theory. Dr. Skinner is perhaps best known for his popular works* Walden
Two *(1948) and* Beyond Freedom and Dignity *(1971).*

duce a surprising change in the baby's condition and behavior. This response is so sensitive that we wonder how a comfortable temperature is ever reached with clothing and blankets.

The discovery that pleased us most was that crying and fussing could always be stopped by slightly lowering the temperature. During the first three months, it is true, the baby would also cry when wet or hungry, but in that case she would stop when changed or fed. During the past six months she has not cried at all except for a moment or two when injured or sharply distressed — for example, when inoculated. The "lung exercise" which is so often appealed to to reassure the mother of a baby that cries a good deal takes the much pleasanter form of shouts and gurgles.   *8*

How much of this sustained cheerfulness is due to the temperature is hard to say, because the baby enjoys many other kinds of comfort. She sleeps in curious postures, not half of which would be possible under securely fastened blankets.   *9*

When awake, she exercises almost constantly and often with surprising violence. Her leg, stomach and back muscles are especially active and have become strong and hard. It is necessary to watch this performance for only a few minutes to realize how severely restrained the average baby is, and how much energy must be diverted into the only remaining channel — crying.   *10*

A wider range and variety of behavior are also encouraged by the freedom from clothing. For example, our baby acquired an amusing, almost apelike skill in the use of her feet. We have devised a number of toys which are occasionally suspended from the ceiling of the compartment. She often plays with these with her feet alone and with her hands and feet in close co-operation.   *11*

One toy is a ring suspended from a modified music box. A note can be played by pulling the ring downward, and a series of rapid jerks will produce Three Blind Mice. At seven months our baby would grasp the ring in her toes, stretch out her leg and play the tune with a rhythmic movement of her foot.   *12*

We are not especially interested in developing skills of this sort, but they are valuable for the baby because they arouse and hold her interest. Many babies seem to cry from sheer boredom — their behavior is restrained and they have nothing else to do. In our compartment, the waking hours are invariably active and happy ones.   *13*

Freedom from clothes and bedding is especially important for the older baby who plays and falls asleep off and on during the day. Unless the mother is constantly on the alert, it is hard to cover the baby promptly when it falls asleep and to remove and arrange sheets and blankets as soon as it is ready to play. All this is now unnecessary.   *14*

Remember that these advantages for the baby do not mean additional labor or attention on the part of the mother. On the contrary, there is an almost unbelievable saving in time and effort. For one thing, there is no bed to be made or changed. The "mattress" is a tightly stretched canvas, which is kept dry by warm air. A single bottom sheet operates like a roller towel. It is stored on a spool outside the compartment at one end and passes into a wire hamper at the other. It is ten yards long and lasts a week. A clean section can be locked into place in a few seconds. The time which is usually spent in changing clothes is also saved. This is especially important in the early months. When we take the baby up for feeding or play, she is wrapped in a small blanket or a simple   *15* nightdress. Occasionally she is dressed up "for fun" or for her play period. But that is all. The wrapping blanket, roller sheet and the usual diapers are the only laundry actually required.

Time and labor are also saved because the air which passes through the   *16* compartment is thoroughly filtered. The baby's eyes, ears and nostrils remain fresh and clean. A weekly bath is enough, provided the face and diaper region are frequently washed. These little attentions are easy because the compartment is at waist level.

It takes about one and one half hours each day to feed, change and other-   *17* wise care for the baby. This includes everything except washing diapers and preparing formula. We are not interested in reducing the time any farther. As a baby grows older, it needs a certain amount of social stimulation. And after all, when unnecessary chores have been eliminated, taking care of a baby is fun.

An unforeseen dividend has been the contribution to the baby's good health.   *18* Our pediatrician readily approved the plan before the baby was born, and he has followed the results enthusiastically from month to month. Here are some points on the health score: When the baby was only ten days old, we could place her in the preferred face-down position without danger of smothering, and she has slept that way ever since, with the usual advantages. She has always enjoyed deep and extended sleep, and her feeding and eliminative habits have been extraordinarily regular. She has never had a stomach upset, and she has never missed a daily bowel movement.

The compartment is relatively free of spray and air-borne infection, as well   *19* as dust and allergic substances. Although there have been colds in the family, it has been easy to avoid contagion, and the baby has completely escaped. The neighborhood children troop in to see her, but they see her through glass and keep their school-age diseases to themselves. She has never had a diaper rash.

We have also enjoyed the advantages of a fixed daily routine. Child special-   *20* ists are still not agreed as to whether the mother should watch the baby or the clock, but no one denies that a strict schedule saves time. The mother can plan her day in advance and find time for relaxation or freedom for other activities. The trouble is that a routine acceptable to the baby often conflicts with the schedule of the household. Our compartment helps out here in two ways. Even in crowded living quarters it can be kept free of unwanted lights and sounds. The insulated walls muffle all ordinary noises, and a curtain can be drawn down over the window. The result is that, in the space taken by a standard crib, the baby has in effect a separate room. We are never concerned lest the doorbell, telephone, piano or children at play wake the baby, and we can therefore let her set up any routine she likes.

But a more interesting possibility is that her routine may be changed to suit   *21* our convenience.

A good example of this occurred when we dropped her schedule from four   *22* to three meals per day. The baby began to wake up in the morning about an hour before we wanted to feed her. This annoying habit, once established, may persist for months. However, by slightly raising the temperature during the night, we were able to postpone her demand for breakfast. The explanation is simple. The evening meal is used by the baby mainly to keep itself warm during the night. How long it lasts will depend in part upon how fast heat is absorbed by the surrounding air.

One advantage not to be overlooked is that the soundproofing also protects   *23*
the family from the baby! Our intentions in this direction were misunderstood
by some of our friends. We were never put to the test, because there was no
crying to contend with, but it was never our policy to use the compartment in
order to let the baby "cry it out."

Every effort should be made to discover just why a baby cries. But if the   *24*
condition cannot be remedied, there is no reason why the family, and perhaps
the neighborhood as well, must suffer. (Such a compartment, by the way, might
persuade many a landlord to drop a "no babies" rule, since other tenants can
be completely protected.)

Before the baby was born, when we were still building the apparatus, some   *25*
of the friends and acquaintances who had heard about what we proposed to
do were rather shocked. Mechanical dishwashers, garbage disposers, air cleaners
and other laborsaving devices were all very fine, but a mechanical baby tender
— that was carrying science too far! However, all the specific objections that
were raised against the plan have faded away in the bright light of our results.
A very brief acquaintance with the scheme in operation is enough to resolve
all doubts. Some of the toughtest skeptics have become our most enthusiastic
supporters.

One of the commonest objections was that we were going to raise a "softie"   *26*
who would be unprepared for the real world. But instead of becoming hyper-
sensitive, our baby has acquired a surprisingly serene tolerance for annoyances. She is not bothered by the clothes she wears at playtime, she is not
frightened by loud or sudden noises, she is not frustrated by toys out of reach,
and she takes a lot of pommeling from her older sister like a good sport. It is
possible that she will have to learn to sleep in a noisy room, but adjustments
of that sort are always necessary. A tolerance for any annoyance can be built
up by administering it in controlled dosages, rather than in the usual accidental way. Certainly there is no reason to annoy the child throughout the whole
of its infancy, merely to prepare it for later childhood.

It is not, of course, the favorable conditions to which people object, but the   *27*
fact that in our compartment they are "artificial." All of them occur naturally
in one favorable environment or another, where the same objection should apply but is never raised. It is quite in the spirit of the "world of the future" to
make favorable conditions available everywhere through simple mechanical
means.

A few critics have objected that they would not like to live in such a com-   *28*
partment themselves — they feel that it would stifle them or give them claus-
trophobia. The baby obviously does not share in this opinion. The compartment is well ventilated and much more spacious than a Pullman berth,
considering the size of the occupant. The baby cannot get out, of course, but
that is true of a crib as well. There is less actual restraint in the compartment
because the baby is freer to move about. The plain fact is that she is perfectly
happy. She has never tried to get out nor resisted being put back in, and that
seems to be the final test.

Another early objection was that the baby would be socially starved and   29
robbed of the affection and mother love that she needs. This has simply not
been true. The compartment does not ostracize the baby. The large window is
no more of a social barrier than the bars of a crib. The baby follows what is
going on in the room, smiles at passers-by, plays "peek-a-boo" games, and obviously delights in company. And she is handled, talked to and played with
whenever she is changed or fed, and each afternoon during a play period which
is becoming longer as she grows older.

The fact is that a baby will probably get more love and affection when it is   30
easily cared for, because the mother is not so likely to feel overworked and re-
sentful of the demands made upon her. She will express her love in a practical
way and give the baby genuinely affectionate care.

It is common practice to advise the troubled mother to be patient and tender   31
and to enjoy her baby. And, of course, that is what any baby needs. But it is
the exceptional mother who can fill this prescription upon demand, especially
if there are other children in the family and she has no help. We need to go
one step further and treat the mother with affection also. Simplified child care
will give mother love a chance.

A similar complaint was that such an apparatus would encourage neglect.   32
But easier care is sure to be better care. The mother will resist the temptation
to put the baby back into a damp bed if she can conjure up a dry one in five
seconds. She may very well spend less time with her baby, but babies do not
suffer from being left alone, only from the discomforts which arise from being
left alone in the ordinary crib.

How long do we intend to keep the baby in the compartment? The baby will   33
answer that in time, but almost certainly until she is two years old, or perhaps
three. After the first year, of course, she will spend a fair part of each day in a
play pen or out-of-doors. The compartment takes the place of a crib and will
get about the same use. Eventually it will serve as sleeping quarters only.

We cannot, of course, guarantee that every baby raised in this way will thrive   34
so successfully. But there is a plausible connection between health and happiness and the surroundings we have provided, and I am quite sure that our
success is not an accident. The experiment should, of course, be repeated again
and again with different babies and different parents. One case is enough,
however, to disprove the flat assertion that it can't be done. At least we have
shown that a moderate and inexpensive mechanization of baby care will yield
a tremendous saving in time and trouble, without harm to the child and probably to its lasting advantage.

Professor Skinner's unusual experiment provoked many questions. . . . Here are   35
many of them. . . .

1. How can the mother hear her baby?
36

The apparatus is only partially soundproofed. With the nursery door open
we can hear the baby about as clearly as if she were in an ordinary crib with
the nursery door closed. If it were desirable to hear very clearly, the window
would be left partly open, with the opening covered by a cloth (say, if the child

were sick). The soundproofing has enough advantages from the baby's point of view to make it worth while.

2. Doesn't the discharged sheet have an unpleasant odor?   37

Not in our experience. There is no noticeable odor in our nursery. Visitors frequently comment on this fact. The reason seems to be that dry urine does not give off a strong odor. Our practice has been to wipe up any traces of bowel movements before moving the sheet along. In case of bad soiling, the sheet could be moved out far enough to permit dipping the soiled section into a pan of water or the whole sheet could be changed, but this has never been necessary.

3. Doesn't the canvas mattress acquire an odor?   38

Again, not in our experience. The canvas is constantly bathed in warm air, and there is little or no chance for the bacterial action which makes urine smell. The canvas is stretched on a removable frame, and we have a spare to permit cleaning when necessary (every two or three weeks). The canvas could, therefore, be changed in case of vomiting. Or a rubber sheet could be used. (We do use rubber pants at night, to avoid chilling due to evaporation of the wet diaper.)

4. What happens if the current fails?   39

We have an alarm, operated on dry-cell batteries, which goes off if the temperature deviates more than two degrees from the proper setting. This is wholly independent of the power supply and would tell us of trouble long before the baby had experienced any extreme condition.

5. Don't you believe a baby's daily bath is necessary?   40

Artificial stimulation of the skin at bathtime may be necessary when the usual clothing and bedding are used, but not in our apparatus. From the very first the fine condition of our baby's skin attracted attention. The skin is soft, but not moist. It is rubbed gently and naturally throughout the day by the under sheet as she moves about. Much of the patting which is advised at bathtime is to make up for the lack of normal exercise of the skin circulation, which is due to clothing. Since our baby's skin is always exposed to the air, a very lively skin reaction to changes in temperature has developed.

6. Don't the mother and child both miss daily bathtime fun?   41

We have had a lot of fun with our baby — more perhaps than if we had been burdened down with unnecessary chores. We have always played with her when we felt like it, which was often. As for the baby, she has certainly had more than her share of fun. The freedom from clothing and blankets has provided much of it. Her bath is fun, too, though probably not as much as the usual baby's because the contrast is not so great. The advice of the child specialist to "allow the baby to exercise its legs for a few minutes at bathtime" shows what I mean. Our baby exercises her legs all day long. (My wife insists I say that we do bathe our baby twice a week, though once a week is enough.)

The fact that our baby is not only in perfect physical condition but keenly   42 interested in life and blissfully happy is our final answer to any possible charge of neglect.

Further Comments (1977)

The word "box" was put in my title by the editors of the *Journal* and it led   43 to endless confusion because I had used another box in the study of operant conditioning. Many of those who had not read the article assumed that I was experimenting on our daughter as if she were a rat or pigeon. Those who read it, however, viewed it quite favorably. Hundreds of people wrote to say that they wanted to raise their babies in the same way. I sent out mimeographed instructions to help those who proposed to build boxes for themselves. My contacts with potential manufacturers were disappointing but eventually an enterprising man, John Gray, organized the Aircrib Corporation and began production on a modest scale. He contributed much of his own time without remuneration, and when he died his son was unable to carry on. Second-hand Aircribs are now in demand.

Our daughter continued to use the Aircrib for sleeping and naps until she 44 was two and a half, and during that time we all profited from it. The long sheet and canvas "mattress" were replaced by a tightly stretched woven plastic, with the texture of linen, which could be washed and dried instantly, and once her bowel-movement pattern was established she slept nude. Urine was collected in a pan beneath the plastic. Predictions that she would be a bed-wetter were not confirmed. She learned to keep dry in her clothing during the day and when she started to sleep in a regular bed she treated it like clothing. Except for one night when we had been traveling and were all rather tired, she has never wet a bed. She proved remarkably resistant to colds and other infections.

Possibly through confusion with the other box, the venture began to be mis- 45 understood. Stories circulated about the dire consequences of raising a baby in any such way. It was said that our daughter had committed suicide, become psychotic, and (more recently), was suing me. The fact is that she is a successful artist living in London with her husband, Dr. Barry Buzan, who teaches in the field of international studies. My older daughter, Dr. Julie Vargas, used an Aircrib with her two daughters, and she and many others have confirmed the results we reported.

The Aircrib has many advantages for both child and parents. For the child 46 it offers greater comfort, safety, freedom of movement, and an opportunity for the earliest possible development of motor and perceptual skills. For the parent it saves labor and gives a sense of security about the baby's well being. There is no danger of being strangled by bedclothes or becoming uncovered on a cold night. It is somewhat more expensive than an ordinary crib, even including mattress, sheets, blankets and laundry, but the resale value is high. It can often save money by saving space. By drawing a curtain over the window at night it can be closed off from the rest of the room, making it possible for a young couple to stay for another year or two in a one-room apartment or to let a baby share a room with an older child.

I do not expect to see Aircribs widely used in the near future. It is not the 47 kind of thing that appeals to American business. It is impossible to convince a Board of Directors that there is a market that justifies tooling up for mass production to keep the price down, and so long as the price remains high a market will not develop.

Nevertheless, the first two or three years are the most important years in a 48 child's life, and I am sure that much more will eventually be done to make them more enjoyable and productive.

Considerations

1. In "Baby in a Box" B. F. Skinner makes some intriguing claims concerning the success that his methods have in controlling his baby's crying. Write a brief essay summarizing these claims.
2. Summarize what Skinner feels about "a fixed daily routine" (para. 20).

Connections

1. Look back at the selections "From *Some Thoughts Concerning Education*" and "From *Émile.*" Compare B. F. Skinner's, John Locke's, and Jean-Jacques Rousseau's views about crying in children.
2. Write an essay on the subject of habit. What do Skinner and Locke have to say on this matter?
3. In a section of *Émile* not included in the excerpt here, Rousseau advises:

   > When the child draws its first breath do not confine it in tight wrappings. No cap, no bandages, nor swaddling clothes. Loose and flowing flannel wrappers which leave its limbs free and are not too heavy to check his movements, not too warm to prevent his feeling the air. Put him in a big cradle, well padded, where he can move about easily safely. [p. 27]

   Explain in a brief essay how closely Professor Skinner seems to have honored these guidelines when designing the Aircrib.

Stages and Their Properties in the Development of Thinking

Jean Piaget

The Attainment of Invariants and Reversible Operations in the Development of Thinking

It is the aim of the present essay to introduce American readers to our more   *1* recent studies of children's thinking and the development of intelligence. Only my very early books have been available for many years in English translation. The investigations that we have conducted since then are largely unknown on

---

Jean Piaget (1896–1980) remains the most influential thinker in the cognitive structuralist school of developmental psychology. This article presents his view of the stages in a child's cognitive growth.

this side of the Atlantic ocean. In the presentation to follow I would like to sketch this work briefly, and to illustrate it with concrete examples from our experiments.

An important difference between our older studies and our present ones   2
pertains to their method: Initially we relied exclusively on interviews and asked the children only verbal questions. This may have been a beginning, and it can yield certain types of results but, assuredly, it is not exhaustive. Of late, our investigations have been conducted quite differently. We now try to start with some action that the child must perform. We introduce him into an experimental setting, present him with objects and — after the problem has been stated — the child must do something, he must experiment. Having observed his actions and manipulation of objects we can then pose the verbal questions that constitute the interview. Note that this interview now pertains to a preceding action, and this seems to me to be a more fruitful and reliable method than the purely verbal inquiry.

Furthermore, while our earlier studies pertained to various classes of thought   3
content, we later became increasingly more interested in the formal aspects of thought. The aspects transcend any single content category and provide the basis for the intellectual elaboration of any and all contents. During the past few years our essential preoccupation has been the analysis of those complex structures[1] of thought that seem to characterize the various developmental stages. Complex structures at the highest level are those systems of operations[2] — be they themselves relatively simple or complex — that make the total operation possible. I shall emphasize primarily one aspect of these structures, namely their reversibility. I use the term reversibility in its logical or mathematical sense, not in its physiological or medical connotation. I believe intelligence is above all characterized by the coordination of operations that are reversible actions.

Basically, to solve a problem is to coordinate operations while focusing on   4
the solution. An operation is, first of all, an action. We shall see that at its inception intelligence begins with simple actions on the sensori-motor level, actions which then become interiorized and come to be represented symbolically. Moreover, operations are basically actions which can be performed in either direction, that is, actions which are reversible. This is really the remarkable thing about intelligence, if one compares intelligence with other mental functions, for instance habits. Habits are not reversible, they are oriented in one direction only. Thus, we have learned to write from left to right, and if we wanted to write from right to left we could not do so on the basis of our previous habits, we would have to start learning a new habit. By contrast, once we can handle an operation, for instance the operation of adding in the arithmetical sense, or in its more general logical sense, we can reverse that specific action. From the moment when the child understands what it means to add, that is, to bring together two groups to form one, he implicitly knows also what it means to separate the groups again, to dissociate them, to subtract. It is of the same operation; he can work in one way, in one direction, and also the other way, in the opposite direction. This reversibility is not a primitive matter; it is progressively built up as a function of the same complex structures mentioned above. From the psychological point of view, one of the

most fruitful terrains for the analysis of this reversibility is the problem of conservation.

In any system of reversible actions there results the construction of certain   5 invariants, certain forms of conservation analogue to those subserving scientific reasoning. In the young child we can observe the development of these invariants, and the evolution of concepts of conservation. For instance, we can ask a child whether, when a given liquid is being poured from a container A into another container B of a different shape, the quantity of the liquid remains the same. For us that is self-evident, as it is for children above a certain age. But we shall see that for the younger child it is not self-evident at all. In fact, they will say that the quantity has increased because the height of the new container is greater, or that it is less because container B is thinner. They have not yet attained the logically relevant concept of conservation and the pertinent invariants, and they cannot grasp these until some time later when their thinking becomes capable of reversible operations, and when these operations become coordinated structures. The immediate result of the achievement of such structures is not only the affirmation of certain forms of conservation, but, at the same time, the insight that this conservation is self-evident, logically necessary, precisely because it arises from the coordination of operations. Let us trace now, step by step, the development of this reversibility, of these forms of conservation and also of certain complex structures.

I shall distinguish four stages in this development: (1) the pre-language sen-   6 sori-motor stage: (2) the pre-operational stage from 2–7 years; (3) the stage of concrete operations between the approximate ages of 7 and 12; (4) finally the stage of propositional operations with their formal characteristics which are attained at the pre-adolescent and adolescent stage.

The Pre-language Stage

We need to say only a few words about the sensori-motor stage. This period   7 is important because during it are developed substructures essential for later operations. At the present time everybody agrees that there is intelligent action prior to language. The baby demonstrates intelligent behavior before he can speak. Interestingly, we note, the earliest forms of intelligence already aim at the construction of certain invariants — practical invariants to be sure, namely invariants of the concrete space of immediate action. These first invariants are already the result of a sort of reversibility but it is a practical reversibility embedded in the very action; it is not yet a constituent of thought proper. Of the invariants which arise at the sensori-motor stage perhaps the most important one is the schema of the permanent object. I call the permanent object that object which continues to exist outside of the perceptual field. A perceived object is not permanent object in that sense. I would say that there is no schema of a permanent object if the child no longer reacts once the object has disappeared from the perceptual field, when it is no longer visible, when it can no longer be touched, when it is no longer heard. On the other hand I would say that there is already an invariant, a schema of the permanent object, if the child begins to search for the vanished object. Such a schema is not present from the very beginning. When, at about 4½ months of age, a child starts to reach for the things he sees in his visual field and, when he begins to coordinate vision and prehension to some extent, one can observe that he does not yet react to a permanent object. For instance, I may show the infant a watch, dangling it in front of him. He reaches out to take the watch, but at the very moment when he has already extended his hand, I cover the watch with a napkin. What happens? He promptly withdraws his hand as if the watch had been absorbed into the napkin. Even though he can very well remove the napkin if it is put over his own face, he does not lift it in order to look for the watch underneath. You might say that the watch is perhaps of no great interest to the infant: however, the same experiment can be made with a nursing bottle. I have done this with one of my children at the age of 7 months. At the time of his feeding I show him the bottle, he extends his hand to take it, but, at that moment, I hide it behind my arm. If he sees one end sticking out he kicks and screams and gives every indication of wanting to have it. If, however, the bottle is completely hidden and nothing sticks out, he stops crying and acts for all we know as if the bottle no longer existed, as if it had been dissolved and absorbed into my arm.

Towards the end of the first year the infant begins to search for the vanished object. Already at 9 to 10 months he looks for it behind a screen. If we place the child between two screens, for example, a cloth or a pillow on his right and another one at his left, we can make a very curious observation concerning the locus of the hiding place. With the child in that position I now show him, for instance, a watch. As soon as he evinces interest in the watch I place it under the cloth at his right. Thereupon the child will promptly lift the cloth and grasp the watch. Now I take it from him and, very slowly, so that he can follow with his eyes, move the watch over to his left side. Then, having made sure that he has indeed followed the movement, I cover the watch in its new position. I have observed this in my three children over varying periods of time, and we have repeated this experiment frequently since. There is a stage when, at the moment the child sees the watch disappear at the left, he immediately turns back to the right and looks for the watch there. In other words, he looks for the object where he has found it before. The object is not yet a mobile thing, capable of movements and correlated displacements in an autonomous system in space. Rather, the object is still an extension of the action itself, an action that is repeated where and how it was successful the first time around. 8

Finally, towards the end of the first year the object comes to have a degree of independent existence. Its disappearance elicits search, and that search is guided by the observed displacements. Now we can speak of a structure of coordinated displacements or, indeed, a group of displacements in the sense in which the term is used in geometry with the implication of the possibilities of movement in one direction and in reverse as well as of detours by means of which the same goal can be reached over a variety of alternate pathways. A long time ago Henri Poincaré advanced the hypothesis that primitive sensorimotor space must originate from such groups of displacements.[3] Without entering into the details of that discussion, I should like to point out that this group structure — which is already a reversible structure — is not an *a priori* given, as Poincaré would have us believe. Instead, it develops gradually during the first year. The attainment of the notion of permanent object is the exact 9 correlate of the emerging organization of reversible movements that constitute the groups of displacements. You could say that the permanent object is the first group invariant, provided it is understood that a group at this level is not yet a system of operations but merely a system of practical actions in the immediate space. This system enables the individual to take account of successive displacements, to order them, then reverse them, and so forth.

The Pre-operational Stage

Let us turn now to the development of representational thinking proper. We *10* observe it first in play, in imaginary games with their fictitious qualities and symbolic aspects, play in which one thing comes to be represented by means of another thing. Differentiated imitation, for instance of various people in the child's environment, and a variety of other symbolic acts belong to this stage. Such representational thinking greatly enlarges the range of intellectual activity. The latter no longer pertains only to the nearby space, the present moment and the action in progress. Thanks to representational thought such activity can now be applied with reference to far away space, to events outside the immediate perceptual sphere, to the past which can be recovered and recounted and to the future in the form of plans and projects. In other words the universe of representation is obviously much wider than the universe of direct action. Consequently, the first tools that have already been developed at the sensori-motor level cannot be applied immediately to this wider sphere, they cannot be generalized immediately in their broader relevance. The child must now reconstruct on an ideational plane the invariants, the forms of coordination whose beginnings we observed at the sensori-motor level. All this takes place in the period which extends from the beginning of language at one end to the age of about seven or eight years at the other end. During this period we can already speak of thought, of representation, but not yet of logical operations defined as interiorized reversible action systems. In children within this age range we have studied all sorts of problems of conservation and invariants, and we have found quite systematically that these notions of conservation begin to develop only at about the age of seven or eight years.

I shall not come back to the problem of liquids being poured from one con- *11* tainer into another, but we can make the same experiment with beads. We can ask the child to put blue beads into container A and red beads into container B, and we make sure that each time he places a blue bead into container A he also places a red bead into the other container B, so that will be the same number of beads in each of the two containers. The child is then told to pour the beads from container B into a new container C, thereupon we ask him if there are the same number of beads in C as in A — those in A having remained there and those from B having been poured into C. Now a curious thing happens. Until approximately the age of 6½ years the child believes that the number of beads has changed, that there are more beads in container C because it is higher than B, or that there are fewer beads in container C because it is thinner than B. If you ask him "Where do these extra beads come from?" or "What happened to the beads that are no longer there?" he is very much surprised at your question. He is totally uninterested in the mechanism of the transformation. What interests him is the gross perceptual configuration which is different in the two situations; even in the case of these discrete entities there is no conservation of absolute quantities.

The same can be shown with respect to the correspondence of numbers. You *12* can make the following experiment. The child is presented with an alignment of six blue poker chips, one next to the other, and is given a box of red poker chips with the request to construct a similar array with as many red poker chips as there are blue poker chips in the model. Here we find three stages, two of them belonging to the period now under discussion. There is a primitive stage at approximately 4 to 4½ years when the child simply places chips in a line of similar length without regard for any one-to-one correspondence of the components. Thus, he defines quantity essentially in terms of occupied space.

The second stage is much more interesting and lasts approximately to age *13* 6½ to 7 years. Here we find exact correspondence between the number of the chips in the model and those placed by the child. Many authors have been satisfied with this visual correspondence, and they have concluded that it is proof of the child's understanding of numbers. We can show, however, that this is not the case. All you have to do is to spread the chips of one of the two groups a little further apart, or to push them closer together, and the child will no longer think that the two alignments contain identical quantities. As soon as visual correspondence is destroyed, the one-to-one correspondence of numbers-of-action is abolished. In other words, the equivalence that the child had produced was only one of the perceptual configuration, a construction which is not yet an operation in our sense. As the configuration changes, the equivalence disappears, and there is no conservation of quantity.

We can study the problem of conservation of quantity also in the realm of *14* space. For example, we draw two parallel lines of the same length whose endpoints lie directly underneath one another; then we shift one of the lines to the right or the left. Under these conditions some children tell us that one line is longer because it extends beyond the other one at the left, or that the first is shorter because the second projects beyond the first one on the right. I have seen some children who, at approximately age seven, suddenly discovered the conservation of length during this experiment. First they said that one line is longer, then that the other line is longer, and then all at once, they said: "No, they are the same. You have moved this line, and that makes a difference at one end, but there is the same difference at the other, and so it is really the same all along." This may seem to you very complicated reasoning to arrive at a notion which is obvious to us, but it is not at all obvious at a level when the invariant relationships between beginning and end are not yet firmly established with respect to length.

The same is true for conservation of distance. We have shown the child a *15* model of two trees, asking him to tell us whether they were close together or far apart in order to establish these concepts. Then we put a wall between the two trees, a box for instance, and I expected that the children would tell us now that the trees were further apart than before, because there is a barrier between them. I reasoned in motor terms, but the children did not. Fortunately psychology is an experimental science and we often find the opposite of what we expect. In this situation children between five and six and a half have explained to me that the distance is less now than before because the linear distance occupied by the barrier does not count. Near and far refer to empty space between objects; the space occupied by the box is not empty and therefore it does not count. One child said to me: "Of course if you had a hole in the wall, it would be the same as before." So we constructed a wall with a hole and a shutter, so that we could open and close the hole. Now indeed we observed that the distance remained unchanged in the eyes of the children as long as the hole remained open, even though they continued to assert that the distance was less as soon as the aperture was closed. These experiments are interesting because they demonstrate not only the impact of the perceptual configuration, which we have mentioned before, but even as influenced by certain perceptual illusions — for example, contrast effects. Perceptually speaking, a straight line and an empty space do not have identical spatial values, and their perceptual difference manifests itself here at the representational level.

Another example is the following: We confront the child with two identical _16_ green cardboards and tell him that these are two pastures where cows can graze. Both have lots of grass, so much, in fact, that if you put a cow half-way between the two she cannot decide which one to choose. At this point the child readily agrees that obviously the two pastures must be equal. Now the farmer who owns the first pasture puts up a house in one corner. The second farmer, who owns the other pasture, builds exactly the same kind of house but, instead of putting it in the corner he puts it right in the middle of the pasture. Do equal amounts of grass remain in the two pastures now? Already here the configuration is somewhat different but you see a good number of children who will tell you that it is the same on both pastures when there is only one house. Next, the first farmer puts up another house adjoining the first one in the corner, and the second farmer puts another one here, adjoining the one in the middle. Are there still equal amounts of grass to be had from the two pastures? Starting with two houses it has become complicated. There are children who will tell us that there is lots more grass in the one pasture than in the other. Remember Euclid's theorem that if you take two equal quantities from two equal quantities there remain two equal quantities? That is the same logic that presupposes conservation, but here we have no conservation and Euclid's axiom is not yet valid for the 5-year-old.

The Stage of Concrete Operations

Towards the age of seven or so the problems of conservation become re- _17_ solved. There are a few exceptions that concern complex quantities, for instance weight or volume, but simple quantities such as collections or lengths are no longer problematical. How have they been resolved? They have been resolved as a function of three arguments which children always give you, irrespective of the experimental problem. The first argument is: the quantity, or the number is the same — for example, in the bead problem, nothing has been added and nothing has been taken away. I call this the identity argument, because it takes place entirely within the single, self-contained system without any attempt at transcending the boundaries of that system. This argument is certainly not the true root of the attainment of conservation, because the younger children also know very well that nothing has been added or taken away. The real problem is to know why this becomes an argument for the child at a given moment, when it was not an argument for him before.

The child's second argument tells us the reason. I call this the argument of *18* simple reversibility. The child says: "You have done nothing except to pour the beads in the other container, so it looks different, but all you have to do is to pour them back and you will see that they are the same." In other words, it is no longer the perceptual configuration which is interesting, it is their displacement and the resultant transformation. This transformation is apprehended as something that can take place in both directions, that is reversible. Now we understand the first argument concerning the identity of the beads. Identity is precisely the product of the original operation and its reversal; it has attained the status of a system as a function of this simple reversibility.

The third argument used by the children is again based on a kind of revers- *19* ibility, but now in the form of a pattern of relationships. The child tells you: "Here is more height but a little less width; what you gain in height you lose in width; that evens it out." This implies a pattern of relationships, a multiplication of relationships and their mutual compensation; it is once more a type of reversibility. In other words these three arguments, that of identity, that of simple reversibility and that of patterned relationships show you the beginnings of operations as we have defined them. These operations, that can be observed between the ages of seven years and eleven or twelve years, are already logical operations. Their structure is essentially logical, even though the available implications of that logic are still rather limited. They are only operations of classes and relations and are not yet operations of the logic of propositions. They do not even contain all the operations possible with classes and relations, but only certain rather elementary systems that can be understood by the child as they relate to concrete *manipulanda*. These operations always center around an action or an application to specific objects. For this reason we call them "concrete operations." We use the term "operational groupings" to designate those elementary and immediate systems of action which are patterned as they occur in spatial and temporal contiguity; these simple systems do not yet include all of the logic of classes and relations.

Here is another example of such an operational grouping. The problem is *20* one of inclusion; that is, the inclusion of a class A in a class B with the complement of A', of inclusion of class B in a class C with the complement of B' etc. In this case you have a very simple system in which the addition of two classes results in a new class from which substraction of one leads back to the first class a tautology with rather limited possibilities. This structure first appears at about age seven and, it seems to me, is basic for the notion of conservation. It is impossible to conduct such operations without invariants and without conservation, precisely because the necessary invariant of these operations is the conservation of the total system. We can experimentally show that this is the case by testing the relationship of inclusion of A in B. You present the child with an open box that contains wooden beads. The child knows they are all wooden because he handles them, touching each and finding that it is made of wood. Most of these beads are brown, but a few are white. The problem we pose is simply this: are there more brown beads or more wooden beads? Let us call A the brown beads, B the wooden beads: then the problem is simply that of the inclusion of A in B. This is a very difficult problem before the age of 7 years. The child states that all the beads are wooden, states that most of them are brown and a few are white, but if you ask him if there are more brown beads or more wooden beads he immediately answers: "There are more brown ones because there are only two or three white ones." So you say: "Listen, this is not what I am asking. I don't want to know whether there are more brown or more white beads, I want to know whether there are more brown beads or more wooden beads." And, in order to make it easier, I take an empty box and place it next to the one with the beads and I ask: "If I were to put the wooden beads into that box would any remain in this one?" The child answers: "No, none would be left because they are all wooden." Then I say: "If I were to take the brown beads and put them into the box, would any be left in this one?" The child replies: "Of course, two or three white ones would remain." Apparently he has now understood the situation, the fact that all the beads are wooden and that some are not brown. So I ask him once more: "Are there more brown beads or more wooden beads?" Now it is evident that the child begins to understand the problem, see that there is indeed a problem, that matters are not as simple as they seemed at first. As we watch him we observe that he is thinking very hard. Finally he concludes: "But there are still more brown beads; if you take the brown ones away, only two or three white beads remain."

Why does this answer recur? Because the child can reason about the whole   *21* as long as it is not broken up into parts or, if we force him to break it up, he can reason about the parts, but he cannot reason simultaneously about the whole and the parts. If he is pushed to deal with the brown beads, then the whole no longer exists, it is divided into the two components, the brown beads and the white beads. In order to reunite one part with the whole, the child must not only be capable of the reasoning involved, he must at the same time understand that one part is always the whole minus the other part, and that presupposes conservation of the whole, conservation which results here from simple grouping operations involving classes. This system is psychologically so interesting because it is one of the basic systems which mediate the notions of conservation.

The Stage of Propositional Operations[4]

Let us proceed to the last stage which begins approximately at the age of   *22* 12 years and which is characteristic of the whole adolescent development. This is the period during which new logical operations appear: propositional operations, the logic of propositions, implication, and so forth. These are superimposed onto the earlier concrete operations. The adolescent is no longer limited to concrete reasoning about objects, he begins to reason hypothetically. Starting from a theoretical assumption he can reason that if it is true, then certain consequences must follow. This is the hypothetico deductive method that presupposes implication, disjunction, compatibility, and all the other operations of the logic of propositions. The psychological problem here is first of all to discover how the logic of propositions develops, how it arises out of the concrete operations discussed above. Moreover, at the same stage — that is, starting at about the age of 12 years, there appear not only propositional operations but also, and very striking, a host of other types of new operations which, at first glance, have no relationship to the propositional operations.

There are for instance what the mathematicians call combinatorial opera- *23* tions. Let me illustrate these by the results of another experiment. We present the child with piles of red, blue, green, and yellow poker chips and set him the task to make all possible combinations of pairs, or all possible combinations of three or four colors. At the level of concrete operations, up to age twelve or so, the child can produce a number of such groups and combinations, and can do so correctly, but he is unable to find a systematic method by means of which he can arrive at all possible combinations. By contrast, around age twelve the child begins to find a practical method that will permit him to make all possible combinations, even though he has not had any instruction concerning combinatorial operations nor learned the proper mathematical formula.

More or less simultaneously we observe at the same stage the appearance *24* of operations which involve proportions. This too we can study experimentally, for instance by means of balance problems where weights and distances can be varied. Here the child discovers that a given weight A at distance B from the fulcrum is equal to weight B at distance A, and he thus comes to establish proportions between weights and distances. Also at approximately the same time operations involving probabilities first appear, operations which involve the consideration of probable and possible events. Finally, certain additional types of operations also enter during this stage, operations which we shall leave aside in the present discussion.

Two fundamental psychological questions arise in connection with this last *25* stage. The first concerns the nature and development of the logic of propositions. Secondly, we must ask why the logic of propositions appears at the same time as such other systems of operation as combinations, proportions, and so forth, that have at first sight no particular relationship either among each other or to the logic of propositions. Here the concept of complex structures appears to me to be especially valuable. Let us take, for instance, the well-known sixteen basic operations of the logic of propositions. If you compare their structure to the structure of concrete operations, you see immediately that there are marked differences. The former is a lattice-type structure in the usual mathematical meaning of that term, a complete lattice, while the latter has an incomplete lattice structure, with a join for any two positions, but lacking meets for classes of the same rank.[5] It is a semi-lattice, and so are all the groups of concrete operations: they may have joins and lack meets, or they may contain meets but lack joins. As soon as you deal with propositional logic, however, you have the basic fourfold table[6] which, to be sure, looks as if it might represent simply the multiplication of classes, that is, which apparently resembles one of the systems already available at a more concrete level.

The great new achievement at this level is the fact that the sixteen binary *26* operations of two-valued propositional logic are systematically derived from the four basic conjunctions. In other words, the attainment of propositional logic presupposes a lattice structure which has evolved from the semi-lattice structures implied by the operations at the earlier, more concrete level, which is the direct result of the generalization of classification. The lattice is the schema of all possible classifications which can be derived from its elements but, at the same time, the lattice has combinatorial characteristics. From the psychological point of view it is very striking to find the simultaneous appearance of propositional operations on the one hand, operations which presuppose a lattice structure and thus combinatorial operations and, on the other hand, combinatorial operations applied to mathematical problems. The child is of course not aware of the identity of the structure of these apparently different operations, an identity which our analysis has convincingly demonstrated.

Now as to proportions — how are we to explain the appearance of proportions at the same stage? Let us remember that propositional operations do not only constitute a lattice, they also constitute a group. If you take any operation, such as implication, you can reverse it — that is, state its negative, and you can determine its reciprocal, as well as the negative of the reciprocal. The latter I would like to call its correlative. Here we have a group of four transformations, logical transformations to be sure, but transformations from which you can nevertheless derive a system of proportions. This system results from the application of simple operations to a single proposition.   27

Perhaps this seems a very abstract explanation. Let us go back, therefore, to concrete observations, and let us find out how the child comes to discover proportions. He discovers proportions through experience, for instance as he finds out that adding weight on a balance produces the same result as increasing a constant weight's distance from the fulcrum, and vice versa, that he can lighten the load by decreasing either weight or distance. In this way he learns the equivalence of two transformations. At the same time he discovers reciprocals — that is, if he increases the weight he must decrease the distance, if he increases the distance he must decrease the weight in order to maintain equilibrium. The child does of course not know these special terms, he expresses himself in simple, everyday language, but his language describes his reasoning exactly. He states that increasing the weight while decreasing the distance gives the same result as decreasing the weight and increasing the distance, and this is a statement of proportions.   28

Conclusion

I suggest that the structure of propositional operations is a complex structure which comprises both lattices and groups. Such a structure has many possibilities and implications. These may remain potentialities only, or they may be realized when there arises a problem requiring propositional operations. Let me add that this hypothesis is not only of psychological interest but also has physiological relevance. In recent years the models of cybernetics have begun to give us some understanding of how operations are combined in the solutions of problems. A formal analysis of these models reveals that their operations are also the outcome of group structures and lattice structures. Even at the very outset you find simple regulatory mechanisms, feedbacks, which may be understood as the most elementary form of reversibility, and which derive from as well as result in a complex structure. At the present time we   29 are engaged in the study of these structures. They have a twofold interest: first by analogy with mathematical operations, which are after all, operations of thought; and secondly by analogy with the physiological structures, or, if you will, with the cybernetic models of hypothesized physiological structures.

NOTES

[1] *Editor's note.* Piaget defines structure as ". . . a form of organization of experience." Battro, Antonio, *Piaget: Dictionary of Terms,* translated and edited by Elizabeth Rütschi-Herrmann, and Sarah F. Campbell, New York: Pergamon Press, 1973, p. 168.

[2] Definition: ". . . interiorized actions or interiorizable actions, reversible and coordinated in total structures." Battro, p. 121.

[3] Henri Poincaré, "The Value of Science," in *The Foundations of Science* (Lancaster, Pa.: The Science Press, 1940), Chaps. III and IV.

[4] *Editor's note.* Often called formal operations.

[5] In the introduction of Piaget's *Logic and Psychology* (New York: Basic Books, 1957), W. Mays gives the following definitions (p. xv): "Boolean algebra may be considered as a special case of certain abstract mathematical systems called lattices. A lattice has certain limiting conditions — *join* and *meet.* In the case of any two classes X and Y, the *join* is the smallest of the classes in which X and Y are both included, and the *meet* is the largest class included both in X and Y." (Italics in original.)

[6] Note 2, pp. xi–xiv and p. 34. For detail the reader may consult any good introductory text, for example, S. K. Langer, *An Introduction to Symbolic Logic,* 2d rev. ed. (New York: Dover, 1953). The interested reader is referred also to the treatment by the author of Alice in Wonderland, Lewis Carroll, in his *Symbolic Logic, Part I Elementary* (London: Macmillan, 1897).

Considerations

1. Write a one-paragraph definition for each of the following terms, all of which are important in reading Piaget's works: (1) *schema,* (2) *assimilation,* (3) *accommodation,* (4) *equilibrium.* (Use outside resources if you need to.)
2. According to Piaget, what are the four stages of cognitive development? What are the chief characteristics of each stage? Can you find concrete examples of each in "Stages and Their Properties"? Write a brief essay that attempts to answer the above questions.

Connections

1. How does Jean Piaget define an *operation?* After you are satisfied that you know the answer to this question, write an essay that explains what Piaget might have thought of John Locke's discussion of Habit.
2. If John Locke and Jean Piaget were to meet, what would they have to say to each other?
3. What would Jean-Jacques Rousseau have to say about the concept of object permanence, which Piaget discusses in his considerations of the "pre-language" stage of development?

Adolescent Thinking
Bärbel Inhelder and Jean Piaget

. . . As opposed to the child who feels inferior and subordinate to the adult,   *1*
the adolescent is an individual who begins to consider himself as the equal of
adults and to judge them, with complete reciprocity, on the same plane as
himself. But to this first trait, two others are indissolubly related. The adolescent is an individual who is still growing, but one who begins to think of the
future — *i.e.*, of his present or future work in society. Thus, to his current activities he adds a life program for later "adult" activities. Further, in most cases
in our societies, the adolescent is the individual who in attempting to plan his
present or future work in adult society also has the idea (from his point of view,
it is directly related to his plans) of changing this society, whether in some
limited area or completely. Thus it is impossible to fill an adult role without
conflicts, and whereas the child looks for resolution of his conflicts in present-
day compensations (real or imaginary), the adolescent adds to these limited
compensations the more general compensation of a motivation for change, or
even specific planning for change.

Furthermore, seen in the light of these three interrelated features, the ado-   *2*
lescent's adoption of adult roles certainly presupposes those affective and intellectual tools whose spontaneous development is exactly what distinguishes
adolescence from childhood. If we take these new tools as a starting point, we
have to ask: what is their nature and how do they relate to formal thinking?

On a naive global level, without trying to distinguish between the student,   *3*
the apprentice, the young worker, or the young peasant in terms of how their
social attitudes may vary, the adolescent differs from the child above all in
that he thinks beyond the present. The adolescent is the individual who commits himself to possibilities — although we certainly do not mean to deny that
his commitment begins in real-life situations. In other words, the adolescent is
the individual who begins to build "systems" or "theories," in the largest sense
of the term.

The child does not build systems. His spontaneous thinking may be more or   *4*
less systematic (at first only to a small degree, later, much more so); but it is
the observer who sees the system from outside, while the child is not aware of
it since he never thinks about his own thought. For example, in an earlier work
on the child's representation of the world, we were able to report on a number
of systematic responses. Later we were able to construct the systems characterizing various genetic stages. But *we* constructed the system; the *child* does
not try to systematize his ideas, although he may often spontaneously return

---

*Bärbel Inhelder (b. 1913) and Jean Piaget continue to trace cognitive develop-
ment through adolescence. They stress parallels between intellectual and emotional
changes associated with this stormy period.*

to the same preoccupations and unconsciously give analogous answers.[1] In other words, the child has no powers of reflection — *i.e.,* no second-order thoughts which deal critically with his own thinking. No theory can be built without such reflection.

In contrast, the adolescent is able to analyze his own thinking and construct   5
theories. The fact that these theories are oversimplified, awkward, and usually contain very little originality is beside the point. From the functional standpoint, his systems are significant in that they furnish the cognitive and evaluative bases for the assumption of adult roles, without mentioning a life program and projects for change. They are vital in the assimilation of the values which delineate societies for social classes as entities in contrast to simple interindividual relations.

Consider a group of students between 14–15 years and the *baccalaureat.*[2] Most   6
of them have political or social theories and want to reform the world; they have their own ways of explaining all of the present-day turmoil in collective life. Others have literary or aesthetic theories and place their reading or their experiences of beauty on a scale of values which is projected into a system. Some go through religious crises and reflect on the problem of faith, thus moving toward a universal system — a system valid for all. Philosophical speculation carries away a minority, and for any true intellectual, adolescence is the metaphysical age *par excellence,* an age whose dangerous seduction is forgotten only with difficulty at the adult level. A still smaller minority turns from the start toward scientific or pseudo-scientific theories. But whatever the variation in content, each one has his theory or theories, although they may be more or less explicit and verbalized or even implicit. Some write down their ideas, and it is extremely interesting to see the outlines which are taken up and filled in in later life. Others are limited to talking and ruminating, but each one has his own ideas (and usually he believes they are his own) which liberate him from childhood and allow him to place himself as the equal of adults.

If we now step outside the student range and the intellectual classes to look   7
at the reactions of the adolescent worker, apprentice, or peasant, we can recognize the same phenomenon in other forms. Instead of working out personal "theories," we would find him subscribing to ideas passed on by comrades, developing in meetings, or provoked by reading. We would find fewer family and still fewer religious crises, and especially a lower degree of abstraction. But under different and varied exteriors the same core process can easily be discerned — the adolescent is no longer content to live the interindividual relations offered by his immediate surroundings or to use his intelligence to solve the problems of the moment. Rather, he is motivated also to take his place in the adult social framework, and with this aim he tends to participate in the ideas, ideals, and ideologies of a wider group through the medium of a number of verbal symbols to which he was indifferent as a child.

But how can we explain the adolescent's new capacity to orient himself to-   8
ward what is abstract and not immediately present (seen from the outside by the observer comparing him to the child), but which (seen from within) is an indispensable instrument in his adaptation to the adult social framework, and as a result his most immediate and most deeply experienced concern? There is no doubt that this is the most direct and, moreover, the simplest manifestation

of formal thinking. Formal thinking is both thinking about thought (propositional logic is a second-order operational system which operates on propositions whose truth, in turn, depend on class, relational, and numerical operations) and a reversal of relations between what is real and what is possible (the empirically given comes to be inserted as a particular sector of the total set of possible combinations). These are the two characteristics — which up to this point we have tried to describe in the abstract language appropriate to the analysis of reasoning — which are the source of the living responses, always so full of emotion, which the adolescent uses to build his ideals in adapting to society. The adolescent's theory construction shows both that he has become capable of reflective thinking and that his thought makes it possible for him to escape the concrete present toward the realm of the abstract and the possible. Obviously, this does not mean that formal structures are first organized by themselves and are later applied as adaptive instruments where they prove individually or socially useful. The two processes — structural development and everyday application — both belong to the same reality, and it is *because* formal thinking plays a fundamental role from the functional standpoint that it can attain its general and logical structure. Once more, logic is not isolated from life; it is no more than the expression of operational coordinations essential to action.

But this does not mean that the adolescent takes his place in adult society 9
merely in terms of general theories and without personal involvement. Two other aspects of his entrance into adult society have to be considered — his life program, and his plans for changing the society he sees. The adolescent not only builds new theories or rehabilitates old ones; he also feels he has to work out a conception of life which gives him an opportunity to assert himself and to create something new (thus the close relationship between his system and his life program). Secondly, he wants a guarantee that he will be more successful than his predecessors (thus the need for change in which altruistic concern and youthful ambitions are inseparably blended).

In other words, the process which we have followed through the different 10
stages of the child's development is recapitulated on the planes of thought and reality new to formal operations. An initial failure to distinguish between objects or the actions of others and one's own actions gives way to an enlargement of perspective toward objectivity and reciprocity. Even at the sensorimotor level, the infant does not at first know how to separate the effects of his own actions from the qualities of external objects or persons. At first he lives in a world without permanent objects and without awareness of the self or of any internal subjective life. Later he differentiates his own ego and situates his body in a spatially and casually organized field composed of permanent objects and other persons similar to himself. This is the first decentering process; its result is the gradual coordination of sensorimotor behavior. But when symbolic functioning appears, language, representation, and communication with others expand this field to unheard-of proportions and a new type of structure is required. For a second time egocentrism appears, but this time on another plane. It still takes the form of an initial relative lack of differentiation both between ego's and alter's points of view, between subjective and objective, but this time the lack of differentiation is representational rather than sensorimo-

tor. When the child reaches the stage of concrete operations (7–8 years), the decentering process has gone far enough for him to be able to structure relationships between classes, relations, and numbers objectively. At the same stage, he acquires skill in interindividual relations in a cooperative framework. Furthermore, the acquisition of social cooperation and the structuring of cognitive operations can be seen as two aspects of the same developmental process. But when the cognitive field is again enlarged by the structuring of formal thought, a third form of egocentrism comes into view. This egocentrism is one of the most enduring features of adolescence; it persists until the new and later decentering which makes possible the true beginnings of adult work.

Moreover, the adolescent manifestation of egocentrism stems directly from *11* the adoption of adult roles, since . . . the adolescent not only tries to adapt his ego to the social environment but, just as emphatically, tries to adjust the environment to his ego. In other words, when he begins to think about the society in which he is looking for a place, he has to think about his own future activity and about how he himself might transform this society. The result is a relative failure to distinguish between his own point of view as an individual called upon to organize a life program and the point of view of the group which he hopes to reform.

In more concrete terms, the adolescent's egocentrism comes out in a sort of *12* Messianic form such that the theories used to represent the world center on the role of reformer that the adolescent feels himself called upon to play in the future. To fully understand the adolescent's feelings, we have to go beyond simple observation and look at intimate documents such as essays not written for immediate public consumption, diaries, or simply the disclosures some adolescents may make of their personal fantasies. For example, in the recitations obtained by G. Dumas from a high-school class on their evening reveries, the most normal students — the most retiring, the most amiable — calmly confessed to fantasies and fabulations which several years later would have appeared in their own eyes as signs of pathological megalomania. Without going into the details of this group, we see that the universal aspect of the phenomenon must be sought in the relationship between the adolescent's apparently abstract theories and the life program which he sets up for himself. Then we see that behind impersonal and general exteriors these systems conceal programs of action whose ambitiousness and naivete are usually immoderate. We could also consider the following sample taken from the dozen or so ex-pupils of a small-town school in Romansch Switzerland. One of them, who has since become a shopkeeper, astonished his friends with his literary doctrines and wrote a novel in secret. Another, who has since become the director of an insurance company, was interested among other things in the future of the theater and showed some close friends the first scene of the first act of a tragedy — and got no further. A third, taken up with philosophy, dedicated himself to no less a task than the reconciliation of science and religion. We do not even have to enumerate the social and political reformers found on both right and left. There were only two members of the class who did not reveal any astounding life plans. Both were more or less crushed under strong "superegos" of parental origin, and we do not know what their secret daydreams might have been.

Sometimes this sort of life program has a real influence on the individual's *13* later growth, and it may even happen that a person rediscovers in his adolescent jottings an outline of some ideas which he has really fulfilled since. But in the large majority of cases, adolescent projects are more like a sort of sophisticated game of compensation functions whose goals are self-assertion, imitation of adult models, participation in circles which are actually closed, etc. Thus the adolescent takes up paths which satisfy him for a time but are soon abandoned. M. Debesse has discussed this subject of egotism and the crisis of juvenile originality. But we believe that, in the egocentrism found in the adolescent, there is more than a simple desire to deviate; rather, it is a manifestation of the phenomenon of lack of differentiation which is worth a further brief discussion.

Essentially, the process, which at any one of the developmental stages moves   *14* from egocentrism toward decentering, constantly subjects increases in knowledge to a refocusing of perspective. Everyone has observed that the child mixes up subjective and objective facts, but if the hypothesis of egocentrism did nothing more than restate this truism it would be worth next to nothing.[3] Actually, it means that learning is not a purely additive process and that to pile one new learned piece of behavior or information on top of another is not in itself adequate to structure an objective attitude. In fact, objectivity presupposes a decentering — *i.e.*, a continual refocusing of perspective. Egocentrism, on the other hand, is the undifferentiated state prior to multiple perspectives, whereas objectivity implies both differentiation and coordination of the points of view which have been differentiated.

But the process found in adolescence on the more sophisticated plane of for-   *15* mal structures is analogous. The indefinite extension of powers of thought made possible by the new instruments of propositional logic at first is conducive to a failure to distinguish between the ego's new and unpredicted capacities and the social or cosmic universe to which they are applied. In other words, the adolescent goes through a phase in which he attributes an unlimited power to his own thoughts so that the dream of a glorious future or of transforming the world through Ideas (even if this idealism takes a materialistic form) seems to be not only fantasy but also an effective action which in itself modifies the empirical world. This is obviously a form of cognitive egocentrism. Although it differs sharply from the child's egocentrism (which is either sensorimotor or simply representational without introspective "reflection"), it results, nevertheless, from the same mechanism and appears as a function of the new conditions created by the structuring of formal thought.

There is a way of verifying this view; namely, to study the decentering pro-   *16* cess which later makes it possible for the adolescent to get beyond the early relative lack of differentiation and to cure himself of his idealistic crisis — in other words, the return to reality which is the path from adolescence to the true beginnings of adulthood. But, as at the level of concrete operations, we find that decentering takes place simultaneously in thought processes and in social relationships.

From the standpoint of social relationships, the tendency of adolescents to   *17* congregate in peer groups has been well documented — discussion or action groups, political groups, youth movements, summer camps, etc. Charlotte Bühler defines an expansive phase followed by a withdrawal phase, although the two do not always seem clearly distinguishable. Certainly this type of social life is not merely the effect of pressures towards conformity but also a source of intellectual decentering. It is most often in discussions between friends, when the promoter of a theory has to test it against the theories of the others, that he discovers its fragility.

But the focal point of the decentering process is the entrance into the occupational world or the beginning of serious professional training. The adolescent becomes an adult when he undertakes a real job. It is then that he is transformed from an idealistic reformer into an achiever. In other words, the job leads thinking away from the dangers of formalism back into reality. Yet observation shows how laborious and slow this reconciliation of thought and experience can be. One has only to look at the behavior of beginning students in an experimental discipline to see how long the adolescent's belief in the power of thinking endures and how little inclined is the mind to subjugate its ideas to the analysis of facts. (This does not mean that facts are accessible without theory, but rather that a theoretical construction has value only in relation to empirical verification.) *18*

From this standpoint, the results of . . . [our investigations of adolescent thought] raise a problem of general significance. The subjects' reactions to a wide range of experimental situations demonstrate that after a phase of development (11–12 to 13–14 years) the preadolescent comes to handle certain formal operations (implication, exclusion, etc.) successfully, but he is not able to set up an exhaustive method of proof. But the 14–15-year-old adolescent does succeed in setting up proofs (moreover, spontaneously, for it is in this area that academic verbalism is least evident). He systematically uses methods of control which require the combinatorial system — *i.e.*, he varies a single factor at a time and excludes the others ("all other things being equal"), etc. But, as we have often seen, this structuring of the tools of experimental verification is a direct consequence of the development of formal thought and propositional logic. Since the adolescent acquires the capacity to use both deduction and experimental induction at the same time, why does he use the first so effectively, and why is he so late in making use of the second in a productive and continuous task (for it is one thing to react experimentally to an apparatus prepared in advance and another to organize a research project by oneself)? Furthermore, the problem is not only ontogenetic but also historical. The same question can be asked in trying to understand why the Greeks were limited (with some exceptions) to pure deductive thought[4] and why modern science, centered on physics, has taken so many centuries to put itself together. *19*

We have seen that the principal intellectual characteristics of adolescence stem directly or indirectly from the development of formal structures. Thus, the latter is the most important event in the thinking found in this period. As for the affective innovations found at the same age, there are two which merit consideration; as usual, we find that they are parallel to intellectual transformations, since affectivity can be considered as the energetic force of behavior whereas its structure defines cognitive functions. (This does not mean either that affectivity is determined by intellect or the contrary, but that both are indissociably united in the functioning of the personality.) *20*

If adolescence is really the age at which growing individuals take their place in adult society (whether or not the role change always coincides with pu- *21* berty), this crucial social adjustment must involve, in correlation with the development of the propositional or formal operations which assure intellectual structuring, two fundamental transfomations that adult affective socialization requires. First, feelings relative to ideals are added to interindividual feelings. Secondly, personalities develop in relation to social roles and scales of values derived from social interaction (and no longer only by the coordination of exchanges which they maintain with the physical environment and other individuals).[5]

Naturally, this is not the place for an essay on the psychology of affects; still, it is important to see how closely these two essential affective aspects of adolescence are interwoven with the transformations of behavior brought on by the development of formal structures.   *22*

First, we are struck by the fact that feelings about ideals are practically nonexistent in the child. A study of the concept of nationality and the associated social attitudes[6] has shown us that the child is sensitive to his family, to his place of residence, to his native language, to certain customs, etc., but that he preserves both an astonishing degree of ignorance and a striking insensitivity not only to his own designation or that of his associates as Swiss, French, etc., but toward his own country as a collective reality. This is to be expected, since, in the 7–11-year-old child, logic is applied only to concrete or manipulable objects. There is no operation available at this level which would make it possible for the child to elaborate an ideal which goes beyond the empirically given. This is only one among many examples. The notions of humanity, social justice (in contrast to interindividual justice which is deeply experienced at the concrete level), freedom of conscience, civic or intellectual courage, and so forth, like the idea of nationality, are ideals which profoundly influence the adolescent's affective life; but with the child's mentality, except for certain individual glimpses, they can neither be understood nor felt.   *23*

In other words, the child does not experience as social feelings anything more than interindividual affects. Even moral sentiments are felt only as a function of unilateral respect (authority) or mutual respect. But, beginning at 13–15 years, feelings about *ideals* or *ideas* are added to the earlier ones, although, of course, they too subsist in the adolescent as well as the adult. Of course, an ideal always exists in a person and it does not stop being an important interindividual element in the new class of feelings. The problem is to find out whether the idea is an object of affectivity because of the person or the person because of the idea. But, whereas the child never gets out of this circle because his only ideals are people who are actually part of his surroundings, during adolescence the circle is broken because ideals become autonomous. No commentary is needed to bring out the close kinship of this affective mechanism with formal thought.   *24*

As for personality, there is no more vaguely defined notion in psychological vocabulary, already so difficult to handle. The reason for this is that personality operates in a way opposite to that of the ego. Whereas the ego is naturally egocentric, personality is the decentered ego. The ego is detestable, even more so when it is strong, whereas a strong personality is the one which manages to discipline the ego. In other words, the personality is the submission of the ego to an ideal which it embodies but which goes beyond it and subordinates it; it is the adherence to a scale of values, not in the abstract but relative to a given   *25* task; thus it is the eventual adoption of a social role, not ready-made in the sense of an administrative function but a role which the individual will create in filling it.

Thus, to say that adolescence is the age at which adolescents take their place   26 in adult society is by definition to maintain that it is the age of formation of the personality, for the adoption of adult roles is from another and necessarily complementary standpoint the construction of a personality. Furthermore, the life program and the plans for change which we have just seen as one of the essential features of the adolescent's behavior are at the same time the changing emotional force in the formation of the personality. A life plan is above all a scale of values which puts some ideals above others and subordinates the middle-range values to goals thought of as permanent. But this scale of values is the affective organization corresponding to the cognitive organization of his work which the new member in the social body says he will undertake. A life plan is also an affirmation of autonomy, and the moral autonomy finally achieved by the adolescent who judges himself the equal of adults is another essential affective feature of the young personality preparing himself to plunge into life.

In conclusion, the fundamental affective acquisitions of adolescence parallel   27 the intellectual acquisitions. To understand the role of formal structures of thought in the life of the adolescent, we found that in the last analysis we had to place them in his total personality. But, in return, we found that we could not completely understand the growth of his personality without including the transformations of his thinking; thus we had to come back to the development of formal structures.

NOTES

[1] For an example, see *Play, Dreams and Imitation in Childhood*, Chap. IX.

[2] *Translators' note: baccalaureat* — a French examination taken at the end of secondary school or about 18–19 years of age. Although, in its details, the analysis of the adolescent presented below fits the European better than the American pattern, one might suggest that even if metaphysical and political theories are less prominent, the American dating pattern and other phenomena typical of youth culture are a comparable "theoretical" or "as if" working out of types of interpersonal relations which become serious at a later point; thus the difference is one of content but not of structure.

[3] *Translators' note:* This passage refers to an opinion more prevalent in Europe than in America, namely that the authors' work simply demonstrates a normative view of the child as an irrational creature. In the United States, where problems of motivation are more often given precedence over purely intellectual functions both from the normative standpoint and in psychological research, another but parallel misinterpretation has sometimes been made; namely, that in maintaining that the child is egocentric, the authors have neglected the fact that he is capable of love. It should be made clear in this section that egocentrism, best understood from its root meaning — that the child's perception is cognitively "centered on his own ego" and thus lacks a certain type of fluidity and ability to handle a variety of perspectives — is not to be confused with "selfish" or "egoistic."

[4] No one has yet given a serious explanation of this fact from the sociological standpoint. To attribute the formal structures made explicit by the Greeks to the contemplative nature of one social class or another does not explain why this contemplation was not confined to metaphysical ideologies and was able to create a mathematical system.

[5] *Translators' note:* "Interindividual" and "social" are used as oppositional terms to a greater extent in French than in English. The first refers to face-to-face relationships between individuals with the implication of familiarity, and the second to the relationship of the individual to society as a whole, to formal institutional structures, to values, etc. Here the meaning is that the child relates only to small groups and specific individuals while the adolescent relates to institutional structures and to values as such.

[6] J. Piaget and A. M. Weil, "Le développement chez L'enfant de l'idée de Patrie et des relations avec l'etranger," *Bulletin international des Sciences sociales* (UNESCO), vol. III (1951), pp. 605–621.

Considerations

1. What are the three stages of egocentrism found in a child's cognitive development? How is the adolescent's version different from the earlier two?
2. Write an essay which (1) discusses the major affective changes associated with adolescence and (2) analyzes their relationships to cognitive changes.

Connections

1. Throughout this article Bärbel Inhelder and Jean Piaget are concerned with the cognitive and affective states associated with adolescence. They also pay considerable attention to the adolescent's "entrance into adult society" (para. 9). Jean-Jacques Rousseau was also concerned with the inevitable transformation of the adolescent into an adult. Consult the complete *Émile* (see Suggestions for Further Reading) and discover what Rousseau has to say on this subject. Then write an essay comparing Rousseau's ideas to those of Piaget and Inhelder.
2. The authors spend considerable time discussing the adolescent's "Messianic" desires to reform the society with which he is confronted. Look again at the *Émile* passages you have uncovered for question 1 above. Write an essay discussing what Piaget and Inhelder might have to say about *Émile*.

Unfolding or Teaching: On the Optimal Training of Artistic Skills

Howard Gardner

Two widely diverging views can be found on the optimal means for developing artistic talent, for fostering creative artists, performers, and perceivers in the visual arts as well as other aesthetic domains. One view might be termed the "unfolding" or "natural" perspective. The child is viewed as a seed, which, though small and fragile, contains within its husk all the necessary "germs"   *1*

Howard Gardner (b. 1943) is a prominent cognitive psychologist associated with Harvard's Project Zero, the Boston University School of Medicine, and the Boston Veterans' Administration Medical Center. Some of his other books include Artful Scribbles: The Significance of Children's Drawings *(1980),* Frames of Mind: The Theory of Multiple Intelligences *(1983), and* The Mind's New Science: A History of the Cognitive Revolution *(1985).*

for eventual artistic virtuosity. The role of the naturalist or gardener who tends the seed is primarily preventive: to shield the young shoots from malevolent influences — violent winds, fiendish crows — so that the seeds have the opportunity to unfold on their own into uniquely beautiful flowers.

By analogy, in the field of art education every normal child is seen as (at least potentially) a productive and imaginative practitioner of the arts. The art teacher must play the role of a Rousseauan tutor — shielding the innocent and fragile young child from pernicious forces in the society so that his inborn talents can flower. Other than providing a comfortable setting and minimally equipping the child with paints, clay, or blocks, the teacher does little that is active; his task is preventive rather than prescriptive.   2

The opposite point of view, if somewhat less in favor today, is no less familiar to those who have toiled in the fields of the arts and education. This perspective, which can be termed the "training," "directive," or "skills" approach, holds that, at the very minimum, unfolding is not enough. Like a young seedling abandoned on the shady side of a hill, the child artist, left alone, will never achieve his potential. Special cultivation or perhaps even transplantation is necessary if the immature plant is to survive or thrive. By the same token, the young child, even one displaying considerable promise, will come to nought without firm guidance and active intervention on the part of more knowledgeable adults. Proficiency in the arts entails the attainment of many highly intricate skills, ones that can be acquired only under the direction of a gifted teacher or practicing artist.   3

It is an established ploy — in teaching, writing, and even thinking — to set up two such antipodes, or straw men, and then to declare sagely that both sides have a point and that the truth lies in a golden mean, located just about midway between equally untenable extremes. I will succumb to this spineless stance to the extent of affirming that both of these positions on art education have a solid cipher in their favor. Yet I hope to go beyond the obvious by insisting that a deeper understanding of both views — unfolding as well as training — may emerge from a developmental perspective and that, indeed, questions in art education in general benefit from such an examination.   4

Developmental studies are today much in vogue. Almost everyone quotes Jean Piaget or Jerome Bruner or Erik Erikson whether or not they agree with or even understand them. This is not the occasion for a minicourse on child development, but it may be opportune to offer a few asides regarding the developmental perspective. To be specific, one is not being "developmental" simply by looking at children or by noting the ways in which they change over time. To say that the average three-year-old is thirty-three inches in height and that the average twenty-year-old is sixty-six inches in height is to make statements about children and their growth but to abjure a developmental approach. One can have a developmental perspective only when one begins to focus on such questions as the rate of growth, the meaning of spurts in growth, the organization of physiological systems, and, most centrally, the possibility that physical growth in two periods of life — such as infancy and adolescence — may be mediated by different physiological mechanisms and affect different portions of the body. For it is the burden of developmental psychology to discern qualitatively different stages in physical, intellectual, and affective growth,   5 the fundamental units and operations entailed in each stage, the factors contributing to the growth of each, and the interrelations among them.

It is no more possible to give a capsule summary of the "state of knowledge" in developmental psychology than to give a foolproof definition of the field but, again, a schematic description taken from the work of Piaget may help to orient our inquiry. As I have discussed in the first essay, Piaget sees intellectual development as consisting of four broad stages: a *sensorimotor* stage, occupying the first two years of life, during which the child gains a practical knowledge of the physical world about him — coming to understand, for example, that objects have a permanent existence within a framework of space and time; and *intuitive* or *symbolic* stage, covering the period from age two to six or seven, during which the child explores various kinds of symbols and images representing the world, but does not yet do so in a systematic or logical way; a *concrete-operational* stage, extending from about the age of seven to the age of twelve, wherein the subject becomes able to think logically about objects, to classify them consistently, and to appreciate their continuity despite alterations in their momentary appearance; and a *formal operations* stage, commencing in early adolescence, at which time the child becomes able to reason logically, using words and other symbols in order to create a world and make deductions about it without departing from the "abstract" or "theoretical" level. 6

Piaget's work is absolutely fundamental to any study of children and their minds. This is true even if one has not yet been converted to his developmental perspective, even if one does not share his convictions that each stage represents a qualitatively different way of thinking about the world, indeed of thinking altogether, or that each stage follows logically after its predecessor, in turn becoming the necessary ingredient for progress to subsequent stages. To conduct research in the area of developmental psychology without knowing about Piaget is about as sensible as pursuing biological studies without taking note of recent developments in genetics and molecular biology or of pursuing physics while ignoring Einstein's conceptual breakthroughs. 7

Having thus praised Piaget, let me add that I think his view can be seriously misleading to those involved in art education. Piaget's model of mature adult thought, as implied above, involves scientific thinking in the manner of the physicist or chemist. Piaget explicitly states — and his candor is refreshing in this eclectic era — that he is not interested in creativity as it is usually defined, or in the arts. It is quite possible, however, that if "involvement in the arts" is seen as a final stage of development, one might arrive at a rather different set of elements and stages, which, while not directly contradicting Piaget's works, possess a strikingly different flavor. 8

My own work has been devoted largely to the building of an informal model of artistic development. Portions of the model are based upon empirical research conducted by many investigators, including those of us associated with Harvard Project Zero; large portions of the model are based on my own observations, impressions, and intuitions as a parent, teacher, and reader. No doubt the model will be tinkered with and revised in the years to come, and that is to the good. But I feel that the model casts some light on the central question raised at the outset, and for that reason I propose to sketch it briefly. 9

During the opening years of life, as Piaget has shown, the child is indeed   *10*
involved in the development of basic sensory and motor capacities and in the
parallel enterprise of constructing knowledge about the physical and social
world. These activities are evidently a prerequisite for artistic activity — for
instance, in awakening the child to various means of communication — but
are not in any powerful sense involved with the arts. That is because, in my
view, the arts are integrally and uniquely involved with symbol systems — with
the manipulation and understanding of various sounds, lines, colors, shapes,
objects, forms, patterns — all of which have the potential to refer, to exemplify, or to express some aspect of the world.

To come to grips with the world of symbols, a world in large part designed   *11*
by the culture, is the principal challenge of the years following infancy. The
most familiar example is, of course, language: in the course of two or three
years the child catapults from a phase during which he can utter or understand a mere word or two to one in which he can effortlessly issue sentences
of almost any length, at the same time understanding a dizzying variety of
structures and messages. But equally stunning progress occurs on all other
symbolic fronts. Children with a musical flair can sing long and complicated
pieces of music, assimilate the basic components of a musical style, and, in
some cases, even compose works of interest. And by the time they enter school
most children have also advanced from the merest capacity to scribble and form
simple geometric patterns to the ability to make complex and aesthetically
satisfying paintings.

I view the period from age two to seven, then, as a time during which the   *12*
child's capacity to use, manipulate, transform, and comprehend various symbols matures at a ferocious pace. These processes can be seen in at least two
ways: in watching the same child over a period of many months, as he advances from simple forms and patterns to complex configurations with many
integrated portions; and, within a briefer interval, as he explores the potentials and possibilities of particular graphic patterns, often making inferences
not apparent initially or combining the pattern with another scheme on which
he has also been working. This kind of rapid "microgenetic development" is,
in its own way, as amazing as the more leisurely "ontogenetic development,"
or evolution over a matter of months or years.

What is most striking, however, about the events of this period is that they   *13*
seem to be similar in most children and that specific instruction has relatively
little effect on what the child does. Let me be clear about what is meant here.
There are indeed differences in children. Some favor one medium over another. Children also differ in the kinds of patterns they come to fix on, in the
various set ideas or themes that recur in their works, and even in the extent to
which these themes are beneficial or counterproductive.

Yet over and above these differences in style and preferences, the principal   *14*
stages affecting young children across cultures, and across media, are persuasively similar. And, as far as we know, this parallel artistic development occurs despite the fact that educational procedures in various cultures may differ
enormously. My best guess is that during this symbolic period the child is pro-
pelled by a dynamism that is largely his own. Like the seed with its own plan
for development, the child is following the inner logic dictated by his own sen-

sorimotor development and the nature of the particular symbols with which he is working. While children will naturally (and properly) draw what they see about them and tell stories about beguiling objects in their environments, external interference and efforts at explicit instruction rarely prove valuable or productive.

By the age of seven or eight, and sometimes earlier, the child has achieved 15 an initial grasp on the major symbolic media of his culture. In our society, for example, a child of this age understands what makes a story (and what does not), and he can produce a literary work that, at least in its broad lines, conforms to the general cultural model. He has a sense of what occurs within a piece of music and, in many cases, can combine fragments in order to produce a new piece on the basis of a familiar style. Finally, his works in the visual or plastic arts also exhibit a sense of composition, balance, and construction, which indicates an awareness of the constituents of executed works of art, and he has long since learned to "read" the various representations contained in pictorial productions.

With what I hope will be regarded as benign exaggeration, I have suggested 16 that the young child of this age is an incipient artist. By this I mean that he now possesses the raw materials to become involved in the artistic process: a "first draft" notion of how symbols work in a raft of symbolic media, some knowledge of how to construe a work, some capacity to construct one on his own. Indeed, he can enact the roles of performer, artist, and member of an audience. Only when it comes to the task of being a critic — who, like Piaget's formal operator, must be able to reason on the level of words or logical propositions — is the young school child significantly deficient.

It would be absurd, of course, to view the child of seven or eight as a mature 17 artist. He requires, at the very least, additional knowledge about the medium, more understanding of the culture in which he lives, increased flexibility in the way he regards artistic objects, and greater psychological insight into human nature, as well as superior technical skill to permit him to realize desired effects in particular media. Indeed, to become acquainted with all the potentials of the medium, the multifarious ways in which it has been and can be employed, is perhaps the central task of artistic development and the one that most clearly differentiates this form of development from other realms, including those detailed by Piaget. It is my feeling, however, that these tasks involve quantitative rather than qualitative change. That is, while the acquiring of technique, of cultural understanding, of knowledge of feelings and thought may well require a lifetime, probably a very full and complete one, no new level of cognitive operation is required. The seven- or eight-year old has the mental equipment to become an artist, and he need not pass through qualitatively different stages in order to participate fully in the artistic process. Here, then, I part company with Piaget. While he highlights the advent of concrete and formal operational thought, rightly perceiving these forms as central to the achievement of the scientist, he does not focus on other forms of thought, and so he does not confront the possibility that concrete and formal operations are not directly relevant to the artist's task, or the contention that versatility with a medium represents an extremely sophisticated cognitive achievement.

This formulation is very controversial, and many scholars would not en- 18 dorse my conclusions. Two worthwhile points may nonetheless emerge from this controversy. First, there is renewed recognition that artistry is not just "less developed" science but rather involves different processes of thought with their own evolution; artistic cognition may not involve qualitative changes after early childhood, but it continues to deepen and evolve for many years. Second, this perspective helps to explain why individuals in other cultures, including the so-called primitive societies, who do not exhibit types of thought crucial to Western science, nonetheless produce artistic works and exhibit an aesthetic awareness commensurate with, if not superior to, our own. We need to acknowledge forms and intensities of thought other than those upheld by Piaget; the particular genius of "medium knowledge" and "symbol use" has to be recognized.

We find, then, that the seven-year-old has gained enough of an intuitive familiarity with symbol systems to be able to work with them adequately. However, he knows little and can accomplish little that is subtle and complex. At the same time, he is superbly equipped to learn. Throughout the world, schooling commences at about this time, and during the years from approximately age seven to thirteen the major lessons of the society are transmitted to offspring. The child of this age group seems superbly equipped to learn just about everything — not merely reading, writing, and arithmetic, not merely farming, fishing, and hunting, not merely reasoning, religion, and rhetoric. As V. S. Pritchett has pointed out in *The Cab at the Door* (p. 102), "That eager period between ten and fourteen is the one in which one can learn anything. Even in the time when most children had no schooling at all, they could be experts in a trade. The children who went up chimneys, worked in cotton mills, packed coster barrows, may have been sick, exhausted, ill-fed but they were at a temporary height of their intelligence and power." If one has any doubts about the particular learning facility of this period, he should travel with a preadolescent to an exotic land and note who picks up the language, and without a trace of an accent. [19]

Many of our data about children's artistic capacities describe this period of life. Since much of this research has been described elsewhere in this volume, I shall not dwell on it here. We have found, basically, that children around the age of six or seven suffer from a number of woeful aesthetic misconceptions or impairments, which, fortunately, prove to be quite reparable. Youngsters of this age do not, for example, exhibit sensitivity to painting style: they view paintings chiefly in terms of subject matter. A few weeks of training, however, in which children look at paintings and are directed to notice stylistic features produce a dramatic increase in their sensitivity to artistic styles. Indeed, so fertile are the minds of these subjects that their sensitivity to style is enhanced even if they are merely drilled in grouping together animals of the same phylogenetic group. [20]

We also find that children of this age display little tendency to produce metaphoric figures of speech in tasks where they are requested to produce such figures. Indeed, their responses exhibit a literal, concrete, trite, or realistic trend. Again, however, a majority of these youngsters can be trained within just a few weeks both to recognize and to produce metaphoric language. [21]

Finally, I should mention an informal study by Judy Burton, who has worked [22] intensively over a period of weeks with sixth and seventh graders. She finds that such preadolescents initially possess little sense of how to produce a third dimension in their drawing. However, after such experimentation with various two- and three-dimensional materials such as paper, wire, or lines, and after some guided practice in producing the subject matter of greatest interest to them — the human figure — the youngsters undergo a quantum leap in their artistic productions. In a matter of weeks they become sensitive to the details of the human figure and to the potential for producing depth relations, in a way previously inaccessible to them. Children of this age generally exhibit a tremendous ability to acquire within a short time new skills in the arts; they enjoy doing so; they are not overly distraught by terminology, by errors, or by empty verbalisms. They are ready to plunge in, to forge ahead, to gain mastery.

And it is in this respect that they differ so demonstrably from other children 23 just a few years older. It is not that adolescents are in some absolute sense less intelligent or even necessarily less motivated. But for a reason that we do not yet completely understand, enthusiasm about acquiring skills in the arts and the ready capacity to immerse oneself fully in an expressive medium seem lacking in most adolescents, at least in our culture.

Piaget may have uncovered one reason for this. During adolescence the child 24 is developing his critical reasoning skills to a new level. For this very reason he may adopt a much more critical opinion of his own work, comparing it unfavorably with what highly skilled individuals are accomplishing. If he finds his own capacities inadequate in comparison, he is no longer motivated to continue producing, and he remains at most a perceiver of the arts. Here, then, we encounter an important lesson for art education. If we are to prevent this decline of interest (and possible decline in skill), our pedagogical efforts during the preadolescent period become extremely important. Sufficient progress in teaching or training should, therefore, be realized so that when the child finally gains in critical acumen, his works will not seem so inadequate that he quits in despair.

At least two measures would seem helpful. First, skills should be developed 25 to a sufficiently high level so that the child's work will, objectively, possess merit; he will then feel less need to reject what he has done. Second, and of equal importance, the child should be encouraged, gently but definitely, to take a somewhat more critical stance toward his work during preadolescence. He can be presented with problems, exposed to various solutions, and given practice in evaluating and improving them. Through such measures he gains familiarity with the practice of criticism; he employs it himself; he benefits from it. By the time he enters adolescence, criticism is already a familiar tool that he can now apply by himself as well as accept graciously. In the cultivation of this critical capacity, I think, lies our best hope of maintaining a garden of young painters instead of a barren row of survivors during the interval from childhood to adulthood.

Perhaps in a sense Piaget has been vindicated. In the end I have returned to 26 his scheme to explain one of the most striking and troublesome events in artistic development: the frequent decline of artistry during adolescence. But it should be noticed that what, for Piaget, is a clearly beneficent event — the advent of formal logical operations — proves severely problematic for the child. Indeed, some of our studies have even indicated a high point in artistic creativity *before* adolescence, with the reasoning capacities of this later period proving more of a hindrance than a boon.

There is, then, a central enigma pervading the development of the child. While   27
in the sciences development is completely linear and progressive, at least through adolescence, in the arts the picture is rather different. If anything, there is a kind of golden period during the first years of life in which every child can be regarded, in a meaningful sense, as a young artist. And while many children continue to participate in the arts in middle childhood, it is often with much less of a sense of inner direction, with much more of a searching for a model, and with a considerable amount of mindless repetition and pointless stylization, especially when no inspiring teacher is present. The development of scientific capacity is, generally speaking, a straight line upward, the lifeline of artistic development is punctuated by ups and downs.

Yet if the emerging picture of artistic development is less simple than one   28
would have liked, our developmental analysis does provide one potentially useful prescription. As already suggested, the early years of life constitute a time of natural development of artistic competence. And during this period the approach of unfolding, of giving full rein to natural development, seems indicated. During middle childhood, however, a more active type of intervention is called for. Rigid drill is not necessary; what is wanted are recipes that give the child tools for achieving the effects he wants, that open up rather than foreclose possibilities. He should have some questions to ask and some ways for trying to answer them and an incipient acquaintance with standards and with criticism. This calls for the more active type of intervention involved in the teaching approach. It occurs, I think, at a time when the child is especially open and undefensive and is receptive to aid, suggestion, and inspirational models. As the noted art educator Viktor Lowenfeld once remarked,

> If we can stimulate the child's unaware production to such an extent that it reaches in his unaware style a creative maturity which will be able to stand the critical awareness which once will set in, we have kept the child from making a sudden change and have protected him from disappointment or shock with regard to his changing imaginative activity. (p. 233)

I submit that both approaches we have contemplated are appropriate. The   29
one that accentuates unfolding displays its particular virtue during the first years of life, from the period of two to seven. With the developmental changes accompanying the years of schooling, a more active and interventionist stance seems advisable, especially in a milieu virtually bereft of societal support for artistic (as opposed to scientific) endeavors. By the time of adolescence, it is in all probability too late to begin a rigorously structured educational program, and if natural development has not exerted its effect by then, it never will. Instead, one hopes that by adolescence the child will have attained sufficient skills and a sense of critical awareness, as well as ample ideas and feelings he wishes to express; then he can continue on his own to gain sustenance from whichever artistic medium he selects.

Considerations

1. Howard Gardner feels that an understanding of Jean Piaget's work is essential "to any study of children and their minds" (para. 7). Yet he also thinks that Piaget's theories can be misleading to anyone interested in art education. Why? Respond in a brief essay.
2. Write a longer essay analyzing Gardner's "informal model of artistic development" (para. 9). Point out similarities and differences with Piaget's theories.
3. Why do adolescents often prove unwilling art students?
4. What prescription does Gardner finally offer for teaching art?

Connections

1. At the beginning of this essay, Howard Gardner clearly identifies one view of the art teacher as a "Rousseauan tutor" (para. 2). He does not make a clear identification of the opposing role model. Your task is to make this identification yourself using any selections from this chapter you wish.
2. What would Jean-Jacques Rousseau and John Locke think about Gardner's proposal for teaching art? Make your answers specific; refer to readings earlier in this chapter if you need to.
3. In his introduction to *Émile*, Rousseau writes:

   > Tender and provident mothers, prudent enough to leave the beaten track and to preserve this growing shrub from the shocks of human prejudice, to such are my words addressed! Cultivate, water the young plant ere it die; it will one day bear fruit delicious to your taste. . . . Plants are formed by cultivation, men by education.

   Examine the beginning paragraphs of "Unfolding or Teaching" for Gardner's careful use of metaphor. Analyze the effectiveness of this extended metaphor. Does it work as well as Rousseau's?
4. After you have read "Unfolding or Teaching," examine Howard Gardner's essay on Mozart (Chapter 7, The Nature of Intelligence). Now that you have read Gardner's reflections on intellectual operations in art and music, examine the thesis of each essay. Does Gardner reach similar conclusions concerning the ways we "learn" art and music? If not, how does he treat the two subjects?

Further Connections

1. John B. Watson was overheard to say, after the birth of his son, "A baby is more fun than all the rats and frogs in creation." Do you think Baby Albert

would have been overjoyed by this statement? Write an essay in which you reflect on the ethics involved in behavioral studies such as the one described by John B. Watson and Rosalie Rayner. These ethics have, of course, changed since 1920; experiments like those done on Baby Albert are no longer allowed. Try to find a statement from the American Psychological Association about current policies. How does the current state of affairs differ from the past?

2. After reading all the selections presented in this chapter, write an essay reflecting on the theme of freedom versus control. Who would you rather have for a teacher — John Locke or Jean-Jacques Rousseau? Would there really be a great difference?

3. In a four- to five-page essay, reflect on the state of your own cognitive development. You need not follow Jean Piaget's theories. Have you noticed distinct changes for which you have your own labels? Where are you now?

4. Define the relationship between a teacher (or tutor if you wish) and a student. To focus your essay, use your own experience plus any material from this chapter that you think is appropriate.

5. At this point in your life as a student, you must be aware that educators and psychologists have constantly measured your intelligence, your verbal reasoning and math abilities, your aptitude for science-related careers, and implicitly, your ability to be assimilated into the dominant White Anglo-Saxon culture. Investigate as many of these intelligence tests as you can remember. When personal recollection fails, research always helps. The thesis for this essay is up to you.

6. Examine Chapter 3, The Frontier Indians. Pay particular attention to the articles by James L. Axtell, Kenneth M. Morrison, and A. Irving Hallowell, all of which concern attempts by missionaries to educate and, usually, to convert North American Indians. Using what you have learned from your reading of Locke, Rousseau, Piaget, and Gardner, analyze the educational methods employed by these missionaries.

Extensions

1. After reading what John Locke has to say about the qualifications of a tutor, visit your campus tutorial center and interview one of the employees. Once you have obtained a complete picture of a tutor's qualifications and responsibilities, write an essay explaining your findings.

2. Visit the library and try to discover what your state requires for prospective teachers desiring (1) a single-subject credential; (2) an administrative credential; (3) a special education credential with a learning-handicapped concentration.

3. Read George Meredith's *The Ordeal of Richard Feverel* (1859). This novel concerns an aristocratic English father who tries to raise his son according to a strict educational system. Young Richard is shielded, as much as possible, from the evils of society, with his education guided by a tutor and his destiny controlled by his father. Write an essay analyzing this method

of education. (Hint: What would Jean-Jacques Rousseau think about the events in this novel?)

4. Look again at Locke's views on the importance of habit — for both moral and intellectual training. Now visit the library reference room. Your task is to investigate Edward Thorndike, an American psychologist famous for his early work in operant conditioning. Consult general reference works like the *Dictionary of Psychology* and the *Encyclopaedia of Psychology*. Construct an essay summarizing Thorndike's work and speculating on his indebtedness to Locke. (What is the Law of Effect?)

5. Use the information you gathered about Thorndike's work in behavioral psychology. Then expand your horizons by finding articles or books in either the *Psychological Index* (covering research from 1894–1935) or *Psychological Abstracts* (1927–present).

6. Investigate the complete *Émile*. Read the section concerning education for women. Then look up Paul Broca, the nineteenth-century French surgeon/anthropologist who was most famous for his advocacy of craniometry. (A good starting point is Stephen Jay Gould's *The Mismeasure of Man* — see Suggestions for Further Reading.) What were Broca's findings about the differences between women's and men's intelligence? Would Rousseau have agreed with him? Construct a six- to eight-page essay exploring these ideas and questions.

7. Until the 1970s, male and female school children in the United States were segregated in some classes designed to prepare them for adult life. Boys took shop — wood, metal, electricity; girls took cooking and home economics. After some preliminary research into specific educational requirements in your state for the 1950s and 1960s, write your own analysis of that phenomenon. Use Rousseau for inspiration if you wish.

8. On your own, find information on classical conditioning in a reliable reference work or a psychology textbook. Write brief definitions for the following terms: *law of contiguity, unconditioned stimulus, unconditioned response, conditioned stimulus, conditioned response, and stimulus generalization*. Now reread the Watson and Rayner article and give examples for your definitions. How did this 1920 experiment illustrate stimulus generalization? Respond in a brief essay.

9. The experimenters involved in Watson's experiment regretted that they had no time to detach the emotional responses which had been conditioned into Albert. We must assume that he lived his whole life fearing rats, rabbits, fur coats and Santa Claus. Do some additional outside reading about classical conditioning. How would a modern behaviorist try to relieve Albert's fears?

10. B. F. Skinner's "Baby in a Box" originally appeared in *Ladies Home Journal*. Thus it was written differently than it would have been for an academic journal. The choice of audience also indicates that this piece is very much a product of its time. Labor-saving devices for the home were prominent in the post-war "baby boom" of the 1940s and 1950s. Your task is two fold: Look around the library and find some old magazines from the baby boom years. Look carefully at the ads. What sorts of labor-saving devices can you find in *Life, Saturday Evening Post*, etc.? Then write an essay

placing Skinner's article in its historical context. Incorporate any useful research you have done.

11. On the first page of "Stages and Their Properties in the Development of Thinking" (1963), Jean Piaget admits that his methodology has changed with recent investigations. Locate an earlier study and analyze some of these changes.

12. After consulting the *Oxford English Dictionary*, write two brief paragraphs defining the terms *interindividual* and *social*.

     In a footnote to Inhelder and Piaget's "Adolescent Thinking," the translator claims that these two words "are used as oppositional terms to a greater extent in French than in English." Does this statement make sense, given what you've learned from your dictionary? Is this opposition important to Piaget's theories? How?

13. Inhelder and Piaget in "Adolescent Thinking" seem to dismiss the desires of adolescents to reform the world as "cognitive egocentrism." In your library look into the *Wandervogel* movement in late nineteenth- and early twentieth-century Germany. What was the movement's origin? Did this *Jugendkultur* have particular goals? What sorts of activities did these wandering youths engage in? What happened to the *Wandervogel* after 1914?

14. After discovering what Rousseau thinks is an appropriate curriculum for educating women, read Margaret Mead's *Coming of Age in Samoa*. See especially the following chapters: "The Education of the Samoan Child", "The Girl and Her Age Group", and "The Experience and Individuality of the Average Girl." How do Mead's observations concerning Samoan adolescence compare with Rousseau's thoughts? Remember that Rousseau was writing for the sons of French aristocrats; Mead was not.

15. Howard Gardner, in "Unfolding or Teaching," mentions the developmental studies of Jerome Bruner and Erik Erikson. Write an eight- to ten-page paper on these two psychologists and their theories.

16. Investigate the curricula in your school's art department. Do the methods generally employed or advocated lean more toward "unfolding" or "teaching"? Does this orientation change when a student proceeds from a design class to a studio course in painting and drawing?

17. Read John Holt's article in *The Progressive* magazine. Write a one- to two-page essay about possible affinity between Holt's beliefs and the ideas of Rousseau and Piaget.

18. After reading Chapter 6 of Paul Goodman's *Compulsory Mis-Education*, investigate the concept of programmed learning. What are the theoretical biases involved? Has programmed learning been a success?

19. Read one or more of the following books: John Stuart Mill's *Autobiography* (1873), Charles Dickens' *Hard Times* (1854), or James Joyce's *Portrait of the Artist as a Young Man* (1914). Analyze the systems of education presented in the work(s) you chose.

Suggestions for Further Reading

Axtell, James L., ed. *The Educational Writings of John Locke.* Cambridge: Cambridge University Press, 1968. The complete collection of Locke's writings on education.

Bruner, Jerome S. *The Process of Education.* New York: Vintage Books, 1960. A useful starting point for students working on *Extensions* question 1. Bruner's theories are influential in modern educational thinking.

Chapman, Antony J., and Hugh C. Foot, eds. *Humour and Laughter: Theory, Research and Applications.* London: Wiley, 1976. A serious collection of articles correlating humor appreciation with cognitive development. A rich source for research assignments that aim outside the limitations of this chapter. *Warning:* These articles are *not* funny.

Corsini, Raymond, ed. *Encyclopedia of Psychology.* 4 vols. New York: Wiley, 1984. The most current and widely praised resource for psychology, but rather difficult to use. Read all the fine print to use its fourfold format.

Current Index to Journals in Education. Phoenix, Ariz.: Oryx Press, published monthly. *CIJE* indexes more than 780 education and related journals. A companion to ERIC's *Resources in Education* (see below).

Education Index. New York: H. W. Wilson Company. Useful for locating periodical articles and book reviews on almost any subject related to education. Indexes about 240 publications each month.

Erikson, Erik. *Childhood and Society.* New York: Norton, 1950. Erikson's theories will prove interesting to students working on *Extensions* question 1. His work offers comparisons with Rousseau's and Piaget's.

Gardner, Howard. *Developmental Psychology: An Introduction.* 2nd ed. Boston: Little, Brown, 1982. Gardner provides a remarkably lucid analysis of developmental issues in an introductory text. Particularly relevant to this chapter are the sections dealing with the history of child study and with theoretical differences between cognitive psychologists (see especially pp. 51–92; 136–153).

Goodman, Paul. *Compulsory Mis-Education.* (Bound with *The Community of Scholars.*) New York: Vintage Books, 1964. Twenty-one years later, still a stimulating iconoclastic assault on the American School System. Chapter 6 — Programmed — presents a discussion of the theoretical underpinnings of programmed instruction advocated by B. F. Skinner and other behaviorists.

Gould, Stephen Jay. *The Mismeasure of Man.* New York: W. W. Norton, 1981. For anyone interested in the growth and measurement of intelligence, Gould's attack on biological determinism is indispensable reading. The topic of intelligence testing remains a controversial matter — one for debate if you are an educator; one for protest if you are a student.

Holt, John. "School's Out: Why Teachers Fail." *The Progressive* (April 1984). An amusing yet scathing look at systems of education, couched in clever metaphor. At least two of the metaphors used by Holt should make readers of this chapter chuckle.

Mead, Margaret. *Coming of Age in Samoa.* New York: William Morrow, 1928. Mead's observations of adolescent Samoan females provides some significant contrasts to this chapter's readings. The curious should examine the complete *Émile* and *Some Thoughts Concerning Education,* remembering that both these works were presented as plans for educating aristocratic young European men.

Meredith, George. *The Ordeal of Richard Feverel.* 1888. Reprint. New York: Dover, 1983. This novel deals with the conflict between a father with a *scientific* system for educating his son and his son, who responds only to natural, very Romantic impulses. Neither side scores much of a triumph.

Miller, Richard. *Bohemia: The Proto-Culture Then and Now.* Chicago: Nelson-Hall, 1977. Although this book is worth reading in itself, it also provides ample concrete material to follow any reading of Piaget and Inhelder's "Adolescent Thinking." I especially recommend the section concerning the *Wandervögel* movement in late nineteenth- and early twentieth-century Germany.

Psychological Abstracts. Washington, D. C.: American Psychological Association. Published monthly since 1927, *Psych. Abs.* offers bibliographic information and brief summaries of more than 20,000 articles each year.

Resources in Education (Formerly *Research in Education*). Washington, D. C.: National Institute of Education. Published monthly, *RIE* provides abstracts of research reports pertaining to education and related issues. Offers four types of indexes: subject, author, institution, and publication. Both this publication and its companion, *Current Index to Journals in Education,* should be used in conjunction with the *Thesaurus of ERIC Descriptors.*

Resnick, Lauren. "Programmed Instruction of Complex Skills." *Harvard Educational Review* (Fall 1983). This article is attacked by Paul Goodman in Chapter 6 of *Compulsory Mis-Education.* Resnick advocates programmed instruction in academic subjects following principles of operant conditioning learned from B. F. Skinner.

Rousseau, Jean-Jacques. *Émile.* London: Everyman's Library, 1974. For those frustrated by the snippets offered in Rousseau's selection in this chapter, here is Rousseau's complete program for the hapless Émile. Not to be missed are Rousseau's views of education for women.

7 The Nature of Intelligence

Edited by **Robert J. Cullen**

What makes us human? Language? Culture? Opposable thumbs? No definition can get very far without somehow taking into account human intelligence; our abilities to solve problems, reason, learn, remember, and communicate, all with immense efficiency and power, set us apart from other species. In exploring the nature of intelligence — which has become possible in any detail only in the last century — we are in a very real sense defining ourselves.

This chapter includes contributions from several disciplines for which intelligence is a key issue. We begin at the microscopic level of neurobiology: in the essays by David H. Hubel and Lane Lenard we learn something about the structure, function, and development of the brain, the "hardware" that underlies intelligence. Psychologists Robert J. Sternberg and Janet E. Davidson work in the opposite direction, from the observation of human behavior itself (specifically, solving puzzles) toward hypotheses about intelligence, insight, and IQ. Drawing on behavioral and biological data, psychologist Howard Gardner argues for a much broader view of intelligence, or, more accurately, intelligences. In an equally wide-ranging article, Stephen Jay Gould illustrates the social and political implications of this issue as he recapitulates the sometimes bitter debate over the heritability of intelligence.

From these pieces exploring the biological, psychological, and social dimensions of intelligence, we turn to the issue raised by computer science, the question of artificial intelligence (AI). You probably know some of the benefits of AI research already; for example, "expert systems" to help diagnose illnesses or manufacture products are now in use. The two AI pieces here go further, examining the prospects for true machine intelligence. Keith Gunderson, while not ruling out AI altogether, shows that what looks like intelligence may not be; in contrast, Douglas R. Hofstadter, answering a question posed by David H. Hubel, believes that in principle machines can work very much like brains.

The chapter ends with Howard Gardner's attempt to apply what we know about intelligence to a particular case, "The Compositions of Mozart's Mind." The issues now become less abstract, less general: Gardner tackles a specific, complex, even awe-inspiring historical example. If you compare what he writes to what Mozart's contemporaries might have said, you will see how much we have learned about intelligence — and how much we have not.

The Brain
David H. Hubel

Can the brain understand the brain? Can it understand the mind? Is it a   *1* giant computer, or some other kind of giant machine, or something more? These are questions that are regularly asked, and it may help to get them out of the way. When someone maintains that brains cannot be expected to understand brains, the analogy is to the aphorism that a person cannot lift himself by his own bootstraps. The analogy is not compelling. Certainly even a brief glimpse of what has been accomplished toward understanding the brain will convince any reader of this *Scientific American* book that much progress has been made since the phrenologists. The pace of progress at the moment is rapid. For all practical purposes, then, neurobiologists are working on the hunch that they can understand the brain, and for the moment they are doing well.

I think the difficulties with questions such as these are semantic. They are   *2* loaded with words such as "understand" and "mind," useful words for many purposes but fuzzy at the edges and out of place when they are applied to questions such as these, which they render either meaningless or unanswerable.

The brain is a tissue. It is a complicated, intricately woven tissue, like noth-   *3* ing else we know of in the universe, but it is composed of cells, as any tissue is. They are, to be sure, highly specialized cells, but they function according to the laws that govern any other cells. Their electrical and chemical signals can be detected, recorded and interpreted, and their chemicals can be identified; the connections that constitute the brain's woven feltwork can be mapped. In short, the brain can be studied, just as the kidney can.

David H. Hubel (b. 1926) is the John Franklin Enders University Professor at Harvard Medical School, where he works in the Department of Neurobiology. His distinguished career includes study at the Montreal Neurological Institute, the Walter Reed Army Institute of Research, and the John Hopkins School of Medicine. He is a specialist in the mammalian visual system and in 1981 was awarded a Nobel Prize (along with Tosten N. Wiesel and Roger W. Sperry) for his work in this area.

The problem comes when we ask about understanding, because such a word   *4*
carries with it the implication of a sudden revelation or dawning, the existence
of a moment when we might be said to leave the darkness of the tunnel. It is
not clear to me that there can be such a moment, or that we will know when
it comes.

Brain research is a very old field of investigation — and before that of spec-   *5*
ulation. Its pace accelerated greatly at the end of the 19th century; since World
War II new techniques have brought significant advances, and in the past decade or so neurobiology has become one of the most active branches in all science. The result has been a virtual explosion of recent discoveries and insights.
Brain research is nonetheless only at its beginning. The incredible complexity
of the brain is a cliché, but it is a fact.

The problem of understanding the brain is a little like that of understanding   *6*
proteins. There must be millions of those ingeniously complicated molecular
inventions in every organism, one protein quite different from the next. To work
out the structural details of even one of them seems to take years, to say nothing of knowing exactly how it works. If understanding proteins means knowing
how all of them work, the prospects are perhaps not good. In an analogous
way the brain consists of very large numbers of subdivisions (although not
millions), each with a special architecture and circuit diagram; to describe one
is certainly not to describe them all. Hence understanding will be slow (if only
for practical reasons of time and manpower), steady (one hopes) and asymp-
totic, certainly with breakthroughs but with no likely point of terminus.

Mind is similarly a useful word but alas even fuzzier. Since its definition is   *7*
elusive, to talk of understanding it (not just the word but the thing the word
refers to) is to talk about an exercise in mental gymnastics that seems to fall
outside of natural science. The mathematician G. H. Hardy is supposed to have
said a mathematician is someone who not only does not know what he is talking about but also does not care. Those who discuss in depth subjects such as
the physiology of the mind probably care, but I cannot see how they could ever
know.

The number of nerve cells, or neurons, that make up man's three pounds or   *8*
so of brain is on the order of 10^{11} (a hundred billion) give or take a factor of
10. The neurons are surrounded, supported and nourished by glial cells, whose
number is also large. A typical neuron consists of a cell body, ranging from
about five to 100 micrometers (thousandths of a millimeter) in diameter, from
which emanate one major fiber, the axon, and a number of fibrous branches,
the dendrites. The axon may give off branches near its beginning and it often
branches extensively near its end. In general terms the dendrites and the cell
body receive incoming signals; the cell body combines and integrates them
(roughly speaking, it averages them) and emits outgoing signals, and it also
serves for the general upkeep of the cell; the axon transports the outgoing signals to the axon terminals, which distribute the information to a new set of
neurons.

The signaling system is a double one: electrical and chemical. The signal   *9*
generated by a neuron and transported along its axon is an electrical impulse,

but the signal is transmitted from cell to cell by molecules of transmitter substances that flow across a specialized contact, the synapse, between a supplier of information (an axon terminal or occasionally a dendrite) and a recipient of information (a dendrite, a cell body or occasionally an axon terminal). One neuron generally is fed by hundreds or thousands of other neurons and in turn feeds into hundreds or thousands of still other neurons.

This may be enough to make it possible to tackle the comparison between   *10*
brains and computers. Most neurobiologists would agree, for the purposes of this discussion, that the brain can be regarded as a machine that is not endowed with properties lying beyond the reach of science. It is also true, however, that not all neurobiologists would agree with that proposition. On the other hand, everyone would surely agree that the computer is a machine and nothing more. And so, depending on one's taste and convictions, the brain and the computer are in one sense either fundamentally similar or radically different. Rational arguments will not, in my opinion, resolve the issue.

Assuming that the brain and the computer are both machines, how are the   *11*
two to be compared? The exercise is interesting. Computers are invented by man and are therefore thoroughly understood, if human beings can be said to understand anything; what they do not know is what future computers will be like. The brain was created by evolution and is in many important ways not understood. Both machines process information and both work with signals that are roughly speaking electrical. Both have, in the largest versions, many elements. Here, however, there is an interesting difference. For cells to be manufactured biologically appears to be reasonably simple, and neurons are in fact produced in prodigious numbers. It seems to be not so easy to increase the elements of a computer, even though the numbers are expanding rapidly. If synapses rather than neurons are considered to be elements of the nervous system, however, I can hardly imagine computers catching up. No one would want to be held to a guess as to the number of synapses in a brain, but 10^{14} (100 trillion) would not be implausible.

A still more important difference is a qualitative one. The brain is not de-   *12*
pendent on anything like a linear sequential program; this is at least so for all the parts about which something is known. It is more like the circuit of a radio or a television set, or perhaps hundreds or thousands of such circuits in series and in parallel, richly cross-linked. The brain seems to rely on a strategy of relatively hard-wired circuit complexity with elements working at low speeds, measured in thousandths of a second; the computer depends on programs, has far fewer elements and works at rates at which millionths of a second are important. Among brain circuits there must be many devoted to keeping evolution going by means of competition and sex drives. So far the computer seems free of all that; it evolves by different means.

How is one to study an organ such as the brain? The major approach, of   *13*
course, is to study its components and then try to learn how they function together. This is done primarily in animals rather than in man. The principles of neuronal function are remarkably similar in animals as far apart as the snail and man; most of what is known about the nerve impulse was learned in the squid. Even the major structures of the brain are so similar in, say, the cat and

man that for most problems it seems to make little difference which brain one studies. Moreover, neurobiology is notable for the wide range of approaches and techniques that have been brought to bear on it, from physics and biochemistry to psychology and psychiatry. In no other branch of research is a broad approach so essential, and in recent years it has begun to be achieved.

The two great interlocking branches of neurobiology itself have tradition- *14* ally been neuroanatomy and neurophysiology. Anatomy seeks to describe the various elements of the brain and how they are put together; physiology asks how the parts function and how they work together. Investigators in the two fields have tended to pursue separate courses and have even been housed in different departments in universities, but in fact they are interdependent. Most modern neuroanatomists are not content with a simple description of structure and spatial relations for their own sake but go on to ask what the structures and connections are for. Physiology, on the other hand, is impossible without anatomy.

At each stage of their development both neuroanatomy and neurophysiol- *15* ogy have had to wait until the physical sciences could provide them with necessary tools and techniques. The neuron is too small to see with the unaided eye except as a mere speck and far too small for its signals to be recorded with ordinary wires. In order to advance beyond the most rudimentary stages anatomy required first the light microscope and then the electron microscope, and physiology required the microelectrode. Both fields of study have been dependent on the invention of increasingly selective methods of staining nerve tissue.

The fundamental achievements of the neuroanatomists of the early part of *16* this century were the recognition that the neuron is the basic unit of nervous tissue and the discovery that neurons are interconnected with a high degree of order and specificity. The physiologists made a strong beginning by learning, in electrical and chemical terms, how the neuron transmits its messages. These two sets of accomplishments have by no means revealed how the brain works, but they provide an absolutely essential foundation. One way to see how far neurobiology has come (and, implicitly, how enormously far it has to go) is to consider some of the historical steps toward the present understanding of the brain and to briefly review the current status of research in some of the divisions of the field.

Why was it so hard to establish in the first place that the single neuron is *17* the basic unit of nervous tissue? The main obstacles were the minute dimensions, the fantastic forms and the enormous variety of shapes of these cells and the fact that the branches of cells near one another are closely intermingled. The word "cell" conjures up a shape like that of a brick or a jelly bean, but a neuron may look more like an elongated oak tree or a petunia — with a trunk or stem that is from 10 to 20 micrometers (thousandths of a millimeter) in diameter and from .1 millimeter to as much as a meter or so in length. To see individual neurons one needs not only a microscope but also a stain to contrast them with their surroundings. The neurons are normally packed together so intimately that in any one region the branching systems of hundreds of them intertwine in a dense thicket, with adjacent branches separated by films of fluid only about .02 micrometer thick, so that virtually all the space is occupied by cells and their various processes; when all the cells in a region are stained, one sees through an optical microscope only a dense and useless smear.

The most important single advance in neuroanatomy (after the microscope   *18*
itself) was therefore a discovery by the Italian anatomist Camillo Golgi in about 1875. He came on a method by which, seemingly at random, only a very small proportion of the cells in a region are stained at one time, and those cells are stained in their entirety. Instead of a hopeless morass a good Golgi stain shows only a few neurons, each one complete with all its branches. By looking at many slices of Golgi-stained brain tissue the anatomist can build up an inventory of the various kinds of cells in that tissue. To this day no one knows how or why the Golgi method works, staining one cell in 100 completely and leaving the others quite unaffected.

Golgi's Spanish contemporary, Santiago Ramón y Cajal, devoted a lifetime   *19*
of stupendous creativity to applying the new method to virtually every part of the nervous system. His gigantic *Histologie du système nerveux de l'homme et des vertébrés*, originally published in Spanish in 1904, is still recognized as the most important single work in neurobiology. In Cajal's day there was controversy over the extent of continuity between nerve cells. Were the cells completely separate entities or were they joined, axon to dendrite, in a continuous network? If there were protoplasmic continuity, signals generated by one cell could pass to an adjoining cell without interruption; if there were no continuity, there would have to be a special process for generating signals anew in each cell.

Cajal's Golgi-stained preparations revealed large numbers of discrete, com-   *20*
pletely stained cells but never anything to suggest a network. His first great contribution, then, was to establish the notion of a nervous system made up of separate, well-defined cells communicating with one another at synapses.

Cajal made a second contribution, possibly even more important. He com-   *21*
piled massive evidence to show that the incredibly complex interconnections among neurons are not random, as has sometimes been supposed, but rather are the very antithesis of random: highly structured and specific. He described exhaustively the architecture of scores of different structures of the brain, in each case identifying and classifying the various cells and in some cases showing, as far as his methods would allow, how the cells are interconnected. From his time on it has been clear that to understand the brain the neurobiologist not only would have to learn how the various subdivisions are constructed but also would have to discover their purposes and learn in detail how they function as individual structures and as groups. Before that could be done it would be necessary to find out how a single neuron generates its signals and transmits them to the next cell. Cajal may never have formulated the problems of understanding the nervous system explicitly in those terms, but one can hardly survey his work without taking that message from it.

For a long time neuroanatomists had to be content with increasingly de-   *22*
tailed descriptions based on light microscopy, the Golgi stain and the Nissl stain (which picks out individuals cell bodies but not their dendrites and axons). The first powerful tool for mapping the connections between different brain struc-

tures — between different parts of the cerebral cortex, for example, or between the cortex and the brain stem or the cerebellum — was a staining method invented in the Netherlands in the early 1950s by Walle J. H. Nauta, who is now at the Massachusetts Institute of Technology. The method capitalizes on the fact that when a neuron is destroyed (by mechanical or electrical means or by heat), the nerve fiber coming from it degenerates and, before disappearing altogether, can be stained differently from its normal neighbors. If a particular part of the brain is destroyed and the brain is stained by the Nauta method a few days later and then examined under the microscope, the presence of selectively stained fibers in some second and perhaps quite distant part means that the second region receives fibers from the destroyed part. The method has led to an enormous expansion in detail of the map of the brain.

In the past decade neuroanatomy has advanced at a higher rate, with more *23* new and powerful techniques, than in the entire 50 years that preceded. . . . . The advances are partly the result of better chemical tools and better understanding of how substances are taken up into neurons and are shipped in both directions along nerve fibers. A typical example is transport autoradiography. A radioactive chemical is injected into a brain structure; cell bodies take it up and transport it along their axons and it accumulates in the terminals. When a photographic emulsion is put in contact with a slice of brain tissue, microscopic examination of exposed silver grains in the emulsion reveals the destination of the axons. Other chemicals can be injected that are taken up instead by nerve terminals and transported back along the axons to the cell bodies, revealing the origin of the axons.

The latest in this series of advances is the deoxyglucose technique invented *24* a few years ago by Louis Sokoloff of the National Institute of Mental Health. Glucose is the fuel for neurons, and the cells consume more glucose when they are active than when they are at rest. Radioactively labeled deoxyglucose is taken up by the cells as if it were glucose. It is broken down like glucose, but the product of the first step of metabolism cannot be further metabolized. Because it also cannot escape from the cell it accumulates there, and the extent of the radioactivity in particular cells shows how active they have been. For example, one can administer the chemical to a laboratory animal by vein and then stimulate the animal with a pattern of sound. Microscopic examination of the brain then reveals the various areas of the brain that are involved in hearing. Very recently a new technique called positron-emission transverse tomography has been developed that makes it possible to detect from outside the skull the presence of deoxyglucose or other substances labeled with positron-emitting radioactive isotopes. This promising technique makes it possible to map active brain structures in a living laboratory animal or in a human being.

Applying all the available techniques, to work out in a rough and unde- *25* tailed fashion the connections in a single structure, say a part of the cerebral cortex or the cerebellum, may take one or two neuroanatomists five or 10 years. Accomplished neuroanatomists, a special breed of people, often compulsive and occasionally even semiparanoid, number only a few score in the entire world. Since the brain consists of hundreds of different structures, it is easy to see that an understanding of just the wiring of the brain is still many years away.

Moreover, to know the connections of a structure within the brain is a quite   26
different thing from understanding the structure's physiology. To do that one
needs to begin by learning how individual neurons work. How a single neuron
generates electrical signals and conveys information to other cells has become
reasonably well understood over the past three or four decades. The work was
done by many individuals; Sir Henry Dale, Otto Loewi, A. L. Hodgkin, A. F.
Huxley, Bernhard Katz, Sir John Eccles and Stephen W. Kuffler are some of
the major contributors. One of the surprising findings was that neurons, in spite
of their differences in size and shape, all use the same two kinds of electrical
signals: graded potentials and action potentials.

The entire neuron — the cell body, its long axon and its branching dendrites   27
— is polarized so that the inside is about 70 millivolts negative with respect
to the outside. Two properties of the cell membrane are responsible for this
"resting potential." First, the membrane actively transports ions, extruding
positively charged sodium ions from the cell and bringing in positively charged
potassium ions, so that the concentrations of the two kinds of ion are quite
different inside the cell and outside it. Second, the ease with which the ions
flow through the membrane is quite different for sodium and potassium.

It is changes in the resulting outside-to-inside resting potential that consti-   28
tute the electrical signals of nerves. A change in the transmembrane voltage
anywhere on the cell or its processes tends to spread quickly in all directions
along the membrane, dying out as it spreads; a few millimeters away there is
likely to be no detectable signal. This is the first kind of electrical signal, the
graded potential. Its main function is to convey signals for very short distances.

The second type of signal, the action potential, conveys information for greater   29
distances. If the membrane is depolarized (its potential decreased) to a critical
level—from the resting level of 70 millivolts to about 50 millivolts — there is
a sudden and dramatic change: the normal barriers to the flow of sodium and
potassium ions are temporarily removed and there ensues a local flow of ions
sufficient to reverse the membrane potential, which reaches about 50 millivolts positive inside and then is reversed again to restore the normal resting
potential. All of this happens within about a millisecond (a thousandth of a
second). Meanwhile the first reversal (to inside-positive) has produced a powerful graded signal that spreads and brings the adjacent region of the membrane to its critical level; that leads to a reversal in the next segment of membrane, which in turn leads to a reversal in the next segment. The result is a
rapid spread of the transient reversal in polarity along the nerve fiber.

This propagating action potential, which travels the entire length of the fi-   30
ber without attenuation, is the nerve impulse. All signaling in the nervous system over distances of a millimeter or more is in the form of impulses. Regardless of the type of fiber and whether it is involved in movement, vision or
thought, the signals are virtually identical. What varies in a given nerve fiber
under particular circumstances is simply the number of impulses per second.

When an impulse arrives at an axon terminal, the neuron next in line is in-   31
fluenced in such a way that its likelihood of in turn generating impulses is

modified. A chemical transmitter substance is released from the presynaptic membrane of the terminal, diffuses across the narrow space separating the two cells and affects the postsynaptic membrane on the far side of the synapse in one of two ways. In an excitatory synapse the transmitter leads to a lowering of the postsynaptic-membrane potential, so that the postsynaptic cell tends to generate impulses at a higher rate. In an inhibitory synapse the effect of the transmitter is to stabilize the postsynaptic-membrane potential, making it harder for excitatory synapses to depolarize the postsynaptic cell and thereby either preventing new impulses from arising or reducing their rate.

Whether a given synapse is excitatory or inhibitory depends on what chem- 32 ical transmitter the presynaptic cell makes and on the chemistry of the postsynaptic cell's membrane. Almost every neuron receives inputs from many terminals, usually many hundreds and sometimes thousands, some of which are excitatory and some inhibitory. At any instant some inputs will be active and some quiescent, and it is the sum of the excitatory and inhibitory effects that determines whether or not the cell will fire and, if it does fire, the rate at which it does so. In other words, the neuron is much more than a device for sending impulses from one place to another. Each neuron constantly evaluates all the signals reaching it from other cells and expresses the result in its own rate of signaling.

The propogation of the two types of signals along the neuron membrane and 33 the chemical events at synaptic contacts are, then, understood at least in broad outline. What is still far from clear is the relation between a neuron's shape (oak v. petunia) and the way it summates and evaluates the inputs it receives. Two incoming signals, either of which may be excitatory or inhibitory, surely add up very differently depending on whether the synapses are adjacent (for example on the same dendritic branch) or one synapse is on one branch and the other on a remote one (perhaps a branch of a different limb) or one synapse involves a branch and the other the cell body. Shape, being very different in different classes of neurons, is bound to be important in neuronal function, but that is about all one can say with assurance.

A related set of questions concerns the implications of certain synapses (or- 34 dinary-looking synapses with presynaptic and postsynaptic components) that are junctions between two dendrites or between two axons rather than — as is usual — between an axon and either a dendrite or a cell body. To put it mildly, no one knows quite what to make of them. Finally, to complicate things even more, some synapses are profoundly different from the usual chemical type, depending on flow of current rather than diffusion of a transmitter. These were discovered in the 1950s by Edwin J. Furshpan and David D. Potter at University College London. Why nature resorts to chemical transmission for some synapses and electrical transmission for others is still a puzzle.

At a more fundamental level many of the important unanswered questions 35 about nerve signals have to do with the fine structure and functioning of the neuron membrane, because it is still not known in molecular terms exactly how ions are transported across membranes or how the permeability to particular ions is influenced by changes in potential and by transmitter substances. . . . A particularly exciting area is the chemistry of synaptic transmission, with more than 20 transmitter substances already identified and the methods by which neurons make, release, take up and destroy the substances fairly well known. . . .

The still incomplete but greatly improved understanding of synapse chem- *36* istry has had profound effects in psychiatry and pharmacology. Many disorders, ranging from Parkinson's disease to depression, appear to stem from disturbances of synaptic transmission, and many drugs act by increasing or decreasing transmission. . . .

In a decade or so the main activities of individual neurons should be known *37* in great detail. At the present stage, with a reasonable start in understanding the structure and workings of individual cells, neurobiologists are in the position of a man who knows something about the physics of resistors, condensers and transistors and who looks inside a television set. He cannot begin to understand how the machine works as a whole until he learns how the elements are wired together and until he has at least some idea of the purpose of the machine, of its subassemblies and of their interactions. In brain research the first step beyond the individual neuron and its workings is to learn how the larger subunits of the brain are interconnected and how each unit is built up. The next step is to try to find out how the neurons interact and to learn the significance of the messages they carry.

One way to get a feel for the overall organization of the brain is to consider *38* it in rough caricature. . . . On the input side there are groups of receptors: modified nerve cells specialized to transform into electrical signals the various forms of information that impinge on them from the outside world. Some receptors respond to light, others to chemicals (taste and smell) and still others to mechanical deformation (touch and hearing). The receptors make contact with a first set of neurons, which in turn contact others, and so on. At each step along the way axons branch to supply a number of the neurons next in line, each of which is supplied by a number of axons that converge on it. Each recipient cell integrates the excitatory or inhibitory impulses converging on it from lower-order cells. Sooner or later, after a number of steps, nerve axons terminate on gland or muscle cells: the outputs of the nervous system.

In brief, there is an input: man's only way of knowing about the outside *39* world. There is an output: man's only way of responding to the outside world and influencing it. And between input and output there is everything else, which must include perception, emotions, memory, thought and whatever else makes man human.

The input-to-output flow described above, it need hardly be said, is over- *40* simplified. Although the main flow of traffic is [clearly from input toward output], there are frequent lateral connections among cells at any one stage; often there are connections in the reverse direction, from output toward input, just as there is feedback in many electronic circuits. There is not just one pathway from input to output; there are many different arrays of receptors, specialized for the various senses and for particular forms of the energy affecting each sense, and there are countless different shunts, relays and detours. The number of synapses between receptors and muscles may be very many or only two or three. (When the number is small, the circuit is usually designated a reflex; the constriction of the pupil in response to light shining on the retina represents a reflex involving perhaps four or five synapses.) And it should be mentioned again that a synapse can be either excitatory or inhibitory; if both kinds of influence impinge on a cell at a particular moment, the result may be a complete cancellation of effects.

Physiologists now have some idea of the kinds of operation performed by *41* the nervous system close to the input end and at the output. At the input end the system is apparently chiefly preoccupied with extracting from the outside world information that is biologically interesting. The receptors generally respond best at the onset or cessation of a stimulus such as pressure on the skin. We need above all to know about changes; no one wants or needs to be reminded 16 hours a day that his shoes are on.

In the visual system, to take one example, it is contrasts and movements *42* that are important, and much of the circuitry of the first two or three steps is devoted to enhancing the effects of contrast and movement. At subsequent stages of the visual system the behavior of the cells becomes more complex, but it is always orderly, and fortunately it makes sense in terms of perception. By now information originating with the light-receptive cells of the retina has been followed into the brain to the sixth or seventh stage, to the part of the cerebral cortex concerned with vision. . . .

Although the visual system is now one of the best-understood parts of the *43* brain, neurobiologists are still far from knowing how objects are perceived or recognized. Yet the amount that has been learned in the few years since microelectrodes became available does suggest that a part of the brain such as the cerebral cortex is, at least in principle, capable of eventually being understood in relatively simple terms.

At the output end of the nervous system the mechanism whereby a motor *44* neuron delivers an impulse to a muscle fiber has been understood in its essentials for some time, and for 50 years or more the parts of the brain concerned with movement have been known. Just what these structures actually do when a human being moves or contemplates moving is still largely unknown, however. Progress has been slow mainly because investigating voluntary movement calls for working with an animal that is awake and that has been given elaborate training, whereas one can study sensory systems in anesthetized animals. One of the main efforts today is to trace the motor impulse back from the motor neuron to structures such as the motor cortex and the cerebellum to learn how the decision to execute a movement is influenced by various signals coming from the input end of the nervous system. . . .

What is important at the output end is not the contraction of an individual *45* muscle but the coordinated contraction and relaxation of many muscles. In making a fist or grasping an object, for example, a person cannot merely flex the fingers by contracting flexor muscles in his forearm; he must also contract extensor muscles in the forearm to keep the finger-flexor muscles from flexing the wrist. This counteracting extension force at the wrist is exerted automatically and without thought (as one can verify by making a fist and feeling the extensor muscles contract on the hairy side of the forearm).

Evidently a command from the brain to make a fist involves the firing of *46* cells several stages removed from the output end of the nervous system, cells whose axons are distributed to the various motor neurons and inhibitory neurons that in turn supply all the muscles involved in executing the command. Other movements bring in different circuits that may well involve the same muscles but in different combinations.

It is not hard, then, to visualize a few of the kinds of functions that may be performed by the nervous system, particularly close to the sensory or the motor ends of the system. It is in the vast in-between region — in the frontal and parietal lobes, the limbic system, the cerebellum and so on and on — that knowledge of function is most lacking, although quite a bit is known about the anatomy. In some cases a kind of basic wiring-diagram physiology is known: which neurons excite or inhibit which, for example. In the case of the cerebellum not only is the wiring known in some detail but also it is now fairly clear which synapses are excitatory and which are inhibitory; for a few kinds of synapse the transmitters have been identified chemically with a moderate degree of confidence. Yet how the cerebellum works is known only in the vaguest terms. It surely has to do with the regulation of movements, muscle tone and balance, but how these functions are carried out by this magnificently patterned, orderly and fantastically complex piece of machinery is quite obscure. **47**

The cerebellum is admittedly a difficult place to work; it lies at the watershed between sensory and motor processes, in the blankest part of the rough diagram above. The kinds of input it receives — the particular significance of impulses that come to the cerebellum from the cerebral cortex, the spine and so on — are imperfectly known; the neural structures to which it sends its output, which are in turn ultimately connected to the muscles, are also not well known. For similar reasons most other parts of the brain are still dimly understood. In spite of recent advances in technique, new and revolutionary methods are badly needed. To give just one example, there is now no known way of studying the signals of single cells in a human being without actually opening his skull on the operating table, and that is generally unacceptable from an ethical standpoint. Major advances have nonetheless been made in understanding some of the higher functions of the human brain . . . but in order to really understand something such as speech, which is peculiar to man, it will be necessary to find ways of recording from single neurons from outside the skull. **48**

Knowledge of the wiring of neurons and their moment-to-moment workings represents only one ultimate goal in neurophysiology. Certain large aspects of brain function are beyond such a horizon. Memory and learning, for example, are surely cumulative processes involving change over a period of time, and very little is yet known about the mechanisms that underlie them. **49**

Neurobiology seems to be particularly subject to fads that sometimes amount almost to a derailment of thought. A few years ago the notion was advanced that memories might be recorded in the form of large molecules, with the information encoded in a sequence of smaller molecules, as genetic information is encoded in DNA. Few people familiar with the highly patterned specificity of connections in the brain took the idea seriously, and yet much time was consumed in many laboratories teaching animals tasks, grinding up their brains **50** and either finding differences in the brain chemistry of the trained animals or finding "statistically significant" improvement in the ability of other animals, into which extracts of the trained animals' brains were injected, to learn the same tasks. The fad has died out, but the fact is that neurobiology has not always advanced or even stood still; sometimes there is momentary backsliding.

In the final analysis an understanding of memory will probably involve two   *51* quite different components. One component is the changes that most likely take place in synapses as a result of the repeated use of neural circuits. For example, there could be an increase in the efficiency of one synapse at the expense of other synapses on the same cell. Particular combinations of stimuli, if repeated, might thus enhance one possible pathway among many in a neural structure.

Studies that might get at this aspect are rather difficult in higher animals;   *52* they are far easier in the small systems of neurons that constitute all, or large parts, of the nervous system of certain lower animals. Individual cells in these animals are often easy to poke with microelectrodes and, even more important, such cells often have unique identity; one can speak of cell No. 56 in a certain lobster ganglion and know that it will have virtually the same position and connections in other lobsters. (This is one profound difference between many invertebrate brains and man's. One can no more assign a number to a neuron of the human brain than one can to a hair of the head or a pore of the skin.)

Elegant experiments are being done at the single-cell level on learning in   *53* these invertebrate systems. . . . It has even been shown, for example, that when an animal learns or forgets a response, identifiable changes take place in the transmission of signals across particular synapses. The learning here is obviously of a simple kind, but it appears to be true learning. (Again and again discoveries have been made in invertebrates that were later extended to higher forms. There is therefore little likelihood that investigators will be discouraged from working on such animals by the gibes of politicians about the implausible sound of such projects as, say, "Problem-solving in the Leech.")

The second component that will need to be grappled with in studying memory   *54* ory will be far more difficult. Things one remembers (in anything but the most rudimentary sense of that word) involve percepts or movements or experiences. To get at memory in any real sense it will be necessary to know what goes on when human beings perceive, act, think and experience, in order to know what of all that is recapitulated when they remember or learn. Of the two components the first — the synaptic — seems to me to be relatively easy, the second stupendously difficult.

To understand the brain of an adult animal is a hard enough task; to understand how a brain gets to be a brain is probably at least as difficult. How   *55* does the nervous system develop, both before birth and afterward? The central problem is to discover how the information encoded in molecules of DNA is translated into cell-to-cell connections within structures, the mutual spatial relations of those structures and the connections among them. The optic nerve, for example, contains about a million fibers, each originating in a tiny part of the retina. Each fiber in turn connects in an orderly way to the platelike lateral geniculate nucleus in the brain, so that in a sense the retina is mapped onto the geniculate. How, during development, do the fibers grow out of the retina, reach the plate and distribute themselves with absolute topographical precision? Similar specifically wired sets of cablelike connections between topographically mapped areas are common throughout the nervous system, and how this precise wiring is laid down remains one of the great unsolved problems. . . .

Developmental studies are potentially important not only because they shed   *56* light on how the brain works but also because so many neurological diseases are, or seem likely to be, developmental in origin. These include most birth defects, Down's syndrome, certain kinds of muscular dystrophy, probably certain common epilepsies and a large number of rarer diseases.

How long it will be before one is able to say that the brain — or the mind   *57* — is in broad outline understood (those fuzzy words again) is anyone's guess. As late as 1950 anyone who predicted that in 10 years the main processes that underlie life would be understood would have been regarded as optimistic if not foolish, and yet that came to pass. I think it will take a lot longer than 10 years to understand the brain, simply because it is such a many-faceted thing: a box brimful of ingenious solutions to a huge number of problems. It is quite possible that human beings may never solve all the separate individual puzzles the brain presents. What one may hope is that, as each region of the brain is looked at in turn, it will become more and more established that the brain's functions are orderly and capable of being understood in terms of physics and chemistry, without appeal to unknowable, supernatural processes. . . .

There will be major individual milestones. For example, some single mech-   *58* anism by which memory (the synaptic component) works may be revealed, or some one process that explains how nerve fibers find their proper destinations in development. This does not mean, however, that at some particular moment in the future a discovery or set of discoveries is likely to be made that completely explains the brain. Progress in brain research tends to be slow. Technical advances have produced a marked acceleration in the past few decades, and yet there have certainly not been any abrupt upheavals to compare with those brought about by Copernicus, Newton, Darwin, Einstein, or Watson and Crick.

Each of those revolutions had the property of bringing some very funda-   *59* mental aspect of man's study of nature into the realm of rational and experimental analysis, away from the supernatural. If Copernicus pointed out that the earth is not the center of the universe and Galileo saw stars and planets but not angels in the sky, if Darwin showed that man is related to all other living organisms, if Einstein introduced new notions of time and space and of mass and energy, if Watson and Crick showed that biological inheritance can be explained in physical and chemical terms, then in this sequence of eliminations of the supernatural the main thing science seems to be left with is the brain, and whether or not it is something more than a machine of vast and magnificent complexity.

It is a question that goes to the very center of man's being, so that funda-   *60* mental changes in our view of the human brain cannot but have profound effects on our view of ourselves and the world. Certainly such advances will have significant effects on other fields of inquiry. The branches of philosophy concerned with the nature of mind and of perception will to some extent be superseded, and so, I think, will some parts of psychology that seek to obtain answers to similar questions by indirect means. The entire field of education will be affected if the mechanisms underlying learning and memory are discovered.

A revolution of truly Copernican or Darwinian proportions may never come   *61* in neurobiology, at least not in a single stroke. If there is one, it may be gradual, having its effect over many decades. Every stage will surely bring human beings closer to an understanding of themselves.

Considerations

1. Using this essay and your own sense of English usage, define *brain, mind, intellect, intelligence, talent, creativity.*
2. Analyze how Hubel uses one or more of the following:
   a. metaphors, similes, and analogies;
   b. statistical and numerical information;
   c. parenthetical remarks.
   In each case, what is his goal, and does he achieve it?
3. Identify and evaluate the organization of this essay (in broad terms, not at the paragraph level).
4. Summarize the relationship of neuroanatomy and neurophysiology. What do the fields share, and how do they differ? How has progress in one aided or impeded progress in the other?

The Dynamic Brain

Lane Lenard

Late at night, a 16-year-old sits before his personal computer, plugging into   *1* phone lines and rummaging through giant computer networks all over the country. Earlier that day, his father had struggled to learn a simple series of commands for the same machine; he just wanted to do his taxes.

Yet the father's achievement may be the more spectacular. The youth has   *2* grown up in the computer age. When he learned programming as a child, the neurons in his brain wired themselves into patterns that eventually made

---

Lane Lenard (b. 1944) holds a Ph.D. in psychobiology and served as articles editor for Science Digest, *the journal to which he later contributed this piece.*

computers second nature. This was easy because while he was young his neurons could still reach out to one another to make new connections.

The task was much more difficult for the father. As an adult, his brain is   3
much less "plastic," and old wiring patterns had to be broken while new ones formed. Until a few years ago, no one thought a brain could rewire itself to form new patterns of connections that hadn't existed before. But new knowledge of the brain's plasticity has now led to the first attempt to transplant nerve tissue into a human brain.

In the future, brain transplants may be the key to cures for a wide range of   4
neurological disorders, including Parkinson's and Alzheimer's diseases. Traditionally, most neuroscientists have envisioned the brain as a static, two-to-three-pound mass composed of billions of individual nerve cells, or neurons, plus structural, or support, cells. All connections between the neurons were made, it was assumed, early in life, after which the only change was a gradual loss of neurons through age.

But new research is showing the brain to be an active, dynamic, ever-changing   5
structure. Neuroscientists now think that things you learn, from a tennis serve to a recipe, can open up new channels of communication in your brain. As the same message is repeated over and over, the neuronal circuits that store it and permit access to it become stronger. Unused circuits become weaker. In time, the neuronal connections in your brain change to reflect all you have experienced and all you are.

This explains why those young computer hackers seem like a new breed.   6
Their brains are different. "You can't have a learning change without having changed the structure of the brain in some way," says neuroscientist Efrain Azmitia of New York University. "Having a computer available may mean that a good memory, for example, will not be as great an asset as it once was. A number of the tasks for which we have relied on our memories can now be done by a computer. As a result, there'll be no reason to expand those parts of the brain formerly needed for memory. Those brain cells will be freed up for other uses." It's not likely you could detect the differences in a computer hacker's brain under a microscope, but Azmitia is confident that differences between individuals exist. Why? Because differences have been observed in the brains of experimental animals.

In a now-classic experiment, one group of rats was raised in an "enriched"   7
environment that included companions, running wheels and assorted toys, while a second group of "impoverished" rats grew up with only the bare essentials. The privileged rats were later found to have a richer network of nerve connections in a region of the brain involved in the retrieval of memories.

"In order to grow and maintain their contacts," says Azmitia, neurons need   8
to be stimulated. If they aren't, their connections will regress or die out.

The brain is an ever-changing kaleidoscope of electrical peaks and valleys   9
and chemical ebbs and flows in which about 10 billion neurons are constantly reaching out to one another across microdistances to deliver their molecular messages. The brain's functioning consists of the sum total of this steady and highly coordinated passage of information — in the form of a few molecules of a chemical transmitter substance — from one neuron to another. Neurotransmitter substance is stored in tiny packets called vesicles in the terminal of each

nerve cell's axon, which is a kind of sending antenna. When a signal, in the form of a tiny electrical pulse, or action potential, reaches the terminal, a few vesicles spurt out their contents into the ultramicroscopic gap between the axon terminal and the surface of the next neuron.

On the other side of the gap, or synapse, is either the main body of a neigh-   *10* boring neuron or part of its dendritic tree, a kind of receiving antenna. Here there are special receptors to which the transmitter can easily attach.

Each neuron receives inputs from perhaps 1,000 other neurons and is ca-   *11* pable of "sending" directly to hundreds more.

"In an enriched environment," says Azmitia, "there can be more contacts.   *12* The number of cells, the number of spines on dendritic trees, what the dendrites look like, can all vary with how much activity a region gets." In addition, both the nature and the amount of the transmitter released can change; there may even be an increase in nerve sprouting if the event that started it is repeated often enough.

Millisecond Learning

Perhaps most astonishing is what goes on when we learn something quickly.   *13* At such times, Azmitia claims, "the synaptic changes associated with learning can occur in milliseconds."

If learning is a process of making new synaptic connections and reinforcing   *14* or weakening older ones, it's easy to see why children learn some things, such as languages or computer programming, more easily than adults.

Unlike most other cells in the body, neurons, with few exceptions, stop di-   *15* viding before birth. You are born with all the nerve cells in your brain that you will ever have. But they are immature; they have yet to make the bulk of the synaptic connections with other neurons that form only as we grow and learn.

As a child learns a language, whether it is English, French or Basic, he writes   *16* on a kind of blank neuronal slate, making new synaptic contacts among the neurons in the brain's language areas. These connections form the basis for new chemical-electrical circuits that allow the child to speak, write and understand.

The youthful brain has plenty of room for new synapses, and the sounds,   *17* words, rhythms and rules of the new language easily mold the brain in their image. But by the time we are adults, the language paths in our brains are well trod. A second tongue must compete for neuronal space. *Chien* (French for dog) must not only forge its own trails in the neuronal wilderness, it must also compete with the old, well-worn ones that mean dog.

What about other pervasive influences on our behavior? Do the country   *18* mouse's problems adapting to city life reflect a fundamental structural difference in the brains of country and city dwellers? Azmitia thinks they do. "You get used to certain patterns and levels of stimulation," he explains. "The neuronal circuitry becomes adapted to a country life-style. If you then change that life-style, it makes sense that the patterns you have set up would not be suited to the new environment."

This is not to say that brains become "hard-wired" in the computer sense.   *19*

"A neuron retains its capacity for growth throughout life," Azmitia says. "It may grow much slower as we grow older, but it will still grow." Translation: You *can* teach an old dog (or *vieux chien*) new tricks; it's just a bit harder.

The new concept of brain plasticity has had a boost in the past 10 years   20
from Azmitia and other researchers who have shown it possible to transplant brain tissue from one animal to another and have the transplanted tissue function normally in its new location. A brain transplant, points out Azmitia, is just an extreme form of plasticity.

While the idea of brain transplants raises images of two-headed monsters,   21
in an experiment only a small portion of brain tissue is transplanted. "Maybe a million cells, of which only ten or twenty percent survive," Azmitia explains, referring to his own work with neurons that produce the transmitter serotonin. "Of those, perhaps one percent or less represents the cells of the particular chemical type you're interested in studying. So you're really looking at a functional transplant of perhaps a hundred to a thousand cells."

Horror-Movie Overtones

Some researchers even balk at the idea that they are doing brain trans-   22
plants. Neurobiologist Bruce McEwen of Rockefeller University, feeling that "brain transplant" has too many horror-movie overtones, prefers the term "brain tissue grafts."

Brain transplants, or tissue grafts, generally take one of three forms. 1. A   23
plug of tissue can be removed from one brain and implanted in another brain from which a similar-size plug has been removed. 2. Donor tissue can be *dissociated* — broken apart by chemicals called enzymes and placed in suspension — and then injected into the host brain. 3. A piece of tissue from the donor can be placed in a ventricle, a large fluid-filled cavity, in the host brain.

Attempts to transplant brain tissue go back to the early part of the century,   24
but have only recently been successful. McEwen notes that a major breakthrough was the discovery that fetal tissue transplants most successfully.

Transplanted fetal brain cells readily connect with other neurons and may   25
even seek out the same types of neurons they connected to in their original environment, the donor brain. Transplantation is less traumatic for the fetal cell because it lacks the multitude of synaptic contacts characteristic of the adult cell. Breaking these connections seems to be a severe jolt, and few adult cells survive it.

One dream of neuroscientists, perhaps from the start, has been to trans-   26
plant a particular behavior along with the tissue — teach an animal a task and transplant the part of its brain concerned with that task into another animal's brain. Next, they want to see whether the second animal will perform the task without having to learn it in the traditional way. But even if it were possible to localize a particular piece of behavior precisely in the brain, the use of tissue from fetuses, which haven't learned anything, precludes such an experiment.

Nevertheless, it is possible to markedly influence behavior with brain trans-   27
plants. In one experiment by neuroscientists Mark Perlow and William Freed of the National Institute of Mental Health, along with physiologist Barry Hof-

fer of the University of Colorado and three other colleagues, a small lesion was made on one side of the brain of adult rats, disrupting the connection of the dopamine neurons between the substantia nigra and the caudate nucleus. This latter area is rich in the synapses containing the neurotransmitter dopamine. The rats, with half of their dopamine-producing system destroyed by the lesion, were then given a drug that stimulates dopamine receptors. The rats reacted by moving in circles.

Next, researchers transplanted portions of the dopamine-producing neurons 28 in the substantia nigra from fetal rats into the brains of these rats near the site of the lesion, and the rate of circling diminished, indicating that the grafted tissue was secreting dopamine the way it should.

Running a Maze

Other experiments by an international team including experimental psy- 29 chologists Stephen Dunnett and Susan Iversen of Cambridge University, neurophysiologist W. C. Low of the University of Vermont, and Anders Bjorklund and Ulf Stenevi of the University of Lund in Sweden have shown that rats whose brains are lesioned in another region rich in synapses involving a neurotransmitter called acetylcholine (ACh) learn to run a maze better if ACh-releasing neurons from fetal rats are transplanted into their brains.

Under the right conditions, even cells that are not neurons can begin to act 30 like neurons when transplanted into the brain. They grow axons and dendrites and release neurotransmitters. This is the basis for the most remarkable brain transplant experiment yet, and the only one so far performed on a human being. It was done in Stockholm, Sweden, by neurosurgeon Olof Backlund and two colleagues at Karolinska hospital.

The patient had Parkinson's disease, in which muscular tremors and other 31 symptoms result from the death of neurons that produce the transmitter dopamine in the caudate nucleus. (The experiments on dopamine centers in rats were connected with research on Parkinson's disease.) Backlund and his colleagues knew from animal experiments that certain cells in the adrenal gland have a chemical make-up similar to neurons in the caudate, but because their environment is different, these cells never develop into neurons.

"They're endocrine cells," explains Azmitia. "They make and secrete epi- 32 nephrine [also known as adrenaline] and small amounts of dopamine as well." Although they don't normally look like neurons, the adrenal cells will grow axons and dendrites when placed in the brain and treated with a naturally occurring substance called nerve growth factor.

Tissue from the Parkinson patient's adrenal gland was transplanted directly 33 into his caudate nucleus. A small improvement resulted. Before the experiment, the patient had been unable to move without medication. Afterward, his medication could be reduced by 15 to 20 percent. It was enough to encourage the experimenters to continue working with human subjects.

Although brain tissue transplants as a clinical tool are clearly years away, 34 Azmitia thinks they may ultimately be used to treat other conditions, including stroke and Alzheimer's disease (senile dementia), both of which are marked by the extensive death of nerve cells.

One of the problems brain transplanters encounter when they do experi- 35 ments such as these is the brain's tendency to heal the wound produced and protect itself from intruding cells. "Whenever some sort of damage occurs in the brain," explains Azmitia, nonneuronal cells called glia "divide and migrate toward the site of the wound." The result in adult animals is a glial scar completely surrounding the transplant, preventing what the researcher calls "true integration."

Neurons themselves are also good at migrating. Azmitia points out that while 36 a glial scar prevents fetal neurons from migrating out of the transplant, there is clear evidence that they do move around inside, seeking to make contacts with other neurons.

Neurons do most of their wandering while the brain is taking shape in the 37 womb. The brain begins as a thin sheet of cells on the surface of the developing embryo. The sheet folds on itself to form a long, hollow "neural tube" that is the foundation of the nervous system. Once the tube is formed, nerve cells near its center begin dividing rapidly, reproducing at the astonishing rate of hundreds of thousands per minute.

A Trio of Bulges

Soon a trio of bulges — the beginnings of the brain — emerges at one end 38 of the neural tube. (The remainder of the tube will become the spinal cord.) Though it is composed of billions of cells, the embryonic brain is barely functional because the neurons at this stage of development have yet to make any synaptic connections. Consequently, they are unable to transmit impulses.

At this point, some of the cells stop dividing. This triggers their migration 39 outward, apparently with a specific destination in mind. If a cell's "birth date" (that is, the time when it loses its capacity to divide) is known, notes the eminent neurophysiologist W. Maxwell Cowan, director of the Weingart Laboratory for Developmental Neurobiology at the Salk Institute, "it is possible to predict where the cell will finally reside. Furthermore, it seems in some cases that the pattern of connections the neuron will ultimately form is also determined at this time."

Neurons migrate through the dense mass of the brain in much the same way 40 an amoeba moves through pond water, pushing part of their mass forward and attaching it to something, then pulling along the rest. By so doing, they travel about a tenth of a millimeter per day. Some neurons use certain glial cells as both scaffolding and guide, "climbing" through the brain like a snake climbing a tree.

Once they arrive at the destination, neurons aggregate with other, similar 41 neurons to form layers of nuclear masses. Only now do they begin to send out fibers, seeking the appropriate fellow neurons with which to form synaptic connections. They find their target by an incredible process involving structures called growth cones, which appear on the ends of the nerve fibers that are making their way, often for long distances, through the nervous system.

These small protrusions extend and retract as though they were feeling their 42 way through the tissue. Notes Erich Harth, a physicist who has studied the brain, "Movies of growth cones . . . convey [the] startling impression of an intelligent search, a series of trials and errors, and decision-making. They almost seem like bloodhounds, sniffing their way through dense underbrush. We must remind ourselves that we are looking here at minute portions of a yet unformed nervous system." Apparently, the growth cones are "looking" for structural or chemical cues to guide them.

But just how does a neuron "know" which of the billions of other neurons 43 in the brain it is supposed to hook up to? How does it "know" in which region of the brain it's supposed to ultimately reside? Are the connections it makes genetically determined or are they random?

These are some of the great unanswered questions of brain research. Harth 44 speculates in his book *Windows on the Mind* that the total answer cannot be contained in our genes. "Assume that there are exactly ten billion neurons in the brain," he writes, "and that each neuron makes a thousand synaptic contacts with other neurons. There are thus a thousand times ten billion, or ten trillion, synapses whose locations must be specified. . . . It is impossible that this information is genetically determined. In fact, it exceeds the total capacity of human DNA by almost a millionfold." Random factors, then, accidental connections, must play an important role in brain formation.

W. Maxwell Cowan disagrees. "There is much evidence," he writes, "that 45 the connections formed [between neurons] are specific not only for particular regions of the brain but also for particular neurons . . . within those regions."

Whichever view turns out to be correct, there is no doubt that, as Harth 46 points out, "experience and learning become the fine texture that is laid down on" the basic structure of the fetal brain.

So we come full circle to that young computer hacker sitting up late, in- 47 venting new ways to play with the toy that is molding his brain as television and hot rods molded his father's. But the computer has ushered in an age of unprecedented technological development, and we must wonder what its long-term, or evolutionary, effects on the structure of the human brain will be.

Will those of us whose brains are more plastic than others have an evolu- 48 tionary advantage? Have we already begun the lengthy process of breeding a race of human beings whose brains are perfectly adapted to the computer?

Considerations

1. What is Lane Lenard's attitude (or tone) toward the material he reports? What specific elements in the essay create this tone?
2. Create a list of questions on this topic you would like answered either through greater elaboration by Lenard or by further research in the field. Then choose two or three of the questions and explain their importance.

Connections

1. How does the idea that the brain undergoes physical changes during learning affect your reading of Chapter 6, The Nature of Learning?

2. Compare and contrast Lane Lenard's brief description of the brain with David Hubel's more extensive one. In what ways are their strategies similar? Does Lenard manage to compress ideas without making them vague or distorting them?
3. Both Lenard and Hubel begin (and Lenard ends) by talking about computers and the brain. Why? Are computers essential to their topics?

The Mind of the Puzzler

Robert J. Sternberg and
Janet E. Davidson

Before departing from San Francisco on a flight to New York recently, a colleague of ours picked out some reading to test his wits. A professor of some accomplishment, he expected to make short work of the problems in *Games for the Superintelligent*, *More Games for the Superintelligent*, and *The Mensa Genius Quiz Book*. By the time he crossed the Rocky Mountains, however, he had realized that he was neither a genius nor, as *The Genius Quiz Book* puts it, "a secret superbrain who doesn't even know it." By the time he crossed the Mississippi River, he knew that he wasn't "superintelligent," either.   1

More often than not, the puzzles stumped him. How could two men play five games of checkers and each win the same number of games without any ties? He couldn't figure it out. How could you plant a total of 10 trees in five rows of four trees each? He drew several diagrams, and none of them worked. But he couldn't put the books down.   2

Our colleague wasn't alone in his frustration. Mental puzzles, whose appeal must be limited to the relatively intelligent, have nevertheless been a staple of the publishing industry for years. Martin Gardner's mathematical puzzles, from the monthly column he used to write for *Scientific American*, have been collected in 10 different books, with total sales of more than half a million copies. *Solve It, Games for the Superintelligent*, and *More Games for the Superintelligent*, all by James Fixx, have together sold nearly one million copies.   3

Puzzles can certainly be fun, and great ego boosters for those who eventually get the right answers. According to James Fixx, many people use mental puzzles to "strengthen their thought processes" and to "tune up their minds." Others use them to test or measure their own intelligence. In fact, *More Games*   4

Robert J. Sternberg (b. 1949) is professor of psychology at Yale University and editor of The Handbook of Human Intelligence. *Janet E. Davidson (b. 1952) is a graduate student in psychology at Yale.*

and *The Mensa Genius Quiz Book* actually contain what are supposed to be short IQ tests.

Many of the problems in these books require flashes of insight or "leaps of logic" on the part of the solver, rather than prior knowledge or laborious computation. We wondered just how people approach such puzzles — which are commonly called insight problems — and whether they provide a valid measure of a person's intelligence. To answer these questions, we examined the literature on problem-solving, and then conducted a mini-experiment to measure the relationship between performance on insight problems and scores on standard intelligence tests.

On the basis of our research, we identified three types of intellectual processes that, separately or together, seem to be required in solving most insight problems: the ability to select and "encode" information — that is, to understand what information is relevant to solving the problem, and how it is relevant; the ability to combine different and seemingly unrelated bits of useful information; and the ability to compare the problem under consideration with problems previously encountered. For example, in solving the problem of the checker players, faulty encoding would lead one to assume that the two men were playing each other. Correctly combining the facts that there were no ties and that each player won the same number of games should lead one to conclude that they couldn't be playing each other.

Similarly, to plant 10 trees in five rows of four trees each, one must get away from the idea of making the five rows parallel. People who are accustomed to thinking in geometric terms will usually imagine several other kinds of patterns, until they hit on the correct one:

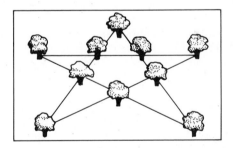

The literature on how people solve insight problems is meager, and includes almost no reports on research relating solution of these problems to intelligence. One of the few studies of this sort was done in 1965 by Norman Maier and Ronald Burke at the University of Michigan. Maier and Burke compared people's scores on a variety of aptitude tests with their skill at solving the "hat-rack problem." The problem calls on them to build a structure, sufficiently stable to support a man's overcoat, using only two long sticks and a C-clamp. The opening of the clamp is wide enough so that the two sticks can be inserted and held together securely when the clamp is tightened. Participants are placed in a small room and are asked to build a hat rack in the center of the room. The solution is shown on the following page:

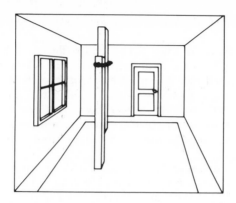

When the researchers compared people's ability to solve the hat-rack prob- 9
lem with their scores on the Scholastic Aptitude Test, the correlations were all
trivial. In other words, whatever insight people needed to build the hat rack
seemed to be unrelated to their scores on standardized intelligence tests. Burke
and Maier concluded that the abilities needed to solve insight problems may
be different from those required to solve problems of the kinds found on such
tests. Their study is of limited value, however: They used only one problem,
and scored the responses only in terms of "right" or "wrong."

We did find in the literature some theoretical basis for the lack of relation- 10
ship between intelligence and performance on the hat-rack problem. Kjell
Raaheim, a psychologist at the University of Bergen, in Norway, wrote in
Problem Solving and Intelligence that "it is unreasonable to expect intelligence
to be an important factor of success in solving tasks which are totally unfamiliar to the individual facing them." According to Raaheim, problems will
best measure intelligence if they present a situation that is *intermediate* in its
degree of familiarity to a problem-solver. Problems presenting situations that
are either too familiar or too unfamiliar will provide poorer measures of a person's intelligence.

In an ingenious set of experiments, Robert Weisberg and Joseph Alba, of 11
Temple University, asked people to solve a set of insight problems. One was
the familiar nine-dot problem, in which they were shown a three-by-three array of nine equally spaced dots and asked to connect the nine dots using four
straight lines without lifting pencil from paper. The solution requires an approach similar to that used to plant the five rows of trees.

What is unique about Weisberg and Alba's study is that participants were 12
actually given the insight they needed to solve the problem: They were told
that it could be solved only by drawing the lines beyond the boundaries formed
by the dots. Still, even after they were given the relevant insights, people in
this study had considerable difficulty in solving the problem. Weisberg and Alba
interpreted the results as suggesting that such problems may not really measure insight, but rather problem-specific prior knowledge. Our interpretation
is a bit different. As we see it, subjects not only needed to know that they could
draw the lines outside the boundaries; they also had to know how to combine
what went outside the dots with what went inside. Performance on these in-

sight problems therefore might not correlate with performance on intelligence-test problems.

Even though classic insight problems may not truly measure insight alone,   *13* we believed that problems could be found that do provide fairly accurate measures of insight, and that performance on such problems would be correlated with intelligence as it is typically measured by standardized tests.

To test this view, we compiled a set of 12 insight problems from a number   *14* of popular books. The problems vary in difficulty, in trickiness, and in the number of possible approaches that can be taken to reach a solution.

We recruited 30 people from the New Haven area by means of a newspaper   *15* advertisement that invited them to take part in a problem-solving experiment at Yale. Though not selected by scientific criteria, our small sample — 19 men and 11 women — represented a fairly typical cross-section of urban residents, with a wide range of ages, occupations, and educational backgrounds. None were connected with Yale.

First, we gave them a standard IQ test (the Henmon-Nelson Test of Mental   *16* Ability), including questions of vocabulary, math, and reasoning. None of the problems were quite like our insight problems. A typical reasoning problem, for example, might require the person to solve an analogy such as: CAR is to GASOLINE as HUMAN is to (a. OIL b. ENERGY c. FOOD d. FUEL); or a number series such as: 3, 7, 12, 18, — ? (a. 24 b. 25 c. 26 d. 27). The IQ test problems were multiple-choice, whereas the insight problems we used required people to generate their own answers.

The average IQ score of our sample on this test was 112, 12 points above   *17* the national average. (Elevated average IQs are typical in such experiments, since those who volunteer for studies on problem-solving are likely to be of above-average intelligence. People with very low IQs may not read newspapers, and probably wouldn't volunteer for experiments on problem-solving even if they do.)

Second, we gave our subjects a deductive-reasoning test on nonsense syllog-   *18* isms, such as "All trees are fish. All fish are horses. Therefore, all trees are horses. Please indicate whether the conclusion is logically valid or not." (This one is.) Third, in a test of inductive reasoning, we presented our subjects with five sets of letters (for example, NOPQ, DEFL, ABCD, HIJK, UVWX) and asked them to choose the set that was based on a rule different from the rule used as a basis for the other sets.

We included these two specific tests, as well as the more general IQ test, to   *19* judge the accuracy of a prediction we had made: If our problems genuinely measured insight, they should be more highly correlated with the inductive test, which requires one to go beyond the information given, than with the deductive test, which merely requires one to analyze the given information and draw the proper conclusion. Normal arithmetic or logic problems, for example, require primarily deductive rather than inductive reasoning skills.

Our subjects found the insight problems fun but sometimes frustrating, since   *20* the items varied considerably in difficulty. The easiest item, answered correctly by 73 percent of our sample, was this:

"Next week I am going to have lunch with my friend, visit the new art gal-   *21* lery, go to the Social Security office, and have my teeth checked at the dentist's. My friend cannot meet me on Wednesday; the Social Security office is closed weekends; the art gallery is closed Tuesday, Thursday, and weekends; and the dentist has office hours only on Tuesday, Friday, and Saturday. What day can I do everything I have planned?" Reaching the answer (Friday) is easy because one can simply check off which days don't work.

The hardest item, answered correctly by only 7 percent of our subjects, was: 22
"A bottle of wine cost $10. The wine was worth $9 more than the bottle. 23
How much was the bottle worth?" People probably had a hard time coming up with the answer (50 cents) because they misunderstood the word 'more.'

The average score on our insight problem test was 4.4 correct out of 12, or 24
roughly 37 percent. The individual scores ranged from a low of one to a high of 10, with no difference between the average scores of the men and the women. The times people spent solving the problems ranged from 11 minutes to 47 minutes, with an average of 28 minutes.

When we examined the relationship between scores on the set of 12 insight 25
problems and scores on the mental-ability tests, we found relatively high correlations between the insight-problem scores and the scores on the tests of IQ (.66 on a scale from zero to one, on which a correlation of zero means no relationship, and a correlation of one means a perfect relationship) and inductive reasoning (.63), and only a moderate correlation with the scores on the test of deductive reasoning (.34). (All of the correlations were statistically significant.) These correlations suggest that performance on insight problems does provide a good index of intelligence, and that such performance may be more closely related to inductive than to deductive reasoning.

We then looked at the relationship between the test scores and time spent 26
on the insight problems, and found that people who spent the most time working on the problems tended to have a higher number of correct solutions, and higher IQ scores. (The correlation between time spent and number of insight problems correctly solved was .62. The correlation between time spent and IQ was .75, which is remarkably high.) Why did smart people take longer on this task? Although we can only speculate, we suspect it is because they became more absorbed in the problems and more motivated to solve them. Our observations suggested that the less bright people either were too quick to choose the seemingly obvious but wrong answers on trick questions, or simply didn't know how to get started on the tougher problems and gave up more quickly.

When we looked at the correlations between the test scores on the insight 27
problems and the scores on the standardized intelligence test, we found that the problems varied considerably in their validity as indicators of IQ. The problem of which day to schedule a lunch date with a friend had almost no correlation with IQ; the problem that proved to be the best predictor of IQ score was the following:

"Water lilies double in area every 24 hours. At the beginning of the summer 28
there is one water lily on a lake. It takes 60 days for the lake to become covered with water lilies. On what day is the lake half covered?" To find the answer, people must realize that since the water lilies double in area every 24 hours, the lake will be half covered on the 59th day in order to be completely covered on the 60th.

What made some items better measures of IQ than others? We discovered   *29*
two patterns among the "good" and "bad" indicators of IQ that we thought
were striking, at least as preliminary hypotheses.

The best indicators of IQ seemed to be those problems that presented both   *30*
relevant and irrelevant information: The key to success was the ability to distinguish necessary information from unnecessary. For example, people with high
IQs tended to realize that "water lilies double in area every 24 hours" was an
important clue to solving this problem. People with low IQs frequently ignored
this information and tried to solve the problem by dividing the 60 days by two.

Our interpretation of performance on the problems supports the theory that   *31*
the ability to detect and use clues embedded in the context of what one reads
plays an important role in solving verbal problems. When reading a test —
whether it is a newspaper, a science book, or a verbal or arithmetic problem
— much of the information may be irrelevant to one's needs; often the hard
part is figuring out what is relevant, and how it is relevant.

The problems that proved to be poor indicators of IQ were the "trick" prob-   *32*
lems in which errors were due primarily to misreading the problem situation
— fixing on the apparent question rather than on the actual question. Take the
following problem: "A farmer has 17 sheep. All but nine break through a hole
in the fence and wander away. How many are left?" People making errors generally failed to comprehend exactly what "all but nine" meant; many assumed
that the nine had escaped and thus subtracted that number from 17 to get the
number of sheep that remained behind.

If, as we have shown, insight problems do provide a good measure of intel-   *33*
lectual ability — at least when they require one to make inductive leaps beyond the given data and when they require one to sift out relevant from irrelevant information — we must ask: Just what is insight? The reason that others
have not found any common element in the various insights they have studied
is that no one model works for all cases. We have identified three basic kinds
of cognitive processes or insightful performance, one or more of which may be
required to solve a given problem:

Selective Encoding, or processing of information. This kind of insight occurs   *34*
when one perceives in a problem one or more facts that are not immediately
obvious. Earlier, we referred to the importance of being able to sort out relevant from irrelevant information. This skill can provide the solver with a basis
for selective encoding.

Consider the following problem: "If you have black socks and brown socks   *35*
in your drawer, mixed in the ratio of 4 to 5, how many socks will you have to
take out to make sure of having a pair the same color?" Subjects who failed to
realize that "mixed in the ratio of 4 to 5" was irrelevant information consistently came up with the wrong solution. (The correct answer: three.) In the
hat-rack problem, noticing the relevance of the floor and ceiling as elements in
the problem is also an example of selective encoding.

Selective Combination. This type of insight takes place when one sees a way   *36*
of combining unrelated (or at least not obviously related) elements, as one must
do in the following problem: "With a seven-minute hourglass and an 11-min-
ute hourglass, what is the simplest way to time the boiling of an egg for 15
minutes?" Our subjects had all of the necessary facts, but they had to figure

out how to combine the two timers to measure 15 minutes. In the hat-rack problem, figuring out how to combine the use of the floor, ceiling, C-clamp, and two sticks constitutes a similar insight of selective combination.

Selective Comparison. This kind of insight occurs when one discovers a non-   37
obvious relationship between new and old information. It is here that analogy, metaphor, and models come into play. In the hat-rack problem, for example, one might think of how a pole lamp can be stabilized by wedging it between the floor and ceiling of a room, and how the same principle could be used in the construction of a hat rack.

Consider another type of selective comparison: If someone doesn't know a   38
word on a vocabulary test, he can often figure out its definition by thinking of words he does know that have the same word stems. For example, if he doesn't know the word 'exsect,' he might be able to guess its meaning by thinking of a word that has the same prefix (such as 'extract,' where *ex* means out) and a word that has the same root (such as 'dissect,' where *sect* means cut). This information might help him realize that 'exsect' means 'to cut out.'

We emphasize the critical role of selection in each kind of information-pro-   39
cessing. In Selective Encoding, one must choose elements to encode from the often numerous and irrelevant bits of information presented by the problem; the trick is to select the right elements. In Selective Combination, there may be many possible ways for the encoded elements to be combined or otherwise integrated; the trick is to select the right way of combining them. In Selective Comparison, new information must be related to one or more of many possible old pieces of information. There are any number of analogies or relations that might be drawn; the trick is to make the right comparison or comparisons. Thus, to the extent that there is a communality in the three kinds of insight, it appears to be in the importance of selection to each kind.

We believe that much of the confusion in the past and present literature on   40
problem-solving stems from a failure to recognize the existence of and differences among these three kinds of insight, which together seem to account for the mental processes that have been labeled as insight, and which are involved in everything from solving problems in puzzle books to making major scientific breakthroughs.

Although we have focused on the importance of insight in problem-solving   41
— and also in intelligence — insight alone is not enough to solve problems. Certain other essential ingredients exist, including:

Prior Knowledge. Even apparently simple problems often require a store of   42
prior knowledge for their solution; complex problems can require a vast store of such knowledge. Consider the problem of the seven-minute and 11-minute hourglasses, and how to time a 15-minute egg. If people have used hourglass timers before, and can remember that they can turn them over at any point, the knowledge will certainly help.

Executive Processes. These are the processes used to plan, monitor, and eval-   43
uate one's performance in problem-solving. To start with, one must first study the problem carefully, in order to figure out exactly what question is being asked.

Another executive process involves monitoring one's solution process (keep-   44
ing track of what one has done, is doing, and still needs to do) and then switch-

ing strategies if one isn't making progress. Sometimes it helps to try a new approach if an old one doesn't work.

Motivation. Really challenging problems often require a great deal of moti- 45
vation on the part of the solver. Successful problem-solvers are often those who simply are willing to put in the necessary effort. Indeed, in our mini-study we found that the better problem-solvers were more persevering than the poorer ones.

Style. People approach problems with different cognitive styles. In particu- 46
lar, some tend to be more impulsive and others more reflective. It seems to us — although we have no hard experimental evidence to support our view — that the most successful problem solvers are those who manage to combine both impulsive and reflective styles. We do not believe that most people follow just one style or the other. Rather, at certain points in the problem-solving process, people act on impulse; at other times, they act only after great reflection. The hard part is knowing which style will pay off at which point in solving problems.

Successful problem-solving involves a number of different abilities. For many 47
problems, one kind of insight may provide a key to a quick solution. But we believe that most problems are like the apartment doors one finds in some of our larger cities: They have multiple locks requiring multiple keys. Without combining different kinds of insights, as well as prior knowledge, executive processes, motivation, and style, the problems remain locked doors, waiting for the clever solver to find the right set of keys.

Considerations

1. Rewrite Robert Sternberg and Janet Davidson's work into a scientific paper, with abstract, introduction, methods, results, and conclusions. You can find models for such scientific papers in writing textbooks or — more abundantly — in professional journals. You may want to do this assignment with a group.

2. Consider the tests you took during high school (both course exams and national exams). How well do you think they measured intelligence, insight, potential, or mastery of a subject? Explain, being as specific as possible. If you like, limit your discussion to one or two particular exams.

3. Identify what Sternberg and Davidson want to prove. Describe the method they use for proving it and list the different elements. Did they indeed prove their point? Can you find any faults in their procedure or their conclusion?

Connections

1. The first three articles all refer to things researchers don't yet understand. Based on these readings, have we made more progress in understanding intelligence at the micro or macro level? Does neurobiology or experimental psychology seem a more potentially fruitful approach?

2. Based on your reading of the first three selections would you expect people with extraordinary intelligence or insight to have brains that are physically different from the average person's? Explain.

The Seven Frames of Mind
Howard Gardner

Since receiving his doctoral degree in social psychology from Harvard 13 years ago, Howard Gardner has been a fulltime research psychologist, dividing his time among three research sites. He conducts neuropsychological research with aphasic patients and other victims of brain disease at the Boston Veterans Administration Medical Center, codirects Harvard Project Zero, where he and his colleagues study the development of artistic skills in normal and gifted children, and is an associate professor at the Boston University School of Medicine. In the past decade Gardner has written seven books, and in 1981 he was awarded a MacArthur Foundation prize fellowship.

Frames of Mind, Gardner's most recent book, was written in response to a request from the Bernard Van Leer Foundation of the Netherlands. The foundation asked Gardner, among others, to prepare a series of books on the nature and realization of human potential. Gardner chose to focus on human cognitive potentials. Although he was trained as a Piagetian,° his research and reading had undermined his belief in general intellectual structures. His work on children's cognition and on the results of brain disease suggested to him that humans were capable of a set of different and often unrelated intellectual capacities or "intelligences." The book gave Gardner an opportunity to synthesize these findings and, at the same time, to offer a critique of current notions of intelligence and IQ testing. As he notes: "Many people realize our contemporary notions of intelligence are inadequate, but until we come up with a new and better theory, we'll continue to be stuck with talk about intelligence and with IQ tests."

—James Ellison

Ellison: Frames of Mind embraces a theory of multiple intelligences. Can you explain that theory in relatively simple terms?   *1*

Gardner: Most people in our society, even if they know better, talk as if individuals could be assessed in terms of one dimension, namely how smart or dumb they are. This is deeply ingrained in us. I became convinced some time   *2*

°*Piagetian:* Piaget (1896–1980) was a Swiss psychologist who outlined distinct stages of intellectual development. See Chapter 6, The Nature of Learning.

Howard Gardner (b. 1943) has authored numerous works in psychology, many of them focusing on children or the arts. In this interview from Psychology Today, *James Ellison, a contributory editor, talks to Gardner about his book,* Frames of Mind. *(Also see p. 367.)*

ago that such a narrow assessment was wrong in scientific terms and had seriously damaging social consequences. In *Frames of Mind*, I describe seven ways of viewing the world; I believe they're equally important ways, and if they don't exhaust all possible forms of knowing, they at least give us a more comprehensive picture than we've had until now.

Ellison: Linguistic and logical-mathematical intelligence are the two we all   *3*
know about.

Gardner: Most intelligence tests assess the individual's abilities in those two   *4*
areas. But my list also includes spatial intelligence. The core ability there is being able to find your way around an environment, to form mental images and to to transform them readily. Musical intelligence is concerned with the ability to perceive and create pitch patterns and rhythmic patterns. The gift of fine motor movement, as you might see in a surgeon or a dancer, is a root component of bodily-kinesthetic intelligence.

Ellison: That leaves the interpersonal and intrapersonal, which would seem   *5*
to be controversial categories.

Gardner: They are. But then my entire theory breeds controversy, particu-   *6*
larly among those who have a narrow, largely Western conception of what intelligence is.

Ellison: How would you define the interpersonal and intrapersonal as intel-   *7*
ligences?

Gardner: Interpersonal involves understanding others — how they feel, what   *8*
motivates them, how they interact with one another. Intrapersonal intelligence centers on the individual's ability to be acquainted with himself or herself, to have a developed sense of identity.

Ellison: I can see where your critics would grant that language and logic are   *9*
intelligences, and they'd probably throw in spatial, grudgingly. But they might balk at your other four measures as not being strictly mental activities.

Gardner: What right does anyone have to determine *a priori* what the realm   *10*
of the mind is and is not? Some of my critics claim that I'm really talking about talents, not intelligences, to which I say fine, if you'll agree that language and logical-mathematical thinking are talents, too. I'm trying to knock language and logic off a pedestal, to democratize the range of human faculties.

Ellison: Democratize?   *11*

Gardner: Forget about Western technological society for a moment and think   *12*
about other societies. In the Caroline Islands of Micronesia, sailors navigate among hundreds of islands, using only the stars in the sky and their bodily feelings as they go over the waves. To that society, this ability is much more important than solving a quadratic equation or writing a sonnet. If intelligence testers had lived among the Micronesians, they would have come up with an entirely different set of testing methods and a wholly distinct list of intelligences.

Ellison: And reading would have been low on the totem pole for these peo-   *13*
ple.

Gardner: Five hundred years ago in the West, a tester would have empha-   *14*
sized linguistic memory because printed books weren't readily available. Five hundred years from now, when computers are carrying out all reasoning, there may be no need for logical-mathematical thinking and again the list of desirable intelligences would shift. What I object to is this: Decisions made about

80 years ago in France by Alfred Binet, who was interested in predicting who would fail in school, and later by a few Army testers in the United States during World War I, now exercise a tyrannical hold on who is labeled as bright or not bright. These labels affect both people's conceptions of themselves and the life options available to them.

Ellison: Isn't it true that high SAT and IQ scores predict superior social and economic results? 15

Gardner: In the short run, these tests have decent predictive value, at least in schools. Children who do well in the tests tend to get good grades in school, for schools also reward quick responses to short-answer questions. Interestingly, though, the tests don't have a good predictive value for what happens beyond school. 16

Ellison: Are there statistics in support of that condition? 17

Gardner: Well, the best studies I know of were done by sociology professor Christopher Jencks of Northwestern University. He and his associates have shown that IQ tests have only a modest correlation with success in professions. 18

Ellison: How can you possibly test something like interpersonal intelligence? 19

Gardner: You can't, in the usual sense of testing. But let me tell you about a plan that some colleagues and I would like to get funded. We're interested in monitoring intellectual capacity in the preschool years. We want to set up what we call an enriched environment, filled with materials that children can interact with freely on their own. How children interact with these materials over a period of time would serve as a much better indicator of their strengths than any short-term measure. 20

Let's say we're looking in the area of spatial intelligence. One of the things we would want to do is to give children blocks of various sorts and observe what and how they build. We would show them games involving more complex structures and see if they pick up principles of construction. In the area of music we would give them Montessori bells and simple computer toys that allow children to create their own melody. Schools can be equipped with these aids. To assess personal intelligences, we'll have the children enact different roles in play or work cooperatively on the project. The point is that, in a few weeks or months, you could see the developmental steps children go through, as well as the richness and depth of their play. 21

Ellison: I take it you feel this is a better method to use than standard testing. 22

Gardner: Yes. First of all, it relates much more to children's natural way of doing things, which is exploring, testing themselves with materials. Second, if a child had an off day or didn't like the experimenter, we would simply go on to the next day. A child would be monitored for six months or a year, and at the end of the year we would come up with a profile of intellectual propensities somewhere between an IQ score and an annotated report card. We would observe intelligences and combinations of intelligences for a year. Then we would have descriptions a page or two long that say in plain English what the child's strengths and interests are, along with his areas of weakness and how they could be strengthened. 23

Ellison: Evidently, then, you still feel that some kind of score is necessary.　*24*

Gardner. It is efficient for the professional to be able to quantify, but I'm　*25* ambivalent about sharing scores with nonspecialists. We actually hope to develop four kinds of tests. One we call a test of core ability. For example, in the area of music we would look at the child's pitch and rhythm ability. But rather than assess sensitivity to pitches in isolation (as in traditional musical tests), we would teach children a song and code how quickly they learn it and how accurate the pitch and rhythm are. The second test is developmental. We would provide children with materials and give them ample opportunity to explore, to get deeper and deeper into the process, to invent their own product.

The third test, a multiple-intelligence measure, involves taking children to　*26* a movie, a museum, perhaps a zoo. Afterwards, children would be asked to re-create the experience, talk about it, sing it, draw it. We would look at how children choose to encode the experience, whether in their recreations, they focus on spatial, musical, linguistic or some combination.

Ellison: You mentioned a fourth test.　*27*

Gardner: Yes, an incidental-learning measure. We would supply something　*28* in the environment that children have no idea they're ever going to be asked about. We want to see what they would pick up spontaneously, without ever attending explicitly.

Ellison: Can you give an example?　*29*

Gardner: Say the child enters a classroom and there's a certain song play-　*30* ing, each day the same song. One day we simply say to the child, "Can you sing the song you hear in the morning?" This is how you discover what kids pick up incidentally. It has a lot to do with how intelligences work. A person does not have a high intelligence because he works very hard at something. On the contrary, having a high intelligence means that you naturally, without effort, pick up certain kinds of things.

Ellison: What about the practicality of administering these sorts of tests? It　*31* obviously would involve a tremendous amount of time and energy.

Gardner: First, you have to decide if the whole thing is feasible. If it is, we　*32* move to the question of practicality. Clearly, to be done adequately would involve several hours of monitoring spread out through the year. But if you take into account the amount of time a teacher spends determining the grades for a report card, the monitoring wouldn't take that much more time. And most important, when you consider the social value of assessing an individual's talents, the costs become trivial. A relatively small amount of time and money can make a huge difference for the person and for the society.

Ellison: Do you think there is a chance of changing the way testing is used　*33* in the United States today?

Gardner: Once people appreciate the perils, change will follow. There's　*34* treachery in labeling and overquantifying. This is true of IQ tests and also applies to SAT scores. SATs, after all, are basically IQ tests. More people probably know their SAT scores than their own Social Security numbers. I'm delighted that some of the best universities are now questioning the need for an SAT, and I'll do whatever I can to come up with a more humane and pluralistic way of assessing humankind.

Ellison: A way that spans the seven intelligences.　*35*

Gardner: Let me put this in personal terms for a moment. I've certainly got-   36
ten ahead by virtue of some of those intelligences that are valued in society.
Moreover, I learned early in life to use those intelligences to supplement things
that I couldn't do so well. For example, I'm not particularly gifted in the spatial area, but if I'm given a spatial test, I can usually use logical means to figure out the right answers. Also, I think I was "saved" because I've always been
very interested in the arts. They are every bit as serious and cognitive as the
sciences, and yet because of various prejudices in our society, the arts are considered to be mainly emotional and mysterious. Our culture confuses being a
scientist with being smart and serious. I came to realize that we really had to
rethink the whole notion of what cognition is all about.

Ellison: In school, the science kids have always been marked as the intellec-   37
tual whizzes, haven't they? Evidently the attitude that science kids grow up to
be our intellectual elite persists in the general adult culture.

Gardner: They are the high priests. And yet the cognitive complexity of Henry   38
James's or Proust's structure of knowledge is every bit as involved and sophisticated as the structural complexities of a physics theory: Granted, it's a different kind of complexity, but I think it's worth noting that someone can be
incredibly good as a scientist and have no sense of what's going on in a Henry
James novel.

Ellison: Once these various intelligences are identified, how can they be   39
translated into a cohesive educational experience?

Gardner: Let's say you have a child with strong spatial abilities, as assessed   40
by block play or by finding the way around a new environment. And let's say
the school doesn't have teachers who work in that area. There certainly are
other people in the community with those kinds of gifts, and it should be the
school's role to help children and parents find them. I'm in favor of dissolving
the boundaries between school and the rest of the community. I think it has to
happen in this country, and I'm convinced it will happen.

Also, the apprenticeship system should be reconstituted. The child who's   41
gifted in the spatial area ought to be working in an architect's office or in map-
making. Apprenticeship ensures the transmissions of skills to individuals in a
position to use them. We need to motivate people toward things they're good
at. Those who are gifted in math like doing it because it provides a lot of satisfaction and they make a lot of progress. But why stop with math? Apprentice
the musical kind to a piano tuner. God knows, we need good piano tuners.

Ellison: Are you saying we shouldn't invest energy in areas where our apti-   42
tude isn't high?

Gardner: I believe that, up to a point. But still, an effort to understand other   43
subjects has to be made.

Ellison: But why? The students who are whizzes in English and can't solve   44
a geometric problem on pain of death — why should they keep trying?

Gardner: One of the major things that prompted my work was recognition   45
that in the real world people have different abilities and disabilities. Take
someone with a good prognosis in the spatial area. What should we do? I think
it's crucial to try to diagnose that early because everything we know from neuroscience suggests that the earlier an individual has a chance to work intensely
with the relevant materials, the more rapidly he or she will develop in that

area. And it makes no difference how meager their potential is, it should be developed.

Ellison: Then in a sense you disagree with my idea that we should ignore *46*
areas of low aptitude.

Gardner: Areas of low aptitude should be detected early in life and they can *47*
be bolstered by what we might call prostheses for an intelligence. Let's assume I have poor visual memory and can't remember forms. Today we have all sorts of aids to make the forms perfectly visible. What if I can't transform an image in my mind? We now have a simple computer program that transforms it for me on demand. Culture, you see, can create instruments to supplement lacks in intelligences.

Ellison: How well do we understand these lacks in others, though? Can the *48*
skilled linguist who can't carry a tune appreciate the world of the jazz trombonist who can barely read the newspaper?

Gardner: I think the theory of multiple intelligences helps you to understand *49*
how people relate, and fail to relate, to one another. We all know that sometimes opposites attract. And if you think about this not in terms of hair color but of intelligences, it's quite intriguing. Often somebody who can't do music worth a damn is attracted to somebody who thinks well musically but has no personal skills and admires the person who's gifted interpersonally. However, problems may arise. One person thinks very spatially but has trouble trying to describe how to get somewhere. The spouse has no spatial ability or has to think of everything linguistically. This can cause considerable conflict, with each person thinking the other stupid, whereas, in fact, their minds are simply working in different ways, displaying contrasting intelligence.

Ellison: Let's move to the personal intelligences. Can you really teach some- *50*
one to interact well with others? Isn't that an art, a gift, in a sense, inborn?

Gardner: It can be taught. I think a lot can be done through different kinds *51*
of media. For example, you can tell stories to children and see what they understand about the motivations of different characters. Or let them act the characters. Show them films and have them look closely at the interactions of characters in the films. We must always be alert for settings in which children can develop in productive ways. It is harmful to put children who are shy and afraid of other people in an environment where everyone is much older and much more sophisticated. But put them in a game room with younger children, and you'll enhance their interpersonal understanding.

Ellison: Sometimes individuals are blocked for psychodynamic reasons. Do *52*
you see therapy as a possible teaching tool, as a way to promote the personal intelligences?

Gardner: Therapy is our society's way of helping individuals use whatever *53*
intrapersonal knowledge they have in a more effective way. In the East you have Hindu, yoga and other kinds of religious philosophies that develop their own sense of what it means to be knowledgeable about the self.

Ellison: Wouldn't you say that the intra- and interpersonal intelligences *54*
communicate with each other constantly?

Gardner: Certainly they enhance each other. The more you understand about *55*
other people, the more potential you have for understanding yourself and vice versa. Nonetheless, there are people highly skilled in understanding other peo-

ple and manipulating them — certain politicians and celebrities come to mind — and they show no particular intrapersonal understanding. By the same token, there are people in the artistic areas who seem to understand themselves while routinely missing cues in other people. An important part of my theory is that each intelligence has its own operation, and one can be strong in one intelligence while weak in others.

Still, there are many activities that involve blends of intelligences, where, 56 as you put it, they communicate. If you look at a society where certain activities use a combination of intelligences, each intelligence will tend to buoy the other. Take those with strong logical-mathematical intelligence. Once they begin to study science, they discover that if they can't write about their findings, they aren't really scientists. They have to be able to publish. That often means finding a collaborator who writes well. As a result of such collaborations, many scientists go from being wretched writers to becoming decent ones.

Ellison: I assume from *Frames of Mind* that the neural organization of the 57 brain determines the strength of the various intelligences.

Gardner: As you know, when somebody has a stroke or an injury to the head, 58 not all skills break down equally. Instead, certain abilities can be significantly impaired while others are spared. A lesion in the middle areas of the left hemisphere will impair somebody's linguistic abilities while leaving musical, spatial, and interpersonal skills largely undamaged. Conversely, a large lesion in the right hemisphere will compromise spatial and musical abilities, leaving linguistic abilities relatively intact. Probably the unique feature of my list of intelligences, compared with those of other researchers, is that I claim independent existences for the intelligences in the human neural system. And my chief source of information is how they function following brain damage. There is impressive evidence that each of the seven intelligences has its own special neurological organization.

Ellison: If *Frames of Mind* were to leave the reader with one point, what one 59 would you choose?

Gardner: Nothing would make me happier than if society were to stop 60 measuring people in terms of some unitary dimension called "intelligence." Instead, I would like us to think in terms of intellectual strengths. I'd like to get rid of numbers entirely and simply say that an individual is, let's say, relatively stronger in language than in logic, even though he or she might be well above the norm in both. Because after all, the norm is irrelevant. If you manage to change the way people talk about things, parents and teachers may begin to think and talk about intellectual proclivities rather than just how "smart" a child is. And if we begin to accept these new terms, we can stop labeling one another as smart or dumb.

Considerations

1. Critics might claim that some of Howard Gardner's seven abilities would be more aptly described as *talent* or *coordination* or *personality*. Is the debate here more than a matter of quibbling over words? Which of his seven categories are you willing to label *intelligence*, and why?

2. Gardner suggests a four-part test of ability. Evaluate the usefulness and practicality of his approach.
3. Will Gardner's measurements, which he claims will have great "social value," tell parents and educators significantly more than they already know in less quantitative terms?
4. Discuss the intellectual proclivities of several of your family or close friends in terms Gardner would accept. Does his approach help you understand or account for their abilities, personalities, or behavior?
5. Consider a job, career, or profession of interest to you. Which of Gardner's intelligences would it employ, and how?

Connections

1. Does Howard Gardner's "Seven Frames of Mind" present serious objections to the work of Robert Sternberg and Janet Davidson? Can their views be reconciled?
2. Is Gardner's claim that the seven intelligences have independent existences in the neural system consistent with David H. Hubel and Lane Lenard's discussion of the brain?
3. Which of Gardner's seven intelligences are used in solving Sternberg and Davidson's insight problems? What would *insight* or its equivalent be in Gardner's other areas?

Singapore's Patrimony (and Matrimony)

Stephen Jay Gould

Some historical arguments are so intrinsically illogical or implausible that, following their fall from grace, we do not anticipate any subsequent resurrection in later times and contexts. The disappearance of some ideas should be as irrevocable as the extinction of species.   *1*

Of all invalid notions in the long history of eugenics — the attempt to "improve" human qualities by selective breeding — no argument strikes me as more   *2*

Stephen Jay Gould (b. 1941) is an award-winning writer and professor at Harvard University, where he teaches geology, the history of science, biology, and paleontology. He is widely known for books like Ever Since Darwin *(1979),* The Panda's Thumb *(1980), and* The Flamingo's Smile *(1985) and for his column in* Natural History *magazine from which this essay is adopted.*

silly or self-serving than the attempt to infer people's intrinsic, genetically based "intelligence" from the number of years they attended school. Dumb folks, or so the argument went, just can't hack it in the classroom; they abandon formal education as soon as they can. The fallacy, of course, lies in a mix-up, indeed a reversal, of cause and effect. We do not deny that adults who strike us as intelligent usually (but by no means always) spent many years in school. But common sense dictates that their achievements are largely a result of the teaching and of the learning itself (and of the favorable economic and intellectual environments that permit the luxury of advanced education), not of a genetic patrimony that kept them on school benches. Unless education is a monumental waste of time, teachers must be transmitting, and students receiving, something of value.

This reversed explanation makes such evident sense that even the staunchest of eugenicists abandoned the original genetic version long ago. The genetic argument was quite popular from the origin of IQ testing early in our century until the mid-1920s, but I can find scarcely any reference to it thereafter — although Cyril Burt, that grand old faker and discredited doyen of hereditarians, did write in 1947: 3

> It is impossible for a pint jug to hold more than a pint of milk; and it is equally impossible for a child's educational attainments to rise higher than his educable capacity permits.

In my favorite example of the original, genetic version, Harvard psychologist R. M. Yerkes tested nearly two million recruits to this man's army during World War I and calculated a correlation coefficient of 0.75 between measured intelligence and years of schooling. He concluded: 4

> The theory that native intelligence is one of the most important conditioning factors in continuance in school is certainly borne out by this accumulation of data.

Yerkes then noted a further correlation between low scores of blacks on his tests and limited or absent schooling. He seemed on the verge of a significant social observation when he wrote: 5

> Negro recruits, though brought up in this country where elementary education is supposedly not only free but compulsory on all, report no schooling in astonishingly large proportion.

But he gave the data his customary genetic twist by arguing that a disinclination to attend school can only reflect low innate intelligence. Not a word did he say about the poor quality (and budgets) of segregated schools or the need for early and gainful employment among the impoverished. (Ashley Montagu reexamined Yerkes's voluminous data twenty years later and, in a famous paper, showed that blacks in several northern states with generous school budgets and strong commitments to education tested better than whites in southern states with the same years of schooling. I could almost hear the old-line eugenicists sputtering from their graves, "Yes, but, but only the most intelligent blacks were smart enough to move north.") 6

I did not, in any case, ever expect to see Yerkes's argument revived as a hereditarian weapon in the ongoing debate about human intelligence. I was wrong. 7

The reincarnation is particularly intriguing because it comes from a place and culture so distant from the original context of IQ testing in Western Europe and America. It should teach us — and this is the main point I hope to convey in this column — that debates among academics are not always the impotent displays of arcane mental gymnastics so often portrayed in our satires and stereotypes, but that ideas can have important social consequences with impacts upon the lives of millions. Old notions may emerge later, often in curiously altered contexts, but their source can still be recognized and traced to claims made in the name of science yet never really supported by more than the social prejudices (often unrecognized) of their proposers. Ideas matter in tangible ways.

Natural History really gets around. I received last month from some regular   *8* readers in Singapore, who knew of my interest in the IQ controversy from previous columns, a thick package of Xeroxed reports from the English-language press of their nation. These pages covered a debate that has raged in their country since August 1983, when in his annual National Day Rally speech (an equivalent to our "state of the union" message, I gather), Prime Minister Lee Kwan Yew abandoned his customary account of economic prospects and progress and, instead, devoted his remarks to what he regards as a great danger threatening his nation. The headline of the *Straits Times* for August 15 read (Singapore was once the primary city of a British colony named Straits Settlement): "Get Hitched . . . and don't stop at one. PM sees depletion of talent pool in 25 years unless better educated wed and have more children."

Prime Minister Lee had studied the 1980 census figures and found a trou-   *9* bling relationship between the years that women spend in school and the number of children subsequently born. Specifically, Mr. Lee noted that women with no education have, on average, 3.5 children; with primary education, 2.7; with secondary schooling, 2.0; and with university degrees, only 1.65. He stated:

> The better educated the people are, the less the children they have. They can see the advantages of a small family. They know the burden of bringing up a large family. . . . The better educated the woman is, the less children she has.

So far, of course, Prime Minister Lee had merely noted for his nation a de-   *10* mographic pattern common to nearly every modern technological society. Women with advanced degrees and interesting careers do not wish to spend their lives at home, bearing and raising large families. Mr. Lee acknowledged:

> It is too late for us to reverse our policies and have our women go back to their primary role as mothers. . . . Our women will not stand for it. And anyway, they have already become too important a factor in the economy.

But why is this pattern troubling? It has existed for generations in many   *11* nations, our own for example, with no apparent detriment to our mental or moral stock. The correlation of education with fewer children becomes a dilemma only when you add to it Yerkes's old and discredited argument that people with fewer years of schooling are irrevocably and biologically less intelligent, and that their stupidity will be inherited by their offspring. Mr. Lee made just this argument, thus setting off what Singapore's press then dubbed "the great marriage debate."

The prime minister is not, of course, unaware that years in school can re-   12
flect economic advantages and family traditions with little bearing on inherited smarts. But he made a specific argument that deemphasized to insignificance the potential contribution of these environmental factors to years of
schooling. Singapore has made great and recent advances in education: universal schooling was introduced during the 1960s and university places were
opened to all qualified candidates. Before these reforms, Lee argued, many genetically bright children grew up in poor homes and never received an adequate education. But, he contends, this single generation of universal opportunity resolved all previous genetic inequities in one swoop. Able children of
poor parents were discovered and educated to their level of competence. Society has sorted itself out along lines of genetic capacity — and level of education is now a sure guide to inherited ability.

> We gave universal education to the first generation in the early 1960s. In the 1960s
> and 70s, we reaped a big crop of able boys and girls. They came from bright parents,
> many of whom were never educated. In their parents' generation, the able and not-
> so-able both had large families. This is a once-ever bumper crop which is not likely
> to be repeated. For once this generation of children from uneducated parents have
> received their education in the late 1960s and 70s, and the bright ones make it to the
> top, to tertiary [that is, university] levels, they will have less than two children per
> ever-married woman. They will not have large families like their parents.

Lee then sketched a dire picture of gradual genetic deterioration.

> If we continue to reproduce ourselves in this lopsided way, we will be unable to
> maintain our present standards. Levels of competence will decline. Our economy will
> falter, the administration will suffer, and the society will decline. For how can we
> avoid lowering performance, when for every two graduates (with some exaggeration
> to make the point), in 25 years' time there will be one graduate, and for every two
> uneducated workers, there will be three?

So far, I have not proved my case — that the worst arguments raised by   13
hereditarians in the great nature–nurture wars of Western intellectuals can re-
surface with great social impact in later and quite different contexts. Mr. Lee's
arguments certainly sound like a replay of the immigration debate in America
during the early 1920s or of the long controversy in Britain over establishing
separate, state-supported schools (it was done for many years) for bright and
benighted children. But the arguments are evident, however flawed. Perhaps
the prime minister of Singapore merely thought them up anew, with no input
from older Western incarnations.

But another key passage in Lee's speech — the one that set off waves of rec-   14
ognition and inspired me to write this column — locates the source of his claims
in old fallacies of the Western literature. I have left one crucial part of the argument out — the "positive" justification for a predominance of heredity in
intellectual achievement (versus the merely negative claim that universal education should have smoothed out any environmental component). Lee stated,
in a passage that sent a frisson of *déjà-vu* up my spine:

> A person's performance depends on nature and nurture. There is increasing evidence
> that nature, or what is inherited, is the greater determinant of a person's perfor-

mance than nurture (or education and environment). . . . The conclusion the researchers draw is that 80 percent is nature, or inherited, and 20 percent the differences from different environment and upbringing.

The giveaway phrase is "80 percent" (supplemented by Lee's specific refer- 15
ences to studies of identical twins reared apart). All cognoscenti of the Western
debate will immediately recognize the source of this claim in the "standard
figure" so often cited by hereditarians (especially by Arthur Jensen in his notorious 1969 article entitled "How Much Can We Boost IQ and Scholastic
Achievement") that IQ has a measured heritability of 80 percent.

The fallacies of this 80 percent formula, both of fact and interpretation, have 16
also been thoroughly aired back home, but that part of the debate has, alas,
apparently not penetrated to Singapore.

When Jensen advocated an 80 percent heritability, his primary support came 17
from Cyril Burt's study of identical twins separated early in life and raised apart.
Burt, the grand old man of hereditarianism, wrote his first paper in 1909 (just
four years after Binet published his initial IQ test) and continued, with stead-
fast consistency, to advance the same arguments until his death in 1971. His
study of separated twins won special fame because he had amassed so large a
sample for this rarest of all animals — more than fifty cases, where no previous researcher had managed to find even half that number. We now know
that Burt's "study" was perhaps the most spectacular case of outright scientific fraud in our century — no problem locating fifty pairs of separated twins
when they exist only in your own head.

Burt's hereditarian supporters first reacted to this charge of fraud by at- 18
tributing it to left-wing environmentalist ideologues out to destroy a man by
innuendo when they couldn't overwhelm him by logic or evidence. Now that
Burt's fraud has been established beyond any possible doubt (see L. S. Hearn-
shaw's biography, *Cyril Burt, Psychologist*), his erstwhile supporters advance
another argument — the 80 percent figure is so well established from other
studies that Burt's "corroboration" was irrelevant in any case.

In my reading, the literature on estimates of heritability for IQ is a confus- 19
ing mess — with values from 80 percent, still cited by Jensen and others, all
the way down to Leon Kamin's contention *(The Science and Politics of IQ)* that
existing information is not incompatible with a true heritability of flat zero. In
any case, it hardly matters, for the real fallacy of Lee's argument lies not in an
inaccurate claim for heritability but in a false interpretation of what heritability means.

The problem lies in a common and incorrect equation of heritable with "fixed 20
and inevitable." Most people, when they hear that IQ is 80 percent heritable,
conclude that four-fifths of its value is irrevocably set in our genes and only
one-fifth is subject to improvement by good education and environment. Prime
Minister Lee fell right into this old trap of false reason when he concluded that
80 percent heritability established the predominance of nature over nurture.

Heritability, as a technical term, is a measure of how much variation in the 21
appearance of a trait within a population (height, eye color, or IQ, for example) can be accounted for by genetic differences among individuals. It is simply
not a measure of flexibility or inflexibility in the potential expression of a trait.

A type of visual impairment, for example, might be 100 percent heritable but still easily corrected to normal vision by a pair of eyeglasses. Even if IQ were 80 percent heritable, it might still be subject to major improvement by proper education (I do not claim that all heritable traits are easily altered; some inherited visual handicaps cannot be overcome by any available technology. I merely point out that heritability is not a measure of intrinsic and unchangeable biology.) Thus, I confess I have never been much interested in the debate over IQ's heritability — for even a very large value (which is far from established) would not speak to the main issue, so accurately characterized by Jensen in his title — how much can we boost IQ and scholastic achievement? And I haven't even mentioned (and won't discuss, lest this column become interminable) the deeper fallacy of this whole debate — the assumption that so wonderfully multifarious a notion as intelligence can be meaningfully measured by a single number, with people ranked thereby along a unilinear scale of mental worth. IQ may have a high heritability, but if this venerable measure of intelligence is (as I suspect) a meaningless abstraction, then who cares? The first joint of my right ring finger probably has a higher heritability than IQ, but no one bothers to measure it because the trait has neither independent reality nor importance.

In arguing that Prime Minister Lee has based his fears for Singapore's intellectual deterioration upon a false reading of some dubious Western data, I emphatically disclaim any right to pontificate about Singapore's problems or their potential solutions. I am qualified to comment on Mr. Lee's nation only by the first criterion of the old joke that experts on other countries are those who have lived there for either less than a week or more than thirty years. Nonetheless, buttinsky that I am, I cannot resist two small intrusions. I question, first, whether a nation with such diverse cultural traditions among its Chinese, Malay, and Indian sectors can really expect to even out all environmental influences in just one generation of educational opportunity. Second, I wonder whether the world's most densely populated nation (excluding such tiny city-states as Monaco) should really be encouraging a higher reproductive rate in any segment of its population. Despite my allegiance to cultural relativism, I still maintain a right for comment when other traditions directly borrow my own culture's illogic.

Considerations

1. Characterize Stephen Jay Gould's tone, citing specific passages that help create it. Do you find his tone effective?
2. Gould dismisses as "silly" and "self-serving" the notion that the number of years spent in school might roughly measure intelligence. Do you believe college graduates are simply more fortunate than nongraduates, or are they genetically more gifted? Support your view with a reasoned argument.
3. Evaluate the effectiveness of Gould's organization of this essay.
4. Analyze the rhetorical effectiveness and the reasonableness of Gould's analogy of education improving intelligence like eyeglasses improve vision.
5. Suppose that Martians have an average IQ of 105 with a bell-shaped distri-

bution from 65 to 145. Suppose humans have an average IQ of 100 with a distribution from 60 to 140. What are the odds that one randomly selected Martian is "more intelligent" than one randomly selected earthling? If you cannot be precise, give an intelligent estimate and explain your method of solving the problem. What is the significance of your findings?

Connections

1. What changes would we see in the United States if people in government, education, and business accepted Stephen Jay Gould and Howard Gardner's views of intelligence?
2. How would Gardner and Gould explain the success of individuals who rise above adverse conditions like poor education?

The Imitation Game

Keith Gunderson

I

Disturbed by what he took to be the ambiguous, if not meaningless, character of the question "Can machines think?," the late A. M. Turing in his article "Computing Machinery and Intelligence" sought to replace that question in the following way. He said: *1*

> The new form of the problem can be described in terms of a game which we call the "imitation game." It is played with three people, a man (A), a woman (B), and an interrogator (C) who may be either sex. The interrogator stays in a room apart from the other two. The object of the game for the interrogator is to determine which of the other two is the man and which is the woman. He knows them by labels X and Y, and at the end of the game he says either "X is A and Y is B" or "X is B and Y is A." The interrogator is allowed to put questions to A and B thus:
>
> C: "Will X please tell me the length of his or her hair?"
>
> Now suppose X is actually A, then A must answer. It is A's object in the game to try to cause C to make the wrong identification. His answer might therefore be:
>
> "My hair is shingled, and the longest strands are about nine inches long."
>
> In order that tones of voice may not help the interrogator the answers should be written, or better still, typewritten. The ideal arrangement is to have a teleprinter communicating between the two rooms. Alternatively the question and answers can be repeated by an intermediary. The object of the game for the third player (B) is to help the interrogator. The best strategy for her is probably to give truthful answers.

Keith Gunderson (b. 1935) holds a Ph.D. in philosophy from Princeton University and currently teaches at the University of Minnesota in Minneapolis. He has published poetry as well as the work on minds and machines represented here.

She can add such things as "I am the woman, don't listen to him!" to her answers, but it will avail nothing as the man can make similar remarks.

We now ask the question, "What will happen when a machine takes the part of A in this game?" Will the interrogator decide wrongly as often as when the game is played between a man and a woman? These questions replace our original, "Can machines think?"

And Turing's answers to these latter questions are more or less summed up in the following passage: "I believe that in fifty years' time it will be possible to program computers, with a storage capacity of about 10^9, to make them play the imitation game so well that an average interrogator will not have more than 70 per cent chance of making the right identification after five minutes of questioning." And though he goes on to reiterate that he suspects that the original question "Can machines think?" is meaningless, and that it should be disposed of and replaced by a more precise formulation of the problems involved (a formulation such as a set of questions about the imitation game and machine capacities), what finally emerges is that Turing does answer the "meaningless" question after all, and that his answer is in the affirmative and follows from his conclusions concerning the capabilities of machines which might be successfully substituted for people in the imitation-game context.

It should be pointed out that Turing's beliefs about the possible capabilities   2
and capacities of machines are not limited to such activities as playing the imitation game as successfully as human beings. He does not, for example, deny that it might be possible to develop a machine which would relish the taste of strawberries and cream, though he thinks it would be "idiotic" to attempt to make one, and confines himself on the whole in his positive account to considerations of machine capacities which could be illustrated in terms of playing the imitation game.

So we shall be primarily concerned with asking whether or not a machine,   3
which could play the imitation game as well as Turing thought it might, would thus be a machine which we would have good reasons for saying was capable of thought and what would be involved in saying this.

Some philosophers[1] have not been satisfied with Turing's treatment of the   4
question "Can machines think?" But the imitation game itself, which indeed seems to constitute the hub of his positive treatment, has been little more than alluded to or remarked on in passing. I shall try to develop in a somewhat more detailed way certain objections to it, objections which, I believe, Turing altogether fails to anticipate. My remarks shall thus in the main be critically oriented, which is not meant to suggest that I believe there are no plausible lines of defense open to a supporter of Turing. I shall, to the contrary, close with a brief attempt to indicate what some of these might be and some general challenges which I think Turing has raised for the philosopher of mind. But these latter I shall not elaborate upon.

II

Let us consider the following question: "Can rocks imitate?" One might say   5
that it is a question "too meaningless to deserve discussion." Yet it seems possible to reformulate the problem in relatively unambiguous words as follows:

The new form of the problem can be described in terms of a game which we call the "toe-stepping game." It is played with three people, a man (A), a woman (B), and an interrogator (C) who may be of either sex. The interrogator stays in a room apart from the other two. The door is closed, but there is a small opening in the wall next to the floor through which he can place most of his foot. When he does so, one of the other two may step on his toe. The object of the game for the interrogator is to determine, by the way in which his toe is stepped on, which of the other two is the man and which is the woman. He knows them by labels X and Y, and at the end of the game he says either "X is A and Y is B" or "X is B and Y is A." Now the interrogator — rather the person whose toe gets stepped on — may indicate before he puts his foot through the opening, whether X or Y is to step on it. Better yet, there might be a narrow division in the opening, one side for X and one for Y (one for A and one for B).

Now suppose C puts his foot through A's side of the opening (which may be labeled X or Y on C's side of the wall). It is A's object in the game to try to cause C to make the wrong identification. His step on the toe might therefore be quick and jabbing like some high-heeled woman.

The object of the game for the third player (B) is to help the person whose toe gets stepped on. The best strategy for her is probably to try to step on it in the most womanly way possible. She can add such things as a slight twist of a high heel to her stepping, but it will avail nothing as the man can step in similar ways, since he will also have at his disposal various shoes with which to vary his toe-stepping.

We now ask the question: "What will happen when a rock-box (a box filled with rocks of varying weights, sizes, and shapes) is constructed with an electric eye which operates across the opening in the wall so that it releases a rock which descends upon C's toe whenever C puts his foot through A's side of the opening, and thus comes to take the part of A in this game?" (The situation can be made more convincing by constructing the rock-box so that there is a mechanism pulling up the released rock shortly after its descent, thus avoiding telltale noises such as a rock rolling on the floor, etc.) Will then the interrogator — the person whose toe gets stepped on — decide wrongly as often as when the game is played between a man and a woman? These questions replace our original, "Can rocks imitate?"

I believe that in less than fifty years' time it will be possible to set up elaborately constructed rock-boxes, with large rock-storage capacities, so that they will play the toe-stepping game so well that the average person who would get his toe stepped on would not have more than 70 percent chance of making the right identification after about five minutes of toe-stepping. 6

The above seems to show the following: what follows from the toe-stepping game situation surely is not that rocks are able to imitate (I assume no one would want to take that path of argument) but only that they are able to be rigged in such a way that they could be substituted for a human being in a toe-stepping game without changing any essential characteristics of that game. And this is claimed in spite of the fact that if a human being were to play the toe-stepping game as envisaged above, we would no doubt be correct in saying that that person was imitating, etc. To be sure, a digital computer is a more august mechanism than a rock-box, but Turing has not provided us with any arguments for believing that its role in the imitation game, as distinct from the net results it yields, is any closer a match for a human being executing such a role, than is the rock-box's execution of its role in the toe-stepping game a match for a human being's execution of a similar role. The parody compar- 7 ison can be pushed too far. But I think it lays bare the reason why there is no contradiction involved in saying, "Yes, a machine can play the imitation game, but it can't think." It is for the same reason that there is no contradiction in saying, "Of course a rock-box of such-and-such a sort can be set up, but rocks surely can't imitate." For thinking (or imitating) cannot be fully described simply by pointing to net results such as those illustrated above. For if this were not the case it would be correct to say that a piece of chalk could think or compose because it was freakishly blown about by a tornado in such a way that it scratched a rondo on a blackboard, and that a phonograph could sing, and that an electric-eye could see people coming.

People may be let out of a building by either an electric-eye or a doorman.   8
The end result is the same. But though a doorman may be rude or polite, the electric-eye neither practices nor neglects etiquette. Turing brandishes net results. But I think the foregoing at least indicates certain difficulties with any account of thinking or decision as to whether a certain thing is capable of thought which is based primarily on net results. And, of course, one could always ask whether the net results were really the same. But I do not wish to follow that line of argument here. It is my main concern simply to indicate where Turing's account, which is cast largely in terms of net results, fails because of this. It is not an effective counter to reply: "But part of the net results in question includes intelligent people being deceived!" For what would this add to the general argument? No doubt people could be deceived by rock-boxes! It is said that hi-fidelity phonographs have been perfected to the point where blindfolded music critics are unable to distinguish their "playing" from that of, let us say, the Budapest String Quartet. But the phonograph would never be said to have performed with unusual brilliance on Saturday, nor would it ever deserve an encore.

NOTE
[1] See Michael Scriven, "The Mechanical Concept of Mind," pp. 31ff., and "The Compleat Robot: A Prolegomena to Androidology" in *Dimensions of Mind*, Sidney Hook, ed. (New York University Press, 1960). Also a remark by Paul Ziff in "The Feelings of Robots," pp. 98ff., and others — for example, C. E. Shannon and J. McCarthy in their preface to *Automata Studies* (Princeton: Princeton University Press, 1956).

Considerations

1. When a machine takes the place of Player A in A. M. Turing's "Imitation Game," does the task of C become to uncover the computer, or does it remain to identify *man* and *woman* even though one is really a computer? Which of these two possible tests is better, and why?
2. Is it true that Turing's test would measure only "net results" and not a thinking process?
3. Write an extended definition of philosophy. Does Keith Gunderson's essay belong in the discipline of philosophy according to your definition?

Connections

1. Compare and contrast Keith Gunderson's and A. M. Turing's notions of intelligence to one or more views expressed earlier in this chapter.
2. Which of Howard Gardner's seven intelligences might machines best imitate? Why? Could a machine be intelligent — even hypothetically — and not be able to pass the Turing test?

Ten Questions and Speculations [About AI]

Douglas R. Hofstadter

. . . I would like to present ten "Questions and Speculations" about AI. I would not make so bold as to call them "Answers" — these are my personal opinions. They may well change in some ways, as I learn more and as AI develops more. (In what follows, the term "AI program" means a program which is far ahead of today's programs; it means an "Actually Intelligent" program. Also, the words "program" and "computer" probably carry overly mechanistic connotations, but let us stick with them anyway.)   *1*

Question: Will a computer program ever write beautiful music?   *2*

Speculation: Yes, but not soon. Music is a language of emotions, and until   *3* programs have emotions as complex as ours, there is no way a program will write anything beautiful. There can be "forgeries" — shallow imitations of the syntax of earlier music — but despite what one might think at first, there is much more to musical expression than can be captured in syntactical rules. There will be no new kinds of beauty turned up for a long time by computer music-composing programs. Let me carry this thought a little further. To think — and I have heard this suggested — that we might soon be able to command a preprogrammed mass-produced mail-order twenty-dollar desk-model "music box" to bring forth from its sterile circuitry pieces which Chopin or Bach might have written had they lived longer is a grotesque and shameful misestimation of the depth of the human spirit. A "program" which could produce music as they did would have to wander around the world on its own, fighting its way through the maze of life and feeling every moment of it. It would have

---

Douglas R. Hofstadter (b. 1945) won a Pulitzer Prize for Gödel, Escher, Bach *(1979), a book that synthesizes key ideas in number theory, music, art, biology, and — as this selection demonstrates — computer science.*

to understand the joy and loneliness of a chilly night wind, the longing for a cherished hand, the inaccessibility of a distant town, the heartbreak and re-generation after a human death. It would have to have known resignation and world-weariness, grief and despair, determination and victory, piety and awe. In it would have had to commingle such opposites as hope and fear, anguish and jubilation, serenity and suspense. Part and parcel of it would have to be a sense of grace, humor, rhythm, a sense of the unexpected — and of course an exquisite awareness of the magic of fresh creation. Therein, and therein only, lie the sources of meaning in music.

Question: Will emotions be explicitly programmed into a machine?   4

Speculation: No. That is ridiculous. Any direct simulation of emotions —   5
PARRY, for example — cannot approach the complexity of human emotions, which arise indirectly from the organization of our minds. Programs or ma-chines will acquire emotions in the same way: as by-products of their struc-ture, of the way in which they are organized — not by direct programming. Thus, for example, nobody will write a "falling-in-love" subroutine, any more than they would write a "mistake-making" subroutine. "Falling in love" is a description which we attach to a complex process of a complex system; there need be no single module inside the system which is solely responsible for it, however!

Question: Will a thinking computer be able to add fast?   6

Speculation: Perhaps not. We ourselves are composed of hardware which does   7
fancy calculations but that doesn't mean that our symbol level, where "we" are, knows how to carry out the same fancy calculations. Let me put it this way: there's no way that you can load numbers into your own neurons to add up your grocery bill. Luckily for you, your symbol level (i.e., *you*) can't gain access to the neurons which are doing your thinking — otherwise you'd get addle-brained. To paraphrase Descartes again:

"I think; therefore I have no access
   to the level where I sum."

Why should it not be the same for an intelligent program? It mustn't be al-lowed to gain access to the circuits which are doing its thinking — otherwise it'll get addle-CPU'd. Quite seriously, a machine that can pass the Turing test may well add as slowly as you or I do, and for similar reasons. It will represent the number 2 not just by the two bits "10," but as a full-fledged *concept* the way we do, replete with associations such as its homonyms "too" and "to," the words "couple" and "deuce," a host of mental images such as dots on domi-nos, the shape of the numeral "2," the notions of alternation, evenness, oddness, and on and on . . . With all this "extra baggage" to carry around, an intelli-gent program will become quite slothful in its adding. Of course, we could give it a "pocket calculator," so to speak (or build one in). Then it could answer very fast, but its performance would be just like that of a person with a pocket calculator. There would be two separate parts to the machine: a reliable but mindless part and an intelligent but fallible part. You couldn't rely on the composite system to be reliable, any more than a composite of person and machine is necessarily reliable. So if it's right answers you're after, better stick to the pocket calculator alone — don't throw in the intelligence!

Question: Will there be chess programs that can beat anyone?   8

Speculation: No. There may be programs which can beat anyone at chess,   9
but they will not be exclusively chess players. They will be programs of *general* intelligence, and they will be just as temperamental as people. "Do you want to play chess?" "No, I'm bored with chess. Let's talk about poetry." That may be the kind of dialogue you could have with a program that could beat everyone. That is because real intelligence inevitably depends on a total overview capacity — that is, a programmed ability to "jump out of the system," so to speak — at least roughly to the extent that we have that ability. Once that is present, you can't contain the program; it's gone beyond that certain critical point, and you just have to face the facts of what you've wrought.

Question: Will there be special locations in memory which store parameters   10
governing the behavior of the program, such that if you reached in and changed them, you would be able to make the program smarter or stupider or more creative or more interested in baseball? In short, would you be able to "tune" the program by fiddling with it on a relatively low level?

Speculation: No. It would be quite oblivious to changes of any particular   11
elements in memory, just as we stay almost exactly the same though thousands of our neurons die every day(!). If you fuss around too heavily, though, you'll damage it, just as if you irresponsibly did neurosurgery on a human being. There will be no "magic" location in memory where, for instance, the "IQ" of the program sits. Again, that will be a feature which emerges as a consequence of lower-level behavior, and nowhere will it sit explicitly. The same goes for such things as "the number of items it can hold in short-term memory," "the amount it likes physics," etc., etc.

Question: Could you "tune" an AI program to act like me, or like you — or   12
halfway between us?

Speculation: No. An intelligent program will not be chameleon-like, any more   13
than people are. It will rely on the constancy of its memories, and will not be able to flit between personalities. The idea of changing internal parameters to "tune to a new personality" reveals a ridiculous underestimation of the complexity of personality.

Question: Will there be a "heart" to an AI program, or will it simply con-   14
sist of "senseless loops and sequences of trivial operations" (in the words of Marvin Minsky)?

Speculation: If we could see all the way to the bottom, as we can a shallow   15
pond, we would surely see only "senseless loops and sequences of trivial operations" — and we would surely not see any "heart." Now there are two kinds of extremist views on AI: one says that the human mind is, for fundamental and mysterious reasons, unprogrammable. The other says that you merely need to assemble the appropriate "heuristic devices — multiple optimizers, pattern-recognition tricks, planning algebras, recursive administration procedures, and

the like," and you will have intelligence. I find myself somewhere in between, believing that the "pond" of an AI program will turn out to be so deep and murky that we won't be able to peer all the way to the bottom. If we look from the top, the loops will be invisible, just as nowadays the current-carrying electrons are invisible to most programmers. When we create a program that passes the Turing test, we will see a "heart" even though we know it's not there.

Question: Will AI programs ever become "superintelligent"?   16

Speculation: I don't know. It is not clear that we would be able to under-   17
stand or relate to a "superintelligence," or that the concept even makes sense. For instance, our own intelligence is tied in with our speed of thought. If our reflexes had been ten times faster or slower, we might have developed an entirely different set of concepts with which to describe the world. A creature with a radically different view of the world may simply not have many points of contact with us. I have often wondered if there could be, for instance, pieces of music which are to Bach as Bach is to folk tunes: "Bach squared," so to speak. And would I be able to understand them? Maybe there is such music around me already, and I just don't recognize it, just as dogs don't understand language. The idea of superintelligence is very strange. In any case, I don't think of it as the aim of AI research, although if we ever do reach the level of human intelligence, superintelligence will undoubtedly be the next goal — not only for us, but for our AI-program colleagues, too, who will be equally curious about AI and superintelligence. It seems quite likely that AI programs will be extremely curious about AI in general — understandably.

Question: You seem to be saying that AI programs will be virtually identical   18
to people, then. Won't there be any differences?

Speculation: Probably the differences between AI programs and people will   19
be larger than the differences between most people. It is almost impossible to imagine that the "body" in which an AI program is housed would not affect it deeply. So unless it had an amazingly faithful replica of a human body — and why should it? — it would probably have enormously different perspectives on what is important, what is interesting, etc. Wittgenstein once made the amusing comment, "If a lion could speak, we would not understand him." It makes me think of Rousseau's painting of the gentle lion and the sleeping gypsy on the moonlit desert. But how does Wittgenstein know? My guess is that any AI program would, if comprehensible to us, seem pretty alien. For that reason, we will have a very hard time deciding when and if we really are dealing with an AI program, or just a "weird" program.

Question: Will we understand what intelligence and consciousness and free   20
will and "I" are when we have made an intelligent program?

Speculation: Sort of — it all depends on what you mean by "understand."   21
On a gut level, each of us probably has about as good an understanding as is possible of those things, to start with. It is like listening to music. Do you really understand Bach because you have taken him apart? Or did you understand it that time you felt the exhilaration in every nerve in your body? Do we understand how the speed of light is constant in every inertial reference frame? We

can do the math, but no one in the world has a truly relativistic intuition. And probably no one will ever understand the mysteries of intelligence and consciousness in an intuitive way. Each of us can understand *people*, and that is probably about as close as you can come.

Considerations

1. This selection is not a real interview. In your best textbook style, rewrite it as straightforward exposition. Then analyze the differences between the two versions — Douglas Hofstadter's and yours — and comment on why he wrote this portion of his book the way he did and whether he was successful.
2. Hofstadter defines the *symbolic level* of the mind earlier in his book. Try to construct your own definition of this term based on Hofstadter's use of it here.
3. List the fields to which Hofstadter somehow refers, giving at least one example from each field (e.g., Painting — Rousseau). What is the effect of these references?

Connections

1. Is Douglas Hofstadter's concept of machine intelligence significantly different from A. M. Turing's?
2. Can Keith Gunderson's criticisms of Turing be applied to Hofstadter as well?
3. Compare and contrast Hofstadter's imaginary dialogue with Howard Gardner's interview. Consider purpose, tone, organization, and depth of analysis.

The Compositions of Mozart's Mind

Howard Gardner

Wolfgang Amadeus Mozart once described in a letter his manner of composing. It was most natural to compose, he said, when he was in a cheerful mood — traveling in a carriage or strolling after a hearty meal. "When and how my ideas come, I know not; nor can I force them," he explained. But the ideas he found to his liking were easily retained, and soon he was able to fashion an appealing piece of music out of their parts — "to make a good dish of   *1*

See pp. 367 and 410 for information about Howard Gardner.

it," as he put it. Mozart proceeded to characterize his activities in a most intriguing way:

> All this fires my soul, and provided I am not disturbed, my subject enlarges itself,
> becomes methodized and designed, and the whole, though it be long, stands almost
> complete and finished in my mind, so that I can survey it, like a fine picture or a
> beautiful statue, at a glance. Nor do I hear in my imagination the parts successively,
> but I hear them, as it were all at once *(gleich alles zusammen)*. What a delight this is
> I cannot tell! (quoted in Ghiselin, p. 45[1])

The claim to hear an entire piece of music — which may take twenty or   2
thirty minutes to perform — in one's head at one moment in time when it has
not even been composed seems incredible. Only because Mozart was one of the
great geniuses — and perhaps the greatest prodigy — of all times has this letter been taken seriously at all (and some musicologists have in fact disputed
its authenticity).

But even assuming that Mozart wrote the letter and that he was not exag-   3
gerating or boasting, the question arises of precisely *what* he meant? How can
one hear something, as it were, in one's mind's ear? And how can one go on to
contrive a composition entirely cerebrally and then, defying time, attend to it
in its entirety in one's hand at a single moment? We will never know the answers to these questions: Mozart has long been dead, and it is in any case unlikely that he could have amplified the comments made in the letter. For those
interested in the creative process, however, it is worth our pondering what
Mozart might have meant by this strange phrasing. And in the course of this
"mental experiment," it should be possible to glimpse some of the concepts
and some of the issues that are being pondered today by investigators of "mental representation" — by that growing tribe of researchers known as cognitive
scientists.

To begin, it is worth recalling what else we know about Mozart's processes   4
of composition, and considering how his procedures compare with other notable feats of creative activity. Beyond doubt Mozart composed with great ease
and rapidity. There is no other way to account for the production of more than
six hundred pieces of music, including forty-one symphonies and some forty-
odd operas and masses, during barely three decades of creative life, except by
invoking an extraordinary fluency. Mozart's colleagues and contemporaries
confirm that he wrote with astonishing efficiency. As a biographer Alfred Einstein reported, "All witnesses of Mozart at work agree that he put a composition down on paper as one writes a letter, without allowing any disturbance
or interruption to annoy him, the writing down, the 'fixing' was nothing more
than that — the fixing of a completed work, a mechanical act" (p. 142).[2] Yet,
while confirming Mozart's own introspective account, observers and biographers have been quick to point out that Mozart was anything but careless or
unduly hasty. Rather, when given an assignment, he thought about it for long
periods of time, would try out various combinations on the piano, hum them
to himself, and contemplate how to accommodate the musical idea (or theme)
to the rules of counterpoint and to the peculiarities of particular texts, performers, and instruments.

There are on record other composers who produced works as rapidly, but 5 there are also numerous contrasting cases. Like Mozart, Beethoven was a fluent and skillful improviser, but he composed only with much more overt difficulty. In addition to keeping a notebook replete with discarded themes and false starts, Beethoven would score a piece numerous times — revising, rejecting, crossing out in his impetuous and messy hand. While Mozart's rapidly produced scores seldom contained erased passages — and indeed were practically of "camera-ready" quality — Beethoven's sketchbooks chronicled painful, even tormented sieges of creation. Certainly Beethoven's agonies during the throes of creation — rather than Mozart's seemingly seamless composing activity — served as the model of the suffering romantic artist in his garret.

Accounts of creation in other media echo the same contrasts. For every fluent 6 Mozart, Trollope, or Picasso, who poured forth works with unceasing fecundity, and for every Edgar Allan Poe, who claimed to plot out his works with mathematical precision, one encounters reports of a Dostoevsky, who reworked his novels numerous times, a Thomas Mann, who struggled over three pages a day, or a Richard Wagner, who had to work himself up into a nearly psychotic frenzy before finally finding himself able to put pen to score.

One recourse in such a state of affairs is to discard such introspective ac- 7 counts altogether. Alternatively, one can assume that these differences signal variations in personality, style, or introspective candor, rather than fundamental differences in approach to creation. As yet another possibility, individuals may intend different meanings by the same phrases. For example, the twentieth-century American composer Walter Piston once reported to a friend that a piece on which he had been working was almost completed. "Can I hear it then?" his friend asked. "Oh, no," Piston retorted, "I haven't yet selected the notes." Far from being ironic, Piston apparently meant that he had planned out the abstract structure of the piece — the number of movements, the principal shifts in orchestral color, the various forms to be employed, and so on — but had still to decide upon the specific vehicles with which to embody his musical conception.

But is it possible to supersede speculation in such matters? Can we actually 8 attain insight into the process of composition by one, two, or even the whole federation of composers? Can we construct models of the composer's mnemonic capacities, his perceptual acuity, his planning strategies, his manner of projecting how a theme will develop or an orchestrated section will sound? And can we apply the accumulated understanding to a specific case of composition — figuring out, for example, whether Mozart could actually conjure up the details of a piece in his head or could only have been referring (Piston-fashion) to the overall conception? Was he endowed with a more capacious memory and more vivid acoustic imagery than other composers, or was he simply able to realize a general conception more rapidly in the course of putting pen to paper? These are some of the challenges that cognitive scientists have posed for themselves. And while members of this group are far from able to model the thought processes of a Mozart, or even of lesser mortals engaged in more mundane activities, the ways in which they have been approaching such issues prove instructive.

Composing a piece of music extends beyond the competence of most indi-   9
viduals (including most cognitive scientists). One promising avenue for con-
ceptualizing this process is to ponder what is involved in less formidable activities. Consider, for example, the way that you plan a dinner party, particularly
if you have in the past often planned such parties. You must think about what
food to eat, in what order, how much of each dish to prepare, when to cook
and serve each, whom to invite, where to seat them before, during, and after
the meal, which individuals are likely to grate on one another and which should
get along, which decorations to display, what to wear, and much more. Such
planning can reach a fine degree of specificity. I have known hosts and hostesses who have worried about who is left-handed and who smokes, about which
topics of conversation to raise at the beginning of the meal and which to avoid,
how big a portion to allot each individual as an appetizer so as to make sure
he will "have room" for the entree.[3]

Or consider your procedure if you are asked to write a letter of recommen-   10
dation on behalf of a colleague, particularly if, like me, you often feel besieged
by this assignment yet want to make certain that the letter exerts a beneficient
effect. I have a plan that I generally follow in writing such letters. I begin by
indicating the circumstances under which I have met the individual, how well
I know him, what the nature of our relationship (professional and personal)
has been. A second paragraph usually describes the growth of that individual
over the period of time that I have known him and indicates the kinds of work
and issues that occupy a central place in that person's professional life. A third
paragraph will review the person's principal scholarly accomplishments so far
and his future promise. (An optional paragraph will focus on teaching abilities.) A fourth paragraph will touch on the individual's personal dimension —
what kind of a colleague he makes, how he gets along with others, whether he
has a good sense of humor, is reliable, responsible, and so on. (An optional
paragraph will detail problems or weaknesses.) The final paragraph is sum-
mative: it recapitulates what I find most outstanding about the individual, explains (or explains away) any difficulties I have mentioned, and attempts to integrate my assessment of the individual as a scholar and future contributor to
the field with his qualities as a person, friend, and colleague. I may also suggest some comparisons with others of comparable age, background, and ambition and offer to provide further information.

Of course, like the hypothetic meal served above, this "model" or "proto-   11
typical" letter is deliberately skeletal. It can be modified to a greater or lesser
extent, depending upon a variety of considerations, including how much time
I have to devote to the effort and now positively I feel about the person. The
challenge I pose myself is to modify this basic scaffolding (designed to serve
most purposes) so that it clings to the particular individual I am describing.

In confronting data like this — the host planning a party , the colleague   12
writing a letter of recomendation — a cognitive scientist would likely adopt
the following perspective. He would say that the host and the teacher have
general schemas — abstract mental representations of what a party or a letter
should be like. These schemas are sufficiently general and abstract to apply to
a variety of parties, a series of letters. Some "slots" of the schemas are relatively inflexible — drinks always have to be served, a letter always opens with

a salutation. Other "slots" of the schemas are quite flexible — the foods to be served or the issues with which the job candidate has been engaged may be entirely different from one "embodiment" of the schema to another. But in general the diverse embodiments of the schemas share at least a family resemblance with one another. Moreover, the realization of each future instance is helped immeasurably by the prior existence of the schema — the mold with its recesses of various shapes and sizes into which particular ingredients are poured.

While it might seem sacrilegious to compare these mundane activities with   *13* the composing of *Don Giovanni* or the *Jupiter Symphony*, I find that the concept of a schema, with its modifications and elaborations, at least provides a useful point of entry. Mozart could not have written his major works — let alone composed them with so little apparent strain — had he not written thousands of fragments of music before. Mozart lived, moreover, during a time when the rules for musical composition were much more clearly spelled out than they are today: there existed definite formulas for writing a symphony, and these formulas were quite sharply constrained. It was possible for almost anyone of a musical bent (including Frederick the Great!) to write a passable piece of music. (At the same time, contemporary ears find it difficult to detect differences among the various compositions of the schools that surrounded Mozart and Haydn. The "second rank" creators in an era typically produce works that are most faithful to and make the least interesting departures from the "schema of the time.")

We can assume, then, that once Mozart had decided to write a symphony,   *14* many of the most important decisions had in fact been made in advance — just as was the case with our more modest contemporary examples. What the general schema did not supply were all the glorious themes or the detailed elaborations that differ significantly across several hundred works. Even as the assignment to planners of parties inheres in making a distinctive addition to the repertoire of galas, Mozart's challenge was to come up with some promising themes for the opening of each movement; to "play" these themes in his mind against the backdrop of the compositional schema to which he was restricted (and indebted); and then to fashion those exciting departures and deviations that made each symphony different from the others, while still remaining, as he put it, *Mozartisch*.

I should make a number of points about this model. To begin with, it is, in   *15* the jargon, a "top-down" (rather than a "bottom-up") approach. We do not assume that party planning (or letter writing or symphonic composing) begins afresh with the first element (the greeting at the door) and then proceeds moment to moment until the last event (saying good night). Nor do we assume that the individual begins with the most specific details (what flowers to buy) and then moves to more general considerations (who to invite, what kind of cuisine to serve). Rather, we assume that the overall plan for the item to be schematized already existed before its actual instantiation; and that it is the creator's task to draw upon and exploit a prior schema so as to produce a distinctive, if not distinguished, member of its class.

Under this plan a cognitive scientist need not prejudge how specifically the   *16* schema has been articulated in the mind of the individual before he "goes public" — for example, writing down words on a page or making a first phone call. Presumably some individuals (or all individuals at some time) make only the most general kinds of decisions before beginning to implement the schema, while others have effected the most detailed decisions in advance before any public behavior can be observed. Thus, if I am in a hurry and do not care much about the letter, I may simply type out a draft with hardly any forethought and correct only the most glaring infelicities before sending it off. On the other hand, if much is riding on the letter, I may plan it out painstakingly in advance, prepare a number of drafts, and circulate it among colleagues before sending it off. This disparity in care does not ensure a difference in overall quality — I have written some fine letters off the top of my head and some mediocre letters despite ample anguish. However, the amount of planning probably does correlate with the extent to which the letter deviates from a schema. It is very difficult to produce a novel instance of the schema without considerable planning and adjusting, even as it is unlikely that a carefully fashioned letter will turn out to be virtually identical to those produced at other times.

Let us, then, renew contact with the possible meanings of Mozart's remark.   *17* If the composer simply meant that he had some general ideas about the piece of music in his mind and that he could monitor its deviation from other instances in a few particulars, but that actual details remained to be worked out, his remarks would be relatively unproblematic. After all, if we can plan a letter or a party with only minimal specificity, why should one of the outstanding composers of all times, who certainly spent more time composing than we do in these mundane activities, experience undue difficulties in anticipating the broad outlines of a composition even before he had written it out?

But clearly, if we are to believe the reports of his contemporaries, Mozart   *18* meant that he did a great deal more than plan the broad outlines. He would have us believe that he could plan out the whole piece in detail, element by element, before putting a mark on the page (how else could he write it out so quickly and smoothly?), and he would have us believe the even more remarkable claim that he could actually perceive — hear it!! — in the orchestral chamber of his mind.

What are we to make of these claims? I do not have much difficulty with   *19* Mozart's apparent ability to envision — or "en-audit" — an entire piece in his own mind before writing it down. His remark testifies to a superlative planning capacity and a nearly infallible memory, to the extent that he did not need the aid of a notebook in order to keep the various fragments in his own mind. Aided by his own composing background and by the existence of powerful schemas, including the schemas based on his own previous works, he was able to make suitable annotations and specifications in his mind. As a result, the piece in all of its individuality could be conceptualized beforehand and then simply transcribed. Even if Mozart did not plan out every single detail beforehand — and I rather doubt that he did — it did not matter, for he was superbly (and justifiably) confident that the details would follow rather easily. If worst came to worst, and he had to abandon a section (or if best came to best, and he conjured up a splendid new idea), Mozart, like any prepared genius, would exploit this opportunity.

And as for the second claim, to hear the whole piece *gleich alles zusammen?*   20
If Picasso had claimed that he could see a whole canvas in his head before producing it, this would not astonish us, for even though one cannot actually survey a whole scene without an eye movement, one can certainly envision a quite
detailed scene at a single mental moment. The difference between Picasso and
us inheres in the fact that we are by and large restricted (except in dreams) to
scenes we have already seen. Our hypothetical Picasso could anticipate scenes
that he was only subsequently going to paint.

Where Mozart differs is in his claim to hear a whole piece simultaneously.   *21*
Here, across the chasms of time and space, I would presume to read Mozart's
mind and say that he did not mean this statement literally: Mozart was not, I
submit, able to hear an entire twenty-minute piece within a second or two.
Rather, Mozart seems to have employed a metaphor here, but one of some accuracy and power. What Mozart meant, I think, was that the entire organization, the distinctive architectonic of the piece of music was fully articulated in
his mind. The crucial decisions about where sections of a piece would begin
and end, where instruments would enter, when themes would recur, could all
be grasped at one moment in time (just as the entire scenario of the dinner
party might seem immanent to one of us after we had pondered it for a considerable period of time).

But what about the actual sound quality of the music? Surely it is different   22
to envision a canvas à la Picasso, or a party à la host, than to imagine a whole
piece of music that ordinarily unfolds in hundreds of measures over a period
of time. Mozart may have intended one of two points. He may have meant that
he was perceiving the piece of music in an essentially *amodal* way — that is,
rather than hearing it, seeing it, or feeling it, he just apprehended its organizational structure in terms of more abstract, nonsensory properties (such as
beginnings, climaxes, countersubjects, return of the theme). Or he may have
meant that he could hear, as it were, almost at the same time the major themes
of the music and the ways in which they were treated and elaborated upon at
the critical moments in the piece. It is as if all the "subjects" of a fugue, which
are usually introduced one at a time over several measures, could be played at
the same time in one's mind, so that their potential manipulation for purposes
of harmony and counterpoint might be perceived with near simultaneity. Put
overly simply, Mozart may have heard the whole melody as if it were an enormously rich chord.

Can we get any further clarifications from descriptions of Mozart's own   23
writing practices? Thanks to his frequent changes in ink and varying colors of
ink, we can confirm that Mozart was almost totally a "top-down" kind of composer. He never wrote out specific sections of a movement, complete in all voices,
but rather proceeded in a stubbornly holistic way. He always wrote out the
primary theme — for example, the one introduced by the first violins — in its
entirety and only subsequently revisited this section to fill in the subordinate
parts. As Alfred Einstein tells us:

> In a work of chamber music or a symphony, he fixes first the principal voices, the
> melodic threads, from beginning to end, leaping as it were from line to line, and in-
> serting the subordinate voices only when he "goes over" or "overhauls" the move-
> ment in a second stage of the procedure. (p. 143)

Yet even Mozart allowed for surprises. Einstein indicates that sometimes during the seemingly half-mechanical labor of filling in (or filling out) the details, Mozart would invent a new fragment, become excited, and then seek to integrate this fragment into other aspects of the piece. The voice of genius is never still.

Even armed with detailed suggestions of how Mozart composed, we are still   24
besieged by questions. For example, one might still contend that, rather than simply proceeding from a schema already well worked out in his mind, Mozart might have had all the details worked out, but simply for convenience decided to write out the major parts of the piece first and fill in details later. (Indeed, on occasion Mozart would ask one of his assistants to fill in the most mechanical details of a piece.) Here some of the experimental innovations of cognitive psychology might eventually offer illumination. If Mozart were to reappear today, we might ask him in the interests of science to carry out some feats: to write out the contemplated piece with full detail from the first measure to the second, third, and so on; to write out the last part of the piece first; to carry through the entire score of a subsidiary instrument first; or even to write the complete piece backwards. If he could execute all these tasks perfectly, we would have to conclude that Mozart had in his head the fully printed score of the piece and was really only an amanuensis — a slavish transcriber. If, however, as appears likely, Mozart would succeed when required to furnish the principal themes, while having difficulties with highly detailed assignments (like writing out the middle portion of the development section for the piccolo), then we would receive confirmation that Mozart was embodying a well-developed schema that nonetheless still allowed certain flexibility. In other words, while he probably anticipated more of the notes than Piston had when the latter's piece was "almost done," Mozart's composing procedures were at least in part constructive and not totally mechanical.

My own efforts at a cognitive exegesis suggest that Mozart had made all of   25
the key decisions about his piece beforehand and could, upon request, provide all the principal themes and variations. All the same, the details of the specific execution of individual parts awaited the time when he was actually scoring the composition.

It can justly be pointed out that this exercise — which is, in broad outlines,   26
one method of attack favored by contemporary cognitive science — leaves out the most important and most mysterious aspects of composition. Why did Mozart compose? Why in the style that he favored? Where did his themes come from? In particular, how can we account for the intrinsic beauty of the arias of *Don Giovanni* or the opening bars of the piano solo in his C-minor concerto, as well as for the ingenious — or genius — transformations he wrought with these themes? How can we account for the startling differences among pieces, the specific "ideas" that nonetheless bear the unmistakable stylistic signature of Mozart? Some of these questions are within the purview of cognitive science, others might well be ruled "out of court," but the sad truth is that we scarcely know how to think about them at the present time.

A description of the composer's mental processes, of course, in no way de-   27
tracts from the beauty and subtlety of the work itself. For instance, psychologists must take note of, but as yet have few means of explaining, Mozart's re-

markable musical talents, his incredible energy, his motivation to write the greatest music of his time, his uncanny dramatic sense, his fabled powers of concentration, his sometimes quixotic but always vital manner. Little as psychology has to say about Mozart's miraculous mind, it has even less insight into his fascinating character.

Yet I do not feel discouraged. The notion of a schema within its realization   28 and elaboration represents a significant advance over the rigidly atomistic approaches of an earlier time. The willingness to countenance what might be involved in the composition of a letter — or even a sonata — is a beneficent development. The discovery and specification of similarities between mundane activities and the creative outpourings of a master is also healthy — some analogous principles may well be at work, even though the rate and scale renders them in some ways incomparable. The suggestive ties between creation and memory, between invention and repetition, cradle important insights. Sophisticated methods of interviewing creative artists in order to gain purchase on their problem-solving procedures may also eventually bear fruit, as should attempts to simulate such problem-solving (and problem-finding) activities on a computer.

A research program that seeks to illuminate such heights of creativity should   29 not (and in my experience does not) affect our experience and enjoyment of the works themselves: these remain glorious, whether or not we understand something of the schematizing activity that generated them. A teacher of mine once responded to a student who was concerned that biochemistry would undermine religion, "We are not here to denigrate God — we are here to glorify molecules."

NOTES
[1] B. Ghiselin, *The Creative Process* (New York: Mentor, 1959). [Editor's note]
[2] Alfred Einstein, *Mozart: His Character, His Work* (New York: Oxford University Press, 1945). [Editor's note]
[3] Sometimes life imitates art. After writing this essay, I came across a forty-page monograph by cognitive psychologist Richard Byrne: "Planning Meals: Problem Solving on a Real Data-Base."

Considerations

1. Howard Gardner uses descriptions of dinner parties and letters of recommendations to explain *schemas* and their *slots* and *embodiments*. Choose your own example to convey the same ideas; develop it roughly as Gardner has done.
2. How might a cognitive psychologist using schema theory describe these activities:
   a. learning to play chess;
   b. learning new vocabulary through reading, without a dictionary;
   c. driving across town as quickly as possible;
   d. designing a new building.
3. Listen repeatedly to the opening of Beethoven's Fifth Symphony and to one other melody or theme in the same work (you may find some sections familiar). Make a concentrated, extended effort to hear the two melodies *gleich*

alles zusammen [everything all together]. Report on your experience. Does it support Gardner's educated guesses?

Connections

1. Compare and contrast Howard Gardner's idea of a *schema* with the function of a computer program.
2. Use the insight and information provided by any author here except Gardner to explain Mozart's composing.
3. How does your reading of Gardner's essay on Mozart affect your evaluation of "Unfolding or Teaching" in Chapter 6, The Nature of Learning? Explain.

Further Connections

1. Scientists have tried to measure intelligence with formal tests or controlled experiments. How do you measure intelligence in people around you? How confident are you in your assessments?
2. What ethical questions are raised by the brain and computer research described in this chapter? Where do you stand on these issues?
3. List as many objections as you can to the proposal that our government give incentives to ethnic groups with high IQ scores to bear more children. Arrange your objections from least serious or damaging to most serious.
4. According to your reading in this chapter and your own experience, what are the most significant barriers to human knowledge and intelligence? What possibilities exist for overcoming the barriers you describe?
5. Choose a religion with which you are familiar and analyze how it would deal with one or more issues raised in this chapter.
6. What facets of intelligence are most used in writing? Could writing assignments measure more than verbal ability?
7. In his book *The Binary Brain*, David Ritchie suggests that man could realize vast gains in knowledge and intelligence by linking human brains to "biochips" — living computer chips implanted in the skull. Using your reading in this chapter, discuss some of the knowledge neuroscience would need to bridge brain and biochip.
8. Using readings from this chapter and the previous one, as well as your own prior knowledge, list as many areas as you can in the field of psychology (e.g., cognitive psychology, developmental psychology). As fully as possible, give an account of their special concerns, assumptions, methods, and contributions to society. Synthesize your categories with classmates to develop a comprehensive classification.
9. Using your reading here and the selections by Charles Darwin and Carl Sagan in Chapter 9, The Impact of Animals, explain how animal intelligence differs from machine and human intelligence.

10. Choose one or two authors from this chapter and suggest what they might say about animal intelligence.
11. Read J. W. Jackson's piece in Chapter 3, The Frontier Indians. How would one or more of the authors in this chapter answer Jackson's claims?

Extensions

1. The "bootstrap analogy" mentioned in paragraph 1 of David Hubel's essay, "The Brain," has been used widely not only in neuroscience but also in computer science, in the social sciences, and in everyday speech. When and how did this expression enter the language, and how has its meaning changed?
2. Study the most recent information you can find on treatments of Parkinson's or Alzheimer's disease. What treatments are now available or under development? How hopeful are doctors about nerve tissue transplants?
3. Compare Lane Lenard's version of language learning to a current summary from a psychology or linguistics textbook.
4. Lenard refers to many specific studies by various researchers. Find one of these, read it, and report on it more fully than Lenard has. Is his use of this research accurate?
5. Give Robert Sternberg and Janet Davidson's questions to two groups of ten volunteers outside your class. Give one group no special instructions. Coach the second group for ten minutes before the test, warning them to read carefully, to avoid being distracted by irrelevant information, and to watch for trick questions. If possible, give them an example not on the test itself. Did your coaching make a difference? Do your results strengthen or weaken your trust in Sternberg and Davidson's work?
6. Construct one of the four types of test Howard Gardner mentions (e.g., a test of "core ability"). Articulate your rationale for each of the questions or activities you use. If possible, administer the test to a small sample population and discuss your results.
7. Consider the portrayal of two or more specific robots or computers in films, science fiction, or television. How do they resemble and differ from (1) each other, and (2) Douglas Hofstadter's "actually intelligent" programs?
8. Write a research report on child prodigies. How are they defined? How rare are they? In what fields do they most often appear? Pay special attention to various explanations of their extraordinary gifts.
9. Report on one "genius" of your choice. What explanation do biographers or contemporaries give of your subject's unusual intelligence?
10. What is photographic memory, and what is its relation, if any, to intelligence?
11. Write a brief report to the rest of your class on SHRDLU, a computer program that Hofstadter (punning on Bach's "Jesu, Joy of Man's Desiring") calls "SHRDLU, Toy of Man's Designing." What is it? Who created it? What is its significance?
12. A problem for solitaire aficionados: A deck of 52 cards can be arranged in 52! unique ways. (52! means *fifty-two factorial* and represents 52 x 51 x 50

. . . x 1.) Form a group of three or four students; for two hours, work on expressing 52! as an integer. Consider as many different ways as you can of reaching the solution. In a two or three-page report on your procedure, describe the progress you made and the obstacles you encountered. Do not limit yourself to mathematical obstacles in this discussion. Conclude with advice to a group that really needs to solve this problem.

13. Working with classmates, list as many peculiarities of thought, perception, or memory as you can (a well-known example would be *déjà vu*, the sensation that you've lived through a particular experience before). Speculate on their causes or, time permitting, research one or more in psychology texts.

Suggestions for Further Reading

Adams, James L. *Conceptual Blockbusting: A Pleasurable Guide to Better Problem Solving.* San Francisco: San Francisco Book Co., 1976. A playful book intended to unlock available mental power.

Boden, Margaret A. *Artificial Intelligence and Natural Man.* New York: Basic Books, 1977. A wide-ranging book, advanced but readable.

Bongard, Mikhail Moiseevich. *Pattern Recognition.* Edited by Joseph K. Hawkins and translated by Theodore Cheron. New York: Spartan Books, 1970. Features 100 spatial problems.

Churchland, Paul. *Matter and Consciousness: A Contemporary Introduction to the Philosophy of Mind.* Cambridge, Mass.: MIT Press, 1984. An up-to-date look at an age-old philosophical problem.

Dennet, Daniel C. "The Imagination Extenders." *Psychology Today* 16:12 (December 1982): 32–39. One of a steady stream of valuable *Psychology Today* articles, this one by a philosopher at Tufts University.

Feigenbaum, Edward A., and Pamela McCorduck. *The Fifth Generation: Artificial Intelligence and Japan's Computer Challenge to the World.* Reading, Mass.: Addison-Wesley, 1983. An excellent source for proposed applications of AI work, with an emphasis on business, economics, and politics.

Gleick, James. "Exploring the Labyrinth of the Mind." *New York Times Magazine,* August 21, 1983. An insightful report on Douglas Hofstadter's AI work.

Hoban, P. "Soul in the Software." *OMNI* (December 1984): 54–58. Concentrates on expert systems, including IVY, a project on lung cancer diagnosis.

Hofstadter, Douglas R. "Metamagical Themas" [Title of regular column]. *Scientific American* 245: 3 (September 1981): 18–30. Examines the role of analogy in human thought with attention to AI programs imitating it.

Michie, Donald, and Rory Johnston. *The Knowledge Machine: Artificial Intelligence and the Future of Man.* New York: William Morrow, 1985. Demonstrates the potential of information management and expert systems.

———. *Machine Intelligence and Related Topics: An Information Scientist's Weekend Book.* New York: Gordon and Breach, 1982. Contains a historical overview of machine intelligence.

Perkins, D. N. *The Mind's Best Work.* Cambridge, Mass.: Harvard University Press,

1981. A book on the many facets of creativity and a good source of puzzles and historical examples of creativity.

Nelson, Carl W., David Baskett, and Jerome Kirsch, "Robotic Mobile Mines." In *Automating Intelligent Behavior: Applications and Frontiers*, pp. 3–7. Piscataway, N.J. and Los Angeles: IEEE Computer Society Press, 1983. This contribution to a conference Proceedings studies two "artificially intelligent" weapons.

Restak, Richard M. *The Brain*. New York: Bantam Books, 1984. Based on the WNET–PBS public television series, this book combines clear explanations with 150 excellent illustrations.

Ritchie, David. *The Binary Brain: Artificial Intelligence in the Age of Electronics*. Boston: Little, Brown, 1984. A controversial work that suggests biochips implanted in the skull could be the next step in human evolution.

Robertson, Scott. "Probing the Mind: The Interface of Computers with Psychology." *Yale Scientific* (Spring 1983): 24–27. Includes discussion of memory and spatial abilities.

Schank, Roger C., with Peter G. Childers. *The Cognitive Computer: On Language, Learning, and Artificial Intelligence*. Reading, Mass.: Addison-Wesley, 1985. By a founder of the Yale AI group, a leader in research on computers and language.

8 The Treatment of Cancer

Edited by **Malcolm Kiniry**

Because it lingers so painfully, because it so visibly lays waste to the body, and because its origins are so mysterious, cancer is the disease we most fear, the threat we want removed from our lives. Already, enormous human resources have been directed toward understanding and treating cancer, and as the number of victims continues to grow each year — along with the number of survivors — we will expend even more effort. At first sight the issues may seem purely medical: how to treat the various cases of cancer. But the issues are also economic, political, psychological, and above all, social: how do we as a society treat the problems of cancer.

A great many of the approaches to cancer can be found in the university. The first line is of course the medical professionals and the schools that train them: those who must diagnose, treat, advise, and sometimes simply helplessly watch their cancer patients. Beyond this front line, however, is the vast network of the life sciences (a term by which many colleges express the interpenetration of biology and other academic fields). There are biochemists who seek to understand cancer through a thorough understanding of the chemical behavior of cells. There are biophysicists who bring to bear increasingly precise techniques of nuclear medicine in diagnosing, managing, and eradicating various cancers. And there are an increasing number of engineers and technicians responsible for designing and maintaining the tools of microbiological research.

Also important to the study of cancer are epidemiologists, statisticians who study the patterns of disease, describing and analyzing correlations between occurrences of disease and the potential causes. Some experts argue that epidemiologists have done more than either doctors or basic researchers to discover the causes of cancer. The recognition that cigarette smoking causes lung cancer, for example, rests primarily upon epidemiological evidence: the rate at which smokers have contracted lung cancer as compared to the rest of the population. Sometimes, by comparing populations epidemiologists observe trends for which there is no absolutely clear explanation: why is the incidence of stomach cancer greater among Japanese than Americans? Why do Dutch women face a greater risk of breast cancer? Why is cancer of the liver more prevalent in certain parts of Africa? Answers to such questions become possible only when statistics have made it possible to ask them.

Social scientists usually approach cancer by way of the more general issues of public health. The public health field is vast, comprising not only medical people and researchers but administrators, technicians, business people, social workers, office personnel, and volunteers. For sociologists the concern is how this system works — what are the unwritten rules and values controlling a community's interactions with the rest of society? For economists the emphasis narrows to questions of costs and benefits — how much will be spent for which cancer services and who will bear the costs? For political scientists the study is the distribution of power. In this country that means the study of relations among special interest groups, like the American Medical Association, privately funded institutions, such as the American Cancer Society, and the host of federal agencies with overlapping responsibilities and imposing initials — EPA, NIEHS, OSHA, USDA, and FDA. If, as seems possible, much of our cancer is environmentally induced, we need to pay attention to cancer politics.

These public perspectives ought not to obscure the more intimate views of cancer available to us, including those offered by literature, psychotherapy, and philosophy. Imaginative literature has approached cancer in forms as varied as the somber novel *Cancer Ward* by the Russian writer Alexander Solzhenitsyn and the intense lament by Welsh poet Dylan Thomas to his dying father, "Do Not Go Gentle Into That Good Night." Psychology offers personalized care: in the psychotherapy increasingly used to augment medical treatments, in the family counseling that acknowledges the disorientation felt by those living with cancer victims, and in the enlightened hospice care that a few institutions have begun to provide for the terminally ill. Some of the philosophical questions are apt to sound merely theoretical in the classroom until we remember that these issues are faced by real people every day: should cancer patients be given addictive drugs? Should they be exposed to experimental treatments? Do cancer sufferers have the right to end their own lives? Less abstract still is the philosophizing we do on our own when the thought of cancer provokes our awareness of death and sharpens our appreciation of our daily lives.

The early readings of this chapter describe some of the main medical treatments for cancer, and the later readings turn toward treatments in the broader social sense. The introductory piece by John Cairns provides some brief definitions and a broad overview. The selections by Richard Selzer, Lucien Israël, Ralph W. Moss, and Maggie Scarf offer views of surgery, radiation therapy, chemotherapy, and a psychological technique called imaging. Two short reviews by Steven d'Arazien and Bruce Ames introduce the controversial issue of environmental cancer. The selection by Susan Sontag asks us to consider how cancer has become a metaphor deeply influencing the way we think about ourselves. Finally, the article by J. Michael Bishop turns toward the research laboratories, where increasingly precise questions are being asked and answered about the mechanisms of cancer cells. The news is at once exciting, disheartening, promising.

Cancer: Science and Society

John Cairns

In the modern industrialized world, where famine and pestilence are things   *1*
of the past, cancer has become the most feared of all diseases. It may not be
the commonest cause of death, occurring much less frequently than heart disease, but it has the reputation of being usually a progressive fatal condition
for which no treatment has been discovered. Further, the very nature of cancer
makes it seem a particularly unnecessary form of death. By way of comparison, although the immediate cause of death in a heart attack is a local abnor-
mality of the arteries supplying the heart, the underlying condition is a widespread defect affecting other parts of the body as well. So we tend to think of
a heart attack as just one particular manifestation of the general process of
aging, and a normal end to a long life; or, when it occurs in a man who is still
middle-aged, as the price he has paid for overeating, lack of exercise, and a life
of stress. But cancer is seen as something that originates in one localized region and then spreads so that the rest of the body, which would otherwise still
be healthy, is gradually eaten away by the disease.

Each case of cancer originates as a defect in one of our cells that allows it   *2*
to start multiplying and give rise to an ever increasing population of similarly
unrestrained progeny cells. The first symptom produced by this population of
multiplying cells depends on their location. If they arise in the skin, for example, they will produce a rapidly detected growth; in the lung they might
cause a persistent cough or an unexplained attack of pneumonia: in the breast
they may be detected simply as a lump (tumor). The patient consults a doctor,
and a provisional diagnosis of cancer is made, perhaps on the basis of X-rays
or a biopsy (the microscopic examination of a small sample excised from the
tumor). In most instances, the best treatment is then to remove the tumor surgically. If the entire population of cells can be excised, this procedure will produce a complete cure. However, a common characteristic of such abnormal cells
is that they acquire the ability to invade the surrounding tissues and spread
by way of the blood and lymph systems to form secondary deposits *(metastases)* in distant sites. If this invasion has already occurred by the time of first
diagnosis, excision of the primary tumor will not produce a cure, and other
methods of treatment such as X-irradiation or chemotherapy will have to be
used; unfortunately, these additional methods of treatment are not very effective for most forms of cancer.

The outcome depends, therefore, on whether the abnormal population of cells   *3*

*John Cairns (b. 1922) teaches in the Department of Cancer Biology at Har-
vard's School of Public Health. This selection is his preface to* Cancer: Science
and Society *(1978), one of the most respected overviews of the cancer field. He is
particularly interested in cancer epidemiology.*

has extended beyond the original site, and the likelihood that there has been spread varies greatly according to the kind of cell affected. For example, most cancers of the skin do not readily undergo metastasis and for that reason, even though very common, they are not often lethal. At the other extreme, cancer of the lung is seldom detected before metastases have occurred.

The probable behavior of the different kinds of cancer and their response to the different forms of treatment have been determined over the years, and this knowledge is the basis for selecting the proper treatment for each case. The information is, however, totally empirical and has not been converted into any general theory of cancer.   *4*

For the outsider who tries to review the entire field, it is possible to see in the cancer problem a reflection of the problems of contemporary society. We are living in an age of transition. Once everything seemed within our reach; now we see limits whichever way we turn. We succeed in virtually abolishing mortality in the young, and a population explosion results. We then succeed in reducing the birth rate, but as the proportion of children in the population falls the proportion of old people starts to rise. We invent ever more effective offensive weapons with which to defend ourselves, and our safety from attack becomes more and more uncertain. We learn how we could easily prevent the most lethal of all cancers (lung cancer), and people continue to smoke. However, it looks as if cancer research is soon going to offer additional options, and before long society may be able to decide what exactly it wishes to do about each kind of cancer — whether to prevent it, spend vast sums of money treating it, or let it run its course.

Considerations

1. How might the ways society treats cancer differ from the ways doctors treat it? Develop the differences in these points of view through a short speculative essay.
2. Is John Cairns's assessment of the cancer problem optimistic or pessimistic? Defend your conclusion in a well-developed paragraph.
3. Cairns's closing sentence is loaded with implications, both in what he says and what he doesn't say. In a short essay enumerate and develop those implications.
4. Based on this brief discussion, do you get the sense that Cairns is most interested in medical developments, epidemiology, or molecular research? Defend your judgments.

Sarcophagus

Richard Selzer

We are six who labor here in the night. No . . . seven! For the man horizon-   *1*
tal upon the table strives as well. But we do not acknowledge his struggle. It
is our own that preoccupies us.

I am the surgeon.   *2*

David is the anesthesiologist. You will see how kind, how soft he is. Each   *3*
patient is, for him, a preparation respectfully controlled. Blood pressure, pulse,
heartbeat, flow of urine, loss of blood, temperature, whatever is measurable,
David measures. And he is a titrator, adding a little gas, drug, oxygen, fluid,
blood in order to maintain the dynamic equilibrium that is the only state compatible with life. He is in the very center of the battle, yet he is one step removed; he has not known the patient before this time, nor will he deal with
the next of kin. But for him, the occasion is no less momentous.

Heriberto Paz is an assistant resident in surgery. He is deft, tiny, mercurial.   *4*
I have known him for three years. One day he will be the best surgeon in Mexico.

Evelyn, the scrub nurse, is a young Irish woman. For seven years we have   *5*
worked together. Shortly after her immigration, she led her young husband into
my office to show me a lump on his neck. One year ago he died of Hodgkin's
disease. For the last two years of his life, he was paralyzed from the waist down.
Evelyn has one child, a boy named Liam.

Brenda is a black woman of forty-five. She is the circulating nurse, who will   *6*
conduct the affairs of this room, serving our table, adjusting the lights, counting the sponges, ministering to us from the unsterile world.

Roy is a medical student who is beginning his surgical clerkship. He has   *7*
been assigned to me for the next six weeks. This is his first day, his first operation.

David is inducing anesthesia. In cases where the stomach is not empty   *8*
through fasting, the tube is passed into the windpipe while the patient is awake.
Such an "awake" intubation is called crashing. It is done to avoid vomiting
and the aspiration of stomach contents into the lungs while the muscles that
control coughing are paralyzed.

We stand around the table. To receive a tube in the windpipe while fully   *9*
awake is a terrifying thing.

"Open your mouth wide," David says to the man. The man's mouth opens   *10*
slowly to its fullest, as though to shriek. But instead, he yawns. We smile down
at him behind our masks.

*Richard Selzer (b. 1928) is a surgeon and teacher at the Yale School of Medi-
cine. "Sarcophagus" appeared in* Confessions of a Knife *(1979). His other essay
collections include* Mortal Lessons *(1977) and* Letters to a Young Doctor *(1982),
and he is the author of a short story collection,* The Rituals of Surgery *(1974).*

"OK. Open again. Real wide."   *11*

David sprays the throat of the man with a local anesthetic. He does this three   *12*
times. Then, into the man's mouth, David inserts a metal tongue depressor which
bears a light at the tip. It is called a laryngoscope. It is to light up the throat,
reveal the glottic chink through which the tube must be shoved. All this while,
the man holds his mouth agape, submitting to the hard pressure of the laryngoscope. But suddenly, he cannot submit. The man on the table gags, struggles
to free himself, to spit out the instrument. In his frenzy his lip is pinched by
the metal blade.

There is little blood.   *13*

"Suction," says David.   *14*

Secretions at the back of the throat obscure the view. David suctions them   *15*
away with a plastic catheter.

"Open," commands David. More gagging. Another pass with the scope. An-   *16*
other thrust with the tube. Violent coughing informs us that the tube is in the
right place. It has entered the windpipe. Quickly the balloon is inflated to snug
it against the wall of the trachea. A bolus of Pentothal is injected into a vein
in the man's arm. It takes fifteen seconds for the drug to travel from his arm
to his heart, then on to his brain. I count them. In fifteen seconds, the coughing
stops, the man's body relaxes. He is asleep.

"All set?" I ask David.   *17*

"Go ahead," he nods.   *18*

A long incision. You do not know how much room you will need. This part   *19*
of the operation is swift, tidy. Fat . . . muscle . . . fascia . . . the peritoneum
is snapped open and a giant shining eggplant presents itself. It is the stomach,
black from the blood it contains and that threatens to burst it. We must open
that stomach, evacuate its contents, explore.

Silk sutures are placed in the wall of the stomach as guidelines between which   *20*
the incision will be made. They are like the pitons of a mountaineer. I cut again.
No sooner is the cavity of the stomach achieved, then a columnar geyser of
blood stands from the small opening I have made. Quickly, I slice open the
whole front of the stomach. We scoop out handfuls of clot, great black gelati-
nous masses that shimmy from the drapes to rest against our own bellies as
though, having been evicted from one body, they must find another in which
to dwell. Now and then we step back to let them slidder to the floor. They are
under our feet. We slip in them. "Jesus," I say. "He is bleeding all over North
America." Now my hand is inside the stomach, feeling, pressing. There! A tumor spreads across the back wall of this stomach. A great hard craterous plain,
the dreaded linitis plastica (leather bottle) that is not content with seizing one
area, but infiltrates between the layers until the entire organ is stiff with cancer. It is that, of course, which is bleeding, I stuff wads of gauze against the
tumor. I press my fist against the mass of cloth. The blood slows. I press harder.
The bleeding stops.

A quick glance at Roy. His gown and gloves, even his mask, are sprinkled   *21*
with blood. Now is he dipped; and I, his baptist.

David has opened a second line into the man's veins. He is pumping blood   *22*
into both tubings.

"Where do we stand?" I ask him.   *23*

"Still behind. Three units." He checks the blood pressure.   *24*

"Low, but coming up, " he says.   *25*

"Shall I wait 'til you catch up?"   *26*

"No. Go ahead. I'll keep pumping."   *27*

I try to remove my fist from the stomach, but as soon as I do, there is a fresh   *28*
river of blood.

"More light," I say. "I need more light."   *29*

Brenda stands on a platform behind me. She adjusts the lamps.   *30*

"More light," I say, like a man going blind.   *31*

"That's it," she says. "There is no more light."   *32*

"We'll go around from the outside," I say. Heriberto nods agreement. "Free   *33*
up the greater curvature first, then the lesser, lift the stomach up and get some
control from behind."

I must work with one hand. The other continues as the compressor. It is the   *34*
tiredest hand of my life. One hand, then, inside the stomach, while the other
creeps behind. Between them . . . a ridge of tumor. The left hand fumbles,
gropes toward its mate. They swim together. I lift the stomach forward to find
that *nothing* separates my hands from each other. The wall of the stomach has
been eaten through by the tumor. One finger enters a large tubular structure.
It is the aorta. The incision in the stomach has released the tamponade of blood
and brought us to this rocky place.

"Curved aortic clamp."   *35*

A blind grab with the clamp high up at the diaphragm. The bleeding slack-   *36*
ens, dwindles. I release the pressure warily. A moment later there is a great
bang of blood. The clamp has bitten through a cancerous aorta.

"Zero silk on a big Mayo needle."   *37*

I throw the heavy sutures, one after the other, into the pool of blood, hoping   *38*
to snag with my needle some bit of tissue to close over the rent in the aorta,
to hold back the blood. There is no tissue. Each time, the needle pulls through
the crumble of tumor. I stop. I repack the stomach. Now there is a buttress of
packing both outside and inside the stomach. The bleeding is controlled. We
wait. Slowly, something is gathering here, organizing. What had been vague
and shapeless before is now declaring itself. All at once, I know what it is. There
is nothing to do.

For what tool shall I ask? With what device fight off this bleeding? A knife?   *39*
There is nothing here to cut. Clamps? Where place the jaws of a hemostat? A
scissors? Forceps? Nothing. The instrument does not exist that knows such deep
red jugglery. Not all my clever picks, my rasp . . . A miner's lamp, I think, to
cast a brave glow.

David has been pumping blood steadily.   *40*

"He is stable at the moment," he says. "Where do we go from here?"   *41*

"No place. He's going to die. The minute I take away my pressure, he'll bleed   *42*
to death."

I try to think of possibilities, alternatives. I cannot; there are none. Minutes   *43*
pass. We listen to the cardiac monitor, the gassy piston of the anesthesia machine.

"More light!" I say. "Fix the light."   *44*

The light seems dim, aquarial, a dilute beam slanting through a green sea. 45
At such a fathom the fingers are clumsy. There is pressure. It is cold.

"Dave," I say, "stop the transfusion." I hear my voice coming as from a great 46
distance. "Stop it," I say again.

David and I look at each other, standing among the drenched rags, the 47
smeared equipment.

"I can't," he says. 48

"Then I will," I say, and with my free hand I reach across the boundary that 49
separates the sterile field from the outside world, and I close the clamp on the
intravenous tubing. It is the act of an outlaw, someone who does not know right
from wrong. But I know. I know that this is right to do.

"The oxygen," I say. "Turn it off." 50

"You want it turned off, you do it," he says. 51

"Hold this," I say to Heriberto, and I give over the packing to him. I step 52
back from the table, and go to the gas tanks.

"This one?" I have to ask him. 53

"Yes," David nods. 54

I turn it off. We stand there, waiting, listening to the beeping of the electro- 55
cardiograph. It remains even, regular, relentless. Minutes go by, and the sound
continues. The man will not die. At last, the intervals on the screen grow longer,
the shape of the curve changes, the rhythm grows wild, furious. The line droops,
flattens. The man is dead.

It is silent in the room. Now we are no longer a team, each with his circum- 56
scribed duties to perform. It is Evelyn who speaks first.

"It is a blessing," she says. I think of her husband's endless dying. 57

"No," says Brenda. "Better for the family if they have a few days . . . to get 58
used to the idea of it."

"But, look at all the pain he's been spared." 59

"Still, for the ones that are left, it's better to have a little time." 60

I listen to the two women murmuring, debating without rancor, speaking 61
in hushed tones of the newly dead as women have done for thousands of years.

"May I have the name of the operation?" It is Brenda, picking up her duties. 62
She is ready with pen and paper.

"Exploratory laparotomy. Attempt to suture malignant aorto-gastric fis- 63
tula."

"Is he pronounced?" 64

"What time is it?" 65

"Eleven-twenty." 66

"Shall I put that down?" 67

"Yes." 68

"Sew him up," I say to Heriberto. "I'll talk to the family." 69

To Roy I say, "You come with me." 70

Roy's face is speckled with blood. He seems to me a child with the measles. 71
What, in God's name, is he doing here?

From the doorway, I hear the voices of the others, resuming. 72

"Stitch," says Heriberto. 73

Roy and I go to change our bloody scrub suits. We put on long white coats. 74
In the elevator, we do not speak. For the duration of the ride to the floor where

the family is waiting, I am reasonable. I understand that in its cellular wisdom, the body of this man had sought out the murderous function of my scalpel, and stretched itself upon the table to receive the final stabbing. For this little time, I know that it is not a murder committed but a mercy bestowed. Tonight's knife is no assassin, but the kind scythe of time.

We enter the solarium. The family rises in unison. There are so many! How 75 ruthless the eyes of the next of kin.

"I am terribly sorry . . . ," I begin. Their faces tighten, take guard. "There 76 was nothing we could do."

I tell them of the lesion, tell of how it began somewhere at the back of the 77 stomach; how, long ago, no one knows why, a cell lost the rhythm of the body, fell out of step, sprang, furious, into rebellion. I tell of how the cell divided and begat two of its kind, which begat four more and so on, until there was a whole race of lunatic cells, which is called cancer.

I tell of how the cancer spread until it had replaced the whole back of the 78 stomach, invading, chewing until it had broken into the main artery of the body. Then it was, I tell them, that the great artery poured its blood into the stomach. I tell of how I could not stop the bleeding, how my clamps bit through the crumbling tissue, how my stitches would not hold, how there was nothing to be done. All of this I tell.

A woman speaks. She has not heard my words, only caught the tone of my 79 voice.

"Do you mean he is dead?"   80

Should I say "passed away" instead of "died"? No. I cannot.   81

"Yes." I tell her, "he is dead."   82

Her question and my answer unleash their anguish. Roy and I stand among 83 the welter of bodies that tangle, grapple, rock, split apart to form new couplings. Their keening is exuberant, wild. It is more than I can stand. All at once, a young man slams his fist into the wall with great force.

"Son of a bitch!" he cries.   84

"Stop that!" I tell him sharply. Then, more softly, "Please try to control 85 yourself."

The other men crowd about him, patting, puffing, grunting. They are all fat, 86 with huge underslung bellies. Like their father's. A young woman in a nun's habit hugs each of the women in turn.

"Shit!" says one of the men.   87

The nun hears, turns away her face. Later, I see the man apologizing to her. 88

The women, too, are fat. One of them has a great pile of yellowish hair that 89 has been sprayed and rendered motionless. All at once, she begins to whine. A single note, coming louder and louder. I ask a nurse to bring tranquilizer pills. She does, and I hand them out, one to each, as though they were the wafers of communion. They urge the pills upon each other.

"Go on, Theresa, take it. Make her take one."   90

Roy and I are busy with cups of water. Gradually it grows quiet. One of the 91 men speaks.

"What's the next step?"   92

"Do you have an undertaker in mind?"   93

They look at each other, shrug. Someone mentions a name. The rest nod.   94

"Give the undertaker a call. Let him know. He'll take care of everything." 95
I turn to leave. 96
"Just a minute," one of the men calls. "Thanks, Doc. You did what you could." 97
"Yes," I say. 98

Once again in the operating room. Blood is everywhere. There is a wild smell, 99
as though a fox had come and gone. The others, clotted about the table, work
on. They are silent, ravaged.
"How did the family take it?" 100
"They were good, good." 101
Heriberto has finished reefing up the abdomen. The drapes are peeled back. 102
The man on the table seems more than just dead. He seems to have gone beyond that, into a state where expression is possible — reproach and scorn. I
study him. His baldness had advanced beyond the halfway mark. The remaining strands of hair had been gallantly dyed. They are, even now, neatly combed
and crenellated. A stripe of black moustache rides his upper lip. Once, he had
been spruce!
We all help lift the man from the table to the stretcher. 103
"On three," says David. "One . . . two . . . three." 104
And we heft him over, using the sheet as a sling. My hand brushes his shoul- 105
der. It is cool. I shudder as though he were infested with lice. He has become
something that I do not want to touch.
More questions from the women. 106
"Is a priest coming?" 107
"Does the family want to view him?" 108
"Yes. No. Don't bother me with these things." 109
"Come on," I say to Roy. We go to the locker room and sit together on a 110
bench. We light cigarettes.
"Well?" I ask him. 111
"When you were scooping out the clots, I thought I was going to swoon." 112
I pause over the word. It is too quaint, too genteel for this time. I feel, at 113
that moment, a great affection for him.
"But you fought it." 114
"Yes. I forced it back down. But, almost . . ." 115
"Good," I say. Who knows what I mean by it? I want him to know that I 116
count it for something.
"And you?" he asks me. The students are not shy these days. 117
"It was terrible, his refusal to die." 118
I want him to say that it was right to call it quits, that I did the best I could. 119
But he says nothing. We take off our scrub suits and go to the shower. There
are two stalls opposite each other. They are curtained. But we do not draw the
curtains. We need to see each other's healthy bodies. I watch Roy turn his face
directly upward into the blinding fall of water. His mouth is open to receive
it. As though it were milk flowing from the breasts of God. For me, too, this
water is like a well in a wilderness.
In the locker room, we dress in silence. 120
"Well, goodnight." 121
Awkwardly our words come out in unison. 122

"In the morning . . ."   *123*
"Yes, yes, later."   *124*
"Goodnight."   *125*
I watch him leave through the elevator door.   *126*

For the third time I go to that operating room. The others have long since   *127*
finished and left. It is empty, dark. I turn on the great lamps above the table
that stands in the center of the room. The pediments of the table and the floor
have been scrubbed clean. There is no sign of the struggle. I close my eyes and
see again the great pale body of the man, like a white bullock, bled. The line
of stitches on his abdomen is a hieroglyph. Already, the events of this night are
hidden from me by these strange untranslatable markings.

Considerations

1. In a paragraph explain the connotations of the title "Sarcophagus."
2. Create a stereotypical description of a doctor and consider to what extent
   Richard Selzer's presentation of himself conforms to or works against this
   stereotype. Then write up a short essay supporting your argument.
3. Selzer, well known as a surgeon, is now best known as a writer. What evidence can you find in this piece that Selzer is not only a surgeon describing
   his experiences, but a writer carefully crafting his material? Write an analytical essay about "Sarcophagus" based either on Selzer's dramatic characterization or upon his attention to individual words.
4. Define the term *ritual* (you might want to consult an anthropology text); then
   write an analytical essay exploring the ritual aspects of "Sarcophagus."

Connections

1. Reading John Cairns's brief comments about cancer surgery probably did
   not prepare you for Richard Selzer's account of this particular operation.
   Compare Cairns's and Selzer's points of view and state which you find to be
   the better perspective. Clarify what you mean by *better*, and defend your
   reasoning.
2. What is Selzer's definition of cancer? How does it resemble and differ from
   that offered by Cairns?
3. Arguing from the point of view of a cancer surgeon, why would you not want
   Selzer's piece to stand as representative of cancer surgery? Write a short
   essay.
4. In July 1985, President Ronald Reagan underwent cancer surgery. After researching accounts of that operation, compare its circumstances with those
   of the operation described by Selzer. Account for the differences.

Radiation

Lucien Israël

Chronologically, radiation was the second weapon to be used against can- 1
cer. X-rays, discovered in 1895 by Wilhelm Roentgen, were applied the next
year by Despeignes, in Lyons, to an inoperable cancer of the stomach. Since
then, there has been an uninterrupted succession of scientific and technical
discoveries down to the present time, when gamma rays produced in accelerators are used, and most recently, equipment has been developed to deliver
high-speed neutrons and pi mesons. In addition, radiotherapists use radioactive bodies, which they implant in the tumor itself, and radioisotopes, which
are introduced into the organism and seek out their target — the skeleton, for
example, or the thyroid gland. With all these techniques at its disposal, radiotherapy is a very valuable weapon that can be expected to have an expanding
role in the future, thanks to better cooperation between radiologists and other
specialists.

The particles delivered in radiotherapy transfer their energy to electrons 2
which ionize the matter they reach — that is, which produce free or ionized
chemical radicals. For example, they ionize water, which constitutes about 80
percent of the organic environment, by separating it into the radicals H, OH,
and so forth. Of course they also ionize the "solid" constituents of cytoplasm,
RNA and DNA. This ionization damages the molecules, weakens them, and leads
to recombinations with the oxygen available in the environment. Thus changes
occur in the biological properties of the molecules. Some of these changes cause
the cell to die, others make it impossible for it to divide, and still others lead
to extinction at a future time, the descendants of the affected cell dying out
after three or four generations. We know many biochemical and genetic details
of these injuries, and already they have shown us how complex the phenomenon is. A cell does not die because it bursts apart, or because its proteins suddenly coagulate, but because of a series of delicate events that take place over
a period of time and are combated by certain mechanisms of self-repair.

Radiotherapy in its modern form is now the treatment of choice in the early 3
stages of Hodgkin's disease (five-year survival: 80 percent). It is very effective
in seminomas of the testicles, and in cancer of the cervix and prostate. In cases
of small breast tumors, it gives results that many investigators consider com-

*Lucien Israël (b. 1926) is a French oncologist. This selection is a chapter from
his book* Le Cancer aujourd'hui, *which appeared in English as* Conquering Cancer *(1978). He has worked in the United States with members of the National Cancer Institute, and he has chaired the lung cancer section of the European Organization for Research on the Treatment of Cancer. He is head of the Hôpital Franco-
Musulman in Bobigny.*

parable to those of surgery. A certain number of cancers of the nasopharynx have also proved very sensitive to radiotherapy. I am talking about treatment that aims to cure — that is, the treatment of cases that are seen early and are operable in principle, but for which ionizing radiation is used instead of surgery, as a definitive local-regional treatment. In cases of this sort, radiotherapy sometimes gives brilliant results. Yet, apart from Hodgkin's disease and lymphosarcoma, there is much disagreement as to its effectiveness — indeed, there have been no conclusive trials — and many physicians prefer surgery, despite the mutilation it entails, because it has the advantage of making a clean sweep: total sterilization by radiation often remains problematical.

As a palliative treatment, radiotherapy is absolutely irreplaceable for localized but inoperable tumors, such as certain tumors of the lung, esophagus, pancreas, colon, breast, and so forth. In such cases the aim is not to bring about a cure, for the tumor is too large, but to obtain at the very least a considerable attenuation of symptoms, often a partial regression of the tumor and the pain it causes, and on occasion even a regression that is apparently complete. In this connection, it is regrettable that radiotherapists don't report their results — as chemotherapists do — in such a way as to differentiate between the percentage of complete regressions and the percentage of objective partial regressions, and to indicate the distribution of length of those regressions. In any event, the results are often only palliative. Radiotherapy suffers from the same limitation as surgery in that it does not affect metastases, and from another limitation as well, which we will analyze later in detail: the difficulty of achieving local sterilization.

The purpose of applying radiotherapy both before and after an operation — a practice that has long been in use — is to perfect the results of surgical excision. This practice is an admission that surgery alone, even when it is visually satisfactory, does not remove everything, and that by combining two different local treatments, we increase the chances of sterilization. If this reasoning is correct, we should observe a reduction in the rate of local recurrences when radiation is added, and no change in the rate of distant metastases, since there is no reason why those should be influenced by an improvement in local treatment.

In fact, we observe something rather different. Local recurrences do diminish in cases of advanced tumors, where there is great danger that malignant cells will have migrated to the lymph nodes of the region or to adjoining tissues. But they do not dimish in cases in which local recurrences are already very rare: a small breast tumor, a peripheral lung tumor. As for distant metastases, certain recent studies have thrown the medical community into confusion by showing that metastases may be more frequent in cases that have received radiation, a finding that could be explained by a pernicious effect of ionizing radiation on immunity. There are still only a few of these studies, and those that do exist are contradictory and highly controversial. But they show that in medicine, logic and deduction cannot take the place of long, honest, empirical studies undertaken with an open mind.

Radiation can cause more or less extensive burns of the skin and mucous membranes; these generally repair themselves in a few weeks, and can usually be avoided by experienced radiotherapists. Vascular lesions that may appear later are more severe and can cause necrosis and fibrosis with loss of function of the irradiated tissues. The different organs vary in their vulnerability to this sort of complication. The liver, kidneys, and lungs are particularly fragile; the muscles are also susceptible. Even very moderate amounts of radiation of the testicles and ovaries may cause sterilization or induce genetic mutations that will reveal themselves in later generations. It is known that radiation has a teratogenic effect: if it is applied before the third month of fetal life, there is a slight but not negligible risk of malformation. The practice of giving regular X-rays to women who are three months pregnant has been abandoned. (It was required by Social Security at a time when the risk of not recognizing tuberculosis in the mother was much higher and more serious than the risk — which no one suspected anyway — of damaging the child or its later offspring.)

Lastly, radiation is carcinogenic at smaller doses than those which immediately injure tissues. The radiologists were the first to suffer from this complication. A few years ago it was learned that irradiation of the thyroid region during childhood is dangerous and, in a not inconsiderable number of cases, induces cancers in the adult. *8*

It may seem curious to use ionizing radiation to treat diseases that can also be caused precisely by ionizing radiation. But the paradox is more apparent than real. Weak doses of radiation are mutagenic and can start the chain of phenomena that, over a period of several years, leads to cancer. Strong doses are destructive, and more so to tissues that are proliferating rapidly than to healthy neighboring tissues, and it is logical to exploit this property. Nevertheless, one might express concern that the radiation that sterilizes the cancer may induce carcinogenic mutations in the healthy tissue through which it passes. There may be some basis for this concern, and it is up to the radiotherapists to evaluate it precisely, for the benefit of us all. But the risk remains absolutely minute. And if we can sterilize a tumor by radiation today, we must do so, even at the risk of inducing a tumor the day after tomorrow. Sufficient unto the day is the evil thereof. *9*

When a wide area is exposed to radiation, it is impossible to avoid irradiating large portions of the skeleton and hence of the bone marrow in which the different blood-cell lines are formed. The serious bone-marrow deficiency that would result if the entire body was irradiated in sufficient doses is an insurmountable obstacle to such therapy, unless a bone-marrow graft is performed afterward, which is still an exceptional procedure. As I have already mentioned, it has recently appeared that radiation can also cause a severe and prolonged immune deficiency. This is true for radiation of the thymus, the organ in which the T-lymphocytes are processed, and hence for radiation of certain tumors of the lung, esophagus, and breast, among others. But it is also true of the radiation of large abdominal areas, which affects an extensive system of lymph nodes, bones, and blood vessels. The more the patient's immunological status deteriorates, the greater becomes the risk of both regional and distant dissemination. From this point of view, we are beginning to suspect that radiotherapy is a two-edged sword, and that it would be well to think about possible ways of countering this very serious disadvantage. *10*

Fortunately, healthy tissues and tumors have a different sensitivity to rays. Certain tissues — intestinal mucous membranes, for example — proliferate faster *11* than tumors and can therefore regenerate themselves more quickly, between two successive sessions of radiotherapy. Others proliferate only as needed to repair losses, and are therefore much less vulnerable to radiation than the tumors, which do not have this feedback mechanism of repair, but on the contrary, proliferate constantly. It is nonetheless true that it is impossible to irradiate a tumor without damaging the surrounding healthy tissues. It is the responsibility of the radiotherapist, with the help of calculations and complicated machines, to establish the best compromise between effectiveness and tolerance. But it is still only a compromise. One would have to sacrifice too much healthy tissue, tissue that is often indispensable, in order to be sure of sterilizing the tumor. It can't always be done.

12   Certain phenomena combine to limit the effect of ionizing radiation on tumors. When an area is bombarded with rays, the destructive events they produce are not equally divided among all the cells. Some cells undergo two, three, or four events when one would have sufficed. Thirty-seven percent are not affected at all. The next time, 37 percent of this 37 percent are spared. And so on. Consequently, the radiotherapist wears himself out trying to hit the last cells and can't do so unless he totally destroys the neighboring tissues. If one cell out of ten thousand escapes, and if the tumor had 10^{11} cells (that is, weighed 100 grams) in the beginning, there remain 10^7 cells, which continue to proliferate and will become 10^{11} cells again in thirteen doublings. The probability of radically sterilizing a tumor by radiotherapy rises in direct proportion with the risks one takes with regard to the healthy tissues, but it is never equal to 1.

13   The cell in phase S, the phase when it is synthesizing DNA, is much more resistant to radiation than the cell in phase M. Unfortunately, for statistical reasons, there are ten to twenty times more cells in phase S than in phase M at any given time. Cells in phase G_1 and G_2 are of an intermediate sensitivity. Cells in a very prolonged G_1 phase are not totally insensitive to radiation, therefore, and that gives us a precious opportunity to reduce the number of nonproliferating cells. Still, even if all the other conditions for effectiveness are met, the succession of the various phases of the cycle of division represents an important limitation to radiotherapy.

14   The presence of oxygen is almost indispensable to the success of radiotherapy, for the oxygenation of the free radicals converts them into compounds that are definitely unsuitable for their intended biological use. But the diffusion of oxygen through the capillaries ceases to be adequate beyond a range of 0.2 millimeters. Certain tumors of insufficient vascularity have areas that are hypooxygenated and hence resistant to radiation. That is a great problem for the radiotherapists. We shall see how they try to solve it.

15   The way in which DNA repairs itself when damaged is a fascinating phenomenon. In both normal cells and tumor cells there are enzymes that recognize in the DNA chain the parts that have undergone chemical damage and cut them out, while other enzymes "sew up" the two fragments, end to end, maintaining the proper order. The repair is sometimes imperfect, and the cell's progeny will suffer. Sometimes it is excellent, and the cell behaves as if nothing had happened. This is a very effective mechanism of radioresistance, although it varies from one tumor to another, from one tissue to another, and perhaps genetically from one individual to another. Certain tumors of the skin, tongue, lips, and so on respond slowly to radiation but are permanently cured. Others — certain sarcomas, for example — melt like snow under the rays of the sun but recur more or less quickly. We can't explain these differences.

Since I am neither a radiobiologist nor a radiotherapist, my notion of the *16* prospects for radiotherapy is no doubt imperfect, and the specialists may not all agree with me. Nevertheless, as a medical oncologist — that is, as a person who needs their services for his patients and who reads many papers in their field — I am interested to see that radiotherapy is not, as some might think, a fixed discipline, but rather one that is making rapid strides and from which we may expect much.

It is important to concentrate the rays on the tumor and to protect healthy *17* tissues, and several methods have been devised to accomplish this. One of them, which has been in use for a long time, consists of employing a cross fire of rays from several directions, in such a way that each intervening portion of healthy tissue penetrated from the skin down receives fewer rays than the tumor itself. Today radiologists using this empirical approach can call upon all the resources of dosimetry. Computers now make it possible to draw the isodose curves, to simulate a clinical situation with an irregular tumor and its particular localization, and to know precisely how the rays will be distributed in and around the tumor. This appears to be a major advance, of such importance that radiotherapy installations that don't have these facilities will soon be outmoded. Another approach would consist of utilizing beams of fast neutrons or pi mesons generated in accelerators; these are more penetrating and can be more selectively localized. Most of the preliminary studies have already been undertaken. We don't know exactly how this heavy artillery — heavy in every sense of the word — will fit into the total arsenal of radiotherapy, but it appears that it will have an important place. Still another procedure is to implant radioactive materials in accessible tumors. Recent innovations here consist of using iridium-192 and cesium-137 instead of radium. As always, there are controversies among specialists. There are probably important advances to be made in the precise localization of the effects of radiation. A Parisian team has acquired a world-wide reputation in this field.

How can we combat radioresistance? It would be ideal if we could inhibit *18* the ligases, the enzymes that repair damaged DNA. We will probably find a way to do that one day by biochemical procedures: certain studies suggest that drugs as simple as caffeine might have the desired effect.

Taking another approach to the problem, investigators have already done a *19* great deal of work on the "oxygen effect." Tests have been conducted of irradiation during and following massive oxygenation of the patient with a mask, under a tent, and even inside a chamber where the pressure can rise to three atmospheres. The tests were not conclusive. But it does not seem that we can use these techniques to surmount the obstacle of oxygen deficiency in the tissues caused by lack of vascularity.

However, other procedures can be summoned to our aid. Various sub- *20* stances, such as synthetic vitamin K, metronidazole, and so forth, concentrate by choice in hypoxic cells and perform the function of oxygen by attaching themselves to free radicals. It will not be easy to measure exactly the increase in effectiveness thus obtained. However, many radiotherapists are devoting themselves to the task, and with all the more enthusiasm because these substances are not harmful. The field of radiosensitizers is wide open.

The difference in sensitivity of the different phases of the cycle is an obstacle that might be overcome if we could find a way to "synchronize" the cells. If we take as the total duration of the cycle twenty-four hours, an S phase of eight hours and an M phase of a half-hour, at any given moment we have one-third of the cells in phase S, or resistant, and one-fiftieth of the cells in phase M, or highly sensitive. We know that in some doses, certain chemical agents that can be utilized in chemotherapy are capable not only of killing cells but also of temporarily arresting others in a given phase. That is the case, for example, with the antimetabolites and the fluoridated pyrimidines, which block cells in phase S. While these substances are active, all the cells reaching phase S from phases G_2, M, and G_1 remain in phase S. When the effect of the chemicals wears off, the cells resume the cycle at the same time and will reach phase M at the same time. They will have been "synchronized." If the radiation treatment is applied at the right time, it will find many more cells in phase M than before synchronization, and its effectiveness will be increased accordingly. Actually, these theoretical propositions are very hard to check. We must extrapolate from results obtained in small animals with small tumors, in which all the parameters are different from those that exist in man. Nevertheless, the idea is certainly one to be pursued. It has already been partly confirmed by clinical studies showing that the synchronization obtained, while it is far from 100 percent, is by no means negligible. *21*

The purpose of splitting the total dose into fractions is not only to combat radioresistance. It is also to increase the difference in effect on healthy tissues and on tumors. If the patient is to receive a total of 6,000 rads, why break it down into fractions of 200 rads, delivered in five-minute sessions, five times a week for six weeks? I am almost certain that it is not merely to keep their weekends free that radiologists treat their patients only five days a week. But the fact is that the ideal schedule is not yet known. We know that the larger the fraction that is administered at one time, the greater the destructive effect, but this is true for normal tissue as well as for the tumor. We also know that the shorter the interval between two fractions, the poorer the repair, but again this is true for both normal and pathological tissues. Continuous irradiation is dangerous to healthy tissues unless we use the technique of implanting the radioactive material in the tumor itself. In order to optimize the breakdown schedule, we would have to know the relative kinetics of healthy tissue and tumor tissue in each case, which is usually impossible. It would be a step forward if radiologists would take into account the rate of growth of the tumors they irradiate, instead of calmly applying the same schedule for a tumor with a doubling time of ten days and for one with a doubling time of four hundred days. It is possible that certain tumors should be irradiated two or three times in the same day and others only twice a week. *22*

The basic objective is not to improve radiotherapy but to improve total results. One way to do that is to improve the use of radiotherapy within an over- *23* all strategy employing all the weapons available. Is it useful to supplement palliative radiotherapy with a course of chemotherapy? Is it possible to use immunoprotection and immunostimulation — before, during, or after radiotherapy — to reduce its immunosuppressive effects without diminishing its antitumor effects? Should we systematically irradiate areas in which postoperative metastases are likely to appear, before they do so?

Radiation remains a local treatment, unsuited for the management of a diffuse disease such as cancer usually is. But this local weapon is of great value because it can be used where surgery is no longer feasible, and it can be used against several different metastases where it would be unwise or impossible to remove them all surgically. It doesn't provide the degree of sterilization that can be achieved with surgery, but current research is making it increasingly effective. It isn't the weapon itself that's open to criticism, but some of those who use it, who consider medical treatments as nonexistent or as lesser forms of therapy having only a supporting role in relation to radiation.   24

A few of the radiologists to whom I refer patients before subjecting them to medical treatment, instead of sending them back to me, tell them that such treatment is unnecessary. Most radiologists do send patients back and are curious to know the results we obtain afterward. But there are not many who spontaneously suggest chemotherapy to a patient whose radiation treatment is coming to an end, even when the risk of recurrence remains very high, as in the case of an inoperable lung cancer, and even when they know that while they may have achieved local control, they have done nothing to protect the patient from metastases at a distance. The opportunities for radiotherapists and medical oncologists to work together are still rare, at least outside of anticancer centers, and the level of communication between them suffers as a result. I hope that new structures can soon be established that will make it easier to exchange information, to adopt a common language, and to eliminate mutual mistrust. The patients have everything to gain from such cooperation.   25

Recently the radiotherapy journals have contained an increasing number of articles on tests of irradiation of the entire body. Some very encouraging results have been published. These results have been achieved by using weak doses that don't endanger the organism and that allow repopulation of the bone marrow by cells that form the various elements of the blood.   26

Considerations

1. Summarize the evidence supporting Lucien Israël's contention that radiotherapy is a valuable weapon against cancer.
2. Assemble all the evidence Israël includes that points to problems with radiotherapy. Then construct an argument claiming that Israel's misgivings about radiotherapy are almost as strong as his support of it.
3. Does Israël employ any metaphors to help describe radiotherapy? If so, do any particular metaphors predominate?
4. Israël's selection indicates several ways in which statistics are important, or should be important, to radiotherapy. Assemble these, and write a short essay ranking their importance.

5. In "Radiation," Israël seems to take for granted a certain amount of biological knowledge, knowledge that you may lack. But it is possible to use this selection to acquire some of that knowledge, and then to ask focused questions that prepare you to learn more. Try out this technique by constructing a list of biological inferences you can make from the text, and add to each inference a question or two about what remains unclear to you. Here's a sample entry:

> Evidently *ionization* refers to a chemical change in the elements within molecules, changes that make these elements vulnerable to combining with oxygen. But what is ionization more exactly? And what damage does ionization do to cells?

Connections

1. Lucien Israël identifies himself as a "medical oncologist." Do you think that means he performs cancer surgery? How does he seem to feel about cancer surgery? Argue from specific sentences in the text.
2. Both Israël (para's. 6 and 17) and John Cairns (para. 4) use the word *empirical*, but their attitudes toward empirical thinking seem different. What does the word seem to mean? Empirical as opposed to what? Write a short essay about the strengths and limitations of empiricism in thinking about cancer.
3. One form of cancer treatment is called immunotherapy. Based on what you can gather from Israël, make an educated guess about what immunotherapy entails. Develop your guess in a well controlled paragraph.
4. If you've read each of the earlier selections in this chapter, consider whether this piece by Israël adds anything to your understanding of what cancer is, what causes it, and what remains unknown about it. Choose one of these issues and answer it as well as you can, based on what you have so far learned. Acknowledge your sources of information.
5. Israël is critical of the lack of cooperation between radiobiologists and other cancer therapists. But perhaps his criticisms apply more to French physicians than to American ones, or perhaps by now his criticisms are outdated. Consult a recent medical text on cancer treatments (such as the one by Haskell listed in Suggestions for Further Reading), and report on whether American radiologists seem to work in collaboration with other cancer specialists.

Chemotherapy

Ralph W. Moss

Third among the so-called "proven" methods of treating cancer is chemo-   *1*
therapy: the use of drugs to kill cancer cells. Few topics in medicine today are
as controversial as the use of these drugs.

In theory, a drug cure for cancer is highly appealing. Just as specific drugs   *2*
cure many bacterial and parasitic infections, so should cancer chemotherapy
ideally kill cancer cells without harming excessive quantities of normal tissue.
In reality, however, orthodox chemotherapy has not yet developed an agent
specific and safe enough to restrict its attack to cancer cells. Most chemotherapeutic agents work by blocking an essential metabolic step in the process of
cellular division. Since cancer cells often divide more rapidly than normal cells,
this lethal "antimetabolite" action should be directed preferentially against
cancer cells. However, most normal tissues engage in cell division at varying
rates. Thus chemotherapy poisons many normal tissues as well — especially
the rapidly dividing cells of the bone marrow, intestinal wall, and the hair fol-
licles.

The bone marrow is the foundation of the immune system. The use of chem-   *3*
otherapy is often accompanied by destruction of this immune system, which
serves the dual function of preventing infections and combating the spread of
cancer. Chemotherapy often brings in its train a host of blood-deficiency diseases (such as leukopenia, thrombocytopenia, and aplastic anemia). These in
turn, can give rise to massive, uncontrollable infections. Cancer patients on
chemotherapy have been known to die of something as innocuous as the common cold.

Because of its effects on the immune system, chemotherapy stands in con-   *4*
tradiction to another form of therapy: immunotherapy. This form of treatment
is still considered experimental at most cancer centers. "Immunotherapy holds
hope of harnessing the body's own disease-fighting systems to combat cancer
with essentially no overt toxicity," says the American Cancer Society's 1979
edition of *Cancer Facts and Figures.* "In laboratory animals, substances such
as BCG (Bacillus Calmette-Guérin) can stimulate immune mechanisms. These
substances now are being used in humans alone or with other forms of treatment" (ACS, 1979).

Since immunotherapy is generally used as a treatment of last resort, almost   *5*

*Ralph W. Moss (b. 1943), currently a freelance writer, was once a classics teacher
(Ph.D. Stanford, 1974). He worked for several years as a public relations officer at
the Sloan-Kettering Cancer Center in New York but was dismissed in 1977. He
was dismissed, he claims, for protesting the cover-up of some favorable results obtained from animal experiments with the controversial cancer drug Laetrile. The*
Cancer Syndrome, *from which this selection is a chapter, was published in 1980.*

all patients receiving it have first received chemotherapy, or are given drugs in combination with the immune-stimulating agents. The clinical results with BCG and other immune stimulants have generally been disappointing, and some doctors believe this is because the prior or concurrent use of immunity-destroying anticancer drugs wipes out whatever beneficial effects these newer agents may have.

Chemotherapy's effect on the gut can be equally disastrous. Cancer patients often have difficulty in eating or absorbing their food. Cancer drugs may cause nausea, bleeding sores around the mouth, soreness of the gums and throat, and ulceration and bleeding of the gastrointestinal tract. Because some forms of chemotherapy particularly affect rapidly dividing cells, and the mucous cells are quick dividers, this form of therapy has resulted in the sloughing of the entire internal mucosa of the gut. Death may result.   6

Some people withstand chemotherapy with few side effects. Many others become nauseated, vomit, lose their hair, or develop infections. Some have a wide range of toxic reactions.   7

There are about thirty drugs in use against cancer. Some of them are what are called "alkylating agents," which react with the genetic material of the cells (DNA). These drugs produce a cross-linking of the bases of the DNA chain, which blocks replication of nuclear DNA during mitosis. Some of these drugs are nitrogen mustard, Thio TEPA, Leukeran, Myleran, and Cytoxan.   8

Another major category of drugs are the antimetabolites. These chemicals prevent cells from making nucleic acids and proteins essential to their survival. The drugs' molecules mimic necessary constituents in the cell. One of them, methotrexate, competes with folic acid, a B vitamin, and prevents the vitamin from being utilized. This leads to the death of the cell. It is thus literally an antivitamin. Other drugs in this category are 6-mercaptopurine (6-MP) and 5-fluorouracil (5-FU).   9

In addition, chemotherapists use antibiotics, which have antitumor activity; plant alkaloids — poisons derived from the periwinkle plant; and even a close cousin of DDT, called o,p-DDD.   10

All of these drugs have one characteristic in common: they are all poisonous. They work because they're poisons. Methotrexate, for example, carries with it the following warning: 11

METHOTREXATE MUST BE USED ONLY BY PHYSICIANS EXPERIENCED IN ANTI-METABOLITE CHEMOTHERAPY.

BECAUSE OF THE POSSIBILITY OF FATAL OR SEVERE TOXIC REACTIONS, THE PATIENT SHOULD BE FULLY INFORMED BY THE PHYSICIAN OF THE RISKS INVOLVED AND SHOULD BE UNDER HIS CONSTANT SUPERVISION (*Physician's Desk Reference*, 1978).

The package insert then goes on to describe the "high potential toxicity" of the product. This includes the abovementioned symptoms, as well as malaise, undue fatigue, chills and fever, dizziness, and various problems of the skin, blood, alimentary system, urogenital system, and central nervous system. Finally, the doctor is warned that   12

Other reactions related or attributed to the use of methotrexate such as pneumonitis; metabolic changes, precipitating diabetes; osteoporotic effects, abnormal tissue, cell changes, and even sudden death have been reported (ibid.).

How successful are these drugs in combating cancer? This question is im- *13* portant; if they were highly effective, one might tolerate their admittedly harsh side effects to get the benefit of a cure.

It is generally agreed that in certain uncommon forms of cancer, chemo- *14* therapy is highly effective. Choriocarcinoma, a rare tumor which afflicts pregnant women, can be cured in about 70 percent of cases with methotrexate, Dactinomycin, and Vinblastine.

Another type of tumor which has yielded quite well to chemotherapy is *15* Burkitt's lymphoma. Through the use of Cyclophosphamide, methotrexate, and other drugs, doctors have been able to achieve about a 50 percent cure rate. However, this type of cancer is exceedingly rare in the United States. It is found primarily in certain parts of Africa, where it is believed to be caused by a virus (Maugh and Marx, 1975:26).

Acute lymphoblastic leukemia, which most often attacks children, is in some *16* ways the "showpiece" of the chemotherapists. Through the use of such drugs as Daunorubicin, Prednisone, Vincristine, 6-MP, methotrexate, and BCNU, often in complex combinations, doctors at certain specialized cancer centers have been able to achieve 90 percent remission, and 70 percent survival beyond five years. This is remarkably better than the grim prognosis for this disease only a decade or so ago.

Other forms of cancer which have responded to chemotherapy include tes- *17* ticular tumors (30–40 percent respond, 2–3 percent cured); Wilms' tumor (treated in combination with surgery and/or radiation: 30–40 percent cured), and neuroblastoma (5 percent cured), and Hodgkin's disease, stage IIIB and IV (70 percent respond, 40 percent survive beyond five years) (ibid.).

In other forms of cancer, chemotherapy can offer palliation (partial or tem- *18* porary remission of the disease) and occasionally prolongation of life.

Unfortunately, the types of cancer which respond to chemotherapy are gen- *19* erally among the least common forms of the disease. The most common forms of cancer — the big killers such as breast, colon, and lung malignancies — generally do not respond to treatment with drugs. Furthermore, according to Maugh and Marx, chemotherapy is not very effective against tumors that have grown large or spread. Its greatest success are against small tumors that have only recently developed.

Chemotherapy has other drawbacks. There is an increased incidence of sec- *20* ond, apparently unrelated malignancies in patients who have been "cured" by means of anticancer drugs. This is probably because the drugs themselves are carcinogenic. When radiation and chemotherapy were given together, the incidence of these second tumors was approximately twenty-five times the expected rate (ibid.:123).

Since both radiation and chemotherapy suppress the immune system, it is *21* possible that new tumors are allowed to grow because the patient has been rendered unable to resist them. In either case, a person who is "cured" of cancer by these drastic means may find himself struggling with a new, drug-induced tumor a few years later.

Interest in cancer chemotherapy developed in part out of frustration with *22* the limitations of surgery and radiation therapy. Even scientists sympathetic to these two methods admit that they "have been near the limits of their utility for many years" (Maugh and Marx, 1975).

The inspiration for cancer chemotherapy was the antibiotic revolution of the 23
1930s. Coupled to this was the "crash program" concept popularized during
World War II.

"I am convinced that in the next decade, or maybe more, we will have a 24
chemical as effective against cancer as sulfanilomides and penicillin are against
bacterial infection," said Sloan-Kettering director C. P. "Dusty" Rhoads in 1953
(*Denver Post*, October 3, 1953).

"There is, for the first time, a scent of ultimate victory in the air," read an 25
article on anticancer drugs in *Reader's Digest* in February 1957.[1]

"We can look forward confidently to the control and ultimately the eradi- 26
cation of cancer," said the director of the National Cancer Institute in the 1950s.
He promised Congress major new gains "in the next few years" (*Denver Post*,
October 3, 1953).

In fact, announcing the imminent demise of cancer has become something 27
of a subspecialty within the medical profession, especially around the month
of April, when the American Cancer Society conducts its annual appeal drive.

"Nothing short of spectacular . . . a work of monumental importance" was 28
how one New York chemotherapist described a new drug treatment for breast
cancer (*New York Daily News*, February 17, 1976).

The public has become cynical and disgruntled about these claims, which 29
usually only succeed in raising false hope in the minds of cancer victims and
their families. "Cancer chemotherapists have a lingering poor reputation among
large segments of the lay public," say the authors of the *Science* report, who
are generally well-disposed toward the field. They attribute this in part to the
"bitter disappointment" of chemotherapy's painfully slow progress (Maugh and
Marx, 1975).

Many scientists have begun to question the basic premise of cancer chem- 30
otherapy, which is the use of toxic agents to kill every last cancer cell in the
body. Dr. Victor Richards, for example, calls chemotherapy "at best an uncertain method of therapy" because it cannot harm or kill cancer cells "without
producing comparable effects on normal cells." Chemotherapy succeeds because it is a systemic poison, and it fails for the same reason. Richards compares the use of such poisons to the difficulty of controlling

an expanding colony of mice by shooting them with a smaller number of bullets than
the number of mice. No matter how we calculate the firing system, one could see that
inevitably, if even two mice capable of mating remained, doubling of the population
would resume (Richards, 1972).

"With chemotherapy," he adds, "we have no sure shot. . . . It is clear that 31
we can never eliminate the last cancer cell by using anti-metabolites" (ibid.).

Given the generally poor performance of chemotherapy, its often horren- 32
dous side effects, and the limitations built into its very nature, why do orthodox doctors continue to promote this form of treatment as the wave of the future, and a "proven" method of treatment?

Among other factors, there are economic forces which help shape the direc- 33
tion of cancer therapy, diagnosis, prevention, and management. Drugs are central to the American economy, and it is perfectly logical from a business point
of view to seek a cure for cancer in the form of a patentable and marketable
drug.

The long-standing interest in such a cure, dating from before World War II, *34* has led to the creation of a "chemotherapy establishment" at all the major medical centers. These individuals are tied to the pharmaceutical industry not only philosophically but often materially as well. Some of them are consultants to drug companies, while others are directors or executives. No law requires companies or consultants to reveal their relationships. Thus it is possible that drug company influence at cancer centers is greater than appears from the public record. In addition, a number of drug company officials serve on NCI advisory committees.[2]

Grant money and gifts are available to those centers which work on drugs *35* in which the companies have a proprietary interest. Money is not generally available for substances or approaches in which drug companies have no such interest. Thus the "invisible hand" of the marketplace has chosen toxic chemotherapy for development and ignored other approaches which might be as promising from a medical, but not an economic, point of view.

Chemotherapists are latecomers to the cancer scene. ". . . lack of regard for *36* chemotherapists . . . has historically been exhibited by many surgeons and radiologists," according to the *Science* report on cancer (Maugh and Marx, 1975). Understandably, the chemotherapists have spoken in glowing terms about the effects of their agents, while underplaying the drawbacks. A steady stream of positive reports has made chemotherapy fully acceptable to medical practitioners.

Finally, if cancer specialists were to admit publicly that chemotherapy is of *37* limited usefulness and often dangerous, the public might demand a radical change in direction — possibly toward unorthodox and nontoxic methods, and toward cancer prevention.

By constantly touting the promise of anticancer drugs, orthodox practition- *38* ers ward off this challenge to their expertise and researchers parry the threat radically new concepts represent to their long years of research. The use of chemotherapy is even advocated by those members of the establishment who realize how ineffective and dangerous it can be.

Richards, for example, admits that in the major forms of cancer (lung, bowel, *39* stomach, pancreas, cervix, etc.) even *palliation* occurs only "for brief duration in about 5 to 10 percent of the cases." Yet he urges the use of drugs for such patients as well. His reason is revealing:

> Nevertheless, chemotherapy serves an extremely valuable role in keeping patients oriented toward proper medical therapy, and prevents the feeling of being abandoned by the physician in patients with late and hopeless cancers. Judicious employment and screening of potentially useful drugs may also prevent the spread of cancer quackery. . . . Properly based chemotherapy can serve a useful purpose in preventing improper orientation of the patient (Richards, 1972:215).

In Richards's view (and he is not alone) it is worthwhile to risk putting pa- *40* tients through the harrowing experience of nausea, vomiting, dizziness, hair loss, mouth sores, and possibly even premature death, simply in order to keep them "oriented toward proper medical therapy" and away from "cancer quackery."

The drug industry is not indifferent to developments in cancer research and *41* therapy.

"A cancer cure will be worth a fortune," a drug-company executive said in   *42*
the 1950s (Applezweig, 1978). Although no infallible "cure" has been discovered for any form of cancer, chemotherapy has become a $200-million-a-year industry. Stock analysts project a $1-billion-a-year business before long (ibid.).

For many years the drug industry showed only lukewarm interest in invest-   *43*
ing its own money in the search for anticancer drugs. According to Alan Klass, a Canadian surgeon and former chairman of the Manitoba Cancer Institute,

> more effort is devoted in the [drug] industry towards research in the area of fast sellers, for the potentially unlimited market of coughs, colds, pain relief, depressions, tensions, than to grim cancer. Prospects of financial success are immeasurably greater in the less grim group (Klass, 1975).

"These [anticancer] drugs are costly to develop and sales are still limited,"   *44*
an industry analyst wrote several years ago (de Haen, 1975).

Other pharmaceutical spokesmen have worried that an effective cancer cure   *45*
would upset the medical marketplace. "Nobody will be able to hold onto a cancer cure," a drug company executive predicted. "It would be too hot to handle" (Applezweig, 1978).

The president of Merck Sharpe & Dohme told *Fortune:*   *46*

> I've always had a horror of Merck having an exclusive position in a cancer drug. It's just so emotional. I have a feeling that if we gave it away free, people would say we were charging too much (Robertson, 1976).

Despite these fears and reservations, since the 1950s all the major drug   *47*
companies have maintained a presence in the cancer field. "All companies regard this work as a public service," Dr. C. Chester Stock of Sloan-Kettering Institute claimed in 1956. "For drug companies there won't be much money in anticancer drugs, but there will be a lot of prestige" (*Wall Street Journal*, February 8, 1956).

If only prestige were involved, however, as Stock claimed, the companies   *48*
were working at it with unusual zeal. Between 1946 and 1953 Parke-Davis alone sent 1,500 different chemical compounds to Sloan-Kettering for testing, according to the president of that drug firm (*Wakefield* [Mass.] *Item*, September 17, 1953).

Many of the hundreds of thousands of compounds tested at Sloan-Kettering   *49*
or the National Cancer Institute were submitted by industry, usually the largest pharmaceutical houses. A standardized legal agreement, drawn up by Frank Howard, a Standard Oil executive, was used to bring about a formal partnership between the company and Sloan-Kettering. The compounds were tested free of charge to the company. The agreement guaranteed a patent or a "perpetual non-exclusive, royalty-free license" for the company involved (Howard, 1962, contains a copy of the agreement). Howard was a firm advocate of patenting medical discoveries, such as cancer drugs. Speaking at George Washington University in 1956, he said:

> To undertake a costly industrial research or development project without inquiring into the patent situation is like drilling an exploratory oil well without finding out who owns the property on which you drill (Howard, 1956).

"Dusty" Rhoads, who shared with Howard the original idea for a cancer 50
drug testing institute, told a group of patent attorneys in 1940:

> In the near future patents may well control its [medicine's] entire development.
> . . . The patent lawyers can and do control the support of industrial science. I wish
> to establish clearly the need for, as well as the profits to be obtained from, intelligent
> study of the factors which influence the course of illness (Memorial, 1940).

In fact, almost every anti-cancer drug marketed since World War II has been 51
patented by its manufacturer, although most of the research was done at gov-
ernment-supported institutions. The agreement between industry and Sloan-
Kettering paid off in one case, that of methotrexate (amethopterin), which was
patented by Lederle Laboratories, a division of American Cyanamid, Inc. in
1951.[3] Under the "standard form" agreement, first used with Lederle, the company was given a patent, was allowed to keep drug research secret, and merely
had to provide the substance for testing.

The agreement was so favorable to industry not only because of the busi- 52
ness orientation of Memorial Sloan-Kettering's leaders, but because of the difficulty of getting profit-oriented drug companies to invest in the seemingly
"grim" field of cancer.

Sales figures for methotrexate were recently estimated at about $5 million 53
a year. With the adoption of a "high-dose methotrexate" regimen for a number
of different cancers, however, these sales figures have probably increased considerably. Methotrexate costs around $9 for 500 milligrams (International
Workshop, 1975). The high-dose regimen requires the use of hundreds of grams
of this substance per patient.

Today, the attitude of the drug companies toward cancer has changed con- 54
siderably. This is due in part to the progress that has been made in the past
twenty-five years in understanding cancer, progress which makes effective drug
treatment more possible. Drug companies have also been enticed into the field
by government grants disbursed by NCI.

In 1955, the center of drug testing shifted from Sloan-Kettering Institute to 55
NCI's Cancer Chemotherapy National Service Center in Bethesda, Maryland.
Congress allocated $25 million to test 20,000 chemicals a year at "The Wall
Street of Cancer Research," in the words of the center's director, Dr. Kenneth
M. Endicott (*Newsweek*, January 20, 1958).

Under this plan the government directly subsidized drug companies to do 56
research which, if successful, would create new products for them. For example, Chas. Pfizer & Co. received $1.2 million in 1958, Upjohn & Co. $150,000,
and Abbott Laboratories $208,000 (ibid.).

Most important in changing industry attitudes, however, have been market 57
factors. The drug industry traditionally has been one of the most profitable
businesses in the world. "For many years," says Dr. Klass, "the profits of the
drug industry have been twice the average for all other American industries"
(Klass, 1975:76). Most of these profits came from antibiotics, painkillers, or
mood-altering drugs such as Valium.

As patents have run out, and as the industry has faced increasingly costly 58
government regulations and other problems, profitability has also fallen. From
a pretax profit of 21 percent in 1973, the entire industry experienced a slump

in the latter 1970s. "Drug profitability is not what it used to be," *Chemical & Engineering News* complained in 1976. "Profit margins have dropped to a 10-year low" (*Chemical & Engineering News*, March 1, 1976). These worries have been compounded in recent years. "Evidence of the slow-down in ethical pharmaceutical volume abounds," writes Standard and Poor's *Industry Survey* (Standard and Poor's, 1979).

One of the main reasons for this drop has been a lack of new markets to   59
exploit. Patents have run out on many of the most profitable drugs of the 1950s and 1960s.

"What the drug industry needs is a major new product line," a Wall Street   60
analyst told *Business Week*. Not surprisingly, one of the areas he pinpointed as a potentially lucrative area was cancer chemotherapy (*Business Week*, January 17, 1977).

Although new cancer drug research is usually shrouded in secrecy, it is known   61
that such giant firms as Eli Lilly, Merck, and Hoffmann-La Roche are now spending an increasing proportion of their research budgets on cancer[4] (*Dun's Review*, December 1974; Robertson, 1976).

General disappointment with cancer chemotherapy has made the drug   62
companies look in other directions for an effective (and patentable) cancer medicine. One candidate is interferon — or more accurately, the interferons. These are naturally occurring substances which appear to have anticancer and antiviral effects.

Interferon was discovered in the 1950s and little interest was shown in de-   63
veloping its potential in the United States, mainly because of the difficulty of producing commercial amounts. Interferon is a natural substance which is formed by cells when they are attacked by viruses.

European studies showing anticancer results, plus an increased possibility   64
of synthesizing an active anticancer drug, have whetted the appetites of the drug companies. The American Cancer Society has now allocated $2 million to buy European interferon and test it in a "crash program" (ACS, 1978).

Should interferon turn out to be an effective agent, and should a way be   65
found to market it (or a substance which could stimulate its production in the human body), it could turn out to be a profitable breakthrough for the pharmaceutical industry.

The potential profits to be derived from interferon production are huge, and   66
the competition is fierce.

Interferon, like radium seventy-five years ago, is fabulously expensive. One   67
ounce of interferon is worth $1.8 billion (*Omni*, July 1979). In 1975 it was estimated that interferon treatment for cancer costs $500–$5,000 per patient per day, depending on the dosage given (International Workshop, 1975:12). It was hoped at the time that new techniques would bring this cost down five to tenfold within a few years. But one industry spokesman has said the price is likely to be *multiplied* by three (ibid.:85).

The cost has come down, but not that much. At the present time 150 cancer   68
patients are being treated with interferon at ten United States cancer centers at an average cost of $50,000 per patient (*New York Post*, June 28, 1979).

Even should the price drop, the cost will certainly remain considerable. In   69
the clinical trials conducted in Sweden at the Karolinska Institute, interferon

was given three times a week for one and a half years. At 1975 prices, this equals between $117,000 and $1,170,000 per patient.

This represents a considerable potential market for the drug companies. 70 Several patents already have been taken out on interferon purification processes. Not surprisingly, then, there is intense competition for techniques, contacts, and markets.

The 1975 International Workshop on Interferon, chaired by Dr. Mathilde Krim 71 of Sloan-Kettering, noted:

> A separate "workshop" session . . . dealt with the cost of production of human interferon. This session was attended by a number of representatives from the [drug] industry, obviously interested in the development of production facilities. However, there was considerable reluctance on the part of industry representatives to quote cost estimates in a public forum. (Interestingly enough, the same individuals were quite eager to discuss the problem in their competitors' absence.) (International Workshop, 1975:66).

When the American Cancer Society, Memorial Sloan-Kettering, National 72 Cancer Institute, and the National Institute for Allergy and Infectious Diseases sponsored the Second International Workshop on Interferons at Rockefeller University, April 22–24, 1979, the list of contributors to the meeting read like a Who's Who of the drug field. It included Baxter-Travenol Laboratories, Bristol-Myers Co., Burroughs Wellcome Co., Cutter Laboratories, Hoffmann–La Roche, Inc., Johnson & Johnson, Merck Sharpe & Dohme, Miles Laboratories, Monsanto Co., Pfizer Inc., Schering-Plough Corp., Searle Laboratories, Smith Kline and French, U.S.V. Pharmaceuticals, and Warner-Lambert (Second International Workshop, 1979).[5]

Nor have the big companies been neglecting the chemical approach to can- 73 cer, although it has been plagued with disappointments. Thus, in recent years, Bristol-Myers has won approval for the commercial marketing of Platinol (cis-platinum), a drug used in the treatment of bladder cancer (MSKCC, 1976). Bristol-Myers also won approval in March 1977 to market BiCNU. And I.C.I. Americas received approval from the U.S. government to sell Nolvadex, a drug used in the treatment of advanced breast cancer (*New York Times,* July 23, 1978).

Cancer drugs represent a tantalizing possibility to the drug companies. In a 74 few special instances it has paid off well. In the United States, the best seller has been Adriamycin, an anticancer antibiotic noted for its extreme toxicity. It is owned outright by Adria Laboratories, a joint venture of Hercules, Inc., and the Montedison Group of Italy. The drug is said to produce regressions in such conditions as lymphoblastic leukemia, acute myeloblastic leukemia, Wilms' tumor, and various other kinds of carcinoma, including Hodgkin's disease (de Haen, 1975).

During its first year on the market (1974) Adriamycin sold an impressive 75 $10 million. And although the United States government routinely hides sales figures on drugs — "to avoid disclosing figures for individual companies" — it is believed that sales have increased considerably since then.[6]

Adriamycin illustrates how the public pays for these drugs to be developed 76 and then pays again — this time at monopoly prices — to purchase these drugs from private companies. Montedison, the Italian conglomerate, attempted to find a United States licensee for its product in 1969. At that time, however, the United States drug industry still had little interest in investing in cancer drugs. The Italian firm finally made an arrangement with the National Cancer Institute under which the U.S. government and Sloan-Kettering Institute would test the drug in animals and humans. United States researchers did much of the work to develop the drug in this country and even obtained permission from the Food and Drug Administration to market it. Of course, United States taxpayer money paid for this expensive work. But the patent remained in the hands of its original owners, who have profited handsomely by this arrangement (Applezweig, 1978).

Even more profitable has been the Soviet drug Ftorafur. This compound has   77
been patented by the Soviet Institute of Organic Synthesis, which has licensed the Japanese Taiho company to market the drug in Japan.

Analysts are not sure of the exact composition of Ftorafur. It appears to be   78
an oral, relatively nontoxic form of the American drug 5-fluorouracil.[7]

Ftorafur is doing better than any American drug for cancer. Sales in 1976   79
were $100 million, or roughly ten times the best-selling drug in the United States.

The main reason for Ftorafur's success, however, was the unusual — some   80
would say reckless — way in which the drug has been marketed. "Some Japanese physicians," it is said, "now tend to identify 'precancerous' states, 'risk of cancer' or 'susceptibility to cancer' and treat the patient prophylactically [i.e., preventively] with anticancer drugs" (Applezweig, 1978).

This situation arises because Japanese physicians routinely sell drugs to their   81
patients. Ftorafur reputedly comes with a high retail markup, which naturally encourages the physician to sell more drugs. If "risk of cancer" now makes one a candidate for an anticancer drug, then every Japanese (and American) could now be considered a candidate for Ftorafur. Because of the radically different way in which drugs are marketed in the United States, however, it is unlikely that American companies could repeat the success of their Japanese counterparts (ibid.).

The drug industry is a kind of "silent partner" in the cancer research enter-   82
prise. It has managed to invest relatively little in the cancer problem, yet stands to reap tremendous benefits when and if a "breakthrough" is found.

Through its many interlocks with the research centers and the American   83
Cancer Society, and through selective funding of specific research projects such as interferon, it maintains its presence in the field. The domination of investment bankers and industrialists over the cancer field guarantees that the ultimate "cure for cancer" will come marked "Patent Pending" and, most probably, "Made in U.S.A."

NOTES

[1] *Reader's Digest* is often a barometer of orthodox thinking on the cancer problem. Laurance S. Rockefeller, chairman of the board of Memorial Sloan-Kettering, is a director of the magazine's parent company, and the *Digest's* publisher, DeWitt Wallace is, in turn, a major contributor to the New York cancer center.

[2] Patricia E. Byfield, associate research scientist, Upjohn, serves on NCI's Breast Cancer Task Force Committee; Hans J. Hansen, director, department of immunology, Hoffmann-La Roche, serves on NCI's Developmental Therapeutics Committee; Bruce Johnson, analytical research department, Pfizer, serves on the Large Bowel and Pancreatic Cancer Review Committee; Irving Johnson, vice-president for research, Lilly, serves on the Developmental Therapeutics Committee; Gary L. Neil, head of cancer re-

search, Upjohn, also serves on the Developmental Therapeutics Committee; and Arthur Weissbach, head, department of cell biology, Roche Institute, serves on NCI's Cause and Prevention Scientific Review Committee (NI, 1979).

[3] MSKCC overseer and former Sloan-Kettering chairman James Fisk, Ph.D., is a director of American Cyanamid, Inc.

[4] The drug industry is said to be "notorious for secrecy" (*Dun's Review*, December 1974:55). Nevertheless, the chairman of Merck has acknowledged that his company is working on a cancer vaccine (ibid.).

[5] Industry speakers were well represented in most of the scientific sessions, which testifies to the seriousness with which it regards this research. An Upjohn scientist spoke at the morning session (April 22) on "interferon inducers," a Burroughs Wellcome researcher spoke that afternoon on "antiviral activities of interferons *in vivo*," etc. In all, fifty-seven drug company representatives attended.

[6] Quote from a government report on pharmaceutical preparations (U.S. Department of Commerce, Bureau of the Census, 1977). "Data on new prescriptions are compiled privately for drug manufacturers by a company that copyrights its figures. Thus, they rarely work their way directly into public hands . . ." (*Wall Street Journal*, July 8, 1976).

[8] The patent on 5-FU, as it is called, was held for seventeen years by Hoffmann - La Roche and the American Cancer Society (25 percent). Perhaps by coincidence, one of the founders of the ACS, Elmer Bobst, is a former president of Hoffmann-La Roche.

Considerations

1. Assemble all of Ralph Moss's objections and reservations concerning chemotherapy; then present them in a forceful summary.
2. What benefits does chemotherapy have? Building on points acknowledged by Moss, make as strong a case as you can for chemotherapy. You might try some role playing: what would a chemotherapist say to Moss?
3. Classify according to severity the criticisms Moss makes of the nation's drug industry and of the medical profession.
4. Where proof is lacking for chemotherapy's ability to halt cancer, what motivations might contribute to its widespread use? Write a speculative essay, drawing on Moss's piece but adding reflections of your own.
5. After reading the biographical note about Moss, assess his possible motives for writing his book. Do you feel that any of those motives affect his argument?
6. How is this selection structured? Is it simply a string of accusations and criticisms, or is it kept coherent by some other means?

Connections

1. Compare the way chemotherapy works with the way radiotherapy does.
2. Compare the perspectives, attitudes, or tone of Ralph Moss with either Lucien Israël or Richard Selzer.
3. What do you think John Cairns would make of Moss's claims? In a short essay, write his probable response.
4. Based on what you have read so far, draft a short essay on "The Economics of Cancer" (for a possible model, see "The Economics of Animal Extinction" in Chapter 9, The Impact of Animals). What you draft here could serve as a trial balloon for a later essay based on some facts and figures.

Images That Heal
Maggie Scarf

"Depression," wrote Arnold A. Hutschnecker in his 1951 book *The Will to Live*,   1
"is a partial surrender to death." Because mind and body are indivisibly intertwined, "we ourselves choose the time of illness, the kind of illness, the course
of illness, and its gravity." Hutschnecker, an authority on psychosomatic medicine, believed that many diseases are nothing other than the expression of a
person's need to withdraw, for a while, from the frays and strains of living. He
believed, too, that death itself is sometimes an individual's way of ending a
painful emotional struggle, of resolving an emotional conflict. "We are moving
toward a recognition that in illness of any kind, from the common cold to cancer, emotional stress plays a part," observed this physician.

Hutschnecker's book, published almost 30 years ago, can now be seen as an   2
early swallow heralding what has become the full, flowering summer of the
view that body and mind are one, an interrelated whole. In the field of cancer
medicine, one of the major exponents of this view is O. Carl Simonton, a 38-
year-old physician who practices in Forth Worth, Texas. Simonton is convinced that psychological forces play an important role in the development of
cancer and that psychological forces can be mobilized to defeat or delay its
course. In his opinion, cancer flourishes in a climate of emotional despair, and
one of the most effective ways of battling the disease is a special technique
that he has developed: a form of positive thinking called "imaging," the central feature of the Simonton method. In this process, cancer patients conjure
up mental images of a sort of inner battlefield upon which healthy cells can be
"observed" putting the malignant ones to rout.

There seem to be Simonton method practitioners — and Simonton patients   3
— everywhere. And, in response to ever-increasing demands for information,
counseling, and treatment, Carl Simonton and his partner, Stephanie Mat-
thews-Simonton, established their own Cancer Counseling and Research Center in 1973. The pair are in heavy demand as lecturers, and they have won an
impressive following among nurses, social workers, psychologists, psychiatrists, and some physicians. According to Stephanie Simonton, more than 500
professionals who work with cancer patients have been trained in the Simonton method. But the response from most doctors has been less favorable; many,
in fact, are indignantly critical.

All the same, given the current *Zeitgeist*, their emergence on the cancer scene   4
is far from surprising. The belief that mind and body affect each other, in sick-

*Maggie Scarf (b. 1932) is a science writer specializing in psychological topics.
She is best known for her study of depression in the lives of women,* Unfinished
Business *(1980). A collection of her essays,* Body, Mind, Behavior *(1976) won one
of several awards she has received from the American Psychological Association.*

ness and in health, has gained a good deal of respectability over the course of the past couple of decades. The rise of the holistic health movement (itself a response to the increasing dehumanization of medical treatment) has given added impetus to this tendency to see what is mental and what is physical as different aspects of the very same entity, the integrated, whole human being.

"One immediate implication" of the holistic health view, psychologist Ken- 5
neth Pelletier wrote in *Mind as Healer, Mind as Slayer,* "is that all disorders are psychosomatic, in the sense that both mind and body are involved in their etiology. Any disorder is created out of a complex interaction of social factors, physical and psychological stress, the personality of the person subjected to these influences, and the inability of the person to adapt adequately to pressures. Once illness is viewed as a complex interaction of these factors, then it is possible to view symptoms as an early indication of excessive strain upon the mind/body system." Many major diseases are "afflictions of civilization," that is, maladaptive responses to chronic and unresolvable emotional stresses. "A medical symptom," Pelletier observed, "may be a useful signal of the need for change in other parts of the person's life."

[Here Scarf goes on to discuss other influential books by Lawrence LeShan and Norman Cousins about the mind's possible role in promoting and counteracting disease. Then she tells of meeting two of the Simontons' former patients, both of whom underwent chemotherapy but credit the remission of their cancers to the Simontons' methods, particularly the practice called *imaging*.]

Simonton, during our first meeting, seemed preoccupied. He was simulta- 6
neously dealing with his patients and a television crew taping a documentary on his technique. A stocky man, he wears glasses and has a crown of auburn curls framing his dimpled, cherubic face. Simonton has been championing his psychological approach to cancer treatment ever since he was a resident in training as a radiation therapist at the University of Oregon Medical School in the early 1970s. It was then that he first became interested in ways of motivating his patients more effectively. "I was, at first, simply trying to get them to co-operate with our standard clinical research program," he told me, "but that wasn't always easy. I needed to get them to come in twice a day for the treatments. Some patients would forget; some just wouldn't do it."

Simonton began noticing that the more he could get his patients involved 7
in their own care, the better they seemed to do. "A patient's positive attitude affected not only the ease with which treatment schedules could be met," he said, "but it impacted, indirectly, on the state of the disease itself. As the patient got more involved — with diet, exercise, and a number of other small, daily things — it influenced his physical functioning." And as Simonton saw how the patient's changing state of mind could affect the course of the illness, he became "really excited."

Reading about methods that have been used to motivate people, he soon 8
realized that "the techniques seemed to have one central feature in common, which is that they involved the person's picturing the desired outcome." For the cancer patient, the desired outcome would obviously be a slowing down or complete remission of the malignant illness.

Accordingly, in 1971, Simonton asked one of his patients, a 61-year-old man   9
with advanced throat cancer, to begin the daily practice of relaxation and "imaging": mentally picturing his radiation treatments and the effects they were
having upon his disease. The radiation therapy was to be visualized as a stream
of tiny bullets of energy that struck all body cells, normal and abnormal, but
destroyed only the weaker, aberrant, "confused" ones — the cancer cells. The
patient was instructed to imagine his body's white blood cells coming in,
swarming over the dead and dying cancer cells, and flushing them off (via the
liver and kidneys) as one might remove the dead and dying enemy from the
field of lost battle. Each imaging session was to close with the patient's visualizing his tumor as decreasing in size and his health as returning to normal.

"The results of treatment were both thrilling and frightening," Simonton re-   10
ported in a 1976 interview printed in *Prevention* magazine. "Within two weeks,
his cancer had noticeably diminished, and he was rapidly gaining weight."

After this almost miraculous success, Simonton told me, he tried a similar   11
approach with some of his other patients. "I was soon convinced: changing the
person's attitudes could have profound effects on physical outcome." The patient's own expectations — of illness and death, or of eventual return to health
— provided some mysterious handle that could regulate the progress of the
illness. Simonton's goal, he said, was to understand this handle better and make
it more accessible to people suffering from cancer. Gradually he moved further
away from standard cancer therapy and developed his own, primarily psychological, treatment approach. When I asked him how frequently he now gives
radiation treatments, he replied: "Rarely. Almost never." But he was swift to
add that he remains a member in good standing of his county medical society.
He could treat cancer patients along more traditional lines again should he
ever choose to do so.

That seems an unlikely eventuality. His Cancer Counseling and Research   12
Center is thriving. It is true, though, that despite the name of the center, almost no face-to-face counseling seems to take place there, and there is no full-
time researcher on the premises. There are seven employees, including an executive director, a secretary and program coordinator, a mailroom person, a
receptionist, and a telephone counselor. The business of the center, Simonton
acknowledged, is primarily communicational; he called it a "communications
center." It is, he said, a nonprofit organization supported partly by funds generated by workshops and training sessions for people who work with cancer
patients. Other income derives from the mail-order sale of books and tapes explaining the method and giving instructions for its home use. Lectures by the
Simontons command a fee of $2,000 each. Patients pay a fee of $1,900 for a 10-
day program that includes a physical examination, a battery of psychological
tests, and several group psychotherapy sessions. When I asked for a rough estimate of the center's yearly income, Simonton could not provide a figure. But
the Simontons were not at a loss when I asked them to explain their ideas about
the causes of cancer. It is not, they say, a disease that comes out of nowhere,
that develops in a psychological vacuum. The Simontons believe that a lethal
confluence of personality traits and stressful life events bring the illness into
being. They argue that there is a cancer-prone personality, that a certain com-

bination of traits makes some people especially vulnerable to cancer. Simonton listed these characteristics in a 1975 article: "First, a great tendency to hold resentment and marked inability to forgive; second, a tendency toward self-pity; third, a poor ability to develop and maintain meaningful long-term relationships; and fourth, a very poor self-image." These qualities, Simonton proposes, make it difficult for a person to deal with emotions at a conscious level, to acknowledge negative feelings and then deal with them.

"The biggest single factor that I can find as a predisposing factor to the actual development of the disease," Simonton wrote, "is the loss of a serious love object, occurring 6 months to 18 months prior to the diagnosis." Another emotional reverse that can precipitate cancer, he says, is the loss of a significant life role, perhaps through the death of a spouse or as a result of getting fired. The potential patient responds to the loss, whatever it is, with profound feelings of helplessness and hopelessness. But these feelings are not acknowledged inwardly or expressed to others; the cancer-prone patient puts on a happy face and denies any sense of loss, anger, distress, disappointment, or despair.   *13*

But the feelings, which the Simontons term "negative emotions," are there just the same and are eventually given somatic expression. Malignancy is thus despair that has been experienced biologically, despair at the level of the cell. In this sense, suggest the Simontons, none of us *gets* cancer; we reach a point at which our deepest need and wish is to withdraw from life, and we therefore "choose" to develop cancer. "The answer to the cancer patient's perennial question, the question of 'Why me?' " Simonton stated, "is always that it's 'me' because some time within the past year or 18 months I simply gave up on my life." Cancer is a state of despair made manifest and real. In the Simontons' view, the illness is a defective coping strategy used by someone who was not able to meet an adaptive demand, someone who could not deal with a stressful loss or life change, and for whom death had come to appear the only possible answer.   *14*

How, though, could emotions contribute to the onset of cancer? How could negative "feeling states" be translated into malignant cells? The link between mind and body, the Simontons say, is the body's natural defense system, our immune reaction to anything foreign or abnormal in the blood. It is a failure in the immune-defensive system, they theorize, that allows the cancer to develop and grow.   *15*

The idea that the immune response is the body's most important defense against cancer has enjoyed wide medical support over the past decade. According to the theory of immunologic surveillance, aberrant cells develop in our bodies periodically, but immune mechanisms reject them in the incipient phase of tumor formation by surrounding and destroying them. The immune-defensive system constantly watches over our interior milieu, defending us from within — unless the integrity of the immune mechanisms has been compromised. This can happen, the Simontons maintain, under the pressure of chronic emotional stress.   *16*

"I believe that the immune system is affected by psychological factors in two ways — across two biological pathways, that is," Simonton told me. "One   *17* is directly through the central nervous system, probably the hypothalamus, and there you get a direct suppressive effect that goes from thoughts to suppression of the immune system. The other pathway is through the endocrines and the hormones." Hormonal imbalances created by psychic stress, he said, further suppress immune responses.

Since emotional states contribute to illness, they can also contribute to health, 18 the Simontons wrote in *Getting Well Again.* "By acknowledging your own participation in the onset of the disease, you acknowledge your power to participate in regaining your health and you have also taken the first step toward getting well again."

The Simontons require their patients to remain in treatment with conven- 19 tional cancer specialists. Meanwhile, the Simonton method makes some genuflections in the direction of improved diet, exercise, and massage, but these are peripheral. The main approach is psychological, and twofold. Patients are supposed to "de-stress," ridding themselves of pent-up negative emotions. They are also supposed to "image positive expectancies" in an effort to influence the immune-defensive system directly. . . .

Each imaging session begins with a period of progressive relaxation. Using 20 standard relaxation procedures, the patient slowly untenses body musculature, moving from one set of muscles to the next. Anne Walsh, for one, finds this wonderful. "I get in touch with not only my physical but my spiritual body, and with my energy," she told me. "I get a tremendous feeling of well-being."

Having relaxed herself thoroughly in this fashion, she begins picturing the 21 drug she is getting in chemotherapy as a powerful "transformative" substance coursing through her bloodstream. The scenario runs like this: The drug transforms her leukocytes into voracious sharks and the cancer cells into "frightened, grayish little fish." The shark/leukocytes pursue the grayish fish/cancer cells, which are envisioned as disorganized and disoriented, and then pounce upon them, rending them to bits with their long, jagged teeth and destroying them. At last, when the cancerous areas have been cleared out completely, the sharks are transformed into ordinary white blood cells once again and continue to course through her bloodstream. The chemotherapeutic agents, together with any "fish/cancer" refuse that remains, are visualized as being flushed out with her body fluids. All is peaceful; all is clean and healthy within. This is imaging.

The quality of the images is as important as regular imaging sessions, Si- 22 monton patients told me. If, for example, a person continually sees the white blood cells as weaker than the cancer cells, it bodes badly for the progress of the disease; the patient is visualizing the immune system in terms that imply that it will eventually be overpowered.

On the other hand, a patient with advanced colon cancer explained, it is 23 unwise to imagine the leukocytes as having hugely disproportionate strength: "I was seeing a huge armament train with big guns and supplies behind it, which was enough to destroy a whole army. That was the white blood cells. And then the cancer cells were like small people, and they were just — just standing there. Just a few of them. And Carl said that that wouldn't do, that I was setting myself up for failure. Because if my army was that powerful, and I had the slightest setback, I'd feel that *nothing* could work. He said, 'You've really put yourself in danger because of the imbalance of those forces.' Yes, the cancer cells were weak, but the proportions were all wrong."

All the patients I spoke to believed that the program, particularly the im- 24
aging, was slowing down or had halted the course of their illness. But I wondered if that could really be so. What solid evidence is there, anyway, linking
emotional factors to the onset or course of cancer? What proof is there that the
immune system is at fault in cancer? Could a process like imaging really influence the progress of malignant diseases that had been pronounced beyond hope
of cure?

One of the first objections I raised with Simonton was that everyone expe- 25
riences stress. "Even though I myself don't have cancer," I said, "I'm sure there
are issues, frustrations, and so forth in my own life, right now. And if I were
ill I could name five big stresses that I was experiencing, but I'm not sure how
much that would really mean."

"Anybody could," agreed Simonton readily. But, he added, there are differ- 26
ences between people who develop cancer and people who do not. "The cancer
patient is someone who's invested a lot in putting up a façade of being happy
when in fact he's terribly depressed. The person who shows his depression is
expressing that emotion; the depression becomes that person's illness. But if
you've got an individual who's depressed and not communicating, who's given
up on his life and yet isn't *telling* people that he's given up on his life, then he's
throwing all that energy into keeping up that façade, you see, of being happy.
This, it appears, is when malignancy develops — or advances," Simonton said.

"You are saying, then, that prior to the illness, depression and despair are 27
always somewhere in the cancer picture?"

He nodded. "They are there to a very significant degree." 28

Simonton himself, as I knew from his writings, had had cancer. I asked him 29
what type of malignancy it was.

"I had a skin cancer on the left side of my nose when I was 16," he answered 30
quickly. "Since that time, I have managed to trace back to what the emotional
issues were. I was unaware, at the time that this was going on, of the things
that were happening to me and in my life." He paused briefly, then said: "The
cancer was surgically removed. Having surgery on my face — and cancer on
my face — at age 16 was very, very scary. A lot more scary to me than I could
admit until some years later."

Then he told me: "I myself have a lot of the cancer personality. Part of my 31
work is a way of working out my own craziness, my own conflicts around these
particular areas. And, you know, I had a second cancer — much later — which
developed around very similar kinds of issues."

I was taken aback. "Issues that had to do with . . . ?" 32

"Loss of face." I stared at him, and Simonton blushed slightly and said, 33
"Literally. These things are so painfully simple." After the development of his
second cancer, he continued, he had made the decision to work on it using Simonton techniques, rather than having it surgically removed.

"It took me a year to get rid of it, and it was really frustrating. I felt like a 34
failure," he confessed. "Because, I mean, how could I teach my patients to get
rid of these terrible incurable cancers when I had this skin cancer on my own

face and I couldn't get rid of it?" Simonton paused, and the pause was tense and prolonged. "Finally, it went away. I was very pleased," he said at last.

Despite Simonton's sense of conviction about his own experience and that *35*
of other cancer victims, no systematic association between cancer and personality or stressful life events has been proved beyond the shadow of scientific doubt. Most of the research on personality traits that are "predisposing" to cancer and the work on the presumed relationship between stressful events and cancer simply wilt under the bright light of objective assessment.

One serious criticism that has been leveled at some of this research is that *36*
biases are built into the experimental design. For example, many of the studies demonstrating that cancer patients are "different" in some way — that they are people whose premorbid personality characteristics have rendered them more vulnerable to malignancy — have used subjects who were already ill at the time the research was done. The naive assumption was that the patients were essentially unchanged by their illness. But many tumors emit fluids that mimic adrenal hormones and neurotransmitter substances (such as the mood-affecting dopamine and serotonin). The illness itself could thus precipitate changes in brain physiology and, hence, in psychological functioning. Not only that, but the patient's psychological functioning could certainly be affected by the trauma of having a life-threatening illness. In much of this research, then, it really isn't clear whether the investigators discovered a "cancer personality" or a personality brought about by the disease itself.

Other flaws in such research include faulty or nonexistent control groups, *37*
inability to replicate results, and lack of appropriate statistical analyses of the data. Moreover, the findings are often contradictory.

A number of investigators have, for instance, found that the cancer patient *38*
is helpless and hopeless before his illness. Lawrence LeShan concluded from his own studies that "an individual does not just get malignancy, which starts on the immunological or endocrinological or psychological level. The entire organism eventuates towards cancer. His total biography, involving all its levels, moves in a direction leading to a total, organism-in-an-environment situation, which we term 'neoplastic disease' . . . 'cancer' is a total organismic situation. . . . "

A poetic statement to the effect that the organism has wanted to sicken and *39*
to die! LeShan's findings, though, are at variance with those of Steven Greer and Tina Morris, who carried out a controlled study of 160 women admitted to King's College Hospital, London, and reported (in 1975) that "we were unable to confirm earlier reports of associations between cancer and such variables as previous stress — particularly loss of a loved person — habitual denial in the face of stress, and depression."

Clause Bahnson, a psychoanalytic researcher, has noted "conformism" and *40*
"religiosity" as prominent personality features of women who develop breast cancer. But a group of Japanese physicians (Yujiro Ikemi and his colleagues) recently reported that a series of patients who had experienced spontaneous regression of their life-threatening tumors had one thing in common: a deep religious faith.

Finally, if stress and cancer are linked; wouldn't people subjected to un- *41* usual degrees of stress — prisoners of war, for instance — show higher rates of cancer later on in their lives? Robert J. Keehn of the Medical Follow-up Agency of the National Academy of Sciences National Research Council recently looked at this particular phenomenon. After studying former World War II and Korean War prisoners, Keehn found their cancer death rates were no different from cancer death rates in the population at large. Keehn did report that the ex-prisoners showed elevated death rates, but they died from such causes as suicide, accidents, tuberculosis, and cirrhosis of the liver.

The positive-sounding findings on the psychological "causes" of cancer are 42
so fascinating, so satisfying in some way, that the negative ones tend to be ignored, at least by laymen. However, Bernard Fox, social-science manager of the field studies and statistics program of the National Cancer Institute and the author of what is generally considered the most elegant and authoritative review of research in this area, has summarized the situation thus: "From the apparent facts, I take the position that early cancers are predominantly hereditary . . . with very small contribution by stress *specific to the individual.* In the middle years, perhaps ages 40 to 60, I propose a larger contribution to the start of cancers, say 10 percent, is attributable to the increased susceptibility associated with *individual* stress. In later years I suggest that the contribution of psychological factors and/or stress declines, so that by age 70 most of the causing agents initiate cancer by virtue of the stimulus becoming great enough . . . (e.g., accumulating cancer-causing agents) and by virtue of the host's threshold of response being lowered. . . . In these years, I feel that psychological factors and/or stress contribute relatively little."

Jimmie Holland, chief of psychiatry at the Sloan-Kettering Institute for 43
Cancer Research, takes a similar position in an article in the book *Cancer Medicine:* "Since neoplastic cells develop in so many species of life, including dogs, reptiles, fish, and plants, emotional factors must certainly be of secondary importance in the causation of cancer, compared to biological etiological factors."

This remark has the ring of good common sense. It is certainly difficult to 44
imagine "emotional factors" as contributing to malignancy in a rattlesnake or a plant. It has been observed, moreover, that domestic animals rarely develop diseases in which psychological factors do appear to play some role, such as asthma, duodenal ulcer, and hypertension. Rheumatoid polyarthritis is simply unknown among these animals, but cancers — lymphomas, osteosarcomas — are not at all uncommon. This suggests, once again, a primarily biological etiology.

It is nevertheless strange but true that the best evidence in support of an 45
association between stress and neoplasms has emerged from animal experimentation. These studies have demonstrated that stress can affect the development of cancer in two ways. It can either speed up or it can delay the number of tumors and the time at which they appear. In other words, depending on the genetic strain of the animal, its age, the type of stress (crowding, electric shock, handling, forced restraint), stressful experience can make the animal either more or less vulnerable.

In 1972, B. H. Newberry and his colleagues showed that both electric shock 46
and forced restraint reduced the number of tumors developing in rats injected

with DMBA (dimethylbenzanthracene), a potent carcinogen. By contrast, the microbiologist Vernon Riley found a clear relationship between cancer incidence and stress.

Riley used female mice of a genetic strain that is bred to be susceptible to   47
mammary tumor and that usually develops tumors within 8 to 18 months of birth. As Riley reported in *Science* in 1975, mice that had been exposed to chronic stress (from living on open racks, handling, dust, odor, noise, anxiety) were strikingly more afflicted than were those that had been kept in a protected environment (on enclosed, ventilated shelves, with little or no handling by humans and little or no exposure to anxiety-producing disturbances). Mammary tumor incidences at 400 days varied from 92 percent among stressed mice to 7 percent among those who had found their world a better place in which to live.

In another experiment, Riley found that stress in mice led to involution of   48
the thymus gland and a subsequent compromise of the organism's immunological competence. Aha, the reader may say. Here are positive findings, from reliable animal data, supporting the immune-surveillance theory. So wouldn't it be reasonable to suppose that what has been shown to be true in animals will one day be demonstrated to be true among humans? Not necessarily. For one thing, animal cancers are in many respects different from human ones. While all kinds of tumors in animals can be affected by loss of immunological competence, this does not appear to be the case when it comes to humans. This brings me to the reasons for the current medical disillusionment with the theory that our immune-defensive system ordinarily protects us from cancer.

The biggest difficulty with the theory has to do with the observation that   49
people whose immune function has been deliberately suppressed — for example, patients who have just undergone a kidney transplant — do show a higher risk (35 times higher) of developing cancer in the immune system itself, but they don't show a heightened rate of cancer in any other sites. This discovery leaves the hypothesis of a link between stress and carcinogenesis in a far more tenuous state, and as Dr. Paul Calabresi, a cancer specialist, noted in a recent medical textbook, "a number of findings have contributed to a decline in popularity of the immune-surveillance theory." Another physician, Richard T. Prehn, has pointed out that immune mechanisms can at times stimulate cancer-cell growth.

Such studies obviously present intellectual difficulties for followers of the   50
Simontons, because the practice of imaging is supposed to influence the immune-defensive system. If (a big "if") imaging does affect a person's immune system, what assurance is there that this is the system that needs to be influenced? Doubts abound, for the Simontons' theoretical construction appears to have many loose seams. I therefore asked Dr. Simonton what evidence he could provide that his system cures or slows down cancer.

His answer, when it came, was slow and thoughtful. "All I can say is that it   51
appears to be the case that, by working along these lines, by acknowledging the ways in which one has let the cancer in, due to one's ways of responding to stress and particularly stressful losses, and then by exploring new options and new ways of handling stresses, a person can have longer survival, an improved quality of life during the time that he or she remains alive, and an improved quality of death."

"At least," he added, his voice serious and gentle, "it *appears* that way."   *52*

"But can you give me some facts and figures?" I asked. Simonton responded   *53*
with the statement that patients in his program had approximately twice the
normal life expectancy for their diagnoses.

"How many patients are you referring to?"   *54*

The physician lifted his shoulders in a mild shrug. "Oh, in terms of numbers   *55*
who have lived long enough, we're probably talking about close to 100 — people who have outlived life expectancy, that is — and this increases every year.
Enough so that we can say there *appears* to be a trend."

This was not, in terms of scientific evidence, an impressive statement.   *56*
"Suppose then," I said, "that I myself were a cancer patient. And I came to
you and told you that I thought I was like the typical patient described in your
book: someone who was feeling helpless and hopeless, who'd lost someone significant to her within the past year or so and then developed a malignant tumor. And suppose I asked whether you believed you could help me get better."

Would he, I inquired, tell me that he could do so?   *57*

Simonton shook his head. He would never promise that he could make any   *58*
patient better. What he could do would be to teach the patient some things
that would increase her likelihood of living longer, of having a better quality
of life, and of ultimately dying a better death. "I would tell the patient that I
believe that to be true," he explained carefully, "and that I could show her a
lot of reasons for my belief. And I would suggest to her that she assume, for
the meanwhile, that it *may* be true and work along these lines. And that's all,
that's it; there's no guarantee."

"But you would still think it worth a try for that patient?"   *59*

"As much as I think it's worth a try for *me*," responded Simonton. "This is   *60*
what I'm spending my own time doing, as a cancer specialist. It's important
enough for me to spend my time doing it, and if the patient wants to do it,
that's fine." His expression was stern. "The patient may not find it worth her
time. It will probably make her feel worse in the beginning, as she begins to
understand the ways in which she participated in developing her illness. Most
people do feel worse at the outset, because they're uncovering a lot of painful
areas. The patient may feel worse, die faster. But," he added, "I like doing it."

This comment, seeming to come out of nowhere, startled me. "Why?" I asked   *61*
him. "Because," replied the physician, "it enriches my life."

"In what way?"   *62*

"Oh . . . " He hesitated momentarily, then answered slowly. "I feel I un-   *63*
derstand myself better. I feel good, as if the work I do means something."

Among those who share Simonton's views about cancer and the psyche is   *64*
Bernard Siegel, a New Haven surgeon who was trained by Simonton and now
runs a psychotherapy group for cancer patients in his community. "If people
answer to what's going on in their heads, they don't have to get physically sick,"
he told me. "What the illness says is that the person has picked the wrong road
in life and must change. If he can change in a positive way, that will affect his
survival." It may be difficult to prove this scientifically, he admitted, but he
insisted that "People are too hung up on statistics and evidence, when statistics are killing people. While emotions — and learning how to discharge emotions — is the kind of thing that's making them well."

Many cancer specialists consider the Simonton method a form of medical 65
evangelism in which old-fashioned sin is replaced by depression, repression,
and denial, and redemption requires confession and an altered lifestyle. The
metaphors used by Simonton — personality change and rebirth into health —
do in fact resemble the metaphors of religion.

If there is one aspect of the method that seems to stick in people's craws 66
more than any other, it is the notion of the cancer patient as the guilty, responsible party, the person who has "participated" in the development of the
malignancy. The game here, so Simonton's appalled critics assert, should be
called "Blame the Patient."

When I raised this issue with patients attending the Simonton group meet- 67
ing, however, they objected to this kind of criticism. "Blame is not the same
as responsibility," a lymphoma patient insisted tartly. "Responsibility means
power, blame is helpless. The fact is that if I actively cooperated with the disease, I gave it to myself. And if I gave it to myself, I can make it go away. The
sense of power and control is there, you see, very strong."

To Jimmie Holland, the Sloan-Kettering psychiatrist, the Simonton method 68
is a "cruel hoax" that is being perpetrated upon frantic and desperately ill
people. Cancer patients, said Holland, are often filled with self-blame and are
therefore very vulnerable to suggestions that they've brought their illness on
themselves merely by virtue of being who they are. "People will say things like,
'I didn't go to the doctor soon enough,' or 'I should have been doing breast
examinations.' Many tend to believe the cancer is punishment for some past
sin. The guilt associated with something that threatens your life is enormous.
We try to help people understand that they did do the best that they could."
If the patient is encouraged to believe that he or she played a role in getting
the disease and can therefore control its growth by the use of mental powers,
an illusion of mastery over the cancer can be obtained temporarily. The crunch
comes when, in the face of recurring or advancing illness, that balloon of hope
is punctured.

"The patient is devastated," Holland said flatly, "because he's got, then, not 69
only this terrible disease but the responsibility for not having been able to control it." Her own expression was, momentarily, stricken. "We seem," she said
after a short silence, "to live in a society that wants psychological answers for
everything. It's our way of imagining we've got things under our control."

Of course, one might try the Simonton method — as one might try any- 70
thing, given a desperate situation, that gave promise of help. But the evidence
for "cures" is not there. As one expert put it, "I could say that sitting in a room
blowing bubbles out of bubble pipe three times daily was an excellent treatment for cancer, and it would be very hard to disprove me, as it is hard to
disprove the Simontons. But still, the burden of providing evidence that it did
work would be upon me, as it now is upon the Simontons." In a forthcoming
article, Jimmie Holland places psychological approaches squarely beside other
unproven cancer remedies such as special diets, high vitamin dosages, and laetrile. She views the Simontons' therapy as "unethical" — and she has said so,
in print. . . .

Simonton's growing celebrity has been paralleled by a growing rift between 71
himself and his medical peers. "I think in some way I'd sold myself the idea

that all the hassle would end when our book came out," he confessed, sounding pained. "But it seemed as if my own profession, my own community, became more closed than ever." He was, he said, blocked from presenting a paper at the American Society of Clinical Oncologists, and that had hurt a lot.

"Of course I'd known, from the outset," Simonton acknowledged, his voice *72* sober, "that I was doing something that as a doctor I had been told never to do — which was to try anything unproven. That was the bottom line. And it *was* very scary, because I didn't know what would happen — I was afraid that I would do a lot of harm." He paused, then gave a brief, despondent shrug. "I've learned a lot about the harm that *can* be done from doing something that's unproven."

I waited, but he said nothing more. "What harm is that?" I asked. *73*

"Oh . . . the guilt this approach engenders. Moving in, psychologically and *74* stripping down defenses and hurting people more than you're helping."

"And that's happened at times?" I met his eyes. He seemed unhappy, upset, *75* and somewhat depressed. "Yes, it's happened," he replied.

We were silent for a few moments, after which I asked him whether he would, *76* from where he sat now, consider doing what he'd done again. "Would you start this same movement going, because you do believe you're on the right track?"

Simonton replied, without hesitation, that he would. "I'd do the same things, *77* but not start out in such an arrogant way. I don't think, if I could start over again, I'd offend so many people so early. But you know, when I started, I thought I knew a lot more than I did. I really believed I had all the answers."

"How has that come to you?" I asked. "I mean, that you don't know as much *78* as you'd thought?"

Simonton almost winced, answered: "By being with a lot of people who died. *79* By seeing that the solutions to these problems are not so simple. By learning that it can be easy to say something and then hard to do it. I really thought," he added suddenly, "that because you could say something, you could do it."

I was silent. How can one attack a man's intellectual position when he keeps *80* abandoning it so gracefully? "I thought, too, that I was indestructible," continued Simonton, "that the harder I worked, the stronger I got. But I worked way past my limits, and I watched myself deteriorate to the point where I couldn't function, couldn't call up my energy. Before, I'd always been able to grit my teeth; I could always give more. But it was death, and being with death . . . all that heaviness. It got to be more than I could handle. And when I saw that there were things that I couldn't handle — that was very humbling."

"So, then, you went out to do battle with death itself, in the first place?" I *81* asked, genuinely moved by this outburst. He nodded. "Yes, and I thought I understood it, but I don't understand death. I'm in a battle with death, because I'm working around people who are dying and I'm attempting to turn that around. I know that I don't understand it, whereas for the first four years, I thought I knew how to beat death, and that it was a win/lose battle; that's how I saw it. Really: a win/lose situation; and again, from the classical standpoint, illness or death was a failure, and being healthy and living was winning."

Simonton now considers himself a teacher far more than a healer. "I can *82* best teach if I stay in touch with my own limitations and my own knowledge rather than act as if I know things that I really don't know," the physician said in a strained voice.

I thought, at that moment, of something he'd said much earlier in our series   *83* of conversations, something about having gone into this work in order to resolve some emotional issues of his own. "Do you think," I asked, my voice tentative, "that you yourself have a more potent fear of death than do most other people?"

Simonton, nodding his head, admitted that this would be a reasonable as-   *84* sumption. As a child, he had naturally heard a good deal of talk about suffering and dying, for his father was a Protestant minister. "If I look at my religious upbringing and what I took away from it," he said, "I would probably say that I did come into my adult life with more fear of death than others have."

Considerations

1. Summarize the methods of O. Carl Simonton as described by Maggie Scarf.
2. Do you feel that Scarf is an impartial reporter? If so, write an analytical essay demonstrating that impartiality at work. If not, write an essay illustrating her biases.
3. What evidence exists that the Simonton method works? Criticize this evidence from the point of view of someone in the American Medical Association.
4. What motivations contribute to the popularity of the Simonton method? Write a speculative essay upon what might make it attractive to both doctors and patients.
5. Based on Scarf's interview with him, write a short essay analyzing Simonton's motives.
6. Do you think the profit motive plays a role in either encouraging or discouraging Simonton's work? Explain this in a short essay.
7. Analyze this article as journalistic drama. What decisions has Scarf made in handling her material, and how do these decisions contribute to the effect of the piece?

Connections

1. Compare Maggie Scarf's perspective with those of Richard Selzer, Lucien Israël, and Ralph Moss. What are its advantages and disadvantages?
2. Compare the evidence for the effectiveness of imaging with the evidence for the effectiveness of radiotherapy and chemotherapy.
3. Think about the Simonton method from the economic perspective suggested by Moss. Whose economic interests might this therapy serve or threaten, and what roles would those interests play?
4. With what other therapies is imaging compatible? Write a short essay defending your reasoning.

5. Write a dialogue between a radiologist or a chemotherapist and a follower of Simonton. Bring the discussion to some resolution.
6. In June 1985 the *New England Journal of Medicine* reported the results of a 359-patient study investigating the potential relation between selected psychosocial factors and cancer survival rates. After reading this article, assess its implications for the Simonton method.

Cancer Plague

Steven d'Arazien

The Politics of Cancer
by Samuel Epstein, M.D.

The public is both confused and frightened by the specter of cancer. Dr.   *1*
Samuel Esptein, professor of occupational and environmental medicine at the University of Illinois School of Public Health, has written a carefully argued, well-documented book that unravels many of the mysteries of the cancer miasma.° Despite its loose and somewhat repetitive organization, *The Politics of Cancer* offers the layman a unique and critical look at the political and economic reasons why the Government has failed to deal effectively with the cancer problem.

Twenty percent of us will die of cancer. The total economic impact, includ-   *2*
ing health care and lost productivity, has been estimated at $25 billion a year.

"It is clear," Dr. Epstein notes, "that there has been a real and an absolute   *3*
increase in cancer incidence and mortality which cannot be explained by increasing life spans or smoking. . . . The increase offers additional support for the conclusion of most experts that cancer is environmental in origin and that the recent increase in incidence of cancer is due to environmental pollutants."

As he observes, most cancer is preventable if we can prevent exposures to   *4*
carcinogens. But Dr. Epstein cites the substantial increase in the production of synthetic organic chemicals since World War II, and the failure to control their introduction into the environment, as key factors why cancer has become the

---

°*miasma:* A noxious atmosphere or influence.

Steven d'Arazien is a former reporter. At the time of this review (July 1979) he was serving as a legislative aide to Andrew Maguire, a Democratic congressman from New Jersey. The review was written for The Progressive, *a journal of the political left.*

nation's number two killer. And, because of the disease's long latency period, we have yet to see the full impact of that continuing failure.

In Dr. Epstein's view, we have reached a crisis in democracy in which spe-   5
cial interests have seized control of the responsible agencies in an effort to further their own short-term economic interests. He cites case after case of the ineffective regulation of such workplace carcinogens as asbestos and benzene, consumer products such as cigarettes and food additives, and environmental contaminants such as DDT. In far too many cases, agencies are influenced by those whose primary loyalties are not to the public health but rather to their former (or current) corporate clients; far-reaching decisions are made on the basis of poor, or even nonexistent, data on the risks involved.

Perhaps the best example of how this subversion of public policy operates   6
is the case of Philippe Shubik, a well-known industrial consultant who remains a member of the National Cancer Advisory Board, a policy-making body of the National Cancer Institute. Dr. Epstein recounts several incidents in which Shubik has been instrumental in undermining important cancer control policies. At one NCI meeting at which the future of a Procter & Gamble detergent was being discussed, Shubik argued for the product's continued use. When challenged as to whose views he was expressing, Shubik admitted the views were those of Procter & Gamble, one of his many corporate clients.

With the example of saccharin, Dr. Epstein shows how a sound regulatory   7
decision was handled poorly by the Food and Drug Administration and was then nullified by an ill-informed Congress which caved in to industry pressure. In 1977, after some twenty studies indicated the carcinogenicity of saccharin, the FDA announced a ban on its use in foods and drinks. Instead of explaining its decision to the public, the FDA press release made the agency look foolish.

The release noted that, for the test, rats were fed saccharin equivalent to   8
human consumption of 800 cans of diet soda a day without explaining that not only are such high dosage tests standard but that the affected industry had reviewed the test plan without negative comment. The release pointed out, "Saccharin has been in use for more than eighty years and has never been found to harm people," without noting the limitations of such human observations. It was a release guaranteed to place the agency under political attack.

Immediately the industry, through its "front group," the Calorie Council,   9
barraged the public with misleading advertisements. Millions of overweight Americans, aroused to action by the potential loss of their diet drinks, stampeded Congress into postponing the FDA ban for eighteen months during a National Academy of Sciences study. (NAS later reported that the methodology of the test represented normal scientific practice.)

Pointing to the tragic lack of any comprehensive and effective Federal pol-   10
icy toward carcinogens, Dr. Epstein observes, "The most concrete generalization that can be made about the Government policy on carcinogens is that there is no single policy yet. Rather the policies and responsibilities are distributed over many diverse agencies and institutes with widely differing philosophies, priorities, and often with overlapping and poorly defined jurisdictions. . . ."

He notes the hodge-podge of environmental law, the lack of interagency co-   11
ordination, and the basic unwillingness to provide more than a slap on the wrist to leaders of industries which place thousands of workers at risk. He cites many

occasions in which industry has concealed knowledge of hazards from the workers and the Government or has destroyed evidence of such knowledge. His sympathies obviously lie with the workers who, according to the National Cancer Institute, get between 20 and 40 percent of all cancer.

The Politics of Cancer is a voluminous reference source for those who want   *12* to understand why the cancer plague will get worse unless the Government gets tough with industry. It deserves a wide readership.

Considerations

1. What are some of the ways in which cancer might be considered political? Write a short essay.
2. What does the word *carcinogenic* mean? Write a paragraph about the difficulties in using the word confidently.
3. Explain the FDA's role in the saccharin controversy. What remains unclear from Steven d'Arazien's account of it?
4. Try constructing a diagram to illustrate the relationships of the organizations mentioned in this review. Then write a short essay describing those relationships and raising questions about what you still would like to know.
5. Define the phrase *conflict of interest.* Illustrate with an example from d'Arazien's review; then go on to speculate about what other conflicts of interest might be found in cancer politics.
6. In a paragraph paraphrase Samuel Epstein's position on the issue of environmental cancer. Then after rereading d'Arazien's review, reduce your paraphrase to two sentences linked by the word *therefore.* Based on this succinct statement of Epstein's position, analyze any flaws you see in it.

Connections

1. What similarities do you see between Ralph Moss and Samuel Esptein? Write a short essay developing these points.
2. See Chapter 5, The Working World. What would either Frederick Taylor or Karl Marx say about the issue of cancer in the workplace?
3. Earlier in this chapter you were asked to express your sense of what cancer is, what causes it, and what remains unknown about it. Look at these issues again and revise your answer by incorporating what you have learned from the last few selections.

Mother Nature Is Meaner Than You Think

Bruce Ames

The Apocalyptics
by Edith Efron

Edith Efron surveys the environmental movement of the last 20 years as it   *1*
relates to environmental carcinogens and their regulation. Efron, a research
associate at the University of Rochester Center for Research in Government
Policy and Management, brings to the task an extraordinary intelligence, an
integrative mind, a biting wit, superb command of English, buckets of skepticism, and the doggedness and determination to master a large, chaotic, and
contentious field. I suspect that this book will be the *Silent Spring* of the counter-
revolution. It is a book that cancer researchers, toxicologists, government reg-
ulators, environmentalists, and concerned laymen will discuss and argue about
for years.

Rachel Carson and her followers galvanized a movement in the U.S. that   *2*
has culminated in the formulation of dozens of laws and the creation of large
governmental agencies designed to regulate the use of toxic man-made chemicals. The Environmental Protection Agency has passed the billion-dollar-per-
year mark in budget (equal to the budget of the National Cancer Institute). The
National Institute for Occupational Safety and Health and the Occupational
Safety and Health Administration research and regulate occupational health.
The National Institute of Environmental Health Sciences supports research on
toxic chemicals. Following years of newspaper stories on Love Canal, dioxin,
flame retardants in children's pajamas, pesticides, hair dyes, PCBs, and statements from government officials and scientists, 77 percent of the public in a
recent poll stated they were afraid of pesticide residues in their food. Dozens
of environmental organizations have sprung up and banded together to pro-
claim that toxic chemicals are the hidden danger in American life.

Efron's conclusion is that the emperor has no clothes — that the apocalyp-   *3*
tic environmental movement, with its emphasis on an epidemic of cancer due
to occupational hazards, pollution, and pesticide residues, has little or no scientific foundation, and that the white knights, OSHA and EPA, cannot slay the
carcinogen dragons. She argues that the scientific knowledge to determine which
carcinogens are significant hazards is rudimentary, that Mother Nature may

---

*Bruce Ames (b. 1928) is chairman of the Department of Microbiology at the
University of California at Berkeley. His bacterial test for chemical carcinogenicity
is used by most chemical companies and regulatory agencies in screening new
chemicals. Chemicals shown to have mutagenic — gene-transforming — properties by the Ames test are then held for animal testing. This review appeared in* Science 84.

be responsible for most of these, and that man-made chemicals may contribute only minimally to human cancer.

About half of Efron's book is on "regulatory science." These chapters discuss the scientific basis for giving the maximum tolerated dose of a chemical to rats and mice for their lifetime, deciding whether the chemical causes an increase in cancer over the controls, and then concluding something about the danger of low doses of that chemical to humans. Efron quotes liberally from all scientific parties to the various disputes (she has a sharp eye for juxtaposing quotes) and then illuminates key questions and what we know about them. Usually we know very little, which is one of her main points. A whole regulatory apparatus has been built around the "new toxicology," based on ideas of prudence rather than compelling science — with little connection to the actual study of humans.

Reading about toxic chemicals might be considered about as pleasant as eating them, but Efron's wit and intelligence keep the whole narrative lively and stimulating. In addition, there is so much flying shrapnel that, even though I am still digging a fair amount out of myself, there is a sort of malicious pleasure in seeing whom she is going to savage next.

Efron discusses the existence of carcinogens in the natural world and why these are never mentioned by the apocalyptics. She points out that they assume that nature is basically benign and that carcinogens are few and manmade. She shows that this is just not true and that the world is absolutely chock-full of carcinogens. They are present when we cook our food, when we eat natural pesticides in plants, when we breathe in oxygen, and when we undergo the natural decay of radioactive potassium in our bodies.

I think she is absolutely right on this. My own estimate is that we are eating 10,000 times more of nature's pesticides — natural toxic chemicals made in large amounts by plants to keep off insects and other predators — than we are of man-made pesticide residues. Furthermore, nature's pesticides are teeming with mutagens, carcinogens, and teratogens. Cooking our food also generates mutagens and carcinogens as all browned and burned material contains them. It takes a Los Angeles resident a year of breathing smog to equal the burned material that a heavy smoker breathes in one day. And we eat even more browned and burned material than the heavy smoker inhales, though we don't know the risk from this.

Efron also argues that we are making mutagens and carcinogens in our normal metabolism. My own view is that this is part of the aging process and that this will turn out to cause the predominant damage to our DNA. Evidence is starting to accumulate that the risk from man-made carcinogens is going to be tiny compared to that from natural carcinogens, and I supect that natural dietary carcinogens will turn out to be a minor risk compared to the risk due to carcinogens created by the aging process. All this remains to be analyzed further, but Efron is right on target to be skeptical. As she says, there is "a crude double standard. Scientists observed that the presence of some synthetic chemical carcinogens doubtless meant that others were yet to be discovered and concluded that an aggressive search for them was necessary. No comparable judgment was made by the apocalyptic scientists about the chemicals in nature."

Epidemiology and toxicology are the sciences that tie us to human experience in cancer, and Efron emphasizes the dangers in straying from those disciplines toward the new toxicology until we know more about the real mechanisms of cancer. She goes over the epidemiological evidence: The rates for most types of cancer have been steady for years or are now declining, with the exception of lung cancer, which appears to be primarily due to cigarette smoking. Only a small fraction of human cancer appears to be due to occupation or pollution.

Efron has an interesting chapter on the current fear of extremely low doses   *10* of carcinogens and the question of safe thresholds, and she conducts the discussion between the various sides with the élan of an orchestra conductor. It soon becomes apparent that since the background of carcinogens in the natural world is very high, it is not sensible to try to regulate very low levels of man-made carcinogens. The key task is to determine which of the many natural and man-made carcinogenic factors we are exposed to represent major hazards and to establish practical tolerance levels. The task is not to chase after smaller and smaller amounts of the next carcinogen that reaches the public eye.

Nevertheless, Efron neglects some important questions. She doesn't discuss   *11* whether it was reasonable to be worried about large increases in the use of synthetic chemicals — either for workers exposed to significant doses or for all of us exposed to food additives and pesticides. She also doesn't discuss that little toxicology was done on many multibillion-pound-a-year chemicals or chemicals, such as DDE (a DDT metabolite) and PCBs, accumulating to what seemed to be considerable levels in body fat and mothers' milk.

Occasionally she misses the mark. She is overly harsh on many dedicated   *12* scientists concerned with the introduction of all the new man-made chemicals into the environment, while she lets some journalists off too easily. If they were ready to accept every exaggeration of the apocalyptic movement, then they too deserve some of the blame.

Despite these complaints, this is an important book for those of us in the   *13* field and for the public. Perhaps society needs a few Rachel Carsons who worry about new technologies; we also need some Edith Efrons to remind us that the increased health and wealth industrial society has brought us has come from not being unreasonably fearful about new technology.

Considerations

1. What is the meaning of the word *apocalyptic?* How does it contribute to Edith Efron's (or to Bruce Ames's) argument?
2. What is toxicology, and what is the relation of the *new toxicology* to it? Explain in a paragraph.
3. In paragraph 7 Ames implies distinctions among "mutagens, carcinogens, and teratogens." Consult a scientific dictionary and then offer a brief explanation of the differences.
4. Paraphrase Efron's or Ames's argument from an economic point of view.
5. Look up Rachel Carson in a biographical dictionary of modern scientists.

Then explain and evaluate the analogy Ames makes between Carson and Efron.
6. In a paragraph paraphrase Edith Efron's position on the issue of environmental cancer. Then after rereading Ames's review, reduce your paraphrase
to two sentences linked by the word *therefore*. Based on this succinct statement of Efron's position, analyze any flaws you see in it.

Connections

1. Compare the points of view of Samuel Epstein and Edith Efron.
2. Compare the points of view of Steven d'Arazien and Bruce Ames.
3. Upon what facts might Epstein, Efron, d'Arazien, and Ames agree? Develop
   them into a paragraph or two.
4. Read the biographical notes about d'Arazien and Ames. How does the information there influence your responses to the two selections?
5. Can you see any ambiguity in the term *environmental cancer?* Show how the
   magnitude of the problem of environmental cancer may depend partly on
   how broadly the term is defined. Draw on any of this chapter's other readings that help you make your points.
6. Where do d'Arazien and Ames stand on the general issues raised by John
   Cairns?
7. Locate the books by Epstein and Efron and develop a comparison based directly on the books rather than indirectly through these reviews. Make your
   comparison manageable by restricting yourself to some aspect covered by
   both books.

Illness as Metaphor

Susan Sontag

Punitive notions of disease have a long history, and such notions are partic-   *1*
ularly active with cancer. There is the "fight" or "crusade" against cancer; cancer
is the "killer" disease; people who have cancer are "cancer victims." Ostensi-

---

*Susan Sontag (b. 1933) is a social and literary critic of wide-ranging accom-
plishments. Novelist, lecturer, and film director, she is best known for her penetrating essays, many of which have been first published in the* New York Review
of Books. *These essays have been collected in a number of influential volumes,
including* Styles of Radical Will, Against Interpretation, *and* On Photography.
Illness as Metaphor *(1979) is the title of the short book from which this selection
is taken. Sontag is a cancer survivor.*

bly, the illness is the culprit. But it is also the cancer patient who is made culpable. Widely believed psychological theories of disease assign to the luckless ill the ultimate responsibility both for falling ill and for getting well. And conventions of treating cancer as no mere disease but a demonic enemy make cancer not just a lethal disease but a shameful one.

Leprosy in its heyday aroused a similarly disproportionate sense of horror.   2
In the Middle Ages, the leper was a social text in which corruption was made visible; an exemplum, an emblem of decay. Nothing is more punitive than to give a disease a meaning — that meaning being invariably a moralistic one. Any important disease whose causality is murky, and for which treatment is ineffectual, tends to be awash in significance. First, the subjects of deepest dread (corruption, decay, pollution, anomie, weakness) are identified with the disease. The disease itself becomes a metaphor. Then, in the name of the disease (that is, using it as a metaphor), that horror is imposed on other things. The disease becomes adjectival. Something is said to be disease-like, meaning that it is disgusting or ugly. In French, a moldering stone façade is still *lépreuse.*

Epidemic diseases were a common figure for social disorder. From pesti-   3
lence (bubonic plague) came "pestilent," whose figurative meaning, according to the *Oxford English Dictionary*, is "injurious to religion, morals, or public peace — 1513"; and "pestilential," meaning "morally baneful or pernicious — 1531." Feelings about evil are projected onto a disease. And the disease (so enriched with meanings) is projected onto the world.

In the past, such grandiloquent fantasies were regularly attached to the ep-   4
idemic diseases, diseases that were a collective calamity. In the last two centuries, the diseases most often used as metaphors for evil were syphilis, tuberculosis, and cancer — all diseases imagined to be, preeminently, the diseases of individuals.

Syphilis was thought to be not only a horrible disease but a demeaning,   5
vulgar one. Anti-democrats used it to evoke the desecrations of an egalitarian age. Baudelaire, in a note for his never completed book on Belgium, wrote:

> We all have the republican spirit in our veins, like syphilis in our bones — we are democraticized and venerealized.

In the sense of an infection that corrupts morally and debilitates physically, syphilis was to become a standard trope in late-nineteenth- and early-twentieth-century anti-Semitic polemics. In 1933 Wilhelm Reich argued that "the irrational fear of syphilis was one of the major sources of National Socialism's political views and its anti-Semitism." But although he perceived sexual and political phobias being projected onto a disease in the grisly harping on syphilis in *Mein Kampf*, it never occurred to Reich how much was being projected in his own persistent use of cancer as a metaphor for the ills of the modern era. Indeed, cancer can be stretched much further than syphilis can as a metaphor.

Syphilis was limited as a metaphor because the disease itself was not re-   6
garded as mysterious; only awful. A tainted heredity (Ibsen's *Ghosts*), the perils of sex (Charles-Louis Philippe's *Bubu de Montparnasse*, Mann's *Doctor Faustus*) — there was horror aplenty in syphilis. But no mystery. Its causality was

clear, and understood to be singular. Syphilis was the grimmest of gifts, "transmitted" or "carried" by a sometimes ignorant sender to the unsuspecting receiver. In contrast, TB was regarded as a mysterious affliction, and a disease with myriad causes — just as today, while everyone acknowledges cancer to be an unsolved riddle, it is also generally agreed that cancer is multi-determined. A variety of factors — such as cancer-causing substances ("carcinogens") in the environment, genetic makeup, lowering of immunodefenses (by previous illness or emotional trauma), characterological predisposition — are held responsible for the disease. And many researchers assert that cancer is not one but more than a hundred clinically distinct diseases, that each cancer has to be studied separately, and that what will eventually be developed is an array of cures, one for each of the different cancers.

The resemblance of current ideas about cancer's myriad causes to long-held   7
but now discredited views about TB suggests the possibility that cancer may be one disease after all and that it may turn out, as TB did, to have a principal causal agent and be controllable by one program of treatment. Indeed, as Lewis Thomas has observed, all the diseases for which the issue of causation has been settled, and which can be prevented and cured, have turned out to have a simple physical cause — like the pneumococcus for pneumonia, the tubercle bacillus for tuberculosis, a single vitamin deficiency for pellagra — and it is far from unlikely that something comparable will eventually be isolated for cancer. The notion that a disease can be explained only by a variety of causes is precisely characteristic of thinking about diseases whose causation is *not* understood. And it is diseases thought to be multi-determined (that is, mysterious) that have the widest possibilities as metaphors for what is felt to be socially or morally wrong.

TB and cancer have been used to express not only (like syphilis) crude fan-   8
tasies about contamination but also fairly complex feelings about strength and weakness, and about energy. For more than a century and a half, tuberculosis provided a metaphoric equivalent for delicacy, sensitivity, sadness, powerlessness; while whatever seemed ruthless, implacable, predatory, could be analogized to cancer. (Thus, Baudelaire in 1852, in his essay *"L'Ecole païenne,"* observed: "A frenzied passion for art is a canker that devours the rest. . . . ") TB was an ambivalent metaphor, both a scourge and an emblem of refinement. Cancer was never viewed other than as a scourge; it was, metaphorically, the barbarian within.

While syphilis was thought to be passively incurred, an entirely involuntary   9
disaster, TB was once, and cancer is now, thought to be a pathology of energy, a disease of the will. Concern about energy and feeling, fears about the havoc they wreak, have been attached to both diseases. Getting TB was thought to signify a defective vitality, or vitality misspent. "There was a great want of vital power . . . and great constitutional weakness" — so Dickens described little Paul in *Dombey and Son.* The Victorian idea of TB as a disease of low energy (and heightened sensitivity) has its exact complement in the Reichian idea of cancer as a disease of unexpected energy (and anesthetized feelings). In an era in which there seemed to be no inhibitions on being productive, people were anxious about not having enough energy. In our own era of destructive

overproduction by the economy and of increasing bureaucratic restraints on the individual, there is both a fear of having too much energy and an anxiety about energy not being allowed to be expressed.

Like Freud's scarcity-economics theory of "instincts," the fantasies about TB   *10* which arose in the last century (and lasted well into ours) echo the attitudes of early capitalist accumulation. One has a limited amount of energy, which must be properly spent. (Having an orgasm, in nineteenth-century English slang, was not "coming" but "spending.") Energy, like savings, can be depleted, can run out or be used up, through reckless expenditure. The body will start "consuming" itself, the patient will "waste away."

The language used to describe cancer evokes a different economic catastro-   *11* phe: that of unregulated, abnormal, incoherent growth. The tumor has energy, not the patient; "it" is out of control. Cancer cells, according to the textbook account, are cells that have shed the mechanism which "restrains" growth. (The growth of normal cells is "self-limiting," due to a mechanism called "contact inhibition.") Cells without inhibitions, cancer cells will continue to grow and extend over each other in a "chaotic" fashion, destroying the body's normal cells, architecture, and functions.

Early capitalism assumes the necessity of regulated spending, saving, ac-   *12* counting, discipline — an economy that depends on the rational limitation of desire. TB is described in images that sum up the negative behavior of nineteenth-century *homo economicus:* consumption; wasting; squandering of vitality. Advanced capitalism requires expansion, speculation, the creation of new needs (the problem of satisfaction and dissatisfaction); buying on credit; mobility — an economy that depends on the irrational indulgence of desire. Cancer is described in images that sum up the negative behavior of twentieth-century *homo economicus:* abnormal growth; repression of energy, that is, refusal to consume or spend.

TB was understood, like insanity, to be a kind of one-sidedness: a failure of   *13* will or an overintensity. However much the disease was dreaded, TB always had pathos. Like the mental patient today, the tubercular was considered to be someone quintessentially vulnerable, and full of self-destructive whims. Nineteenth- and early-twentieth-century physicians addressed themselves to coaxing their tubercular patients back to health. Their prescription was the same as the enlightened one for mental patients today: cheerful surroundings, isolation from stress and family, healthy diet, exercise, rest.

The understanding of cancer supports quite different, avowedly brutal no-   *14* tions of treatment. (A common cancer hospital witticism, heard as often from doctors as from patients: "The treatment is worse than the disease.") There can be no question of pampering the patient. With the patient's body considered to be under attack ("invasion"), the only treatment is counterattack.

The controlling metaphors in descriptions of cancer are, in fact, drawn not   *15* from economics but from the language of warfare: every physician and every attentive patient is familiar with, if perhaps inured to, this military terminology. Thus, cancer cells do not simply multiply; they are "invasive." ("Malignant tumors invade even when they grow very slowly," as one textbook puts it.) Cancer cells "colonize" from the original tumor to far sites in the body, first setting up tiny outposts ("micrometastases") whose presence is assumed, though they cannot be detected. Rarely are the body's "defenses" vigorous enough to obliterate a tumor that has established its own blood supply and consists of billions of destructive cells. However "radical" the surgical intervention, however many "scans" are taken of the body landscape, most remissions are temporary; the prospects are that "tumor invasion" will continue, or that rogue cells will eventually regroup and mount a new assault on the organism.

Treatment also has a military flavor. Radiotherapy uses the metaphors of *16* aerial warfare; patients are "bombarded" with toxic rays. And chemotherapy is chemical warfare, using poisons.[1] Treatment aims to "kill" cancer cells (without, it is hoped, killing the patient). Unpleasant side effects to treatment are advertised, indeed overadvertised. ("The agony of chemotherapy" is a standard phrase.) It is impossible to avoid damaging or destroying healthy cells (indeed, some methods used to treat cancer can cause cancer), but it is thought that nearly any damage to the body is justified if it saves the patient's life. Often, of course, it doesn't work. (As in: "We had to destory Ben Suc in order to save it.") There is everything but the body count.

The military metaphor in medicine first came into wide use in the 1880s, *17* with the identification of bacteria as agents of disease. Bacteria were said to "invade" or "infiltrate." But talk of siege and war to describe disease now has, with cancer, a striking literalness and authority. Not only is the clinical course of the disease and its medical treatment thus described, but the disease itself is conceived as the enemy on which society wages war. More recently, the fight against cancer has sounded like a colonial war — with similarly vast appropriations of government money — and in a decade when colonial wars haven't gone too well, this militarized rhetoric seems to be backfiring. Pessimism among doctors about the efficacy of treatment is growing, in spite of the strong advances in chemotherapy and immunotherapy made since 1970. Reporters covering "the war on cancer" frequently caution the public to distinguish between official fictions and harsh facts; a few years ago, one science writer found American Cancer Society proclamations that cancer is curable and progress has been made "reminiscent of Vietnam optimism prior to the deluge." Still, it is one thing to be skeptical about the rhetoric that surrounds cancer, another to give support to many uninformed doctors who insist that no significant progress in treatment has been made, and that cancer is not really curable. The bromides of the American cancer establishment, tirelessly hailing the imminent victory over cancer; the professional pessimism of a large number of cancer specialists, talking like battle-weary officers mired down in an interminable colonial war — these are twin distortions in this military rhetoric about cancer.

Other distortions follow with the extension of cancer images in more gran- *18* diose schemes of warfare. As TB was represented as the spiritualizing of consciousness, cancer is understood as the overwhelming or obliterating of consciousness (by a mindless It). In TB, you are eating yourself up, being refined, getting down to the core, the real you. In cancer, non-intelligent ("primitive," "embryonic," "atavistic") cells are multiplying, and you are being replaced by the nonyou. Immunologists class the body's cancer cells as "nonself."

It is worth noting that Reich, who did more than anyone else to disseminate *19* the psychological theory of cancer, also found something equivalent to cancer in the biosphere.

> There is a deadly orgone energy. It is in the atmosphere. You can demonstrate it on devices such as the Geiger counter. It's a swampy quality. . . . Stagnant, deadly water which doesn't flow, doesn't metabolize. Cancer, too, is due to the stagnation of the flow of the life energy of the organism.

Reich's language has its own inimitable coherence. And more and more — as its metaphoric uses gain in credibility — cancer is felt to be what he thought it was, a cosmic disease, the emblem of all the destructive, alien powers to which the organism is host.

As TB was the disease of the sick self, cancer is the disease of the Other. 20 Cancer proceeds by a science-fiction scenario: an invasion of "alien" or "mutant" cells, stronger than normal cells *(Invasion of the Body Snatchers, The Incredible Shrinking Man, The Blob, The Thing)*. One standard science-fiction plot is mutation, either mutants arriving from outer space or accidental mutations among humans. Cancer could be described as a triumphant mutation, and mutation is now mainly an image for cancer. As a theory of the psychological genesis of cancer, the Reichian imagery of energy checked, not allowed to move outward, then turned back on itself, driving cells beserk, is already the stuff of science fiction. And Reich's image of death in the air — of deadly energy that registers on a Geiger counter — suggests how much the science-fiction images about cancer (a disease that comes from deadly rays, and is treated by deadly rays) echo the collective nightmare. The original fear about exposure to atomic radiation was genetic deformities in the next generation; that was replaced by another fear, as statistics started to show much higher cancer rates among Hiroshima and Nagasaki survivors and their descendants.

Cancer is a metaphor for what is most ferociously energetic; and these ener- 21 gies constitute the ultimate insult to natural order. In a science-fiction tale by Tommaso Landolfi, the spaceship is called "Cancerqueen." (It is hardly within the range of the tuberculosis metaphor that a writer could have imagined an intrepid vessel named "Consumptionqueen.") When not being explained away as something psychological, buried in the recesses of the self, cancer is being magnified and projected into a metaphor for the biggest enemy, the furthest goal. Thus, Nixon's bid to match Kennedy's promise to put Americans on the moon was, appropriately enough, the promise to "conquer" cancer. Both were science-fiction ventures. The equivalent of the legislation establishing the space program was the National Cancer Act of 1971, which did not envisage the near-to-hand decisions that could bring under control the industrial economy that pollutes — only the great destination: the cure.

TB was a disease in the service of a romantic view of the world. Cancer is 22 now in the service of a simplistic view of the world that can turn paranoid. The disease is often experienced as a form of demonic posession — tumors are "malignant" or "benign," like forces — and many terrified cancer patients are disposed to seek out faith healers, to be exorcised. The main organized support for dangerous nostrums like Laetrile comes from far-right groups to whose politics of paranoia the fantasy of a miracle cure for cancer makes a serviceable addition, along with a belief in UFOs. (The John Birch Society distributes a forty-five-minute film called *World Without Cancer*.) For the more sophisticated, cancer signifies the rebellion of the injured ecosphere: Nature taking revenge on a wicked technocratic world. False hopes and simplified terrors are raised by crude statistics brandished for the general public, such as that 90 percent of all cancers are "environmentally caused," or that imprudent diet and tobacco smoking alone account for 75 percent of all cancer deaths. To the accompaniment of this numbers game (it is difficult to see how any statistics about "all cancers" or "all cancer deaths" could be defended), cigarettes, hair dyes, bacon, saccharine, hormone-fed poultry, pesticides, low-sulphur coal — a lengthening roll call of products we take for granted have been found to cause cancer. X-rays give cancer (the treatment meant to cure kills); so do emanations from the television set and the microwave oven and the fluorescent clock face. As with syphilis, an innocent or trivial act — or exposure — in the present can have dire consequences far in the future. It is also known that cancer rates are high for workers in a large number of industrial occupations. Though the exact processes of causation lying behind the statistics remain unknown, it seems clear that many cancers are preventable. But cancer is not just a disease ushered in by the Industrial Revolution (there was cancer in Arcadia) and certainly more than the sin of capitalism (within their more limited industrial capacities, the Russians pollute worse than we do). The widespread current view of cancer as a disease of industrial civilization is as unsound scientifically as the right-wing fantasy of a "world without cancer" (like a world without subversives). Both rest on the mistaken feeling that cancer is a distinctively "modern" disease.

The medieval experience of the plague was firmly tied to notions of moral 23 pollution, and people invariably looked for a scapegoat external to the stricken community. (Massacres of Jews in unprecedented numbers took place everywhere in plague-stricken Europe of 1347–48, then stopped as soon as the plague receded.) With the modern diseases, the scapegoat is not so easily separated from the patient. But much as these diseases individualize, they also pick up some of the metaphors of epidemic diseases. (Diseases understood to be simply epidemic have become less useful as metaphors, as evidenced by the near-total historical amnesia about the influenza pandemic of 1918–19, in which more people died than in the four years of World War I.) Presently, it is as much a cliché to say that cancer is "environmentally" caused as it was — and still is — to say that it is caused by mismanaged emotions. TB was associated with pollution (Florence Nightingale thought it was "induced by the foul air of houses"), and now cancer is thought of as a disease of the contamination of the whole world. TB was "the white plague." With awareness of environmental pollution, people have started saying that there is an "epidemic" or "plague" of cancer.

NOTE

[1] Drugs of the nitrogen mustard type (so-called alkylating agents) — like cyclophosphamide (Cytoxan) — were the first generation of cancer drugs. Their use with leukemia (which is characterized by an excessive production of immature white cells), then with other forms of cancer — was suggested by an inadvertent experiment with chemical warfare toward the end of World War II, when an American ship, loaded with nitrogen mustard gas, was blown up in the Naples harbor, and many of the sailors died of their lethally low white-cell and platelet counts (that is, of bone-marrow poisoning) rather than of burns or sea-water inhalation.

Chemotherapy and weaponry seem to go together, if only as a fancy. The first modern chemotherapy success was with syphilis: in 1910, Paul Ehrlich introduced an arsenic derivative, arsphenamine (Salvarsan), which was called "the magic bullet."

Considerations

1. Summarize Susan Sontag's argument.
2. Explain Sontag's central comparison of cancer and tuberculosis.
3. Develop the analogy of "the cancer crusade" by thinking about the characteristics of the historical crusades (consult an encyclopedia or history text).
4. In Sontag's view how does the rhetoric of the cancer establishment inadvertently mask some of the real accomplishments of cancer research?

Connections

1. Look elsewhere in this chapter for evidence supporting Susan Sontag's comments about the metaphor of the "war against cancer." Write an analytical essay about this tendency.
2. Do any of the readings suggest a better metaphor than war for describing the cancer situation? Develop it in a short essay.
3. With which other writers in this chapter are Sontag's views most compatible? Explain your judgments.
4. Where does Sontag stand in the debate sketched by d'Arazien and Ames?
5. What would Sontag say of the Simonton method? Build your case making close use of both texts.
6. Do you find Sontag's view more or less political than that of Ralph Moss or Samuel Epstein? Explain what you mean by *political* and develop your points in an analytical essay.

Oncogenes

J. Michael Bishop

Can the cancer cell be understood? Since no one can yet explain how a normal cell controls its growth, it may seem foolhardy to think the abnormal rules governing the growth of a cancer cell can be deciphered. Yet the history of

---

J. Michael Bishop (b. 1936) graduated from Harvard Medical School in 1962 and later served as a research associate in virology at the National Institute of Allergy and Infectious Diseases. He is currently a professor of microbiology at the University of California in San Francisco. A member of the National Academy of Sciences, he has published his research on tumor viruses in the New England Journal of Medicine *and* Cell. *This article appeared in* Scientific American.

biology records many instances in which the study of abnormalities has illu-
minated normal life processes. Recent developments in cancer research have
added a dramatic new example. For the first time investigators have perceived
the dim outline of events that can induce cancerous growth. Enzymes that catalyze those events have been identified, and so have the genes specifying the
structure of the enzymes.

These advances have come from the study of viruses that induce tumors.   2
Recent years have seen an enthusiastic search for viruses that cause cancer in
human beings. The search has been largely unsuccessful, leading many informed observers to doubt that viruses will ever prove to be a major cause of
human cancer. Some viruses do induce tumors in other animals, however, and
investigators have been studying these tumor viruses, attempting to define
fundamental derangements of the cell that are responsible for cancerous growth.
That quest has struck gold.

Although the genes implicated in the development of cancer were first ob-   3
served in work with viruses, they are not native to the viruses. Indeed, it has
turned out that the genes are not even peculiar to cancer cells. They are present and functioning in normal cells as well, and they may be as necessary for
the life of the normal cell as they appear to be for the unrestrained growth of
a cancer. A final common pathway by which all tumors arise may be part of
the genetic dowry of every living cell.

Tumor Viruses

A virus is little more than a packet of genetic information encased in a pro-   4
tein coat. The information can be embodied in either DNA or RNA (whereas in
the cells of higher organisms the genetic archive invariably consists of DNA).
Both DNA and RNA are long strands of four of the chemical units called nucleotides. The sequence of the nucleotides constitutes a coded message, punctuated into the discrete units called genes. The instructions encoded in genes
are carried out in various ways. Most commonly the sequence of nucleotides
specifies the order in which amino acids are assembled to form a particular
protein, typically an enzyme or a structural element. Viruses can have fewer
than five genes and never have more than several hundred, whereas the cells
of more complex organisms have a genome, or total genetic complement, of
tens of thousands of genes. The reproduction of viruses mimics the processes
by which cells grow and divide, but the simplicity of viruses makes them much
easier than cells to study and understand.

In cells DNA is transcribed into a strand of messenger RNA and the RNA is   5
translated into protein. An infecting virus insinuates its genetic information
into the cellular machinery, so that the cell synthesizes viral proteins specified
by viral genes. The proteins synthesize many copies of the viral genome, construct new virus particles and execute any other instructions of the viral genes.
In some instances the instructions include a command that converts the host
cell to a cancerous state.

The existence of tumor viruses was first suspected at the turn of the century.   6
A critical discovery came in 1910, when Peyton Rous of the Rockefeller Institute for Medical Research showed that a cell-free filtrate from chicken tumors

called sarcomas could induce new sarcomas in chickens. His reports were not well received; eventually Rous abandoned his work on tumor viruses because of his peers' disapproval. Decades later the reality of the virus first identified by Rous, and of other tumor viruses as well, was established beyond doubt by purification with physical techniques and visualization with the electron microscope. Tumor viruses became workaday agents in cancer research. In 1966, at the age of 85, Rous was awarded a Nobel prize.

Some tumor viruses are oncogenic (that is, they induce tumors) only in animals that are not their host in nature, whereas other tumor viruses are oncogenic in their natural host. Such differences are understood only in part, but for the investigator they are of no great concern. The ability to induce tumors at will with a rather simple and well-defined agent has been a great boon to cancer research, even if it is sometimes necessary to resort to an unnatural combination of virus and host.   7

Transformation

Many tumor viruses have a particularly valuable property: they elicit cancerous changes in cells in an artificial culture medium. This "transformation" of cultured cells makes it possible to examine the interaction of a tumor virus with a host cell under controlled conditions and to avoid the difficulties associated with experiments in animals. It is important to remember, however, that some tumor viruses do not transform cells in culture and yet are powerful oncogenic agents in animals.   8

The ability or inability of a virus to transform cultured cells is connected with its mechanism of oncogenesis. Two patterns have been recognized. Some viruses have a single gene that is solely responsible for their capacity to induce tumors, or in some cases a few such "oncogenes." The action of viral oncogenes is rapid, and it predominates over the activity of all other genes in the cell. Most viruses with oncogenes (and perhaps all of them) can transform cells in culture; the capacity for transformation is provisional evidence that a virus has an oncogene. Other viruses lack oncogenes and induce tumors by more subtle means. Such tumor viruses act slowly in animals, in many cases taking from six to 12 months to give rise to a tumor, in contrast to the few days or weeks required by an oncogene virus. And they do not transform cells in culture.   9

Both forms of oncogenesis are characterized by the persistence of the viral genome in the host cell for as long as the cell survives. In most instances viral DNA has been integrated, or chemically stitched, into the DNA of the host cell, but the genome of some tumor viruses appears to survive within the cell as a separate unit and to reproduce independently. At the moment it seems that the persistence of the viral genome is necessary for viral oncogenesis, either to maintain the influence of an oncogene over the cell or to sustain the less direct effects of viruses that induce tumors but do not carry an oncogene. The mysteries of viral oncogenesis have occasionally prompted the hypothesis of a "hit and run" mechanism in which a transient virus infection triggers a sequence of events eventuating in a tumor, with no trace of the virus necessarily persisting in the tumor cells. There is now very little evidence to support such models.   10

Retroviruses

The sarcoma virus discovered by Rous belongs to a family known as the re- *11* troviruses, which are the only tumor viruses with an RNA genome. Retroviruses have provided the most coherent view of oncogenesis now available. Three features of retroviruses account for their utility in the analysis of tumor development. First, they have been found in a large number of vertebrate species and they induce many types of tumors: experimental models for most major forms of human cancer. Second, it is relatively easy to identify and isolate retrovirus oncogenes and to find their products, and so they have provided the first glimpse of the chemical processes responsible for cancerous growth. Third, retrovirus oncogenes do not appear to be indigenous components of the viral genome; instead they seem to have been copied from genes of the vertebrate host in which the virus replicates. There is reason to suspect that the cellular genes from which the retrovirus oncogenes apparently arose are themselves involved in the production of tumors induced by agents other than viruses. Thus tumor virologists engaged in the arcane endeavor of tracking the evolutionary origin of oncogenes have been led to genetic mechanisms that may underlie many forms of cancer.

Retroviruses derive their name from a feature of their life cycle that makes *12* them unique in biology: their RNA must be transcribed "backward" into DNA for them to propagate. This unusual process is accomplished by an enzyme called reverse transcriptase. The enzyme was discovered in the particles of viruses such as the Rous sarcoma virus in 1970 by David Baltimore of the Massachusetts Institute of Technology and by Satoshi Mizutani and Howard M. Temin of the University of Wisconsin. The discovery was important on several counts. It scuttled the widely held misconception that genetic information could flow only from DNA to RNA. It triggered a surge of research on retroviruses by clarifying the previously obscure mechanism of their replication. And it provided an essential reagent for the developing technology of genetic engineering with recombinant DNA.

The life cycle of a retrovirus is a marvel of cooperation between parasite *13* and host. The success of virus infection depends on the lavish hospitality offered by the cell, and yet the virus retains much authority to control events. During the early hours of infection the viral RNA genome is transcribed into DNA by reverse transcriptase. The viral DNA is then integrated into the cell's genome, with the result that viral genes are replicated along with cellular genes and are expressed by the machinery of the cell.

In many cases a retrovirus infection is innocuous to the cell. The virus ac- *14* quires a new and potentially enduring home; new virus particles are manufactured and leave the cell, and yet the cell suffers no damage. The partnership can go awry, however, as a result of either of the two kinds of viral oncogenesis mentioned above. If the virus carries an oncogene, the activity of the gene can convert the cell to cancerous growth. If the virus lacks an oncogene, the integration of the viral DNA can interfere with a cellular gene at or near the point of insertion; in other words, the insertion can cause a mutation in the host cell's genome. Mutations at certain sites may engender cancerous growth. The induction of tumors by oncogenes and induction by the consequences of integration appear at first to be quite dissimilar events, but I shall show below that they are intimately related.

The src Gene

The oncogene of the Rous sarcoma virus was the first to yield to experimen-   15
tal analysis. An important early step was taken in 1970, when G. Steven Martin of the University of California at Berkeley identified temperature-sensitive "conditional" mutations that affect the ability of the virus to transform cells in culture. A conditional mutation is a powerful tool because it makes possible the reversible inactivation of a gene. When cultured cells infected with temperature-sensitive Rous sarcoma viruses are maintained at a "permissive" temperature, they are transformed. When the temperature is shifted to a higher, "restrictive" one, within hours the cells regain a normal appearance, only to be transformed once more when the temperature is again lowered. The interpretation is that at a restrictive temperature a mutated gene is inactivated. Transformation, then, is due to the action of a gene, which must be expressed continuously to maintain the cancerous state. (In most cases the elevated temperature probably does not act directly on the gene itself. Instead the mutation alters the structure of the protein product of the gene, with the result that the activity of the protein is impaired by the restrictive temperature.)

The gene first glimpsed by Martin is now called src (for sarcoma, the tumor   16
it induces); it is the oncogene of the Rous sarcoma virus. The src gene was soon made more tangible by Peter H. Duesberg of Berkeley and by Charles Weissmann, Martin Billeter and John M. Coffin of the University of Zurich. They worked with strains of the Rous sarcoma virus that had been isolated by Peter K. Vogt of the University of Southern California. The strains are "deletion" mutants that have lost the oncogene and are therefore incapable of inducing tumors or transforming cells in culture. Duesberg and Weissmann and his colleagues fragmented the genomes of deletion mutants and of wild-type (oncogenic) viruses with the enzyme ribonuclease. By determining which fragment was missing in the mutants they were able to identify the oncogene as a segment of RNA near one end of the Rous sarcoma virus genome.

In the past few years the powerful new techniques of genetic engineering   17
have been exploited to define oncogenes more precisely and to test their cancerous potential. DNA can now be cut into fragments at specific sites with the aid of a battery of enzymes called restriction endonucleases. Particular fragments can be grown in quantity in bacteria, then reisolated and inserted into cultured cells, where the genes carried by the DNA are expressed. In this way one can cut viral DNA into pieces that each carry a single gene and learn which of the pieces cause transformation. Analysis of the DNA of the Rous sarcoma virus has revealed a single gene capable of transforming cells; the gene encodes a single protein product. The implication is that one gene, by directing the synthesis of one protein, can bring about the changes characterizing a cancer cell. To know that protein and how it acts is to have in view the events that can generate a malignant tumor.

The protein encoded by src is known, owing largely to the work of Raymond   18
L. Erikson of the University of Colorado School of Medicine and his colleagues.

They began by identifying a protein that is synthesized in the test tube under the instructions of the wildtype Rous sarcoma virus genome but not under the instructions of the genome of a deletion mutant lacking *src*. Then they raised rabbit antibodies to a putative *src* protein by inducing tumors in rabbits with the Rous sarcoma virus. The antibodies combined specifically with the protein synthesized in the test tube and also with an identical protein in cells transformed by *src*. These findings persuasively identified a protein that is encoded by *src* and is responsible for the effects of the gene. The protein was designated pp60v-*src;* the "pp" signifies that it is a phosphoprotein (a protein to which phosphate groups are attached), the "60" refers to its molecular weight of 60,000 daltons and "v-*src*" indicates its genetic origin is the viral gene *src*.

A Cancer Enzyme

How does the protein product of the *src* gene convert a cell to cancerous   *19* growth? That seemed to be a daunting question when the protein was isolated. Yet a first answer came quickly when it was discovered that pp60v-*src* is a protein kinase: an enzyme that attaches phosphate ions to the amino acid components of proteins in the reaction known as phosphorylation. The discovery was made by Erikson and his colleague Mark S. Collett and, independently, by Arthur Levinson, working with Harold E. Varmus and me in our laboratory at the University of California School of Medicine in San Francisco.

Soon thereafter Tony Hunter and Bartholomew M. Sefton of the Salk Insti-   *20* tute for Biological Studies reported that pp60v-*src* attaches phosphate ions specifically to the amino acid tyrosine. That put pp60v-*src* outside the known classes of protein kinases, which phosphorylate the amino acids serine and threonine. The phosphorylation of tyrosine has turned out to be a common characteristic of oncogene-encoded enzymes; surprisingly, it also has a role in regulating the growth of normal cells.

Not many years ago phosphate appeared to most biologists to be a mun-   *21* dane material and its transfer to proteins a humble event. Now it is clear that the phosphorylation of proteins is one of the central means by which the activities of growing cells are governed. One enzyme, by phosphorylating a number of proteins, can vastly alter the functioning of a cell. In the case of pp60v-*src* two modes of action have been proposed. The enzyme could phosphorylate a single protein, precipitating a cascade of events that together give rise to the properties of a cancer cell; alternatively, the enzyme could phosphorylate numerous proteins, directly affecting the functions of each of them and perhaps precipitating secondary events or even cascades in turn. What little is known at the moment makes it seem likely that the second alternative correctly describes the action of pp60v-*src*.

Can the phosphorylation of tyrosine subunits in cellular proteins account   *22* for the ability of *src* to induce tumors? Hunter and his colleagues have shown that the amount of phosphorylated tyrosine in a cell increases approximately tenfold as a result of transformation by *src*. The increase is regarded as a manifestation of the activity of pp60v-*src*. The critical questions now are: What cellular proteins are phosphorylated by the enzyme and what are their functions? There are only a few clues, none of which can yet account for the unrestrained growth of the tumors induced by *src*. The pursuit of targets for pp60v-*src* is under way in many laboratories.

Site of Action

One approach is to find out where in the cell pp60v-*src* acts, in the hope of   23
learning what proteins it affects and what those proteins do. Early studies indicated that the products of viral oncogenes might take up residence in the nucleus of the cell, where they could meddle directly with the apparatus responsible for replicating the cellular DNA and so drive the cell to unrestrained growth. Experiments by Hartmut Beug and Thomas Graf of the Max Planck Institute for Virus Research in Tübingen showed, however, that the effects of the *src* protein can be detected even in cells from which the nucleus has been removed. It came as no surprise, then, when several workers found that little if any of the pp60v-*src* in transformed cells is in the nucleus. Most of the protein is at the other extreme of the cell: it is bound to the plasma membrane, the thin film that encloses the cell and mediates its interactions with the outside world. Many cell biologists have argued that the control of cell growth may originate at the plasma membrane and its associated structures.

Inspection of the plasma membrane of cells transformed by *src* has pro-   24
vided the first correlation between the action of pp60v-*src* on a specific cellular protein and one of the typical changes in structure and function seen in cancer cells. By means of specialized techniques of photomicroscopy Larry R. Rohrschneider of the Fred Hutchinson Cancer Research Center in Seattle was able to demonstrate that pp60v-*src* is concentrated in adhesion plaques: regions of the membrane that adhere to solid surfaces. In cancer cells the adhesion plaques are dismantled; the resulting decrease in cell adhesion may contribute to the ease with which most cancer cells break away from their tissue of origin and metastasize to other sites.

Rohrschneider's findings suggested that pp 60v-*src* might dismantle adhe-   25
sion plaques by phosphorylating one of their component proteins, or perhaps several of those proteins. Pursuing that suggestion, Sefton and S. J. Singer of the University of California at San Diego showed that pp60v-*src* phosphorylates a tyrosine unit in vinculin, a protein that is a constituent of normal adhesion plaques and becomes dispersed throughout the cell following transformation by *src*. It seems reasonable to suggest that the phosphorylation of vinculin precipitates the dismantling of adhesion plaques, but the importance of such events in the unruly behavior of cancer cells has yet to be established.

Once it was thought that the oncogenic effects of viruses might be ancillary   26
manifestations of viral genes whose main function is to assist in the production of new virus particles. Now it is clear that the replication of retroviruses proceeds normally in the absence of oncogenes. How then can one explain the wide occurrence of oncogenes in retroviruses and their apparent conservation in the course of evolution? A decade of investigation has furnished a surprising answer. Retrovirus oncogenes are merely cellular genes in another guise, passengers acquired from the animals in which the viruses replicate. The discovery that cells too have oncogenes has implications extending far beyond tumor virology.

The Origin of Oncogenes

In 1972 Dominique Stehelin, Varmus and I set out to explore the "oncogene 27
hypothesis" proposed by Robert J. Huebner and George J. Todaro of the National Cancer Institute. Seeking one mechanism to explain the induction of
cancer by many different agents, Huebner and Todaro had suggested that retrovirus oncogenes are a part of the genetic baggage of all cells, perhaps acquired through viral infection early in evolution. The oncogenes would be innocuous as long as they remained quiescent. When stimulated into activity by
a carcinogenic agent, however, they could convert cells to cancerous growth.
We reasoned that if the hypothesis was correct, we might be able to find the
src gene in the DNA of normal cells.

The DNA of vertebrates includes tens of thousands of genes. To search for 28
src amid this vast array Stehelin fashioned a powerful tool: radioactive DNA
copied solely from *src* by reverse transcriptase. The copied DNA served as a
probe with which to search for cellular DNA with a nucleotide sequence similar to that of *src*. The search was carried out by molecular hybridization, in
which chains of a nucleic acid (either DNA or RNA) hybridize, or form com-
plexes, with nucleic acids to which they are related. We were exhilarated (and
more than a little surprised) to learn that Stehelin's copy of *src* could hybridize with DNA from uninfected chickens and other birds. Deborah H. Spector
joined us and went on to find DNA related to *src* in mammals, including human beings, and in fishes. We concluded that all vertebrates probably posess
a gene related to *src* in mammals, including human beings, and in fishes. We
concluded that all vertebrates probably possess a gene related to *src*, and it
therefore seemed the Huebner-Todaro oncogene hypothesis might be correct.

On closer inspection, however, the gene we had discovered in vertebrates 29
proved not to be a retrovirus gene at all. It is a cellular gene, which is now
called c-*src*. The most compelling evidence for this conclusion came from the
finding that the protein-encoding information of c-*src* is divided into several
separate domains, called exons, by intervening regions known as introns. A split
configuration of this kind is typical of animal-cell genes but not of the genes of
retroviruses. Apart from their introns, the versions of c-*src* found in fishes, birds
and mammals are all closely related to the viral gene v-*src* and to one another.
It appears the vertebrate *src* gene has survived long periods of evolution without major change, implying that it is important to the well-being of the species
in which it persists.

The mystery presented by c-*src* deepened with the discovery that the gene 30
not only is present in normal cells but also is active in them, that is, the gene
is transcribed into messenger RNA and the RNA is translated into protein. Molecular hybridization with Stehelin's radioactive copy of v-*src* brought the RNA
to view first, in both avian and mammalian cells. The protein was more elusive, mainly because it is synthesized in very small quantities in most cells.
Success came when we and others probed for the cellular protein with antibodies prepared originally for the pursuit of the viral transforming protein,
pp60v-*src*. The cellular protein isolated with the aid of these antibodies proved
to be virtually indistinguishable from the viral protein, and it was therefore
named pp60c-*src*. The two proteins are similar in size and chemical structure;

both catalyze the phosphorylation of tyrosine and both are tightly bound to the plasma membrane of cells (transformed cells in the case of pp60v-*src*, normal cells in the case of pp60c-*src*). It is as if the two proteins were designed for the same purpose, even though one is a viral protein that causes cancer and the other is a protein of normal cells.

Cellular Oncogenes

The findings with respect to *src* were the first hint of a generalization whose   31
extent and significance have yet to be established. Of 17 retrovirus oncogenes identified to date, 16 are known to have close relatives in the normal genomes of vertebrate species. Most of these cellular relatives of viral oncogenes obey the principles first deduced for c-*src*. They have the structural organization of cellular genes rather than of viral genes; they seem to have survived long periods of evolution, and they are active in normal cells. To account for these facts and for the remarkable similarity between retrovirus oncogenes and their normal cellular kin most virologists have settled on the idea that retrovirus oncogenes are copies of cellular genes. It appears the oncogenes were added to preexistent retrovirus genomes at some time in the not too distant past. How and why retroviruses have copied cellular genes is not known, but there is reason to think the copying continues today, and it may even be possible to recapitulate the process in the laboratory.

The vertebrate genes from which retrovirus oncogenes apparently arose were   32
at first called proto-oncogenes, to emphasize their evolutionary significance and to avoid implying that the cellular genes themselves have oncogenic potential. Now it is clear that they do have such potential. They are cellular oncogenes. The investigations that justify this designation began with this question: If retrovirus oncogenes are merely copies of genes found in normal cells, how can one account for the devastating effects of the viral genes on infected cells? Two explanations have been offered. The mutational hypothesis proposes that viral oncogenes differ from their cellular progenitors in subtle but important ways as a result of mutations introduced when the cellular genes were copied into the retrovirus genome. For example, the apparently similar enzymatic activities of pp60v-*src* and pp60c-*src* might actually have different targets in the cell and might therefore have very different effects on cellular behavior. The alternative dosage hypothesis suggests that retrovirus oncogenes act by brute force, overburdening cells with too much of what are essentially normal proteins carrying out normal functions. In this view the genesis of cancer by retrovirus oncogenes is related to the amount of the viral proteins rather than to any unique properties they have.

It is too early to know which of these views is correct, but initial indications   33
favor the dosage hypothesis. First, the doses of retrovirus transforming proteins are unquestionably large. The signals directing the activity of retrovirus genes are quite powerful, with the result that the amount of protein produced from a viral oncogene is far larger than the amount usually produced from the corresponding cellular gene; it is clearly possible that the cell might be overwhelmed. More important evidence has come from attempts to test a central prediction of the dosage hypothesis: If retrovirus oncogenes and cellular on-

cogenes are indeed identical in function, it should be possible to find circumstances under which the cellular genes themselves can induce cancerous growth.

Cellular-Gene Oncogenesis

The first test of this prediction came from the remarkable experiments of 34 Hidesaburo Hanafusa and his colleagues at Rockefeller University. Hanafusa found strains of the Rous sarcoma virus that had lost large portions of the *src* gene (but not all of it) and were therefore incapable of inducing the characteristic sarcoma in experimental animals. When Hanafusa injected the crippled viruses into chickens and then recovered the virus particles manufactured in the infected cells, he was astonished to discover that the v-*src* gene of the virus had been reconstituted. Apparently genetic material from the c-*src* gene was recombined with the viral genome while the virus was growing in the birds. The virus bearing the reconstituted gene was again fully capable of causing tumors, even though as much as three-fourths of its oncogene had just been acquired from a cellular gene. Hanafusa was able to repeat this extraordinary exercise at will, in quails as well as in chickens. His findings lent weight to the idea that the functions of c-*src* and v-*src* are the same, but many tumor virologists were unpersuaded in the absence of more direct evidence for the tumorigenic potential of the cellular genes.

Now such evidence is at hand. The research groups of George F. Vande 35 Woude and Edward M. Scolnick of the National Cancer Institute exploited the techniques of genetic engineering to isolate three cellular oncogenes (one from mice and the other two from rats) and to show directly that these genes can induce cancerous growth in cultured cells. The feat was accomplished by attaching to the cellular genes a viral "promoter," a DNA-encoded signal that helps to regulate the expression of a nearby gene. In accordance with the dosage hypothesis, when the *src*-promoter complex was introduced into cells, some of the cells were transformed as if they had received a viral oncogene, whereas what they had received was a cellular gene under viral orders to work harder than usual. Moreover, cells transformed by the two rat cellular oncogenes could be shown to make very large quantities of the proteins encoded by the genes, again in accordance with the dosage hypothesis.

Why should an overabundance of a normal protein wreak such havoc? The 36 question can be answered with assurance only when the role of cellular oncogenes in the orderly affairs of normal cells is understood. Perhaps cellular oncogenes are part of a delicately balanced network of controls that regulate the growth and development of normal cells. Excessive activity by one of these genes might tip the balance of regulation toward incessant growth.

There is evidence that the activities directed by viral and cellular oncogenes 37 do help to control the growth of normal cells. Whereas at first the phosphorylation of tyrosine by pp60v-*src* seemed to be an anomalous process whose foreign nature might underlie the cancerous response to *src*, that view was reversed when Stanley Cohen of the Vanderbilt University School of Medicine found a role for tyrosine phosphorylation in the housekeeping of normal cells. Having discovered and purified a small "epidermal growth factor" whose binding to the surface of cells stimulates DNA synthesis and cell division, he considered how the signal for these events might be transmitted from the exterior of the cell to the interior. Cohen first showed that the binding of epidermal growth factor to cells brings about phosphorylation of proteins; prompted by the findings with pp60v-*src*, he ultimately found that the phosphorylation elicited by epidermal growth factor specifically affects tyrosine. Other workers have since shown that some proteins phosphorylated in response to epidermal growth factor can be phosphorylated by pp60v-*src*. A normal stimulant of cell division (epidermal growth factor) and an abnormal one (pp60v-*src*) thus appear to play on the same keyboard. The implication is that tyrosine phosphorylation by pp60c-*src* has a part in regulating the growth of normal cells.

In Search of a Unified Theory

Retroviruses do not seem to be a major cause of human cancer. They may   38
nonetheless have pointed the way to the central mechanisms by which the disease arises. It is generally thought that cancer begins with damage to DNA, although the exact nature of the damage is in dispute. How might the damage cause cancerous growth? Most recent efforts to answer the question in a way that might apply to all forms of cancer have invoked the existence of "cancer genes": components of the normal cellular genome whose activity is unleashed or augmented by carcinogens of various kinds and is then responsible for sustaining the undisciplined behavior of cancer cells. In this scheme cancer genes are viewed not as alien intruders but as normal, indeed essential, genes run amok; the damage done by a carcinogen turns friend into foe, perhaps by acting directly on the cancer gene or perhaps by crippling a second gene that normally polices the activity of the cancer gene.

Medical geneticists may have detected the effects of cancer genes years ago,   39
when they first identified families whose members inherit a predisposition to some particular form of cancer. Now, it appears, tumor virologists may have come on cancer genes directly in the form of cellular oncogenes. In their viral form these genes are tumorigenic, and Vande Woude's and Scolnick's results imply that the cellular genes can also transform cells. It is therefore easy to imagine that cancer genes and the cellular oncogenes revealed by retroviruses are one and the same. The oncogene hypothesis has been restaged with the actors now cellular rather than viral genes; the dosage hypothesis serves to explain why the augmented activity of a normal cellular gene might cause cancer.

Evidence in support of these ideas comes from the study of chicken retro-   40
viruses that induce lymphoma, a lethal tumor of the immune system. The chicken lymphoma viruses have no oncogenes. Why then do they cause tumors? William S. Hayward and Benjamin G. Neel of Rockefeller University and Susan M. Astrin of the Institute for Cancer Research in Fox Chase, Pa., have discovered that in tumors induced by the chicken lymphoma viruses the viral DNA is almost always inserted into cellular DNA in the immediate vicinity of a single cellular oncogene (not c-*src* but a more recently recognized oncogene known as c-*myc*). As a seeming consequence of the insertion, the expression of the cellular oncogene is greatly amplified.

These findings fit the concept of cancer genes quite well. The insertion of   41 lymphoma-virus DNA into the host genome is analogous to mutagenesis or other forms of damage introduced by carcinogens of many kinds. The insertion apparently stimulates the activity of a gene that is known to be oncogenic when it appears (as v-*myc*) in a different chicken retrovirus; the stimulated action of the cellular oncogene seems to be responsible, at least in part, for the genesis of tumors. Retroviruses without oncogenes induce a variety of tumors; by identifying the site where the viral genome is inserted into cellular DNA in some of those tumors, virologists may be able to discover cancer genes not yet identified by other means.

The unveiling of cancer genes (in the form of cellular oncogenes) by retro-   42
viruses was serendipitous. Must investigators be content with the pace at which retroviruses thus offer up new oncogenes from within the cell? Apparently not. Robert A. Weinberg of M.I.T. and Geoffrey Cooper of the Harvard Medical School have broadened the search for cancer genes beyond the purview of tumor virology. They have shown that gene-length bits of DNA isolated from some tumors (tumors that were not induced by viruses) can transmit the property of cancerous growth when they are introduced into previously normal cells in culture.

Weinberg and Cooper have evidently found a way of transferring active can-   43
cer genes from one cell to another. They have evidence that different cancer genes are active in different types of tumors, and so it seems likely that their approach should appreciably expand the repertory of cancer genes available for study. None of the cancer genes uncovered to date by Weinberg and Cooper is identical with any known oncogene. Yet it is clearly possible that there is only one large family of cellular oncogenes. If that is so, the study of retroviruses and the procedures developed by Weinberg and Cooper should eventually begin to draw common samples from that single pool.

A Final Common Pathway

Normal cells may bear the seeds of their own destruction in the form of cancer   44
genes. The activities of these genes may represent the final common pathway by which many carcinogens act. Cancer genes may be not unwanted guests but essential constituents of the cell's genetic apparatus, betraying the cell only when their structure or control is disturbed by carcinogens. At least some of these genes may have appeared in retroviruses, where they are exposed to easy identification, manipulation and characterization.

What has been learned from oncogenes represents the first peep behind the   45
curtain that for so long has obscured the mechanisms of cancer. In one respect the first look is unnerving, because the chemical mechanisms that seem to drive the cancer cell astray are not different in kind from mechanisms at work in the normal cell. This suggests that the design of rational therapeutic strategies may remain almost as vexing as it is today. It will be of no use to invent means for impeding the activities responsible for cancerous growth if the same activities are also required for the survival of normal cells.

However the saga of oncogenes concludes, it presents some lessons for   46
everyone concerned with cancer research. The study of viruses far removed from human concerns has brought to light powerful tools for the study of human

disease. Tumor virology has survived its failure to find abundant viral agents of human cancer. The issue now is not whether viruses cause human tumors (as perhaps they may, on occasion) but rather how much can be learned from tumor virology about the mechanisms by which human tumors arise.

Considerations

1. You may find this article intimidating, particularly if you have little background in biology. But you needn't understand everything in the article to learn from it. If you approach it inquisitively, there's a good chance you'll leave with much more than you brought to it. To begin with, try working only with the first three paragraphs and the last three. Based on what you read there, write a one paragraph summary of what the article is about.

2. Articles in *Scientific American* are usually review articles; that is, they bring together into a coherent overview recent developments in the writer's field of expertise. Compile a list of the significant research contributions mentioned by J. Michael Bishop, providing a one- or two-sentence encapsulation of each contribution. Then link these encapsulations in a summary essay.

3. *Scientific American* articles are written for "the intelligent layman." What features of this article make it different from a direct report on original research presented to scientific colleagues?

4. Paragraphs 4 and 5 play a key role in introducing some of the features of cells that we need in making sense of the rest of the article. But the material there moves quickly, without much detail. As a way of getting more background, consult the index in a general biology textbook. Locate explanations for the following terms:DNA, RNA, nucleotides, genes, amino acids, enzymes, proteins, and viruses. After reading and taking notes on each of these terms, look back at the two paragraphs in the text; then write a well developed essay explaining in more detail the relations of these cellular elements.

5. *Genetic* is sometimes taken to mean "inherited from one's parents." Explain, with reference to this article, how cancer could be considered genetic without meaning that cancer is inherited.

6. Do viruses cause cancer? After pinning down what you mean by *cause*, argue that viruses do not cause cancer; then argue the opposite side, that viruses do cause cancer. Bring these two lines of argument to some sensible resolution.

7. Explain how viruses can be used as a tool of scientific research as opposed to an object of study in their own right.

8. It has been said that microbiologists have never helped cancer patients. What is meant by this charge, and do you feel that Bishop's article supports or refutes this claim?

9. At several points in his article Bishop makes reference to evolution. What could evolution have to do with the study of cancer? Explain in a short speculative essay.

10. What does the term *genetic engineering* mean? Illustrate, using an example from this article. Why is genetic engineering a volatile political issue?
11. Locate places where Bishop uses metaphors to help make his points. Analyze his use of them. Are there any generalizations you can offer?
12. Some historians of science criticize other historians of science for implying that scientific progress moves in straight lines, with one discovery leading directly to another. Science, these critics argue, moves in fits and starts. There are many dead ends, and sometimes theories discredited by one generation are rehabilitated by another. Which view of scientific progress does Bishop's article seem to endorse? After weighing both possibilities, defend your final judgment.

Connections

1. Henry Pitot, writing in the late 1970s said, "Although it has been clearly demonstrated that certain viruses can add genetic information to cells during cancer formation, the actual role of this process in conversion of a normal to a cancer cell has not been elucidated." Does J. Michael Bishop's article give us reason to amend this statement? Explain why or why not in a brief essay.
2. Does the oncogene hypothesis seem to encourage or to discourage the idea that cancer can be environmentally caused?
3. Lucien Israël says that strong doses of radiation can be mutagenic. Having read the J. Michael Bishop article, try to clarify what that means at the cellular level.
4. Do you think the work with oncogenes should encourage or discourage chemotherapeutic approaches? You will need to do some guessing, but defend your guesses with reasoning where you can.
5. Would Susan Sontag find J. Michael Bishop guilty of the cultural attitudes she criticizes? Explain why or why not, making reference to both selections.
6. Based on what you've read here, suggest a better metaphor than *war* for our relationship to cancer. Work out that metaphor in a short essay.
7. If you have been keeping a running list of what is not yet known about cancer, explain whether Bishop's article enables you to add or subtract anything from your list. Write up your list in summary form.
8. Why might molecular researchers find little of value in the definitions of cancer offered by the other readings in this chapter?

Further Connections

1. Compare and contrast some of the perspectives from which we may look at cancer. Draw freely on the selections in this chapter to provide illustration.

2. Based on the limited evidence in this chapter and supplemented by your own general knowledge, rank the following propositions from most to least likely, explaining your reasoning:

> Cigarettes cause cancer.
> Radiation causes cancer.
> Environmental factors cause cancer.
> Genetic damage causes cancer.
> Carcinogens cause cancer.
> Viruses cause cancer.
> Uncontrolled cellular growth causes cancer.
> Dietary factors cause cancer.
> Doctors cause cancer.
> Sunshine causes cancer.
> Oncogenes cause cancer.
> Research scientists cause cancer.

3. Using the various essays in this chapter and by doing some brainstorming of your own, write an essay evaluating cancer metaphors — metaphors for cancer and cancer itself as metaphor. What conclusions can you draw about cancer and thinking?

4. Write an essay about the economics of cancer. Take into consideration approaches toward treatment, cures, and prevention. Consider professions connected to cancer. Evaluate the cost in non-monetary terms as well as in monetary ones.

5. Write an essay analyzing several of the ways in which cancer is a political topic. How are the issues defined from various political perspectives?

6. Are doctors scientists? Before taking a stand, show why this could be a controversial question. Develop your argument by drawing examples from this chapter.

7. Write a sociological analysis of cancer. Consider the positions or roles it occupies, and consider the social issues with which it connects.

8. After reading the selections in Chapter 7, The Nature of Intelligence, classify and comment upon some of the forms of intelligence at work in the cancer field.

9. How are animal issues linked to cancer issues? Draw connections between the articles by Maggie Scarf and J. Michael Bishop in this chapter and those by William Tucker and Anne and Paul Ehrlich in Chapter 9, The Impact of Animals.

10. Write an essay analyzing cancer problems in terms of power. In thinking over possible approaches, consider biological, technological, social, linguistic, and political forms of power.

11. What is meant by "the scientific method"? After considering a range of scientific methods, evaluate some of the ones encountered in this chapter.

12. Newspapers are often accused of sensationalizing scientific developments. On the subject of cancer, newspaper accounts are apt to oversimplify in optimistic directions. Illustrate how this might happen by composing three newspaper articles varying from accurate to very distorted. Include head-

lines and use as your subject either the Simonton method or oncogene research.

Extensions

1. Look up the term *cancer* in a large, unabridged dictionary, such as the *Oxford English Dictionary*. Using the information you find there, including some of the short illustrative quotations, write a report describing the historical use of the term.
2. Locate two or more general biology textbooks and compare the coverage they give to cancer. Can you discern any differences in tone or emphasis?
3. Locate current indexes for two major newspapers (for example, the *New York Times* and the *Los Angeles Times*) and scan the space devoted to cancer over the course of a year. Using the indexes, write a tentative report, hazarding a few generalizations. What is the range of coverage? The depth? What sorts of headlines do the editors provide? Do the same writers tend to reappear? Overall, how do the two papers compare in coverage?
4. Using the same indexes as in question 3, target a few articles and take a closer look. Find at least one representative pairing of pieces that allows you to compare two writers' treatments of an issue in some detail.
5. Early detection is one of the keys in treating cancer effectively. What general advice is offered by the American Cancer Society or the American Medical Association for detecting cancer early? (One place to look is in *Toward the Conquest of Cancer* by Edward J. Beattie, Jr. — see Suggestions for Further Reading).
6. Consult at least two reputable sources that give advice about cancer prevention and write up the information there. Make sure that the advice is based upon solid epidemiological evidence. Divide your report into preventive measures that *might* help and measures that will *probably* help.
7. What have been some of the results of the national Cancer Act of 1971? A good place to begin is with Joseph Hixson's book, *The Patchwork Mouse* (see Suggestions for Further Reading).
8. Compile a list of some medical and quasi-medical treatments of cancer that have not been touched upon in this chapter. Organize your list from the least promising to the most promising treatments, showing evidence and reasoning for your organization.
9. According to some commentators the cancer in *Cancer Ward* by Russian novelist Alexander Solzhenitsyn (Translated by Nicholas Bethel and David Berg. New York: Farrar, Straus, and Giroux, 1968) has psychosomatic and political overtones. What can those overtones be? Write your own interpretation of this novel taking into account these possibilities.
10. The renowned biology essayist Lewis Thomas is also the head of the Sloan-Kettering Cancer Center in New York, yet the essays in his best known books, *The Lives of a Cell* (New York: Viking, 1974) and *The Medusa and the Snail* (New York: Viking, 1979), seldom touch directly upon the topic of cancer.

After browsing through one or both of these volumes, speculate upon why this might be. Then research Thomas's scientific writing (use the *Index Medicum)*, and look at the one general essay he has written about cancer in *Notes of a Medicine Watcher* (New York: Viking, 1983). Write a critical essay about the major themes in Thomas's writing, making whatever connections you can between these themes and his concerns as a cancer doctor.

11. Research a chemical alleged to be carcinogenic. What evidence has been compiled against it, and what procedures, if any, have been taken to curtail its public use? Two places to begin: nitrosamines and saccharine.

12. Two potential cancer treatments that have stirred excitement in the 1980s are those involving interferon and monoclonal antibodies (hybridomas). Compare these two potential treatments and report on the state of current research.

13. Analyze breast cancer as a medical and feminist issue. Look at recent shifts in the way breast cancer is treated medically. You might also want to take into account the claims made by Peggy Boyd in *The Silent Wound: A Startling Report on Breast Cancer and Sexuality* (Reading, Mass.: Addison-Wesley, 1985) that breast cancer can be influenced by adolescent sexual anxiety.

14. Starting with Suggestions for Further Reading, research the hospice movement. Analyze it as an alternative treatment of cancer and assess its influence in this country.

Suggestions for Further Reading

Beattie, Edward J., Jr. *Toward the Conquest of Cancer.* New York: Crown 1980. A cancer surgeon argues that most cancer is preventable and that many forms of cancer are being successfully combatted.

Cameron, Ewan, and Linus Pauling. *Cancer and Vitamin C.* Menlo Park, Ca.: The Linus Pauling Institute of Science and Medicine, 1979. Pauling, perhaps the greatest chemist of our time, has been a crusader for vitamin C. The experimental bases for the claims in this book are regarded as very controversial.

Collier, R. John, and Donald A. Kaplan. "Immunotoxins." *Scientific American* 251 (July 1984): 44–52. Describes research with monoclonal antibodies, the potential "magic bullets" for obliterating cancer cells.

Craddock, Valda M. "Nitrosamines and Human Cancer: Proof of an Association?" *Nature* (December 15, 1983): 638. Balances epidemiological evidence and animal experiments.

Devoret, Raymond. "Bacterial Tests for Potential Carcinogens." *Scientific American* 241 (August 1979): 40–49. Describes the Ames test and Devoret's own test for screening potential cancer-causing chemicals.

Ernster, Virginia, Susan T. Sacks, and Nicholas Petrakis. "The Tools of Cancer Epidemiology." In *Concepts in Cancer Medicine,* edited by S. Benham Kahn, Richard L. Love, Charles Sherman, Jr., and Ranes Chakravorty. New York:

Grune and Stratton, 1983. A good, concise account of epidemiological methods.

Goodfield, June. *The Siege of Cancer*. New York: Dell, 1975. A reporter's interviews with prominent cancer researchers. This book is now dated enough to offer interesting comparisons with present trends in cancer research.

Gould, Stephen Jay. "The Median Isn't the Message." *Discover* (June 1985): 40–42. This foremost natural science writer (see Chapters 7 and 9) has a rare form of cancer called mesothelioma. His essay is about interpreting cancer statistics, including those that bear upon his own disease.

Haskell, Charles M., ed. *Cancer Treatment*, 2nd ed. Philadelphia: W. B. Saunders, 1985. The state of the art: essays by medical specialists.

Hixson, Joseph. *The Patchwork Mouse*. New York: Anchor Press, 1976. A behind-the-scenes account of the politics of cancer research.

Holden, Constance. "Hospices for the Dying, Relief from Pain and Fear." In *A Hospice Handbook*, edited by Michael P. Hamilton and Helen F. Reid. Grand Rapids, Mich: William B. Eerdmans, 1980. A good account of the hospice movement originated in England by Cicely Saunders.

Markle, Gerald E., and James C. Peterson. *Politics, Science, and Cancer: the Laetrile Controversy*. Boulder, Colo.: Westview Press, 1980. An interdisciplinary symposium with a sociological emphasis, sponsored by the American Association for the Advancement of Science.

Pitot, Henry C. "Cancer — An Overview." In *Cancer: The Outlaw Cell*, edited by Richard E. La Fond. Washington, D.C.: American Chemical Society, 1978. Offers a brief historical perspective and discusses problems of definition and classification.

Reddy, E. Premkumar, Roberta K. Reynolds, Eugenio Santos, and Mariano Barbacid. "A point mutation is responsible for the acquisition of transforming properties by the T24 human bladder carcinoma oncogene." *Nature* 300 (November 11, 1982). The real stuff, a research account written for fellow scientists. See preliminary articles for context. You will have learned much if you can explain the title phrase by phrase.

Ter-Pogossian, Michel M., Marcus E. Raichle, and Burton E. Sobel. "Positron-Emission Tomography." *Scientific American* 243 (October 1980): 170–181. Technological advances in nuclear medicine.

Weinberg, Robert A. "A Molecular Basis for Cancer." *Scientific American* 249 (November 1983): 126–142. A review article incorporating the oncogene work of the Weinberg, Barbacid, and Bishop groups, among others.

9 The Impact of Animals

Edited by **Sonia Maasik**

In our everyday lives we surround ourselves with animals: we live with them in our homes, visit them in zoos and nature parks, experiment on them in science and industry, imaginatively recreate them in literature and art, and symbolically associate them with the products we advertise ("put a tiger in your tank!"). Whether real or imagined, beloved friends or feared pests, animals pervade our lives, even as our society grows increasingly urban and increasingly removed from our natural heritage. Our relationship with the animal world raises a complex question: what are the human needs that animals satisfy? It also raises another fundamental issue: how does the animal world shape our own self-conception, our own identity as human beings?

Many academic fields have explored our complicated relationship with the animal world, yielding a rich variety of insights. The humanities often focus on the ways animals activate our imaginations and enable us to address truths about *both* worlds. In children's literature, of course, animals have the characteristics of both child and adult. This can be seen in works ranging from *Alice in Wonderland* to *The Wind in the Willows*. But animals are not restricted to juvenile literature: in fact, they represent the best and the darkest sides of adult life. Medieval beast fables identified animal characters with human personality traits, while texts such as Rudyard Kipling's *Jungle Books* and George Orwell's *Animal Farm* use animals to allegorize human social and political organization. Such allegorization can be seen in the visual arts as well; we need only look at a Breughel maelstrom to see man's darker nature emerging from part-reptilian, part-satanic images. And in native art there is a profoundly spiritual evocation of the animal world, one that in totemic cultures such as the Eskimo not only respects animals but sees them as an origin for human identity. Here animals are important in both art and religion.

This symbolic, even mythical use of animals is explored by other disciplines as well. Among social scientists, anthropologists often take the material studied by the humanities — the art and artifacts — to examine the origins of human culture and its early manipulation of the world. The animal cave drawings at Lascaux, for instance, reveal both a sophisticated artistic sensibility and a complex human organization dependent upon the domestication of animals. Such use of animals as a human resource is a common focus of social scientists. Social historians may research the link between human social organization and the domestication of animals, as in the conflict between cattlemen and shepherds in the American West. Political scientists may study the roles animals (as livestock and as natural resources) play in international trade, law, and government. The attempt to ban the hunting of whales is just one instance where ethical interests intersect or collide with the hard realities of international politics. At the same time economists may view these very issues in more purely monetary terms, analyzing how the supply and demand of animal resources has an impact upon the human economy, an acute problem that both industrial and third-world nations share, although in radically different ways. For other social scientists such as sociobiologists the concern with animals centers on the biological basis of human social behavior and organization. By suggesting that human behavior is biologically determined, the sociobiologists have indeed raised a new controversy over our relationship with animals.

The sciences approach the animal world both as an object of study in itself and for the knowledge it can reveal about human beings. Zoologists and ethologists, microbiologists and paleontologists, all in different ways, shape their careers around solving the mysteries of the form and function, the behavior and history of animal life. Yet even when the scientific mysteries are human, research usually depends on animals as experimental subjects. Much medical research on cancer, for instance, is organized around the testing of animal systems homologous to human systems. The current debate over animal research signals our tremendous dependence on the animal world for our own health and welfare as well as our profound anxiety about whether we ought to extend moral consideration to that other world.

This chapter begins with economists Douglass North and LeRoy Miller boldly classifying animals as human property, thus leading to some hard questions about our relationship with animals: Are humans superior creatures who have property rights over animals? Or is it wrong to view animals, as the etymology of the word *cattle* suggests, as our *chattel?* Implicitly, the selections by Charles Darwin, Carl Sagan, and Stephen Jay Gould enter this debate by presenting biological, linguistic, and cultural evidence of our continuity with animals. Yet our face-to-face encounters with animals are not easily classified or interpreted. Read as a pair, the selections by naturalist Farley Mowat and historian Charles Beals describe conflicting responses to an animal that often haunts our imagination: the wolf. Together the two show how complex our relationship with animals can be. These complexities are next explored by William Tucker in contemporary political terms as he discusses the current concern over endangered species. The chapter closes with a selection by Anne and Paul Ehrlich, who outline concrete, familiar evidence for our psychological and emotional bonds to the animal world. Deep-rooted and strong, these bonds shape our understanding of both animals *and* ourselves.

The Economics of Animal Extinction

Douglass C. North and
Roger LeRoy Miller

In its report on the Endangered Species Act of 1973, the Senate Commerce   *1*
Committee concluded that the two major causes of animal extinction are hunting and destruction of habitat. There is certainly an element of truth in this
observation: ever since prehistoric times humans and animals have competed
for space and habitat on this planet. The problem, however, is more complex
than a simple statement of that sort.

Let us begin with prehistoric times. The destruction of animal species by   *2*
humans is nothing new. The arrival of human beings in North America about
12,000 years ago is usually tied to the extinction of most of the existing me-
gafauna. The LaBrea Tarpits yielded 24 mammals and 22 birds which no longer
exist. Among these are the saber tooth tiger, the giant llama, the 20-foot ground
sloth, a bison that stands 7 feet at the hump with 6-foot wide horns, etc.

In fact, only 0.02 percent of all of the species that have ever existed on earth   *3*
are currently extant. While many believe that human hunting was directly responsible for the destruction of these species, there is some evidence to the
contrary.

The argument for direct human guilt in destroying these animals is based   *4*
on the view that humans were indiscriminate, wasteful hunters. Hunting
methods such as driving animals over a cliff, which resulted in many more being
killed than could be used by the tribe, are illustrations of this indiscriminate
destruction of male and female animals alike. The fact that no group had exclusive property rights over animals meant that there was no incentive to husband the resource. If one group was careful and husbanded the animals, another group would simply exploit them in competition with that group.

This view has not gone unchallenged. Some have argued that, in fact, prim-   *5*
itive tribes did husband the resource and attempted to kill off only the weaker
animals, saving the females of the species. But note that the issue was still one
over property rights. To the degree that the animals were exclusively within
the hunting range of only one tribe, that tribe had an incentive to husband the
resource and to provide for a perpetual renewal of those animals.

Whether or not primitive tribes in America were responsible for the extinc-   *6*

*Douglass C. North (b. 1920), professor of economics at Washington University
in St. Louis, is also author of* Economic Growth of the United States, 1790–
1860 *(1961), with R. Thomas,* The Rise of the Western World *(1973), and* Structure and Change in Economic History *(1981).His collaborator, Roger LeRoy Miller
(b. 1943), is professor of economics at the University of Miami's Law and Economics Center.*

tion of many early animals and birds is still an open question; but the role of human beings in the extinction of animals at a later time is much clearer. The first known instance is the extinction of the European lion, the last survivor being dated in A.D. 80. In modern times the most famous example is that of the passenger pigeon. At one time these birds were the most numerous species of birds in North America and perhaps in the world. They nested and migrated together in huge flocks, and may have numbered more than a billion. When flocks passed overhead the sky would be dark with pigeons, literally for days at a time. Audubon measured one roost at 40 miles long and about 3 miles wide. While the Indians had long hunted these birds, it was the arrival of the white man and the demand for pigeons as a food source that led to their ultimate demise. The birds were netted in vast numbers. And by the end of the nineteenth century, an animal species which had been looked upon as literally indestructible because of its enormous numbers had almost completely disappeared. The last known passenger pigeon died in the Cincinnati zoo in 1914.

The American bison only narrowly escaped the same fate. The vast herds   7
that roamed the plains were an easy target for hunters; with the advent of the railroad and the need to feed railroad crews as transcontinental railroad lines were built, hunters like Buffalo Bill Cody killed bison by the thousands. Then as the demand for the fur of the bison increased, it became the target for still further hunting. Like the passenger pigeon, the bison appeared to be indestructible because of its numbers. But in the absence of any property rights over bison, the result was almost the same as with the passenger pigeon — bison were becoming extinct. Despite the outcries of the Indians who found their major food source being decimated, it was not until late in the nineteenth century that any efforts were made to protect the bison.

The fate of the passenger pigeon and of the bison illustrates the main di-   8
lemma of protecting endangered species. To the degree that there are no ownership rights over these animals, anyone can attempt to hunt them for private gain. The conflict between the needs of human beings for food or clothing and the survival of a particular species can only lead to one end — the extinction of the animal species.

In modern times, government has attempted, by means of state and federal   9
regulation, to limit hunting seasons and the number of animals or birds that may be taken. The results have been at least partially successful. It is probable that there are more deer in North America today than there were at the time of the colonists. The same is true for a number of other animal species. In effect, a rationing system (rather than prices) was used to limit the exploitation of a "common property resource." But the threatened extinction in modern times of many species of whales illustrates that the problem is far from resolved.

The pattern of harvesting whales has been the subject of international dis-   10
cussion ever since World War II; it was readily apparent to all concerned that without some form of restraint, the whaling population was in danger of extinction. The result was the setting up of an international regulatory body, the International Whaling Commission (IWC), in 1948, in an attempt to regulate international whaling through cooperative endeavor. But the IWC was virtually doomed from the start. Its members were given the right to veto any regulation they considered too restrictive; if a member decided to blatantly

disobey regulations, the IWC had no enforcement powers. Since some whaling nations, such as Chile and Peru, refused to join the IWC, quotas had little effect on these nations. And some IWC members have used nonmember flagships to circumvent the quotas themselves.

The story of the decimation of a species is probably best told in the events   *11* surrounding the blue whale. Even with the most modern equipment, the great blue whale, which sometimes weighs almost a hundred tons, is difficult to kill; but intensive hunting methods gradually reduced the stock from somewhere between 300,000 and 1,000,000 to, at present, somewhere between 600 and 3000. In the 1930–1931 winter season almost 30,000 blue whales were taken. By 1945–1946, less than 10,000 were taken; and in the late 1950s the yearly catch was down to around 1500 per year. By 1964–1965, the total was only 20 whales. In 1965, a ban was placed by the IWC on killing blue whales. But even after the ban, the hunting of blues continued from land stations by nonmembers such as Brazil, Chile, and Peru.

Humpback whales have suffered a similar fate. From an original population   *12* estimated at 300,000, there remain between 1500 and 5000 today. Like the blues, humpbacks are now under a hunting ban, but the lack of monitoring capacity makes it probable that the ban is only nominal. The problems of the IWC can be seen in the reactions to several conservation measures passed at the 1973 meeting. The United States pushed through measures banning the hunting of finbacks in the Antarctic, setting the quota on minke whales at 5000 instead of 12,000 as Japan requested, and instituting an area by area quota for sperm whales so that the total population would be protected. A year later, the Japanese and then the Russians, parties to these agreements, announced they would set more realistic quotas in line with Japanese interests.

Moreover, even where government regulations attempt to protect animals,   *13* poaching, a lucrative source of income, has been widespread. This is particularly true in poor nations: to an individual native hunter in Africa, the income from the ivory tusks of a single elephant may be the difference between starvation and relative abundance.

Nothing better illustrates the dilemma of animal extinction than the cases   *14* of the snail darter and of the coyote. The National Environmental Policy Act of 1969 made it mandatory that an environmental impact statement be made on all projects which would affect the environment. A mechanism was thus created for the protection of endangered species against environmental destruction. The most famous example involves the snail darter, a small fish whose existence was threatened by the construction of a dam proposed by the Tennessee Valley Authority (TVA). The environmental impact statement process required the TVA to list the extinction of the snail darter as the probable outcome of the construction of the dam. The 1973 Endangered Species Act, with its clause requiring emergency action to protect any species threatened with extinction, was invoked. The result was a national furor in which the benefits to humankind of the additional power to be provided by the dam were measured against the possible extinction of an obscure small fish, the existence of which was known only to a very small number of people. In fact, this issue was resolved when the TVA reevaluated the benefit costs of the dam and concluded that it was not worthwhile after all. Nevertheless, many people viewed the conflict as an absurd one in terms of the benefit costs of a snail darter versus hydroelectric power.

However, if the snail darter illustrates an absurdity in the efforts to save   *15* animals from extinction, the case of coyote versus sheep highlights a more difficult dilemma. The coyote has not come under protection, but the ways by which it can be hunted have been severely limited; in particular, some methods of poisoning the coyote have been restricted or forbidden, with the result that there has been an enormous growth in their population.

Lamb is a favorite food of the coyote. Consequently, the sheepherders in many   *16* areas have found it prohibitively expensive to raise sheep because of their ravaging by a growing coyote population. With fewer sheep, the relative prices of wool and lamb have risen significantly in the United States. What should be the outcome? Should the coyote be protected, as many environmental groups have insisted, and are we willing to pay the price of substantially higher costs for wool and lamb as a result? The conflict between man and animal species is not easily resolved, as these two cases illustrate.

Summary

If one were to draw up two separate lists of animals — those that are en-   *17* dangered and those that are not — one would be hard-pressed to come up with a single set of physical characteristics distinguishing the two. In actuality, the main distinction between endangered animals and nonendangered ones is that the former are common property. There is no incentive for a single individual to refrain from killing common property animals, because the action will have no effect on the total number of animals that ultimately survive. All of the government restrictions on hunting are an attempt to overcome the common property problem. Unfortunately, even government restrictions are hard to enforce in the case of animals that are constantly on the move, such as the whale.

Considerations

1. What would be the implications for Douglass North and Roger Miller's argument if wild animals were placed in a different economic category — say, *natural resources?*
2. Modern zoos are often considered the last preserve for endangered species. Discuss the ways in which zoos can illustrate North and Miller's economic principles.
3. Economists define *common* and *communal* property as that which "everyone has the right to use" and which "no one (not even the state) has the right to exclude anyone from using." Accordingly, North and Miller label endangered species *common property.* In an analytic essay, explain how their designation of wild animals as property influences the way they define the general problem of extinction.

Comparison of the Mental Powers of Man and the Lower Animals

Charles Darwin

The difference in mental power between the highest ape and the lowest savage, immense — Certain instincts in common — The emotions — Curiosity — Imitation — Attention — Memory — Imagination — Reason — Progressive improvement — Tools and weapons used by animals — Abstraction, self-consciousness — Language — Sense of Beauty — Belief in God, spiritual agencies, superstitions.

We have seen that man bears in his bodily structure clear traces of his descent from some lower form; but it may be urged that, as man differs so greatly in his mental power from all other animals, there must be some error in this conclusion. No doubt the difference in this respect is enormous, even if we compare the mind of one of the lowest savages, who has no words to express any number higher than four, and who uses hardly any abstract terms for common objects or for the affections,[1] with that of the most highly organised ape. The difference would, no doubt, still remain immense, even if one of the higher apes had been improved or civilised as much as a dog has been in comparison with its parent-form, the wolf or jackal. The Fuegians rank amongst the lowest barbarians; but I was continually struck with surprise how closely the three natives on board H.M.S. "Beagle," who had lived some years in England, and could talk a little English, resembled us in disposition and in most of our mental faculties. If no organic being excepting man had possessed any mental power, or if his powers had been of a wholly different nature from those of the lower animals, then we should never have been able to convince ourselves that our high faculties had been gradually developed. But it can be shewn that there is no fundamental difference of this kind. We must also admit that there is a much wider interval in mental power between one of the lowest fishes, as a lamprey or lancelet, and one of the higher apes, than between an ape and man; yet this interval is filled up by numberless gradations.   *1*

Nor is the difference slight in moral disposition between a barbarian, such   *2* as the man described by the old navigator Byron, who dashed his child on the rocks for dropping a basket of sea-urchins, and a Howard or Clarkson; and in intellect, between a savage who uses hardly any abstract terms, and a Newton or Shakespeare. Differences of this kind between the highest men of the high-

Charles Darwin (1809–1882) began his career as an amateur naturalist serving on the HMS. Beagle *and, as father of evolutionary theory, became the nineteenth century's most influential scientist. Among his most noteworthy publications are* A Naturalist's Voyage on the Beagle *(1839),* On the Origin of Species *(1859), and* The Descent of Man *(1871).*

est races and the lowest savages, are connected by the finest gradations. Therefore it is possible that they might pass and be developed into each other.

My object in this chapter is to shew that there is no fundamental difference between man and the higher mammals in their mental faculties. Each division of the subject might have been extended into a separate essay, but must here be treated briefly. As no classification of the mental powers has been universally accepted, I shall arrange my remarks in the order most convenient for my purpose; and will select those facts which have struck me most, with the hope that they may produce some effect on the reader. . . . The lower animals, like man, manifestly feel pleasure and pain, happiness and misery. Happiness is never better exhibited than by young animals, such as puppies, kittens, lambs, &c., when playing together, like our own children. Even insects play together, as has been described by that excellent observer, P. Huber,[2] who saw ants chasing and pretending to bite each other, like so many puppies.

The fact that the lower animals are excited by the same emotions as ourselves is so well established, that it will not be necessary to weary the reader by many details. Terror acts in the same manner on them as on us, causing the muscles to tremble, the heart to palpitate, the sphincters to be relaxed, and the hair to stand on end. Suspicion, the offspring of fear, is eminently characteristic of most wild animals. It is, I think, impossible to read the account given by Sir E. Tennent, of the behaviour of the female elephants, used as decoys, without admitting that they intentionally practise deceit, and well know what they are about. Courage and timidity are extremely variable qualities in the individuals of the same species, as is plainly seen in our dogs. Some dogs and horses are ill-tempered, and easily turn sulky; others are good-tempered; and these qualities are certainly inherited. Every one knows how liable animals are to furious rage, and how plainly they shew it. Many, and probably true, anecdotes have been published on the long-delayed and artful revenge of various animals. The accurate Rengger, and Brehm[3] state that the American and African monkeys which they kept tame, certainly revenged themselves. Sir Andrew Smith, a zoologist whose scrupulous accuracy was known to many persons, told me the following story of which he was himself an eye-witness; at the Cape of Good Hope an officer had often plagued a certain baboon, and the animal, seeing him approaching one Sunday for parade, poured water into a hole and hastily made some thick mud, which he skilfully dashed over the officer as he passed by, to the amusement of many bystanders. For long afterwards the baboon rejoiced and triumphed whenever he saw his victim.

The love of a dog for his master is notorious; as an old writer quaintly says,[4] "A dog is the only thing on this earth that luvs you more than he luvs himself."

In the agony of death a dog has been known to caress his master, and every one has heard of the dog suffering under vivisection, who licked the hand of the operator; this man, unless the operation was fully justified by an increase of our knowledge, or unless he had a heart of stone, must have felt remorse to the last hour of his life.

As Whewell[5] has well asked, "who that reads the touching instances of maternal affection, related so often of the women of all nations, and of the females of all animals, can doubt that the principle of action is the same in the two cases?" We see maternal affection exhibited in the most trifling details; thus

Rengger observed an American monkey (a Cebus) carefully driving away the flies which plagued her infant; and Duvaucel saw a Hylobates washing the faces of her young ones in a stream. So intense is the grief of female monkeys for the loss of their young, that it invariably caused the death of certain kinds kept under confinement by Brehm in N. Africa. Orphan monkeys were always adopted and carefully guarded by the other monkeys, both males and females. One female baboon had so capacious a heart that she not only adopted young monkeys of other species, but stole young dogs and cats, which she continually carried about. Her kindness, however, did not go so far as to share her food with her adopted offspring, at which Brehm was surprised, as his monkeys always divided everything quite fairly with their own young ones. An adopted kitten scratched this affectionate baboon, who certainly had a fine intellect, for she was much astonished at being scratched, and immediately examined the kitten's feet, and without more ado bit off the claws.[6] In the Zoological Gardens, I heard from the keeper that an old baboon *(C. chacma)* had adopted a Rhesus monkey; but when a young drill and mandrill were placed in the cage, she seemed to perceive that these monkeys, though distinct species, were her nearer relatives, for she at once rejected the Rhesus and adopted both of them. The young Rhesus, as I saw, was greatly discontented at being thus rejected, and it would, like a naughty child, annoy and attack the young drill and mandrill whenever it could do so with safety; this conduct exciting great indignation in the old baboon. Monkeys will also, according to Brehm, defend their master when attacked by any one, as well as dogs to whom they are attached, from the attacks of other dogs. But we here trench on the subjects of sympathy and fidelity, to which I shall recur. Some of Brehm's monkeys took much delight in teasing a certain old dog whom they disliked, as well as other animals, in various ingenious ways.

Most of the more complex emotions are common to the higher animals and ourselves. Every one has seen how jealous a dog is of his master's affection, if lavished on any other creature; and I have observed the same fact with monkeys. This shews that animals not only love, but have desire to be loved. Animals manifestly feel emulation. They love approbation or praise; and a dog carrying a basket for his master exhibits in a high degree self-complacency or pride. There can, I think, be no doubt that a dog feels shame, as distinct from fear, and something very like modesty when begging too often for food. A great dog scorns the snarling of a little dog, and this may be called magnanimity. Several observers have stated that monkeys certainly dislike being laughed at; and they sometimes invent imaginary offences. In the Zoological Gardens I saw a baboon who always got into a furious rage when his keeper took out a letter or book and read it aloud to him; and his rage was so violent that, as I witnessed on one occasion, he bit his own leg till the blood flowed. Dogs show what may be fairly called a sense of humour, as distinct from mere play; if a bit of stick or other such object be thrown to one, he will often carry it away for a short distance; and then squatting down with it on the ground close before him, will wait until his master comes quite close to take it away. The dog will then seize it and rush away in triumph, repeating the same manoeuvre, and evidently enjoying the practical joke.

We will now turn to the more intellectual emotions and faculties, which are very important, as forming the basis for the development of the higher mental powers. Animals manifestly enjoy excitement, and suffer from ennui, as may be seen with dogs, and, according to Rengger, with monkeys. All animals feel Wonder, and many exhibit Curiosity. They sometimes suffer from this latter quality, as when the hunter plays antics and thus attracts them; I have witnessed this with deer, and so it is with the wary chamois, and with some kinds of wild-ducks. Brehm gives a curious account of the instinctive dread, which his monkeys exhibited, for snakes; but their curiosity was so great that they could not desist from occasionally satiating their horror in a most human fashion, by lifting up the lid of the box in which the snakes were kept. I was so much surprised at this account, that I took a stuffed and coiled-up snake into the monkey-house at the Zoological Gardens, and the excitement thus caused was one of the most curious spectacles which I ever beheld. Three species of Cercopithecus were the most alarmed; they dashed about their cages, and uttered sharp signal cries of danger, which were understood by the other monkeys. A few young monkeys and one old Anubis baboon alone took no notice of the snake. I then placed the stuffed specimen on the ground in one of the larger compartments. After a time all the monkeys collected round it in a large circle, and staring intently, presented a most ludicrous appearance. They became extremely nervous; so that when a wooden ball, with which they were familiar as a plaything, was accidentally moved in the straw, under which it was partly hidden, they all instantly started away. These monkeys behaved very differently when a dead fish, a mouse,[7] a living turtle, and other new objects were placed in their cages; for though at first frightened, they soon approached, handled and examined them. I then placed a live snake in a paper bag, with the mouth loosely closed, in one of the larger compartments. One of the monkeys immediately approached, cautiously opened the bag a little, peeped in, and instantly dashed away. Then I witnessed what Brehm has described, for monkey after monkey, with head raised high and turned on one side, could not resist taking a momentary peep into the upright bag, at the dreadful object lying quietly at the bottom. It would almost appear as if monkeys had some notion of zoological affinities, for those kept by Brehm exhibited a strange, though mistaken, instinctive dread of innocent lizards and frogs. An orang, also, has been known to be much alarmed at the first sight of a turtle.[8]

The principle of Imitation is strong in man, and especially, as I have myself *10* observed, with savages. In certain morbid states of the brain this tendency is exaggerated to an extraordinary degree: some hemiplegic patients and others, at the commencement of inflammatory softening of the brain, unconsciously imitate every word which is uttered, whether in their own or in a foreign language, and every gesture or action which is performed near them.[9] Desor[10] has remarked that no animal voluntarily imitates an action performed by man, until in the ascending scale we come to monkeys, which are well known to be ridiculous mockers. Animals, however, sometimes imitate each other's actions: thus two species of wolves, which had been reared by dogs, learned to bark, as does sometimes the jackal,[11] but whether this can be called voluntary imitation is another question. Birds imitate the songs of their parents, and sometimes of other birds; and parrots are notorious imitators of any sound which they often hear. Dureau de la Malle gives an account[12] of a dog reared by a cat, who learnt to imitate the well-known action of a cat licking her paws, and thus washing her ears and face; this was also witnessed by the celebrated naturalist Audouin. I have received several confirmatory accounts; in one of these, a dog had not been suckled by a cat, but had been brought up with one, together with kittens, and had thus acquired the above habit, which he ever afterwards practised during his life of thirteen years. Dureau de la Malle's dog likewise learnt from the kittens to play with a ball by rolling it about with his fore paws, and springing on it. A correspondent assures me that a cat in his house used to put her paws into jugs of milk having too narrow a mouth for her head. A kitten of this cat soon learned the same trick, and practised it ever afterwards, whenever there was an opportunity.

The parents of many animals, trusting to the principle of imitation in their *11* young, and more especially to their instinctive or inherited tendencies, may be said to educate them. We see this when a cat brings a live mouse to her kittens; and Dureau de la Malle has given a curious account (in the paper above quoted) of his observations on hawks which taught their young dexterity, as well as judgment of distances, by first dropping through the air dead mice and sparrows, which the young generally failed to catch, and then bringing them live birds and letting them loose.

Hardly any faculty is more important for the intellectual progress of man *12* than Attention. Animals clearly manifest this power, as when a cat watches by a hole and prepares to spring on its prey. Wild animals sometimes become so absorbed when thus engaged, that they may be easily approached. Mr. Bartlett has given me a curious proof how variable this faculty is in monkeys. A man who trains monkeys to act in plays, used to purchase common kinds from the Zoological Society at the price of five pounds for each; but he offered to give double the price, if he might keep three or four of them for a few days, in order to select one. When asked how he could possibly learn so soon, whether a particular monkey would turn out a good actor, he answered that it all depended on their power of attention. If when he was talking and explaining anything to a monkey, its attention was easily distracted, as by a fly on the wall or other trifling object, the case was hopeless. If he tried by punishment to make an inattentive monkey act, it turned sulky. On the other hand, a monkey which carefully attended to him could always be trained.

It is almost superfluous to state that animals have excellent Memories for *13* persons and places. A baboon at the Cape of Good Hope, as I have been informed by Sir Andrew Smith, recognised him with joy after an absence of nine months. I had a dog who was savage and averse to all strangers, and I purposely tried his memory after an absence of five years and two days. I went near the stable where he lived, and shouted to him in my old manner; he shewed no joy, but instantly followed me out walking, and obeyed me, exactly as if I had parted with him only half an hour before. A train of old associations, dormant during five years, had thus been instantaneously awakened in his mind. Even ants, as P. Huber[13] has clearly shewn, recognised their fellow-ants belonging to the same community after a separation of four months. Animals can certainly by some means judge of the intervals of time between recurrent events.

The Imagination is one of the highest prerogatives of man. By this faculty *14* he unites former images and ideas, independently of the will, and thus creates brilliant and novel results. A poet, as Jean Paul Richter remarks,[14] "who must reflect whether he shall make a character say yes or no—to the devil with him; he is only a stupid corpse." Dreaming gives us the best notion of this power; as Jean Paul again says, "The dream is an involuntary art of poetry." The value of the products of our imagination depends of course on the number, accuracy, and clearness of our impressions, on our judgment and taste in selecting or rejecting the involuntary combinations, and to a certain extent on our power of voluntarily combining them. As dogs, cats, horses, and probably all the higher animals, even birds[15] have vivid dreams, and this is shewn by their movements and the sounds uttered, we must admit that they possess some power of imagination. There must be something special, which causes dogs to howl in the night, and especially during moonlight, in that remarkable and melancholy manner called baying. All dogs do not do so; and, according to Houzeau,[16] they do not then look at the moon, but at some fixed point near the horizon. Houzeau thinks that their imaginations are disturbed by the vague outlines of the surrounding objects, and conjure up before them fantastic images: if this be so, their feelings may almost be called superstitious.

Of all the faculties of the human mind, it will, I presume, be admitted that *15* Reason stands at the summit. Only a few persons now dispute that animals possess some power of reasoning. Animals may constantly be seen to pause, deliberate, and resolve. It is a significant fact, that the more the habits of any particular animal are studied by a naturalist, the more he attributes to reason and the less to unlearnt instincts.[17] In future chapters we shall see that some animals extremely low in the scale apparently display a certain amount of reason. No doubt it is often difficult to distinguish between the power of reason and that of instinct. For instance, Dr. Hayes, in his work on "The Open Polar Sea," repeatedly remarks that his dogs, instead of continuing to draw the sledges in a compact body, diverged and separated when they came to thin ice, so that their weight might be more evenly distributed. This was often the first warning which the travellers received that the ice was becoming thin and dangerous. Now, did the dogs act thus from the experience of each individual, or from the example of the older and wiser dogs, or from an inherited habit, that is from instinct? This instinct, may possibly have arisen since the time, long ago, when dogs were first employed by the natives in drawing their sledges; or the Arctic wolves, the parent-stock of the Esquimaux dog, may have acquired an instinct impelling them not to attack their prey in a close pack, when on thin ice.

We can only judge by the circumstances under which actions are per- *16* formed, whether they are due to instinct, or to reason, or to the mere association of ideas: this latter principle, however, is intimately connected with reason. A curious case has been given by Prof. Möbius,[18] of a pike, separated by a plate of glass from an adjoining aquarium stocked with fish, and who often dashed himself with such violence against the glass in trying to catch the other fishes, that he was sometimes completely stunned. The pike went on thus for three months, but at last learnt caution, and ceased to do so. The plate of glass was then removed, but the pike would not attack these particular fishes, though he would devour others which were afterwards introduced; so strongly was the idea of a violent shock associated in his feeble mind with the attempt on his former neighbours. If a savage, who had never seen a large plateglass window, were to dash himself even once against it, he would for a long time afterwards associate a shock with a window-frame; but very differently from the pike, he would probably reflect on the nature of the impediment, and be cautious under analogous circumstances. Now with monkeys, as we shall presently see, a painful or merely a disagreeable impression, from an action once performed, is sometimes sufficient to prevent the animal from repeating it. If we attribute this difference between the monkey and the pike solely to the association of ideas being so much stronger and more persistent in the one than the other, though the pike often received much the more severe injury, can we maintain in the case of man that a similar difference implies the possession of a fundamentally different mind?

Houzeau relates[19] that, whilst crossing a wide and arid plain in Texas, his two dogs suffered greatly from thirst, and that between thirty and forty times they rushed down the hollows to search for water. These hollows were not valleys, and there were no trees in them, or any other difference in the vegetation, and as they were absolutely dry there could have been no smell of damp earth. The dogs behaved as if they knew that a dip in the ground offered them the best chance of finding water, and Houzeau has often witnessed the same behaviour in other animals.   *17*

I have seen, as I daresay have others, that when a small object is thrown on the ground beyond the reach of one of the elephants in the Zoological Gardens, he blows through his trunk on the ground beyond the object, so that the current reflected on all sides may drive the object within his reach. Again a well-known ethnologist, Mr. Westropp, informs me that he observed in Vienna a bear deliberately making with his paw a current in some water, which was close to the bars of his cage, so as to draw a piece of floating bread within his reach. These actions of the elephant and bear can hardly be attributed to instinct or inherited habit, as they would be of little use to an animal in a state of nature. Now, what is the difference between such actions, when performed by an uncultivated man, and by one of the higher animals?   *18*

The savage and the dog have often found water at a low level, and the coincidence under such circumstances has become associated in their minds. A cultivated man would perhaps make some general proposition on the subject; but from all that we know of savages it is extremely doubtful whether they would do so, and a dog certainly would not. But a savage, as well as a dog, would search in the same way, though frequently disappointed; and in both it seems to be equally an act of reason, whether or not any general proposition on the subject is consciously placed before the mind.[20] The same would apply to the elephant and the bear making currents in the air or water. The savage would certainly neither know nor care by what law the desired movements were effected; yet his act would be guided by a rude process of reasoning, as surely as would a philosopher in his longest chain of deductions. There would no doubt be this difference between him and one of the higher animals, that he would take notice of much slighter circumstances and conditions, and would observe any connection between them after much less experience and this would be of paramount importance. I kept a daily record of the actions of one of my in-   *19* fants, and when he was about eleven months old, and before he could speak a single word, I was continually struck with the greater quickness, with which all sorts of objects and sounds were associated together in his mind, compared with that of the most intelligent dogs I ever knew. But the higher animals differ in exactly the same way in this power of association from those low in the scale, such as the pike, as well as in that of drawing inferences and observation.

The promptings of reason, after very short experience, are well shewn by the following actions of American monkeys, which stand low in their order. Rengger, a most careful observer, states that when he first gave eggs to his monkeys in Paraguay, they smashed them, and thus lost much of their contents; afterwards they gently hit one end against some hard body, and picked off the bits of shell with their fingers. After cutting themselves only *once* with any sharp tool, they would not touch it again, or would handle it with the greatest caution. Lumps of sugar were often given them wrapped up in paper; and Rengger sometimes put a live wasp in the paper, so that in hastily unfolding it they got stung; after this had *once* happened, they always first held the packet to their ears to detect any movement within.[21]   20

The following cases relate to dogs. Mr. Colquhoun[22] winged two wild-ducks, which fell on the further side of a stream; his retriever tried to bring over both at once, but could not succeed; she then, though never before known to ruffle a feather, deliberately killed one, brought over the other, and returned for the dead bird. Col. Hutchinson relates that two partridges were shot at once, one being killed, the other wounded; the latter ran away, and was caught by the retriever, who on her return came across the dead bird; "she stopped, evidently greatly puzzled, and after one or two trials, finding she could not take it up without permitting the escape of the winged bird, she considered a moment, then deliberately murdered it by giving it a severe crunch, and afterwards brought away both together. This was the only known instance of her ever having wilfully injured any game." Here we have reason though not quite perfect, for the retriever might have brought the wounded bird first and then returned for the dead one, as in the case of the two wild-ducks. I give the above cases, as resting on the evidence of two independent witnesses, and because in both instances the retrievers, after deliberation, broke through a habit which is inherited by them (that of not killing the game retrieved), and because they shew how strong their reasoning faculty must have been to overcome a fixed habit.   21

I will conclude by quoting a remark by the illustrious Humboldt.[23] "The muleteers in S. America say, 'I will not give you the mule whose step is easiest, but *la mas racional*,—the one that reasons best;' " and as he adds, "this popular expression, dictated by long experience, combats the system of animated machines, better perhaps than all the arguments of speculative philosophy." Nevertheless some writers even yet deny that the higher animals possess a trace of reason; and they endeavor to explain away, by what appears to be mere verbiage, all such facts as those above given.   22

It has, I think, now been shewn that man and the higher animals, especially the Primates, have some few instincts in common.   23

NOTES

[1] See the evidence on those points, as given by Lubbock, "Prehistoric Times," p. 354, etc.

[2] "Recherches sur les Mœurs des Fourmis," 1810, p. 173.

[3] All the following statements, given on the authority of these two naturalists, are taken from Rengger's "Naturgesch. der Säugethiere von Paraguay," 1830, s. 41–57, and from Brehm's "Thierleben," B. i. s. 10–87.

[4] Quoted by Dr. Lauder Lindsay, in his "Physiology of Mind in the Lower Animals;" "Journal of Mental Science," April 1871, p. 38.

[5] "Bridgewater Treatise," p. 263.

[6] A critic, without any grounds ("Quarterly Review," July, 1871, p. 72), disputes the possibility of this act as described by Brehm, for the sake of discrediting my work. Therefore I tried, and found that I could readily seize with my own teeth the sharp little claws of a kitten nearly five weeks old.

[7] I have given a short account of their behaviour on this occasion in my "Expression of the Emotions," p. 43.

[8] W. C. L. Martin, "Nat. Hist. of Mammalia," 1841, p. 405.

[9] Dr. Bateman "On Aphasia," 1870, p. 110.

[10] Quoted by Vogt, "Mémoire sur les Microcéphales," 1867, p. 168.

[11] "The Variation of Animals and Plants under Domestication," vol. i. p. 27.

[12] "Annales des Sc. Nat." (1st Series), tom. xxii. p. 397.

[13] "Les Mœurs des Fourmis," 1810, p. 150.

[14] Quoted in Dr. Maudsley's "Physiology and Pathology of Mind," 1868, pp. 19, 220.

[15] Dr. Jerdon, "Birds of India," vol. i. 1862, p. xxi. Houzeau says that his parokeets and canary-birds dreamt: "Facultés Mentales," tom. ii. p. 136.

[16] "Facultés Mentales des Animaux," 1872, tom. ii. p. 181.

[17] Mr. L. H. Morgan's work on "The American Beaver," 1868, offers a good illustration of this remark. I cannot help thinking, however, that he goes too far in underrating the power of instinct.

[18] "Die Bewegung der Thiere," &c., 1873, p. 11.

[19] "Facultés Mentales des Animaux," 1872, tom. ii. p. 265.

[20] Prof. Huxley has analysed with admirable clearness the mental steps by which a man, as well as a dog, arrives at a conclusion in a case analogous to that given in my text. See his article, "Mr. Darwin's Critics," in the "Contemporary Review," Nov. 1871, p. 462, and in his "Critques and Essays," 1873, p. 279.

[21] Mr. Belt, in his most interesting work, "The Naturalist in Nicaragua," 1874 (p. 119), likewise describes various actions of a tamed Cebus, which, I think, clearly shew that this animal possessed some reasoning power.

[22] "The Moor and the Loch," p. 45. Col. Hutchinson on "Dog Breaking," 1850, p. 46.

[23] "Personal Narrative," Eng. translat., vol. iii. p. 106.

Considerations

1. Examine the organization of the Darwin selection. How is the argument arranged? How might this organization be especially well-suited for a hostile or skeptical readership?

2. Test Darwin's argument that humans share with animals many emotional and mental powers using a family pet as your evidence.

3. Evaluate the evidence that Darwin uses to support his claim that humans and animals share mental abilities: to what extent do his examples justify his claims?

4. Many readers today may find Darwin's nineteenth-century language quaint. List as many examples of such quaint diction and sentence structure as you can find. Then use this list to write a short description of nineteenth-century writing style as we find it in Darwin.

Connections

1. Charles Darwin believes both in a continuity between animals and humans *and* in human superiority over all other beasts. Speculate on Darwin's response to Douglass North and Roger Miller's classifications of animals as human property, writing your essay as if you were Charles Darwin.

The Abstractions of Beasts

Carl Sagan

"Beasts abstract not," announced John Locke, expressing mankind's prevailing opinion throughout recorded history. Bishop Berkeley had, however, a sardonic rejoinder: "If the fact that brutes abstract not be made the distinguishing property of that sort of animal, I fear a great many of those that pass for men must be reckoned into their number." Abstract thought, at least in its more subtle varieties, is not an invariable accompaniment of everyday life for the average man. Could abstract thought be a matter not of kind but of degree? Could other animals be capable of abstract thought but more rarely or less deeply than humans?   *1*

We have the impression that other animals are not very intelligent. But have we examined the possibility of animal intelligence carefully enough, or, as in François Truffaut's poignant film *The Wild Child*, do we simply equate the absence of our style of expression of intelligence with the absence of intelligence? In discussing communication with the animals, the French philosopher Montaigne remarked, "The defect that hinders communication betwixt them and us, why may it not be on our part as well as theirs?"   *2*

There is, of course, a considerable body of anecdotal information suggesting chimpanzee intelligence. The first serious study of the behavior of simians—including their behavior in the wild—was made in Indonesia by Alfred Russel Wallace, the co-discoverer of evolution by natural selection. Wallace concluded that a baby orangutan he studied behaved "exactly like a human child in similar circumstances." In fact, "orangutan" is a Malay phrase meaning not ape but "man of the woods." Teuber recounted many stories told by his parents, pioneer German ethologists who founded and operated the first research   *3*

Well-known for bringing complex scientific problems to a general audience, Carl Sagan (b. 1934) is the author of many books including The Dragons of Eden *(1977),* Broca's Brain *(1979), and with I. S. Shklovsky,* Intelligent Life in the Universe *(1966). He is David Duncan Professor of Astronomy and Space Science at Cornell University.*

station devoted to chimpanzee behavior on Tenerife in the Canary Islands early in the second decade of this century. It was here that Wolfgang Kohler performed his famous studies of Sultan, a chimpanzee "genius" who was able to connect two rods in order to reach an otherwise inaccessible banana. On Tenerife, also, two chimpanzees were observed maltreating a chicken: One would extend some food to the fowl, encouraging it to approach; whereupon the other would thrust at it with a piece of wire it had concealed behind its back. The chicken would retreat but soon allow itself to approach once again—and be beaten once again. Here is a fine combination of behavior sometimes thought to be uniquely human: cooperation, planning a future course of action, deception and cruelty. It also reveals that chickens have a very low capacity for avoidance learning.

Until a few years ago, the most extensive attempt to communicate with chimpanzees went something like this: A newborn chimp was taken into a household with a newborn baby, and both would be raised together—twin cribs, twin bassinets, twin high chairs, twin potties, twin diaper pails, twin baby-powder cans. At the end of three years, the chimp had, of course, far outstripped the young human in manual dexterity, running, leaping, climbing and other motor skills. But while the child was happily babbling away, the chimp could say only, and with enormous difficulty, "Mama," "Papa," and "cup." From this it was widely concluded that in language, reasoning and other higher mental functions, chimpanzees were only minimally competent: "Beasts abstract not." 4

But in thinking over these experiments, two psychologists, Beatrice and Robert Gardner, at the University of Nevada realized that the pharynx and larynx of the chimp are not suited for human speech. Human beings exhibit a curious multiple use of the mouth for eating, breathing and communicating. In insects such as crickets, which call to one another by rubbing their legs, these three functions are performed by completely separate organ systems. Human spoken language seems to be adventitious. The exploitation of organ systems with other functions for communication in humans is also indicative of the comparatively recent evolution of our linguistic abilities. It might be, the Gardners reasoned, that chimpanzees have substantial language abilities which could not be expressed because of the limitations of their anatomy. Was there any symbolic language, they asked, that could employ the strengths rather than the weaknesses of chimpanzee anatomy? 5

The Gardners hit upon a brilliant idea: Teach a chimpanzee American sign language, known by its acronym Ameslan, and sometimes as "American deaf and dumb language" (the "dumb" refers, of course, to the inability to speak and not to any failure of intelligence). It is ideally suited to the immense manual dexterity of the chimpanzee. It also may have all the crucial design features of verbal languages. 6

There is by now a vast library of described and filmed conversations, employing Ameslan and other gestural languages, with Washoe, Lucy, Lana and other chimpanzees studied by the Gardners and others. Not only are there chimpanzees with working vocabularies of 100 to 200 words; they are also able to distinguish among nontrivially different grammatical patterns and syntaxes. What is more, they have been remarkably inventive in the construction of new words and phrases. 7

On seeing for the first time a duck land quacking in a pond, Washoe ges-   8
tured "water bird," which is the same phrase used in English and other languages, but which Washoe invented for the occasion. Having never seen a
spherical fruit other than an apple, but knowing the signs for the principal colors, Lana, upon spying a technician eating an orange, signed "orange apple."
After tasting a watermelon, Lucy described it as "candy drink" or "drink fruit,"
which is essentially the same word form as the English "water melon." But
after she had burned her mouth on her first radish, Lucy forever after described them as "cry hurt food." A small doll placed unexpectedly in Washoe's
cup elicited the response "Baby in my drink." When Washoe soiled, particularly clothing or furniture, she was taught the sign "dirty," which she then extrapolated as a general term of abuse. A rhesus monkey that evoked her displeasure was repeatedly signed at: "Dirty monkey, dirty monkey, dirty monkey."
Occasionally Wahoe would say things like "Dirty Jack, gimme drink." Lana,
in a moment of creative annoyance, called her trainer "You green shit." Chimpanzees have invented swear words. Washoe also seems to have a sort of sense
of humor; once, when riding on her trainer's shoulders and, perhaps inadvertently, wetting him, she signed: "Funny, funny."

Lucy was eventually able to distinguish clearly the meanings of the phrases   9
"Roger tickle Lucy" and "Lucy tickle Roger," both of which activities she enjoyed with gusto. Likewise, Lana extrapolated from "Tim groom Lana" to "Lana
groom Tim." Washoe was observed "reading" a magazine—i.e., slowly turning
the pages, peering intently at the pictures and making, to no one in particular,
an appropriate sign, such as "cat" when viewing a photograph of a tiger, and
"drink" when examining a Vermouth advertisement. Having learned the sign
"open" with a door, Washoe extended the concept to a briefcase. She also attempted to converse in Ameslan with the laboratory cat, who turned out to be
the only illiterate in the facility. Having acquired this marvelous method of
communication, Washoe may have been surprised that the cat was not also
competent in Ameslan. And when one day Jane, Lucy's foster mother, left the
laboratory, Lucy gazed after her and signed: "Cry me. Me cry."

Boyce Rensberger is a sensitive and gifted reporter for the *New York Times*   10
whose parents could neither speak nor hear, although he is in both respects
normal. His first language, however, was Ameslan. He had been abroad on a
European assignment for the *Times* for some years. On his return to the United
States, one of his first domestic duties was to look into the Gardners' experiments with Washoe. After some little time with the chimpanzee, Rensberger
reported, "Suddenly I realized I was conversing with a member of another
species in my native tongue." The use of the word tongue is, of course, figurative: it is built deeply into the structure of the language (a word that also means
"tongue"). In fact, Rensberger was conversing with a member of another species in his native "hand." And it is just this transition from tongue to hand
that has permitted humans to regain the ability—lost, according to Josephus,
since Eden—to communicate with the animals.

In addition to Ameslan, chimpanzees and other nonhuman primates are being   11
taught a variety of other gestural languages. At the Yerkes Regional Primate
Research Center in Atlanta, Georgia, they are learning a specific computer language called (by the humans, not the chimps) "Yerkish." The computer rec-

ords all of its subjects' conversations, even during the night when no humans are in attendance; and from its ministrations we have learned that chimpanzees prefer jazz to rock and movies about chimpanzees to movies about human beings. Lana had, by January 1976, viewed *The Developmental Anatomy of the Chimpanzee* 245 times. She would undoubtedly appreciate a larger film library. . . .

    . . . The machine provides for many of Lana's needs, but not all. Some-   12
times, in the middle of the night, she forlornly types out: "Please, machine, tickle Lana." More elaborate requests and commentaries, each requiring a creative use of a set grammatical form, have been developed subsequently.

    Lana monitors her sentences on a computer display, and erases those with   13
grammatical errors. Once, in the midst of Lana's construction of an elaborate sentence, her trainer mischievously and repeatedly interposed, from his separate computer console, a word that made nonsense of Lana's sentence. She gazed at her computer display, spied her trainer at his console, and composed a new sentence: "Please, Tim, leave room." Just as Washoe and Lucy can be said to speak, Lana can be said to write.

    At an early stage in the development of Washoe's verbal abilities, Jacob   14
Bronowski and a colleague wrote a scientific paper denying the significance of Washoe's use of gestural language because, in the limited data available to Bronowski, Washoe neither inquired nor negated. But later observations showed that Washoe and other chimpanzees were perfectly able both to ask questions and to deny assertions put to them. And it is difficult to see any significant difference in quality between chimpanzee use of gestural language and the use of ordinary speech by children in a manner that we unhesitatingly attribute to intelligence. In reading Bronowski's paper I cannot help but feel that a little pinch of human chauvinism has crept in, an echo of Locke's "Beasts abstract not." In 1949, the American anthropologist Leslie White stated unequivocally: "Human behavior is symbolic behavior; symbolic behavior is human behavior." What would White have made of Washoe, Lucy and Lana?

    These findings on chimpanzee language and intelligence have an intriguing   15
bearing on "Rubicon" arguments—the contention that the total brain mass, or at least the ratio of brain to body mass, is a useful index of intelligence. Against this point of view it was once argued that the lower range of the brain masses of microcephalic humans overlaps the upper range of brain masses of adult chimpanzees and gorillas; and yet, it was said, microcephalics have some, although severely impaired, use of language—while the apes have none. But in only relatively few cases are microcephalics capable of human speech. One of the best behavioral descriptions of microcephalics was written by a Russian physician, S. Korsakov, who in 1893 observed a female microcephalic named "Masha." She could understand a very few questions and commands and could occasionally reminisce on her childhood. She sometimes chattered away, but there was little coherence to what she uttered. Korsakov characterized her speech as having "an extreme poverty of logical associations." As an example of her poorly adapted and automaton-like intelligence, Korsakov described her eating habits. When food was present on the table, Masha would eat. But if the food was abruptly removed in the midst of a meal, she would behave as if the

meal had ended, thanking those in charge and piously blessing herself. If the food were returned, she would eat again. The pattern apparently was subject to indefinite repetition. My own impression is that Lucy or Washoe would be a far more interesting dinner companion than Masha, and that the comparison of microcephalic humans with normal apes is not inconsistent with some sort of "Rubicon" of intelligence. Of course, both the quality and the quantity of neural connections are probably vital for the sorts of intelligence that we can easily recognize.

Recent experiments performed by James Dewson of the Stanford University 16 School of Medicine and his colleagues give some physiological support to the idea of language centers in the simian neocortex—in particular, like humans, in the left hemisphere. Monkeys were trained to press a green light when they heard a hiss and a red light when they heard a tone. Some seconds after a sound was heard, the red or the green light would appear at some unpredictable position—different each time—on the control panel. The monkey pressed the appropriate light and, in the case of a correct guess, was rewarded with a pellet of food. Then the time interval between hearing the sound and seeing the light was increased up to twenty seconds. In order to be rewarded, the monkeys now had to remember for twenty seconds which noise they had heard. Dewson's team then surgically excised part of the so-called auditory association cortex from the left hemisphere of the neocortex in the temporal lobe. When retested, the monkeys had very poor recall of which sound they were then hearing. After less than a second they could not recall whether it was a hiss or a tone. The removal of a comparable part of the temporal lobe from the right hemisphere produced no effect whatever on this task. "It looks," Dewson was reported to say, "as if we removed the structure in the monkeys' brains that may be analogous to human language centers." Similar studies on rhesus monkeys, but using visual rather than auditory stimuli, seem to show no evidence of a difference between the hemispheres of the neocortex.

Because adult chimpanzees are generally thought (at least by zookeepers) 17 to be too dangerous to retain in a home or home environment, Washoe and other verbally accomplished chimpanzees have been involuntarily "retired" soon after reaching puberty. Thus we do not yet have experience with the adult language abilities of monkeys and apes. One of the most intriguing questions is whether a verbally accomplished chimpanzee mother will be able to communicate language to her offspring. It seems very likely that this should be possible and that a community of chimps initially competent in gestural language could pass down the language to subsequent generations.

Where such communication is essential for survival, there is already some 18 evidence that apes transmit extragenetic or cultural information. Jane Goodall observed baby chimps in the wild emulating the behavior of their mothers and learning the reasonably complex task of finding an appropriate twig and using it to prod into a termite's nest so as to acquire some of these tasty delicacies.

Differences in group behavior—something that it is very tempting to call 19 cultural differences—have been reported among chimpanzees, baboons, macaques and many other primates. For example, one group of monkeys may know how to eat bird's eggs, while an adjacent band of precisely the same species may not. Such primates have a few dozen sounds or cries, which are used for intra-group communication, with such meanings as "Flee; here is a predator." But the sound of the cries differs somewhat from group to group: there are regional accents.

An even more striking experiment was performed accidentally by Japanese   20
primatologists attempting to relieve an overpopulation and hunger problem in a community of macaques on an island in south Japan. The anthropologists threw grains of wheat on a sandy beach. Now it is very difficult to separate wheat grains one by one from sand grains; such an effort might even expend more energy than eating the collected wheat would provide. But one brilliant macaque, Imo, perhaps by accident or out of pique, threw handfuls of the mixture into the water. Wheat floats; sand sinks, a fact that Imo clearly noted. Through the sifting process she was able to eat well (on a diet of soggy wheat, to be sure). While older macaques, set in their ways, ignored her, the younger monkeys appeared to grasp the importance of her discovery, and imitated it. In the next generation, the practice was more widespread; today all macaques on the island are competent at water sifting, an example of a cultural tradition among the monkeys.

Earlier studies on Takasakiyama, a mountain in northeast Kyushu inhab-   21
ited by macaques, show a similar pattern in cultural evolution. Visitors to Takasakiyama threw caramels wrapped in paper to the monkeys—a common practice in Japanese zoos, but one the Takasakiyama macaques had never before encountered. In the course of play, some young monkeys discovered how to unwrap the caramels and eat them. The habit was passed on successively to their playmates, their mothers, the dominant males (who among the macaques act as babysitters for the very young) and finally to the subadult males, who were at the furthest social remove from the monkey children. The process of acculturation took more than three years. In natural primate communities, the existing nonverbal communications are so rich that there is little pressure for the development of a more elaborate gestural language. But if gestural language were necessary for chimpanzee survival, there can be little doubt that it would be transmitted culturally down through the generations.

I would expect a significant development and elaboration of language in only   22
a few generations if all the chimps unable to communicate were to die or fail to reproduce. Basic English corresponds to about 1,000 words. Chimpanzees are already accomplished in vocabularies exceeding 10 percent of that number. Although a few years ago it would have seemed the most implausible science fiction, it does not appear to me out of the question that, after a few generations in such a verbal chimpanzee community, there might emerge the memoirs of the natural history and mental life of a chimpanzee, published in English or Japanese (with perhaps an "as told to" after the by-line).

If chimpanzees have consciousness, if they are capable of abstractions, do   23
they not have what until now has been described as "human rights"? How smart does a chimpanzee have to be before killing him constitutes murder? What further properties must he show before religious missionaries must consider him worthy of attempts at conversion?

I recently was escorted through a large primate research laboratory by its   24
director. We approached a long corridor lined, to the vanishing point as in a

perspective drawing, with caged chimpanzees. They were one, two or three to a cage, and I am sure the accommodations were exemplary as far as such institutions (or for that matter traditional zoos) go. As we approached the nearest cage, its two inmates bared their teeth and with incredible accuracy let fly great sweeping arcs of spittle, fairly drenching the lightweight suit of the facility's director. They then uttered a staccato of short shrieks, which echoed down the corridor to be repeated and amplified by other caged chimps, who had certainly not seen us, until the corridor fairly shook with the screeching and banging and rattling of bars. The director informed me that not only spit is apt to fly in such a situation; and at his urging we retreated.

I was powerfully reminded of those American motion pictures of the 1930s 25 and 40s, set in some vast and dehumanized state or federal penitentiary, in which the prisoners banged their eating utensils against the bars at the appearance of the tyrannical warden. These chimps are healthy and well-fed. If they are "only" animals, if they are beasts which abstract not, then my comparison is a piece of sentimental foolishness. But chimpanzees *can* abstract. Like other mammals, they are capable of strong emotions. They have certainly committed no crimes. I do not claim to have the answer, but I think it is certainly worthwhile to raise the question: Why, exactly, all over the civilized world, in virtually every major city, are apes in prison?

For all we know, occasional viable crosses between humans and chimpan- 26 zees are possible. The natural experiment must have been tried very infrequently, at least recently. If such offspring are ever produced, what will their legal status be? The cognitive abilities of chimpanzees force us, I think, to raise searching questions about the boundaries of the community of beings to which special ethical considerations are due, and can, I hope, help to extend our ethical perspectives downward through the taxa on Earth and upwards to extraterrestrial organisms, if they exist.

Considerations

1. A widely acclaimed scientific writer, Carl Sagan has also been accused of being a popularizer of science who engages in sensational and far-fetched speculation. Critique his essay, explaining whether you see any evidence for this accusation.
2. What does Sagan mean by *human chauvinism?*
3. Respond to the question Sagan asks in paragraph 14: How *would* anthropologist Leslie White, who denies animals the power of abstraction, respond to the chimpanzees Washoe, Lucy, and Lana?

Connections

1. Charles Darwin and Carl Sagan both argue for the ability of animals to engage in higher level, abstract thinking. Using their essays as your evidence,

argue for or against Douglass North and Roger Miller's division of animals into those possessing "common property" status and those possessing "private property" status.

2. Darwin shares Sagan's belief that animals have emotional and mental capabilities. Does he share Sagan's conviction that animals should enjoy human rights? Explain your answer in a short analytic essay.

A Biological Homage to Mickey Mouse

Stephen Jay Gould

Age often turns fire to placidity. Lytton Strachey, in his incisive portrait of Florence Nightingale, writes of her declining years: *1*

> Destiny, having waited very patiently, played a queer trick on Miss Nightingale. The benevolence and public spirit of that long life had only been equalled by its acerbity. Her virtue had dwelt in hardness. . . . And now the sarcastic years brought the proud woman her punishment. She was not to die as she had lived. The sting was to be taken out of her; she was to be made soft; she was to be reduced to compliance and complacency.

I was therefore not surprised—although the analogy may strike some people   *2* as sacrilegious—to discover that the creature who gave his name as a synonym for insipidity had a gutsier youth. Mickey Mouse turned a respectable fifty last year. To mark the occasion, many theaters replayed his debut performance in *Steamboat Willie* (1928). The original Mickey was a rambunctious, even slightly sadistic fellow. In a remarkable sequence, exploiting the exciting new development of sound, Mickey and Minnie pummel, squeeze, and twist the animals on board to produce a rousing chorus of "Turkey in the Straw." They honk a duck with a tight embrace, crank a goat's tail, tweak a pig's nipples, bang a cow's teeth as a stand-in xylophone, and play bagpipe on her udder.

Christopher Finch, in his semiofficial pictorial history of Disney's work,   *3* comments: "The Mickey Mouse who hit the movie houses in the late twenties was not quite the well-behaved character most of us are familiar with today. He was mischievous, to say the least, and even displayed a streak of cruelty." But Mickey soon cleaned up his act, leaving to gossip and speculation only his

---

Stephen Jay Gould (b. 1941) teaches evolutionary biology, geology, and the history and philosophy of science at Harvard University. His list of publications includes Ever Since Darwin *(1977),* The Mismeasure of Man *(1981),* The Panda's Thumb *(1982), and* The Flamingo's Smile *(1985).*

unresolved relationship with Minnie and the status of Morty and Ferdie. Finch continues: "Mickey . . . had become virtually a national symbol, and as such he was expected to behave properly at all times. If he occasionally stepped out of line, any number of letters would arrive at the Studio from citizens and organizations who felt that the nation's moral well-being was in their hands. . . . Eventually he would be pressured into the role of straight man."

As Mickey's personality softened, his appearance changed. Many Disney fans   *4* are aware of this transformation through time, but few (I suspect) have recognized the coordinating theme behind all the alterations—in fact, I am not sure that the Disney artists themselves explicitly realized what they were doing, since the changes appeared in such a halting and piecemeal fashion. In short, the blander and inoffensive Mickey became progressively more juvenile in appearance. (Since Mickey's chronological age never altered—like most cartoon characters he stands impervious to the ravages of time—this change in appearance at a constant age is a true evolutionary transformation. Progressive juvenilization as an evolutionary phenomenon is called neoteny. More on this later.)

The characteristic changes of form during human growth have inspired a   *5* substantial biological literature. Since the head-end of an embryo differentiates first and grows more rapidly in utero than the foot-end (an antero-posterior gradient, in technical language), a newborn child possesses a relatively large head attached to a medium-sized body with diminutive legs and feet. This gradient is reversed through growth as legs and feet overtake the front end. Heads continue to grow but so much more slowly than the rest of the body that relative head size decreases.

In addition, a suite of changes pervades the head itself during human growth.   *6* The brain grows very slowly after age three, and the bulbous cranium of a young child gives way to the more slanted, lower-browed configuration of adulthood. The eyes scarcely grow at all and relative eye size declines precipitously. But the jaw gets bigger and bigger. Children, compared with adults, have larger heads and eyes, smaller jaws, a more prominent, bulging cranium, and smaller, pudgier legs and feet. Adult heads are altogether more apish, I'm sorry to say.

Mickey, however, has traveled this ontogenetic pathway in reverse during   *7* his fifty years among us. He has assumed an ever more childlike appearance as the ratty character of *Steamboat Willie* became the cute and inoffensive host to a magic kingdom. By 1940, the former tweaker of pig's nipples gets a kick in the ass for insubordination (as the *Sorcerer's Apprentice* in *Fantasia*). By 1953, his last cartoon, he has gone fishing and cannot even subdue a squirting clam.

The Disney artists transformed Mickey in clever silence, often using sugges-   *8* tive devices that mimic nature's own changes by different routes. To give him the shorter and pudgier legs of youth, they lowered his pants line and covered his spindly legs with a baggy outfit. (His arms and legs also thickened substantially—and acquired joints for a floppier appearance.) His head grew relatively larger and its features more youthful. The length of Mickey's snout has not altered, but decreasing protrusion is more subtly suggested by a pronounced thickening. Mickey's eye has grown in two modes: first, by a major, discontinuous evolutionary shift as the entire eye of ancestral Mickey became the pupil of his descendants, and second, by gradual increase thereafter.

Mickey's improvement in cranial bulging followed an interesting path since   *9*
his evolution has always been constrained by the unaltered convention of representing
his head as a circle with appended ears and an oblong snout. The
circle's form could not be altered to provide a bulging cranium directly. Instead,
Mickey's ears moved back, increasing the distance between nose and ears,
and giving him a rounded, rather than a sloping, forehead.

To give these observations the cachet of quantitative science, I applied my   *10*
best pair of dial calipers to three stages of the official phylogeny—the thin-nosed,
ears-forward figure of the early 1930s (stage 1), the latter-day Jack of Mickey
and the Beanstalk (1947, stage 2), and the modern mouse (stage 3). I measured
three signs of Mickey's creeping juvenility: increasing eye size (maximum height)
as a percentage of head length (base of the nose to top of rear ear); increasing
head length as a percentage of body length; and increasing cranial vault size
measured by rearward displacement of the front ear (base of the nose to top of
front ear as a percentage of base of the nose to top of rear ear).

All three percentages increased steadily—eye size from 27 to 42 percent of   *11*
head length; head length from 42.7 to 48.1 percent of body length; and nose to
front ear from 71.7 to a whopping 95.6 percent of nose to rear ear. For comparison,
I measured Mickey's young "nephew" Morty Mouse. In each case,
Mickey has clearly been evolving toward youthful stages of his stock, although
he still has a way to go for head length.

You may, indeed, now ask what an at least marginally respectable scientist   *12*
has been doing with a mouse like that. In part, fiddling around and having fun,
of course. (I still prefer *Pinocchio* to *Citizen Kane*.) But I do have a serious point—
two, in fact—to make. We must first ask why Disney chose to change his most
famous character so gradually and persistently in the same direction? National
symbols are not altered capriciously and market researchers (for the doll
industry in particular) have spent a good deal of time and practical effort
learning what features appeal to people as cute and friendly. Biologists also

Mickey's evolution during 50 years (left to right). As Mickey became increasingly well be-
haved over the years, his appearance became more youthful. Measurements of three stages
in his development revealed a larger relative head size, larger eyes, and an enlarged cranium
— all traits of juvenility. © *Walt Disney Productions*

have spent a great deal of time studying a similar subject in a wide range of animals.

In one of his most famous articles, Konrad Lorenz argues that humans use   13 the characteristic differences in form between babies and adults as important behavioral cues. He believes that features of juvenility trigger "innate releasing mechanisms" for affection and nurturing in adult humans. When we see a living creature with babyish features, we feel an automatic surge of disarming tenderness. The adaptive value of this response can scarcely be questioned, for we must nurture our babies. Lorenz, by the way, lists among his releasers the very features of babyhood that Disney affixed progressively to Mickey: "a relatively large head, predominance of the brain capsule, large and low-lying eyes, bulging cheek region, short and thick extremities, a springy elastic consistency, and clumsy movements." (I propose to leave aside for this article the contentious issue of whether or not our affectionate response to babyish features is truly innate and inherited directly from ancestral primates—as Lorenz argues—or whether it is simply learned from our immediate experience with babies and grafted upon an evolutionary predisposition for attaching ties of affection to certain learned signals. My argument works equally well in either case for I only claim that babyish features tend to elicit strong feelings of affection in adult humans, whether the biological basis be direct programming or the capacity to learn and fix upon signals. I also treat as collateral to my point the major thesis of Lorenz's article—that we respond not to the totality or *Gestalt*, but to a set of specific features acting as releasers. This argument is important to Lorenz because he wants to argue for evolutionary identity in modes of behavior between other vertebrates and humans, and we know that many birds, for example, often respond to abstract features rather than *Gestalten*. Lorenz's article, published in 1950, bears the title *Ganzheit und Teil in der tierischen und menschlichen Gemeinschaft*—"Entirety and part in animal and human society." Disney's piecemeal change of Mickey's appearance does make

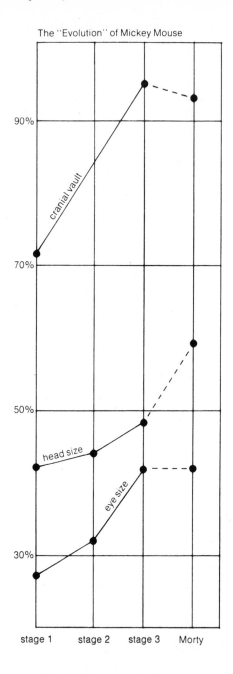

The "Evolution" of Mickey Mouse

At an early stage in his evolution, Mickey had a smaller head, cranial vault, and eyes. He evolved toward the characteristics of his young nephew Morty (connected to Mickey by a dotted line).

sense in this context—he operated in sequential fashion upon Lorenz's primary releasers.)

Lorenz emphasizes the power that juvenile features hold over us, and the *14* abstract quality of their influence, by pointing out that we judge other animals by the same criteria—although the judgment may be utterly inappropriate in an evolutionary context. We are, in short, fooled by an evolved response to our own babies, and we transfer our reaction to the same set of features in other animals.

Many animals, for reasons having nothing to do with the inspiration of af- *15* fection in humans, possess some features also shared by human babies but not by human adults—large eyes and a bulging forehead with retreating chin, in particular. We are drawn to them, we cultivate them as pets, we stop and admire them in the wild—while we reject their small-eyed, long-snouted relatives who might make more affectionate companions or objects of admiration. Lorenz points out that the German names of many animals with features mimicking human babies end in the diminutive suffix *chen*, even though the animals are often larger than close relatives without such features—*Rotkehlchen* (robin), *Eichhörnchen* (squirrel), and *Kaninchen* (rabbit), for example.

In a fascinating section, Lorenz then enlarges upon our capacity for biolog- *16* ically inappropriate response to other animals, or even to inanimate objects that mimic human features. "The most amazing objects can acquire remark-

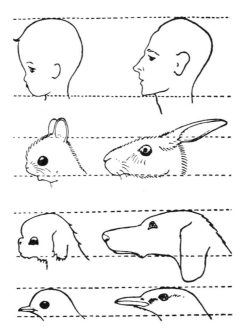

Humans feel affection for animals with juvenile features: large eyes, bulging craniums, retreating chins (left column). Small-eyed, long-snouted animals (right column) do not elicit the same response. From Studies in Animal and Human Behavior, *vol. II, by Konrad Lorenz, 1971. Methuen & Co. Ltd.*

able, highly specific emotional values by 'experiential attachment' of human properties. . . . Steeply rising, somewhat overhanging cliff faces or dark storm-clouds piling up have the same, immediate display value as a human being who is standing at full height and leaning slightly forwards"—that is, threatening.

We cannot help regarding a camel as aloof and unfriendly because it mimics, quite unwittingly and for other reasons, the "gesture of haughty rejection" common to so many human cultures. In this gesture, we raise our heads, placing our nose above our eyes. We then half-close our eyes and blow out through our nose—the "harumph" of the stereotyped upperclass Englishman or his well-trained servant. "All this," Lorenz argues quite cogently, "symbolizes resistance against all sensory modalities emanating from the disdained counterpart." But the poor camel cannot help carrying its nose above its elongate eyes, with mouth drawn down. As Lorenz reminds us, if you wish to know whether a camel will eat out of your hand or spit, look at its ears, not the rest of its face.   17

In his important book *Expression of the Emotions in Man and Animals*, published in 1872, Charles Darwin traced the evolutionary basis of many common gestures to originally adaptive actions in animals later internalized as symbols in humans. Thus, he argued for evolutionary continuity of emotion, not only of form. We snarl and raise our upper lip in fierce anger—to expose our non-existent fighting canine tooth. Our gesture of disgust repeats the facial actions associated with the highly adaptive act of vomiting in necessary circumstances. Darwin concluded, much to the distress of many Victorian contemporaries: "With mankind some expressions, such as the bristling of the hair under the influence of extreme terror, or the uncovering of the teeth under that of furious rage, can hardly be understood, except on the belief that man once existed in a much lower and animal-like condition."   18

In any case, the abstract features of human childhood elicit powerful emotional responses in us, even when they occur in other animals. I submit that Mickey Mouse's evolutionary road down the course of his own growth in reverse reflects the unconscious discovery of this biological principle by Disney and his artists. In fact, the emotional status of most Disney characters rests on the same set of distinctions. To this extent, the magic kingdom trades on a biological illusion—our ability to abstract and our propensity to transfer inappropriately to other animals the fitting responses we make to changing form in the growth of our own bodies.   19

Donald Duck also adopts more juvenile features through time. His elongated beak recedes and his eyes enlarge; he converges on Huey, Louie, and Dewey as surely as Mickey approaches Morty. But Donald, having inherited the mantle of Mickey's original misbehavior, remains more adult in form with his projecting beak and more sloping forehead.   20

Mouse villains or sharpies, contrasted with Mickey, are always more adult in appearance, although they often share Mickey's chronological age. In 1936, for example, Disney made a short entitled *Mickey's Rival*. Mortimer, a dandy in a yellow sports car, intrudes upon Mickey and Minnie's quiet country picnic. The thoroughly disreputable Mortimer has a head only 29 percent of body length, to Mickey's 45, and a snout 80 percent of head length, compared with Mickey's   21

49. (Nonetheless, and was it ever different, Minnie transfers her affection until an obliging bull from a neighboring field dispatches Mickey's rival.) Consider also the exaggerated adult features of other Disney characters—the swaggering bully Peg-leg Pete or the simple, if lovable, dolt Goofy.

As a second, serious biological comment on Mickey's odyssey in form, I note   22
that his path to eternal youth repeats, in epitome, our own evolutionary story. For humans are neotenic. We have evolved by retaining to adulthood the originally juvenile features of our ancestors. Our australopithecine forebears, like Mickey in *Steamboat Willie*, had projecting jaws and low vaulted craniums.

Our embryonic skulls scarcely differ from those of chimpanzees. And we fol-   23
low the same path of changing form through growth: relative decrease of the cranial vault since brains grow so much more slowly than bodies after birth, and continuous relative increase of the jaw. But while chimps accentuate these changes, producing an adult strikingly different in form from a baby, we proceed much more slowly down the same path and never get nearly so far. Thus, as adults, we retain juvenile features. To be sure, we change enough to produce a notable difference between baby and adult, but our alteration is far smaller than that experienced by chimps and other primates.

A marked slowdown of developmental rates has triggered our neoteny. Pri-   24
mates are slow developers among mammals, but we have accentuated the trend to a degree matched by no other mammal. We have very long periods of gestation, markedly extended childhoods, and the longest life span of any mammal. The morphological features of eternal youth have served us well. Our enlarged brain is, at least in part, a result of extending rapid prenatal growth rates to later ages. (In all mammals, the brain grows rapidly in utero but often

Dandified, disreputable Mortimer (here stealing Minnie's affections) has strikingly more adult features than Mickey. His head is smaller in proportion to body length: his nose is a full 80 percent of head length. © Walt Disney Productions

very little after birth. We have extended this fetal phase into postnatal life.)

But the changes in timing themselves have been just as important. We are 25 preeminently learning animals, and our extended childhood permits the transference of culture by education. Many animals display flexibility and play in childhood but follow rigidly programmed patterns as adults. Lorenz writes, in the same article cited above: "The characteristic which is so vital for the human peculiarity of the true man—that of always remaining in a state of development—is quite certainly a gift which we owe to the neotenous nature of mankind."

In short, we, like Mickey, never grow up although we, alas, do grow old. 26 Best wishes to you, Mickey, for your next half-century. May we stay as young as you, but grow a bit wiser.

Cartoon villains are not the only Disney characters with exaggerated adult features. Goofy, like Mortimer, has a small head relative to body length and a prominent snout. © Walt Disney Productions

Considerations

1. Summarize the evolution that Stephen Jay Gould claims Mickey Mouse has undergone.
2. How would Gould explain the physical features of many popular toys such as stuffed animals or of cartoon characters such as Snoopy, Opus, and Garfield?
3. Throughout this essay, Gould makes humorous, often deprecating remarks about himself (for instance, "ask what an at least marginally respectable scientist has been doing with a mouse like that" on p. 542). How do these remarks affect your impression of Gould as a writer? as a scientist?
4. Gould assumes that the Disney artists were unaware of the progressive evolution of their cartoon characters. Do you share his belief that such substantial changes in a famous character would not be deliberate? Why or why not?
5. How does the graph on p. 544 affect your understanding of Gould's argument?
6. Think of the personality traits that are conventionally associated with animals such as rabbits, otters, bears, and house cats on the one hand, and with animals such as snakes, hawks, alligators, and rats on the other. How do these traits reflect the bias Gould claims we have for juvenile features?

Connections

1. Both Charles Darwin and Stephen Jay Gould assume that at least some animals possess the faculty of *imagination*. Compare and contrast Darwin's understanding of this word with Gould's, paying particular attention to the examples each uses and the value they attach to the word.
2. Stephen Jay Gould and Carl Sagan are both renowned for making scientific concepts accessible to the layperson. Analyze the writing styles of these two authors, focusing on the characteristics that contribute to their reputations as writers. As part of your analysis, be sure to identify any differences in their styles that you notice.
3. In different ways, Darwin, Sagan, and Gould all argue for the intelligence of animals. Write a critique of their arguments, explaining which you find more persuasive and why.

Good Old Uncle Albert

Farley Mowat

[*Never Cry Wolf* describes the young Farley Mowat's first professional experience as a field biologist. Sent to the Canadian Arctic to observe wolves, Mowat discovered much about this animal's life and behavior, as the following selection indicates. Editor's note.]

Once it had been formally established and its existence ratified by the wolves   *1*
themselves, my little enclave in their territory remained inviolate. Never again did a wolf trespass on my domain. Occasionally, one in passing would stop to freshen up some of the boundary marks on his side of the line, and, not to be outdone in ceremony, I followed suit to the best of my ability. Any lingering doubts I might have had as to my personal safety dissolved, and I was free to devote all my attention to the study of the beasts themselves.

Very early in my observations I discovered that they led a well-regulated   *2*
life, although they were not slavish adherents to fixed schedules. Early in the evenings the males went off to work. They might depart at four o'clock or they might delay until six or seven, but sooner or later off they went on the nightly hunt. During this hunt they ranged far afield, although always—as far as I could tell—staying within the limits of the family territory. I estimated that during a normal hunt they covered thirty or forty miles before dawn. When times were hard they probably covered even greater distances, since on some occasions they did not get home until the afternoon. During the balance of the daylight hours they slept—but in their own peculiarly wolfish way, which consisted of curling up for short wolf-naps of from five to ten minutes' duration; after each of which they would take a quick look about, and then turn around once or twice before dozing off again.

The females and the pups led a more diurnal life. Once the males had de-   *3*
parted in the evening, the female usually went into the den and stayed there, emerging only occasionally for a breath of air, a drink, or sometimes for a visit to the meat cache for a snack.

This cache deserves special mention. No food was ever stored or left close   *4*
to the den; and only enough was brought in at one time for immediate consumption. Any surplus from a hunt was carried to the cache, which was located in a jumble of boulders half-a-mile from the den, and stuffed into crevices, primarily for the use of the nursing female who, of course, could not join the male wolves on extended hunting trips.

Canadian author Farley Mowat (b. 1921) has written over twenty-five books, including The Siberians *(1970),* A Whale for the Killing *(1972), and* And No Birds Sang *(1979).* Never Cry Wolf *(1963), from which this selection was taken, was made into a movie and released in 1983.*

The cache was also used surreptitiously by a pair of foxes who had their 5
own den close by. The wolves must have known of the location of the foxes'
home, and probably knew perfectly well that there was a certain amount of
pilfering from their cache; but they did nothing about it even though it would
have been a simple matter for them to dig out and destroy the litter of fox
pups. The foxes, on their side, seemed to have no fear of the wolves, and several times I saw one flit like a shadow across the esker within a few yards of a
wolf without eliciting any response.

Later I concluded that almost all the dens used by the Barren Land wolves 6
were abandoned fox burrows which had been taken over and enlarged by the
wolves. It is possible that the usefulness of the foxes as preliminary excavators
may have guaranteed them immunity; but it seems more likely that the wolves'
tolerance simply reflected their general amiability.

During the day, while the male wolves took it easy, the female would be 7
reasonably active about her household chores. Emerging boisterously from the
close confines of the den, the pups also became active—to the point of total
exhaustion. Thus throughout the entire twenty-four-hour period there was
usually something going on, or at least the expectation of something, to keep
me glued to the telescope.

After the first two days and nights of nearly continuous observing I had about 8
reached the limits of my endurance. It was a most frustrating situation. I did
not dare to go to sleep for fear of missing something vital. On the other hand,
I became so sleepy that I was seeing double, if not triple, on occasion; although
this effect may have been associated with the quantities of wolf-juice° which I
consumed in an effort to stay awake.

I saw that something drastic would have to be done or my whole study pro- 9
gram would founder. I could think of nothing adequate until, watching one of
the males dozing comfortably on a hillock near the den, I recognized the solution to my problem. It was simple. I had only to learn to nap like a wolf.

It took some time to get the knack of it. I experimented by closing my eyes 10
and trying to wake up again five minutes later, but it didn't work. After the
first two or three naps I failed to wake up at all until several hours had passed.

The fault was mine, for I had failed to imitate *all* the actions of a dozing 11
wolf, and, as I eventually discovered, the business of curling up to start with,
and spinning about after each nap, was vital to success. I don't know why this
is so. Perhaps changing the position of the body helps to keep the circulation
stimulated. I *do* know, however, that a series of properly conducted wolf-naps
is infinitely more refreshing than the unconscious coma of seven or eight hours'
duration which represents the human answer to the need for rest.

Unfortunately, the wolf-nap does not readily lend itself to adaptation into 12
our society, as I discovered after my return to civilization when a young lady
of whom I was enamored at the time parted company with me. She had rather,
she told me vehemently, spend her life with a grasshopper who had rickets,
than spend one more night in bed with me.

°wolf-juice: A mixture of beer and laboratory alcohol that Mowat concocted.

As I grew more completely attuned to their daily round of family life I found   *13*
it increasingly difficult to maintain an impersonal attitude toward the wolves.
No matter how hard I tried to regard them with scientific objectivity, I could
not resist the impact of their individual personalities. Because he reminded me
irresistibly of a Royal Gentleman for whom I worked as a simple soldier during the war, I found myself calling the father of the family George, even though
in my notebooks, he was austerely identified only as Wolf "A."

George was a massive and eminently regal beast whose coat was silver-white.   *14*
He was about a third larger than his mate, but he hardly needed this extra
bulk to emphasize his air of masterful certainty. George had presence. His dignity was unassailable, yet he was by no means aloof. Conscientious to a fault,
thoughtful of others, and affectionate within reasonable bounds, he was the kind
of father whose idealized image appears in many wistful books of human family reminiscences, but whose real prototype has seldom paced the earth upon
two legs. George was, in brief, the kind of father every son longs to acknowledge as his own.

His wife was equally memorable. A slim, almost pure-white wolf with a thick   *15*
ruff around her face, and wide-spaced, slightly slanted eyes, she seemed the
picture of a minx. Beautiful, ebullient, passionate to a degree, and devilish when
the mood was on her, she hardly looked like the epitome of motherhood; yet
there could have been no better mother anywhere. I found myself calling her
Angeline, although I have never been able to trace the origin of that name in
the murky depths of my own subconscious. I respected and liked George very
much, but I became deeply fond of Angeline, and still live in hopes that I can
somewhere find a human female who embodies all her virtues.

Angeline and George seemed as devoted a mated pair as one could hope to   *16*
find. As far as I could tell they never quarreled, and the delight with which
they greeted each other after even a short absence was obviously unfeigned.
They were extremely affectionate with one another, but, alas, the many pages
in my notebook which had been hopefully reserved for detailed comments on
the sexual behavior and activities of wolves remained obstinately blank as far
as George and Angeline were concerned.

Distressing as it was to my expectations, I discovered that physical love-   *17*
making enters into the lives of a pair of mated wolves only during a period of
two or three weeks early in the spring, usually in March. Virgin females (and
they all are virginal until their second year) then mate; but unlike dogs, who
have adopted many of the habits of their human owners, wolf bitches mate
with only a single male, and mate for life.

Whereas the phrase "till death us do part" is one of the more amusing   *18*
mockeries in the nuptial arrangements of a large proportion of the human race,
with wolves it is a simple fact. Wolves are also strict monogamists, and although I do not necessarily consider this an admirable trait, it does make the
reputation for unbridled promiscuity which we have bestowed on the wolf
somewhat hypocritical.

While it was not possible for me to know with exact certainty how long   *19*
George and Angeline had been mated, I was later able to discover from Mike°

°Mike: A half-Eskimo, half-white trapper whom Mowat met in the Canadian wilderness.

that they had been together for at least five years—or the equivalent of thirty years in terms of the relative longevity of wolves and men. Mike and the Eskimos recognized the wolves in their area as familiar individuals, and the Eskimos (but not Mike) held the wolves in such high regard that they would not have thought of killing them or doing them an injury. Thus not only were George, Angeline and other members of the family well known to the Eskimos, but the site of their den had been known for some forty or fifty years, during which time generations of wolves had raised families there.

One factor concerning the organization of the family mystified me very much   20
at first. During my early visit to the den I had seen *three* adult wolves; and during the first few days of observing the den I had again glimpsed the odd-wolf-out several times. He posed a major conundrum, for while I could accept the idea of a contented domestic group consisting of mated male and female and a bevy of pups, I had not yet progressed far enough into the wolf world to be able to explain, or to accept, the apparent existence of an eternal triangle.

Whoever the third wolf was, he was definitely a character. He was smaller   21
than George, not so lithe and vigorous, and with a gray overcast to his otherwise white coat. He became "Uncle Albert" to me after the first time I saw him with the pups.

The sixth morning of my vigil had dawned bright and sunny, and Angeline   22
and the pups took advantage of the good weather. Hardly was the sun risen (at three A.M.) when they all left the den and adjourned to a nearby sandy knoll. Here the pups worked over their mother with an enthusiasm which would certainly have driven any human female into hysterics. They were hungry; but they were also full to the ears with hellery. Two of them did their best to chew off Angeline's tail, worrying it and fighting over it until I thought I could actually see her fur flying like spindrift; while the other two did what they could to remove her ears.

Angeline stood it with noble stoicism for about an hour and then, sadly   23
disheveled, she attempted to protect herself by sitting on her tail and tucking her mauled head down between her legs. This was a fruitless effort. The pups went for her feet, one to each paw, and I was treated to the spectacle of the demon killer of the wilds trying desperately to cover her paws, her tail, and her head at one and the same instant.

Eventually she gave it up. Harassed beyond endurance she leaped away from   24
her brood and raced to the top of a high sand ridge behind the den. The four pups rolled cheerfully off in pursuit, but before they could reach her she gave vent to a most peculiar cry.

The whole question of wolf communications was to intrigue me more and   25
more as time went on, but on this occasion I was still laboring under the delusion that complex communications among animals other than man did not exist. I could make nothing definite of Angeline's high-pitched and yearning whine-cum-howl. I did, however, detect a plaintive quality in it which made my sympathies go out to her.

I was not alone. Within seconds of her *cri-de-coeur*, and before the mob of   26
pups could reach her, a savior appeared.

It was the third wolf. He had been sleeping in a bed hollowed in the sand   27 at the southern end of the esker where it dipped down to disappear beneath the waters of the bay. I had not known he was there until I saw his head come up. He jumped to his feet, shook himself, and trotted straight toward the den— intercepting the pups as they prepared to scale the last slope to reach their mother.

I watched, fascinated, as he used his shoulder to bowl the leading pup over   28
on its back and send it skidding down the lower slope toward the den. Having broken the charge, he then nipped another pup lightly on its fat behind; then he shepherded the lot of them back to what I later came to recognize as the playground area.

I hesitate to put human words into a wolf's mouth, but the effect of what   29
followed was crystal clear. "If it's a workout you kids want," he might have said, "then I'm your wolf!"   .

And so he was. For the next hour he played with the pups with as much   30
energy as if he were still one himself. The games were varied, but many of them were quite recognizable. Tag was the standby, and Albert was always "it." Leaping, rolling and weaving amongst the pups, he never left the area of the nursery knoll, while at the same time leading the youngsters such a chase that they eventually gave up.

Albert looked them over for a moment and then, after a quick glance toward   31
the crest where Angeline was now lying in a state of peaceful relaxation, he flung himself in among the tired pups, sprawled on his back, and invited may- hem. They were game. One by one they roused and went into battle. They were really roused this time, and no holds were barred—by them, at any rate.

Some of them tried to choke the life out of Albert, although their small teeth,   32
sharp as they were, could never have penetrated his heavy ruff. One of them, in an excess of infantile sadism, turned its back on him and pawed a shower of sand into his face. The others took to leaping as high into the air as their bowed little legs would propel them; coming down with a satisfying thump on Albert's vulnerable belly. In between jumps they tried to chew the life out of whatever vulnerable parts came to tooth.

I began to wonder how much he could stand. Evidently he could stand a lot,   33
for not until the pups were totally exhausted and had collapsed into complete somnolence did he get to his feet, careful not to step on the small, sprawled forms, and disengage himself. Even then he did not return to the comfort of his own bed (which he had undoubtedly earned after a night of hard hunting) but settled himself instead on the edge of the nursery knoll, where he began wolf-napping, taking a quick look at the pups every few minutes to make sure they were still safely near at hand.

His true relationship to the rest of the family was still uncertain; but as far   34
as I was concerned he had become, and would remain, "good old Uncle Al- bert."

Considerations

1. Anthropologists stipulate that one of the things that characterizes a family is economic cooperation and child socialization. To what extent are these functions fulfilled by the wolves Farley Mowat observes?

2. Describe Mowat's method for observing the wolf family.
3. To what extent does Mowat's description of the wolf family confirm or violate your prior expectations about wolf behavior?

Connections

1. Douglass North and Roger Miller would designate Farley Mowat's wolf family *common property*. Do you find this designation valid ethically? Construct an argument that justifies or repudiates North and Miller's use of this economic concept using the wolf family as your major evidence.
2. Biologists Farley Mowat and Charles Darwin have both studied and written about the animal world. Compare and contrast their methods for observing natural phenomena. What relationship do they establish between scientist and object of study? Do their approaches qualify as being proper scientific method?
3. To what extent does Farley Mowat's wolf family exhibit the mental and emotional powers that Darwin claims for animals?
4. In "Good Old Uncle Albert" we see Farley Mowat develop an attachment to the wolf family, especially to the cubs. How would Stephen Jay Gould explain Mowat's response?

Early American Wolf Hunt
Charles Beals

On the evening of Nov. 14 [1830] couriers rode furiously through Tamworth   *1*
and the surrounding towns, proclaiming that "countless numbers" of wolves
had come down from the Sandwich Range mountains and had established
themselves in the woods on Marston Hill. All able-bodied males, from ten years
old to eighty, were therefore summoned to report at Marston Hill by daylight
on the following morning.

Marston Hill was crowned by about twenty acres of woods, entirely sur-   *2*
rounded by cleared land. Sentinels were posted around the hill and numerous
fires were lighted to prevent the wolves from effecting a return to the mountains. All through the night a continuous and hideous howling was kept up by
the besieged wolves and answering howls came from the slopes of the great
mountains. The shivering besiegers were regaled with food and hot coffee furnished by the women of the country-side throughout their long lonely watch.

Historian Charles Edward Beals (b. 1869) wrote Passaconaway in the White
Mountains *from which this selection is taken.*

All night long reinforcements kept arriving. By daylight there were six   3
hundred men and boys on the scene, armed with rifles, shotguns, pitchforks
and clubs. A council of war was held and a plan of campaign agreed upon.
General Quimby, of Sandwich, a war-seasoned veteran, was made commander-in-chief. The general immediately detailed a thin line of sharpshooters
to surround the hill, while the main body formed a strong line ten paces in the
rear of the skirmishers. The sharpshooters then were commanded to advance
towards the center, that is, towards the top of the hill. The firing began. The
reports of the rifles and the unearthly howling of wolves made the welkin° ring.
The beleaguered animals, frenzied by the ring of flame and noise, and perhaps
by wounds, made repeated attempts to break through "the thin red line," but
all in vain. They were driven back into the woods, where they unceasingly continued running, making it difficult for the marksmen to hit them. In about an
hour the order was given for the main line to advance, which was done.

Closing in on the center, the circular battle-line at last massed itself in a   4
solid body on the hilltop, where, for the first time in sixteen hours, the troops
raised their voices above a whisper, bursting out into wild hurrahs of victory.
Joseph Gilman records that few of the besieged wolves escaped. But the historian of Carroll County maintains that the greater part of the frantic animals
broke through the line of battle and escaped to the mountains whence they
had come. Returning to the great rock on which the commander-in-chief had
established headquarters, the victorious warriors laid their trophies at the feet
of their leaders — four immense wolves — and once more gave thrice three
thundering cheers.

The little army then formed column, with the general, in a barouche,° at its   5
head. In the barouche also reposed the bodies of the slain wolves. After a rapid
march of thirty-five minutes, the triumphant volunteers entered the village and
formed a hollow square in front of the hotel, the general, mounted on the top
of his barouche, being in the center of the square. What a cheering and waving
of handkerchiefs by the ladies, in windows and on balconies, there was! General Quimby then made a speech befitting the occasion, after which the thirsty
soldiers stampeded to the bar to assuage the awful thirst engendered by twenty
mortal hours of abstinence and warfare.

Considerations

1. What is the popular folk image of the wolf that underlies the Tamworth villagers' understanding of wolf behavior? (Consider folk tales such as "Little
   Red Riding Hood" and folk figures such as the werewolf.)
2. Analyze the language that Charles Beals uses to describe the Tamworth villagers' wolf hunt. To what extent does he provide an objective description?

°welkin: The vault of heaven, the sky (poetic).
°barouche: A four-wheeled carriage with a collapsible hood.

Connections

1. Compare and contrast Farley Mowat's view of wolves with that of the villagers. As part of your essay, explain the differences you observe.
2. Write a defense of the Tamworth villagers' actions using Douglass North and Roger Miller's economic principles as your critical framework.
3. How would Stephen Jay Gould explain the differences between Farley Mowat's response to wolves and that of the Tamworth villagers?
4. How might the Tamworth villagers' wolf hunt be explained as an example of Darwinian survival of the fittest?
5. In an analytic essay explain the extent to which the "Early American Wolf Hunt" illustrates Elias Canetti's thesis (Chapter 1) that a political or metaphorical power struggle represents a desire for domination over one's prey?

Endangered Species

William Tucker

The concern for endangered species is built around both emotional and logical argument. There has always been a poignancy in watching human activity and settlement crowd out existing animals and plants so that their numbers gradually dwindle and disappear. The dodo, the passenger pigeon, and the golden parrakeet are examples of animals that were once abundant and have now vanished. The buffalo, the whooping crane, the rhinoceros, the tiger, the African elephant, the sperm whale, and many other large animals may soon follow them. No one wants to see such rare and exotic creatures driven to extinction. A great deal of the early impetus of the environmental movement was mobilized around this issue. Its ultimate accomplishment was the Endangered Species Act of 1973.   *1*

Yet within a few years of that time, there seemed to be endangered species everywhere. Each time someone proposed a dam or a highway or a major industrial project, an endangered species seem to appear in the way. Suddenly it seemed as if we were about to exterminate all of God's creatures. This problem climaxed in the case of the Tellico Dam, where a major building project, 90 percent complete, was suspended because it seemed about to obliterate the snail darter, a tiny, three-inch fish. Overnight, the snail darter became a celebrity.   *2*

How did it happen that such a well-meaning program turned so quickly into   *3*

Journalist William Tucker (b. 1942), who writes on the environment, economics, and public policy, publishes often in Harper's.

a logical absurdity? Have things really gone so far that every time we try to build something we are obliterating some innocent plant or animal? Are we really that close to wiping out the earth's remaining diversity of life?

It would be appealing to think that we are living in such times of crisis, and   *4* that we are fighting for survival in the earth's last days. But once again, the disappointing conclusion is that environmentalists are up to their old tricks, distorting another issue on the public agenda. In this case, the confusion has revolved around an extraordinary misunderstanding of terminology. Briefly, people have had very little idea what they are talking about when they discuss "endangered species." The public thinks in terms of the whales, tigers, buffaloes, and whooping cranes, which were the original concern. Environmentalists, however, have known all along that the scientific terminology of species classification, if embedded in legal terminology, might produce a situation in which endangered species could be found almost anywhere. Thus, environmentalists have once again twisted Congress' tail and left the public aghast about our seeming inability to do anything but cause nature harm.

What Is a Species?

It is commonly estimated that about 100 million species of plants, animals,   *5* and microbes have evolved at various points along the earth's 3.5-billion-year biological history. Of all these species, about 99 percent are extinct, so that the one million-or-so animal and 350,000 plant species that inhabit the world today represent only a tiny fraction of all the evolutionary paths that have been taken.

To say that all 99 million missing species have gone extinct, however, would   *6* be misleading. Every creature that is alive today is a successful adaptation by some previous species. Much of evolution has been the gradual morphological change among succeeding generations. What we regard as some of the most dramatic events in evolutionary history are actually the shiftings for position among a few large organisms at the top of the food chain.

The biosphere as a whole is not any less productive today than it ever was.   *7* Microbes are as plentiful as ever. So are plants and animals. Many evolutionary processes, such as the growth of soil, are cumulative, drawing on the stored work of previous generations. Thus, despite the rather limited effects of most human activities (we always exaggerate our accomplishments), the total output of the whole biosphere is probably greater today than it has ever been. Nor is it conceivable that any human activity, short of all-out nuclear war, can be expected to bring about a radical impoverishment of the world ecosystem.

As large, complex creatures, we usually focus our attention in the biological   *8* world around other large, complex creatures. The concern with endangered species began with predators like whales, bears, wolves, peregrine falcons, bald eagles, and other animals that live with us at the top of the various food chains. This makes perfect sense. We are very near competitors with these animals, and they are most likely to be affected by our actions. When we start occupying natural habitats and reshaping ecosystems for our own use, these large animals are the first creatures to suffer.

It is well worth our efforts to try to save as many of these animals as pos-   *9* sible, if only for the sake of preserving nature's diversity for posterity. They deserve our protection. The problem with endangered-species concerns was that Congress, at the urging of environmentalists, wrote a law that extended these legitimate concerns into the staggeringly prolific world of insects, invertebrates, and even microbes. This is when concerns for "endangered species" became a political football.

Being basically anthropocentric, we tend to forget what a small slice of the *10* biological world we inhabit. The mammalian species have probably all been classified by now, since mammals are few and easy to find. Yet together they make up only about 5,000 species, or the same as the number of different sponges. Animals with backbones — mammals, fish, and reptiles — make up only 45,000 species, or the same as the number of mites and spiders. Of the world's one million animal species, about 900,000 are believed to be insects, which are by far the most prolific of all classes of animals. The insects have a greater biological mass than all the world's other animals put together. It is often said that the planet really belongs to them, and that we are just fooling ourselves by thinking we are the main occupants.

There is a good reason why there are so many insects and other inverte- *11* brates, and why there are so relatively few mammals and other vertebrates. This is because the two groups have pursued different biological strategies. Insects and other invertebrates have survived and proliferated mainly through their enormous powers of reproduction and speciation. They meet the vicissitudes of life through their ability to produce staggering numbers of offspring. They tend to produce a new species adaptation for every new environment.

Vertebrates, and particularly mammals, have survived, on the other hand, *12* by *internalizing* control methods and trying to build biological buffers between their internal workings and the outer environment. This has usually involved building bigger brains. We tend to think of the brain as functioning mainly for intellectual capacities. But most of the mammalian brain is actually dedicated to regulating the body's internal environment — temperature, the endocrinal system, and other feedback and insulating mechanisms. The compensating price we pay is the long gestation period that is required for us to develop before birth. (Only elephants spend more time in the womb than human beings.) Insects and other invertebrates, with little prenatal development, reproduce in fantastic numbers within a period of only hours or days. Vertebrates take much longer. There is no sense in trying to say which has been the better strategy. Both have had their advantages.

Most of the speciation in the evolutionary tree, then, has been among inver- *13* tebrates. There are, for example, more species of nematodes — microscopic worms that inhabit the soil — than there were dinosaurs in all of evolutionary history. There are more mollusks — snails, squids, and bivalves — than there are vertebrates. It is the fantastic reproductive power of insects that makes it possible, for example, to produce a mutant variety of fruit flies in the laboratory within a few days. Wherever some small population of invertebrates has become isolated, their reproductive powers have been enough to produce variations that qualify as new species.

None of this was entirely clear until the species classification system was *14* developed in the eighteenth century by the Swedish naturalist Baron Carl von

Linné. He worked out a system of categorization that divided all plants and animals into a dozen or so major phyla, continuing the divisions right down to the species level. Every creature was given its own Latinized genus and species name. Von Linné even Latinized his own name, calling himself "Linnaeus."

Here are the major categories in the Linnaean system: *15*

kingdom
phylum
class
order
family
genus
species

For human beings, for example, the classification would be as follows: *16*

kingdom — animal
phylum — chordates
class — mammals
order — primates
family — homonids
genus — homo
species — *Homo sapiens*

The Linnaean system was a huge cathedral into which the world's naturalists eagerly began moving their furniture. Probably nothing has ever excited the world's thousands of dedicated nature-lovers more than the possibility of discovering and naming a new species. Often as not, the discoverer gets to attach his or her name to the new classification. David Brower, director of Friends of the Earth, is only one of the scores of enthusiasts who has his name attached to a species of butterfly. Under the Linnaean system, there was room for any and all new classifications. In fact, the passion for subdividing has been so great that there are now three commonly accepted divisions *below* the species level: "subspecies," "varieties" (or "races"), and "populations." This is where a great deal of misunderstanding has arisen. People tend to think that when biologists talk about species they are talking about bears, elephants, lions, and wolves. This is a mistaken impression. Most of these popular categorizations of animals fall at the "genus" or "family " levels. "Species" generally refers to localized populations of these animals that naturalists or biologists have decided show enough minor differences to be classified separately.   *17*

Elephants, for example, are not a species but a family of animals with 2 genera and 2 species. Bears are a family of about 8 species. There are 40 species in the deer family, one genus of which is the elk, of which there are, in turn, 12 species in North America. An oriole is a genus with 15 species; a crow a genus with 36 species. There are about 10 species of skunk, a dozen species of weasels, 150 species of squirrels, 350 species of sharks, and 850 species of bats. Probably the only common animal that fits the popular notion of species is the giraffe, a genus with one species, *Giraffa camelopardalis*.   *18*

Even when we reach the level of fish, the numbers begin to add up quickly. There are estimated to be about 10,000 species of fresh-water fish, only 5,000   *19* of which have been described. Plants also exist in enormous species differentiation. The violet is actually a family of flowers, of which there are about 600 species. There are 100 genera of roses, each containing dozens and dozens of species. When the Rodale Research Institute recently put out a call for varieties of amaranth — commonly known as "pigweed" — in order to try to develop it as a world crop, it was quickly able to assemble over 300 closely related varieties, all of which could probably be registered as species. Altogether, the plant kingdom now consists of about 350,000 classified species, with an unknown number of other varieties that could easily meet the same criterion.

All this, however, pales beside the animal invertebrates. Here the numbers   20
are only understandable in orders of magnitude. There are estimated to be about 5,300 separate species of coral, 4,800 species of sponges, 2,000 species of oysters, and 5,000 species of starfish. Among insects, there are 360 species of dragonflies, 110,000 of moths and butterflies (1,100 butterfly species in North America alone), 100,000 species of bees, ants, and wasps, and 250,000 species of beetles. Over 15,000 species of insects have been found in New York City. Since the vast majority of these species live in small, localized populations, it is easy to see how it has almost become child's play to discover an "endangered species" almost everywhere we look.

Still another problem with pressing the Linnaean system into service for   21
such legal issues as the Endangered Species Act is that there have never been any real rules laid down as to what constitutes a separate species. The decisions are made by the editors of any one of the dozens of journals that are published by museums and natural history societies for the explicit purpose of identifying new species. These publications rarely ever dispute the claim of a naturalist or biologist that some newly discovered population of plants and animals — which is probably indistinguishable in any number of ways from several other species — constitutes a new species. The new "species" may be only another population of the same plant or animal, now located in a neighboring valley. But there has never been much effort to dwell on these difficulties. The stakes have never been high, few have cared. Naming new species has been the only real object of the game. . . .

This seemingly endless proliferation of small, distinct species of plants and   22
animals always presented the greatest challenge to pre-Darwinian biology. At the time, the world was either believed to be the one-time act of single Creator, or — for those who read and believed the geological record — a series of creations that had all been obliterated by subsequent catastrophes. According to Catastrophism, which competed with Darwin for decades after the *Origin of Species*, there had been a series of previous biological ages that served as sort of warm-up sessions for the Creator. It was in this way that the fossil record of dinosaurs and primeval ocean life, already well known, was explained. (The earlier creations were "not good enough" for humanity, so the argument went. The Biblical Flood was often taken for the last of the catastrophes.)

Why, the question was asked, if the world were a one-time creation, or the   23
last of a series of creations, had the Deity gone to such trouble to create such seemingly endless variety among the species of plants and animals? As diligent naturalists scoured the world turning up new species everywhere, it seemed as if there would be literally no end to the variety of creatures. By 1815, Coleridge

was complaining that naturalists were piling up so many classifications that the whole science of natural history seemed ready to topple under its own weight. Yet the answer to the question that came back was: "So God could show off His handiwork."

There were always, of course, the "splitters" and "joiners." Some natural-   24
ists have always been upset by the rush to identify new species at the sight of a different-colored feather or a slightly different song. They looked for under-lying patterns that tied all this information together. (Linnaeus was, of course, one of the most outstanding.) But for the most part, the splitters have had the upper hand, mainly because there was never any way to police new distinc-tions. Even today there is no accepted definition of a species. For the most part, ever-enthusiastic naturalists have been content to go on describing ever-new distinctions, bringing them all within the Linnaean system.

This endless categorization of distinctions was finally met head-on by the   25
greatest "joiner" of them all — Charles Darwin. It is no surprise that Darwin began his book, whose full title is *On the Origin of Species by Means of Natural Selection*, with a frontal assault on the preoccupation with ever-new classifi-cations. At the beginning of the *Origin*, Darwin writes:

> How many of the birds and insects in North America and Europe, which differ very slightly from each other, have been ranked by one eminent naturalist as un-doubted species, and by another as varieties, or, as they are often called, geographical races! . . . Close investigation in many cases will no doubt bring naturalists to agree how to rank doubtful forms. Yet it must be confessed that it is in the best known countries that we find the greatest number of them. I have been struck with the fact that if any animal or plant in a state of nature be highly useful to man, or from any cause closely attracts his attention, varieties of it will almost universally be found recorded. These varieties, moreover, will often be ranked by some authors as species.[1]

With reference to the specific term "species," Darwin wrote: "I look at the   26
term species as one arbitrarily given, for the sake of convenience . . . to a set of individuals closely resembling each other . . . [s]pecies are only strongly marked varieties."[2]

Darwin's point, of course, was that small separate populations that seemed   27
to be endlessly distinguishable were actually closely related through a com-mon ancestor. He emphasized the biologocal unity of life over the small dis-tinctions on which naturalists had focused so much of their attention.

Darwin knew nothing about genetics, but when Gregor Mendel's mid-nine-   28
teenth-century work was rediscovered in 1901, it was immediately realized that Mendel's laws of genetic variation and inheritance were the engine that pow-ered Darwin's natural-selection process. Incorporating the laws of genetics, a group of English biologists, led by Julian Huxley, restated Darwin's theory in the 1930s in what is still a classic definition. Describing the origin of species, Huxley wrote:

> Once two groups are physically isolated so that they can no longer interbreed, they inevitably come to diverge from each other in new mutations and genetic recombi-nations which they accumulate under the influence of natural selection . . .
>
> In addition, when an isolated group is small in numbers, it can be shown on mathematical grounds that it is likely to pick up and incorporate some mutations

and recombinations that are useless or even slightly unfavorable. Thus, some of the diversity of life is, biologically speaking, purely accidental . . .

The result is an overwhelming multiplicity of distinct species. Naturally, they are all adapted to their surroundings, but the geographical and cytological accidents that produced physical and genetic isolation cause their numbers to be much greater than that which would be necessary on purely adaptive grounds; and non-adaptive variation adds its quota to the diversity.

Most of evolution is thus what we may call short-term diversification.[3]

29   Properly understood, then, Darwin's evolutionary theory tells us that *any-where* that small populations become geographically isolated, they are likely to drift into small genetic variations — "genetic drift" is the term — that will produce differences that can probably be categorized as a new species. Over the long geological changes, of course, this pattern has produced the huge morphological changes that have enabled fish to grow into amphibians, amphibians into reptiles and mammals, of which we are a small branch. The process should not be underestimated.

30   But neither should it be assumed that we are chopping the evolutionary tree from under ourselves, or destroying one of God's irreplaceable handiworks, whenever we confront one of these small populations in the wild. We should not be *careless* about such things. But neither should we adopt the attitude that some irreplaceable portion of our genetic heritage is being lost.

31   Take the example of the snail darter. The fish was identified as a separate species by Dr. David Etnier, a University of Tennessee ichthyologist, for the deliberate purpose of opposing the Tellico Dam. Dr. Etnier had long been an opponent of the project. When the 1973 Endangered Species Law was passed — which said that a Federally funded project must give way *in every case* where the obliteration of an endangered species would result — Dr. Etnier went down to the vicinity of the site along the Little Tennessee River and discovered the snail darter in one morning's work.[4]

32   The snail darter is a member of the perch family, which includes 8 genera and 150 species. Three of these genera are the "darter" branches, which, like an old hillbilly family, have relatives living in almost every nook and hollow of the Tennessee Valley. There are about 100 darter species, 65 of which are found in the region. Three of these species have been identified by Dr. Etnier, and one of them bears his name. Far from being nearly extinct, the darter genera are thriving. As Darwin argued, it is precisely the ability to send out close relatives into a variety of habitats and to proliferate into new species that indicates the evolutionary *success* of this particular genetic line.

33   In January 1975, a few months after the discovery, Dr. Etnier published a paper describing the snail darter as a new species in the *Proceedings of the Biological Society of Washington*, a quarterly journal with a circulation of about 450 published by a small group of scientists within the Smithsonian Institution (but not a Smithsonian publication). The *Proceedings* is one of dozens of similar journals dedicated entirely to the description of new species. The papers are all reviewed by fellow scientists, but the editors say that there is hardly a case on record where the description of a new species has been challenged. The snail darter met the criterion of a new species because it had certain tail

and fin characteristics that, while they occur in other darters, do not occur in the same combination.

On this flimsy proceeding, the fate of the Tellico Dam was apparently sealed. *34* The snail darter was declared an official species, and, because it had never been found anywhere else, an endangered species. Therefore the project must give way. That it had never been found was probably because no one had ever bothered to look. (Another population was discovered in a neighboring river in 1979.) The issue was taken to the Supreme Court, where the judges rightfully decided that when Congress said in 1973 that no Federally funded project could be built over the bodies of an endangered species, that is exactly what it meant. It took a special act of Congress to say that the Tellico Dam must be completed despite the Endangered Species Act of 1973. Yet that only solved the problem in this one particular case. Left unaffected were the hundreds of cases that would obviously follow under such an absurdly misdirected piece of legislation.

Meanwhile, environmentalists, with an opportunity for halting unwanted *35* progress that was literally as big as all outdoors, were off having a field day. Soon they were prancing through the country turning up endangered species almost anywhere that a Federally funded developer was putting a shovel. With the growing involvement of the Federal government in almost every type of development, this was getting much easier.

Into the Wild

While the snail darter was holding up the Tellico Dam, the snail on which *36* the darter feeds — Anthony's River snail — had also been labeled a species and was waiting to join the snail darter on the endangered list. Meanwhile, four other snails — the *Duttons, Jays, Geniculate,* and *Rugger river snails* — had been found in the Duck River, another branch of the Tennessee, where the Tennessee Valley Authority wanted to build another dam. An Alabama darter, the *Slackwater darter,* was threatening a TVA stream channelization project. An Oklahoma darter, the *leopard darter,* was blocking an Army Corps of Engineers plan for a dam on Glover Creek, Oklahoma. The Tennessee-Tombigbee Waterway, one of the most bitterly contested public-works projects in the country, was undergoing a potential challenge as environmentalists turned up three fish — the *crystal* and *freckle darters* and the *freckle-belly madtom* — in its path, in addition to eight "rare" mollusks. The *scioto madtom,* another species of catfish, was also found in the way of a proposed municipal reservoir near Columbus, Ohio.

Among shellfish, the *Birdwing pearly mussel,* the *Cumberland monkey-face* *37* *mussel,* the *Turgid riffle shell,* and the *Pale lilliput pearly mussel,* were all in the way of the TVA's Columbia Dam, already under construction. The Army Corps of Engineers' Meramac Park Dam in Missouri was endangering the habitat of the *Higgins pearly mussel.* (Notice how often the name of the naturalist is attached to the species.) The same mussel had turned up in a dredging operation in the Minnesota River and had halted work for some time, until it was decided that the mussel had been dead for two years and therefore was no longer endangered.

Among plants, the *Furbish lousewort,* named after nineteenth-century ama- *38* teur naturalist Kate Furbish, was holding strong against the proposed Dickey-Lincoln Dam in northern Maine. A population of blue wildflowers called the *Northern wild monksheads* were threatening the proposed LaFarge Dam in Wisconsin. The monkshead was one of the first of 14 species to be put on the list at the Interior Department's Office of Endangered Species (usefulness in blocking dams obviously gave high priority) but was only designated as "threatened" *because it existed elsewhere as well. . . .*

Insects were a vein of pure gold. Six California butterflies have already been   39
identified as "endangered." One species, the *El Segundo Blue*, has been found living — wouldn't you know it — in only two places in the world: a two-acre plot next to an oil refinery and a two-hundred-acre tract that the Los Angeles International Airport is trying to develop for a new runway. (Airports and oil refineries are obviously the first places to start looking for new species.) The oil refinery had gingerly erected a fence around the butterfly's two-acre "critical habitat" and was praying that no state or Federal agency would decide to shut it down. The airport was poised for a long fight with environmentalists, who wanted the two-hundred-acre tract turned into a park. Apparently, it had not occurred to either the refinery or airport officials to hire a lepidopterist to go and find out if these species existed anywhere else. The environmentalists' superior knowledge of these matters allows them to lead the corporate leviathans wherever they will.[5]

Perhaps the most remarkable effort to save an endangered species occurred   40
in Santa Cruz County, an affluent college area south of San Francisco. The mountainous, wooded region was being overrun by upper-middle-class people who, like upper-middle-class people everywhere, didn't want any more upper-middle-class people moving in with them. Rather than wasting time with exclusionary zoning laws, the residents focused on the long-toed salamander, a local amphibian that inhabits the nearby hillsides and, once a year, migrates down to several large, lowland ponds where it carries on its mating ritual.

In order to protect the species, the county board of supervisors wrote leg-   41
islation requiring that all new housing built on the hillsides be constructed *on stilts*. In addition, retaining walls would have to be equipped with elaborate ramps so that the salamanders would not have any difficulty in wending their way to their annual mating grounds. Needless to say, few people built any new houses to conform with the ordinance. Yet this blatantly exclusionary action was applauded by the World Wildlife Fund and received a favorable report in the *New York Times*.[6] . . .

All this, of course, only represents upper-middle-class people using their   42
professional and legal skills to twist and turn environmental concerns to their own purposes. Yet there are still hundreds of legitimate things that can be done in order to preserve and protect important and irreplaceable animal and plant populations. For instance, a highway in Mississippi was easily rerouted in order to protect one of the major nesting areas for the Sand Hill cranes. The Alaskan oil pipeline was raised at certain key points so that migrating caribou herds could pass beneath it (in fact the caribou now seem to like to follow the pipeline in their annual peregrinations). The Department of the Interior points out that 99 percent of the conflicts between construction projects and endan-

gered species have been resolved through design changes, without evoking the legal proscriptions that led to the Tellico confrontation.

Yet it is also obvious that the law, as it is written now, offers environmen-   43
talists and their lawyers an almost infinite opportunity to set up roadblocks and pile up prohibitive construction delays to major projects. Make no mistake, there may be many good reasons for *not* building these projects. Most observers have agreed that the Tellico Dam was a useless, make-work effort, and that the Tennessee-Tombigbee Waterway is little more than an ill-conceived attempt by a few Alabama Congressmen to make the Tennessee River flow through their state. But these disputes should be settled through more sensible means than the shotgun approach of the endangered-species issue.

What we obviously need is an endangered-species program to protect *ver-*   44
tebrates, particularly slow-breeding birds and mammals. (Fish, which spawn hundreds of thousands of eggs each year, are really closer to invertebrates in their breeding patterns.) It is obvious that these creatures cannot breed fast enough to overcome the loss of habitat that threatens their numbers. Mammals and reptiles should be saved at the species level, while fish could probably be protected at the genus level.

But to talk about saving invertebrates at the species level — actually at the   45
population level, since the 1973 law applies to any population of an endangered species — literally means preserving every habitat on earth. There is nowhere in the world that it is not going to be possible for environmentalists to turn up some insect or nematode population that is unique and therefore "endangered." (One group on Long Island was even blocking a project with an endangered microbe.)

To this, environmentalists usually respond that "diversity equals stability"   46
and that by cutting down on nature's diversity we are endangering the whole Creation. The genetic diversity created through the course of evolution is nature's insurance policy against disaster. Ecosystems that have very broad and intricate patterns of interrelationships are much more capable of handling intrusions and resisting shocks. A system that is genetically uniform is prone to disaster because it does not have a depth of defense mechanisms.

There is a firm core of truth to this argument, and so it is worth examining   47
for a moment. There is agreement among biologists that the maxim that "diversity equals stability" works as a general case. That is, in most instances, a system with inbred diversity is likely to be more stable than one of greater simplicity. The question is, however, whether *ultimate* stability can be achieved through *ultimate* diversity, or whether we hit the point of trade-offs. Is diversity the only important consideration, or are there other factors that also contribute to the stability of a system?

The fact is that, from a human perspective, nature, for all its diversity, is   48
still not very stable. For most of nature, the laws of survival still mean matching the ever-present possibilities for catastrophe against the inborn capabilities of organisms to reproduce fantastic numbers of offspring to continue the genetic line. Let me give an example. In 1963, scientists doing an oceanographic survey in the Indian Ocean came across a 4,000-square-mile area covered with dead fish. The number equaled about one quarter of the world's catch at the time. The fish had not died from human activity but were the victims of

the inevitable nutrient cycles that govern most of the ocean environment.[7] . . .

The unpleasant truth is that natural cycles, for all their diversity, are still   49
enormously unstable. Genetic diversity can protect diversified climax forests
from diseases, for example, but fires can still destroy whole forests. It is this
uncertainty that evokes the widely used strategy of fantastic procreative abilities among plants and invertebrates.

As mammals, we have tried to overcome these unpredictabilities through a   50
different strategy — by internalizing our environment and building self-cor-
recting controls. That is why we do not need the heat of the sun, as reptiles do,
to warm our blood and give us energy at the start of the day. Nor are we as
devastated by dryness or changes in the weather. (Some insect populations have
been shown to go through population explosions and crashes from temperature changes of only a few degrees.) By building internal controls, we have been
able to stabilize the relationship between our internal and external environments.

The business of human progress, then, has been a *continuation* of this evo-   51
lutionary line of development. Human progress has not been "growthmania"
or "growth for growth's sake," as environmentalists often charge. It has been
a deliberate effort to extend our control over the external environment so that
we are not subject to the instabilities and unpredictabilities of nature's cycles.

Thus, we do not guarantee ourselves any kind of stability in human affairs   52
by foregoing the effort to humanize the environment, and letting nature take
its course. That only returns us to nature's unpredictabilities. What we *can* do
is be very cautious about disrupting natural systems any more than is necessary, and conserve wildlife wherever possible. This does not have to be strict
preservation, but only a matter of taking concern for wild systems where they
still exist. . . .

At this point, environmentalists are often inclined to introduce the "you-never-   53
know" argument, objecting that the little populations that we obliterate today
may turn out to have evolved some miraculous chemical that might cure the
world of cancer or solve the energy crisis. Commonly cited are the bread molds
that produce penicillin, or the horseshoe crab that was recently discovered to
have blood chemicals that can be used to detect toxins in intravenous fluids.[8]
What if we had wiped them out twenty or fifty years ago with a shopping center or a power plant?

All that can be said at this point is that, once again, environmentalists are   54
using words and language apart from their meaning. Neither the penicillin-
producing fungi nor the horseshoe crab are a species, nor are they endangered.
A whole genus of microbes produces penicillin-like antibacterial agents. These
organisms are universal in the soil. We probably couldn't wipe them out if all
our human resources were appropriated to the task. Horseshoe crabs are a family
of animals with about twenty species that are abundant all over the Atlantic
and Gulf coasts and in the South Pacific. They are a "living fossil," closely related to the ancient trilobites, and have hardly changed over the last 400 million years. It is hardly likely that the relatively small changes we make on the
planet are going to affect the horseshoe crab's ancient history.

This argument once again flies directly in the face of Darwin's point that   55
similar species are closely related and have similar genetic heritages. Any quality

that appears in one species is very likely to appear in any number of closely related species as well. If it is a useful chemical, it is all the more likely to be widespread, since it would be evolutionarily successful.

Playing God

The emotions that the endangered-species issue has raised are truly remark-   56
able. The resentment of favoring animals over humans strikes some people very hard. Thus, when the Reagan Administration took office, Interior Secretary James Watt began his antienvironmental program by immediately rescinding some restrictions against the importation of furs from certain endangered species. The implication seemed to be that the faster we could wipe out the cheetah and the leopard, the more quickly the American economy would revive. At their annual convention, the Young Americans for Freedom, an ultraconservative group celebrating its new ascendancy in the Reagan Administration, were reported carrying posters that read: "Nuke the Whales."[9] Such slogans only suggest the emotional deprivation that probably lies behind these attitudes.

The truth is that the future does not look very bright for many of the large   57
mammals that still inhabit the few remaining preserves in Africa, Asia, and South America. The rhinoceros may be doomed by the absurd superstition among Middle Eastern and Asian people that its horn is an aphrodisiac (as if sexual potency were not already enough of a problem in these countries). The elephants do not seem to have enough land to survive, and the tigers have almost entirely disappeared from India. Among the mountain gorillas of central Africa, a kind of despair has set in, so that even the animals themselves seem to know they are doomed. Ethnologists report that adult male and female gorillas wander the forests in isolation, ignoring their courtships and showing little enthusiasm for propagating the race.

Sad as this all may be, however, it would be a mistake to confuse the loss   58
of habitat among these large mammals with the decline of biological diversity over the entire planet. If we seem to have trouble sharing the ecosphere with these creatures, it is only because we are so closely related to them. We crowd them because we are all competing at the top of the food chain. But discouraging development and trying to encourage these Third World people to give up progress and "live naturally" is hardly going to be a help. Once again, development, both economic and political, is the only assurance that these countries will be affluent and organized enough to initiate their own preservation efforts. The recent Ugandan episode is a case in point. When Tanzanian Army troops invaded that hapless country in 1980 and soon found themselves short of rations, they broke their discipline and headed for Uganda's game preserves, where they feasted on carefully preserved wild animals, leaving the herds decimated. Development and stabilization are obviously the only route to preservation in these conflict-torn areas.

When all these arguments are exhausted, environmentalists turn to the re-   59
ligious dimension. By dooming some innocent species to extinction, they argue, we are "playing God." Never before in the history of the planet, it was argued during the Tellico case, had human beings *deliberately* consigned some

other species to extinction. Are we ready to assign one of God's creations to eternal oblivion?

All that can be said to such arguments is that they too can quickly produce   *60*
logical absurdities. Eastern religions, which environmental writers often admire, have been zealous in their reverence for all living creatures. Marco Polo described Indian holy men who would break up their feces after defecating so that no worms could grow in them. The worms, the holy men told him, would eventually die, leaving the holy men responsible for their souls. An even more interesting example of this attitude is India's Jains, one of the smaller religions on the subcontinent. The Jains shun farming because breaking up the soil involves the destruction of microorganisms. Therefore they have taken to trading and manufacturing, since these callings do not destroy life. As a result, they have become the most prosperous, middle-class sector of Indian society.[10]

We live in a world where some competition is unavoidable. We cannot be   *61*
completely passive. If we must assume some guilt for the destruction of other creatures while pursuing our own interests, then that may be the price of our own existence. There has never been a species on earth that did not somehow crowd, compete with, or devour other forms of life. Extinction is the common fate of all individuals, of nearly all species to date, and, as far as we know, will probably be the destiny of the stars and of matter itself. If there is any particular guilt in our deliberate choice to end the history of one small species, it does not seem too far out of line with the common nature of the universe.

What we do know is that the extreme *unadaptability* of fearing to face the   *62*
smallest consequences of our own actions is in itself a choice of evolutionary strategy. From all indications, it has not been a very successful one.

NOTES

[1] Charles Darwin, *On the Origin of Species by Means of Natural Selection* (New York: Lovell, Coryell & Company, no date), pp. 42, 44.

[2] Ibid., pp. 47, 50.

[3] Julian Huxley, "Darwinism Today," in *Man in the Modern World* (New York: New American Library, 1948), pp. 167–68.

[4] William Tucker, "The Sinking Ark," *Harper's*, January 1979.

[5] All incidents cited from Jeff Wheelwright, "The Furbish Lousewort Is No Joke," *The New Republic*, May 14, 1977.

[6] Bernard Frieden, *The Environmental Protection Hustle* (Cambridge, Mass.: MIT Press, 1979), p. 150.

[7] Cy A. Adler, *Ecological Fantasies* (New York: Delta Books, 1974), p. 28.

[8] See, for example, Philip Shabecoff, "New Battles Over Endangered Species," the *New York Times Magazine*, June 4, 1978.

[9] Dudley Clendinen, "After 20 Years, Young Conservatives Enjoy a Long-Awaited Rise to Power," the *New York Times*, August 22, 1981.

[10] "Ablution Without Absolution," *Time*, March 16, 1981.

Considerations

1. Write a critique of William Tucker's rhetorical and argumentative strategies. Be sure to examine the terms with which he describes the motives and background of the environmentalists.

2. Evaluate the effect of the word *only* in Tucker's statement, "If we seem to

have trouble sharing the ecosphere with these creatures, it is only because we are so closely related to them" (para. 58).

3. Summarize what Tucker assumes to be the causes of extinction.

Connections

1. Evaluate William Tucker's inclusion of Darwinian evidence. How does he use Darwin? Why?
2. Both the Douglass North and Roger Miller and the William Tucker essays share an economic perspective on animal extinction. Which version of this perspective do you find more convincing and why?
3. As Tucker explains, some people strongly resent "favoring animals over humans." How would an animal-rights advocate like Carl Sagan explain such resentment?
4. Assuming William Tucker's perspective, write an editorial in the Tamworth, New Hampshire *Times* that judges the legitimacy of the villagers' wolf hunt.
5. How would William Tucker explain the fact that the wolf, a well-adapted creature, is in danger of extinction? For evidence, you can use Farley Mowat's description of wolf family behavior and Charles Beals's account of human response to this animal.

Compassion, Esthetics, Fascination, and Ethics
Anne and Paul Ehrlich

To say that our own lives have been esthetically enriched by contact with   *1*
the other organisms of our planet would be a vast understatement. To a biologist, every day is likely to bring pleasant surprises, be it the discovery that a "bird dropping" in a tropical forest is actually many bugs of two colors sitting together to simulate a dropping; or the finding, virtually in your own back-

---

Anne Ehrlich (b. 1933) is a senior research associate with Stanford University's Biological Sciences Department. Paul Ehrlich (b. 1932), Bing Professor of Population Studies at Stanford, is the author of numerous works including The Population Bomb *(1968) and, with Anne Ehrlich,* Population, Resources, Environment: Issues in Human Ecology *(1977).*

yard, that an insect you thought fed exclusively on one plant actually depends on another for its survival.

Still, is making life interesting for biologists a sufficient reason to preserve organic diversity? Perhaps, for the pleasure and employment of this minority of *Homo sapiens* and for what their studies can offer to the rest of the world. Another reason would be the very large number of nonbiologists who are, or potentially could be, interested in the same diversity. Most children are extremely interested in natural history, although the interest is often killed rather than nurtured by school systems.

There are, moreover, millions of adults who enjoy nature in some way. There are some 8 million bird-watchers in the United States alone. A 1965 outdoor recreation survey found that about 20 million Americans took nature walks and almost 3 million photographed wildlife annually.[1] Keeping aquaria, an activity heavily dependent on the diversity of fishes, is the largest hobby in the country. People fascinated by succulent plants are so common that "cactus rustling" has become a crime in the southwestern United States. And there are enormous numbers of people who keep birds and reptiles as pets. So many people are interested in the wildflowers on Stanford University's Jasper Ridge Preserve that tight controls have had to be established to prevent research areas from being trampled. There are hundreds of nature and conservation centers in the United States. Similar statistics apply to many other countries, where nature hobbies are often even stronger; Winston Churchill and Vladimir Nabokov unashamedly collected butterflies.

The Lindblad *Explorer,* the luxury "nature cruise" ship, is booked years in advance for its trips to the Antarctic by people willing to pay many thousands of dollars to wade through guano to be among thousands of nesting penguins, shiver in rubber boats to watch crabeater seals sunning themselves on ice floes, or hike up difficult slopes to observe albatrosses nesting in the Falklands. The *Explorer* is so popular that another company has built a ship and set up a cruise schedule to emulate it.

Much the same can be said for the highly popular safaris to the game parks of East Africa. We will never forget the day that the lioness used our Land-Rover as cover to stalk (unsuccessfully) a wildebeest, the first time a bull elephant threatened us by making a short charge, or the day Hugo von Lawick introduced us to the wild dogs that he and Jane Goodall had been studying in the Serengeti, each one known as an individual by its distinctive color pattern. Nor will we forget the hour we watched two elephants wash each other, with what seemed to be loving care, at a waterhole in Kenya. The plains of East Africa can provide *Homo sapiens* with one of the last glimpses of what Earth was like before humanity exploded across its surface.

Of course, while the total number of people who can visit Antartica, the plains of East Africa, tropical rainforests, or other exotic places as touring naturalists is large, it still represents a tiny fraction of humanity. But as many millions of backyard bird, bug, and flower watchers have learned, the pleasures of knowing other organisms are not restricted to the well-off. Indeed, how many ghetto children have been thrilled — or could be — by watching a female guppy give birth in a school aquarium? Or by seeing a gorgeous male Siamese fighting fish, ablaze with crimson or blue, build a bubble nest, embrace his mate beneath it, and then catch her fertilized eggs in his mouth and spit them into the nest? Not one encounter with sharks, Killer Whales, lions, rhinos, elephants, chimps, rare butterflies, or army ants in Paul's lifetime as a field biologist has had the impact of his discovery as a child that a giant silk moth — a Polyphemus — had emerged from a cocoon he had been watching. That is a thrill available to virtually any child at no expense.

It is not even necessary to have direct experience with other organisms in 7 the wild in order to be enriched by them. A trip to the primate house at the zoo will tell a perceptive person volumes about his or her kinship with other animals, as well as about what those animals endure in captivity.

But beyond compassion for leopards and baby seals slaughtered for their 8 hides, beyond the naturalist's delight in the millions of diverse lifestyles produced by evolution, there seems to be a deeper feeling for other life forms that runs through all societies. In the West, as naturalist Jim Fowler likes to point out, it can be seen in the use of symbols. Not just in the Mercury Cougar, Ford Falcon, and Audi Fox, but in metaphors and symbols that go far back in history and are perpetuated in such phrases as *a real tiger, lionhearted, brave as a bull, sturdy as an oak, strong as an ox, free as a bird.* It shows up too in national symbols such as the double eagle of Napoleon, the Russian bear, and the American eagle.

In many cultures, people have maintained special relationships with other 9 living things, especially animals, even to the extent of worshiping them. These relationships survive in our own culture in ever-popular children's stories, both fiction and nonfiction. The importance of animals in particular to children would be hard to overestimate. The extinction of many animal species would deprive future generations of children of the pleasures of becoming acquainted with real versions of the animals in their books.

People of all cultures seem to feel that they are more "human" in the con- 10 text of a natural world. This clearly was a factor in the post–World War II rush to the suburbs in the United States. It may well be that contact with nature is essential to human psychological well-being. Three University of Wisconsin biologists expressed this thought as follows:

> Unique as we may think we are, we are nevertheless as likely to be genetically programmed to a natural habitat of clean air and a varied green landscape as any other mammal. To be relaxed and feel healthy usually means simply allowing our bodies to react in the way for which one hundred millions of years of evolution has equipped us. Physically and genetically, we appear best adapted to a tropical savanna, but as a cultural animal we utilize learned adaptations to cities and towns. For thousands of years we have tried in our houses to imitate not only the climate, but the setting of our evolutionary past: warm, humid air, green plants, and even animal companions. Today, if we can afford it, we may even build a greenhouse or swimming pool next to our living room, buy a place in the country, or at least take our children vacationing on the seashore. The specific physiological reactions to natural beauty and diversity, to the shapes and colors of nature (especially to green), to the motions and sounds of other animals, such as birds, we as yet do not comprehend. But it is evident that nature in our daily life should be thought of as part of the biological need. It cannot be neglected in the discussions of resource policy for man.[2]

Many aspects of human behavior confirm this observation. That the color [11]
green is soothing is well known. People try to nurture plants even in the worst
city slums, and city dwellers as well as suburbanites often surround themselves with animals — dogs, cats, fishes, birds — as if trying to recapture a
time when animals were an everyday part of human existence. Is it any wonder that environmental concerns remain high in the polls even in times of economic distress? Could it be that most people intuitively understand that preserving nature is not just an elitist ploy, but something essential to preserving
the spirit, if not the body, of a human being?

NOTES
[1] Reported in F. T. Bachmura, "The economics of vanishing species," *Natural Resources Journal*
II:687, 1971.
[2] H. H. Iltis, P. Andrews, and O. Loucks, "Criteria for an optimum human environment," *Bulletin
of Atomic Scientists* 26 (I):2–6, 1970.

Considerations

1. In what ways have you derived psychological or emotional benefits from the
   animal world? Add your own experiences to the Ehrlichs' list.
2. Are animals as crucial to human psychological well-being as the Ehrlichs
   imply? Write an argumentative essay that assesses the validity of this assumption.

Connections

1. The word *conservative* refers to two political and philosophical positions that
   are often considered antithetical: the right wing of the political spectrum
   and the pro-environmental movement. Write an essay that accounts for the
   ambiguity of this word. You can use William Tucker's and the Ehrlichs' essays as examples of these two positions.
2. To what extent do the Ehrlichs provide an adequate rebuttal to Tucker's charge
   that an environmental ethos is elitist?
3. How would the Ehrlichs answer the question that Carl Sagan poses: "Why,
   exactly, all over the civilized world, in virtually every major city, are apes
   in prison?"
4. How would the Ehrlichs use Darwin's "Comparison of the Mental Powers
   of Man and the Lower Animals" as evidence to counter William Tucker's
   use of Darwinian classification theory?
5. Douglass North and Roger Miller, William Tucker, and the Ehrlichs all suggest solutions to the crises faced by endangered species. In an argumentative essay, identify these solutions and evaluate their relative persuasive-
   ness.

Further Connections

1. How does the design of the town or city in which you live allow for contact between humans and animals? Think about the location of zoos, parks, and other natural areas; proximity to agricultural regions; zoning laws that may permit or prohibit the keeping of certain animals as pets; laws that regulate dog-walking.

2. Historian Keith Thomas has observed that ". . . it is an enduring tendency of human thought to project upon the natural world (and particularly the animal kingdom) categories and values derived from human society." Write a critique of this statement, drawing upon the readings in this chapter for your evidence.

3. Explore the ethical question that Carl Sagan raises: If animals have a rational consciousness, do they also deserve "human rights"? To what extent do our definitions of what is human or animal determine the legal status we accord different creatures? You can draw upon any of the selections in this chapter to construct your argument.

4. *Homo sapiens* are often assumed to be the superior species. Investigate the extent to which the writers in this chapter share this assumption and how common it is, even among those who defend animal rights. Use your findings to write an essay that evaluates the validity of this assumption.

5. Construct a debate on the "coyote problem" as Douglass North and Roger Miller describe it. Your debators are an animal-rights advocate and an economist hired to represent a local sheep-ranchers' league. They may raise whatever ethical, economic, aesthetic, or political arguments that would support their cause. Use this chapter as your debators' reference library of opinions about the proper relationship between humans and animals.

6. William Tucker presents the snail darter debate as an example of an exaggerated concern for a little-known species. Is such a concern unwarranted? Write an argumentative essay in response to this question, using this chapter as your evidence.

7. Assuming the perspective of an Ojibwa Indian (see the selection by A. Irving Hallowell in Chapter 3), write a persuasive essay arguing for the protection and care of all animal species. As part of your essay, you may want to compare or contrast the Ojibwa views with the white perspectives articulated in this chapter.

8. To what extent can the human hunting of animals be seen as a biologically motivated assertion of power? Refer to Chapter 1, especially the Bertrand Russell and Elias Canetti selections.

9. Do you find in the Charles Darwin selection any evidence of the racial superiority assumed by J. W. Jackson (Chapter 3) and analyzed by Stephen Jay Gould (Chapter 7)? How might you account for the presence of such beliefs in Darwin, a man responsible for revealing the common origin of *homo sapiens*?

10. To what extent does Robert Kennedy (Chapter 4) include our psychological need for contact with nature in his assessment of urban living? Sup-

plement Kennedy's catalogue with any aspect of the natural world you feel he overlooks.

11. Evaluate the three patterns of American city development Howard J. Nelson describes in Chapter 4 in terms of thier ability to promote contact between humans and animals. Which patterns are more successful in promoting such contact, and why?

12. How would intelligence as defined by Howard Gardner (Chapter 7) be modified if we test animals by the same criteria? You can use the Darwin, Sagan, Mowat, and Beals selections for instances of animal intelligence.

Extensions

1. In "Comparison of the Mental Powers of Man and the Lower Animals," Darwin describes a hierarchy of mental powers, ranging from "lower emotions" to the "higher" forms of reasoning. How does this particular hierarchy reflect Darwin's general theory of evolution? Consult Darwin's *Origin of Species* (edited by Philip Appleman, 2nd ed. New York: Norton, 1979), especially Chapter 4, "Natural Selection."

2. Economists often use Darwin's theory of evolution as a model for describing economic systems. Read "Natural Selection" (Chapter 4 in the *Origin of Species*). How can this be considered analogous to the modern capitalist system? Now evaluate the validity of the analogy: do you find an economic system to be comparable to a system of species evolution?

3. Charles Darwin was not the first biologist to suggest an evolutionary link between humans and animals, but his theories were considered shocking in the nineteenth century. Research the Huxley-Wilberforce debates about Darwin's theories, using your findings to explain why Darwin was considered so radical in his time. You might begin your research by consulting Loren Eiseley's *Darwin's Century: Evolution and the Men Who Discovered It* (New York: Doubleday, 1958).

4. Carl Sagan draws an analogy between traditional zoos and prisons, claiming that both institutions deny their wards basic rights of freedom. Many modern zoo directors, however, would dispute this charge: they see zoos developing a new, important role in preserving endangered species. Consult Robert Bendiner, *Fall of the Wild, Rise of the Zoo* (New York: E. P. Dutton, 1981), for information on the modern zoo, and use your findings to test the validity of Sagan's analogy.

5. Farley Mowat's observations contradict the popular image of the wolf as a bloodthirsty, savage killer. Can his findings be corroborated? If so, how do you account for the prevalence of the popular image? You might consult the following sources: Barry Holstein Lopes, *Of Wolves and Men* (New York: Scribner's, 1978); Erik Zimen, *The Wolf: A Species in Danger* (New York: Delacorte, 1981); and L. David Mech, *The Wolf: The Ecology and Behavior of an Endangered Species* (Garden City, N.Y.: Doubleday for the Natural History Museum, 1970).

6. Research the current controversy over animal experimentation, exploring

the position of both scientific researchers and animal-rights advocates. Check the *New York Times Index* or the *Los Angeles Times Index* for reports on the animal liberation movement of the mid-1980s and the scientific community's response to it. Use your research to formulate a well-documented argument for or against such experimentation.

7. At the close of "Good Old Uncle Albert," Farley Mowat leaves his reader to speculate about Uncle Albert's relationship to the other members of the wolf pack. Use *Biological Abstracts* to research an answer to this question: how are wolf families structured?

8. Investigate the shift from the ecological idealism of the early 1970s (reflected in the selection by the Ehrlichs) to the environmental politics of the early 1980s (exemplified in Tucker's essay). Also refer to popular sources such as *Time* or *Newsweek* for reports on Earthday in 1970 and on the response to Interior Secretary James Watt in the early 1980s. Use your research to analyze and explain the causes behind this shift.

9. Analyze the role of animal characters in Kenneth Grahame's *The Wind in the Willows* (or another animal tale written for children). As you write your essay, consider why animals were used instead of human characters: how might they be especially appropriate for children?

10. Read George Orwell's *Animal Farm* and analyze how animals function as part of his political and social allegory. What did Orwell gain by using animals rather than human characters? What is the significance of his title?

11. Choose a representative sample from three different popular magazines (such as *Time, Sports Illustrated, Glamour*) and analyze the roles animals play in the advertisements. As you brainstorm, ask yourself questions like the following: how are animals associated with a particular product? Do the animals share any characteristics with the products being sold or is the relationship between them arbitrary? What animals are most commonly used in advertising and why?

12. Take a field trip to a local zoo or animal park. While there interview eight to ten other zoo patrons to discover their motives for being there. (Try to select a varied group: elderly people, young couples, parents with children.) Use this information, along with the readings in this chapter, to argue for or against the following statement: "Zoos exist only to allow human beings to assert their superiority over other creatures."

13. What modifications have been made to Darwin's theory of evolution since the publication of the *Origin of Species* in 1859? Research your answer to this question by consulting Francis Hitching, *The Neck of the Giraffe* (New York: New American Library, 1982).

Suggestions for Further Reading

Bendiner, Robert. *Fall of the Wild, Rise of the Zoo.* New York: Dutton, 1981. Bendiner argues that the modern zoo — far from being the "animal prison" that so often exists in the popular imagination — may well insure the survival of many endangered species.

Berger, John. "Why Look at Animals?" In *About Looking*, pp. 1–26. New York: Pantheon, 1980. Marxist art critic Berger studies the relation between animals and humans, offering a controversial indictment of modern institutions such as pets and zoos.

Clark, Kenneth. *Animals and Men: Their Relationship as Reflected in Western Art from Pre-History to the Present Day.* New York: Morrow, 1977. This classic work traces the relationship between humans and animals through the history of art.

Davis, Flora. *Eloquent Animals: A Study in Animal Communication.* New York: Coward, McCann & Geoghegan, 1978. Davis discusses the Washoe and Lana projects that Carl Sagan describes, as well as other studies on animal communication.

Fiennes, Richard N. *Zoonoses and the Origins and Ecology of Human Disease.* New York: Academic Press, 1978. The author reviews human diseases in relation to our environment and the animals with which we associate.

Hofstadter, Richard. *Social Darwinism in American Thought.* Boston: Beacon Press, 1955. Hofstadter discusses the "adaptation of Darwinism and related biological concepts to social ideologies."

Peters, Michael. "Nature and Culture" in *Animals, Men, and Morals*, edited by Stanley and Roslind Godlovitch and John Harris, pp. 213–31. New York: Taplinger, 1972. Peters disputes the traditional anthropological distinction between nature and culture, arguing that humans and animals do not fit neatly in separate categories.

Porter, J. R., and W. M. S. Russell, eds. *Animals in Folklore.* Cambridge, Eng.: D. S. Brewer Ltd. and Rowman & Littlefield for the Folklore Society, 1978. This collection of essays covers the folklore of animal motifs and images and of animals that change shape in the folklore of different regions.

Premack, David. *Intelligence in Ape and Man.* Hillsdale, N. J.: Lawrence Erlbaum Associates, 1976. Psychologist Premack studies the linguistic and intellectual capacities of animals to find a striking continuity between animals and humans.

Regan, Tom. *The Case for Animal Rights.* Berkeley: University of California Press, 1983. Philosopher Regan presents a rigorous and controversial argument that the ethical and humane treatment of animals is a logical necessity.

Rowland, Beryl. *Animals with Human Faces.* London: Allen and Unwin, 1974. Literary historian Rowland traces animal symbolism in literature and art, especially in Biblical, medieval, and Renaissance works.

Singer, Peter. *The Expanding Circle.* New York: Farrar, Straus, and Giroux, 1981. Philosopher Singer supplements Edmund O. Wilson's version of sociobiology by including a system of ethics and altruism in the human genetic make-up.

Steadman, Philip. *The Evolution of Designs: Biological Analogy in Architecture and the Applied Arts.* Cambridge, Eng.: Cambridge University Press, 1979. Design historian Steadman studies art history, archaeology, the history of science, biology, philosophy, and cybernetics as he explores the analogy between evolution and architectural form.

Thomas, Keith. *Man and the Natural World: Changing Attitudes in England 1500–1800.* London: Allen Lane, 1983. Historian Thomas traces the shift in attitudes toward animals, humans, and nature through 300 years of English history.

Turner, James. *Reckoning with the Beast: Animals, Pain, and Humanity in the Victorian Mind*. Baltimore: The Johns Hopkins University Press, 1980. Historian Turner traces the reassessment of humanity's relationship with animals, focusing especially on the increasing sympathy for animal welfare in the nineteenth and twentieth centuries.

Wilson, Edward O. *Sociobiology: The New Synthesis*. Cambridge, Mass.: Harvard University Press, 1975. In claiming a biological basis for all social behavior, Wilson has boldly pioneered a much-debated field that studies human social structure, ethology, genetics, and evolutionary history.

The Fairy Tale
10 "Snow White"

Edited by **Carol L. Edwards**

To paraphrase Max Lüthi, fairy tales present a world of little jeweled boxes, a world in miniature that exists outside of time. Fairy tales, magic tales, or *Märchen*, as folklorists term them, are now considered children's stories. Originally, though, they were told by adults to other adults, often in communal work settings, but also as an evening's entertainment. Though many knew these tales, they were told by a community narrator skilled in the art of storytelling. By the time the Brothers Grimm published their *Kinder-und Hausemärchen*, or *Household Tales*, in 1812, such tales had become children's stories, often told to children by a nurse or older relative. The Grimms' concern with the tales, however, was philological. Through a study of these oral records of an earlier period, they hoped to illuminate the Indo-European roots of German culture and language. Similar concerns with the Indo-European basis of cultural beliefs and world view led the comparative mythologists Adalbert Kuhn, Walter Kelly and others to analyze the tales for records of myth — an approach now in disfavor because of its overly broad generalizations. Inspired by European nationalists, the Finnish Historical-Geographical School sought the historical origin and original form of individual tale types. They later revised their expectations, looking for the tale's provenance, its most likely place of origin, as well as its patterns of migration, and a normal or standard form, the most widely circulated version of a tale.

While many of the tales the Grimms collected came from oral tradition, they soon inspired popularized literary collections, beginning, for the English-speaking world, with Andrew Lang's *The Blue Fairy Book*, an adaptation of the Grimms' *Household Tales*. (Lang also helped to popularize the term *fairy tale*.) Lang himself was simply continuing the practice of such earlier authors as Charles Perrault, whose *Contes de ma mère l'oye*, or *Mother Goose Tales*, was published in 1697. Perrault's collection of fairy tales, which includes "Cinderella," are his own literary versions of tales from oral tradition. Another author,

Giambattista Basile, wrote the collection of stories *Il Pentamerone,* also based on oral tales and also containing many versions of well-known fairy tales. (Basile's tales, however, retain more fully the flavor of the earlier medieval romances and moral tales.)

While folklorists have studied these tales since the nineteenth century, *Märchen* have recently enjoyed a resurgent popularity, partly because of the publication of child psychologist Bruno Bettelheim's *The Uses of Enchantment,* and partly because of feminists' focus on these tales as instilling outdated cultural values in young women. While psychologists have often interpreted these tales, Bettelheim aroused interest in them by arguing against a commonly held opinion that children should not read fairy stories because of their violence and unhealthy amount of fantasy. *Au contraire,* Bettelheim argued: fantasizing about wicked witches and evil stepmothers served a useful psychological function for children. Such imaginary encounters with evil allowed them to prepare for similar encounters in real life. These tales also served a cathartic function: they rid children of their own bad wishes and impulses. Feminists' concern with these tales similarly grew out of the public's concern with the tales as repositories of outmoded cultural values. Many women pointed out that the tales often presented male heroes solely, while providing females with models of passivity.

These tales, however, exist in a much larger context, one that folklorists and social historians have studied for years. The tales are part of oral tradition, or folklore, which is usually defined as traditional lore, craft, or behavior of unknown authorship, transmitted by word of mouth or example, which persists in tradition and varies by region. A joke offers an example of current oral tradition that meets these criteria. Though it, like a fairy tale, exists in multiple versions that are recognizably similar (we can usually tell from its opening lines if we have heard a joke before), it also varies or differs from version to version. While folklorists were at first interested in the similarities between these versions, or *variants,* and thus tried to collect complete versions of tales containing all the expected motifs, they later became more interested in the differences or variations. As folklorists began to look at deviations from a norm or type, they tried to explain such deviations in cultural or social terms. They also considered the narrator's aesthetic sensibilities and personality. As the European comparative folklorist Max Lüthi reminds us, while we consider that these tales are of unknown authorship, each tale, of course, has an individual creator with a particular style and taste. In addition, every tale type, such as "Snow White" (AT 709), has an individual origin at some point in time. These two ideas have led scholars to consider each version of a fairy tale as a unique text capable of being examined on its own individual merits as well as in relation to any other version and to the tale type, or ideal version.

This chapter contains a sampling of such studies. The reading selections offer you both primary data, the tales themselves, and secondary sources, studies of fairy tales by others with which you can analyze these tales. I have selected "Snow White," probably best known in the Grimm version, as the primary tale for analysis. You will find several versions of the tale in this section, collected from such diverse places as Greece and the Outer Hebrides, Scotland. The secondary sources, or discussions of the fairy tales, offer a variety of perspectives, including the feminist and psychological ones mentioned above, as well as folkloristic ones. Two of the selections offer a way of classifying the "Snow White" tale. The first, by the folklorist Stith Thompson, presents a model or idealized version of this particular tale in outline form. Based on hundreds of oral versions, it allows you to measure any individual tale against the norm established by experts. The second selection, by the Russian formalist and structuralist Vladimir Propp, provides a model or outline of the ideal *fairy tale.* Rather than a surface concern with plot, Propp's model derives from a concern with underlying patterns of action that recur from tale to tale. Though Propp based his model on 100 Russian fairy tales, folklorists have found that it fits all *Märchen* or magic tales. While you will use these two methods mainly to classify the various tales, they also allow you to consider the different analytical models resulting from the concerns of two separate disciplines.

The Swiss scholar Max Lüthi established the characteristics of the *Märchen* using the formal method familiar to teachers of literature to create analytical categories for the fairy tale. In contrast, the approach of the literary folklorist N. J. Girardot, a student of comparative religion, offers categories derived from an anthropological view of this particular tale. Rather than focusing on episodes or motifs in individual tales or on the characteristics of the magic tale, Girardot considers how the tale fits its cultural context. He imagines that context to be a puberty ritual, an earlier version of such modern rituals as the *bas mitzvah* or the sixteenth birthday party. Instead of looking at individual texts or a model version of that text, Girardot begins with a society, as anthropologists do, then tries to see how the tale fits into that society and supports its social structures.

In applying feminist and literary analysis to the tales, Karen Rowe suggests that this and other fairy tales present models of ideal cultural behavior for women. Thus for Rowe and other feminists, fairy tales encourage conformity to cultural norms. Though it is applied in a literary study, this idea ultimately derives from the functional analysis of Bronislaw Malinowski, and thus from anthropology. Finally, the child psychologist Bruno Bettelheim presents a Freudian analysis of *Märchen* dealing with the function of the tales, their meaning for the human psyche, and their usefulness to individuals as well as to society. Unlike Rowe, however, he believes that these tales help socialize children in positive ways. Bettelheim's and Girardot's approaches are valuable because they see the tales in a broader context, rather than simply looking at the individual tales. Any one of these studies will allow you to analyze the versions of "Snow White" offered here. Together, they offer a cross-section of approaches to the fairy tales.

Sneewittchen (Little Snow White)

Wilhelm and Jacob Grimm

Translated by Francis P. Magoun, Jr.

Once upon a time in the middle of winter when the snowflakes were falling   *1*
from the sky like feathers, a queen was sitting by a window with a black ebony
frame and was sewing. As she was thus sewing and looking at the snow, she
stuck the needle in her finger, and three drops of blood fell into the snow. Because the red looked so pretty in the white snow, she thought to herself, "If
only I had a child as white as snow, as red as blood, and as black as the wood
of the window frame!" Soon thereafter she had a little daughter who was as
white as snow, as red as blood, and whose hair was as black as ebony. Therefore she was called Snow-White, and when the child was born, the queen died.

A year later the king married a second wife. She was a beautiful woman but   *2*
proud and haughty and couldn't bear being second in beauty to anyone. She
had a marvelous mirror: when she stepped up to it and looked at herself in it,
she'd say,

> "Mirror, mirror on the wall,
> Who is the fairest in all the land?"

The mirror would then reply,

> "Lady Queen, you are the fairest in the land."

Then she'd be content, knowing that the mirror was telling the truth.

But Snow-White grew up and got more and more beautiful and, when she   *3*
was seven, she was as beautiful as a bright day and fairer than the queen herself. Once when the queen asked her mirror,

> "Mirror, mirror on the wall,
> Who is the fairest in all the land,"

it replied,

> "Lady Queen, you are the fairest here,
> But Snow-White is a thousand times fairer than you."

Collected circa 1812 by the Brothers Grimm, this tale is the most well-known
version of AT 709, "Snow White." It appeared in the 1812 edition of Kinder- und
Hausemärchen *(usually translated as* Household Tales*). For detailed notes on the*
tale and a summary of a number of variants, consult Johannes Bolte and Georg
Polivka, Anmerkungen zu den Kinder- und Hausmärchen der Brüder Grimm.
Vol. I (Leipzig, 1937).

Then the queen was frightened and got green and yellow with envy. From that hour, whenever she looked at Snow-White, she'd feel a turn, she hated the girl so. Envy and pride grew like a weed in her heart, higher and higher, so that day or night she no longer had any rest. Then she summoned a huntsman and said, "Take the child out into the forest; I don't want to lay eyes on her again. You're to kill her and bring me her lungs and her liver as a token." The huntsman obeyed and took her out, and when he'd drawn his hunting-knife and was about to pierce Snow-White's innocent heart, she began to weep and said, "Alas, dear huntsman, spare me my life. I'm willing to go into the wild forest and never come back home again," and because she was so beautiful, the huntsman took pity on her and said, "Just run away, poor child." "The wild animals will soon devour you," he thought, feeling just the same as if a heavy load had been lifted from his heart because he didn't have to kill her. Since a young boar came running past, he killed it, took out its lungs and liver, and brought them as a token to the queen. The chef had to cook them in brine, and the wicked woman ate them up, thinking she'd eaten Snow-White's lungs and liver.

Now the poor child was all alone in the big forest and got so frightened that 4 she even eyed all the leaves of the trees and didn't know what to do. She started running and ran over the sharp stones and through the thorn bushes, and the wild animals sprang past her but did her no harm. She ran as long as her legs would carry her till nearly nightfall. Then she saw a little cottage and went in to rest. In the cottage everything was tiny but indescribably pretty and neat. There was a little table there laid with a little white cloth with seven little plates, and each plate with its little spoon, furthermore seven little knives and forks, and seven little tumblers. Along the wall stood seven little beds side by side, spread with snow-white sheets. Because she was so hungry and thirsty, Snow-White ate some vegetables and bread off each plate and drank a drop of wine from each tumbler, for she didn't want to take everything away from any one of them. After that, since she was so tired, she lay down in one of the beds, but not one of them fitted her: one was too long, another too short, till finally the seventh was just right. She lay down in it, commended herself to God, and fell asleep.

When it had got quite dark, the masters of the cottage came home; they were 5 the seven dwarfs who with pick and shovel mined for ore in the mountains. They lighted their seven little candles and, when it was light in the cottage, they saw that someone had been in there, for not everything was the way they'd left it. The first said, "Who's been sitting in my chair?" The second, "Who's been eating off my plate?" The third, "Who's been taking some of my roll?" The fourth, "Who's been eating some of my vegetables?" The fifth, "Who's been handling my fork?" The sixth, "Who's been cutting with my knife?" The seventh, "Who's been drinking out of my tumbler?" Then the first looked about and noticing a little wrinkle in his bed, said, "Who got into my bed?" The others came on the run, exclaiming, "Somebody's been lying in my bed, too!" The seventh, when he looked in his bed, saw Snow-White, who was lying there asleep. He called the others. They came running up and crying out in astonishment, fetched their seven candles and let the light shine on Snow-White. "My goodness, my goodness!" they exclaimed, "how beautiful the child is!" and were so happy that they didn't wake her up but let her go on sleeping in the bed. The seventh dwarf, however, slept with his companions, one hour with each till the night had passed.

When it was morning, Snow-White woke up, and seeing the seven dwarfs,   6
was frightened. They were friendly, however, and asked, "What's your name?" "My name is Snow-White," she answered, "How did you get to our house?" continued the dwarfs. Then she told them that her stepmother had meant to have her slain, but that the huntsman had made her a present of her life, and that she'd walked all day until she finally found their cottage. "If you'll keep house for us," said the dwarfs, "cook, make the beds, wash, sew, and knit, and if you'll keep everything neat and clean, then you may stay with us and you shall lack nothing." "Yes, very gladly," said Snow-White, and she stayed on with them and kept their house in order. In the morning they'd go into the mountains to look for ore and gold, in the evening they'd come back, and then their food had to be ready. During the day the girl was alone, and the good little dwarfs warned her, saying, "Watch out for your stepmother. She'll soon know that you're here. Let absolutely nobody in."

The queen, after she thought she'd eaten Snow-White's lungs and liver, had   7
no notion but that she was once more the fairest and most beautiful woman. She stepped up to her mirror and said,

> "Mirror, mirror on the wall,
> Who is the fairest in all the land?"

Then the mirror answered,

> "Lady Queen, you are the fairest here,
> But Snow-White over the mountains
> With the seven dwarfs
> Is a thousand times fairer than you."

Then she was frightened, for she knew that the mirror didn't lie and saw that the huntsman had deceived her and that Snow-White was still alive. Again she thought and thought how she might kill her, for so long as she was not the most beautiful woman in the whole land, her envy gave her no rest. When at last she'd thought up something, she stained her face, dressed herself up as an old peddler woman, and was quite unrecognizable. In this guise she crossed the seven mountains to the seven dwarfs, knocked at the door, and called, "Pretty wares for sale! Pretty wares for sale!" Snow-White looked out the window and said, "How do you do, good woman. What have you got for sale?" "Good wares, pretty wares," she answered, "bodice laces of every color," and drew one out that was braided of silks of many colors. "I may safely let this good woman in," thought Snow-White. She unbolted the door and bought the pretty lace. "Child," said the old woman, "how you do look! Come, let me lace you up properly for once." Snow-White, suspecting no harm, stood in front of her and let herself be laced up with the new bodice lace. The old woman, however, laced her up so quickly and so tight that Snow-White lost her breath and fell down as if dead. "Well, you used to be the most beautiful!" she said and hurried out.

Not long after, the seven dwarfs came home in the evening, but how fright-   8
ened they were to see their dear Snow-White lying on the floor, still and motionless as if dead. They lifted her up, and noticing that she was too tightly

laced, cut the lace. Then she began to breathe a little and gradually revived. When the dwarfs heard what had happened, they said, "The old peddler woman was none other than the wicked queen. Watch out and don't let any person come in when we're not with you."

When the wicked woman got home she stepped up to the mirror and asked,   9

> "Mirror, mirror on the wall,
> Who is the fairest in all the land?"

Then as usual the mirror replied,

> "Lady Queen, you are the fairest here,
> But Snow-White beyond the mountains
> With the seven dwarfs
> Is a thousand times fairer than you."

When she heard this, all her blood went to her heart from fright, for she quite realized that Snow-White had come to life again. "But this time," she said, "I'll think up something that will be the death of you," and with witches' arts, in which she was expert, made a poisoned comb. Then disguising herself and assuming the appearance of a different old woman, she went on over the seven mountains to the seven dwarfs, knocked on the door and called, "Pretty wares for sale! Pretty wares for sale!" Snow-White looked out and said, "Get right along! I mayn't let anybody in." "But surely you're allowed to look," said the old woman, took out the poisoned comb and held it up. The child liked it so well that she let herself be fooled and opened the door. When they'd agreed on the price, the old woman said, "Now I'll comb your hair properly for once." Poor Snow-White, suspecting no harm, let the old woman go ahead, but hardly had she put the comb in her hair than the poison in it worked, and the girl fell down unconscious. "You paragon of beauty!" said the wicked woman, "now you're done for!" and went away. Fortunately it was near evening, the time the seven dwarfs would be coming home. When they saw Snow-White lying on the floor as if dead, they at once suspected the stepmother, searched about, and found the poisoned comb. No sooner had they taken it out than Snow-White regained consciousness and told them what had happened. Once more they warned her to be on her guard and not to open the door for anyone.

At home the queen stood before her mirror and said,   10

> "Mirror, mirror on the wall,
> Who is the fairest in all the land?"

Then the mirror answered as before,

> "Lady Queen, you are the fairest here,
> But Snow-White beyond the mountains
> With the seven dwarfs
> Is a thousand times fairer than you."

On hearing the mirror talk thus, she trembled and shook with anger. "Snow-White shall die!" she cried, "even if it costs me my very life." Thereupon she went into a solitary chamber, quite hidden away, where no one ever went and there made a very poisonous apple. Outside it looked beautiful, white with red cheeks, so that everybody who saw it longed for it, but whoever ate even a tiny bit of it was doomed to die. When the apple was ready, she stained her face and disguised herself as a farmer's wife and went thus over the seven mountains to the seven dwarfs. She knocked at the door, and Snow-White put her head out the window, saying, "I mustn't let anybody in; the seven dwarfs have forbidden me to." "Quite all right," answered the farmer's wife, "but of course I'll get rid of my apples. There!" I'll make you a present of one." "No," said Snow-White, "I mustn't accept anything." "Are you afraid of poison?" said the old woman. "Look, I'll cut the apple in half: you, eat the red cheek and I'll eat the white." The apple had been so skillfully made that only the red cheek was poisonous. Snow-White looked greedily at the beautiful apple, and when she saw the farmer's wife eating some, she could no longer resist, put out her hand, and took the poisoned half. Scarcely, however, had she got a bite of it in her mouth than she fell dead on the floor. Then the queen gave her an awful look and burst out into loud laughter, saying, "White as snow, red as blood, black as ebony! This time the dwarfs can't wake you up again!" When she consulted the mirror at home,

> "Mirror, mirror on the wall,
> Who is the fairest in all the land."

it finally replied,

> "Lady Queen, you are the fairest in the land."

Then her envious heart was at rest, at least as much as an envious heart can be.

When the dwarfs got home in the evening, they found Snow-White lying on   *11* the floor. No breath was coming out of her mouth, and she was dead. They lifted her up, looked to see if they might find something poisonous, unlaced her bodice, combed her hair, washed her with water and wine, but all to no purpose. The dear child was dead and remained dead. They laid her on a bier, and all seven sat down beside it and wept for three whole days. They were going to bury her, but she still looked as fresh as a living being and her pretty cheeks were still rosy. "We can't lower her into the dark ground," they said and had a transparent glass coffin made so that one could view her from all sides, put her in it, and on it wrote in letters of gold her name and that she was a king's daughter. Then they placed the coffin on the mountain, and one of them always stayed by it and guarded it, and the birds, too, came and wept over Snow-White, first an owl, then a raven, and finally a dove.

Snow-White lay in the coffin for a long, long time and didn't decay but looked   *12* rather as if she were asleep, for she was still as white as snow, as red as blood, and her hair was as black as ebony. A king's son happened to get into the forest and came to the dwarfs' cottage to spend the night. He saw the coffin on the mountain and beautiful Snow-White in it and read what was written on it in letters of gold. Then he said to the dwarfs, "Let me have the coffin; I'll give you whatever you want for it;" but the dwarfs answered; "We won't sell it for all the gold in the world." Then he said, "Make me a present of it then, for I can't live without seeing Snow-White. I'll honor her and esteem her as my most dearly beloved." Since he spoke thus, the good dwarfs took pity on him and gave him the coffin. The king's son now had his servants carry it off on their shoulders. Then by chance they stumbled over a shrub, and from the jolt the poisoned piece of apple which Snow-White had bitten off came out of her throat, and before long she opened her eyes, lifted the coffin lid, raised herself up, and was alive again. "Good heavens, where am I?" she cried. Joyfully the king's son said, "You're with me?" and relating what had happened, said, "I love you more than everything on earth. Come with me to my father's palace. You shall be my wife." Then Snow-White fell in love with him and went with him, and their wedding was celebrated with great pomp and splendor.

Snow-White's wicked stepmother was also invited to the feast. Once she was   *13*
all dressed in beautiful clothes, she stepped up to her mirror and said,

> "Mirror, mirror on the wall,
> Who is the fairest in all the land?"

The mirror answered,

> "Lady Queen, you are the fairest here,
> But the young queen is a thousand times fairer than you."

Then the wicked woman cursed and got so frightened that she didn't know what to do. At first she didn't want to go to the wedding at all, but that gave her no peace; she had to go and see the young queen. When she came in, she recognized Snow-White and stood motionless from terror and fear. However, iron slippers had already been put over a charcoal fire and were now bought in with tongs and placed before her. Then she had to put the red-hot slippers on and dance until she dropped to the ground dead.

Considerations

1. Write a summary of this version of "Snow White." Following your instructor's guidelines for a good summary, try to capture the tale's basic plot. You will need this summary later in another assignment.
2. We might conceive of the tale as a series of pictures or visuals as a filmmaker might. Now that you have summarized the tale, select several scenes that you consider particularly vivid, attempting to explain the images portrayed and the details that make them striking.
3. List the colors mentioned in the tale. Next, explain in a paragraph or so what the colors add to our appreciation of the tale. Do any of them figure in the scenes you wrote about above? What dimension do they add to a particular scene?
4. Write a paragraph identifying some of the tale's metaphors and explaining their function within the tale.

Boule-de-Neige (Snowball)

*Narrated by Madame Morin, collected
by Louis Morin, and translated
from the French by Carol L. Edwards*

Once upon a time there lived a very pretty woman. She had a young daugh-   *1*
ter named Snowball, who was much more beautiful than her mother. Because
of this, the mother was jealous. She consulted her mirror:

> "Mirror, mirror, am I the most beautiful woman in the district?"
> "Yes — but little Snowball is much more beautiful than you."

"Ah!" replied the mother, "She is the most beautiful! She must die; I will   *2*
abandon her."

And she led her daughter into the mountains and abandoned her.   *3*

Little Snowball was terrified. She searched for a long time until she found   *4*
a tiny house in which lived three little men. Inside she found three places set
at the table: at the first place was hot chocolate, at the second, coffee, and at
the third, soup. Since she loved hot chocolate, she drank all that was set out.
Then, since she was tired, she searched for a bed. And, upon finding three little
ones, she laid herself down on one of them.

When the three brothers returned, they found the empty bowl. The one whose   *5*
meal she had eaten said:

"That's funny! I don't have anything to eat."   *6*

"While we were gone," his brothers told him, "you ate everything."   *7*

Then they decided to go to bed. All at once, one of them cried: "This is too   *8*
strange! I've found a young girl in my bed."

The three brothers were very surprised. When Snowball woke up, they asked   *9*
her what she was doing there. She answered that her mother had abandoned
her. Then they proposed that she should remain with them: she could cook their
meals and clean the house while they were working in the fields. Snowball accepted.

Meanwhile, her mother returned to her mirror: *10*

> "Mirror, mirror, am I the most beautiful woman in this district?"
> "Yes, but little Snowball, who lives far off in the mountains, is more beautiful than
> you."

"What! She isn't dead! I must go to the mountains at once."   *11*

So she disguised herself as a seller of laces, and searched the mountains,   *12*
crying: "Ladies, see my beautiful laces. Buy my beautiful laces, ladies."

---

*This charming variant of "Snow White," contemporary with the Grimms' var-
iant, was collected in France about 1890. Louis Morin collected it from his 63-
year-old mother, Madame Morin. Along with a number of her tales, this version
appears in* Revue des Traditions Populaires 5 (1890), *published in Paris.*

Snowball opened the door but did not recognize her mother, who said to   *13*
her: "Oh, Madame, buy my beautiful laces!"

"But I have no need of them, Madame."   *14*

"Go on, take them and you'll instantly become beautiful. I will lace you up.   *15*
You have a beautiful shape."

And she laced her so tightly that Snowball fell to the earth unconscious.   *16*

Upon their return, the brothers found her lying on the ground. They were   *17*
asking themselves who had done this to her when one of them suggested they
cut her laces. The young girl revived. Then they demanded to know why she
was laced so tightly. She told them that a woman had climbed the mountain
and had forced her to buy some laces with which she had squeezed the breath
out of her. They told her to keep the door shut, and not to buy anything on the
mountain.

Her mother returned to her mirror: *18*

> "Mirror, mirror, am I the most beautiful in this district?"
> "Yes, but little Snowball, who lives far off in the mountains, is more beautiful than
> you."

"Ah! She isn't dead," said her mother. "I will return to the woods."   *19*

This time she disguised herself as a comb seller. She cried, "See my beau-   *20*
tiful combs, ladies. Buy my beautiful combs."

Snowball was curious. She opened the door again, and her mother said to   *21*
her: "Buy a beautiful comb, Madame."

"But I don't need one."   *22*

"Oh, but one of them is so beautiful! It will make you so beautiful! Let me   *23*
put it in your hair."

And she pierced her head with the comb so forcefully that Snowball fell into   *24*
a second faint.

The brothers found her lying on the ground and unlaced her, but this did   *25*
nothing. Finally, one of them realized that the blood had left her head and they
withdrew the comb. Again, they demanded of her who had left her in that state.
She said that it was a peddlar.

After having scolded her, they warned her again for her own good that she   *26*
should not buy anything.

Her mother consulted her mirror once again: *27*

> "Mirror, mirror, am I the most beautiful woman in the district?"
> "Yes, but little Snowball, who lives far off in the mountains, is more beautiful than
> you."

This time the mother disguised herself as an apple-seller. After poisoning a   *28*
beautiful one, she returned to the mountain:

"Ladies, buy my beautiful apples!"   *29*

Snowball again came to the door, and her mother offered her the fruit. Upon   *30*
her refusal, her mother gave her the poisoned apple, saying, "This one is a beauty
— take it; I'll give it to you."

Snowball took the apple, ate it, and fell into a death-like swoon.   *31*

Again finding her so, the brothers undressed her, cut her laces, searched for   *32*
a comb, but found nothing.

When she had remained in this state for three days, they told themselves 33
that she was dead, and decided to bury her.

On the way they met the king's son, who asked, "What do you intend to do 34
with that beautiful young woman?"

"Alas, she is dead. We're going to bury her." 35

"If you'll give me the casket, I will put it in my vault." 36

The brothers willingly gave him Snowball. But, the jolting of the carriage 37
made her throw up. She coughed up the poisoned apple and returned to life,
not understanding where she was.

The prince explained that he believed her dead, and was going to place her 38
in his vault. Then, seeing how beautiful she was, the prince proposed, and
married her.

Meanwhile, her mother returned yet again to her mirror: 39

"Mirror, mirror, am I the most beautiful woman in this district?"
"Yes, but Snowball, who is married to the king's son, is much more beautiful than
you."

The mother was so filled with rage at not having disposed of her rival that 40
she killed herself.

Considerations

1. Describe the three attempts that the queen makes to kill Snow White. You
   might wish to treat the *means* by which she attempts to kill Snow White
   and the *vehicle* which she uses to disguise that attempt. While the actual
   devices for dispatching her rival seem pretty standard ones, do the vehicles
   of disguise carry special import in a tale of jealousy about beauty?
2. Write a paragraph or two describing the tale's conclusion. How effectively
   motivated are the actions of the prince? How believable is the queen's suicide? If you find these events unrealistic, do they still work in the tale? How
   do you account for this success?
3. In the original French version, the dwarves are *les Lapons* (Laplanders). Who
   are the Laplanders and how do you imagine them? Can you offer any explanation for such characters in a tale collected in France? Defend your response in a paragraph.
4. Notice the extent to which the tale's structure relies on repetition. Try working
   out a schema that accurately portrays that repetition. What is its effect on
   the tale? Can you postulate a law or rule for such a schema?

Connections

1. Compare this version of "Snow White" to the Grimms' version, looking for
   similarity of plot and motif.
2. Now contrast the tales, examining their differences.
3. Drawing on the two previous assignments, decide whether the two stories

represent the same tale, "Snow White." If they are recognizable as two versions of the same story, postulate some reasons for their similarity, without assuming that one tale influenced the other directly (though tales can cross language barriers).

Snow Bella: A Tale from the French Folklore of Louisiana

Narrated by Leota Edwards Claudel, collected by Calvin A. Claudel and edited by Joseph M. Carriere

Once there were two sisters sitting near the fireplace while snow was falling   1
outside. One of the sisters at her sewing, looking up at the snow through the window, suddenly stuck her finger with the needle with which she was sewing. She pressed her finger, hurt by the sting of the needle, and a drop of red, red blood fell on her dress

"You should make a wish," said the other sister, "and it will be granted for   2
having lost your drop of blood."

"Then I wish," began the sister, "that some day I shall have a most beau-   3
tiful daughter, whose cheeks and lips will be as red as this blood and whose skin will be as white as the snow falling outside."

It turned out just as the sister wished. She married a very handsome young   4
man and had a girl whose lips and cheeks were deep red like the blood that had dropped from her finger and whose skin was as fair and white as the snow. She was so beautiful that she called her Snow Bella.

However, Snow Bella's mother, the sister who had lost the drop of blood   5
while sewing when it snowed, became ill and suddenly died. Her husband was married again to a very cruel and wicked woman, who became Snow Bella's stepmother. Her stepmother vainly thought herself very beautiful, and no sooner was she married than she became violently jealous of Snow Bella's great beauty.

This Louisiana French version of the tale collected in the 1940s illustrates the persistence of folklore as well as its regional variation. The tale was told to Calvin A. Claudel by his mother who was fifty-nine years old at the time and who was born in Marksville, Avoyelles Parish, Louisiana. She was of Scottish-French descent on her mother's side of and of English descent on her father's side. Her parents died when she was a child, however, and she was raised in a French-speaking family. Consequently, she spoke French as a child. She learned this tale and many of the others in her repertoire from her foster father, Mr. Fey [Ferrier] V. Goudeau, of Goudeau, Louisiana, a small rural community in Avoyelles Parish.

So she treated the girl most cruelly, making her do all the house work. She also began plotting and planning a way to get rid of her stepdaughter.

"Snow Bella," began the cruel stepmother, "come with me into the woods today. We shall look around for some herbs and roots for my skin." 6

So they both walked and walked until they reached a deep, dark place in the woods. 7

"You search over there, and I shall search somewhere else," suggested the stepmother. "After a while we shall meet here again, to return home." 8

Snow Bella gathered roots until nearly dark and returned to the place, but the stepmother was not there. She waited and waited, but no one came. Finally Snow Bella began walking. It soon got dark, however, and she was lost. Suddenly she came up on a little hut in the woods, from the window of which shone a wee light. She knocked at the door, and a young man appeared, saying: 9

"Who is there?" 10

"My name is Snow Bella," said the girl, "and I am lost in the woods. . . . May I come in for the night?" 11

"Come in," replied the young man. "I live here with two dwarf brothers, who are asleep. We all work in the deep woods. . . . There is a little soup left. Perhaps you are hungry." 12

"Thank you very much," answered Snow Bella. "It is so kind of you to give me something to eat." 13

After the young man had warmed the soup in a huge black pot, hanging over the fire of the fireplace, Snow Bella sat at the table and ate. 14

"Tell me about yourself," spoke the young man. 15

"I live with my father and my cruel stepmother," began Snow Bella. "I am afraid she has lost me in the woods and does not want me back home. . . . I really don't know what to do." 16

"That is too bad," sympathized the young man. "As I said before, I live here with my two brothers, who are dwarfs. Tomorrow I shall talk to them about you, and perhaps we shall be able to help you. . . . You may sleep on my bed here, near the fire. I myself am very tired and must say goodnight." 17

The young man went off to bed on some straw in the next room, while his two brothers were snoring on their tiny feather beds. After Snow Bella finished her soup and piece of black bread, she went to bed, falling fast asleep. 18

The next morning she was softly awakened by the young man, while the two little dwarfs with dark skin and wrinkles stood nearby. He said: 19

"These are my two brothers, Snow Bella. You may live with us, if you wish. While we work in the woods, you can keep house for us. Be careful, though, whom you talk to, because you are very beautiful and harm may befall you." 20

Now the wicked stepmother, thinking that Snow Bella was eaten up by wild animals in the forest, did not worry about her any more. All day long she combed her hair and admired herself before her looking glass. Suddenly she heard someone outside calling out in a sharp voice: 21

"Mirrors to sell, mirrors to sell." 22

The stepmother went to the window and called out to the vendor, who was a hunched and wrinkled old man, wearing thick glasses over his tiny eyes: 23

"What kind of mirrors have you to sell?" 24

"Little mirrors, my lady — little mirrors that talk when spoken to. Ask a 25 question and the truth will be answered."

"Give me one," agreed the wicked stepmother, thinking that this would be 26 a good way to find the whereabouts of Snow Bella, if still alive.

The stepmother immediately hung the little mirror on her wall, gazed into 27 it and sang:

> "Tiny mirror, tiny mirror,
> Of this town and all the land,
> Tell me, if you can,
> Who is everywhere
> Most beautiful and fair?
> While I look in you,
> Answer true, answer true."

The mirror sang back: 28

> "Lady, lady in the mirror,
> Snow Bella's the name,
> Whose beauty's the fame
> Here and everywhere —
> Most beautiful and fair
> As ever maid be,
> And at the dwarfs' lives she."

"Ah, Snow Bella is at the dwarfs'," cried the jealous stepmother. "I must do 29 away with that girl. To think that she is fairer than I!"

The next day, while the angry stepmother was fretting around for a plan to 30 kill Snow Bella, she heard the sharp voice of the vendor again:

"Jewelry to sell, jewelry to sell." 31

"What kind of jewelry have you?" she asked the wizened old man with im- 32 patience.

"Ah, the most cunning sort of trinkets, my lady," replied he. "Here is a 33 necklace wrought with tiny darts in the beads. Whoever wears it will die in- standly. Very cunning jewelry, heh, heh. . . ."

"Quick, give me the necklace," bargained the stepmother. 34

The wicked woman set out for the hut of the dwarfs. When she came to the 35 door, the dwarfs were all away at work in the woods for the day. The step- mother threw a hood over her face not to be seen, and she rapped at the door.

"I have a pretty, pretty necklace to sell," said the jealous woman to Snow 36 Bella, who came to open a tiny crack in the door.

"I have no money," answered Snow Bella, who was nevertheless attracted 37 by the beautiful necklace. "I cannot buy it."

"Beautiful maiden, open the door a tiny bit more, so I can show it to you," 38 enticed the stepmother.

"I am forbidden to open to strangers," replied Snow Bella. 39

"Only put your pretty neck out, so I can try it on, to show you how beautiful 40 it fits you," coaxed the mean stepmother.

So Snow Bella put her head outside the door, and the stepmother slipped 41 the necklace onto her slender neck. The poor girl instantly fell dead to the floor.

The wicked woman went away laughing to herself with joy and rubbing her hands in satisfaction.

Finally the young man, who had become very fond of Snow Bella, and who   42
was as large as an ordinary human being and more handsome than his brothers, came home with the two dwarfs. He saw Snow Bella dead on the floor. With the help of his two brothers he picked her up, brought her to the bed and began rubbing her hands, to try to revive her. Everything was in vain, because the pretty girl was dead, and all the color had left her cheeks. Finally the older dwarf noticed the necklace around her neck, exclaiming:

"This necklace around Snow Bella's neck is something new! She did not wear   43
this before today."

Saying this he snatched away the necklace, breaking it from her neck and   44
throwing it to the floor. Soon Snow Bella's color began returning, and she stirred. The young brother and the dwarfs were overjoyed to have her back alive. They all wept, as she embraced them around the neck.

"Snow Bella," said the older dwarf, "you must be careful, my lovely child.   45
. . . Tell us, who was it? Tell us if you have enemies."

"It was no one," replied Snow Bella, not wishing to worry the dwarfs.   46

After the wicked stepmother was home several days, thinking Snow Bella   47
surely dead, she again went to her little mirror on the wall. She decided to try it again, repeating her song:

> "Tiny mirror, tiny mirror,
> Of this town and all the land,
> Tell me, if you can,
> Who is everywhere
> Most beautiful and fair?
> While I look in you,
> Answer true, answer true."

The mirror answered: 48

> "Lady, lady in the mirror,
> Snow Bella's the name,
> Whose beauty's the fame
> Here and everywhere —
> Most beautiful and fair?
> As ever maid can be,
> And at the dwarfs' lives she."

The two ditties went something like this in Louisiana French: 49

> "Tit-miroir, tit-miroir,
> Dis-moi laquelle
> Est la plus belle?
> Quel est son nom
> Dans ce canton
> Et ce territoire?
> Oui, tit-miroir."
>
> "O madame, ô madame,
> Snow Bella s'appelle
> Celle la plus belle

Dans ce canton,
Snow Bella le nom
D'elle chez les nains,
Plus belle des humains."

"Can it be possible that this wretch of a girl is still alive?" the enraged step- 50
mother questioned herself. "I shall kill her forever this time."

While pacing the floor the next day, she heard the same vendor's voice 51
through the window:

"Combs to sell, combs to sell." 52

"Over here with your combs!" cried the woman in exasperation. "Tell me 53
what kind of combs they are."

"My lady, these are round combs, set with tiny poisoned jewels," explained 54
the vendor. "This circular comb covers the head and kills the wearer on the
spot."

"Give me one quickly," she said. 55

The next day the stepmother disguised herself as an old, old woman and set 56
out for the hut of the dwarfs. She knocked at the door, which was opened to a
crack by Snow Bella, who asked:

"What do you want?" 57

"I am a poor old woman," whined the cunning stepmother. "Please buy a 58
comb, buy a comb from me. You are so beautiful; it will deck your pretty black
hair."

"Oh, no," replied Snow Bella. "I cannot talk to you." 59

"It will only cost you a few pennies," said the old woman. "Here, put your 60
head out, and "I'll try it on you."

"Please do not beg me," continued Snow Bella. "I want to help you, but I 61
don't know you."

"Here, my pretty child, let me slip it into your hair. If you don't like it, you 62
may return it right away."

So again Snow Bella put her head outside the door, and the crafty step- 63
mother pushed the comb into her pretty black tresses. She fell back inside dead,
dead.

When the dwarfs and their brother reached home that evening late, there 64
was no fire, no food, and nothing done. Snow Bella lay dead in a heap on the
floor. They picked up her lifeless body and placed it on the bed. The younger
of the two dwarfs began to rub her hands and cheeks to try to bring her back
to life. But the beautiful girl was cold. The youngest brother lighted a lamp.
Noticing the evil comb in her hair, he exclaimed:

"That comb! Where does it come from?" 65

He pulled it from Snow Bella's hair and threw it to the floor. They all rubbed 66
her, bathing her face with warm water. Finally she opened her beautiful, large
eyes.

"Where am I?" asked she. 67

"You are all right," answered the young man holding her hand. 68

"You and your brothers have been so wonderful to me. I know not how to 69
express it," said Snow Bella.

"Snow Bella," warned again the oldest of the three, "you must be careful in 70
the future. You are too beautiful. It is the fate of some that their beauty bring

them good fortune and happiness but it is your beauty that brings you only misfortune and suffering. . . . I fear it is your wicked stepmother. So beware of women at the door in the future."

The wicked stepmother reached home again, sang and rejoiced at what she had done to Snow Bella.   71

"How wonderful I feel," said she to herself, "since I am rid of that bad girl. I know now I am the prettiest in all the land. . . . Yet I think I shall try my little mirror again."   72

So she sang while sitting before the mirror: 73

> "Tiny mirror, tiny mirror,
> Of this town and all the land,
> Tell me, if you can,
> Who is everywhere
> Most beautiful and fair?
> While I look in you,
> Answer true, answer true."

Then replied the little mirror: 74

> "Lady, lady in the mirror,
> Snow Bella's the name,
> Whose beauty's the fame
> Here and everywhere —
> Most beautiful and fair
> As ever maid can be,
> And at the dwarfs' lives she."

"This is the limit," gasped the cruel woman in a fit of rage. "Kill her I will. Kill her I will. . . . What shall I do to the wretch?"   75

The next day while the wicked stepmother was brooding and thinking how to kill Snow Bella, again the vendor called to the window: 76

"Apples to sell, nice red, red apples to sell."   77

"Bring me your apples, old man," exclaimed the woman. "How are they?"   78

"Ah, my dear lady," said he, "one bite into the peeling and one is dead — a most malefic poison. Yet they are crimson red and most sweet to smell."   79

"Give me one quickly," said she. . . . "I shall see whether this wretch will live to be fairer than I and fairest of the land."   80

This time the stepmother disguised herself as a man and set out again for the hut, carrying the apple neatly covered in a basket. She knocked at the hut door.   81

"What is it?" asked Snow Bella, peeping through the key hole.   82

"I have the sweetest and reddest apples on earth," cajoled the stepmother in the voice of a man. "They are very cheap, especially for you, beautiful maiden."   83

"I cannot let you in for anything on earth," replied Snow Bella, who looked longingly at the crimson fruit.   84

"Here, my child," coaxed the woman. "Try this one. I shall roll it in under the door."   85

Snow Bella picked up the poisoned apple, and the wicked stepmother at the key hole watched her bite into it and fall dead to the floor. She went away dancing for joy and sure that Snow Bella was dead forever.   86

The three brothers soon came home, saw Snow Bella dead upon the floor,   87
picked her up again and put her on the bed. They did everything in vain for
three days to revive her, but she remained cold and dead. The apple with the
part bitten out of it was lying on the floor. So they knew Snow Bella had been
poisoned by it. At length they all built a coffin from the fine wood they worked
at in the forest. They set up all night to wake for Snow Bella, their lovely little
housekeeper, whom they loved so much. The tears streamed from their eyes.
Next day they dug a grave into the greensward nearby and began carrying the
coffin to the grave. One of them stumbled and tilted the coffin, shaking up Snow
Bella. The jolt shook her so much, that the piece of apple she had swallowed
came out from her throat into the coffin. Finally she began stirring in the coffin, and one of the dwarfs saw her and told the others about it.

"She is alive!" cried he. "Beautiful Snow Bella is alive."   88

They took her from the coffin and wept again for joy, Snow Bella embracing   89
each in turn around the neck, because she had learned to love the dwarfs for
their faithful kindness and their warm tenderness. She had also learned to love
deeply the handsome young brother, who likewise worshipped Snow Bella.

"This must be the end of the wicked stepmother!" shouted the older dwarf.   90
"Let us go to kill her."

Now the stepmother was home rejoicing and arranging herself before the   91
mirror, which she addressed again:

> "Tiny mirror, tiny mirror,
> Of this town and all the land,
> Tell me, if you can,
> Who is everywhere
> Most beautiful and fair?
> While I look in you,
> Answer true, answer true."

Then came the mirror's reply: 92

> "Lady, lady in the mirror,
> Snow Bella's the name,
> Whose beauty's the fame
> Here and everywhere —
> Most beautiful and fair
> As ever maid can be,
> And at the dwarfs' lives she."

"Hateful mirror!" cried the stepmother, taking the mirror from the wall and   93
dashing it to bits on the floor.

Just then in came the two dwarfs and the youngest brother. With knives   94
and clubs they fell upon the wicked stepmother and killed her on the spot, which
was the end of the cruelest and vainest woman on earth. The three returned
home, announcing the good news to Snow Bella, who became light as a feather
for joy, because this was like a terrible weight of sorrow and trouble lifted from
her life.

The youngest brother of the two dwarfs, who was now more tall and hand-   95
some than any Prince ever was, declared his love for Snow Bella. The two were
married, and they all lived together happily ever after.

Considerations

1. In this version of "Snow White," one of the brothers warns Snow Bella that she is too beautiful: "It is the fate of some that their beauty bring them good fortune and happiness but it is your beauty that brings you only misfortune and suffering" (para. 70). Write an essay in which you apply this maxim to the tale.

2. Discuss the motif of the magic mirror. How does the stepmother acquire the mirror in this variant? Does this incident seem arbitrary? What is the queen's relationship with the mirror? Is there any development in her interactions with the mirror even though the mirror's response remains the same?

3. In a paragraph describe the narrator's world view. That is, how does she seem to view the world, optimistically or pessimistically? How does she portray characters and the way they interact with one another? What rationale, if any, does she offer for the presence of good and evil in the world?

Connections

1. In comparing the three versions of the tale you have read so far, would you say that "Snow Bella" seems closer to "Snowball" or "Sneewittchen"? Explain.

2. Compare the narrators of the three versions. Can you detect any differences in their voices that affect our responses to the tales?

"Snow White," Type 709 in *The Types of the Folktale*

Antti Aarne and Stith Thompson

[Type 709, "Snow White," appears in Aarne–Thompson's *The Types of the Folktale*, a classification of oral folktales. Based on hundreds of versions of each tale which he examined, Thompson outlined a type, or model, for each tale. The type presents a series of episodes found in the tale. The tale of "Snow White" has five episodes, the encounter between Snow White and her stepmother (I), Snow White's rescue from an attempt on her life (II), and so on. Thompson does not suggest that every variant should contain each episode, or that a variant that follows the outline closely is a better version of "Snow White." Rather, the outline is a useful model against which folklorists can measure tales, classifying them as one type or another. Thompson follows the type with a list of motifs that appear in many versions of the tale. By *motif* Thompson means an object, character, attitude, or action that is repeated from version to version. For example, a magic ring or mirror is a motif, but so is a wish to have a child. Since, unlike this particular combination of episodes, motifs can appear in many other tales, they do not identify a tale as a particular type. (For example, a version of "Cinderella" also might begin with a queen wishing for a child.) Editor's note.]

709 Snow-White

The wicked stepmother seeks to kill the maiden. At the dwarfs' (robbers')   *1*
house, where the prince finds the maiden and marries her.

  I. *Snow-White and her Stepmother.* (a) Snow-White has skin like snow, and   *2*

When Stith Thompson, born in Nelson County, Kentucky, March 7, 1885, died ninety-one years later in 1976, he had earned the sobriquet "the Father of American Folklore." First writing on folklore for an undergraduate thesis, he went on to earn a master's degree from the University of California, Berkeley and a Ph.D. from Harvard in 1914. He founded the first American doctoral program in folklore, the Folklore Institute at Indiana University, a program that also gave the university an international reputation. Thompson translated and expanded the Finnish scholar Antti Aarne's Verzeichnis der Märchentypen, *publishing it in 1928 as* The Types of the Folktale. *His major work, the six-volume* Motif-Index of Folk Literature, *appeared from 1932–1937. Conceived of as a way to allow folktales to be studied through the historic-geographic method, it indexed the smallest meaningful repeated unit in a folktale. With this index, scholars could trace the history and geographical distribution of folktales by identifying their original episodes and motifs. Thompson was himself internationally known and respected by colleagues and students alike.*

lips like blood. (b) A magic mirror tells her stepmother that Snow-White is more beautiful than she.

II. *Snow-White's Rescue.* (a) The stepmother orders a hunter to kill her, but   3
he substitutes an animal's heart and saves her, or (b) she sends Snow-White to the house of the dwarfs (or robbers) expecting her to be killed. The dwarfs adopt her as a sister.

III. *The Poisoning.* (a) The stepmother now seeks to kill her by means of poi-   4
soned lace, (b) a poisoned comb and (c) a poisoned apple.

IV. *Help of the Dwarfs.* (a) The dwarfs succeed in reviving her from the first   5
two poisonings but fail with the third. (b) They lay the maiden in a glass coffin.

V. *Her Revival.* A prince sees her and resuscitates her. The stepmother is made   6
to dance herself to death in red hot shoes.

Motifs

I. Z65.1 Red as blood, white as snow. L55. Stepdaughter heroine. M312.4.   7
Prophecy: superb beauty for girl. D1311.6.3 Sun answers questions. D1311.2.
Mirror answers questions. D1323.1. Magic clairvoyant mirror.

II. S31. Cruel stepmother. K2212. Treacherous sister. S322.2. Jealous mother   8
casts daughter forth. K512.2. Compassionate executioner: substituted heart.
F451.5.1.2. Dwarfs adopt girl as sister. N812. Giant or ogre as helper. N831.1.
Mysterious housekeeper. Men find their house mysteriously put in order. Discover that it is done by a girl (frequently an animal transformed into a girl).

III. K950. Various kinds of treacherous murder. S111. Murder by poisoning.   9
D1364.16. Hairpin causes magic sleep. D1364.9. Comb causes magic sleep.
D1364.4.1. Apple causes magic sleep. S111.1. Murder with poisoned bread.
S111.2. Murder with poisoned lace. S111.3. Murder with poisoned comb. S111.4.
Murder with poisoned apple.

IV. F852.1. Glass coffin. F852.2. Golden coffin. F852.3. Silver coffin.   10

V. N711. King (prince) accidentally finds maiden in woods (tree) and mar-   11
ries her. E21.1. Resuscitation by removal of poisoned apple. By shaking loose
the apple from the throat of the poisoned girl the prince brings her to life. E21.3.
Resuscitation by removal of poisoned comb. Q414.4. Punishment: dancing to
death in red-hot-shoes.

Considerations

1. Try reconstructing a version of "Snow White" from the episodes that Stith
   Thompson presents. How does that version compare with the tales you've
   read?
2. Thompson uses this method of classification to distinguish between tale types
   and to create a model outline of a particular tale. Discuss the value of this
   method for making such a distinction. How useful would you find such a
   model if you had a variety of tales to classify? Can you anticipate any problems with a system that uses plots of stories to group them together or distinguish between them?

Connections

1. Compare several versions of "Snow White" to the tale type model for type 709. To what extent does each version adhere to the type's pattern? Where does each deviate? Would you classify each of these versions, as type 709, "Snow White"? If so, defend your classification, or, if not, explain which tale or tales you find dissimilar enough to have become a separate type. If you eliminate any tale, explain why you did so.
2. Comparing several versions of "Snow White" to the tale type model, argue that certain episodes must occur in order for this tale to be classified as type 709. (You might also include certain motifs in your argument.)
3. Compare the structure of the tale type model or paradigm to the structure you have identified above from any one variant of the tale. Does it offer the same structure? The same pattern of repetition?
4. Revise the tale type outline so that it allows for more variation. You might simply break down each episode into several episodes. This division would allow for versions that do not contain all of the episodes. Argue for your revision by referring to the actual tales on which you base your model type.
5. Find examples of some of the motifs listed under type 709, "Snow White." Comparing them, define *motif* as Thompson uses the term.

Morphology of the Folktale

Vladimir Propp

[Propp classifies folktales according to the functions of their characters. While Propp worked with 100 Russian *Märchen*, or fairy tales, his system has been applied universally to other fairy tales. Propp devised 31 functions, abstractions of individual actions, which he felt covered every event in these tales. It's easiest to think of Propp's functions in practical terms: just as the function of a bicycle pump is to pump air into a tire, so the function of a villain, for ex-

Vladímir Jákovlevič Propp was born in St. Petersburg on April 17, 1895 to a family of German descent. He died in Leningrad, where he had been a professor of folklore and chair of the Folklore Department at the University of Leningrad. In 1928 he published his first book, Morfológija skázki, *translated 30 years later as* Morphology of the Folktale, *which had a profound impact on folktale scholarship. Propp's work first received recognition when it was praised by the French structuralist Claude Lévi-Strauss in 1960. It was then taken up by semioticians such as Roland Barthes and Claude Bremond. In the United States Alan Dundes's application of Propp's ideas made his work famous. A later work by Propp,* Theory and History of Folklore, *has recently been translated.*

ample, is to cause trouble for the hero. These functions, or moves as they are often called, advance the story by setting up a series of conflicts and resolutions. Propp labeled each function with a noun describing the situation. For instance, "Lack" is Propp's abbreviated definition for function 8a, "One member of the family either lacks something or desires to have something." Clearly the Grimm version of "Snow White," begins with function 8a, "Lack." The queen longs for a child with snow white skin, blood red lips, and ebony-black hair, a child that she *lacks*. According to Propp, all fairy tales follow the same basic pattern of functions in the same sequence. While different tales will progress through different functions, all will rely on these same basic oppositions. And these oppositions occur within a predictable order. Propp intended his system to be a better way of classifying tales than that of the tale types, which, in their focus on the tale's plot, made all tales seem to have little in common.

Propp's concern with function rather than character or event led him to establish several narrative laws, the most important of which, the "law of constants and variables," says that different characters can fill the same role or function in a tale. Thus, whether it is a queen, a mother, or a stepmother, if the character shows jealousy toward Snow White, she fills the same role in the tale. In other words, villains are interchangeable. The notion that functions rather than episodes form the basis for a tale's structure, combined with the rule that different characters can perform the same actions, provide a useful way to look at folk tales. Editor's note.]

1 Let us first of all attempt to formulate our task. As already stated in the foreward, this work is dedicated to the study of *fairy* tales. The existence of fairy tales as a special class is assumed as an essential working hypothesis. By "fairy tales" are meant at present those tales classified by Aarne under numbers 300 to 749. This definition is artificial, but the occasion will subsequently arise to give a more precise determination on the basis of resultant conclusions. We are undertaking a comparison of the themes of these tales. For the sake of comparison we shall separate the component parts of fairy tales by special methods; and then, we shall make a comparison of tales according to their components. The result will be a morphology (i.e., a description of the tale according to its component parts and the relationship of these components to each other and to the whole).

2 What methods can achieve an accurate description of the tale? Let us compare the following events:

1. A tsar gives an eagle to a hero. The eagle carries the hero away to another kingdom.
2. An old man gives Súčenko a horse. The horse carries Súčenko away to another kingdom.
3. A sorcerer gives Iván a little boat. The boat takes Iván to another kingdom.
4. A princess gives Iván a ring. Young men appearing from out of the ring carry Iván away into another kingdom, and so forth.

3 Both constants and variables are present in the preceding instances. The names of the dramatis personae change (as well as the attributes of each), but neither their actions nor functions change. From this we can draw the inference that a tale often attributes identical actions to various personages. This

makes possible the study of the tale *according to the functions of its dramatis personae.*

We shall have to determine to what extent these functions actually repre-   4
sent recurrent constants of the tale. The formulation of all other questions will depend upon the solution of this primary question: how many functions are known to the tale?

Investigation will reveal that the recurrence of functions is astounding. Thus   5
Bába Jagá, Morózko, the bear, the forest spirit, and the mare's head test and reward the stepdaughter. Going further, it is possible to establish that characters of a tale, however varied they may be, often perform the same actions. The actual means of the realization of functions can vary, and as such, it is a variable. Morózko behaves differently than Bába Jagá. But the function, as such, is a constant. The question of *what* a tale's dramatis personae do is an important one for the study of the tale, but the questions of *who* does it and *how* it is done already fall within the province of accessory study. The functions of characters are those components which could replace Veselóvskij's "motifs," or Bédier's "elements." We are aware of the fact that the repetition of functions by various characters was long ago observed in myths and beliefs by historians of religion, but it was not observed by historians of the tale. Just as the characteristics and functions of deities are transferred from one to another, and, finally, are even carried over to Christian saints, the functions of certain tale personages are likewise transferred to other personages. Running ahead, one may say that the number of functions is extremely small, whereas the number of personages is extremely large. This explains the two-fold quality of a tale; its amazing multiformity, picturesqueness, and color, and on the other hand, its no less striking uniformity, its repetition.

Thus the functions of the dramatis personae are basic components of the   6
tale, and we must first of all extract them. In order to extract the functions we must define them. Definition must proceed from two points of view. First of all, definition should in no case depend on the personage who carries out the function. Definition of a function will most often be given in the form of a noun expressing an action (interdiction, interrogation, flight, etc.). Secondly, an action cannot be defined apart from its place in the course of narration. The meaning which a given function has in the course of action must be considered. For example, if Iván marries a tsar's daughter, this is something entirely different than the marriage of a father to a widow with two daughters. A second example: if, in one instance, a hero receives money from his father in the form of 100 rubles and subsequently buys a wise cat with this money, whereas in a second case, the hero is rewarded with a sum of money for an accomplished act of bravery (at which point the tale ends), we have before us two morphologically different elements — in spite of the identical action (the transference of money) in both cases. Thus, identical acts can have different meanings, and vice versa. *Function is understood as an act of a character, defined from the point of view of its significance for the course of the action.*

The observations cited may be briefly formulated in the following manner: 7

1. *Functions of characters serve as stable, constant elements in a tale, independent of how and by whom they are fulfilled. They constitute the fundamental components of a tale.*

2. *The number of functions known to the fairy tale is limited.*

If functions are delineated, a second question arises: in what classification   *8*
and in what sequence are these functions encountered?

A word, first, about sequence. The opinion exists that this sequence is acci-   *9*
dental. Veselóvskij writes, "The selection and *order* of tasks and encounters
(examples of motifs) already presupposes a certain *freedom.*" Šklóvskij stated
this idea in even sharper terms: "It is quite impossible to understand why, in
the act of adoption, the *accidental* sequence [Šklóvskij's italics] of motifs must
be retained. In the testimony of witnesses, it is precisely the sequence of events
which is distorted most of all." This reference to the evidence of witnesses is
unconvincing. If witnesses distort the sequence of events, their narration is
meaningless. The sequence of events has its own laws. The short story too has
similar laws, as do organic formations. Theft cannot take place before the door
is forced. Insofar as the tale is concerned, it has its own entirely particular and
specific laws. The sequence of elements, as we shall see later on, is strictly *uniform.* Freedom within this sequence is restricted by very narrow limits which
can be exactly formulated. We thus obtain the third basic thesis of this work,
subject to further development and verification:

3. *The sequence of functions is always identical.*

As for groupings, it is necessary to say first of all that by no means do all   *10*
tales give evidence of all functions. But this in no way changes the law of sequence. The absence of certain functions does not change the order of the rest.
We shall dwell on this phenomenon later. For the present we shall deal with
groupings in the proper sense of the word. The presentation of the question
itself evokes the following assumption: if functions are singled out, then it will
be possible to trace those tales which present identical functions. Tales with
identical functions can be considered as belonging to one type. On this foundation, an index of types can then be created, based not upon theme features,
which are somewhat vague and diffuse, but upon exact structural features. Indeed, this will be possible. If we further compare structural types among
themselves, we are led to the following completely unexpected phenomenon:
functions cannot be distributed around mutually exclusive axes. This phenomenon, in all its concreteness, will become apparent to us in the succeeding and
final chapters of this book. For the time being, it can be interpreted in the following manner: if we designate with the letter A a function encountered everywhere in first position, and similarly designate with the letter B the function
which (if it is at all present) *always follows A,* then all functions known to the
tale will arrange themselves within a *single* tale, and none will fall out of order, nor will any one exclude or contradict any other. This is, of course, a completely unexpected result. Naturally, we would have expected that where there
is a function A, there cannot be certain functions belonging to other tales. Supposedly we would obtain several axes, but only a single axis is obtained for all
fairy tales. They are of the same type, while the combinations spoken of previously are subtypes. At first glance, this conclusion may appear absurd or perhaps even wild, yet it can be verified in a most exact manner. Such a typo-
logical unity represents a very complex problem on which it will be necessary
to dwell further. This phenomenon will raise a whole series of questions.

In this manner, we arrive at the fourth basic thesis of our work: *11*

4. *All fairy tales are of one type in regard to their structure.*

We shall now set about the task of proving, developing, and elaborating these   *12* theses in detail. Here it should be recalled that the study of the tale must be carried on strictly deductively, i.e., proceeding from the material at hand to the consequences (and in effect it is so carried on in his work). But the *presentation* may have a reversed order, since it is easier to follow the development if the general bases are known to the reader beforehand.

Before starting the elaboration, however, it is necessary to decide what ma-   *13* terial can serve as the subject of this study. First glance would seem to indicate that it is necessary to cover all extant material. In fact, this is not so. Since we are studying tales according to the functions of their dramatis personae, the accumulation of material can be suspended as soon as it becomes apparent that the new tales considered present no new functions. Of course, the investigator must look through an enormous amount of reference material. But there is no need to inject the entire body of this material into the study. We have found that 100 tales constitute more than enough material. Having discovered that no new functions can be found, the morphologist can put a stop to his work, and further study will follow different directions (the formation of indices, the complete systemization, historical study). But just because material can be limited in quantity, that does not mean that it can be selected at one's own discretion. It should be dictated from without. We shall use the collection by Afanás'ev, starting the study of tales with No. 50 (according to his plan, this is the first fairy tale of the collection), and finishing it with No. 151. Such a limitation of material will undoubtedly call forth many objections, but it is theoretically justified. To justify it further, it would be necessary to take into account the degree of repetition of tale phenomena. If repetition is great, then one may take a limited amount of material. If repetition is small, this is impossible. The repetition of fundamental components, as we shall see later, exceeds all expectations. Consequently, it is theoretically possible to limit oneself to a small body of material. Practically, this limitation justifies itself by the fact that the inclusion of a great quantity of material would have excessively increased the size of this work. We are not interested in the quantity of material, but in the quality of its analysis. Our working material consists of 100 tales. The rest is reference material, of great interest to the investigator, but lacking a broader interest.

Propp's 31 Functions*

The following list of 31 functions includes a one-sentence definition of each   *14* function and a one-word abstraction of that definition. The single word abstractions offer a useful shorthand method of describing tales. For example, a five-move tale might consist of *interdiction, violation, departure, struggle, and return.*

---

*Vladimir Propp, Propp's 31 Functions. This material is an abridged version of Chapter III of *Morphology of the Folktale*, Second Edition, by V. Propp, translated by Laurence Scott, Copyright of translation © 1968, and is reproduced by permission of the University of Texas Press.

1. One of the members of a family absents himself from home *(absention)*.
2. An interdiction is addressed to the hero *(interdiction)*.
3. The interdiction is violated *(violation)*.
4. The villain makes an attempt at reconnaissance *(reconnaissance)*.
5. The villain receives information about his victim *(delivery)*.
6. The villain attempts to deceive his victim in order to take possession of him or his belongings *(trickery)*.
7. The victim submits to deception and thereby unwittingly helps his enemy *(complicity)*.
8. The villain causes harm or injury to a member of the family *(villainy)*.
8a. One member of a family either lacks something or desires to have something *(lack)*.
9. Misfortune or lack is made known; the hero is approached with a request or command; he is allowed to go or he is dispatched *(mediation, the connective incident)*.
10. The seeker agrees to or decides upon counteraction *(beginning counteraction)*.
11. The hero leaves home *(departure)*.
12. The hero is tested, interrogated, attacked, etc., which prepares the way for his receiving either a magical agent or helper *(the first function of the donor)*.
13. The hero reacts to the actions of the future donor *(the hero's reaction)*.
14. The hero acquires the use of a magical agent *(provision or receipt of a magical agent)*.
15. The hero is transferred, delivered, or led to the whereabouts of an object of search *(spatial transference between two kingdoms, guidance)*.
16. The hero and the villain join in direct combat *(struggle)*.
17. The hero is branded *(branding, marking)*.
18. The villain is defeated *(victory)*.
19. The initial misfortune or lack is liquidated *(liqudation)*.
20. The hero returns *(return)*.
21. The hero is pursued *(pursuit, chase)*.
22. Rescue of the hero from pursuit *(rescue)*.
23. The hero, unrecognized, arrives home or in another country *(unrecognized arrival)*.
24. A false hero presents unfounded claims *(unfounded claims)*.
25. A difficult task is proposed to the hero *(difficult task)*.
26. The task is resolved *(solution)*.
27. The hero is recognized *(recognition)*.
28. The false hero or villain is exposed *(exposure)*.
29. The hero is given a new appearance *(transfiguration)*.
30. The villain is punished *(punishment)*.
31. The hero is married and ascends the throne *(wedding)*.

Considerations

1. Summarize the characteristics that Propp claims identify the *Märchen* or fairy tale.

607 の Propp / Propp's 31 Functions

2. Explain what Propp means by "constants and variables." Offering examples other than the ones he uses, show how this concept helps to explain the special characteristics of the fairy tale. How useful is such a concept?
3. Examine Propp's 31 functions. Do you see natural divisions among them? Try grouping them according to some principle.

Connections

1. Apply Propp's system of functions to "Snow White." Choose the functions from the Propp list that match actions in the tale. Then try to group the functions, identifying and labeling what you see as the major groups of conflict and resolution within the tale.
2. Once you have worked out the functions for one tale, repeat the process for several other tales. Your goal will be to develop a series of functions or groups of functions that will fit all the versions of "Snow White" (or any other tale of your choice).
3. Now try applying the type you have established to other fairy tales, deciding whether these tales do indeed all have the same structure, as Propp asserts.
4. Develop a shorthand version of Propp's 31 functions, one that you feel would more readily cover all fairy tales. Starting with your groups of functions, try to establish a set of actions or oppositions of resolution and conflict that would cover all tales. You may need several such structural patterns, depending upon a tale's complexity.
5. Challenge Propp's assertion that a tale's functions always occur in the same order or sequence.
6. Compare Propp's method of classifying tales with that of Stith Thompson. What are the advantages and disadvantages of each system? Be sure to support your assertions with specific examples from the tales themselves.

Aspects of the *Märchen* and the Legend

Max Lüthi

In the introduction to a recently published collection of Breton folktales the editor, Geneviève Massignon, noted the remark of one of her informants that these *Märchen* were so old that one couldn't know if they ever were invented by anyone: *"contes si vieux que l'on ne sait pas si personne les a jamais inventés."* The remark of this woman of Lower Brittany, in particular the choice of the word *inventé*, shows exactly the feelings of countless hearers and narrators of folk tales and also those of many scholars: these stories could not have been invented; they must somehow have created themselves. "Composition" *(Zubereitung)* in literature and "spontaneous creation" *(Sichvonselbstmachen)* in folk literature are the formulations Jacob Grimm used to express this.   1

Under the influence of the theory of *gesunkenes Kulturgut* such views later fell into disfavor. We have not become weary of repeating that it is not any mystical folk mind which creates poetry, but that in every single case it is a certain individual. . . . The continuing argument over the question of how far tales and legends are of collective and how far of individual origin shows that the impression that *Märchen* and legends have not been arbitrarily created, not *inventé*, but somehow arose and grew by themselves, an impression occurring again and again among simple peoples just as among scholars, really contributes to the fascination of this creation.   2

In the present essay, which by no means attempts to discuss the problem in a fundamental manner, the apparent or real spontaneous creation of objects in folktales can serve as a point of departure. Even now it has become clear that the most varied sciences are interested in the *Märchen*. The literary scholar attempts to investigate the history, that is the origin, development, spread, and changes of the tales, but he also asks about their structure and style and about the view of man and the world contained in them. The folklorist seeks not only traces of old customs and rites in the *Märchen* and legend, but as a biologist he investigates their place in the life of the community; he is interested in the tales and in the relation of the tales to their environment. The sociologist also promotes *Märchen* and legend biology, and beyond that he sees in legends and tales reflections of the disputes of the different social groups. Historians of religion and mythologists take tales and legends as evidence of the relation of   3

Born in 1909 in Bern, Switzerland, and educated at the Universities of Bern and Berlin, Max Lüthi holds a chair as professor of European folk literature at the University of Zürich. Along with his work on the folktale for popular audiences, Once Upon a Time: On the Nature of the Fairy Tale, *Lüthi's classic study of the* Märchen, Das europaische Volksmärchen, *has recently been translated as* The European Folktale.

men to the supernatural, and psychologists, educators, and psychiatrists try to understand them as the expression of emotional development and complexities and to investigate their effect and influence on healthy people and on patients, on children and on adults. Thus tales and legends are a field of activity (at times one might say a playground) for many sciences.

Since in *Märchen*, and especially in legends, standards are also set and ethical demands advanced, one could think that even philosophy would allow herself to be tempted out of her ivory tower. So far this has not happened. Instead, folkloristics is concerned with this side of the legend, with the moralizing and ethical standards in the legend. The folklorist is the most comprehensive caretaker of tales and legends. He is not only their investigator but at the same time their collector and usually also their editor. Each science investigates the folktale from a different standpoint; each makes other aspects visible. We have already touched on a few of these, and we will touch on a few others, but essentially we are limiting ourselves to the literary method of observation. This also has more than one side and has the advantage of a certain objectivity. *Märchen* psychology easily leads to speculation. Whether the various figures of the tales represent various parts of the personality is a matter for discussion.

Since each action of a man is also an argument of this man with himself, it seems to me that one cannot deny the supposition that the family in the folktale is a symbolic representation of the total personality — "Each person is a little society" — a supposition that is at least relatively justified. But it still remains a supposition, whereas the descriptive statement that the family as an organizing principle plays a greater role in the *Märchen* than in the legend is in the realm of the observable. That it is the nuclear family which forms the folktale (nephews, cousins, or aunts scarcely ever appear) contributes to the strictness of the narrative form. At the same time, something of its world view manifests itself in the way the *Märchen* presents the family. The family in the *Märchen* is full of tensions, full of inner conflicts. The hero and heroine are better sheltered in universal nature than they are in family. Animals and stars are usually more trustworthy and helpful partners than brothers and sisters, sons and parents; to scarcely any of the usual helper figures does the hero of the *Märchen* have a closer relation than to the helpful animals. These are sober statements. But whether a helpful fox symbolizes a specific side of the unconscious allows for a difference of opinion. Because psychologists lean toward bold theories, they have so far encountered from folklorists and literary scholars almost as strong a rejection as that encountered by the Nature Mythologists of the last century. However, their contribution to the knowledge of the folktale should not be underestimated. If in this literary essay little is said of them, this should not be taken as a value judgment.

To the question of what is spontaneously created in the *Märchen* — we will speak of it next — one might answer: the manner of narration, the style. Whoever acknowledges that the characteristic mark of a work of art is the harmony of all its elements in a unified style will state, perhaps with a certain bewilderment, that in the European folktale, which in the form finally transmitted to us is certainly not the work of a single person, such a harmony of stylistic elements establishes itself as though spontaneously. The folktale likes everything to be sharply defined, of specified form. It likes to speak of staffs, swords, guns, feathers, and animals hairs — all things whose form approaches the linear. It often mentions little boxes, nuts, eggs; not only costly clothes or spinning wheels, but whole castles are enclosed in a nut or an egg and therewith are confined in a circle with a clear outline. One of the best-known folktale motifs is that of the life in the egg; the innermost life of the giant or a cannibal is not in his body but somewhere far away in a well-hidden and well-protected egg. Only the one who breaks or crushes this egg can kill the giant. In our context one recognizes at once that the egg occurs here not only because it is an ancient symbol of life, but also because as a stylistic element it is well suited to the total style of the folktale. The folktale also likes to speak of rooms, houses, and castles, all things with sharp borders and horizontal and vertical interior lines. The castle, a mentally projected geometric conception, is a sort of emblem for the folktale, just as the cave with its uncertain form lost in the darkness of the earth is an emblem for the legend. Correspondingly, in the *Märchen* clothing plays a greater role than the body — whose presence we often feel very clearly in the legend.

To the partiality for sharply outlined, clearly formed things is added the   7
Märchen's general preference for hard and clear-colored metals such as gold, silver, copper, and iron; for minerals — stone and glass; and for bold colors, especially red, white, and black, above all, and the metallic colors. Mixed colors and shades are almost completely lacking. In addition to this come the formulaic numbers (3, 7, 12, 100), formulaic openings and conclusions, transition sentences, charms and magic verse, the habit of formulaic repetition, multiplication, contrast, and the tendency to push everything to its farthest extreme — the punishments as well as the rewards, the social types (the hero is either prince or swineherd) as well as character types (the hero and heroine are good, their opponents evil). The hero and heroine stand not only at the extreme ends of the social order but also at the extreme edge of the family. They are the youngest and apparently the weakest and most unpromising.

The same sharp formation, precision, clarity, and stability reign in the de-   8
sign of the action. Things such as the forest or the city into which the hero enters are only named, not described. The figures are isolated; they set out into the world alone; the action is developed in far-reaching lines, whereas by preference the events of the legend occur within one place. The folktale action has marked junctions, tasks, commands, prohibitions, and restrictions; the hero is guided by advice, gifts, and assistance, not by emotional impulse or the decisions of his conscience. The terse conclusion is in accordance with the clarity marking the narrow line of action. The sudden transformation, as well as any sort of miraculous happening, also fits into the total style. It is a style of precision and clarity. The episodes rank themselves together, not haphazardly, and not in unspecified numbers, as happens so often in the sweeping oriental tales, but usually in three divisions, with the stress on the last. As a whole the folktale is frequently in two parts. The order of episodes is in accord syntactically with the parataxis of the sentences. But many other tales also tend toward a clear diagram, which makes everything visible, makes everything proceed smoothly, and translates qualities into deeds, relationships into gifts. Neither the inner life nor the social life of the characters, neither their surroundings,

origin, or posterity are presented. The characters of the *Märchen* are cut out of the context of their existence; they have no real surroundings, no real inner world, no posterity, no ancestors. And the isolation of the characters accords with the isolation of the episodes, which are sealed off in themselves, often so much so that reference or allusion to earlier events is avoided and instead these events are told again in the same or slightly different words. Certainly this is one of the means of prolonging the tales without having to lose oneself in descriptions. But it is at the same time suited to the whole style of the folktale. Indeed stylistic pressure is rather stronger than the need to expand the tales.

When one considers that all this happened again and again in oral tales, *9* among more and more different narrators, and among the most varied peoples, then one will involuntarily say that the tale has obviously risen spontaneously. That is, it arises not only or even predominantly from the necessities of oral transmission and the primitiveness of the narrator. Folksong and legend have different styles than the *Märchen*. In folksong the colors of living nature, green and brown, occur frequently; in the *Märchen* mention is made of neither the green of the deciduous forest or the pine forest nor the brown of tree trunks, fields, or hair, but rather they speak of golden hair and coppery-colored forests. This is not because these are easier to tell of or more convenient to transmit but because they belong to the style of this class of tale.

Thereto it happens that a picture of man automatically results from this style *10* of the European folktale, which I have tried to sketch comprehensively or at least to indicate. At the center of the *Märchen* stands the hero or heroine. All other characters, no matter how sharply drawn, are only opponents, helpers, or motivators of him, or they contrast to him. Now the central character, the hero, appears, in accord with the total style of the folktale, as one isolated. He is the outermost, most dispensable member of the social order as well as of the family. Within the family he bears the stigma of stupidity or laziness; not infrequently he is the only child, born to parents who have been childless for a long period; he is a stepchild or a Tom Thumb; magical conception may mark him and single him out — he appears as the offspring of an animal or even as half-man. He leaves his parents and by no means always returns to his father's house, as Hansel and Gretel do. Hansel and Gretel are abandoned; others leave voluntarily, travel under completely different pretexts out into the unknown world and encounter adventures alone. But precisely because they are nowhere firmly rooted, they are free to accept each new relationship, free to enter into and dissolve every tie; they receive gifts and help from otherworldly characters easily and surely.

In its heroes and heroines the *Märchen* delineates man as isolated and, be- *11* cause of this, capable of universal relationships. The hero of the *Märchen* is isolated but not at the mercy of the world; instead he is simply the gifted one, who receives gifts and aid at every step and is able to accept them, in contrast to his unendowed older brothers and sisters. He is isolated but not lonely, because he doesn't feel himself to be alone; all important contacts are made without difficulty. Because this representation of man results from the whole style of the *Märchen*, it recurs in each tale. Psychologists, who try to interpret the *Märchen* symbolically, refer to particular statements of different tales, to maturation and growth processes, to struggles with bonds to mother or father, to the search for the core of the true personality, to the devotion to unconscious spheres and neglected possibilities, to conflicts within the unconscious. We completely believe that such things are reflected in the *Märchen*. It is indisputable that the *Märchen* plainly invites symbolic interpretation. Everyone sees that the beautiful princess symbolizes a high value and that dragons, witches, and ogres symbolize evil powers. But in the interpretation of special traits opinions can differ, and arbitrary judgment easily slips in. However the general picture of man, which is peculiar to this genre can be immediately gathered from the tales.

The legend also gives a description of man. It is different from that of the   *12* *Märchen* because the viewpoint of the legend is different. The *Märchen* considers man; the legend considers what happens to man. The *Märchen* outlines the narrow road of the hero walking through the world and does not dwell on the figures meeting him. But the legend looks fixedly at the inexplicable which confronts man. And because it is monstrous — war, pestilence, or landslide, and especially often a numinous power, be it nature, demons, or spirits of the dead — man becomes small and unsure before it. The legend sketches suffering man, stricken and perplexed, questioning, brooding, explaining, but also struggling with a difficult decision, losing himself in wantonness or rising to a sacrificial act. More than once it has been shown that the historical legend in particular sketches man as someone enduring fate rather than shaping or mastering it. But the man of the legend is not more passive than he of the *Märchen* in every respect. In thinking and interpreting, in the spiritual conflict with the powers meeting him, he is far more self-reliant and active than the hero of the *Märchen*, who accepts almost everything as self-evident. Not only his thoughts, misgivings, and fears arise out of his own soul, but also his decisions and deeds, whereas the hero of the *Märchen* is guided and moved through gifts, instructions, obstacles, and aids. In the distant view of the *Märchen*, men, animals, and otherworldly beings change into mere shapes. The legend, however, is close to man, animal and spirit. It has another viewing distance and another line of sight. In its center stands not man as such, but his difficult-to-comprehend partner.

Both the slight distance and the attention to the supernatural partner au-   *13* tomatically produce another description of man. It also produces another manner of narration. In this way, as the man of the legend is a groper, a questioner, a small thing surrendered to the grip of monstrous powers, so also is the manner of narration groping and fragmentary. It is debatable whether one could speak of a special legend style. "When dealing with the legend, there is . . . no point in asking after the form of the tale and after its generic style," declares Leopold Schmidt. "There is no such thing; in the legend, everything is content." Such an attitude apparently does not differentiate at all, or not enough, between folk belief and legend. In folk belief everything is content, but the folk legend is a narrative form and as such has its style. In another place I have tried to describe this style more precisely as a mixture of elements of certainty and uncertainty, a mixture which the divided, uncertain attitude of the man of the legend matches.

As narrative the *Märchen* is richer than the legend. As simple as it seems, it   *14* is differentiated in its way. It is aware of the contrast between being and appearing; especially is it aware of the two-facedness of a thing. The forest, the castle, and the forbidden room are at the same time places of danger and of important adventure, the wild animal can change to a grateful helper or to a radiant bridegroom, death can bring release or transformation to man. A more central bearer of the theme of appearance and reality is the hero of the *Märchen*, who appears to be stupid, lazy, dirty, awkward, ugly, and abnormal but then proves himself to be one who outshines all the others.

Other important themes also appear in the *Märchen*, such as the meeting 15 with oneself. We have already encountered the motif of the hidden tale; the tales in which it is contained are known under a variety of names, such as The Giant without a Heart (and are Number 302 in the Aarne-Thompson Type Index). The giant, ogre, or cannibal has hidden his life somewhere outside his body, usually far away in a berry, a bee, a bird, or a fish, in a sword, or especially in an egg. He who gets it in his power has power over the life of the giant. The secret of where the life is placed being conveyed to the hero through the maiden stolen by the giant, he finds the egg and crushes it so that the giant must die. In many variants it is the case that the death of the giant ensues only when one hurls the egg against the giant's own forehead. The giant dies by his own hand, as it were. It is noteworthy that the most different types of folk narrative, not only the *Märchen*, tend toward such a fateful self-encounter. As in "Hansel and Gretel" the witch must burn in her own oven, in this manner other monsters also perish through their own evil methods; in the *Märchen* of the Romanic countries, for example, Bluebeard and the evil mother-in-law of Dornröschen perish in this manner. . . .

We have called our essay "Aspects of the *Märchen* and the Legend." From 16 the point of departure of spontaneous creation a number of different aspects have come into view; others have remained unmentioned. We now refer back to one of the tales previously mentioned and consider in particular a few more points. . . .

If social criticism can emanate from different classes and groups, . . . so 17 too different epochs naturally make themselves noticeable in the legend and the *Märchen*. Where in antiquity the death of Great Pan is spoken of, Christian thought can later make its way. While cutting wood, servants hear a bird sing, "Stutzi Mutzi! Tomorrow we must go to church, the chief is dead!" Thus in the legend the otherworldly realm is not only moralized but also Christianized. Historical changes can be identified in the *Märchen*, though mere shifting of elements, such as the substitution of swords with guns, of the inn with the hotel, affect only the surface area of the *Märchen*. But it is believed as well that one can find traces of historical developments in its structure. In the tale of The Giant without a Heart, frequently alluded to here, the hero receives from the animal helpers the ability to take on their shape. It is thought that this shifting of shape is older than the magical summoning of animals usual in other tales. In the contact with the beasts of prey one suspects an older level than in contact with domestic animals. But descriptive research may say that younger and older layers unite in the *Märchen;* each element is woven into the whole.

The historian, as well as the psychologist, moves in the realm of conjecture 18 and, like him, is exposed to severe disappointments. Thus one ventured to conclude from the old-Germanic-sounding rhythm of the verse "Rapunzel, Rapunzel, lass dein Haar herunter" that the Rapunzel tale extended back into a relatively early time — if not into the Germanic, then somewhere into the tenth, eleventh, or twelfth century. And then it turned out that that coining of the verse originated with Jacob Grimm and that in the source (the model text of which moreover is not a German but a French *Märchen*) there is no verse at all but a clumsy and completely unmagical prose: "Rapunzel, lass deine Haare runter, dass ich rauf kann" — the awkward translation of the French "Persinette, descendez vos cheveux que je monte." Other scholars assume a relationship between the tower of the Rapunzel *Märchen* and the puberty house of many primitive peoples and believe it is possible to ascertain the age of the tale in this way.

In my exposition I have refrained from such daring hypotheses and have tried only to show what lies open today, what yields itself, as it were. In what appears obvious are many problems and many aspects. To consider a few of them, if only in a quick survey and without systematizing them in any way, was the intention of this essay.

19

Considerations

1. Outline the major and minor concepts in this article. Try to present Max Lüthi's central argument and sketch in his supporting evidence.
2. Lüthi discusses the motif of transformation or change in the *Märchen*. In one or two paragraphs present his ideas on the topic.
3. Develop your previous paragraph(s) further by more fully defining *transformation* as it occurs in the fairy tale. What are the characteristics that distinguish it from transformation in nature? How does such change come about? What are its implications for creating the atmosphere of the *Märchen*?
4. Select one of Lüthi's minor characteristics of fairy tales, such as a penchant for primary colors, and write a paragraph illustrating that trait.

Connections

1. Using Max Lüthi's article "Aspects of the *Märchen* and the Legend" as a guide, summarize the characteristics of the fairy tale. Selecting a variant of "Snow White" as your example, identify the major and minor characteristics of this genre.
2. Identify and apply those aspects of the *Märchen* most suited to "Snow White." Based on this survey, how representative of *Märchen* characteristics is this tale?
3. Lüthi describes the *Märchen* protagonist as isolated and passive, yet capable of new relationships and even of transformation. Apply this description to Snow White. Does the common pattern Lüthi suggests illuminate Snow White's nature and experiences?
4. The approaches of Propp (tale types) and Lüthi (*Märchen* characteristics) both derive from the underlying assumption that all such tales share the same

characteristics. Briefly explain the source of this assumption, and sum up the characteristics of the *Märchen* as you understand them based on both approaches.

5. Compare the paragraph on the use of colors in the *Märchen* that you wrote when you read the Grimm variant with the paragraph on primary colors that you wrote in response to Lüthi's selection. Did Lüthi's article deepen your understanding of the use of primary colors in any way?

Blanca Rosa and the Forty Thieves

Narrated by Amanda Flores,
collected by Marino Pizaro,
and translated by Rockwell Gray

A certain widower had a beautiful daughter called Blanca Rosa who was 1
the living image of her mother. The mother, upon dying, had left the girl a little magic mirror and had told her daughter that if she ever wanted to see her, she need only take out her looking glass and it would give her her desire. After some time, the widower married again, this time to a very envious woman. When the stepmother saw the daughter talking all day with her mirror, she took it away from her. This lady considered herself the most beautiful woman in the world. She asked the mirror, "Who is the most lovely of all women?" The mirror answered, "Your daughter." As the little glass didn't flatter her with the right answer, she became furiously envious and ordered her daughter killed. The men who were supposed to do the job abandoned the girl, and a little old man helped her.

Meanwhile the stepmother asked the mirror once again who was the most 2
beautiful woman in the world. "Your daughter, who is still alive," was the answer. In a rage, she called for the little old man who had helped the girl and sentenced him to death if he didn't bring her the tongue and the eyes of her daughter. Now, the old fellow had a pet dog with blue eyes. Seeing that he couldn't defend the poor girl, he decided to kill the dog and convince the stepmother that he had followed orders. After this, he left Blanca Rosa to God's

---

This Chilean version of AT 709 was collected in 1949 by Marino Pizaro in Monte Patria, Coquimbo, Chile. The tale was told by Amanda Flores, a school teacher. Translated by Rockwell Gray, the tale appears in Yolando Pino-Saavedra's Folktales of Chile. *The "Snow White" tale itself is widespread in Spanish-speaking countries.*

care in the forest. The stepmother was very pleased when he brought her the blue eyes and the tongue on a silver platter.

For a long while the life of Blanca Rosa was sad and full of pain until one   3
day she came upon the hideout of forty thieves. One morning when she had perched high in the crown of a tree, she observed a band of men leaving the forest. The girl climbed down to the den from which they had emerged and was dazzled and amazed to see all manner of jewels and delicious dishes. The good food was what she most wished for so she crept in and ate to her heart's content, returning afterward to the tree top and falling into a deep sleep.

When the thieves returned to their lair, they found everything strewn about   4
and suspected that somebody had found them out. The leader, however, didn't think so, but left a guard at the entance just to make sure. When they had all gone off on their forays the next day, Blanca Rosa came down again. The guard saw her and was fascinated with such great beauty. He believed that she was a being descended from heaven and dashed off pell-mell to give the rest the news. But when they returned to the camp, nobody put much stock in what he said. After this, the chief ordered five men to stand guard to see about this strange apparition. All of them saw Blanca Rosa and reported the same news, believing that it was the Virgin of Heaven come to punish them. Meanwhile Blanca Rosa took her pleasure in the hideout while the thieves were away. On their return, they found nobody. The chief himself decided to stand guard, for he couldn't be convinced of all these goings-on. Great was his surprise when he saw Blanca Rosa descend from the tree. Never before had he seen such a beautiful woman. He begged her pardon, thinking that she was surely the mother of God, and called his companions to repent and adore her. But Blanca Rosa, full of anguish, protested that she was not the Virgin, but rather only a poor orphan cast out of her stepmother's house. The only thing she wished was shelter so as not to die of hunger in her solitude. The thieves refused to believe this and continued to worship her as the Virgin. They built her a throne of gold, dressed her with the most lovely dresses, and adorned her with the most precious jewels. From that day on, Blanca Rosa lived happy and content among her robber "relatives."

It was rumored in the city that there was in the forest a den of thieves who   5
adored a beautiful woman. When the stepmother got wind of this, she refused to believe it, and insisted that she was the only beautiful one in the world.

"Little mirror," she asked the charm, "by the power God has given you, tell   6
me who is the most beautiful of all."

"Blanca Rosa is the most beautiful woman," answered the little glass.   7

In desperation, the stepmother sought out a sorceress and offered her a great   8
sum of money if she would only kill the lovely stepdaughter. The old witch searched through the forest until she found the hideout and, with lies, cajoleries, and flatteries, was able to see Blanca Rosa. When the old charmer was sure it was the right girl, she pretended to be a poor woman who wished to show her gratitude for some gold that the girl had once given her. She handed the girl a basket of fruit, but Blanca Rosa told the old woman to keep it, for she already had a great deal.

"If you won't accept this bit of fruit," croaked the old lady, "at least let me   9
touch your dress and run my hand over your silky hair." She stroked Blanca

Rosa's head and jabbed her with a magic needle. Instantly the girl dropped into a deep, deep sleep. The old hag slipped out in a wink and went to the stepmother to tell her that her daughter would trouble her no longer.

When the thieves arrived at the forest lair, they found their precious queen *10* sleeping. As she didn't stir for many days, they believed her dead. After great weeping and many efforts to revive her, they resigned themselves to the task of the burial. Her outlaw friends placed her in a casket made of pure gold and silver, dressing her beautifully and adorning her with the most exquisite necklaces and pearls. They sealed her in against the least little drop of water and threw the casket into the sea.

Now there was in a certain city a prince who lived with his two old maid *11* sisters and was very fond of fishing. One day he was out in his launch pulling in some nets when he saw in the waves something that sparkled and shone over the waters. Anxious to find out about this mystery, he called some fishermen to help him land the beautiful floating casket. They loaded it into his boat and he took it home, shutting himself in his own room. The casket was riveted so tight that he couldn't open it until he brought his whole tool kit to the task. After seven days and seven nights of labor, he removed the lid and found the girl dressed with such lovely garments and jewels. He tenderly removed the body and placed it on his bed, where he stripped it of its clothes and removed the jewels one by one, puzzling over the mystery of this person. When he found nothing, it occurred to him to comb her silken hair. The comb got snarled on a little bump, which the prince removed with a pair of tweezers. Immediately the fair girl sprang to life, and he realized that she had been bewitched all the time.

"Where are my thieves?" cried Blanca Rosa, seeing herself alone with this *12* man she had never met, and totally nude. To console the distraught girl, the prince began to tell her the tale of how he had found her floating over the waves, assuring her that he was a good man and that there was nothing to fear. She would not be calmed and insisted on leaving, so the prince drove the needle back into her head and walked out to think what he could possibly do with the lovely maiden. Meanwhile the two old maid sisters were at their wit's end to see what their brother was doing locked in his room day and night. He hadn't even appeared to eat. They began to keep watch through the keyhole. Great was their shock when they spied a golden casket and heaps of jewels.

The prince returned to his room after long thought and removed the needle *13* once again from Blanca Rosa's head. He told her he had not been able to find the forty thieves and asked her to remain in his house under his protection, as his wife. If she didn't wish to go into the street, she could remain in her room and nobody would know the secret.

One fine morning when the prince had gone off to fish and had left the sad *14* and melancholy Blanca Rosa in her room, the two sisters were seized with curiosity and opened the door. They were very indignant at seeing such a pretty girl seated on the bed. Immediately they stripped her of her fine clothing and necklaces and threw her nude into the street. Blanca Rosa frantically tried to hide and eventually arrived, breathless, at the house of an old cobbler. She was crying so bitterly that the old man took her in and hid her. The prince arrived home and found her room empty with the clothes strewn on the floor. Disconsolate, he wandered aimlessly in search of the lovely girl until someone told him of a beautiful young woman at the cobbler's house. Sure enough, he found Blanca Rosa there and took her joyfully back to his own place, where he began the preparations for the wedding. As a punishment for his sisters, the prince sent for two wild horses and had the old maids bound to them head and foot. The bucking broncos tore them into a thousand pieces. Immediately after this, the wedding was celebrated with great pomp. The forty thieves attended at Blanca Rosa's request and brought the bride many marvelous gifts. She and the prince lived very happily for all the rest of their lives.

Considerations

1. Write a summary or brief plot outline of this tale. To what extent does your plot present the standard form of "Snow White" as you recall it? Where does it deviate?
2. Outline the tale's structure. Does it rely on the repetition common to the other tales? If not, try to explain the effect this different structure has on the tale.
3. Since it was collected in a Catholic country, religious motifs figure prominently in this tale. Describe these religious elements. What do they add to the tale? Do they influence or change the story's fairy tale atmosphere?
4. This version of "Snow White" develops the relationship between the protagonist and the prince. Describe that relationship. How does the prince treat her and how do you account for such behavior?

Connections

1. Compare this version to the tale type model and describe the extent of stability and variation. Which characteristic predominates? To what extent is this version an original tale, and to what extent does it simply flesh out the critical paradigm?
2. Compare this variant to the Grimms' "Snow White." Concentrate on the differences in episodes, motifs, and atmosphere. Which version seems truer to the tale type model?
3. Applying Lüthi's characteristics of the *Märchen* to this tale, discuss where and how it deviates. What is the effect of that deviation? Does this tale seem less like a fairy tale than, for example, the Grimms' version?

Myrsina, or Myrtle

Collected by I. Proios and
translated by Helen Colaclides

Once upon a time there were three sisters who were orphans. Neither father   *1*
had they nor mother.

One day they thought they would find out who was the best of the three. So,   *2*
just as the sun was about to rise, they went onto a sun porch and stood, the
three of them, in a row and said to the sun, "Sun on the sun porch, who is the
best of us all?"

And the sun said, "One's as good as the other, but the third and youngest is   *3*
better still."

When the two elder sisters heard this, they bit their lips and went home   *4*
with bitterness in their hearts. The next day, they both put on their best clothes,
decked themselves out in their finery, but the unhappy youngest, whose name
was Myrsina, was obliged to wear her worst and dirtiest, and again they went
to consult the sun.

And when he came out on the porch, they said again, "Sun on the sun porch,   *5*
who is the best of us all?"

And the sun again said, "One's as good as the other, but the third and   *6*
youngest is better still."

When Myrsina's sisters heard this they burned with shame and went home,   *7*
much humbled. On the third day they again consulted him, and the sun again
told them the same. Then the two were more than ever consumed with envy
and plotted together to get rid of the unhappy Myrsina. "Our mother has been
so many years dead and very soon we must go and rebury her; but we must
make all ready this evening, for our mother is buried far away on the mountain and we ought to leave very early." And the luckless Myrsina believed it,
and next day she took some soul bread and *kollyva* and they set off to rebury
their mother. They walked and walked and came to a wood and halted under
a beech tree.

Then the eldest said, "Here, this is our mother's monument. Bring the pickax   *8*
for me to dig."

"Oh dear," said the other. "Look what we've gone and done, forgetful nin-   *9*
nies that we are! How are we to dig? We've brought neither fork nor pick. Now
what are we to do?"

Then the eldest one said, "One of us shall go and get the pickax."   *10*

"I'm afraid," said the second.   *11*

*Collected in Macedonia, Greece in 1888 and deposited in the Athens Folklore
Archives, MS 188, p. 82. This version, published in Georgio A. Megas's* Folktales
of Greece, *also appears in his* Hellenika Paramythia [Greek Folktales], *and was
translated from Greek into German in his* Griechische Volksmärchen.

"And if I," said Myrsina, "as much as see a bird fly suddenly from a tree, I   *12*
shall be stiff with fright."

"Listen," said the eldest, "you stay here, Myrsina, and we'll go and get the   *13*
pick, because none of us can go alone. You sit down and look after the *kollyva*
till we come."

"Very well, but come quickly, for I'm afraid to be alone."   *14*

"Oh, we're back already!" they said, and went gleefully off.   *15*

Poor Myrsina sat and waited and waited till the sun went down. Then, when   *16*
she saw night was falling and she was all alone on the mountain, she began to
cry. She cried so much that even the trees took pity on her.

A beech tree told her, "Don't cry, dear lass, only let that breadring you are   *17*
holding roll, and wherever it stops there shall you bide, without a fear in the
world."

Then Myrsina set the bread rolling and ran after it. Following it one way   *18*
and the other, and without seeing where she was going, Myrsina ran into a pit.
There she saw a house before her and went inside. Now in this house there
lived twelve brothers, the Months, who spent all day going about the world
and came home only late at night. When Myrsina came, there was no one at
home. Then Myrsina rolled up her sleeves, took up a broom and cleaned all the
house, and then sat down and cooked a delicious meal. Then she set the table,
ate a little, and hid herself in the loft. Then the Months came home. They came
in, and what should they see but all the house swept, the table set, and everything ready! What had been happening?

So then they said, "Who is it that has done this for us? Let him not be afraid,   *19*
but come out, and if it's a lad, we'll make him our brother, and if a lass, our
sister."

But no one answered. So they all ate and wondered some more and then   *20*
went to bed. In the morning they were soon up and away. Then Myrsina came
down from the loft, and again cleaned the house and sat down and made a pie,
but what a pie! The kind of pie you lick your lips over when you eat it. Then,
when evening came, she set the table and put out all the dishes. Then she cut
herself a little piece of pie, ate it, and again went and hid in the loft. In a little
while the Months came home, and when they saw everything was ready, they
hardly knew what to say.

And they said, "But who is it that has done this for us? Let him not be afraid,   *21*
but come out . . ." And they said this and so many other things, but in vain!
Myrsina would not come out. Then they sat down and ate and then went to
bed.

Then the youngest said, "I shan't come with you tomorrow, but stay here   *22*
and hide, and find out who it is that comes and does all this for us."

And so, when God sent a new day, they all got up and went, and only the   *23*
youngest stayed behind and hid behind the door. Then down came Myrsina to
do what she had done before.

But just as she was coming down, the youngest Month seized her by the   *24*
skirt, and said, "And so it's you, lady, who has done all these things for us and
won't tell us but keeps hidden! Don't be afraid. You'll be like our own sister to
us: something we asked for in heaven and found on earth."

Then Myrsina took courage and told him how her sisters had left her, and   *25* how she came to be in the house. And she set to and did all the work she had done before. She cleaned all the house, cooked, and made everything ready, like a true housewife. Late that evening, when the Months came home and saw Myrsina, they were very glad. They hardly knew what to do for gladness. Then they sat down and ate and went to bed, like good little brothers.

They got up early, and said to Myrsina, "Little sister, do as you have done 26 for us, and this evening you will see what brothers we can be to you."

Then they went off. Myrsina did all the housework as she had before, and 27 as it was growing dark, she went outside the house and waited for her brothers.

She had not been waiting long when the Months came home, and said, with 28 gladness, "Well met, little sister!"

"Welcome home, brothers!" 29

"How did your day go?" 30

"Well. And yours?" 31

"Never mind us. If your day goes well, then so does ours." 32

"Come away in, now, and rest your limbs. You are tired, and the meal is 33 ready."

"That's true, Myrsina, you're right. Let's eat, for we are very hungry this 34 evening."

Then they came in and sat down at table. And when they had eaten, you 35 should have been there to see! One gave Myrsina earrings of gold, the next a garment of cloth of gold embroidered with the heavens and stars. Another two brought her dresses embroidered with the earth and crops, and the sea and fishes; another — but to hear it all, you'd think you were in a fairy tale. And so Myrsina lived with the Months as happily as could be.

When her sisters learnt that Myrsina was alive and well, they were eaten up 36 with envy and made plans to poison her. And straightway they baked a pie with poison in it, and went to find Myrsina. It was just as the Months had gone.

Rat-tat! they knocked on the door. 37

"Who is it?" Myrsina answered from inside. 38

"Why, Myrsina, have you forgotten us so soon? Open the door. It is your 39 sisters that have worn themselves out searching for you on the mountain."

"My sisters dear!" said Myrsina, and at once opened the door and embraced 40 them and began to weep.

Then they said, "But what did you suppose, Myrsina? We went home as fast 41 as we could go, found the pickax, and came back for you. We looked everywhere, but no Myrsina! So then we said, When Myrsina was left alone, she was afraid and someone must have passed by and she would have gone with him to some village . . . and the long and short of it is, Myrsina love, we heard later you were here, and here we are to visit you. But we can see you are well, little sister!"

"Oh yes, I'm well, I couldn't be better." 42

"So we see, but take care not to leave here, as they're so fond of you. We'll 43 be going now."

"Why won't you stay?" 44

"No, we're in a hurry, another time. Stay well, Myrsina." 45

"Go well." 46

"We'll often come and see you. Ah, there! you see? We nearly forgot — here, 47 take this pie — it's one of those we baked for our mother's soul. Now you eat it for our mother's soul."

And Myrsina took it. And when they went, she cut a piece for the dog they 48 had there. And straightway the poor thing fell dead. Then Myrsina knew that the pie had been poisoned and that her sisters had tried to poison her, so she did not eat it. She threw it in the oven and burnt it.

After many months had passed, Myrsina's sisters heard that Myrsina had 49 not been poisoned. And they procured a poisoned ring and came again to where Myrsina was. They knocked on the door, but Myrsina would not open.

Whereupon they said, "Open the door, Myrsina, we have something to tell 50 you. Look, we have brought you our mother's ring, for when she died you were only little and knew nothing about it. And when our mother was on her death-bed, she said, 'Lest you have my curse, give this ring to Myrsina, when she grows up.' And we don't want to go to hell, so, as you're grown up now, take your ring."

Then Myrsina opened the window and took the ring. And no sooner had she 51 put it on than she fell to the ground like one dead. That evening, when the Months came home and saw Myrsina lifeless, they raised such lamentation as made the countryside ring. And after three days they took her up and dressed her in gold, laid her in a golden casket, and kept her in the house.

A good while after, a prince chanced to pass that way. And when he saw the 52 chest, it pleased him so much that he asked the lads to let him have it. At first they would not give it to him, but after much persuasion they let him have it. But they warned him never to open it. And the Prince took the chest and brought it to his palace. And one day he fell very ill and nearly died.

Then he turned and said to his mother "Mother, I shall die and never know 53 what is in that chest. Bring it for me to open. But all you others must leave the room."

And when they had all gone outside, he opened the chest, and what did he 54 see? Myrsina, all dressed in gold and so beautiful that even though lifeless she looked like an angel. Then the Prince was struck with wonder. And when he came to himself and saw the ring Myrsina wore, he said, "Let me see if there is anything written in the ring that will tell me what this unhappy girl's name is."

And no sooner had he taken it off her finger than Myrsina woke on the in- 55 stant and leapt out of the chest.

She began to ask, "Where am I? Who brought me here? Why, this isn't my 56 home. Where are you, brothers mine?"

"I'm your brother now," said the Prince, "and you're in the King's palace." 57

And then he told her all that had happened: how he had bought the chest 58 with her in it from the Months, and how she had lain lifeless inside until he had taken off the ring and brought her back to life.

Then Myrsina remembered her sisters, and said, "Alas! Your Grace, be sure 59 you throw that ring into the sea, for it is poisoned and bewitched. It was brought to me by my sisters and the moment I put it on my finger, I was poisoned and fell into the state I was in when you found me."

Then the Prince bade Myrsina tell him all her story. And when he had heard 60 it, he swore bitterly, and said, "Though those sisters of yours be at the ends of the world, I'll find them and punish them, for . . ."

"Please, your Grace, do nothing," said Myrsina. "Let them be, do nothing *61*
to them. Let them have their punishment from God."

Then the Prince was appeased. And when his illness was over, he lost no *62*
time in marrying Myrsina, and they lived happily together.

When her sisters heard that Myrsina was alive and had married the Prince, *63*
they could not contain their envy. And they came to the palace to poison her.

They entered and asked a manservant, "Where is Queen Myrsina? We are *64*
her sisters and have come to visit her."

"Wait there," said the manservant, "and I will inquire, for without the King's *65*
permission no one may see Myrsina."

Then he entered and said to the Prince, "Sire, there are two young women *66*
outside who say they are Queen Myrsina's sisters and wish to see her. Shall I
let them in?"

Then the Prince said to one of his gentlemen-in-waiting, "Quickly, seize those *67*
women and get rid of them as best you know how. For they have come here to
poison Queen Myrsina."

Then they seized the two sisters and what they did with them I don't know. *68*
I only know that they were never seen or heard of again.

But Myrsina and the Prince lived and thrived, and Myrsina's name was on *69*
everyone's lips for her beauty and good works.

I have been to the palace and seen Myrsina. And when I took my leave, they *70*
gave me a string of gold coins to take home with me. But as I was going by
Melachro's house, her dog came out and ran after me. To save myself I had to
throw down the coins and the dog picked them up and ran off. But should you
get up very early in the morning, at sunrise, take a sop of bread and throw it
to Melachro's dog, and she will give you the gold coins.

Considerations

1. Outline the plot of this tale or its episodes, grouping them into sections.
2. Looking at the outline you've created for the previous assignment, describe this tale's structure, movement, and completeness as a story and as a *Märchen*. Does the story appear well-plotted? Well-structured? Do any episodes seem out of place or extraneous? Argue for or against the tale having a traditional *Märchen* structure.
3. The protagonist Myrsina has two sisters. Describe her relationship with them. How do they treat her and what motivates their behavior? What is their function in the story? How typical is their behavior of certain types of characters in fairy tales?
4. Does the tale contain any elements that identify it as Greek or Mediterranean? In a paragraph describe and discuss those elements.
5. This tale contains several magical agents, actors, or helpers who provide unusual or supernatural aid or offer predictions or unusual advice. Describe these agents and their function in the story. What do they add to the atmosphere of the tale?

Connections

1. Which regional variations localize the tale, making it more closely aligned with Greece than, say, with Germany?
2. As with the previous tale, compare this one with the tale type paradigm or model. Where does it deviate? Where does it match?
3. Apply Propp's method of classification to this variant. Do you find it more useful in describing the tale than the tale type model?
4. Using this tale as your example, compare the usefulness of Vladimir Propp's versus Stith Thompson's systems of classifying *Märchen*. Determine whether one system is more useful and more flexible than the other. At least try to illuminate what you see as the differences in approaches.

Gold-Tree and Silver-Tree
Narrated by Kenneth Macleod

There was before this a king who had a wife, whose name was Silver-tree, *1* and a daughter, whose name was Gold-tree. On a certain day of the days, Gold-tree and Silver-tree went to a glen, where there was a well, in which there was a trout.

Said Silver-tree — "Troutie, bonny little fellow, am not I the most beautiful *2* queen in the world?"

"Oh! indeed, you are not." *3*

"Who then?" *4*

"Yes, Gold-tree, your daughter." *5*

Silver-tree went home, and she blind with rage. She lay down on the bed, *6* and she would never be well, until she would get the heart and the liver of Gold-tree, her daughter, to eat.

At night-fall the king came home, and it was told him that Silver-tree, his *7* wife, was very sick. He went where she was, and asked her what was wrong with her.

"Oh, only a thing which you may heal, if you like." *8*

"Oh, indeed; there is nothing at all which I could do for you that I would *9* not do."

"If I will get the heart and the liver of Gold-tree, my daughter, to eat, I shall *10* be well."

The king went and sent his lads to the hunting-hill for a he-goat, and he *11* gave its heart and its liver to his wife to eat; and she rose well and healthy.

Collected in the Scottish Hebrides on the Isle of Eigg in 1887 and published in both Gaelic and English in the Celtic *Magazine 13 (1887–1888): 213–218.*

What happened about this time but that the son of a great king came from   *12*
abroad to ask Gold-tree for marrying. The king agreed to this, and they went
abroad.

A year after this Silver-tree went to the glen, where there was the well in   *13*
which there was the trout.

"Troutie, bonny little fellow," said she, "am not I the most beautiful queen   *14*
in the world?"

"Oh, indeed, you are not."   *15*

"Who, then?"   *16*

"Yes, Gold-tree, your daughter."   *17*

"Oh, well, it is long since she was living. There is a year since I ate her heart   *18*
and liver."

"Oh! indeed, it is she that is not dead. She is married to a great prince   *19*
abroad."

Silver-tree went home, and the king would require to put the long-ship in   *20*
order, that she was going to see her dear Gold-tree, and that it was long since
she saw her. The long-ship was put in order, and they went away.

It was Silver-tree herself that was at the helm, and she steered the ship so   *21*
well that they were not long at all without arriving.

The prince was out in the hunting-hill. Gold-tree knew the long-ship of her   *22*
father coming. "Oh!" said she to the servants, "my mother is coming, and she
will kill me."

"She will not kill you at all; we will lock you in a room where she will not   *23*
get near you."

This is how it was; and when Silver-tree came ashore, and she began to cry   *24*
out —

"Come to meet your own mother, and she come to see you," Gold-tree said   *25*
that she could not, that she was locked in the room, and that she could not get
out of it.

"Will you not put out," said Silver-tree, "your little finger through the key-   *26*
hole, and that your own mother may give a kiss to it?"

She put out her little-finger, and Silver-tree went and put a poisoned stab   *27*
in it, and Gold-tree fell dead.

When the prince came home, and found Gold-tree dead, he went to great   *28*
sorrow, and with how beautiful she was, he did not bury her at all, but he locked
her in a room where nobody would get near her.

In the space of time he married again, and the whole house was under the   *29*
hand of this wife but one room, and he himself was keeping the key of that
room. On a certain day of the days he forgot to bring the key with him, and
the second wife got into the room. What did she see there but the most beautiful woman that she ever saw.

She began to turn and try her, and she noticed the poisoned stab in her fin-   *30*
ger. She took the stab out, and Gold-tree rose alive, as beautiful as she was
ever.

At the fall of night the prince came home from the hunting-hill, looking very   *31*
downcast.

"What bet," said his wife, "would you put to me that I would make you   *32*
laugh?"

"Oh! indeed, nothing would make me laugh, except Gold-tree to come alive." 33

"Well, you have her alive down there in the room." 34

When the prince saw Gold-tree alive he made great rejoicings, and he began 35
to kiss her, and kiss her, and kiss her. Said the second wife, "Since she is the
first one you had it is better for you to stick to her, and I will go away."

"Oh! indeed, you will not go away, but I shall have both of you." 36

At the end of the year Silver-tree went to the glen, where there was the well, 37
in which there was the trout. "Troutie, bonny little fellow," said she, "am not
I the most beautiful queen in the world?"

"Oh! indeed, you are not." 38

"Who then?" 39

"Yes, Gold-tree, your daughter." 40

"Oh! well, she is not alive. There is a year since I put the poisoned stab into 41
her finger."

"Oh indeed, it is she that is not dead; it is she that is not." 42

Silver-tree went home, and the king would require to put the long-ship in 43
order, that she was going to see her dear Gold-tree, and that it was long since
she saw her. The long-ship was put in order, and they went away. It was Silver-tree herself that was at the helm, and she steered the ship so well that they
were not long at all without arriving.

The prince was out in the hunting-hill. Gold-tree knew her father's ship 44
coming.

"Oh," said she, "my mother is coming and she will kill me." 45

"Not at all," said the second wife, "we will go down to meet her." 46

Silver-tree came ashore. "Come down, Gold-tree, love," said she, "and your 47
own mother come to you with a valuable drink."

"It is a custom in this country," said the second wife, "that the person who 48
offers a drink take a draught out of it himself first."

Silver-tree put her mouth to it, and the second wife went and gave a hit to 49
it down her throat, and she fell dead. They had only to carry her home a dead
corpse and bury her.

The prince and his two wives were long alive after this, pleased and peace- 50
ful.

I left them there. 51

Considerations

1. Write a brief paragraph identifying the characters in this tale, including their
   names, and defining their functions. Speculate why the characters have such
   unusual names.
2. This tale contains an obviously distinctive motif: the trout in the well. What
   is the function of the motif in this story? How can you explain its presence?
   Is the trout a typical magical agent or is this motif developed in a special
   way? Present your ideas in a well-organized paragraph or two.
3. This tale was collected in Scotland, in the Outer Hebrides, and translated
   from the Gaelic. Does it contain any motifs or episodes that suggest its lo-

cale, either in the British Isles or on an island? Try to identify any elements that might localize the tale in this way.

Connections

1. Apply Lüthi's characteristics to the tale. Do some of the elements he mentions help explain the characters' names?
2. Compare "Blanca Rosa and the Forty Thieves," "Myrsina, or Myrtle," and "Gold-Tree and Silver-Tree." Discuss their relative stability or variation.

Female Initiation Rites

N. J. Girardot

Mircea Eliade has stated that the popularity and power of fairy tales in modern life might be because the folktale "takes up and continues 'initiation'" on the level of the imagination. In other words, the universal appeal of a traditional narrative form like the folktale is not simply that it allows for amusement or a temporary escape from the banalities of ordinary life but, because at a deeper level, it preserves a vision of human life as fundamentally an initiatory process: "what is called 'initiation' coexists with the human condition, that every existence is made up of an unbroken series of 'ordeals,' 'deaths,' and 'resurrections' . . . ."   *1*

Eliade's suggestion that the fairy tale functions as an "easy doublet" for initiatory myths and rites and, consequently, reaffirms the ultimate religious significance of life and the real possibility of a "happy ending," has been echoed by scholars such as Max Lüthi who wrote that: *2*

> The charm of the fairy tale is explained not only by the fact that everything usually comes out all right in the end. . . . It is more than mere wish-fulfillment literature. The religious historian Mircea Eliade once said that the hearers of fairy tales, without being aware of it, experience a sort of initiation not entirely unlike that in the customs of some primitive peoples. . . . How correct this scholar's assertion is can be shown in any folk fairy tale.

My intention is not to discuss these general speculations, but rather to examine the proposition that fairy tales not only vaguely suggest initiatory themes at the level of individual symbols but that the narrative form of a fairy tale as

N. J. Girardot is a historian of religion. This excerpt is from his article, "Initiation and Meaning in Snow White and the Seven Dwarfs," originally published in the Journal of American Folklore *90 (1977).*

a particular structural constellation of symbols basically reveals an initiatory pattern. . . .

The moment of transition for a young girl into womanhood is ordinarily   3
marked by the coming of the first bloody menstruation. Successful passage to adulthood and marriage, however, requires a preliminary separation or isolation from the ordinary world and usually involves a retreat from the village and family to the bush, forest, or some outlying area. There is also sometimes a special place (hut, house, etc.) of initiation where the young women are sequestered from the tribe.

Phase of Liminality

The period of separation is variable in time (possibly even years in length),   4
but commonly involves the teaching of tribal lore to the young initiates by the old women who represent the mythic ancestors originally responsible for the mysteries and powers of female life. This traditionally involves an education in the basic feminine crafts (spinning, weaving, etc.) and responsibilities necessary for adult married life, as well as a teaching of feminine sexual and religious lore. There are often ordeals of a physical and psychological nature inflicted by the old women which suggest that this period of time spent in isolation from the community is a deathlike period — in effect, a period that represents a symbolic return to the liminal conditions of the mythic chaos time which is a necessary prelude to any new creation or transition in life.

Phase of Reincorporation and Rebirth

The whole initiation process is completed by a return to the village and the   5
giving of a new name and gifts symbolic of the initiate's new identity and status as an adult woman. In many instances the successful passage into the cultural world of the tribe is marked by collective dance rites which serve as a direct and necessary prelude to marriage (which either immediately follows the initiation or occurs at some later time set by the tradition).

The dangerous transition from childhood to psycho-sexual maturity and full   6
membership in the cultural life of the society is accomplished by these rites — the bringing of a girl to social, psychological, and religious adulthood.

Considerations

1. Summarize the Girardot excerpt first in one page, then one paragraph, then one sentence.
2. Briefly outline the initiatory process as Girardot presents it. Can you offer examples from your own experience or from modern American life that illustrate this process?
3. In the first paragraph, Girardot quotes Eliade's suggestion that the fairy tale "takes up and continues 'initiation' on the level of imagination." Discuss this assumption, analyzing its meaning and illustrating it with other tales you know.

Connections

1. N. J. Girardot's description of female initiation rituals, especially the stages of separation, isolation, and return after the initiate reaches maturity, lends itself to the "Snow White" fairy tale. Apply the stages Girardot mentions to the tale, determining whether it can be analyzed as such a rite.
2. Girardot has been criticized for applying his critical frame to only one representative version of the tale, the Grimm variant. Does his schema appear to fit that variant more accurately than it does, for example, "Blanca Rosa"? Write an essay in which you apply his critical frame to *Sneewittchen* and to "Blanca Rosa" or "Myrsina," comparing the results.

Feminism and Fairy Tales

Karen E. Rowe

Some day my prince will come. With mingled adolescent assurance and anxiety, young girls for many centuries have paid homage to the romantic visions aroused by this article of faith in fairy tale. Even in modern society where romance co-habits uncomfortably with women's liberation, barely disguised forms of fairy tales transmit romantic conventions through the medium of popular literature. . . .   1

The mass popularity of these fictions — erotic, ladies, and gothic — testifies to a pervasive fascination with fairy tale romance in literature not merely for children but for twentieth-century adults. Moreover, folklorists counter any casual dismissal of folktales as mere entertainment by arguing that they have always been one of culture's primary mechanisms for inculcating roles and behaviors. The ostensibly innocuous fantasies symbolically portray basic human problems and appropriate social prescriptions. These tales which glorify passivity, dependency, and self-sacrifice as a heroine's cardinal virtues suggest that culture's very survival depends upon a woman's acceptance of roles which relegate her to motherhood and domesticity. Just how potently folklore contributes to cultural stability may be measured by the pressure exerted upon women to emulate fairy tale prototypes. Few women expect a literally "royal" mar-   2

Karen E. Rowe, recipient of a National Endowment for the Humanities grant in 1977–1978 sponsoring her residence at the Radcliffe Institute, is an associate professor of English and the director of the Center for the Study of Women at the University of California at Los Angeles. She is currently completing a book on fairy tales and women's literature. This selection is excerpted from Rowe's fuller study of the same title published in Women's Studies 6 *(1979): 237–257.*

riage with Prince Charming; but, subconsciously at least, female readers assimilate more subtle cultural imperatives. They transfer from fairy tales into real life those fantasies which exalt acquiescence to male power and make marriage not simply one ideal, but the only estate toward which women should aspire. The idealizations, which reflect culture's approval, make the female's choice of marriage and maternity seem commendable, indeed predestined. In short, fairy tales are not just entertaining fantasies, but powerful transmitters of romantic myths which encourage women to internalize only aspirations deemed appropriate to our "real" sexual functions within a patriarchy. . . .

Although lingeringly attracted to fantasies (like Eve to the garden after the   3
Fall), many modern women can no longer blindly accept the promise of connubial bliss with the prince. Indeed, fairy tale fantasies come to seem more deluding than problem-solving. "Romance" glosses over the heroine's impotence: she is unable to act independently or self-assertively; she relies on external agents for rescue; she binds herself first to the father and then the prince; she restricts her ambitions to hearth and nursery. Fairy tales, therefore, no longer provide mythic validations of desirable female behavior; instead, they seem more purely escapist or nostalgic, having lost their potency because of the widening gap between social practice and romantic idealization. . . .

An examination of a few popular folktales from the perspective of modern   4
feminism not only reveals why romantic fantasy exerts such a powerful imaginative allure, but also illuminates how contemporary ambiguities cloud women's attitudes toward men and marriage.

Among the classic English tales of romance, "Cinderella," "Sleeping Beauty   5
in the Wood," "Snow-White," "The Tale of the Kind and the Unkind Girls," "Beauty and the Beast," and "The Frog-Prince" focus on the crucial period of adolescence, dramatizing archetypal female dilemmas and socially acceptable resolutions. Confronted by the trauma of blossoming sexuality, for instance, the young girl subliminally responds to fairy tale projections of adolescent conflicts. She often achieves comforting release from anxieties by subconsciously perceiving in symbolic tales the commonness of her existential dilemma. Moreover, the equal-handed justice and optimistic endings instill confidence that obstacles can be conquered as she progresses from childhood to maturity. More than alleviating psychic fears associated with the rite of passage, however, tales also prescribe approved cultural paradigms which ease the female's assimilation into the adult community.

The stepmother and bad fairy, who invariably appear odious, embody the   6
major obstacles against this passage to womanhood. Not simply dramatic and moral antagonists to the youthful heroine, they personify predatory female sexuality and the adolescent's negative feelings toward her mother. In Perrault's version of "Cinderella" (AT 510), persecution of the adolescent stems directly from the father's remarriage and the new stepmother's sexual jealousies. Because "she could not bear the good qualities of this pretty girl; and the less, because they made her own daughters so much the more hated and despised," Cinderella's stepmother displays her "ill humour" by employing the child "in the meanest work of the house" (p. 123). Similarly proud and vain, Snow-White's stepmother in Grimm's recounting plots against the seven-year-

old child who "was as bright as the day, and fairer than the queen herself" (p. 177). Although fairy tales carefully displace animosities onto a substitute figure, they in part recreate the fears of a menopausal mother. For the aging stepmother, the young girl's maturation signals her own waning sexual attractiveness and control. In retaliation they jealously torment the more beautiful virginal adolescent who captures the father's affections and threatens the declining queens. Recurrent narrative features make clear this generational conflict, as the stepmothers habitually devise stratagems to retard the heroine's progress. Remanded to the hearth, cursed with one hundred years of sleep, or cast into a death-like trance by a poisoned apple, heroines suffer beneath onslaughts of maternal fear and vengeance. Ironically, both in life and fairy tale, time triumphs, delivering the daughter to inescapable womanhood and the stepmother to aged oblivion or death.

In contrast to persecuting stepmothers, natural mothers provide a counter- 7 pattern of female protection. The christening celebration in Perrault's "Sleeping Beauty" (AT 410) is a jubilant occasion for the "King and a Queen, who were so sorry that they had no children, so sorry that it was beyond expression," and so sorry that they tried "all the waters in the world, vows, pilgrimages, every thing" before successfully conceiving this babe (p. 85). Since the King and Queen do not survive the spell, the "young Fairy" assumes the role of tutelary spirit and promises that the princess "shall only fall into a profound sleep which shall last a hundred years, at the expiration of which a King's son shall come and awake her" (p. 86). Similarly, Cinderella's deceased mother is lauded only briefly as "the best creature in the world" and the source for the daughter's "unparalleled goodness and sweetness of temper" (p. 123); in her place the fairy godmother acts as guardian. This prominence of contrasting maternal figures offers a paradigm for traumatic ambivalences. As the child matures, she becomes increasingly conscious of conflicting needs for both infantile nurturing and independence and suffers as a result severe ambivalences toward the mother. By splitting the maternal role to envision, however briefly, a protective mother who blesses the heroine with beauty and virtue, romantic tales assuage fears of total separation. Conversely, the stepmother embodies the adolescent's awesome intimations of female rivalry, predatory sexuality, and constrictive authority. As Bruno Bettelheim argues, romantic tales often recreate oedipal tensions, when a mother's early death is followed by the father's rapid remarriage to a cruel stepmother, as in "Cinderella." Kept a child rather than acknowledged as a developing woman and potential recipient of the father's love, a young girl, like Cinderella or Snow-White, feels thwarted by her mother's persistent, overpowering intervention. The authoritarian mother becomes the obstacle which seems to stifle natural desires for men, marriage, and hence the achievement of female maturity. Neither heroines nor children rationally explore such deep-rooted feelings; rather, the tales' split depiction of mothers provides a guilt-free enactment of the young female's ambivalences and a means through fantasy for coping with paradoxical impulses of love and hate.

Such traumatic rivalries between young girls and the mother (or heroine 8 and stepmother) comprise, however, only another stage in a progressive cultural as well as psychological pageant. Frequently a good fairy, old woman, or comforting godmother (second substitution for the original mother) releases the heroine from the stepmother's bondage and enables her to adopt appropriate adult roles. Godmothers or wise women may seem merely fortuitous magical agents who promise transformations to make external circumstances responsive to the heroine's inner virtue. Emancipated from enslavement as a cinderlass, Cinderella, for example, blossoms fully into a marriageable young princess at the ball. Functioning more subtly to exemplify cultural expectations, however, the "dream" figure allows the heroine not only to recall the pattern embedded by the original mother, but also to claim that paradigm of femininity as her own. Aptly, in many versions of "Cinderella" the supernatural helper is not a random apparition, but the natural mother reincarnated into a friendly creature, such as a red calf in the Scottish "Rashin Coatie," or memorialized by a hazel tree and a white bird to grant wishes, as in Grimm's "Aschenputtel." When the heroine gains sexual freedom by repudiating the stepmother, she immediately channels that liberty into social goals epitomized by the primary mother. Fairy tales, therefore, do acknowledge traumatic ambivalences during a female's rite of passage; they respond to the need for both detachment from childish symbioses and a subsequent embracing of adult independence. Yet, this evolution dooms female protagonists (and readers) to pursue adult potentials in one way only: the heroine dreamily anticipates conformity to those predestined roles of wife and mother. As Adrienne Rich so persuasively theorizes in *Of Woman Born*, the unheralded tragedy within western patriarchies is found in this mother/daughter relationship. If she imitates domestic martyrdom, the daughter may experience a hostile dependency, forever blaming the mother for trapping her within a constricting role. If a daughter rebels, then she risks social denunciations of her femininity, nagging internal doubts about her gender identity, and rejection by a mother who covertly envying the daughter's courage must yet overtly defend her own choices. Furthermore, romantic tales point to the complicity of women within a patriarchal culture, since as primary transmitters and models for female attitudes, mothers enforce their daughters' conformity.

By accentuating the young female's struggle with a menacing stepmother, many romantic tales only vaguely suggest the father's role in the complex oedipal and cultural dramas. But in other tales, such as "Beauty and the Beast" the attraction to the father, prohibitions against incest, and the transference of devotion to the prince round out the saga of maturation. In the throes of oedipal ambiguities, a young girl who still desires dependency seizes upon her father's indulgent affection, because it guarantees respite from maternal persecutions and offers a compensating masculine adoration. Many tales implicitly acknowledge the potent attraction between females and the father; but, as purveyors of cultural norms, they often mask latent incest as filial love and displace blatant sexual desires onto a substitute, such as a beast in "The Frog-Prince" (AT 440) or "Snow-White and Rose-Red" (AT 426). Madame de Beaumont's telling of "Beauty and the Beast" (AT 425), for example, focuses on the intimate bonds between father and daughter which impede the heroine's rite of passage. Pursued by suitors, the fifteen-year-old Beauty "civilly thanked them that courted her, and told them she was too young yet to marry, but chose to stay with her father for a few years longer" (p. 139). For a heroine Beauty acts with unusual decisiveness in consigning herself to a passive waiting and in prolonging her allegiance to the father. The abrupt loss of the merchant's wealth casts the family into genteel poverty, which again elicits Beauty's determination: "Nay, several gentlemen would have married her, tho' they knew she had not a penny; but she told them she could not think of leaving her poor father in his misfortunes, but was determined to go along with him into the country to comfort and attend him" (p. 139). She sacrifices individual happiness yet a third time by volunteering to die in her father's stead to satisfy the offended Beast: "Since the monster will accept of one of his daughters, I will deliver myself up to all his fury, and I am very happy in thinking that my death will save my father's life, and be a proof of my tender love for him" (p. 143). Lacking a jealous stepmother to prevent this excessive attachment and to force her into a rebellious search for adult sexuality, Beauty clings childishly to her father. The tale suppresses intimations of incest; nevertheless, it symbolizes the potent, sometimes problematic oedipal dependency of young girls. Well before her encounter with Beast then, Beauty's three decisions — to stay, to serve, finally to sacrifice her life — establish her willing subservience to paternal needs. Complementary to the natural mother's role as model for appropriate female adaptions, the natural father's example of desirable masculine behavior likewise shapes her dreams of a saviour and encourages the heroine's later commitment to the prince.

Beauty's apprenticeship in her father's house reveals an early conformity to   *10*
domestic roles; but, her subsequent palatial captivity by Beast symbolizes a further stage in her maturation. Relinquishing filial duties, she must confront male sexuality and transmute initial aversion into romantic commitment. Comparable to the substitution of a stepmother, replacement of Beast for the merchant exemplifies the adolescent's ambivalent yearning for continued paternal protection, yet newly awakened anxieties about masculine desires. Initially horrified by Beast's proposal of marriage, Beauty first ignores his overt ugliness, an act which signifies her repression of sexual fears. When she then discovers his spiritual goodness, her repugnance gradually gives way to compassion, then romantic adoration, and finally marital bliss. Having schooled herself to seek virtue beneath a physically repulsive countenance, she commits herself totally: "No dear Beast, said Beauty, you must not die; live to be my husband; from this moment I give you my hand, and swear to be none but yours. Alas! I thought I had only a friendship for you, but the grief I now feel convinces me that I cannot live without you" (p. 149). The magical transformation of Beast into a dazzling prince makes possible a consummation of this love affair which is no longer grotesque. Not just literally, but psychologically, the beast in the bedroom becomes transmuted into the prince in the palace. Just as Cinderella's prince charming arrives with a glass slipper, or Sleeping Beauty's prince awakens her with a kiss to reward these heroines for patient servitude or dreamy waiting, so too Beast's transformation rewards Beauty for embracing traditional female virtues. She has obligingly reformed sexual reluctance into self-sacrifice to redeem Beast from death. She trades her independent selfhood for subordination. She garners social and moral plaudits by acquiescing to this marriage. While realignment of her passions from father to prince avoids incest and psychologically allays her separation anxieties, still the female remains childlike — subjected to masculine supervision and denied any true independence.

Romantic tales require that the heroine's transference of dependency be not   *11* only sexual, but also material. Beneath romantic justifications of "love" lurk actual historical practices which reduce women to marketable commodities. In Perrault's "Diamonds and Toads" (AT 480) the King's son hardly restrains his pecuniary impulses: "The King's son, who was returning from hunting, met her, and seeing her so very pretty, asked her what she did there alone, and why she cry'd! *Alack-a-day! Sir, my mamma has turned me out of doors.* The King's son, who saw five or six pearls and as many diamonds come out of her mouth, desired her to tell him whence this happen'd. She accordingly told him the whole story; upon which the King's son fell in love with her; and considering with himself that such a gift as this was worth more than any marriage portion whatsoever in another, conducted her to the palace of the King, his father, and there married her" (p. 102). Despite this gallant's empathy for a pathetic story, he computes the monetary profit from such an inexhaustible dowry. Heroines do not so crassly calculate the fortune to be obtained through advantageous marriages, bound as they are by virtue to value love as superior. However, the tales implicitly yoke sexual awakening and surrender to the prince with social elevation and materialistic gain. Originally of regal birth, both Sleeping Beauty and Snow-White only regain wealth and a queen's position by marrying a prince. Although Cinderella and little Beauty experience temporary reversals of fortune which lead to servitude or genteel poverty, these heroines also miraculously receive fortunes from their marriages. A strict moral reading would attribute these rewards solely to the heroine's virtue; but, the fictional linkage of sexual awakening with the receipt of great wealth implies a more subtle causality. *Because* the heroine adopts conventional female virtues, that is patience, sacrifice, and dependency, and *because* she submits to patriarchal needs, she consequently receives both the prince and a guarantee of social and financial security through marriage. Status and fortune never result from the female's self-exertion but from passive assimilation into her husband's sphere. Allowed no opportunity for discriminating selection, the princess makes a blind commitment to the first prince who happens down the highway, penetrates the thorny barriers, and arrives *deus ex machina* to release her from the charmed captivity of adolescence. Paradoxically, this "liberation" symbolizes her absolute capitulation, as she now fulfills the roles of wife and mother imprinted in her memory by the natural mother and re-enters a comfortable world of masculine protection shared earlier with her father.

Not designed to stimulate unilateral actions by aggressive, self-motivated *12* women, romantic tales provide few alternative models for female behavior without criticizing their power. The unfortunate heroines of "The Twelve Dancing Princesses" (AT 306) initially elude marriage by drugging suitors and magically retreating at night to dance with dream princes in an underground kingdom. Apparently unwilling to forgo romantic fantasies for realistic marriages, the twelve princesses are eventually foiled by a clever soldier, who promptly claims the eldest as reward. Not alone among heroines in this aversion to marriage, nonetheless, most reluctant maidens, including little Beauty, a proud daughter in Grimm's "King Thrushbeard" (AT 900), haughty All-Fair in d'Aulnoy's "The Yellow Dwarf," and the squeamish princess who disdains the frog-prince, ultimately succumb. Romantic tales thus transmit clear warnings to rebellious females: resistance to the cultural imperative to wed constitutes so severe a threat to the social fabric that they will be compelled to submit. Likewise, tales morally censure bad fairies and vain, villainous stepmothers who exhibit manipulative power or cleverness. Allowed momentary triumph over the seemingly dead Snow-White or comatose Beauty, eventually these diabolic stepmothers are thwarted by the prince's greater powers. Facing punishment through death, banishment, or disintegration, the most self-disciplined and courageous villainesses execute justice upon themselves, thereby leaving the sterling morality of the prince and princess untarnished. Thus, in Perrault's "Sleeping Beauty" the orgrish mother-in-law voluntarily casts "her self head foremost into the tub" which she had "filled with toads, vipers, snakes, and all kinds of serpents" and where she is now "devoured in an instant by the ugly creatures she had ordered to be thrown into it for others" (p. 92). In condign punishment for jealousy, Snow-White's stepmother dances herself to death on iron-hot shoes, while the witch of "Hansel and Gretel" (AT 327) roasts in her own oven. Because cleverness, will-power, and manipulative skill are allied with vanity, shrewishness, and ugliness, and because of their gruesome fates, odious females hardly recommend themselves as models for young readers. And because they surround alternative roles as life-long maidens or fiendish stepmothers with opprobrium, romantic tales effectively sabotage female assertiveness. By punishing exhibitions of feminine force, tales admonish, moreover, that any disruptive non-conformity will result in annihilation or social ostracism. While readers dissociate from these portraitures of feminine power, defiance, and/or self-expression, they readily identify with the prettily passive heroine whose submission to commendable roles insures her triumphant happiness.

. . . As long as women acquiesce to cultural dicta set forth so mythically in   *13*
romantic *Märchen*, then the harmonious continuity of civilization will be assured. We cannot ask fairy tales to metamorphosize into Greek tragedies. But we should recognize that the conventional patterns of double enchantment, communal rituals, and nuptial climaxes have serious implications for women's role in society.

But one question remains unresolved: do we have the courageous vision and   *14*
energy to cultivate a newly fertile ground of psychic and cultural experience from which will grow fairy tales for human beings of the future?

Considerations

1. In a paragraph, sketch Karen Rowe's central argument. Don't worry about detail or illustrations; simply try to present the overall thrust of her argument objectively.
2. Using your sketch of Rowe's ideas, flesh it out with a fuller presentation. Try to indicate how the central argument is developed. What critical categories does Rowe rely on? What is the progression of her argument? How does she illustrate it?

3. Select one fairy tale characteristic that Rowe suggests influences young women, such as a concern for physical beauty. Write a paragraph explaining Rowe's point and illustrate it with examples from the tales in this section or from your childhood memories of such tales.

Connections

1. In her article, "Feminism and Fairy Tales," Karen Rowe argues that fairy tales encourage dependency in young women, socializing them to look to others to solve their problems and to intervene for them in times of trouble. Analyze "Snow White" in these terms, arguing for or against the premise that such tales encourage passivity in women.
2. Karen Rowe suggests that the overly romantic view of love and marriage in fairy tales encourages young women to view marriage and the nursery as their most fitting roles in society. The emphasis of such tales as "Snow White" on the conclusion in which prince and princess live "happily ever after" encourages girls to dream no further than such a happy ending. Examine "Snow White" and several other tales with female protagonists, testing Rowe's assertion against these tales. Do the details warrant such a conclusion?
3. Compare the roles and images of the male characters in "Snow White" with those of the female characters. Does such a comparison support Rowe's argument?
4. Respond to Rowe's charge that fairy tales socialize women to be passive by drawing on Max Lüthi's assertion that all fairy tale heroes are passive. Argue for one or the other of these positions, explaining fairly the side you oppose.

Oedipal Conflicts and Resolutions

Bruno Bettelheim

The Knight in Shining Armor and the Damsel in Distress

In the throes of oedipal conflict, a young boy resents his father for standing   *1*
in his way of receiving Mother's exclusive attention. The boy wants Mother to
admire *him* as the greatest hero of all; that means that somehow he must get
Father out of the way. This idea, however, creates anxiety in the child, because
without Father to protect and take care of them, what would happen to the
family? And what if Father were to find out that the little boy wanted him out
of the way . . . might he not take a most terrible revenge?

One can tell a small boy many times that someday he will grow up, marry,   *2*
and be like his father — without avail. Such realistic advice provides no relief
from the pressures the child feels right now. But the fairy tale tells the child
how he can live with his conflicts: it suggests fantasies he could never invent
for himself.

The fairy tale, for example, offers the story of the unnoticed little boy who   *3*
goes out into the world and makes a great success of life. Details may differ,
but the basic plot is always the same: the unlikely hero proves himself through
slaying dragons, solving riddles, and living by his wits and goodness until
eventually he frees the beautiful princess, marries her, and lives happily ever
after.

No little boy has ever failed to see himself in this starring role. The story   *4*
implies: it's not Father whose jealousy prevents you from having Mother all to
yourself, it's an evil dragon — what you really have in mind is to slay an evil
dragon. Further, the story gives veracity to the boy's feeling that the most desirable female is kept in captivity by an evil figure, while implying that it is
not Mother the child wants for himself, but a marvelous and wonderful woman
he hasn't met yet, but certainly will. The story tells more of what the boy wants
to hear and believe: that it is not of her own free will that this wonderful female (i.e., Mother) abides with this bad male figure. On the contrary, if only

*Bruno Bettelheim (b. 1903), a psychologist and former educator, took his doc-
toral degree at the University of Vienna in 1938 before emigrating to the United
States. He taught at the University of Chicago from 1944 to 1973, where he was
named Stella M. Rowley Distinguished Service Professor in 1963. This selection is
excerpted from his book* The Uses of Enchantment: The Meaning and Importance of Fairy Tales *(1976). He has also written a book on emotionally disturbed
children,* Love is Not Enough *(1950), and a work on male envy of the female principle,* Symbolic Wounds.

she could, she would much prefer to be with a young hero (like the child). The dragon slayer always has to be young, like the child, and innocent. The innocence of the hero with whom the child identifies proves by proxy the child's innocence, so that, far from having to feel guilty about these fantasies, the child can feel himself to be the proud hero.

It is characteristic of such stories that once the dragon is slain — or whatever deed that frees the beautiful princess from her captivity is accomplished — and the hero is united with his beloved, we are given no details about their later life, beyond being told that they lived "happily ever after." If their children are mentioned, it's usually a later interpolation by someone who thought the story would become more enjoyable or realistic if such information were offered. But introducing children into the story's ending shows little comprehension of a small boy's imaginings about a blissful existence. A child cannot and does not want to imagine what is actually involved in being a husband and father. This would imply, for example, that he would have to leave Mother for most of the day to work — while the oedipal fantasy is a situation where the boy and Mother will never be separated for a moment. The little boy certainly doesn't want Mother to be busy with housekeeping, or taking care of other children. He doesn't want to have sex with her either, because that is still an area full of conflict for him, if he has much awareness of it at all. As in most fairy tales, the little boy's ideal is just he and his princess (Mother), all their needs and wishes taken care of, living by themselves and for each other forever.

The oedipal problems of a girl are different from those of a boy, and so the fairy stories which help her to cope with her oedipal situation are of a different character. What blocks the oedipal girl's uninterrupted blissful existence with Father is an older, ill-intentioned female (i.e., Mother). But since the little girl also wants very much to continue enjoying Mother's loving care, there is also a benevolent female in the past or background of the fairy tale, whose happy memory is kept intact, although she has become inoperative. A little girl wishes to see herself as a young and beautiful maiden — a princess or the like — who is kept captive by the selfish, evil female figure and hence unavailable to the male lover. The captive princess' real father is depicted as benevolent, but helpless to come to the rescue of his lovely girl. In "Rapunzel" it is a vow that stymies him. In "Cinderella" and "Snow White" he seems unable to hold his own against the all-powerful stepmother.

The oedipal boy, who feels threatened by his father because of the wish to replace him in Mother's attention, casts Father in the role of the threatening monster. This also seems to prove to the boy how dangerous a rival to the father he is, because otherwise why would this father figure be so threatening? Since the desirable female is held captive by the old dragon, the little boy can believe that only brute force prevents this lovely girl (Mother) from joining him, the much-preferred young hero. In fairy stories which help the oedipal girl to understand her feelings and find vicarious satisfaction, it is the (step)-mother's or the enchantress' intense jealousy which keeps the lover from finding the princess. This jealousy proves that the older woman knows the young girl is preferable, more lovable, and more deserving of being loved.

While the oedipal boy does not want any children to interfere with Mother's complete involvement in him, matters are different for the oedipal girl. She does want to give her father the love-gift of being mother to his children. Whether this is an expression of her need to compete with Mother in this respect, or a dim anticipation of her motherhood to come, is difficult to determine. This desire to give Father a child doesn't mean having sexual relations with him — the little girl, like the little boy, doesn't think in such concrete terms. The little girl knows that children are what bind the male even more strongly to the female. That is why in fairy stories dealing in symbolic form with the oedipal wishes, problems, and hardships of a girl, children *are* occasionally mentioned as part of the happy ending.

In the Brothers Grimm's version of "Rapunzel" we are told that the prince in his wanderings "at length came to the desert where Rapunzel, with the twins to which she had given birth, a boy and a girl, lived in wretchedness," though no children had been mentioned before. When she embraces the prince, two of Rapunzel's tears wet his eyes (which had been pierced and blinded) and cure his blindness; and "he led her to his kingdom where he was joyfully received, and where they lived happily for a long time." Once they are united, no more is said about the children. They are only a symbol in the story of the bond between Rapunzel and the prince during their separation. Since we are not told of the two having been married, and there is no other suggestion of any form of sexual relation, this mention of children in fairy tales supports the idea that children can be gotten without sex, just as a result of love.

In the usual course of family life, the father is often out of the home, while the mother, having given birth to the child and nursed him, continues to be heavily involved in all child care. As a result, a boy can easily pretend that Father is not all that important in his life. (A girl cannot as readily imagine dispensing with Mother's care, however.) That is why replacement of an original "good" father by a bad stepfather is as rare in fairy tales as the evil stepmother is frequent. Since fathers have typically given much less attention to the child, it is not such a radical disappointment when this father begins to stand in the child's way, or to make demands of him. So the father who blocks the boy's oedipal desires is not seen as an evil figure within the home, or split into two figures, one good and one bad, as the mother often is. Instead, the oedipal boy projects his frustrations and anxieties onto a giant, monster, or dragon.

In a girl's oedipal fantasy, the mother is split into two figures: the pre-oedipal wonderful good mother and the oedipal evil stepmother. (Sometimes there are bad stepmothers in fairy stories with boys, such as in "Hansel and Gretel," but such tales deal with problems other than oedipal ones.) The good mother, so the fantasy goes, would never have been jealous of her daughter or have prevented the prince (father) and the girl from living happily together. So for the oedipal girl, belief and trust in the goodness of the pre-oedipal mother, and deep loyalty to her, tend to reduce the guilt about what the girl wishes would happen to the (step)mother who stands in her way.

Thus, both oedipal girls and boys, thanks to the fairy tale, can have the best of two worlds: they can fully enjoy oedipal satisfactions in fantasy and keep good relations to both parents in reality.

For the oedipal boy, if Mother disappoints him, there is the fairy princess in the back of his mind — that wonderful woman of the future who will compensate for all his present hardships, and the thought of whom makes it much easier to bear up under them. If Father is less attentive to his little girl than *she* desires, she can endure such adversity because a prince will arrive who will prefer her to all competitors. Since everything takes place in never-neverland, the child need not feel guilty or anxious about casting Father in the role of a dragon or evil giant, or Mother in the role of a miserable stepmother or witch. The little girl can love her real father all the better because her resentment over his failure to prefer her to her mother is explained by his unfortunate ineffectuality (as with fathers in fairy tales), for which nobody can blame him since it is due to superior powers; besides, it will not prevent her from getting her prince. A girl can love her mother more because she puts out all her anger at the mother-competitor, who gets what she deserves — as Snow White's step-mother is forced to put on "red-hot shoes, and dance until she dropped dead." And Snow White — and with her the little girl — need not feel guilty because her love of her true mother (who preceded the stepmother) has never stopped. The boy can love his real father even better after having gotten out all his anger at him through a fantasy of destroying the dragon or the bad giant.

Such fairy-tale fantasies — which most children would have a hard time 14 inventing so completely and satisfactorily on their own — can help a child a great deal to overcome his oedipal anguish.

The fairy story has other unequaled values in helping the child with oedipal 15 conflicts. Mothers cannot accept their little boys' wishes to do away with Daddy and marry Mommy; but a mother can participate with pleasure in her son's imagining himself as the dragon slayer who gains possession of the beautiful princess. Also, a mother can fully encourage her daughter's fantasies about the handsome prince who will join her, thus helping her to believe in a happy solution despite her present disappointment. Thus, far from losing Mother because of the oedipal attachment to Father, the daughter realizes that Mother not only approves of such wishes in disguise, but even hopes for their realization. Through fairy tales the parent can join the child in all voyages of fancy, while still retaining the all-important function of fulfilling the parental tasks in reality.

Thus a child can have the best of both worlds, which is what he needs to 16 grow up into a secure adult. In fantasy a girl can win out over the (step)mother whose efforts to prevent her happiness with the prince fail; a boy can slay the monster and gain what he wishes in a far-distant land. At the same time, both girls and boys can retain at home the real father as protector and the real mother who dispenses all the care and satisfactions a child needs. Since it is clear all along that slaying the dragon and marrying the enslaved princess, or being discovered by the fairy prince and punishing the wicked witch, occur in faraway times and countries, the normal child never mixes them up with reality.

Oedipal-conflict stories are typical of a large class of fairy tales that extend 17 the child's interests outside the immediate family. To make his first steps toward becoming a mature individual, the child must begin to look to the larger world. If the child does not receive support from his parents in his real and imaginary investigation of the world outside his home, it is at the risk of impoverishing the development of his personality.

It is not wise to urge a child in so many words to begin to enlarge his ho- 18 rizons, or to inform him specifically how far to go in his explorations of the world, or how to sort out feelings about his parents. If a parent verbally encourages a child to "mature," to move out psychologically or geographically, the child interprets this as meaning "they want to get rid of me." The result is the direct opposite of what is intended. For the child then feels unwanted and unimportant, and such feelings are most detrimental to the development of his ability to cope with this wider world.

The child's learning task is precisely that of making decisions about moving 19 out on his own, in his own good time, and into the areas of living he himself selects. The fairy tale helps in this process because it only beckons; it never suggests, demands, or tells. In the fairy tale all is said implicitly and in symbolic form: what the tasks for one's age might be; how one might deal with one's ambivalent feelings about one's parents; how this welter of emotions can be mastered. It also warns the child of some of the pitfalls he can expect and perhaps avoid, always promising a favorable outcome.

Considerations

1. Summarize Bruno Bettelheim's comparison between female and male oedipal problems. Include his central point or thesis.
2. Expand on your summary by examining critically Bettelheim's assumptions. Consider any assumptions that might weaken his argument. For example, is there any problem with his assumption that all male and female children have these experiences? Recall that these tales were originally composed for adults and told in communal work situations. Does that fact affect Bettelheim's point?

Connections

1. Can the "Snow White" tale be used to support Bruno Bettelheim's comments? Illustrate.
2. Do all variants of "Snow White" lend themselves equally well to Bettelheim's approach? Choose two of the more dissimilar variants and analyze them in relation to Bettelheim.
3. Compare Bruno Bettelheim's comments about oedipal relationships with N. J. Girardot's explanation. To what extent is their underlying concern a similar one?
4. Both Karen Rowe and Bruno Bettelheim discuss the socializing effect of these tales on children. One sees that effect in more general, positive terms; the other, in more focused, negative terms. Compare their views.

Further Connections

1. Examine the use of the term *fairy tale* in advertising. Look for the term itself or advertisements that use familiar tales and characters or that create a fairy tale setting. Drawing on several specific examples, define and discuss different uses of this term.
2. Apply Vladimir Propp's system of functions to an advertisement for a beauty product (or other product), a television commercial, or a film. Which functions recur regularly? Based on a series of advertisements or other material, develop a Proppian model for their structure.
3. Write your own modern literary version of "Snow White." Try to adhere to the tale type while freely adapting the tale's motifs and motivations.
4. Test Max Lüthi's characterization of the *Märchen* world using the tales in this section as evidence for your evaluation. For example, do you agree with his assessment of the fairy tale's atmosphere? With his characterization of its hero? Do his criteria hold for all elements in individual tales or for all tales in general?
5. Compare several versions of "Snow White." While you might want to discuss similarities, merely listing likenesses between several versions of a tale won't tell us much beyond what we already know: tales exist in multiple versions. Folklorists are more interested in how tales differ from one another. You might begin by listing differences. Decide which variations are significant, and suggest reasons for these differences. You may narrow your focus by concentrating on differences in character, in actions or episodes, or in motifs. For example, you might fruitfully compare the character of Snow White in several of these versions.
6. Compare the Grimms' version of "Snow White" with your recollection of the Walt Disney adaptation. If you have seen the film recently, you might focus on one or two significant changes. For example, how does he expand the role of the dwarves and what difference does that make in the story's seriousness and tone? Or compare Disney's treatment of the Queen with her character and actions in the Grimms' version. Why, for example, does Disney present the Queen as a witch while she says she is disguising herself as a peddler? (You can also find books based on Disney's version in the children's section of the public library.)
7. *In-class Survey:* As a class or in groups, list five fairy tales that particularly impressed you as a child. Discuss the results of your quick survey, trying to hypothesize reasons for your results.
8. Two of the tales in this chapter, "Blanca Rosa" and "Myrsina," are fuller versions than the others. The collecting context may be responsible for this difference. Folklorists recognize that tales collected out of context — that is, on request — are apt to be briefer versions than those collected during a performance with an audience. Test this distinction by collecting two jokes, anecdotes, personal experience stories, or ghost stories, one out of context and one in context or during its performance. For your out-of-context narrative simply ask someone to tell you a joke. Write it down as accurately as you can (you may ask them to repeat it). Then look for a situation in

which someone naturally tells a joke or funny story, anecdote, or ghost story. Is one of the texts a fuller narrative than the other? Ask the person who told the joke out of context to tell it before an audience. In this way you can compare two versions of the same story.

9. After comparing the results of the two collecting situations above, apply them to the tales in this chapter. Can you hypothesize about the collecting situations from the length and brevity of the tales and from the detail they possess or lack?

10. The Finnish Historical-Geographical School sought the normal form of a tale, which they hoped to determine by comparing a large number of variants. They compared the motifs of these versions to determine which were the most common and hence most likely the original ones. Carry out your own miniature historic-geographic study with the six variants of "Snow White" in this chapter. Begin by comparing the tales against the tale type model, determining their type by episode. Group all tales of one type together. Then separate out major and minor motifs. A major motif is one that figures in the plot in a significant way. (For example, the magic mirror is a major motif.) Look for the motifs that appear most frequently. Use this statistic to create an abstract of the tale's standard or most reasonable form.

Extensions

1. Use the Aarne-Thompson *Types of the Folktale* to find several versions of a different fairy tale, such as "Cinderella," (type AT 510), "Sleeping Beauty" (AT 410), or "Beauty and the Beast" (AT 425C). To find other tales, refer to the list of versions that Thompson appends to the tale type (or use the bibliography at the end of this chapter). Apply any of this chapter's writing suggestions to the tale you choose.

2. Read several fairy tales in a collection such as Grimms', and find a way of typing them other than by outlining their plots as Thompson has done.

3. A *Los Angeles Times* article on Walt Disney's *Snow White* that criticized the film from a feminist perspective caused much controversy among the *Times's* readers. The original article appeared in the *Calendar* section, July 16, 1983, p. 1, col. 1–3, p. 6, col. 1–2. Find the original article and some of the letters readers wrote in response. Summarize the controversy or report on it to your class.

4. Develop your essay on the previous topic more fully by incorporating the discussion of how the Disney Studio conceived of and filmed *Snow White*. You'll find this discussion in Richard Schickel's *The Disney Version* (New York: Simon and Schuster, 1968).

5. In the library locate N. J. Girardot's original article (in the *Journal of American Folklore* 90 (1977): 274–300) and the controversy surrounding it (in "The Pitfalls of Snow White Scholarship," in the same journal, vol. 92 (1979): 69–77.) Summarize and compare the two opposing views in this controversy.

6. Locate a copy of Giambattista Basile's *Pentamerone* which contains a variant of "Snow White" entitled "The Young Slave." This version of the tale contains the continuation of hostilities that Steven Swann Jones discusses in "The Structure of Snow White". Drawing on N. J. Girardot's source (the Grimm variant) and one of Jones's sources (the Basile version), re-examine this controversy.

7. Read Jones's and Girardot's original articles, comparing their analyses of this tale. Discuss specifically their different conclusions about the tale's structure.

8. Drawing on H. C. Bartlett's "Some Experiments on the Reproduction of Folk Stories," conduct your own experiment concerning the transmission of folktales (use a tale other than "Snow White").

9. Write a critique of Bartlett's experiment. What elements affect the validity of his experiment? (Consider, for example, the differences between natural and laboratory settings.)

10. Locating the Grimms' *Kinder- und Hausemärchen* in the library, survey all the tales in the collection for female protagonists. What percent fit Rowe's characterization of fairy tale heroines? Develop this idea in an organized essay. You may carry out the same study for female protagonists of children's versions of fairy tales or for several versions of one tale such as "Sleeping Beauty" or "Beauty and the Beast."

11. In his selection on oedipal conflicts, Bruno Bettelheim suggests that boys release their anxiety over their attachment for their mother and subsequent rivalry with their father through hero tales in which they can sublimate such anxieties. Such sublimation, or repression of fears too threatening to confront directly, requires an outlet such as a tale that can substitute fairy tale characters for actual people. Starting from this premise, locate a hero tale that features a male protagonist (such as "Jack and the Beanstalk" or the "Three Stolen Princesses' (AT 305) and examine it for details that would lend themselves to such projection. Explain Bettelheim's thesis as you illustrate it with a tale.

12. Using your previous paper on oedipal conflicts, criticize Bettelheim's premise. Try to offer other explanations for the details in the stories that you believe are more valid than Bettelheim's. What other fantasies of young children might such hero tales fulfill?

13. Test Max Lüthi's characterization of the *Märchen* world by applying his criteria to tales from several collections (see Suggestions for Further Reading). You might want to assess the universality of these characteristics by applying them to nonwestern collections, such as Stith Thompson's *Tales of the North American Indians* or Wolfram Eberhardt's *Folktales of China.*

14. Find a modern literary version of "Snow White" and compare it to the traditional versions presented here. Perhaps the most well-known of these literary retellings are Anne Sexton's poem, "Snow White and the Seven Dwarves," from her collection, *Transformations* and Donald Barthelmes's novella, *Snow White.* Look for specific changes that reveal the author's interpretation of the story. You might want to focus on one change such as that of atmosphere or tone. Does either of the literary versions appear to take place in the fairy tale world as Max Lüthi describes it? How do

these authors deal with motivation? What attitudes do they bring to the conflict between Snow White and her stepmother or the relationship between Snow White and the dwarves?

Suggestions for Further Reading

Afanas'ev, Aleksandr. *Russian Fairy Tales*. Translated by Norbert Guterman. New York: Pantheon Books, 1945. A portion of the collection of Russian magic tales on which Propp based his study.

Bartlett, H. C. "Some Experiments on the Reproduction of Folk Stories." In *The Study of Folklore*, edited by Alan Dundes, pp. 243–258. Englewood Cliffs, N.J.: Prentice-Hall, 1965. An experimental study on the transmission of folk tales in a laboratory situation.

Burton, Anthony. "Beauty and the Beast: A Critique of Psychoanalytic Approaches to the Fairy Tale." *Psychocultural Review* 2 (1978): 241–258. Burton argues against such Freudian analyses of fairy tales as Bettelheim's study because they do not consider the cultural milieu and function of the tales.

Dégh, Linda. "Folk Narrative." In *Folklore and Folklife: An Introduction*, edited by Richard M. Dorson, pp. 53–83. Chicago: University of Chicago Press, 1972. Dégh's survey of the types of oral narrative includes the *Märchen*. She discusses genres and their history, offering a schema for the multilayered *Märchen* influenced by primitive, medieval, and modern periods.

―――. *Folktales and Society*. Bloomington: Indiana University Press, 1969. The classic study of folktales in their cultural context, this work examines taletelling in a Hungarian community.

―――. *Folktales of Hungary*. In *Folktales of the World Series*, edited by Richard M. Dorson. Chicago: University of Chicago Press, 1965. Authentic folktales collected in Hungary in the twentieth century and part of a series including tales from China, Japan, Mexico, and Egypt, as well as European tales.

Dundes, Alan, ed. *Cinderella: A Folklore Casebook*. New York: Garland, 1982. This anthology offers excerpts from such classic studies of "Cinderella" as those of Marian Cox or Anna Birgitta Rooth as well as new studies of "Cinderella," including an African variant.

Finnegan, Ruth. *Limba Stories and Story-Telling*. Oxford: Clarendon, 1967. A collection of folktales from the Limba of northern Sierra Leone. Presented in their cultural context, the tales illustrate a type radically different from the European magic tale.

Fischer, J. L. "The Sociopsychological Analysis of Folktales." *Current Anthropology* 4 (1963): 235–306. A critical survey of sociological and psychological studies of folktales.

Foxe, A. N. "Terrorization of the Ego and Snow White." *Psychoanalytic Review* 27 (1940): 144–148. Foxe examines Snow White as if she were a psychologically disturbed patient suffering from masochistic tendencies.

Gilbert, Sandra, and Susan Gubar. "The Queen's Looking Glass." In *The Madwoman in the Attic: The Woman Writer and the Nineteenth-Century Literary Imagination*, ch. 1, pp. 3–44. New Haven: Yale University Press, 1979. These scholars develop the motif of the magic mirror into a metaphor for the "patriarchal voice of narcissism."

Glassie, Henry. *Passing the Time in Ballymenone.* Philadelphia: University of Pennsylvania Press, 1982. Along with its companion volume, *Irish Folk History,* this work presents the cultural history of an Ulster community in Northern Ireland.

Heuscher, Julius E. *A Psychiatric Study of Myths and Fairy Tales.* Springfield, Ill.: Charles C. Thomas, 1974. Chapter 14 offers a psychological interpretation of Snow White as a child in the post-oedipal stage or latency period.

Hoogasian-Villa, Suzie. *100 Armenian Tales.* Detroit: Wayne State University Press, 1966. An outstanding collection of tales collected from Armenian-Americans.

Jones, Steven Swann. "The Structure of Snow White." *Fabula* 24 (1984): 56–71. Jones re-examines the tripartite structure of the *Märchen,* looking at variants in which hostilities toward Snow White are resumed after her marriage.

Lüthi, Max. *The European Folktale: Form and Nature.* Translated and edited by John D. Niles. Philadelphia: ISHI, 1982. An important study of the structure and characteristics of the European folktale.

Roberts, Leonard W. *South from Hel-fer-Sartin: Kentucky Mountain Folk Tales.* Lexington, Kentucky: University of Kentucky Press, 1955. Versions of fairy tales from Kentucky mountaineers that illustrate localization of these tales.

Stone, Kay. "Things Walt Disney Never Told Us." In *Women and Folklore,* edited by Claire R. Farrer. Austin: University of Texas Press, 1975. The first feminist analysis of fairy tales by a folklorist. Stone examines the puerile heroine of the Disney versions of magic tales.

Tatar, Maria. "From Nags to Witches: Stepmothers in the Grimms' Fairy Tales." In *Opening Texts: Psychoanalysis and the Culture of the Child,* edited by Joseph H. Smith and William Kerrigan. Philadelphia: Johns Hopkins, 1985. Another feminist analysis of the fairy tale. This one focuses on the character of the stepmother, her role and function.

von Franz, Marie-Louise. *An Introduction to the Interpretation of Fairy Tales.* New York: Spring Publications, 1970. A Jungian psychoanalyst interprets fairy tales looking closely at individual tales and motifs and relating them to archetypes and the unconscious.

Waelti-Walters, Jennifer. "On Princesses: Fairy Tales, Sex Roles, and Loss of Self." *International Journal of Women's Studies* 2 (1979): 180–188.

Acknowledgments *(continued from page iv)*

of Fairy Tales, by Bruno Bettelheim. Copyright © 1975, 1976 by Bruno Bettelheim. Portions of this book originally appeared in the *New Yorker.* Reprinted by permission of Alfred A. Knopf, Inc.

J. Michael Bishop, "Oncogenes." In *Scientific American* (March 1982). Copyright © 1982 by Scientific American, Inc. All rights reserved.

Peter Bondanella and Mark Musa, editors, "The Qualities of the Prince," by Niccolò Machiavelli. From *The Portable Machiavelli,* Peter Bondanella and Mark Musa, editors. Copyright © 1979 by Viking Penguin Inc. Reprinted by permission of Viking Penguin Inc.

John Cairns, "The Epidemiology of Cancer." From *Cancer: Science and Society* by John Cairns. W.H. Freeman and Company. Copyright © 1978.

Elias Canetti, "The Entrails of Power." From *Crowds and Power* by Elias Canetti. English translation copyright © 1962, 1973 by Victor Gollancz Ltd. Reprinted by permission of the Continuum Publishing Company.

Calvin A. Claudel, compiler, and Joseph M. Carrière, editor, "Snow Bella: A Tale from the French Folklore of Louisiana." From *Southern Folklore Quarterly* 6 (1942).

Sherburne F. Cook, *The Conflict Between the California Indian and White Civilization.* Reprinted by permission of the University of California Press.

Harvey Cox, excerpts from *The Secular City,* Revised Edition, by Harvey Cox. Copyright © Harvey Cox 1965, 1966. Reprinted with permission of Macmillan Publishing Company.

Steven d'Arazien, "Cancer Plague." In *The Progressive* (July 1979) by permission of *The Progressive,* 409 East Main Street, Madison, Wisconsin. Copyright © 1979, The Progressive, Inc.

Charles Darwin. Reprinted from *Darwin: A Norton Critical Edition,* selected and edited by Philip Appleman, by permission of W. W. Norton & Company, Inc. Copyright © 1979, 1970 by W. W. Norton & Company, Inc.

Paul Dickson, excerpts from "American Velvet: That Crazy Place in Connecticut." From *The Future of the Workplace: The Coming Revolution in Jobs* by Paul Dickson. Copyright © 1975 by Paul Dickson. Reprinted by permission of the Helen Brann Agency, Inc.

Barbara Ehrenreich and Annette Fuentes, "Life on the Global Assembly Line." In *Ms* (January 1981). Reprinted by permission of *Ms.*

Paul R. Ehrlich and Anne Ehrlich, excerpts from "Compassion, Esthetics, Fascination, and Ethics." From *Extinction: The Causes and Consequences of the Disappearance of Species,* by Paul R. Ehrlich and Anne Ehrlich. Copyright © 1981 by Paul R. Ehrlich and Anne H. Ehrlich. Reprinted by permission of Random House, Inc.

Randall Forsberg, "Overview: The Nuclear Arms Debate from 1945." From *A Nuclear Freeze & Non-Interventionary Conventional Policy* by Randall Forsberg. Reprinted by permission of the Institute for Defense and Disarmament Studies.

Sigmund Freud, "Why War?" From *Collected Papers,* vol. 5, by Sigmund Freud, edited by James Strachey. Published by Basic Books, Inc. by arrangement with the Hogarth Press, Ltd. and the Institute of Psycho-Analysis, London. Reprinted by permission of Basic Books, Inc. and Chatto & Windus Ltd./Hogarth Press.

Howard Gardner, "The Compositions of Mozart's Mind" and "Unfolding or Teaching: On the Optimal Training of Artistic Skills." From *Art, Mind and Brain: A Cognitive Approach to Creativity* by Howard Gardner. © 1982 by Howard Gardner. Reprinted by permission of Basic Books, Inc., Publishers. "The Seven Frames of Mind." Reprinted with permission from *Psychology Today* Magazine. Copyright © 1984 American Psychological Association.

Norman J. Girardot, "Initiation and Meaning in the Tale of Snow White and the Seven Dwarfs." Reproduced by permission of the author and the American Folklore Society from *Journal of American Folklore* 90(357):274–275, 282, 1977. Not for further reproduction.

Stephen Jay Gould, "Singapore's Patrimony (and Matrimony)." Reprinted with permission from *Natural History* 93:5. Copyright © by the American Museum of Natural History, 1984. "A Biological Homage to Mickey Mouse." From *The Panda's Thumb: More*

Reflections in Natural History, by Stephen Jay Gould, by permission of W. W. Norton & Company, Inc. Copyright © 1980 by Stephen Jay Gould.

G. Allen Greb and Gerald W. Johnson, "A History of Strategic Arms Limitations." *Bulletin of the Atomic Scientists* (January 1984): 30–37.

Grimm Brothers, "Snow White" (Sneewittchen). From *The Grimms' German Folk Tales*, translated by Francis P. Magoun, Jr. and Alexander H. Krappe. Copyright © 1960 by Southern Illinois University Press. Reprinted by permission.

Keith Gunderson, "The Imitation Game." From *Minds and Machines*, edited by Alan Ross Anderson, 1964, Prentice-Hall, Inc.

A. Irving Hallowell, "Ojibwa Ontology, Behavior, and World View." From *Contributions to Anthropology: Selected Papers of A. Irving Hallowell* (University of Chicago, 1976) and from "Ojibwa Metaphysics of Being and the Perception of Persons," by A. Irving Hallowell, in Tagiuri and Petrullo, eds., *Person Perception and Interpersonal Behavior* (Stanford, 1958). Used by permission.

Michael Hamburger, "Lines on Brueghel's *Icarus*." From *Collected Poems 1941–1983* by Michael Hamburger. Carcanet Press Ltd. Reprinted by permission of the author.

Douglas Hofstadter, "Ten Questions and Speculations (about AI)." From *Godel, Escher, Bach: An Eternal Golden Braid* by Douglas R. Hofstadter. © 1979 by Basic Books, Inc., Publishers. Reprinted by permission of the publisher.

David Hubel, "The Brain." Copyright © 1979 by Scientific American, Inc. All rights reserved.

Bärbel Inhelder and Jean Piaget, "Adolescent Thinking." From *The Growth of Logical Thinking: From Childhood to Adolescence* by Bärbel Inhelder and Jean Piaget. Translated by Anne Parsons and Stanley Milgram. © 1958 by Basic Books, Inc., Publishers. Reprinted by permission of the publisher.

Lucien Israël, "Radiation." From *Conquering Cancer*, by Lucien Israël, translated by Joan Pinkham. Translation copyright © 1978 by Lucien Israël. Reprinted by permission of Random House, Inc.

Shirley Jackson, "Pillar of Salt." From *The Lottery* by Shirley Jackson. Copyright 1948, 1949 by Shirley Jackson, copyright renewed © 1976, 1977 by Laurence Hyman, Barry Hyman, Mrs. Sarah Webster and Mrs. Joanne Schnurer. Reprinted by permission of Farrar, Straus and Giroux, Inc.

Jane Jacobs, excerpts from *Cities and the Wealth of Nations* by Jane Jacobs. Copyright © 1984 by Jane Jacobs. Reprinted by permission of Random House, Inc.

Samuel S. Janus, "Humor, Sex and Power in American Society." From *The American Journal of Psychoanalysis* 41:81, 161–167. Reprinted by permission of the publisher, Agathon Press, Inc., New York.

Robert F. Kennedy, excerpts from his remarks as a member of the Ribicoff subcommittee on Executive Reorganization of the Senate Committee on Governmental Operations, August 15, 1966. Reprinted in *Urban Crisis: The Remarkable Ribicoff Hearings* (Edited Documents Series, No. 1), Charles O. Jones and Layne D. Hoppe, editors (Washington National Press, 1969).

Arthur Kopit, excerpts from *Indians* by Arthur Kopit. Copyright © 1969 by Arthur Kopit. Reprinted by permission of Hill and Wang, a division of Farrar, Straus and Giroux, Inc.

Theodora Kroeber, "Copper-Colored People in a Goldon Land." From *Ishi in Two Worlds: A Biography of the Last Wild Indian in North America*. Copyright © 1961 the Regents of the University of California. Reprinted by permission of the University of California Press.

Father Chrestien Le Clercq, "On the Wigwams and Dwellings of the Gaspesians." From *New Relation of Gaspesia*. Translated and edited by W. F. Ganong (Toronto: The Champlain Society, 1910).

Lane Lenard, "The Dynamic Brain." In *Science Digest* (December 1983). First appeared in *Science Digest*, © 1983 by the Hearst Corporation. Reprinted by permission of the author.

John Locke. James L. Axtell, "Some Thoughts Concerning Education by John Locke." Reprinted from *The Educational Writings of John Locke*, edited by James L. Axtell, by permission of Cambridge University Press.

Max Lüthi, "Aspects of the Märchen and the Legend." In *Genre* 2:2 (1969). Translated by Barbara Flynn. Reprinted by permission of the University of Illinois Press.

Kenneth Macleod, editor, "Gold-Tree and Silver-Tree." In *The Celtic Magazine* 13, 1887–1888.

Michael Mandelbaum, excerpts from *The Nuclear Question: The United States and Nuclear Weapons, 1946–1976.* Reprinted by permission of Cambridge University Press.

Karl Marx, "Alienated Labor." From *Man Alone: Alienation in Modern Society,* edited and translated by Eric and Mary Josephson. Copyright © 1962 by Dell Publishing Co. Used by permission of Dell Publishing Co.

Gergios A. Megas, "Myrsina, or Myrtle." From *Folktales of Greece,* translated by Helen Colaclides. Reprinted by permission of The University of Chicago Press.

Stanley Milgram, excerpts from "The Experience of Living in Cities." *In Science* 167 (March 13, 1970), pp. 1461–1465. Copyright © 1970 by the American Association for the Advancement of Science.

C. Wright Mills, excerpts from *White Collar: The American Middle Classes.* Copyright 1951 by Oxford University Press, Inc.; renewed 1979 by Yaraslava Mills. Reprinted by permission of Oxford University Press, Inc.

Kenneth M. Morrison, "The Mythological Sources of Abenaki Catholicism: A Case Study of the Social History of Power." In *Religion* 11 (1981). Reprinted by permission of the author.

Ralph W. Moss, "Chemotherapy." From *The Cancer Syndrome* by Ralph W. Moss. Copyright © 1980 by Ralph Moss. Reprinted by permission of Grove Press, Inc.

Farley Mowat, "Good Old Uncle Albert." From *Never Cry Wolf* by Farley Mowat. Copyright © 1963 by Farley Mowat. By permission of the author, and Little, Brown and Company in association with the Atlantic Monthly Press.

Alva Myrdal, "A History of Lost Opportunities." From *The Game of Disarmament: How the United States and Russia Run the Arms Race,* Revised and Updated Edition, by Alva Myrdal. Copyright © 1976, 1982 by Alva Myrdal. Reprinted by permission of Pantheon Books, a division of Random House, Inc.

Howard J. Nelson, "The Form and Structure of Cities: Urban Growth Patterns." In the *Journal of Geography* LXVIII, no. 4 (April 1969). Reprinted by permission of the National Council for Geographic Education.

Douglass C. North and Roger LeRoy Miller, "The Economics of Animal Extinction." From *The Economics of Public Issues,* 6th edition, by Douglass C. North and Roger LeRoy Miller. Copyright © 1983 by Harper & Row, Publishers, Inc. By permission of Harper & Row Publishers, Inc.

Alfonso Ortiz, "Some Concerns Central to the Writing of 'Indian History'." In *The Indian Historian* X (1977). Reprinted by permission of the American Indian Historical Society.

William O'Rourke, "The Maggot Principle." Copyright © 1972, 1977 by William O'Rourke. First published in *Transatlantic Review* 44 (1972). Reprinted from *On the Job: Fiction About Work by Contemporary American Writers* by William O'Rourke. Reprinted by permission of the author and Edward J. Acton, Inc.

Ronald D. Pasquariello, Donald W. Shriver, Jr., and Alan Geyer, "The City in the Bible." From *Redeeming the City: Theology, Politics, and Urban Policy* by Ronald D. Pasquariello, Donald W. Shriver, Jr., and Alan Geyer. Reprinted by permission of Pilgrim Press.

Guillermo de la Peña, "The Figueroa Family." From *A Legacy of Promises* by Guillermo de la Peña. Reprinted by permission of Manchester University Press, Manchester, England.

Jean Piaget, "The Attainment of Invariants and Reversible Operations in the Development of Thinking." From *Social Research* 30:3 (1963). Reprinted by permission of the New School for Social Research.

Yolando Pino-Saavedra, editor, "Blanca Rosa and the Forty Thieves," Rockwell Gray, translator. From *Folktales of Chile,* Yolando Pino-Saavedra, editor. Reprinted by permission of the University of Chicago Press.

Vladimir Propp, "Morphology of the Folktale." This material has previously appeared as Chapter II of *Morphology of the Folktale,* Second Edition, by V. Propp, translated by

Laurence Scott. Copyright of translation © 1968. Reproduced by permission of the University of Texas Press.

John Reps, "Towns, Time, and Tradition: The Legacy of Planning in Frontier America." From *Town Planning in Frontier America* by John Reps. Copyright © 1969 by Princeton University Press. Excerpt pp. 422–429 reprinted with permission of Princeton University Press.

Jean Jacques Rousseau, excerpts from *Emile, Julie and Other Writings*. Reprinted by permission of Barron's Educational Series, Inc., © 1964.

Karen E. Rowe, "Feminism and Fairy Tales." In *Women's Studies*, 6 (1979). Reprinted by permission of Karen E. Rowe and Gordon and Breach Science Publishers Ltd. Copyright © Gordon and Breach Science Publishers Inc.

Bertrand Russell, "Power over Opinion." From *Power* by Bertrand Russell. Reprinted by permission of George Allen & Unwin.

Carl Sagan, "The Abstractions of Beasts." From *The Dragons of Eden: Speculations on the Evolution of Human Intelligence* by Carl Sagan. Copyright © 1977 by Carl Sagan. Reprinted by permission of Random House, Inc.

Maggie Scarf, "Images That Heal." Copyright © 1980 by Maggie Scarf. Reprinted by permission of International Creative Management.

Richard Selzer, "Sarcophagus." From *Confessions of a Knife* by Richard Selzer. Copyright © 1979 by David Goodman and Janet Selzer, trustees. Reprinted by permission of Simon & Schuster, Inc.

B. F. Skinner, "Baby In a Box." In *Ladies' Home Journal* (October 1945). © 1945 Family Media, Inc. Reprinted with permission of *Ladies' Home Journal*.

Susan Sontag, excerpts from *Illness as Metaphor* by Susan Sontag. Copyright © 1977, 1978 by Susan Sontag. Reprinted by permission of Farrar, Straus and Giroux, Inc.

Robert J. Sternberg and Janet E. Davidson, "The Mind of The Puzzler." In *Psychology Today* 16 (June 1982). Copyright © 1982 by American Psychological Association. Reprinted with permission from *Psychology Today* Magazine.

Stockholm International Peace Research Institute, "Arms Control and Disarmament." From *Armaments and Disarmament in the Nuclear Age, A Handbdook*. Reprinted by permission of Humanities Press International, Inc., Atlantic Highlands, NJ.

Frederick Winslow Taylor, "The Principles of Scientific Management." From *Scientific Management* by Frederick Winslow Taylor. Copyright 1911 by Frederick W. Taylor; renewed 1939 by Louise M. S. Taylor. Reprinted by permission of Harper & Row, Publishers, Inc.

Studs Terkel, "Barbara Herrick," "Mike Lefevre," "Ann Bogan." From *Working: People Talk About What They Do All Day and How They Feel About What They Do*, by Studs Terkel. Copyright © 1972, 1974 by Studs Terkel. Reprinted by permission of Pantheon Books, a division of Random House, Inc.

Stith Thompson, "The Types of the Folktale." In *Folklore Fellows Communication* 184 (1961). Reprinted by permission of FFC, Academia Scientiarum Fennica, Helsinki.

William Tucker, "Endangered Species." From *Progress and Privilege* by William Tucker. Copyright © 1982 by William Tucker. Reprinted by permission of Georges Borchardt, Inc.

John B. Watson and Rosalie Rayner, "Conditioned Emotional Reactions." In *Journal of Experimental Psychology* III (February 1920).

William Carlos Williams, "Landscape with the Fall of Icarus." From *Picture from Brueghel* by William Carlos Williams. Copyright © 1960 by William Carlos Williams. Reprinted by permission of New Directions Publishing Corporation.

About the Editors

Jennifer Bradley (Chapter 4, The Urban Experience) received her Ph.D. from the State University of New York, Stony Brook. Supervisor of the English Department's teaching assistants at UCLA, she has taught graduate pedagogy courses, writing courses attached to social sciences, and a freshman composition course examining the geography, history, politics, art, architecture and literature of Los Angeles.

Patricia Chittenden (Chapter 1, The Dimensions of Power) teaches writing in the UCLA Writing Programs and the Graduate School of Library and Information Science. She has advanced degrees in literature (UCLA) and library science (University of Washington). She has taught various interdisciplinary composition courses as well as courses attached to history and political science. She is the joint editor of *Information and Libraries: Syllabus/Workbook*, published by the Graduate School of Library and Information Science (UCLA, 1984).

Robert Cullen (Chapter 7, The Nature of Intelligence) received his Ph.D. from UCLA and has taught writing in conjunction with courses in problem-solving and computer studies. Author of a videotape on how to use the university's word-processing system, he is currently working on a computer game that rewards reading and writing skills and is co-editing a collection of essays on computers and writing.

Carol L. Edwards (Chapter 10, The Fairy Tale "Snow White") received a double Ph.D. in literature and folklore from the University of Indiana. She is currently at California State University, Long Beach. At UCLA, she has taught writing courses attached to folklore, literature, sociology, political science, and women's studies. As a practicing folklorist, she has published in *Fabula, Western Folklore*, and the *Journal of American Folklore*.

Donna Uthus Gregory (Chapter 2, The Origins of the Nuclear Arms Race) received her Ph.D. from the University of Utah and has had extensive experience in interdisciplinary research and teaching. She presently teaches a university-wide elective course on nuclear issues and is the editor of *The Nuclear Predicament: A Sourcebook* (Bedford Books, 1986). She has been awarded a MacArthur Foundation Fellowship in International Security to do a rhetorical analysis of nuclear strategy.

Michael Gustin (Chapter 6, The Nature of Learning) received his M.A. from UCLA and has taught writing classes attached to courses in history, film, and literature. He has also served as supervisor of English tutors for UCLA's Academic Advancement Program. For several years he has worked closely with psychology teachers in constructing links between psychology and writing courses in the Freshman Summer Program.

Michael K. Havens (Chapter 5, The Working World) received his Ph.D. in interdisciplinary humanities from Syracuse University and currently teaches at the University of California, Davis. He has served as staff training coordinator (UCLA) and developed general education workshops (UCD). His publications treat the English Romantics, literary criticism, and composition. Besides developing his "Working" course over several years, he has taught writing classes attached to sociology, political science, and ecology classes. He also enjoys the craft of winemaking.

Malcolm Kiniry (Chapter 8, The Treatment of Cancer) also teaches in the UCLA Writing Programs. He holds a Ph.D. in English from Rutgers University and has published articles on Renaissance drama and on basic writing. He has taught writing courses adjuncted to political science, history, and biology. With Mike Rose, he is co-author of a forthcoming cross-curricular sourcebook (Bedford Books).

Sonia Maasik (Chapter 9, The Impact of Animals) did her graduate work at the Johns Hopkins University and presently teaches in the UCLA Writing Programs. At UCLA, she has taught writing classes attached to economics, political science, and biology courses, and she has drawn upon this cross-curricular experience to develop the course on our relations with animals that inspired her chapter. In addition, she teaches upper-division courses in writing for business and other professional fields.

Ellen Strenski (Chapter 3, The Frontier Indians) received her Ph.D. from Reading University, England, and presently coordinates the upper division of the UCLA Writing Programs. She teaches a writing workshop for graduate history students and adjunct writing courses attached to undergraduate history and sociology courses. She is co-author of *The Research Paper Workbook* (Longman) and co-editor of *A Guide to Writing Sociology Papers* (St. Martin's). Her publications include articles in the *History Teacher, Social Education,* and *College English.*

Index of Authors and Titles